Innovative Applications of Big Data in the Railway Industry

Shruti Kohli
University of Birmingham, UK

A.V. Senthil Kumar
Hindusthan College of Arts and Science, India

John M. Easton
University of Birmingham, UK

Clive Roberts
University of Birmingham, UK

A volume in the Advances in Civil and Industrial
Engineering (ACIE) Book Series

Published in the United States of America by
  IGI Global
  Engineering Science Reference (an imprint of IGI Global)
  701 E. Chocolate Avenue
  Hershey PA, USA 17033
  Tel: 717-533-8845
  Fax: 717-533-8661
  E-mail: cust@igi-global.com
  Web site: http://www.igi-global.com

Library of Congress Cataloging-in-Publication Data

Names: Kohli, Shruti, 1978- editor.
Title: Innovative applications of big data in the railway industry / Shruti
  Kohli [and three others], editors.
Description: Hershey, PA : Engineering Science Reference, [2018]
Identifiers: LCCN 2017016448| ISBN 9781522531760 (hardcover) | ISBN
  9781522531777 (ebook)
Subjects: LCSH: Railroads--Management. | Railroads--Technological
  innovations. | Big data.
Classification: LCC TF507 .I537 2018 | DDC 385.0285/57--dc23 LC record available at https://lccn.loc.gov/2017016448

This book is published in the IGI Global book series Advances in Civil and Industrial Engineering (ACIE) (ISSN: 2326-6139; eISSN: 2326-6155)

British Cataloguing in Publication Data
A Cataloguing in Publication record for this book is available from the British Library.

All work contributed to this book is new, previously-unpublished material. The views expressed in this book are those of the authors, but not necessarily of the publisher.

For electronic access to this publication, please contact: eresources@igi-global.com.

Advances in Civil and Industrial Engineering (ACIE) Book Series

Ioan Constantin Dima
University Valahia of Târgovişte, Romania

ISSN:2326-6139
EISSN:2326-6155

MISSION

Private and public sector infrastructures begin to age, or require change in the face of developing technologies, the fields of civil and industrial engineering have become increasingly important as a method to mitigate and manage these changes. As governments and the public at large begin to grapple with climate change and growing populations, civil engineering has become more interdisciplinary and the need for publications that discuss the rapid changes and advancements in the field have become more in-demand. Additionally, private corporations and companies are facing similar changes and challenges, with the pressure for new and innovative methods being placed on those involved in industrial engineering.

The **Advances in Civil and Industrial Engineering (ACIE) Book Series** aims to present research and methodology that will provide solutions and discussions to meet such needs. The latest methodologies, applications, tools, and analysis will be published through the books included in **ACIE** in order to keep the available research in civil and industrial engineering as current and timely as possible.

COVERAGE

- Ergonomics
- Transportation Engineering
- Urban Engineering
- Operations research
- Materials Management
- Structural Engineering
- Engineering Economics
- Hydraulic Engineering
- Quality Engineering
- Construction Engineering

IGI Global is currently accepting manuscripts for publication within this series. To submit a proposal for a volume in this series, please contact our Acquisition Editors at Acquisitions@igi-global.com or visit: http://www.igi-global.com/publish/.

Titles in this Series

For a list of additional titles in this series, please visit: www.igi-global.com/book-series

Dynamic Stability of Hydraulic Gates and Engineering for Flood Prevention
Noriaki Ishii (Osaka Electro-Communication University, Japan) Keiko Anami (Osaka Electro-Communication University, Japan) and Charles W. Knisely (Bucknell University, USA)
Engineering Science Reference • copyright 2018 • 660pp • H/C (ISBN: 9781522530794) • US $245.00 (our price)

Handbook of Research on Trends and Digital Advances in Engineering Geology
Nurcihan Ceryan (Balikesir University, Turkey)
Engineering Science Reference • copyright 2018 • 765pp • H/C (ISBN: 9781522527091) • US $345.00 (our price)

Intelligent Vehicles and Materials Transportation in the Manufacturing Sector Emerging Research and Opportunities
Susmita Bandyopadhyay (University of Burdwan, India)
Engineering Science Reference • copyright 2018 • 230pp • H/C (ISBN: 9781522530640) • US $155.00 (our price)

Recent Advances in Applied Thermal Imaging for Industrial Applications
V. Santhi (VIT University, India)
Engineering Science Reference • copyright 2017 • 306pp • H/C (ISBN: 9781522524236) • US $205.00 (our price)

Performance-Based Seismic Design of Concrete Structures and Infrastructures
Vagelis Plevris (Oslo and Akershus University College of Applied Sciences, Norway) Georgia Kremmyda (University of Warwick, UK) and Yasin Fahjan (Gebze Technical University, Turkey)
Engineering Science Reference • copyright 2017 • 320pp • H/C (ISBN: 9781522520894) • US $205.00 (our price)

Engineering Tools and Solutions for Sustainable Transportation Planning
Hermann Knoflacher (Vienna University of Technology, Austria) and Ebru V. Ocalir-Akunal (Gazi University, Turkey)
Engineering Science Reference • copyright 2017 • 374pp • H/C (ISBN: 9781522521167) • US $210.00 (our price)

Design Solutions and Innovations in Temporary Structures
Robert Beale (Independent Researcher, UK) and João André (Portuguese National Laboratory for Civil Engineering, Portugal)
Engineering Science Reference • copyright 2017 • 503pp • H/C (ISBN: 9781522521990) • US $200.00 (our price)

Modeling and Simulation Techniques in Structural Engineering
Pijush Samui (National Institute of Technology Patna, India) Subrata Chakraborty (Indian Institute of Engineering Science and Technology (IIEST), Shibpur, India) and Dookie Kim (Kunsan National University, South Korea)
Engineering Science Reference • copyright 2017 • 524pp • H/C (ISBN: 9781522505884) • US $220.00 (our price)

701 East Chocolate Avenue, Hershey, PA 17033, USA
Tel: 717-533-8845 x100 • Fax: 717-533-8661
E-Mail: cust@igi-global.com • www.igi-global.com

Table of Contents

Section 1
Concepts and Approaches

Section 2
Innovations and Technologies

Section 3
Big Data and Text Mining

Section 4
Applications and Use Cases

Detailed Table of Contents

Section 1
Concepts and Approaches

  Diego Galar, Lulea University of Technology, Sweden & TECNALIA, Spain
  Dammika Seneviratne, Lulea University of Technology, Sweden & TECNALIA, Spain
  Uday Kumar, Lulea University of Technology, Sweden

Railway systems are complex with respect to technology and operations with the involvement of a wide range of human actors, organizations and technical solutions. For the operations and control of such complexity, a viable solution is to apply intelligent computerized systems, for instance, computerized traffic control systems for coordinating airline transportation, or advanced monitoring and diagnostic systems in vehicles. Moreover, transportation assets cannot compromise the safety of the passengers by only applying operation and maintenance activities. Indeed, safety is a more difficult goal to achieve using traditional maintenance strategies and computerized solutions come into the picture as the only option to deal with complex systems interacting among them and trying to balance the growth in technical complexity together with stable and acceptable dependability indexes. Big data analytics are expected to improve the overall performance of the railways supported by smart systems and Internet-based solutions. Operation and Maintenance will be application areas, where benefits will be visible as a consequence of big data policies due to diagnosis and prognosis capabilities provided to the whole network of processes. This chapter shows the possibilities of applying the big data concept in the railway transportation industry and the positive effects on technology and operations from a systems perspective.

  John M. Easton, University of Birmingham, UK

In recent years, the UK railway industry has struggled with the effects of poor integration of data across ICT systems, particularly when that data is being used across organizational boundaries. Technical progress is being made by the industry towards enabling data sharing, but an open issue remains around how the costs of gathering and maintaining pooled information can be fairly attributed across the stakeholders who draw on that shared resource. This issue is particularly significant in areas such as Remote Condition Monitoring, where the ability to analyse the network at a whole-systems level is being blocked by the business cases around the purchase of systems as silos. Blockchains are an emerging technology that have the potential to revolutionize the management of transactions in a number of industrial sectors. This chapter will address the outstanding issues around the fair attribution of costs and benefits of data sharing in the rail industry by proposing blockchains as a forth enabler of the rail data revolution, alongside ESB, ontology, and open data.

Chapter 3

Alper M. Selver, Dokuz Eylul University, Turkey
Enes Ataç, Dokuz Eylul University, Turkey
Burak Belenlioglu, Kentkart, Turkey
Sinan Dogan, Kentkart, Turkey
Yesim E. Zoral, Dokuz Eylul University, Turkey

This chapter reviews the challenges, processing and analysis techniques about visual and LIDAR generated information and their potential use in big data analysis for monitoring the railway at onboard driver support systems. It surveys both sensors' advantages, limitations, and innovative approaches for overcoming the challenges they face. Special focus is given to monocular vision due to its dominant use in the field. A novel contribution is provided for rail extraction by utilizing a new hybrid approach. The results of this approach are used to demonstrate the shortcomings of similar strategies. To overcome these disadvantages, dynamic modeling of the tracks is considered. This stage is designed by statistically quantifying the assumptions about the track curvatures presumed in current railway extraction techniques. By fitting polynomials to hundreds of manually delineated video frames, the variations of polynomial coefficients are analyzed. Future trends for processing and analysis of additional sensors are also discussed.

Chapter 4

Swastikaa Moudgil, Chandigarh College of Engineering and Technology, India
Ashim Bhasin, Chandigarh College of Engineering and Technology, India
Ankit Gupta, Chandigarh College of Engineering and Technology, India

The present competitive world of transport particularly the rail industry is driven by automation and centralization. New ways are being devised each day by the operators and managers to improve efficiency, operational safety, and risk control. Big Data and its multiple applications play a significant role in developing ways of analyzing and evaluating the rail data gathered and using it to enhance the transport industry. Wayside train Monitoring System is a field that is slowly gaining popularity through the different methods it provides to handle the big Data of the transport industry. It can measure the operational performance of rolling stock and infrastructure assets as well as the direct surroundings. The chapter addresses the problem of overall safety and optimum cost of railways transportation. Consequently, the chapter aims to resolve the following issues: How can the rail industry leverage the enormous amount of data available? How can industry players benefit from the data and use it to understand the real needs of travelers?

Section 2
Innovations and Technologies

Chapter 5

Stijn Verstichel, Ghent University, Belgium

Wannes Kerckhove, Ghent University, Belgium

Thomas Dupont, Ghent University, Belgium

Jabran Bhatti, Televic Rail NV, Belgium

Dirk Van Den Wouwer, Televic Rail NV, Belgium

Filip De Turck, Ghent University, Belgium

Bruno Volckaert, Ghent University, Belgium

To this day, railway actors obtain information by actively hunting for relevant data in various places. Despite the availability of a variety of travel-related data sources, accurate delivery of relevant, timely information to these railway actors is still inadequate. In this chapter, we present a solution in the form of a scalable software framework that can interface with almost any type of (open) data. The framework aggregates a variety of data sources to create tailor-made knowledge, personalised to the dynamic profiles of railway users. Core functionality, including predefined non-functional support, such as load balancing strategies, is implemented in the generic base layer, on top of which a use case specific layer – that can cope with the specifics of the railway environment – is built. Data entering the framework is intelligently processed and the results are made available to railway vehicles and personal mobile devices through REST endpoints.

Chapter 6

Gaurav Ahlawat, Panjab University, India

Ankit Gupta, Chandigarh College of Engineering and Technology, India

Avimanyou K Vatsa, University of Missouri, USA

Many attempts have been made to derive insights and any useful information about the behavior of the passengers traveling using different data analytics approaches and techniques. The different ways the researchers have tried to model the travel behavior and also their attempt to measure the behavioral changes at an individual level will be discussed in this chapter. The insights derived using these methods can help policy makers and the authorities to make necessary and important changes to the railways. The transit systems of the Railways provide us with the data, which is analysed using different techniques and methodologies and derived insights from.

Chapter 7
Myneni Madhu Bala, Institute of Aeronautical Engineering, India
Venkata Krishnaiah Ravilla, Institute of Aeronautical Engineering, India
Kamakshi Prasad V, JNTUH, India
Akhil Dandamudi, NIIT University, India

This chapter discusses mainly on dynamic behavior of railway passengers by using twitter data during regular and emergency situations. Social network data is providing dynamic and realistic data in various fields. As per the current chapter theme, if the twitter data of railway field is considered then it can be used for enhancement of railway services. Using this data, a comprehensive framework for modeling passenger tweets data which incorporates passenger opinions towards facilities provided by railways are discussed. The major issues elaborated regarding dynamic data extraction, preparation of twitter text content and text processing for finding sentiment levels is presented by two case studies; which are sentiment analysis on passenger's opinions about quality of railway services and identification of passenger travel demands using geotagged twitter data. The sentiment analysis ascertains passenger opinions towards facilities provided by railways either positive or negative based on their journey experiences.

Chapter 8
Hamid Barkouk, Abdelmalek Essaâdi University, Morocco
El Mokhtar En-Naimi, Abdelmalek Essaâdi University, Morocco

The VANET (Vehicular Ad hoc Network) is a collection of mobile nodes forming a temporary network on variable topology, operating without base station and without centralized administration. Communication is possible between vehicles within each other's radio range as well as with fixed components on road side infrastructure. The characteristics of VANET network that distinguishes it from other ad hoc networks, such as high mobility and communication with the infrastructure to support security or comfort applications, have prompted researchers to develop models and mobility specific protocols. The main goal of this chapter is firstly to compare the performance of three Ad hoc routing protocols: OLSR, AODV and DSDV, and secondly to examine the impact of varying mobility, density and pause time on the functionality of these protocols. The results of this chapter demonstrate that AODV have better performance in terms of Throughput and Packets Delivery Rate (PDR), whereas OLSR have best performance in terms of Packet Delivery Time (Delay).

Section 3
Big Data and Text Mining

Chapter 9
Arun Solanki, Gautam Buddha University, India
Ela Kumar, Indira Gandhi Delhi Technical University for Women, India

Delhi Metro passengers had a difficult time mostly on Monday morning as trains on the busy corridors are delayed due to technical problems or track circuit failure. This study found different factors like power failure, weather, rider load, festive season, etc. which are responsible for the delay of Delhi Metro. Due to these factors, Metro got delayed and run at a reduced speed causing much inconvenience to the people, who are hoping to reach their offices on time. Delhi Metro data are received from different sources which may be structured (timings, speed, traffic), semi-structured (images and video) and unstructured (maintenance records) form. So, there is heterogeneity in data. Except for this data, the feedback or suggestion of a rider is vital to the system. Nowadays riders are using social media like Facebook and Twitter very frequently. Three-tier architecture is proposed for the delay analysis of Delhi Metro. Different implementation techniques are studied and proposed for the social media module and delay prediction modules for the proposed system.

Chapter 10

David Golightly, University of Nottingham, UK
Robert J. Houghton, University of Nottingham, UK

Social media plays an increasing role in how passengers communicate to, and about, train operators. In response, train operators and other rail stakeholders are adopting social media to contact their users. There are a number of opportunities for tapping this big data information stream through the overt use of technology to analyse, filter and present social media, including filtering for operational staff, or sentiment mapping for strategy. However, this analysis is predicated on a number of assumptions regarding the manner in which social media is currently being used within a railway context. In the following chapter, we present data from studies of rail social media that shed light on how big data analysis of social media exchange can support the passenger. These studies highlight important factors such as the broad range of issues covered by social media (not just disruption), the idiosyncrasies of individual train operators that need to be taken into account within social media analysis, and the time critical nature of information during disruption.

Chapter 11

Kanza Noor Syeda, Lancaster University, UK
Syed Noorulhassan Shirazi, Lancaster University, UK
Syed Asad Ali Naqvi, Lancaster University, UK
Howard J Parkinson, Digital Rail Limited, UK
Gary Bamford, Digital Rail Limited, UK

Due to modern powerful computing and the explosion in data availability and advanced analytics, there should be opportunities to use a Big Data approach to proactively identify high risk scenarios on the railway. In this chapter, we comprehend the need for developing machine intelligence to identify heightened risk on the railway. In doing so, we have explained a potential for a new data driven approach in the railway, we then focus the rest of the chapter on Natural Language Processing (NLP) and its potential for analysing accident data. We review and analyse investigation reports of railway accidents in the UK, published by the Rail Accident Investigation Branch (RAIB), aiming to reveal the presence of entities which are informative of causes and failures such as human, technical and external. We give an overview of a framework based on NLP and machine learning to analyse the raw text from RAIB reports which would assist the risk and incident analysis experts to study causal relationship between causes and failures towards the overall safety in the rail industry.

Section 4
Applications and Use Cases

Chapter 12

Shaik Rasool, MJCET, India
Uma Dulhare, MJCET, India

Indian Railways is the largest rail network in the world, can be plays an essential role in the development of infrastructure areas such as coal, electric power, steel, concrete and other critical industries. Indian government has started concentrating on the modernization of the railways through huge investment. Internet of Things(IoT) is vital attention to expansion and excellence. The chapter will commence with the past history of rail transport in India Further section will support the IoT which is another great trend in technology. The later section of the chapter will give attention to how Internet of things could expertise the railroad industry, introducing a remedy which will be made to modernize aging sites at railroads, improve basic safety. The railway can help the passenger to utilize fewer interruptions in the event that's what they need. There's a large number of things that require to be watched and the railway can run as a completely digital service, without having to have people walking the tracks, it brings cost benefits and increased safety for the workforce.

Chapter 13

Shruti Kohli, University of Birmingham, UK
Shanthini Muthusamy, University of Birmingham, UK

Transportation systems are designed to run in normal conditions. The occurrence of planned works, unscheduled major events or disturbances can affect the transportation services that intended to provide and as a result, the disruptive nature may have a significant impact on the operation of the transport modes. This chapter focuses on the impact of disruptions in the multimodal transportation using the available open data. The enablers (key variables) of the datasets are taken into account to evaluate the service performance of each transport mode and its influence on other transport modes in case of disturbances. The high-volume, streaming data collected for a long time is a good potential use case for applying text mining techniques on big data. This chapter provides an insight into research being carried out for developing capabilities to store and analyze multi-modal data feeds for predictive analysis.

Chapter 14

Emanuele Fumeo, University of Genoa, Italy
Luca Oneto, University of Genoa, Italy
Giorgio Clerico, University of Genoa, Italy
Renzo Canepa, Rete Ferroviaria Italiana S.P.A., Italy
Federico Papa, Ansaldo STS S.P.A., Italy
Carlo Dambra, Ansaldo STS S.P.A, Italy
Nadia Mazzino, Ansaldo STS S.P.A., Italy
Davida Anguita, University of Genoa, Italy

Current Train Delay Prediction Systems (TDPSs) do not take advantage of state-of-the-art tools and techniques for extracting useful insights from large amounts of historical data collected by the railway information systems. Instead, these systems rely on static rules, based on classical univariate statistic, built by experts of the railway infrastructure. The purpose of this book chapter is to build a data-driven TDPS for large-scale railway networks, which exploits the most recent big data technologies, learning algorithms, and statistical tools. In particular, we propose a fast learning algorithm for Shallow and Deep Extreme Learning Machines that fully exploits the recent in-memory large-scale data processing technologies for predicting train delays. Proposal has been compared with the current state-of-the-art TDPSs. Results on real world data coming from the Italian railway network show that our proposal is able to improve over the current state-of-the-art TDPSs.

Preface

The emerging field of big data science has already begun to revolutionise both the service sector and retail industries, enabling companies to gain a deeper understanding of their customer's habits, their logistical operations, and their supply chains. To date however, the penetration of these technologies into more traditional heavy industries, such as the railways, has been limited.

The potential benefits offered to the railway industry by the application of big data technologies are huge, ranging from more efficient management of assets and infrastructure, through improved connectivity with other transport modes and a greater understanding of passenger demand, to data-led approaches to critical, long-term issues such as safety management.

To date, the railway industry has mainly focused on the collection of data describing its assets and operations; installing condition monitoring equipment, building detailed GIS models of the infrastructure, and publishing data on vehicle movements; however, moves to install modern signaling systems and traffic management, along with other innovations including a cross-industry DRACAS, will soon trigger rapid growth in the availability of operational data. As the volume, variety, and velocity of data available grows, and industry stakeholders begin to rely on it for their decision-making processes, a need is emerging for robust, scalable tools that can efficient mine the data and produce new business intelligence.

ORGANISATION OF CHAPTERS

The book has been divided into four sections: "Concepts and Approaches", "Innovations and Technologies", "Big Data and Text Mining", and "Applications and Use Cases". Altogether the book contains 14 manuscripts covering a wide range of topics of interest to the rail industry, including:

Chapter 1 focuses on the application of big data technologies in the area of operations and maintenance of the railway. It considers the complex, cyber-physical architecture of the railway system and how it relates to the industrial Internet of Things, before discussing how big data techniques and open source toolkits can be applied to asset management within the railways, and the positive impacts such technologies could have.

Chapter 2 looks at the problem of attribution of costs and benefits of data collection from railway assets, when the data is used to benefit other stakeholders within the industry. It proposes the use of blockchains, the distributed ledger technology underpinning the Bitcoin cryptocurrency, as a method for monetizing these data exchanges, and considers how the technology would sit alongside the other main elements of the railway data revolution, including ESBs, ontologies, and linked open data.

Chapter 3 reviews the challenges around managing multi-sensor generated big data for monitoring the railway, and its use in onboard driver advisory systems. It surveys a range of sensor technologies, looking at design, intended use, and practical limitations, before moving on to identify the added value provided by each sensor. The chapter then draws this information together into a new hybrid approach, which employs multi-scale edge detection and fusion followed by dynamic modelling of the tracks.

Chapter 4 provides a detailed description of working with Wayside Train Monitoring Systems, which use big data derived from the rolling stock and from infrastructure assets to assess operational performance. It looks at how the industry can leverage the potentially huge amounts of data generated by these systems, and provides cases studies to illustrate their value.

Chapter 5 looks at the big data problem from the perspective of the passenger, and considers how the range of information resources used during a typical multimodal journey can be effectively integrated and tailored to their needs. It addresses the challenge of data interoperability, and presents an open-source framework supporting agile development in the transport sector.

Chapter 6 discusses the research being done to predict the behaviour of passengers during journeys. It examines how data collected through smart cards can be used to validate passenger behaviour models, and presents a case study around Transport for London.

Chapter 7 looks at how passenger behaviour changes in emergency situations by considering data from the social media platform Twitter. It discusses how social media data is leveraged by railway companies, and provides a case study using data from cities in India.

Chapter 8 looks at the interface between rail and road transport, and discusses how the VANET system can be used within the Intelligent Transport System.

Chapter 9 makes use of data mining techniques to provide insight into delays impacting on Delhi Metro services. This study identified a range of contributory factors, including power failure, weather, passenger loading, and festivals, which are responsible for the delay of Delhi Metro.

Chapter 10 returns to the theme of social media as a tool to aid the understanding of passenger behaviours. The authors present data from studies that shed light on how big data analysis of social media exchange can support the passenger. These studies highlight important factors such as the broad range of issues covered by social media (not just disruption), the idiosyncrasies of individual train operators that need to be taken into account during analysis of social media data, and the time critical nature of information during the disruption.

Chapter 11 discusses the application of natural language processing in the analysis of railway safety data. The authors make use of accident investigation reports published by the Rail Accident Investigation Branch (RAIB) in the UK, with the aim of identifying entities that are instrumental in causing accidents, including human, technical and external factors.

Chapter 12 describes recent investment by the Indian Railways in the IoT, with a particular focus on how the technologies could be employed to modernize the aging infrastructure, and improve safety.

Chapter 13 explains how big data technologies can be used in the mining of public data feeds to gain additional insights into the operation of multi-modal transportation systems. The chapter considers the impact of disruptions to the multimodal transportation network, as determined from the available open data. The system captures big data in real time from Transport for London and Network Rail service providers, processes that data, store the results in MongoDB enabling the use of text mining analysis to identify significant disruption factors.

Chapter 14 describes the application of big data technologies to the prediction of train delays in Italian rail network. The authors present a data-driven Train Delay Prediction System (TDPS) for large-scale railway networks, which exploits the most recent big data technologies, learning algorithms, and statistical tools. They then propose a fast learning algorithm for Shallow and Deep Extreme Learning Machines that fully exploits the recent in-memory large-scale data processing technologies for predicting train delays. Results are presented based on real world data coming from the Italian railway network.

AIMS OF THE BOOK

Over the last few years there has been a great deal of discussion within the industry around the shape the railways will take in the decades to come. Much of the debate has focused on the arrival of new, digital technologies that will replace the systems the industry has relied on until now, and what the impact of those changes might be in terms of passenger experience, the operation of the network, safety and security, and business processes. This book introduces the key topics driving big data usage in the rail industry. It discusses the challenges faced by rail companies striving to provide passengers with safe, reliable, cost effective services, and the approaches to data-driven decision-making they use to support them in the future.

The editors hope that through the collection of manuscripts on the applications of big data technologies in the railways presented in this book, the reader will gain a comprehensive understanding of the potential these technologies offer the industry, and the scope for future developments of the approaches in the years to come.

Shruti Kohli
University of Birmingham, UK

A. V. Senthil Kumar
Hindusthan College of Arts and Science, India

John M. Easton
University of Birmingham, UK

Clive Roberts
University of Birmingham, UK

Acknowledgment

The editors would like to thank all those who have contributed to, or reviewed material for this book, for their hard work, time, and dedication.

Shruti Kohli
University of Birmingham, UK

A. V. Senthil Kumar
Hindusthan College of Arts and Science, India

John M. Easton
University of Birmingham, UK

Clive Roberts
University of Birmingham, UK

Section 1
Concepts and Approaches

Chapter 1
Big Data in Railway O&M:
A Dependability Approach

Diego Galar
Lulea University of Technology, Sweden & TECNALIA, Spain

Dammika Seneviratne
Lulea University of Technology, Sweden & TECNALIA, Spain

Uday Kumar
Lulea University of Technology, Sweden

ABSTRACT

Railway systems are complex with respect to technology and operations with the involvement of a wide range of human actors, organizations and technical solutions. For the operations and control of such complexity, a viable solution is to apply intelligent computerized systems, for instance, computerized traffic control systems for coordinating airline transportation, or advanced monitoring and diagnostic systems in vehicles. Moreover, transportation assets cannot compromise the safety of the passengers by only applying operation and maintenance activities. Indeed, safety is a more difficult goal to achieve using traditional maintenance strategies and computerized solutions come into the picture as the only option to deal with complex systems interacting among them and trying to balance the growth in technical complexity together with stable and acceptable dependability indexes. Big data analytics are expected to improve the overall performance of the railways supported by smart systems and Internet-based solutions. Operation and Maintenance will be application areas, where benefits will be visible as a consequence of big data policies due to diagnosis and prognosis capabilities provided to the whole network of processes. This chapter shows the possibilities of applying the big data concept in the railway transportation industry and the positive effects on technology and operations from a systems perspective.

INTRODUCTION

Industry 4.0 symbolizes a fourth generation of industrial activity as a result of the fourth industrial revolution characterized by smart systems and Internet-based solutions, Landscheidt et al. (2016). The first revolution took place in the 19th century, when production was mechanized. This meant that production

DOI: 10.4018/978-1-5225-3176-0.ch001

was moved from the home or small workshops to large factory units and a new social class was born; the working class. The second revolution occurred in the last century when the production was electrified and parts and processes were standardized. The archetype of this revolution is Ford's assembly line. The digitization of production is usually called the third revolution marked by introduction of programmable logic controllers (PLC) in late 1960s.

The fourth industrial revolution relies on ICT evolution and data driven decision making processes by the means of big data. Two of the characteristic features of Industry 4.0 are computerization with the help of cyber-physical systems and intelligent factories that are based on the concept of "internet of things" (Amadi, 2010). Cyber-physical systems are integrated computer-based or digital components that monitor and control physical devices, also called embedded systems (Le, 2016). These systems communicate over a network usually based on internet technology, creating an "internet of things" (as opposed to social media that could be described as "internet of persons"). Combining these two concepts, we get a distributed network of embedded systems communicating with each other in an ad hoc and dynamic way. In today's competitive environment, there are unmistakable signs that human beings, organizations, cities, systems and so on are increasingly becoming interconnected, instrumented and intelligent.

The transportation sector and especially the railway have not ignored industry 4.0 and adapted most of the positive inputs, as has the aircraft industry (traditional driver of advanced O&M methodologies by the means of massive data capturing).

This is leading to improved quality of services, new savings, enhanced resource utilization and efficiency. This has also facilitated the development of the new services and business models based on the capability of industrial internet and the analytics capabilities provided by big data. Indeed, big data provides a foundation for the next generation of transportation technologies based on the use of advanced information logistics analytics to transform the current state of the art railway platforms into a network of collaborative communities seamlessly moving freight and passengers and delivering services in a planned way. It symbolizes the current trend of automation and data exchange in the transportation sector striving to adopt and adapt the new and emerging technologies to achieve new levels of effectiveness and efficiency.

Big data in railways include necessary stakeholders who instrument, interconnect and finally provide intelligence to the railway system. It means that the complete big data architecture will be comprised of cyber-physical systems, the Internet of things and cloud computing in order to have a real big data environment providing "smart railways". In fact, one of the application areas which created more expectations is a better operation and maintenance in the form of self-learning and smart systems that predict failure, make diagnoses, and trigger maintenance actions. These systems are already having high demands on data access and data quality and use multiple data sources to extract relevant information with further analytics, Lee et al. (2014). Several research projects have focused on the cyber-physical approach for developing intelligent O&M management systems for failure detection, diagnostics and prognostics, Kroll et al. (2014), Sankavaram et al. (2013) and Syed et al. (2012). So far, the main application area has been process and manufacturing industries, but it is pretty obvious that these services have a huge potential in other areas like the railway sector due to the complexity and huge amount of data generated and captured with high quality standards.

Big data analytics in railway O&M are expected to utilize the advanced technologies for predictive analytics and provides decisions based on feasibility. Therefore, big data for O&M services involves data collection, analysis, visualization and decision making for assets. Big data in O&M also addresses a common Achilles heel in asset management: a better assets status forecasting, commonly called prognosis. The estimation of the remaining useful life constitutes the basis for any operation or maintenance service in order to check the probability of mission accomplishment by the asset (Galar et al., 2012).

The 'Big data' approach can be applied to diverse sources of information and create new services based on the ontologies exploited and knowledge discovery performed (Baglee et al., 2014). This adoption of Big data may pave the ground for better Operation and Maintenance policies bridging the gap between them considering that O&M have been historically optimized in independent silos. In summary, the foundation of big data in railway O&M is built around the concepts of interconnectivity, instrumentation and intelligence for the assets by the means of successful proven technologies such industrial internet, cloud computing or industrial Internet of Things (IoT).

INSTRUMENTATION AND INTERCONNECTION

Internet of Things

The Internet of Things (IoT) is a collective term for the developments whereby machinery, vehicles, goods, appliances, clothes and other things and creatures (including humans), is equipped with tiny sensors and computers. IoT could be defined as a dynamic network infrastructure with self-configuring capabilities based on standard interoperable communication protocols where physical and virtual things have identities, physical attributes, and virtual personalities and use intelligent interfaces, and are seamlessly integrated into the information network. In short, the Internet of Things (IoT) is the network of everything—devices, vehicles, buildings and other items embedded with electronics, software, sensors, and network connectivity that enables these objects to collect and exchange data.

Industrial Internet

Industrial internet can be defined as the new and emerging technologies for managing interconnected machines and systems between its physical assets and computational capabilities (Lee et al., 2014).

The Industrial Internet of Things (IIoT) is the use of Internet of Things (IoT) technologies in manufacturing incorporating machine-to-machine communication, big data analytics, harnessing of the sensor data and robotics and automation technologies that have existed in industrial settings for years.

There are three main elements of Industrial Internet:

- **Intelligent Machines:** New ways of connecting myriad of machines, facilities, fleets and networks with advanced sensors, controls and software applications.
- **Advanced Analytics:** Harnessing the power of physics-based analytics, predictive algorithms, automation and deep domain expertise in material science, electrical engineering and other key disciplines required to understand how machines and larger systems operate.
- **People:** Connecting people, whether they work in industrial facilities, offices, hospitals or on the move, at any time to support more intelligent design, operations, maintenance as well as higher quality service and safety. Connecting and combining these elements offers new opportunities across firms and economies.

The Industrial Internet starts with embedding sensors and other advanced instrumentation in an array of machines from the simple to the highly complex. This allows the collection and analysis of an enormous amount of data, which can be used to improve machine performance, and inevitably the efficiency of the systems and networks that link them. Even the data itself can become "intelligent," instantly knowing which users it needs to reach.

The three main components of this concept are intelligent devices, intelligent systems, and digital instrumentation to industrial machines. These represent the first step in the Industrial Internet Revolution.

Several forces at work to make machines and collections of machines more intelligent are costs of deployment (instrumentation, Internet of Things), computing power (nanotechnology) and advanced analytics (Big Data Analytics).

The specific domain of railways with pervasive computer and connection via the train bus where most of the subsystems and their respective sensors are accessible is one of the most promising domains in this regard. Indeed, the interconnection by data buses inside the vehicle of different subsystems with different OEMs open the doors and create new insights for global optimization in a system of system approach replacing the old approach of local optima with reduced scope for O&M of the whole asset and its desired function.

Cyber-Physical Architecture

Cyber-Physical Systems (CPS) is defined as transformative technologies for managing interconnected systems between its physical assets and computational capabilities (Kans and Gill, 2016). The 5-level CPS structure, namely the 5C architecture, provides a step-by-step guideline for developing and deploying a CPS for manufacturing application (Liggins et al., 2015).

- **Smart Connection:** Acquiring accurate and reliable data from machines and their components is the first step in developing a Cyber-Physical System application. The data might be directly measured by sensors or obtained from controller or vehicle/track side systems such as ERP, MES, SCM and CMMS.
- **Data-to-Information Conversion:** Meaningful information to be inferred from the data. In recent years, extensive focus has been applied to develop these algorithms specifically for prognostics and health management applications. By calculating health value, estimated remaining useful life etc., the second level of CPS architecture brings context-awareness to machines.
- **Cyber:** The cyber level acts as central information hub in this architecture. Information is being pushed to it from every connected machine to form the machines network.
- **Cognition:** Implementing CPS on this level generates thorough knowledge of the monitored system. Presentation of the acquired knowledge to expert users supports the correct decision.
- **Configuration:** The configuration level is the feedback from cyber space to physical space and acts as supervisory control to make machines self-configure and self-adaptive. This stage acts as resilience control system (RCS) to apply the corrective and preventive decisions, which have been made in cognition level, to the monitored system.

Figure 1. Architecture of CPS
Source: Liggins et al., 2015

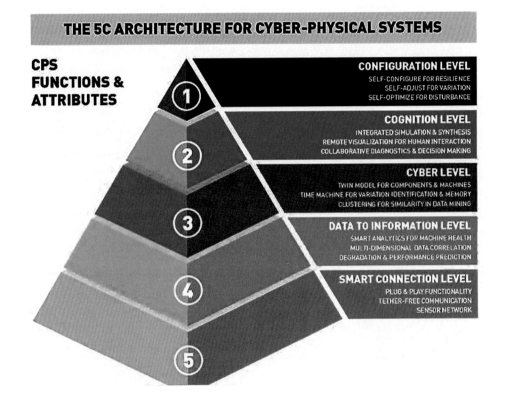

Cloud Computing

According to National Institute of Standards and Technology definition of cloud computing V15, dated 10-7-2009 (NIST, 2009), cloud computing is a model for enabling convenient, on-demand network access to a shared pool of configurable computing resources (for example, networks, servers, storage, applications, and services) that can be rapidly provisioned and released with minimal management effort or service provider interaction. Talking in terms of a cloud for industrial services cloud computing can be seen as a broad array of web-based services aimed at allowing users to obtain a wide range of functional capabilities on a 'pay-as-you-go' basis that previously required tremendous hardware and software investments and professional skills to acquire. Cloud computing is the realization of the earlier ideals of utility computing without the technical complexities or complicated deployment worries.

Therefore, the cloud is just a set of hardware, networks, storage, services, and interfaces that enables the delivery of computing as a service. For maintenance, the cloud seems to be the solution, given the large amounts of dispersed data in different repositories. The end user (maintenance or operators for infrastructure or rolling stock) do not really have to know anything about the underlying technology. The data collection and distribution applications may be dispersed throughout the network and data may be collected at a number of locations.

Figure 2 illustrates a simplified functional block diagram of data flow and communication associated with or used by the asset cloud. In particular, the diagram includes the data collection and distribution system which receive data from numerous data sources.

The cloud can maintain and store these data in the central working data store. At the same time, a user interface can provide a powerful analysis tool because of its ability to integrate layout, inventory, conditions, maintenance input, weather etc.

BIG DATA STATE OF THE ART

This section is divided into six parts to fully explain the state of the art in Big Data techniques relevant to the railway sector. Thus, the characteristics of current available commercial tools and the most recent outcomes from the scientific community in predictive algorithms, scalable data structures, data acquisition and communication and visualization and research outcomes in big data techniques applied to the railway operation and maintenance will be described.

Characteristics of Current Available Commercial and Open Source Tools

Big Data software tools: EU VisMaster and Zikopoulos (2011) have performed a deep survey in the visual analytics (VA) and Big Data tools currently available. The summary is described in the following points:

Figure 2. Services provided by the asset cloud

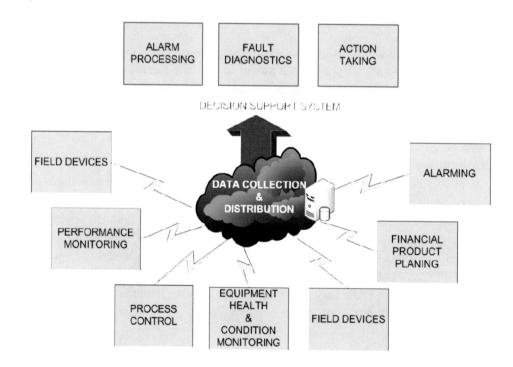

- **Open Source Toolkits:** A number of open-source VA toolkits exist; each covers a specific set of functionalities for visualization, analysis and interaction. For example, InfoVis Toolkit, Prefuse, Improvise and JUNG. Using existing toolkits for required functionality instead of implementing from scratch provides much efficiency while developing new VA solutions, although the level of O&M, development and user community support of open source toolkits can vary drastically. Besides, a relatively high amount of programming expertise and effort is often required to integrate these components into a new system.

- **Commercial VA Systems:** Tableau, Spotfire, QlikView, JMP, Visual Analytics, Centrifuge Jaspersoft, Board and ADVIZOR are the most relevant Big Data commercial software. They consist of long-standing software suites, which have developed out of core database or statistical data analysis suites. Common tasks of BD systems include reporting of historic and current data, performing analysis (intelligence) of data, and publishing prediction capabilities including what-if analysis.

The summary provided by Zikopoulos 2011 allows to easily draw the following conclusions:

1. There is already an important ecosystem (at least 10 very complete commercial SW tools and a similar number of open source tools) for Big Data processing. Most of them share similar features.
2. There is an important limitation in the predictive algorithms. Most of the commercial SW tools do not provide these algorithms, and those which provide them are based on simple linear predictive models such as ARIMA, Holt-Winter or Multi Variable Linear Regression.
3. Hardly all the "input information formats" are excel files, CVS and GIS.
4. The visualization techniques are limited to "control centre" standard statistical charts, georelated data and network description through tree maps. However, real time information is not displayed and neither data to maintenance personnel on-field.

The leading programming paradigm for Big Data is MapReduce. Although its fundamentals have roots in the LISP functional paradigm, the term was coined much more recently, in 2004, by Google MapReduce. While some papers were published, Google's software remained private. Then some researchers interested in the idea began to develop an open-source version. This effort, led by Dog Cutting, ended with a framework written in Java and called Hadoop.

Hadoop has become a framework for distributed storage and distributed processing of very large datasets on computer clusters built from commodity hardware. Two key ideas behind Hadoop are robustness and ease of use. A fundamental assumption is that hardware will probably fail and the system should face that. On the other hand, the functional decomposition of the problems in terms of map, shuffle and reduce modules to provide a general framework within with a linear scalability is possible with almost zero effort from the programmer.

The core of Apache Hadoop consists of a storage component, Hadoop Distributed File System (HDFS), and a processing module. Out of the core functionality a rich ecosystem of applications and tools have been or are currently being developed. Commercial support and added services are provided by a number of private corporations, e.g. Cloudera, HortonNetworks, MapR, However, the leading development is hosted within the Apache Software Foundation ApacheSF, who has boosted its development, and application. It also hosts a number of related projects: Ambari, Avro, Cassandra, Hbase, Hive, Mahout, Pig, and ZooKeeper, to name a few.

In addition, many other vendors that traditionally offer software for data processing and analysis are developing specific adaptations of Hadoop to their respective platforms, e.g. IBM, SAS or SAP.

While very effective when properly applied, the MapReduce paradigm is not universal and suffers from several limitations. For example, some of the best-known Data Mining techniques cannot easily be implemented within its framework, such as the Support Vector Machines. It does not work well for algorithms like Iterative Graph, Gradient Descent or Expectation Maximization. Some efforts have arisen to overcome these limitations. For example, extensions for particular cases, like Pregel (Google proposal for iterative graph algorithms) or Stanford's Graph Processing System.

The most effective of those newcomers is Spark. Spark was initially developed at UC Berkeley, and afterwards become a new project under the ApacheSF. Spark can access and manage a variety of data source, with a focus on HDFS, but can also connect too many other relational and non-relational database systems and data formats. So, it does not provide a new storage component. However, in contrast to Hadoop disk-based processing, Spark provides in-memory computation primitives which can boost the performance up to 100 times faster for suitable applications. In particular, it is well suited to deploy machine learning and data mining algorithms. This so clear that the previous effort to develop a Machine Learning Library on pure Hadoop, called Mahout, has been frozen in favor of native component of Spark, the MLlib, and Machine Learning Library.

Spark has become the current state-of-the-art in Big Data Processing. Anyway, this is a field in constant change and a host of open-source proposals are being developed exploring different aspects.

Big Data Techniques Applied to Railway Maintenance

This section describes first the already available SW tools to aid maintenance of the railway system and then the most important contributions from the research community in this field. Currently, SW tools to aid maintenance of the railway system can be divided in two families; on one hand, the SW tools from the rolling stock manufacturers, which to some degree are usually responsible for the operation and maintenance of the vehicles, and on the other hand, the SW tools for the infrastructure managers.

In the first family, we could include tools provided by ALSTOM, CAF or SIEMENS. They all provide similar features, for example, ALSTOM publishes the following features:

- Information management (e.g. documentation, staff, spare, task scheduling for corrective and predictive maintenance).
- Condition-based monitoring (CBM) based on vehicle parameters which are radio transmitted to a ground-based server. Unfortunately, the information to monitor is very limited to a set of parameters with very limited prediction capabilities. In general, the parameters are more alarms than performance indicators.
- Predictive data analytics for maintenance (HealthHub): algorithms to predict the future state of a given component. Monitors asset health and uses advanced data analytics to predict their remaining useful life and replace assets on a truly as-needed basis. Unfortunately, the algorithms are very limited by the amount of data available and only simple statistical regressions are provided.
- Optimization algorithms to reduce the cost of the component lifecycles. Optimization is very limited because they rely on predictive algorithms which are not accurate enough.

In the second family, different IT service providers have general purpose solutions which are typically customized for the infrastructure operator. Apart from the Integral Asset Management (IAM) service concept released by SIEMENS and probed successfully in several large infrastructures (e.g. Madrid Barajas Airport), ILOG® from IBM, RAMSYS from MERMEC group, it is worth highlighting the Maintenance Management System of THALES (6618NetTrac). This SW application provides a wide range of features such as:

- Information management (e.g. documentation, staff, spare, task scheduling for corrective and predictive maintenance)
- Condition monitoring (on-line and off-line). Unfortunately, the information to monitor is very limited to a set of parameters with very limited prediction capabilities. In general, the parameters are more alarms than performance indicators.
- Visualization (web technologies and mobile devices environment). The visualization is very limited to standard charts and reports. Advanced visualization systems to aid field work is not provided.

THALES also publishes prediction capabilities but it is limited by the reduced amount of information available and the underlying algorithm is basically a statistical correlation.

In conclusion, currently available SW tools to aid maintenance of railway systems cannot be considered Big Data technology since the sources of information actually analysed are very limited (some hundreds of MB) to either the infrastructure or the fleet. Therefore, the predictive algorithms are not accurate enough nor scalable and consequently the optimization capabilities could be significantly enhanced. Moreover, the visualization techniques are limited to different types of standard charts which give little information when dealing with Big Data in a control centre, and they do not provide "context dependent" advanced visual information to field workers.

In summary, during the last fifteen years the research community, led by Europe, has developed several projects aiming to reduce the operation and maintenance expenses of assets. Regarding the use of Big Data for predicting component failures, it is worth mentioning the following research projects:

- **Learning to Predict Train Wheel Failures:** In Kroll (2014) the goal was to optimize maintenance and operation of trains employing decision trees and Naïve Bayes. Through indirect measurement and a prediction algorithm the project achieved a predicting accuracy of 97% of wheel failures while maintaining a reasonable false alert rate (8%). Like in previous cases, the sources of information were limited since no information from the type of material, the operational information of the vehicle or the conditions of the rail was used.
- **Railway Track Geometry Defect Modelling:** Deterioration, Derailment Risk and Optimal Repair (Qing, 2012) where the goal is to predict railway track geometry defect by means of a method based on three steps:
  ◦ Track deterioration model to study the degradation of Class II geo-defects;
  ◦ A survival model to assess the derailment risk as a function of the track condition;
  ◦ An optimization model under uncertainty for track repair decisions. This research project states that this methodology based on Big Data technology can reduce 20% of the total composite cost on average.
- **Predictive Maintenance Sensor Rich but Uncertain Information Quality Environment Case Study in Railroad (IBM, 2013):** The objectives are to increase network velocity by either reduc-

ing the number of derailments (attributed to mechanical -car and locomotive- faults as primary cause) and reducing intermediate maintenance calls due to false positives/alarm (by 5% from current level). The methodology employed is based on SVM (Support Vector Machine a machine learning algorithms). The presented results reveal a saving of 5% in O&M associated costs.

- **Facilitating Maintenance Decisions on the Dutch Railways Using Big Data:** The ABA Case Study Niekamp (2015) developed by the TU Delft and published recently in 2014 IEEE international conference on Big Data. This research project employs up to 1TB of data for identifying and predicting rail degradation.

The analysis of the state of the art of the research community reveals huge potential savings and this is encouraging the work in this research line. However, there is a huge distance from research to the commercial solutions in terms of technology. The research projects have not coped with the problem from a holistic point of view. The sources of information do not combine all possibilities such as track-side sensing, vehicle sensing, maintenance site information, weather conditions or fleet operational conditions. Moreover, most of the information is analyzed off-line and there are no specific tools for big data visualization (not in control centers or in field work).

SYSTEMS COMPLEXITIES IN RAILWAY TRANSPORTATION

Systems thinking is a way to understand a complex phenomenon by defining the system characteristics, its boundaries and components, and by describing the interactions between the components in the system. The systems thinking has its origins in the general systems theory developed in the 1940s as a reaction to the emerging need for new approaches to problem solving in the modern world, Sandra (2005). Instead of focusing on separate items or occurrences, these are seen as parts of a bigger whole; the system. Today, the systems approach is applied in virtually every category of science. Natural science such as biology studies ecosystems, social science studies human interactions, engineering science studies mechanical systems and computer science studies human-computer systems. Systems science and its applications can roughly be divided into two categories: hard systems and soft systems. Hard systems apply mathematical methods and simulations for quantifying the system and the interactions between components in the system. Operational research and management research are examples of hard systems approaches. The soft systems approach is applied for problems that are hard to quantify, such as those involving human interactions and conflicting viewpoints.

Railway in general is a system with a high level of complexity especially with respect to technology and operations. From the technological point of view the rail-way consists of a number of physical objects, both rolling equipment and fixed, that interact with each other. Operational conditions, usage and weather conditions are examples of variables that affect the technical systems and their performance. The performance of the technical systems in turn affects the operations. The technical objects interact with human beings, both employees with specific roles and passengers, in the creation of the main service; transportation. In addition, the objects have to be coordinated in time and space with capacity as a delimiting variable. The operations must reach the goals of punctuality, reliability, safety, and health and environment. The planning, coordination and control take place on the organizational level, where different actors and organizations interact. It is thus obvious that the railway is an excellent object for systems studies.

The railway sector has undergone big changes since the 1980's when the national railway organizations comprising infrastructure and rolling stock were deregulated and split into two parts, operators and infrastructure managers. Operators, both passengers and freight became responsible for the traffic and the infrastructure manager became responsible for the fixed assets. These companies all over the world were privatized and the traffic was fully deregulated. In this situation, the number of train-kilometers has increased steadily, mainly for passenger trains. Meanwhile, the number of actors in the railway transport industry has increased. More advanced technology in trains as well as in infrastructure and increased speed have changed the railway transportation industry. The railway transportation is a highly complex activity with respect to organization, operations and technology.

Organizational Complexity

The organizational complexity of the railway has previously been studied mainly using qualitative, or soft, approaches. Busby (2006), Amadi et al. (2010) and Gustafson et al. (2013) use a qualitative approach for understanding risk behavior and to increase safety in railway, while Kyriakidis et al. (2015) use a quantitative approach for understanding risk behavior of operators. In Nishikawa (2014), the organisational change process in Japanese railway is described from an organization cultural perspective.

For each of the four main processes identified in Figure 3 (build, manage, maintain and operate) a number of functions are found. These functions support the main activity labelled "Transportation service" on the far right. The functions are planned and coordinated horizontally to reach this, but a vertical coordination is also required. Coordinated investments are often found on the strategic level, i.e. on the

Figure 3. Main functions of the railway system

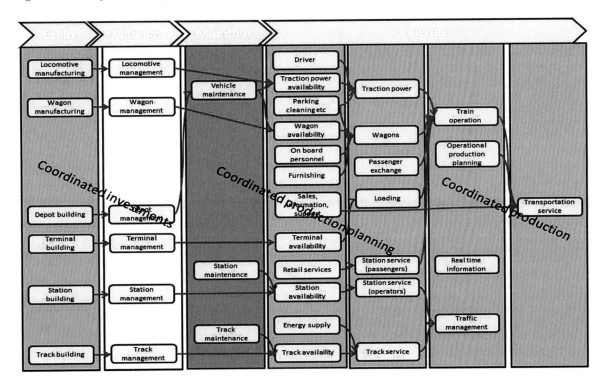

long-term planning scale, while the coordinated production planning is in the annual to weekly horizon, i.e. on the tactical level. Coordinated production is a daily operational matter. Coordinating all actors and functions within the main processes is a complex problem, with respect to both information flow and decision making. Because of the high number of actors involved in the timetabling process, there are long lead times in the planning. The timetable process for instance is a yearlong process, from the first application of capacity utilisation in February to April, to the detailed time plan in October, which is translated into the operational timetable that takes effect in December, Taneia (2012).

Operational Complexity

For addressing the operational complexity in the railway, the hard systems approach has been applied in various research, such as Moore (1993), Michalos (2016) and Kans et al. (2016). These researchers propose models for capacity, cost and schedule optimisation based on different operational research methods. The operational complexity occurs during the "operate" phase of the value chain, and especially the early stage of this phase, when assets are made available for the production. The ability to have assets available when needed is directly affected by the efficiency of maintenance, see Figure 1. The ability to provide assets when needed is a scheduling problem. Many actors have to be coordinated, for instance train owners, operators, infrastructure managers, and regulatory bodies. When put into an extraordinary situation, such as the winter season 2009 / 2010 with heavy snowfall causing delays and cancellation of trains, the complexity of the organization was one of the factors that created additional negative impact, SIS (2014). The seasonal changes are an additional factor of operational complexity, as well.

From 2000 there was a significant increase in railway transport. Especially the major routes and routes in major cities are experiencing very high capacity utilisation. This created several operational problems. The most direct is the timetabling of major bottlenecks. The speed is also reduced and this affects punctuality. Moreover, the higher capacity utilization affects the possibility of performing maintenance, which in turn affects the safety. As an example, postponed maintenance caused the derailment of a freight train south of Stockholm the 12th of November 2013, Amadi (2014). This incident affected the traffic for over one week. Therefore, maintenance windows should be considered as key factors in this complex system for smoother operation and higher customer satisfaction.

Technical Complexity

The technical complexity of the railway system has been addressed mainly using the hard systems approach. Lutchman et al. (2006) propose a model for the prediction of wheel and rail wear. In Johansson and Hassel (2010) static and functional properties of interdependent technical railway infrastructure systems are modelled, and the results could be used for vulnerability analysis. A tool for energy and wear simulation and optimisation of train traction and braking systems is proposed by Perko et al. (2016). Olsson et al. (2015) address one of the complexities in railway, i.e. the interaction between rolling elements and railway infrastructure. This complexity makes it hard to create reliable wear models. Lack of reliable models for deterioration and for assessing the condition of Swedish railway infrastructure is one of the deficiencies reported in Rong et al. (2015). The railway is a large networked system where different fixed and rolling elements interact. This diversity of technological solutions and age of the infrastructure add to the complexity. Today, the infrastructure managers simply do not know the true condition of the full railroad network. In addition, due to the interactions of technical systems and components, it is hard to assess the true cause of failure, Penna (2014), which in turn affects the detection of the true cause of train delays.

BIG DATA FOR O&M: A NEW DOMAIN FOR KNOWLEDGE DISCOVERY

The use of big Data Analytics is a standard (e.g. bank sector or pharmaceutical sector). For these sectors, there are also a great number of software tools and IT services that cover most of the end user needs. Some successful implementations of Big Data have been summarized in Whyte et al. (2016). Most businesses or industrial processes (parts of the supply chain) have not yet incorporated the Big Data concept, either for the lack of specific tools (real time communication, scalable data structures, complex predictive algorithms or visualizations tools) or the excessive cost to involve all the required stakeholders.

Whyte et al. (2016) define big data as: datasets that could not be perceived, acquired, managed, and processed by traditional Information Technology and software/hardware tools within a tolerable time. IBM researchers (Zikopoulos and Eaton, 2011) have modeled big data in terms of 3V properties: Volume, amount of data; Variety, unstructured data coming from multiple sources; and Velocity, high rate of data generation. In Lomotey and Deters (2014) this model has been extended into 5V, by adding: Value, understanding the cost and value of the data; and Veracity, the need to check accuracy of the data and data cleaning. Data Mining is one of the processes for Knowledge Discovery that aims in creation of new knowledge. Lomotey and Deters (2014) propose an Analytics-as-a-Service tool for Knowledge Discovery in Big Data. It has been indicated that existing data mining techniques have been designed for structured and schema oriented data storages. The proposed approach aims to perform topic and terms mining from unstructured data silos. In a McKinsey & Company report (Meier et al., 2010) the value that creative and effective utilization of big data could create are summarized: in U.S. medical industry it may surpass 300 billion USD; retailers may improve their profit by more than 60%. Meanwhile, the EU could save over 100 billion EUR by utilizing big data to improve the efficiency of government operations.

Big Data in Asset Management

Data produced in asset management can be described in terms of the 5Vs described by Zikopoulos and Eaton (2011) and Lomotey and Deters (2014). Data from sensors like accelerometers or acoustic sensors can be acquired at a velocity of tens of thousands of samples per second per each measuring point. Having hundreds or thousands of those points, a big volume of data is being produced. Some maintenance related data are structured while some are not, such as free text comments for performed maintenance actions or failure reports. Moreover, data from different systems are in different formats. This is the source of variety of data in asset management. This data has potential value when properly employed in asset management, but in order to achieve this, there is a need to assess and manage the veracity of the data, i.e. the data uncertainty. Finally, it is important to understand the value of data, i.e. how data can enable efficiency and effectiveness in maintenance management, for instance for improved decision making, and to choose the most cost-effective means to process the data is important.

Data mining in big asset data can discover knowledge in terms of new patterns and relations not visible at a glance. The big data approach enables incorporation of contextual information in Maintenance Decision Support Systems (Galar et al., 2015). One example of useful knowledge that could be discovered is root cause of failure. This can provide an input for design improvement, as well as for more accurate maintenance planning.

Supporting an effective maintenance decision making process needs a trusted DSS based on knowledge discovery. The process of knowledge discovery will essentially consist of; data acquisition, to obtain relevant data and manage its content; data transition, to communicate the collected data; data fusion, to compile data and information from different sources; data mining, to analyze data to extract information and knowledge; and information extraction and visualization, to support maintenance decision; as shown in Figure 4. Figure 4 illustrates a maintenance decision based on real time data using data fusion and big data analytics and context sensing to get real time decisions and solutions for maintenance problems.

The integration of data, recorded from a multiple-sensor system, together with information from other sources to achieve inferences is known as data fusion (Liggins & Hall, 2017). Data fusion is a prerequisite when handling data from heterogeneous sources or from multiple sensors. Knowledge discovery when applied for maintenance decision support uses eMaintenance concept for integrating the data mining and knowledge discovery. To get the right decision for the context sensing is a must as illustrated in Figure 5. However, development of eMaintenance for industrial application faces a number of challenges which can be categorised into: 1. Organisational; 2. Architectural; 3. Infrastructural; 4. Content and Contextual; and 5. Integration (Karim, et al, 2016). Indeed, big data in O&M domain utilize the advanced technologies for the predictive analytics and provides decisions based on feasibility.

eMaintenance Solutions and Big Data

The on-going industrial digitalization provides enormous capabilities for railway industry to collect vast amount of data and information, from various processes and data sources such as operation, maintenance, and business processes. However, having accurate data and information available is one the prerequisites in maintenance knowledge discovery. Beside the collecting data and information, another challenge is to understand the patterns and relationships of these data useful and relevant for maintenance decisions. To deal with the challenges arising out of high volume of data generated by railway sector both infra and rolling stock, big data, advanced tools are developed and implemented so that data can be systematically processed into information and facilitate decision making with more information in real time. The concept is captured within the framework of eMaintenance solutions and maintenance analytics as a crucial part of a wider and ambitious concept called the asset management.

Figure 4. A generic maintenance information process

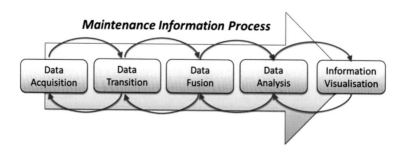

Figure 5. eMaintenance solution

Since there is no standard definition we define eMaintenance as a concept that connects all the stake holders, integrates their requirements and facilitates optimal decision making on demand or in real time to deliver the planned and expected function and services from the assets and minimizes the total business risks.

eMaintenance Challenges

e-Maintenance is the facilitator of the O&M processes by the means of ICT solutions and especially big data analytics. Indeed eMaintenance is the adaptation of big data analytics for O&M due to the special characteristics of this process, vey uncommon and entirely different from health, banking, etc.

It represents services that are aimed for managing maintenance-related information. The e-Maintenance services can be utilized during all system lifecycle phases for different purposes, such as maintenance preparation, execution, assessment and also knowledge management. Hence, it is believed that a proper eMaintenance solution should be approached from a holistic perspective. Its design should be based on appropriate strategies, methodologies and technologies (e.g., service-orientation). To identify them, however, is a very challenging task. Some of the challenges to be met are the following: Organizational challenges mainly focus on aspects related enterprise resource management. Examples of these challenges are: 1. restructuring of the organizations involved in maintenance; 2. planning of resources (e.g. material, spare-part); 3. information management; 4. knowledge management; and 5. management of heterogeneous organizations.

Architectural challenges deal with issues related to the overall architecture of eMaintenance solutions. Some of these challenges are: 1. development of a framework for development of eMaintenance; 2. development of models for decentralized data processing and analysis; 3. development of service model for decentralized data analysis; 4. development of model based prognostic tools; 5. development of model aimed for data and information visualization to support Human-Machine Interaction; and 6. development of model aimed for distributed data storage capability.

Infrastructural challenges address with issues related to provision of necessary technologies and tools that are required to meet needs and requirements when services, according to SOA, are developed, implemented and managed in an enterprise. Example of these are: 1. network infra-structure (e.g. wired and wireless); 2. authentication of services and users; 3. authorization of services and users; 4) safety and security mechanism; 5. maintainability of eMaintenance services; 6. availability performance management; and tracing and tracking mechanism.; and 7. provision of mechanism aimed for documentation and archiving

Content and contextual challenges are mainly related to data and information provided through the eMaintenance services. Some of these challenges are: 1. provision of appropriate ontology through which

Figure 6. O&M decision process incorporating knowledge discovery by the means of big data

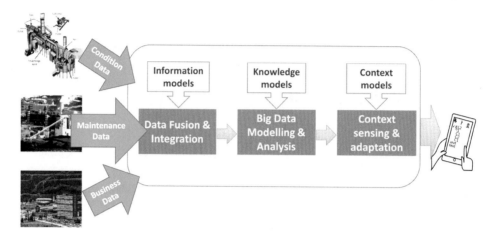

data from data sources (e.g. process data, product data, condition monitoring data, and business data) can smoothly and seamlessly be integrated; 2. provision of quality assurance mechanism that ensures that required data quality is fulfilled and visualized, in order to increase the quality of decision making; 3. mechanism for sensing user's current situation in order to adapt information to user's context; 4. provision of mechanism for describing various context; 5. mechanism to manage uncertainty in data sets; and 6. provision of mechanism for pattern recognition.

Integration challenges address issues related to coordination, orchestration, and integration of services and data managed by the eMaintenance solution. Some of these challenges are related to: 1. management, interaction and interactivity of services; 2. configuration management of eMaintenance services; 3. enablement of integration capability across a multi-platform and technologies.

Big Data Analytics and Knowledge Discovery in O&M

Within O&M, the process of automating the decision support and through knowledge discovery forms important parts of the decision support system looking for failure free operations. The process of knowledge discovery will essentially consist of: data acquisition from intelligent devices, to obtain relevant data and manage its content; data transition, to communicate the collected data; data fusion, to compile data and information from different sources; data mining, to analyses data to extract information and knowledge; and information extraction and visualization, to support maintenance decision in real time.

Data mining in big asset data can discover knowledge in terms of new patterns and relations not visible at a glance. The big data approach enables incorporation of contextual information in Maintenance Decision Support Systems (Galar et al., 2015). Conceptually, KDD refers to a multiple step process that can be highly interactive and iterative in the following (Fayyad & Uthurusamy, 1995; Wang, 1997).

Artificial intelligent techniques have advanced knowledge management, including knowledge acquisition, knowledge repositories, knowledge discovery, and knowledge distribution. Knowledge acquisition captures tacit and explicit knowledge from domain experts, while knowledge repositories formalize the outcomes of knowledge acquisition and integrate knowledge in distributed corporate environments. Knowledge discovery and mining approaches explore relationships and trends in the knowledge repositories to create new knowledge (Le et al., 2016).

In data integration, multiple sources or multiple data types can be integrated. By integrating multiple sources of the same data type, it is possible to compare parameters and by that retrieve an indication on the quality of the data, integrating multiple data types enables a more thorough analysis utilizing the relation between the data types and their behavior. The last step, Data visualization, is the interface between the user and the cloud by the means of web service (Figure 7).

This includes any interaction from the user. As previously mentioned, this turns into quite a complex task due to the varying character of the customers and their users. The information to visualize and the relevancy in the information will differ a lot depending on customer characteristics

Expectations From Big Data Analytics in O&M Domain Analytics

The on-going industrial digitalization provides enormous capabilities for industry to collect vast amount of data and information i.e. railway Big Data, from various processes and data sources such as operation, maintenance, and business processes. However, having accurate data and information available is one the prerequisites in maintenance knowledge discovery. Beside the collecting data and information, another puzzle is to understand the patterns and relationships of these data useful and relevant for maintenance decisions.

Hence, the purpose of big data in O&M for railways is provide analytics which aim to facilitate operation and maintenance actions through enhanced understanding of data and information. These analytics focus in new knowledge discovery addressing the process of discovery, understanding, and communication of maintenance data from four time-related perspectives. These time related perspective match with the determination of the past, present and future state, summarized by Gartner (2012) in four questions, as it can be seen in Figure 8. What happened, why it happened, what will happen and how can we make it happen are the issues involving the determination of the state of an asset. The questions are ordered by the value of the information given by each of them, in such a way that the former has the less value and the latter the higher value. Nevertheless, obtaining this valuable information requires more and more resources as the difficulty to achieve the goals proposed by the questions is higher. The last question will be in the spotlight in the coming future in order to decide how to take advantage of a

Figure 7. Interface between the user and the cloud

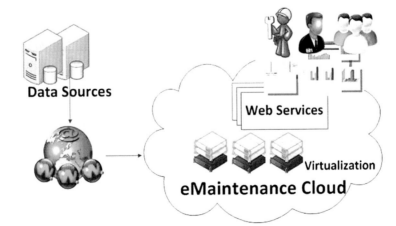

Figure 8. The way to prescriptive analysis
Source: Gartner, 2012.

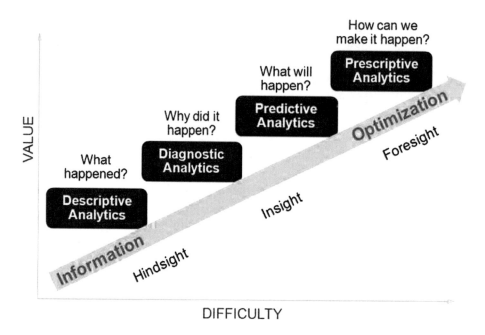

future opportunity or mitigate a future risk, getting information about the implications of each decision option. The selection of the best option, based on some given parameters, will provide a meaningful tool for improving maintenance planning and production scheduling.

- **Descriptive Analytics (Monitoring):** It focuses to discover and describe what happened in the past; and why something happened; In this phase access to data related to system operation, system condition, and expected condition is highly important. Another important aspect in order understand the relationship of events and states during the descriptive analytics is time and time frame associated with each specific log.
- **Diagnostic Analytics:** It explains the possible reasons for faults or failures, i.e., the why question and the where since diagnosis is defined by EN13306 as the fault detection, identification and localization.
- **Predictive Analytics:** It focuses to estimate what will happen in the future; The Maintenance Predictive Analytics phase of MA aims to answer: "What will happen in the future?" but also why will it happen? In this phase, the outcome from 'Descriptive Analytics' is used. Additionally, in this phase, availability of reliability data and maintainability data is necessary beside the data used in descriptive phase. In addition, in order to predict upcoming failure and fault there is a need to provide business data such as planned operation and planned maintenance to this phase.
- **Prescriptive Analytics:** Which addresses what need to be done next. The Prescriptive Analytics phase aims to answer: "What needs to be done?" When dealing with Maintenance Analytics (MA) provision of appropriate information logistics is essential. The main aim of information logistics is to provide just-in-time information to targeted users and optimization of the information supply process, i.e. making the right information available at the right time and at the right point of

location (Heuwinkel et al., 2003; Haseloff, 2005). Solutions for in-formation logistics need to deal with: I) time management, which addresses 'when to deliver'; II) content management, which refers to 'what to deliver'; III) communication management, which refers to 'how to deliver'; IV) con-text management, which addresses 'where and why to deliver' (Heuwinkel et al., 2003; Haseloff, 2005).

Expectations and Challenges of Big Data for Railway O&M

The objective of big data in railways are mostly foreseen as enablers of Big Data technologies in the fields of predictive algorithms from heterogeneous data sources, scalable data structures, real-time communications and visualizations techniques. This fundamental research is challenging in a sector such as the infrastructure assets maintenance and specifically to the railway environment in three different areas: railway system component degradation prediction modelling, railway infrastructure and vehicle maintenance cost prediction modelling, and infrastructure and vehicle condition monitoring.

Specifically, the objectives of the Big Data in railways follow these points:

- Real time predictive algorithms from heterogeneous data sources that will cope with privacy preserved processing, feature and instance selection, discretization, data compression, ensemble classifiers and regression models, and spatial and temporal alignment of data.
- Scalable data structures based on cross-domain data sources acquisition by means of a virtualization layer between data acquisition process and data analytics. This also includes new solutions that combine new databases capabilities to integrate heterogeneous data sources on a high-performance accessing system based on Cloud.
- Enabling Big Data Communications by means of open interface gateways with monitoring systems providing timestamp and position synchronization, heterogeneous communication support, including mobility and aggregation, and priority protocols for real-time transmission of information.
- Application of visualization techniques of info graphics and virtual/augmented reality (see Figure 9).

THE POSITIVE EFFECTS OF BIG DATA ANALYTICS ON THE RAIL-WAY TRANSPORTATION SYSTEM

This section discusses on how big data analytics can overcome organizational, operational and technical complexities in railway industries. The economic and human being effects are organizational effects, but it would be good to highlight effects on the information handling too.

Effects on Technology

Currently deployed Traffic Management Systems (TMS) are combinations of various sub-systems with limited integration and non-standardised interfaces and display rules. In this scenario, the dramatic change will come in the way of a seamless, fully-automated TMS enabling integration with railway related services and other modes of transport.

Figure 9. Application of visualization techniques of info graphics and virtual/augmented reality

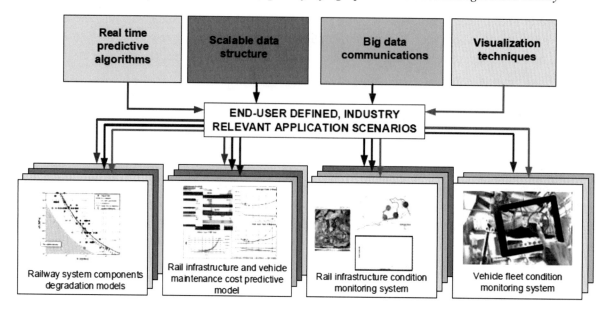

However, the disparate number and nature of current transportation assets with distributed non-integrated and non-standardised asset registers makes the integration of data sources extremely difficult and therefore the network asset status information cannot be widely understood or exploited to inform TMS decision making (Galar, et al. 2012). Even more challenging is the integration with other information domains like maintenance related services, energy resources etc., which must be done manually. In summary operation and maintenance are completely disconnected in terms of incoming data sources and further decision making (Parida, et al. 2011).

For this purpose, new 'Business Intelligence' (BI) approaches from other sectors where success is already proven may provide Big data analytics as a technology trigger in order to harmonize and create single sources of data with accepted, adopted and exportable taxonomies and ontologies cross over infrastructure managers, contractors and service providers (Thaduri, et al, 2014). It is relevant to mention the need of 'Big data' approach to diverse sources of information and create new services based on the ontologies exploited and therefore knowledge discovery performed (Baglee, et al. 2014). This adoption of BI and Big data may pave the ground for a real Operation and Maintenance policy in transportation bridging the gap between them.

In fact, all these new O&M services lead to a common Achiles heel in asset management and specifically in transportation: a better assets status forecasting, commonly called prognosis. The estimation of the remaining useful life constitutes the basis for any operation or maintenance service in order to check the probability of mission accomplishment by the asset (Galar et al., 2012). The figure 10 below shows a common scenario where a vehicle merges its status with the infrastructure condition in order to forecast the asset condition and verify the user scenario selected in the onboard computer. The analytics are expected to provide relevant info regarding the probability of getting the desired destination according to the current condition of the car and other information sources like road condition weather etc. Relevant information regarding maintenance planning, spare parts and inspection may be provided as well and sent to the closest workshops.

Effects on Operations

Big data will enable a more automated, interoperable, interconnected and advanced traffic management systems; scalable and upgradable systems, utilising standardised products and interfaces, enabling easy migration from legacy systems; the wealth of data and information on assets and traffic status; information management systems adding the capability of nowcasting and forecasting of critical asset statuses. Indeed, the positive effects of forecasting asset status don´t provide benefits just for maintenance planning but also for traffic management.

Therefore, one of the main advantages of Big data in railways will be the improvement of the traffic operation and management by the means of side benefits also gotten with the deployment big data analytics such as:

- A standardised approach to information management and dispatching system enabling an integrated Traffic Management System (TMS).
- An Information and Communication Technology (ICT) environment supporting all transport operational systems with standardised interfaces and with a plug and play framework for TMS applications.
- An advanced asset information system with the ability to 'nowcast' and forecast network asset statuses with the associated uncertainties from heterogeneous data sources.

Figure 10. Big data applied in railway transportation as a fusion of vehicles and infrastructure sources

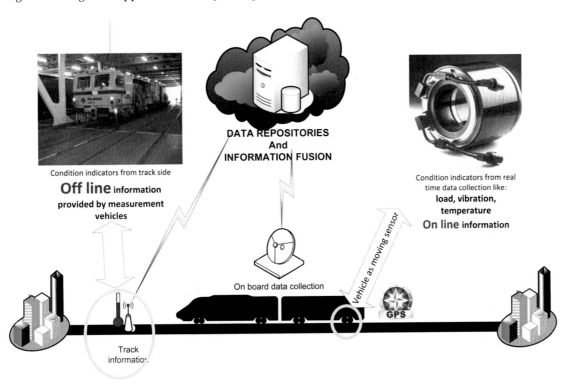

For these reasons, a transportation system with big data analytics capabilities should be able to provide advanced automated, interoperable and interconnected; scalable and upgradable traffic management systems. All these goals will be achieved utilizing standardized products and interfaces enables easy migration from legacy systems since big data is expected to have a smooth transition from earlier attempts, failed initiatives and proprietary systems. The new traffic service that is based on the prognosis is shown in Figure 11.

Organizational Effects (Effects on Economy and Human Beings)

Big data in railway will contribute to achieve the objectives of the Transport White Paper. In this document EU members state that "Transport is fundamental to our economy and society. Mobility is vital for the internal market and for the quality of life of citizens as they enjoy their freedom to travel. Transport enables economic growth and job creation: it must be sustainable in the light of the new challenges we face. Transport is global, so effective action requires strong international cooperation".

Considering that many European companies are world leaders in infrastructure, logistics, and traffic management systems and manufacturing of transport equipment – but as other world regions are launching huge, ambitious transport modernization and infrastructure investment programs, it is crucial that European transport continues to develop and invest to maintain its competitive position. For this purpose, a sustainable maintenance of the infrastructure and the vehicles is a "must" as a crucial tool in the European agenda.

Figure 11. New O&M services provided by prognosis in railway big data context

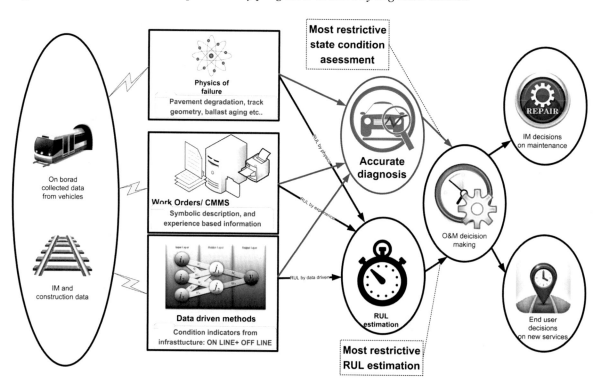

Therefore, big data analytics in railway will provide specific benefits as follows:

- **Long-Term Needs and Socio-Economic Growth:** Big data will develop common methodology for improving infrastructure capacity, safety and environmental impacts.
- **Smarter Railway Processes:** SMARTness in transportation is closely related to operation and maintenance methodologies aiming for self-configuration, self-maintenance and self-repair systems in order to maximize capacity and utilization of the assets minimizing shutdowns. Therefore instrumented, interconnected and intelligent assets will be maintained in a very different way from traditional policies.
- **System Integration, Safety, and Interoperability:** New O&M policies by the means of big data outcomes will provide open cross borders with higher interoperability by the means of harmonization in RAMS analysis and calculations, increased safety as a consequence of increased reliability, and finally a common way to integrate systems creating complex assets as system of systems but in such a way that reliability is not affected by the complexity along the international corridors.

Last but not least, the potential benefits of Big data analytics in Energy and sustainability for the railway domain are not disregard. It is already proven that better O&M reduces energy consumption and therefor improves the carbon fingerprint of the assets both rolling stock and infrastructure, thus big data in railway will optimize operation and maintenance methodologies in a holistic approach, considering the entire life cycle of the asset in a cradle to grave approach and contributing to the sustainability of the transportation system in a significant way.

REFERENCES

Amadi-Echendu, J. E., Brown, K., Willett, R., & Mathew, J. (Eds.). (2010). Definitions, concepts and scope of engineering asset management. In Engineering Asset Management Review (Vol. 1). Springer. doi:10.1007/978-1-84996-178-3

Baglee, D., & Marttonen, S. (2014, January). The need for Big Data collection and analyses to support the development of an advanced maintenance strategy. In *Proceedings of the International Conference on Data Mining (DMIN)* (p. 3). The Steering Committee of The World Congress in Computer Science, Computer Engineering and Applied Computing (WorldComp).

Galar, D., Kans, M., & Schmidt, B. (2016). Big Data in Asset Management: Knowledge Discovery in Asset Data by the Means of Data Mining. In *Proceedings of the 10th World Congress on Engineering Asset Management (WCEAM '15)* (pp. 161-171). Springer International Publishing. doi:10.1007/978-3-319-27064-7_16

Galar, D., Palo, M., Van Horenbeek, A., & Pintelon, L. (2012). Integration of disparate data sources to perform maintenance prognosis and optimal decision making. Insight-non-destructive testing and condition monitoring, 54(8), 440-445.

Galar, D., Thaduri, A., Catelani, M., & Ciani, L. (2015). Context awareness for maintenance decision making: A diagnosis and prognosis approach. *Measurement, 67*, 137–150. doi:10.1016/j.measurement.2015.01.015

Gartner. (n. d.). Gartner IT Glossary. Retrieved from http://www.gartner.com/it-glossary/big-data/

Haseloff, S. (2005). Context awareness in information logistics.

Heuwinkel, K., Deiters, W., Konigsmann, T., & Loffeler, T. (2003, May). Information logistics and wearable computing. In *Proceedings of the 23rd International Conference on Distributed Computing Systems Workshops* (pp. 283-288). IEEE. doi:10.1109/ICDCSW.2003.1203568

Hipkin, I. (2001). Knowledge and IS implementation: Case studies in physical asset management. *International Journal of Operations & Production Management*, 21(10), 1358–1380. doi:10.1108/01443570110404763

Hirsch, M., Opresnik, D., Zanetti, C., & Taisch, M. (2013, September). Leveraging Assets as a Service for Business Intelligence in Manufacturing Service Ecosystems. In *Proceedings of the 2013 IEEE 10th International Conference on e-Business Engineering (ICEBE)* (pp. 162-167). IEEE. doi:10.1109/ICEBE.2013.25

Ingwald, A., & Kans, M. (2016). Service management models for railway infrastructure, an ecosystem perspective. In *Proceedings of the 10th World Congress on Engineering Asset Management (WCEAM '15)* (pp. 289-303). Springer International Publishing. doi:10.1007/978-3-319-27064-7_28

Kans, M., & Ingwald, A. (2016). Business Model Development Towards Service Management 4.0. Procedia CIRP, 47, 489-494.

Karim, R., Westerberg, J., Galar, D., & Kumar, U. (2016). Maintenance Analytics–The New Know in Maintenance. *IFAC-PapersOnLine*, 49(28), 214–219. doi:10.1016/j.ifacol.2016.11.037

Khosrowshahi, F., Ghodous, P., & Sarshar, M. (2014). Visualization of the modeled degradation of building flooring systems in building maintenance. *Computer-Aided Civil and Infrastructure Engineering*, 29(1), 18–30. doi:10.1111/mice.12029

Kroll, B., Schaffranek, D., Schriegel, S., & Niggemann, O. (2014, September). System modeling based on machine learning for anomaly detection and predictive maintenance in industrial plants. In Proceedings of 2014 IEEE Emerging Technology and Factory Automation (ETFA) (pp. 1-7). IEEE doi:10.1109/ETFA.2014.7005202

Landscheidt, S., & Kans, M. (2016). Method for Assessing the Total Cost of Ownership of Industrial Robots. *Procedia CIRP*, 57, 746–751. doi:10.1016/j.procir.2016.11.129

Le, T., & Jeong, H. D. (2016). Interlinking life-cycle data spaces to support decision making in highway asset management. *Automation in Construction*, 64, 54–64. doi:10.1016/j.autcon.2015.12.016

Lee, J., Kao, H. A., & Yang, S. (2014). Service innovation and smart analytics for industry 4.0 and big data environment. Procedia CIRP, 16, 3-8.

Liggins, M. II, Hall, D., & Llinas, J. (Eds.). (2017). *Handbook of multisensor data fusion: theory and practice*. CRC press.

Lomotey, R. K., & Deters, R. (2014, April). Towards knowledge discovery in big data. In *Proceedings of the 2014 IEEE 8th International Symposium on Service Oriented System Engineering (SOSE)* (pp. 181-191). IEEE. doi:10.1109/SOSE.2014.25

Lutchman, R. (2006). Sustainable asset management: linking assets, people, and processes for results. DEStech Publications, Inc.

Meier, H., Roy, R., & Seliger, G. (2010). Industrial product-service systems—IPS 2. *CIRP Annals-Manufacturing Technology, 59*(2), 607–627. doi:10.1016/j.cirp.2010.05.004

Michalos, G., Sipsas, P., Makris, S., & Chryssolouris, G. (2016). Decision making logic for flexible assembly lines reconfiguration. *Robotics and Computer-integrated Manufacturing, 37*, 233–250. doi:10.1016/j.rcim.2015.04.006

Moore, J. F. (1993). Predators and prey: A new ecology of competition. *Harvard Business Review, 71*(3), 75–83. PMID:10126156

Niekamp, S., Bharadwaj, U. R., Sadhukhan, J., & Chryssanthopoulos, M. K. (2015). A multi-criteria decision support framework for sustainable asset management and challenges in its application. *Journal of Industrial and Production Engineering, 32*(1), 23–36. doi:10.1080/21681015.2014.1000401

Olsson, N. O., & Bull-Berg, H. (2015). Use of big data in project evaluations. *International Journal of Managing Projects in Business, 8*(3), 491–512. doi:10.1108/IJMPB-09-2014-0063

Park, S., Park, S. I., & Lee, S. H. (2016). Strategy on sustainable infrastructure asset management: Focus on Korea′s future policy directivity. *Renewable & Sustainable Energy Reviews, 62*, 710–722. doi:10.1016/j.rser.2016.04.073

Penna, R., Amaral, M., Espíndola, D., Botelho, S., Duarte, N., Pereira, C. E., . . . Frazzon, E. M. (2014, July). Visualization tool for cyber-physical maintenance systems. In *Proceedings of the 2014 12th IEEE International Conference on Industrial Informatics (INDIN)* (pp. 566-571). IEEE. doi:10.1109/INDIN.2014.6945575

Perko, I., & Ototsky, P. (2016). Big Data for Business Ecosystem Players. *Naše gospodarstvo [Our economy], 62*(2), 12-24.

Rong, K., Hu, G., Lin, Y., Shi, Y., & Guo, L. (2015). Understanding business ecosystem using a 6C framework in Internet-of-Things-based sectors. *International Journal of Production Economics, 159*, 41–55. doi:10.1016/j.ijpe.2014.09.003

Sankavaram, C., Kodali, A., & Pattipati, K. (2013, January). An integrated health management process for automotive cyber-physical systems. In *Proceedings of the 2013 International Conference on Computing, Networking and Communications (ICNC)* (pp. 82-86). IEEE. doi:10.1109/ICCNC.2013.6504058

SIS, SS-ISO 55000:2014, Asset management – Overview, principles and terminology. (2014).

Syed, B., Pal, A., Srinivasarengan, K., & Balamuralidhar, P. (2012, December). A smart transport application of cyber-physical systems: Road surface monitoring with mobile devices. In *Proceedings of the 2012 Sixth International Conference on Sensing Technology (ICST)* (pp. 8-12). IEEE.

Taneja, J., Katz, R., & Culler, D. (2012, April). Defining cps challenges in a sustainable electricity grid. In *Proceedings of the 2012 IEEE/ACM Third International Conference on Cyber-Physical Systems (IC-CPS)* (pp. 119-128). IEEE. doi:10.1109/ICCPS.2012.20

Thaduri, A., Galar, D., & Kans, M. (2016). Maintenance 4.0 in Railway Transportation Industry. In *Proceedings of the 10th World Congress on Engineering Asset Management (WCEAM '15)* (pp. 317-331). Springer International Publishing.

Tiddens, W. W., Braaksma, A. J. J., & Tinga, T. (2015). The adoption of prognostic technologies in maintenance decision making: A multiple case study. *Procedia CIRP*, *38*, 171–176. doi:10.1016/j.procir.2015.08.028

Wang, G., Gunasekaran, A., Ngai, E. W., & Papadopoulos, T. (2016). Big data analytics in logistics and supply chain management: Certain investigations for research and applications. *International Journal of Production Economics*, *176*, 98–110. doi:10.1016/j.ijpe.2016.03.014

Whyte, J., Stasis, A., & Lindkvist, C. (2016). Managing change in the delivery of complex projects: Configuration management, asset information and big data. *International Journal of Project Management*, *34*(2), 339–351. doi:10.1016/j.ijproman.2015.02.006

Zikopoulos, P., & Eaton, C. (2011). *Understanding big data: Analytics for enterprise class hadoop and streaming data*. McGraw-Hill Osborne Media.

Chapter 2
Blockchains:
A Distributed Data Ledger for the Rail Industry

John M. Easton
University of Birmingham, UK

ABSTRACT

In recent years, the UK railway industry has struggled with the effects of poor integration of data across ICT systems, particularly when that data is being used across organizational boundaries. Technical progress is being made by the industry towards enabling data sharing, but an open issue remains around how the costs of gathering and maintaining pooled information can be fairly attributed across the stakeholders who draw on that shared resource. This issue is particularly significant in areas such as Remote Condition Monitoring, where the ability to analyse the network at a whole-systems level is being blocked by the business cases around the purchase of systems as silos. Blockchains are an emerging technology that have the potential to revolutionize the management of transactions in a number of industrial sectors. This chapter will address the outstanding issues around the fair attribution of costs and benefits of data sharing in the rail industry by proposing blockchains as a forth enabler of the rail data revolution, alongside ESB, ontology, and open data.

INTRODUCTION

In recent years, many railways worldwide have undergone a revival, with growth in passenger numbers driven by factors such as traffic congestion, and a desire to work during travel time. The United Kingdom's railway network is the oldest in the world, and has been steadily growing in popularity; between the years of 1991 and 2011 passenger numbers across the network rose by 67% (Office of Rail Regulation, 2011). This significant growth in demand for rail travel has put pressure on the industry to make better use of the available capacity on the rail network; however, with changes to the underlying physical infrastructure being both disruptive and hugely costly, the industry is being forced to consider alternative approaches to generating the additional capacity required.

DOI: 10.4018/978-1-5225-3176-0.ch002

One option that is being actively pursued is the greater use of digital technologies in support of railway operations. It is hoped that through digitization of the railway, and the introduction of improved information-driven alternatives to current traffic management, signaling, and maintenance systems, the industry will be able to support up to one billion extra passenger journeys per year by 2030 (Digital Railway, 2017).

This chapter will examine the issues around the digital revolution in UK rail, with a particular focus on the dual challenges of poor integration of information, and the mechanisms by which costs may be equitably distributed around the various stakeholders in the industry for the collection, maintenance, and distribution of data used for the benefit of other parties. The chapter will begin by explaining the challenge facing the industry, before moving on to propose a solution in the form of blockchains, the distributed ledger technology that underpins the cryptocurrency Bitcoin. Finally, the chapter will conclude with a discussion of some of the outstanding issues posed by the work, and the enabling steps that will need to take place so that the industry is ready to take advantage of the technology when it reaches mainstream implementation, expected to be in around five to ten years' time (Gartner Inc., 2016).

Background

In recent years, the UK railway industry has struggled with the effects of poor integration of data across Information and Communications Technology (ICT) systems, particularly when that data is being used across organizational boundaries. The problem is far from unique to rail, and has been seen globally in many other infrastructure-led sectors; the National Institute of Science and Technology in the US has reported that in 2002 alone the US capital facilities industry could have saved around $15.8 billion (1% - 2% of annual revenue) through improved information interoperability (Gallaher, O'Conor, Dettbarn, & Gilday, 2004). Translated into the context of the UK railways this would amount to potential savings of between £82 million and £164 million for the financial year 2013 – 2014 (Tutcher, Easton, & Roberts, 2017).

To illustrate the scale of the problem facing the rail industry, consider Figure 1. Figure 1 shows the subset of shared information systems, not owned or operated by Network Rail (the infrastructure manager), used by stakeholders in the UK rail industry. The figure has been produced based on data from the 2015 update of the National Information Systems catalogue, originally released in 2011 by the Rail Safety and Standards Board (Brewer, 2011). In the figure individual ICT systems, represented by vertices, are divided into classes by function and labeled by color; crime and security related systems in green, customer / commercial systems in yellow, operational systems in red, planning in purple, rolling stock in grey, safety in orange, and supply chain and R&D systems in cyan. The arcs linking the systems denote data interfaces between them, and these are also colored; manual interfaces (requiring human data entry) are shown in red, interfaces based on the download and subsequent upload of a file are shown in blue, and fully automated interfaces are shown in green. The nature of interfaces shown in grey was unknown at time of preparation of the figure.

The complex web of interactions between systems shown in Figure 1 is typical of railway systems across Europe, and is an inevitable product of the business environment in which the systems developed. The nationalised railways of the 1960s, 70s, and 80s, meant that the very early ICT systems used to manage railway operations were, quite naturally, developed to work in the context of vertically-integrated railway systems. As the railways began to become privatised in the early 1990s, these vertically integrated architectural models persisted for legacy systems (and the updates to them), but newer ICT systems and

Figure 1. The shared information systems, not owned by Network Rail, used by the UK rail industry
Derived from the UK National Information Systems Catalogue for non-Network Rail Systems, 2015 release.

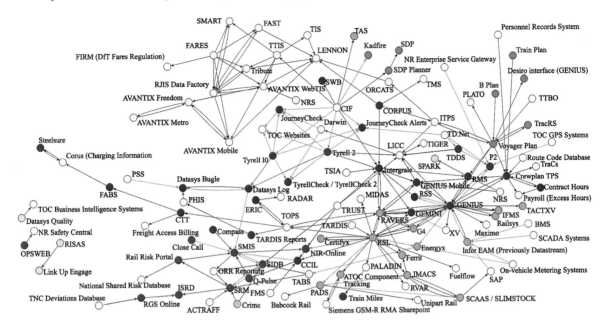

particularly those being developed for information exchange over the web, began to be specified and procured in-house by individual stakeholders, a move that led to a proliferation of similar ICT platforms across the wider industry. Data began to be drawn from second and third hand sources, usually due to ease of access within an organisation or as a result of additional local annotations, and this led to the formation of the web of interconnected platforms we see today.

By 2011, the issue of poor integration between ICT systems in UK rail had become so pronounced that a government funded review of the value for money offered by the industry found that:

The effectiveness of the industry's Information Systems is inhibited by a suite of legacy systems that are expensive to run, unable to communicate with new technology and encourage users to develop a wide range of bespoke local systems to overcome limitations. Many legacy systems were created and managed in company silos, with only a few systems crossing industry boundaries (McNulty, 2011)

The industry response to the report's findings was swift, and a year later it published a national strategy document, the Rail Technical Strategy (RTS), which envisaged a future where:

The businesses in the industry are information-rich and use that information effectively to enhance and drive decision-making processes. Advanced and appropriate decision support tools are in place and in use on a daily basis. … The industry realizes the value of its data for customer and internal purposes and improves its costs, attractiveness and performance as a consequence (TSLG, 2012)

Since the publication of the RTS in 2012, the UK rail industry has been steadily working towards the implementation of these goals. Drawing from a combination of best practice in modern ICT system design, the outcomes of nationally and European-funded research projects with an interest in system architecture e.g. InteGRail (Shingler, Fadin, & Umiliacchi, 2008), ON-TIME (Albrecht & Dasigi, 2016), Capacity4Rail (Schmitt, Létourneaux, De Keyzer, & Crompton, 2016), and IN2RAIL (Zanella & Pinasco, 2016), and programs specifically designed to support the digitalization of the industry e.g. the cross-industry Digital Railway program, the groundwork has been laid for a number of key technical enablers. These have included steps towards the creation of an Enterprise Service Bus (ESB) to ease the movement of data between systems while minimizing the number of interfaces, the development of rail industry ontologies to ensure data content is maintained across system boundaries, and the provision of public open data feeds that enable third-party application developers to support passengers through innovative new services.

As progress has been made towards the delivery of technical solutions to the problems of data integration in UK rail, other, less tangible issues have been brought to the fore. Key amongst these is the question of how, once the industry has the ability make its data ubiquitously available, the costs of gathering and maintaining pooled information can be fairly attributed across the stakeholders who draw on that shared resource. In areas where this issue is particularly sensitive, such as the provision of effective cross-industry Remote Condition Monitoring (RCM) systems, detailed work on the development of contractual frameworks that support the creation of business cases for this type of data sharing has already taken place e.g. RSSB's T1010 project (Newcombe & Tucker, 2016); however, further technical work is needed to realize the benefits inherent to these approaches.

Supporting the Equitable Distribution of Cross-Industry Data Costs in the Digital Railway

This chapter will attempt to resolve the outstanding issues around the fair attribution of costs and benefits of data sharing in the rail industry by proposing a forth enabler of the rail data revolution, blockchains. Sitting alongside the technical work already in progress within the industry on ESB, ontology, and linked open data, and supporting the contractual frameworks being developed by groups such as RSSB, blockchains will serve as a non-volatile, permanent record of data transactions, allowing the accurate, automated attribution of fair payments to individual stakeholders, based on the utilization of data they are gathering by the industry, and the value of any derived information. The discussion will be framed around the cross-industry RCM problem, however, the tools proposed should be equally valuable in any data sharing scenario involving multiple stakeholders within or external to the industries boundaries.

The Problem of Cross-Industry Remote Condition Monitoring

Remote Condition Monitoring is now a well-understood concept in the rail industry worldwide, and specific use cases, such as the instrumentation of points to predict upcoming failures, have become commodity systems for Infrastructure Managers. Despite this, it is still common for systems to be specified and purchased as stand-alone installations rather than as part of a wider ecosystem of sensors, making it difficult to combine the results from multiple monitoring systems. This stems from an underlying difficultly with forming a business case around the benefits of interfaces for the integration of RCM data with other systems, particularly when the beneficiary of that integration is likely to be a different stakeholder in the industry.

The problems of a lack of information integration are particularly evident in use cases where data from sensors installed on vehicles are being used to measure the condition of trackside infrastructure and *vice-versa*. A good example of this can be found in the case of on-bogie inertial measurement systems; track geometry measurements are usually taken by specialist measurement trains fitted with high-accuracy, safety critical equipment capable of obtaining absolute positions for any measurements. Running these trains requires the booking of dedicated train paths (preventing those paths from being used by passenger and freight services), and the measurement services themselves do not generate revenue. Because of this, detailed measurements of the track are only taken at relatively long intervals, ranging from periods of weeks on busy routes, to months or even annually on less well utilized tracks.

Inertial measurement equipment mounted on the bogies of passenger services has the potential to provide useful low-resolution monitoring of the degradation in asset condition between the safety-critical asset inspections; this would enable maintenance to be better planned, and potentially avoid the need to introduce emergency speed restrictions on the section of line, saving the industry money, and ensuring that passengers arrive at their destinations on time. However, the business case for this work would need to allow for equipment installation costs on-vehicle (which would fall to the owner of the vehicle, in the UK this would be one of the Rolling Stock Operating Companies, or ROSCOs), and maintenance costs (these would rest with the Train Operating Company, or TOC), for a benefit in terms of reduced delay charges to the Infrastructure Manager, who in the scenario outlined would not yet have directly incurred any of the costs. Further confusing this situation are operational and contractual issues around short franchise periods for some TOCs, making it difficult to ensure pay-back on investment even if fees are levied for the upkeep of equipment, and the remaining lifespan of some older rolling stock, which may mean upgrades would not be cost-effective for ROSCOs.

Rail is far from unique in terms of the difficulties it has leveraging full value from its sensor installations. Indeed, the clear majority of industrial sensors are specifically deployed for use in the context of a single application, and within a closed network (Wörner & von Bomhard, 2014). This is in stark contrast to the vision of an "Internet of Things", where smart devices produce data that can be used by stakeholders to build up a more holistic vision of a physical system operating at scale.

The Industry Response to the Data Integration Challenge

The rail industry is aware of the challenge it faces around the integration of data across stakeholders, and from the technical perspective the groundwork has already been laid for future solutions. In the operations arena for example, the industry is looking towards the inclusion of live RCM data in the traffic management process. This will enable traffic management systems to predict when assets are likely to fail, isolate the routes that the failure will block, and automatically re-plan the working timetable to minimize the disruption caused. To that end, European research work in projects including ON-TIME (Albrecht & Dasigi, 2016), Capacity4Rail (Schmitt et al., 2016) and IN2RAIL (Zanella & Pinasco, 2016), has proposed the use of Enterprise Service Bus architectures for future railway traffic management platforms, enabling systems and services contributing data to communicate via a single common message bus, rather than via a large number of dedicated point-to-point interfaces.

Alongside the work on connecting systems, a focus has also been placed on handing the description of the data itself with work on semantic data models for the rail industry, originally begun over a decade ago by the InteGRail project (Shingler et al., 2008), finally being adopted. These ontology models are currently expected to be ready for use in the UK during Control Period 6, between 2020 and 2025 (Network Rail Limited, 2013). The addition of contextual information by data models such as ontologies gives a number of benefits in large-scale IT systems, first and foremost amongst these is the ability to encode business logic as rules within the models, allowing data conversions to be performed on the fly as data is requested, and decoupling that logic from the applications using the data resources (Tutcher et al., 2017). Further to this, the models help support the provision of data to third parties as four or five star linked open data, the gold standard from data provision on the semantic web.

Moving into the business and contractual arena, the Rail Safety and Standards Board has done a significant amount of work within the T1010 project into contractual frameworks that can begin to support business cases for cross-industry RCM systems (Newcombe & Tucker, 2016). Here, the team have begun to capture the organizational relationships between the various stakeholders involved in the purchase and operation of such systems, and outlined the provisions that should be considered when drawing up contracts between them. A toolkit has also been produced that guides industry stakeholders through the process.

The projects and initiatives discussed above show the extent to which the UK rail industry is actively working to solve the cross-industry RCM data problem. The approaches being developed are impacting on the problem from both the implementational and contractual perspectives, but before they meet in the middle and form an overall solution, a bridge between the two will be needed. This bridge must be able to implement the contractual provisions laid out by projects such as T1010, and do so within the technical constraints specified by IN2RAIL, the Digital Railway program, and others. In this work, we propose that this bridging technology should be the blockchain.

A DISTRIBUTED DATA LEDGER FOR THE RAIL INDUSTRY

What Are Blockchains?

Blockchains are an emerging technology that have the potential to revolutionize the management of transactions in a number of industrial sectors. Originally used as the basis for the cryptocurrency Bitcoin (Nakamoto, 2008), blockchains are virtual ledgers that can be used to record transactions between the actors in a complex system, and allow audits to take place on those operations. Transactions between actors, who are uniquely identified using public-key cryptography, are grouped together and recorded in blocks each of which is identified by a hash value. The blocks are then linked together to form a chain of events over time. Before a new block can be added to the chain, two things must happen – firstly, the transaction must be verified by another party in the network using the public keys in the ledger (this provides proof that the sender currently owns the resource being transferred), and secondly a new, valid hash must be formed for the new block. This is done competitively by the other actors in the network with the first to form a valid hash receiving recompense for the work done, and ensures that the validating party is not always the first actor to respond to the request – an important security feature that prevents collusion between senders and verifiers (Witte, 2016). This process is known as mining.

Blockchains are decentralised with the entire non-volatile chain replicated on every server in the network; the majority of parties within the network (according to a definition of majority defined by the specific implementation) must accept a new transaction for the chain it forms to be valid, a fact that is inherent in the longest chain currently existing in the network being retained (Milani, García-Bañuelos, & Dumas, 2016), and as a result blockchains are not subject to overall control by any single party (Brandon,

2016). As a direct result of their distributed nature, blockchains, once started, are very difficult to disrupt and so provide a resilient, scalable basis for recording the exchange of resources between stakeholders.

Blockchains may be public (open for all to join), or private (only open to those on a whitelist). While there are savings in computational overheads to be gained from an open chain, in the first instance at least it is likely that the security requirements industry would drive any vendor towards a private blockchain solution.

A key feature that differentiates blockchains from other ledger-based systems, is the lack of explicit trust either between the parties involved in the transaction, or in the form of a centralized "trusted" authority or regulator. Instead, a combination of the open, non-volatile record provided by the blockchain itself, and the cryptographic security provided by the signing of transactions with unique keys, means that "trust" within a blockchain is inherent to the interests of the majority of participants in the network. For this reason, the blockchain is expected to be a major stimulus for the Internet of Things (Wörner & von Bomhard, 2014), where potentially huge numbers of data providing sensors, owned by a range of individuals and companies will provide data to users as needed. This situation is of course not dissimilar to the multi-stakeholder environment of the railway industry, and has led insiders to suggest that going forwards RCM of the railway network will increasing just become an "Internet of Railway Things" (IoRT) based on commodity hardware and software.

Smart Contracts

The utility of a blockchain can be further extended by the use of smart contracts. Smart contracts are uniquely addressable scripts that exist within the blockchain, allowing multistep processes to be carried out in much the same way as a stored procedure in a database (Christidis & Devetsikiotis, 2016). A typical example of a smart contract in a railway context might involve Stakeholder A creating a contract with 3 functions; the first function, a deposit function protected by Stakeholder A's private key, would allow money to be added to the contract account. The second function, a trade function that is open to all, would enable a predefined volume and type of data to be "sold" by a stakeholder (Stakeholder B) in exchange for some (or all) of the money already deposited by Stakeholder A, for example "one unit of currency for 3 units of data". The third and final function, again protected by Stakeholder A's private key, would allow the deposited resources to be withdrawn, that is to say it would allow Stakeholder A to recover any remaining money, along with the resources bought from Stakeholder B.

By publishing a smart contract on the blockchain stakeholders can exchange resources with providers they do not know or trust, secure in the knowledge that the transaction record will be permanently recorded in the chain; the only caveat to this is that while a new block is still in the top few entries of the chain, there is a slim chance that the whole blockchain may be replaced by a longer branch from elsewhere in the network, thus it is advisable to wait for an additional four to five blocks to be added to the head of the chain before releasing the goods that have been exchanged.

Similar functionality to that described above, with a blockchain network and smart contracts underpinning the exchange of data between sensors and actors in an IoT ecosystem, has also been proposed in detail by Zhang and Wen (Zhang & Wen, 2017), and in the field of cloud-based manufacturing by Bahga and Madisetti (Bahga & Madisetti, 2016). The latter also includes discussions of many other key industrial functions, such as supply chain management, and how the blockchain can be further leveraged to support these tasks.

Micropayments

Although a virtual currency might work within the core of the industry, the reality of an environment as diverse as rail is that any enabler of cross-industry data will ultimately need to be based on real currency. In recent years, authors have proposed approaches to the commoditization of sensor data based on micropayments (Robert, Kubler, & Traon, 2016). At the time of writing much of this work is still in its infancy, and significant further development is needed before this can be proven to be suitable for leveraging in an industrial context; however, a number of mechanisms for such payments are coming to the marketplace, including several backed by recognized and trusted providers such as VISA and PayPal.

Blockchains as an Enabler of Enhanced Security in the Internet of Things

Security of IoT nodes, particularly in relation to the firmware they are running, is a known issue in the cyber security community. In industrial Cyber Physical Systems (CPS), systems that contain both software control and physical actuation, there is commonly a reluctance on the part of operators to update firmware on remote devices if the current version is believed to be working; this often stems from the risk of introducing a new error into the system with the new firmware, that could lead to a reduction in the availability of the physical asset, however difficulties in managing the update process, and in obtaining up-to-date firmware for older hardware (CPS normally have operating lifetimes measured in decades) also factor in these decisions (Stouffer, Pillitteri, Lightman, Abrams, & Hahn, 2015).

The use of blockchain technology in the management of updates to IoT nodes has been proposed within the literature (Lee & Lee, 2017), and the non-volatile nature of the blockchain does offer strong benefits in this area. In particular, the use of the blockchain to provide validation and integrity checking information on the current version of a device's firmware in a distributed context enables both checking of firmware updates for tampering as they arrive at the IoT device (because the files are subject to verification, they can be distributed by scalable file sharing technologies such as torrenting), and the avoidance of problems caused by expired download URLs over time.

Applications of the Blockchain in Industry

Blockchains are currently enjoying what Gartner Inc. define as "the peak of inflated expectation" (Gartner Inc., 2016), that point in the technology acceptance curve where, thanks to exposure in the popular press and online, many industries are investing in the technology but the inevitable practical limitations have not yet been found. To date, potential applications have been identified in industries as diverse as finance (Collomb & Sok, 2016), healthcare (Azaria, Ekblaw, Vieira, & Lippman, 2016; Irving & Holden, 2016), smart cities and the sharing economy (Biswas & Muthukkumarasamy, 2016; Huckle, Bhattacharya, White, & Beloff, 2016; Sun, Yan, & Zhang, 2016), and the Intelligent Transport System (Yuan & Wang, 2016).

Challenges Facing the Blockchain Community

The permanent nature of blockchain records is, of course, a double-edged sword, with recent research from Germany highlighting one of the more troubling aspects of the technology. In the study, researchers looked at the transactional history of the blockchain underpinning Bitcoin for the period from its launch to July 2016 (Matzutt et al., 2016). Using heuristics designed to detect non-transactional content, they found that around 0.8% of the content was not directly related to transactions, a proportion of which was illegal content of various forms (files, images, software, and links to other material), content which due to the non-volatile nature of the blockchain itself, could now not be deleted. More disturbingly, because the blockchain is designed to be replicated to machines within the network, the illegal content would be distributed to machines owned by innocent users.

Management of Reputation in the Blockchain

One approach to addressing the problem of incorrect or out-of-date data within the blockchain would be to include an element of reputation in the chain, whereby users known to be misusing the system would receive a demerit against their reputation. Such a system has been proposed by Dennis and Owenson (Dennis & Owen, 2015), although at time of writing it is not thought to have been implemented in any of the prototype systems from major cloud providers.

CONCLUSION

In this chapter, RCM data from railway assets has been used as an analogy to support a discussion of how blockchains can serve as the forth enabler of the big data revolution in the rail industry. While the cross-industry exchange of RCM data is an obvious candidate for a trial of the technology within the UK railways, the arguments presented here would apply equally strongly to any scenario where industry data was being gathered by one stakeholder, but then leveraged by another.

The advantages that blockchain offers the industry in the area of data integration across platform boundaries are many and obvious; blockchains will allow rail industry stakeholders to monetize their data assets, to exchange those assets in a way that can be audited by reviewing the transactions records within the blockchain, and to realize the business rules arrived at from work such as RSSBs T1010 project within the framework of the blockchain as smart contracts.

Despite the advantages that the blockchain offers, care will need to be taken to ensure that any roadmap towards adoption is well planned, and undertaken with a view to the risks involved. Although the blockchain is inherently secure over the medium to long-range timeframe the size of the network of machines involved in a blockchain matters, and in practice can have a significant impact on the security and immutability of the chain in the very short term. This is primarily related to the rate at which proof-of-work can be demonstrated – transactions become nearly impossible to change once more than 3 or 4 blocks have been appended to the chain beyond their location, but before that, with sufficient effort, exploits do exist that would allow the chain to be altered. In the context of UK rail this would mean that, at the very least, several of the major stakeholders would need to be actively working with the blockchain for it to be a viable solution, resilient to the loss of data and secure from tampering.

Although estimates currently put blockchain technology around 5 – 10 years from mainstream implementation (Gartner Inc., 2016), the major cloud providers such as IBM are already providing protytpe blockchain implementations for R&D use. Further to this, the Bitcoin blockchain has now been running for nearly a decade, and while there have been some teething difficulties, such as the issue of recorded illegal content reffered to in the chapter, the technology is developing very rapidly.

Given the traditionally long technology acceptance cycle in the rail industry, now is therefore the appropriate time for the industry to begin to trial and work with the blockchain if it is to help shape the mainstream solutions, integrate support for them into research prototypes from projects such as IN2RAIL, and to ready itself to gain the maximum possible benefits from them as they are commercially released.

REFERENCES

Albrecht, T., & Dasigi, M. (2016). ON-TIME: A Framework for Integrated Railway Network Operation Management. In *Traffic Management* (pp. 167–181). Hoboken, NJ, USA: John Wiley & Sons, Inc. doi:10.1002/9781119307822.ch12

Azaria, A., Ekblaw, A., Vieira, T., & Lippman, A. (2016). MedRec: Using Blockchain for Medical Data Access and Permission Management. In *2016 2nd International Conference on Open and Big Data (OBD)* (pp. 25–30). IEEE. doi:10.1109/OBD.2016.11

Bahga, A., & Madisetti, V. K. (2016). Blockchain Platform for Industrial Internet of Things. *Journal of Software Engineering and Applications*, *9*(10), 533–546. doi:10.4236/jsea.2016.910036

Biswas, K., & Muthukkumarasamy, V. (2016). Securing Smart Cities Using Blockchain Technology. In *Proceedings of the 2016 IEEE 18th International Conference on High Performance Computing and Communications; IEEE 14th International Conference on Smart City; IEEE 2nd International Conference on Data Science and Systems (HPCC/SmartCity/DSS)* (pp. 1392–1393). IEEE. doi:10.1109/HPCC-SmartCity-DSS.2016.0198

Brandon, D. (2016). The Blockchain: the future of business information systems? *International Journal of the Academic Business World*, *10*(2), 33–41.

Brewer, J. (2011). *National Information Systems Catalogue for Non-Network Rail Systems*. Retrieved from www.sparkrail.org

Christidis, K., & Devetsikiotis, M. (2016). Blockchains and Smart Contracts for the Internet of Things. *IEEE Access*, *4*, 2292–2303. doi:10.1109/ACCESS.2016.2566339

Collomb, A., & Sok, K. (2016). Blockchain / Distributed Ledger Technology (DLT): What Impact on the Financial Sector? *Communications & Stratégies*, (103), 93–111. Retrieved from https://search.proquest.com/docview/1841718518

Dennis, R., & Owen, G. (2015). Rep on the block: A next generation reputation system based on the blockchain. In *Proceedings of the 2015 10th International Conference for Internet Technology and Secured Transactions (ICITST)* (pp. 131–138). IEEE. doi:10.1109/ICITST.2015.7412073

Digital Railway. (2017). Digital Railway - Frequently Asked Questions. Retrieved from http://digital-railway.co.uk/resources/

Gallaher, M. P., O'Conor, A. C., Dettbarn, J. L., & Gilday, L. T. (2004). Cost Analysis of Inadequate Interoperability in the U.S. Capital Facilities Industry. *NIST*. doi:10.6028/NIST.GCR.04-867

Gartner, Inc. (2016). Gartner's 2016 Hype Cycle for Emerging Technologies Identifies Three Key Trends That Organizations Must Track to Gain Competitive Advantage. Retrieved May 29, 2017, from http://www.gartner.com/newsroom/id/3412017

Huckle, S., Bhattacharya, R., White, M., & Beloff, N. (2016). Internet of Things, Blockchain and Shared Economy Applications. *Procedia Computer Science, 98*, 461–466. https://doi.org/10.1016/j.procs.2016.09.074

Irving, G., & Holden, J. (2016). How blockchain-timestamped protocols could improve the trustworthiness of medical science. *F1000 Research, 5*, 222. doi:10.12688/f1000research.8114.2 PMID:27239273

Lee, B., & Lee, J.-H. (2017). Blockchain-based secure firmware update for embedded devices in an Internet of Things environment. *The Journal of Supercomputing, 73*(3), 1152–1167. doi:10.1007/s11227-016-1870-0

Matzutt, R., Hohlfeld, O., Henze, M., Rawiel, R., Ziegeldorf, J. H., & Wehrle, K. (2016). POSTER. In *Proceedings of the 2016 ACM SIGSAC Conference on Computer and Communications Security - CCS'16* (pp. 1769–1771). New York, New York, USA: ACM Press. doi:10.1145/2976749.2989059

McNulty, R. (2011). *Realising the Potential of GB Rail: Final Report of the Rail Value for Money Study : Detailed Report.* UK Department for Transport. Retrieved from http://assets.dft.gov.uk/publications/report-of-the-rail-vfm-study/realising-the-potential-of-gb-rail.pdf

Milani, F., García-Bañuelos, L., & Dumas, M. (2016). *Blockchain and business process improvement.* Retrieved from http://www.bptrends.com/bpt/wp-content/uploads/10-04-2016-ART-Blockchain-and-Bus-Proc-Improvement-Milani-Garcia-Banuelos-Dumas.pdf

Nakamoto, S. (2008). *Bitcoin: A Peer-to-Peer Electronic Cash System.* Retrieved from https://bitcoin.org/bitcoin.pdf

Network Rail Limited. (2013). *Network Rail Technical Strategy.*

Newcombe, S., & Tucker, G. (2016). Enabling greater use of cross-industry remote condition monitoring. In *Proceedings of the International Conference on Railway Engineering (ICRE 2016).* Institution of Engineering and Technology. doi:10.1049/cp.2016.0520

Office of Rail Regulation. (2011). *National Rail Trends 2010 - 2011 Yearbook.* Retrieved from http://www.orr.gov.uk/__data/assets/pdf_file/0017/3482/nrt-yearbook-2010-11.pdf

Robert, J., Kubler, S., & Le Traon, Y. (2016). Micro-billing Framework for IoT: Research & Technological Foundations. In *Proceedings of the 2016 IEEE 4th International Conference on Future Internet of Things and Cloud (FiCloud)* (pp. 301–308). IEEE. doi:10.1109/FiCloud.2016.50

Schmitt, L., Létourneaux, F., De Keyzer, I., & Crompton, P. (2016). CAPACITY4RAIL: Toward a Resilient, Innovative and High-capacity European Railway System for 2030/2050. In *Materials and Infrastructures 2* (pp. 105–114). Hoboken, NJ, USA: John Wiley & Sons, Inc. doi:10.1002/9781119318613.ch8

Shingler, R., Fadin, G., & Umiliacchi, P. (2008). From RCM to predictive maintenance: the InteGRail approach. In *Proceedings of the 4th IET International Conference on Railway Condition Monitoring (RCM 2008)* (pp. 17–17). IEE. doi:10.1049/ic:20080324

Stouffer, K., Pillitteri, V., Lightman, S., Abrams, M., & Hahn, A. (2015). *Guide to Industrial Control Systems (ICS) Security.* doi:10.6028/NIST.SP.800-82r2

Sun, J., Yan, J., & Zhang, K. Z. K. (2016). Blockchain-based sharing services: What blockchain technology can contribute to smart cities. *Financial Innovation, 2*(1), 26. doi:10.1186/s40854-016-0040-y

TSLG. (2012). *The Rail Technical Strategy 2012.* Retrieved from https://www.rssb.co.uk/library/future railway/innovation-in-rail-rail-technical-strategy-2012.pdf

Tutcher, J., Easton, J. M., & Roberts, C. (2017). Enabling Data Integration in the Rail Industry Using RDF and OWL: The RaCoOn Ontology. *ASCE-ASME Journal of Risk and Uncertainty in Engineering Systems, Part A. Civil Engineering (New York, N.Y.), 3*(2). doi.org/10.1061/AJRUA6.0000859

Witte, J. H. (2016). The Blockchain: A Gentle Four Page Introduction. Retrieved from http://arxiv.org/abs/1612.06244

Wörner, D., & von Bomhard, T. (2014). When your sensor earns money. In *Proceedings of the 2014 ACM International Joint Conference on Pervasive and Ubiquitous Computing Adjunct Publication - UbiComp '14 Adjunct* (pp. 295–298). New York, New York, USA: ACM Press. doi:10.1145/2638728.2638786

Yuan, Y., & Wang, F.-Y. (2016). Towards blockchain-based intelligent transportation systems. In *Proceedings of the 2016 IEEE 19th International Conference on Intelligent Transportation Systems (ITSC)* (pp. 2663–2668). IEEE. doi:10.1109/ITSC.2016.7795984

Zanella, G. L., & Pinasco, M. (2016). *Deliverable D8.1 Requirements for the Integration Layer.* Retrieved from http://www.in2rail.eu/download.aspx?id=9c5d1b91-17bc-4a17-8d0a-283332c96ab4

Zhang, Y., & Wen, J. (2017). The IoT electric business model: Using blockchain technology for the internet of things. *Peer-to-Peer Networking and Applications, 10*(4), 983–994. doi:10.1007/s12083-016-0456-1

KEY TERMS AND DEFINITIONS

Blockchain: A distributed ledger made up of transaction blocks, each identified by a unique hash value. Block identifiers include the identifier of the block preceding them within their own hash value, along with the content of their transactions. This places both the block and the transactions in an unambiguous sequence and ensures data is unaltered going forwards.

Enterprise Service Bus: An architectural model in the IT industry under which software services communicate with each other via a common messaging channel (the message bus). The advantage of a bus-based model is that each service has a single interface to the message bus, rather than multiple interfaces to each of the other services it needs to communicate with.

Hash Value: The output of a one-way function that takes as an input an alpha-numeric sequence, and outputs a derived sequence of known length. The hashing process is almost impossible to reverse engineer, and therefore the original data can only be forcibly recovered by attempting to hash random sequences, a process that is computational unfeasible for all but very few sequences.

Internet of Things: The network of smart devices capable of creating and delivering data on the state of the world, and their own functionality, in real or near-real time.

Sharing Economy: The predominantly online, peer-to-peer market for the temporary use of goods or services; examples of the sharing economy include the renting of spare rooms in houses via Airbnb, or the very short-term lease of a nearby car from services such as Car2Go.

Smart Contract: A uniquely addressable segment of code stored on the blockchain that enables a complex function (such as the purchase of data) to be performed automatically. Functions within the smart contract are commonly triggered by transactions being sent to it.

Transaction: The transfer of a resource between a sender and a recipient within the blockchain.

Chapter 3
Visual and LIDAR Data Processing and Fusion as an Element of Real Time Big Data Analysis for Rail Vehicle Driver Support Systems

Alper M. Selver
Dokuz Eylul University, Turkey

Enes Ataç
Dokuz Eylul University, Turkey

Burak Belenlioglu
Kentkart, Turkey

Sinan Dogan
Kentkart, Turkey

Yesim E. Zoral
Dokuz Eylul University, Turkey

ABSTRACT

This chapter reviews the challenges, processing and analysis techniques about visual and LIDAR generated information and their potential use in big data analysis for monitoring the railway at onboard driver support systems. It surveys both sensors' advantages, limitations, and innovative approaches for overcoming the challenges they face. Special focus is given to monocular vision due to its dominant use in the field. A novel contribution is provided for rail extraction by utilizing a new hybrid approach. The results of this approach are used to demonstrate the shortcomings of similar strategies. To overcome these disadvantages, dynamic modeling of the tracks is considered. This stage is designed by statistically quantifying the assumptions about the track curvatures presumed in current railway extraction techniques. By fitting polynomials to hundreds of manually delineated video frames, the variations of polynomial coefficients are analyzed. Future trends for processing and analysis of additional sensors are also discussed.

DOI: 10.4018/978-1-5225-3176-0.ch003

INTRODUCTION

Recognition of the objects and obstacles in front of a train is an essential component of railway driver support systems, which are supposed to generate an alarm to notify the driver or controllers in case of a dangerous and/or unexpected situation (Lenior, Janssen, Neerincx, & Schreibers, 2006). The essence of such security systems is getting more important as innovative approaches for autonomous trains and personal rapid transfer systems are being considered for transportation such as (Ultra Global Personal Rapid Transit Systems, 2011). Being an emerging element of railway condition monitoring (Chen & Roberts, 2006; Hodge, O'Keefe, & Weeks, 2015), there are various purposes of these systems such as obstacle identification and collision prevention (Ruder, Mohler, & Ahmed, 2003; Wohlfeil, 2011), obstacle-free range detection (Maire & Bigdeli, 2010), self-localization (Maire, 2007), near-miss event analysis (Aminmansour, 2014), road sign and signaling recognition (Kastrinaki, Zervakis, & Kalaitzakis, 2013). Each of these applications requires different processing approaches and pipelines. For instance, obstacle detection needs to be done in real time to prevent collisions, while near-miss event analysis can be performed offline at a later time. In order to develop systems that completely satisfy the requirements imposed by these applications, diverse types of sensors are needed. Most commonly used devices are cameras including monocular ones combined with zoom (Nassu & Ukai, 2012), infrared (Razaei & Sabzevari, 2009), thermal (Berg, Öfjäll, Ahlberg, & Felsberg, 2015), Bird's eye (Wang et al., 2015) and stereo view systems (Ohta, 2005) etc.). Other devices consist of radio-frequency identification (RFID) (Mašck, Kolarovksi, & Čamaj, 2016), radar (GSM-Railway based passive (He et al., 2016), millimeter wave (Yan, Fang, Li et al., 2016), light detection and ranging (LIDAR) (Jwa & Sonh, 2015)), ultrasonic devices (Sinha & Feroz, 2016), laser (Amaral, Marques, Lourenço et al., 2016) or other types of sensors (Cañete, Chen, Diaz, Llopis, & Rubio, 2015).

These sensors are employed to detect and identify the objects in front of the train or the obstacles on the rails before an accident occurs. In conventional systems, each sensor speaks for itself and monitors the scene individually. If one of the sensors detects a risk, it activates an alarm to warn the driver. Unfortunately, this direct approach can lead to a significant number of false positives (i.e. incorrect alarms) and even worse, false negatives (i.e. missed risks) (Chen & Roberts, 2006). In such systems, the advantages of integral capabilities of the collective data processing for combined sensor information are simply ignored. As a result, the possibility of obtaining an overall picture of the forthcoming scene is lost. Thus, these numerous sensors should be utilized together and new strategies to integrate the data acquired by them should be developed in order to obtain high accuracy and robustness at all scenarios. Moreover, because of the wide variety of operating conditions, these systems should have feasible properties such as being low-cost, ease of deployment, and simplicity of operation.

Due to the differences at their data acquisition principles, these sensors can provide complimentary information, which used to examine the complete aspects of the scene if properly integrated. Besides collection, storage and transmission issues, which revolutionize the database and communication technologies (Hodge et al., 2015; Cañete, Chen, Diaz, Llopis, & Rubio, 2015; Masson, Berbineau, 2017; Aguirre et al., 2017; Buggy et al., 2016), the analysis and processing of this multi-sensor generated big data should be handled with care by using proper preventive measures in order to keep all vital information, while effectively reducing the enormous amount of data (Schiavo, 2016). In a more general perspective, the collected information should be pre-processed to integrate different sources in order to enable efficient data analysis (Thaduri, Galar, & Kumar, 2015). Because of the wide variety of sensors, the collected data have varying characteristics with respect to noise, redundancy, consistency, and other sensor related parameters. In a broad sense, the pre-processing for analysis can be divided into three steps as elimination, reduction, and integration (Chen, Mao, Zhang, & Leung, 2014), which are discussed with examples at the last section of this chapter.

After the pre-processing, either big data analysis can be applied to the composite data or the information from each sensor is analyzed individually and then, their results can be combined. In both cases, unique and distinct limitations of each sensor under practical conditions should be carefully handled. For example, standard cameras are sensitive to the factors that affect visibility such as inverse illumination, shadows, rust, vegetation and clustered rails, while LIDAR is extremely sensitive to noise, which drops down the signal to noise ratio (SNR) drastically as measurement distances increase. Standard and zoom cameras have no usability inside tunnels or at night, while LIDAR and ultrasonic devices have very limited use under heavy rain. These challenges necessitate the use of different techniques for analysis. For instance, recent studies, which focus on camera based rail extraction and obstacle detection, conclude that the pixel based image processing techniques have limited performance to successfully cover all challenges. Therefore, polynomial fitting or geometric modeling, both of which would take advantage of smoothness, slow changing characteristics and parallel construction of left and right rails, should be used to obtain the final result. On the other hand, LIDAR data at low SNR values should be analyzed by multi-scale or multi-resolution techniques, such as wavelets, in order to eliminate the effects of noise while preserving important information. Here, a mature signal processing field is being explored to determine the most suitable analysis techniques to be employed at multi-sensor generated big data for railway driver support systems.

In addition to the above-mentioned problems and challenges, there are other factors, which might affect the design of a system. A good example might be the online processes, which should be completed almost in real time without using any explicit knowledge about the train speed or the camera parameters. For instance, a train traveling with 100 km/h and require 400 meters to stop (i.e. 14.4 seconds) need to determine an obstacle approximately about 800 meters ahead (i.e. 28.8 seconds), such that the driver would have a reaction time after the warning. These durations change based on train speed and the chosen methods should satisfy the given computational requirements.

To sum up, this chapter reviews the challenges, pre-processing and analysis techniques for monitoring the rails during a journey by taking camera as the principle and LIDAR as the secondary sensors. Their individual use, practical limitations, innovative designs for fusion and approaches for overcoming the challenges are surveyed. Added value of each sensor is explored considering their performances on obstacle detection. Their complementary properties, which can be merged to obtain a better system, are investigated. A novel multi-scale edge detection strategy is provided for rail extraction and the results of this approach are used to demonstrate the shortcomings of similar strategies, which dominate the related field. Then, to overcome these disadvantages, dynamic modeling of the tracks is studied. Based on the statistical analyses performed on hundreds of manually delineated rail tracks, a novel approach is also proposed to regulate the output of any rail extraction algorithm. By considering the result of such an algorithm as an initial model for tracks, the developed approach approximates it to the closest analytic representation, definition which is found by statistical analysis on parametric representation of tracks. Finally, possibilities and potential use of adding other sensors are discussed together with their computational burden.

CAMERA BASED SYSTEMS

Camera based approaches are the most widely analyzed application of obstacle detection. In this section, it is aimed to point out the common characteristics of different methods and propose solutions to their shortcomings. Therefore, the section is organized as follows:

1. By analyzing a large collection of publicly available cabin view videos, which represent diverse routes from several countries, a list about the challenges of video processing is obtained. Here, two assumptions are considered:
   a. The detection algorithms are designed to find the rails prior to obstacles and
   b. At least some parts of the rails are visible in a fraction of consecutive frames. For instance, tunnels can completely block the view or the visual information would be useless due to lack of brightness inside a tunnel. Such cases are excluded from this discussion.
2. In addition to a general literature review on rail extraction, the fundamental strategy of multi-scale edge detection methods, which lies underneath most of the approaches proposed in the literature, is discussed. It is stressed that even if different tools are employed for extraction, many of the short-comings of this strategy are common. To illustrate them with examples, the details of a selected one is presented. Thus, the properties of one of the most common strategies (i.e. multi-scale edge detection) and its shortcomings are summarized.
3. The assumptions used in literature for extracting rails are collected and their usability is validated. Such an analysis is done for the first time by carrying out statistical analysis in order to quantitatively measure the variations in rail geometry. Here, the main focus is to check the acceptability of the current assumptions, which are commonly used in several algorithms, and conclude on their pros and cons.
4. At the end of this section, a new method to represent the rail geometry using polynomial coefficient estimation is proposed. It is designed in such a way that it can be used by any rail extraction method, which should use its result for initialization of the polynomials. Thus, a post-processing framework is provided to overcome the challenges faced in general.

Challenges of Camera Vision

In order to give examples on some of the challenges, the first and the third rows of Figure 1 illustrate video frames from different routes and the second row shows the maximum response of the image to an edge-detector (i.e. combined response of 2D Gabor filters at multiple scales and directions). The frames are chosen among many to represent multiple challenges in a single frame. The first challenge is the variations of illumination, which cause alternating characteristics for rails. For instance, non-uniform illumination causes varying brightness levels for rails, which affect the filter responses such that instantaneous changes or discontinuities can occur based on the kernel size. All of the images at Figure 1 are affected from this while it is most apparent in Figure 1.c, where only the tracks at the middle of the frame are bright due to local illumination. The position of the sun has also a significant illumination effect, which creates polynomial rails instead of linear ones due the brightness variations in Figure 1.e. The shadow of a train or other objects around the rails can preclude the visibility of the rails (Figures 1.a and 1.b) and cause edge detection problems as given in Figure 1.f, where the shadow-daylight border

Figure 1. Examples for the challenges of rail extraction

(a)   (b)   (c)

(d)   (e)   (f)

(g)   (h)

has the strongest edge response in the Region of Interest (ROI). The shadow itself can be detected as an edge and it also can impair the integrity of the visual appearance of the rails (Figure 1.d).

The second challenge is the weather conditions. It can be hard to extract rails after snow if it causes discontinuous appearance of rail tracks. On the other hand, snow might increase performance by creating stronger edge information due to higher contrast between dark rail and bright environment. Here, it should be noted the filter responses might change sign since the rails might appear brighter than the environment when reflections of sunlight is considerably high (Figure 1.a). Rain is another challenging weather condition, during which the rain drops can create semi-transparent barriers over edge information (Figure 1.e). The third challenge is the condition of the camera during the journey. External effects such as flies or other environmental particles can leave dirt in front of or on the camera lens, which would partly block the view and harden the rail detection process (Figure 1.b). The blurring effect due to the constant vibrations of the locomotive together with the train speed is another factor in this group of challenges (Figure 1.g).

Next, the condition of the rails introduces other challenges. Rails can be covered by rust and in such cases; the filter responses of the rails can decrease dramatically. In some cases, even the appearance of the left and right rails with respect to their environment might be different (Figure 1.f). The vegetation around the rails also introduce similar problem. The effect of these rail and environmental conditions increase and might cause blurry edges and poor contrast especially at remote corners of the frame. Finally, the railway crossing, where the unknown trajectory of the train leads to possibility of several potential tracks, creates a challenge of extraction of all routes for consideration (Figure 1.h).

Considering the above challenges, one of the most critical issues is the sensitivity of an approach to the fine tuning of its parameters. In other words, a robust method, which can operate under various conditions, is needed in order to generalize the performance. Although several methods are proposed, such robustness has not been achieved yet.

Despite the severe challenges they face, vision based algorithms are one of the key elements of driver assistance systems. Accordingly, rail extraction and obstacle detection is studied extensively using many techniques of the image processing field. Proposed strategies include feature-classifier systems and their integration with other approaches such as combining Histogram of Gradient (HOG) feature and region-growing algorithm (Qi, Tian, & Shi, 2013) and TF-IDF (term frequency-inverse document frequency) like transform followed by classifier decisions on superpixels (Teng, liu, & Zhang, 2016). The extended applications, which have similar objectives, search for automatic obstacle detection on catenaries (Möller, Hulin, Krötz, & Sarnes, 2001) such as birds (Wu, Yuan, Peng, Ngo, & He, 2016) use application specific parameters for different techniques such as histogram projections (Bai & Jung, 2015), deep learning (Mancini, Costante, Valigi, & Ciarfuglia, 2016), or by iteratively selecting local maxima in the gradient image using a sliding window approach (Espino & Stanciulescu, 2012).

Considering the requirements introduced by real time analysis of big data, one of the most promising approaches for rail extraction is to include an edge detection step such as the analysis of the eigenvalues of local grey value gradients (Wohfeil, 2011), dynamic hysteresis thresholding local high-pass filtering results (Nassu & Ukai, 2012; Ross, 2012). Edge extraction should be finalized by merging the preliminary edges using appropriate fusion mechanisms such as the Hough transform to obtain longer lines (Kaleli & Akgul, 2009) The edge extraction can be performed in parallel to different pre-defined regions of the scene to achieve real-time performance.

Recently, multi-scale strategies are shown to achieve this performance in a systematic manner (Selver, Er, Belenlioglu, & Soyaslan, 2016). This novel approach is further extended here by employing collection of edges extracted by using 2-D Gabor wavelets and taking the maximum responses over all filters at each scale and direction for merging. First, each frame is divided into four sub-regions in order to group varying thicknesses and curvatures of the rails. The region at the top, namely the horizon, does not contain any rail information. The region at the bottom, namely "near", has the thickest rail appearance. The rails at the two regions between "near" and "horizon", namely "far" and "remote", consists of tracks that are getting thinner as the distance from the camera increases. Moreover, their curvature varies in a wider range as they reach out from "near" region to "remote". This information can be used to build up a filter bank having adequate space-frequency localizations and orientations for each region.

For instance, the curvature of the rail tacks is very limited at "near" region such that they can be considered as straight lines having orientation inside the range ±15°. On the other hand, the tracks in the "near" region have the thickest appearance in the image and, therefore scaling parameter of the filter should be adjusted accordingly. In a systematic manner, these orientations and scales are determined by Gabor wavelets, which are chosen due to their superior performance on analyzing non-stationary and inhomogeneous signals. The Gabor wavelet is a directional tool and it can be tuned to specific frequencies and therefore, it allows edge detection together with noise filtering in a single step. The Gabor wavelet is composed of a complex exponential multiplied by a Gaussian that can be defined as $g(x,y) = e^{jk\left(x^2+y^2\right)}e^{-\left(x^2\varepsilon^{-1}+y^2\right)/a^2}$. Here, ε is called the elongation parameter and k determines the frequency of the complex exponential. In this study, the value of ε is fixed to 5, while k is selected as 3, 4 and 5 for "near", "far" and "remote" regions, respectively. Rotation and axis scaling operations are applied using transformations $\dot{x} = x\cos\theta + y\sin\theta$ and $\dot{y} = -x\sin\theta + y\cos\theta$ where $\dot{x}$ and $\dot{y}$ are the rotated axes in the clockwise direction by θ. Some of the selected ones among the entire filter bank are given in Figure 2.a.

The overall response image is obtained by calculating the maximum moduli of the filter outputs over all angles (Figure 2.b). A post-processing step is applied to obtain the candidate pixels in binary form without any discontinuities and missing parts. First, thresholding is applied and the highest 10% percent of

Figure 2. Gabor filter bank at different scales and orientations and their application for extracting the rails

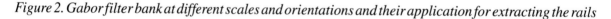

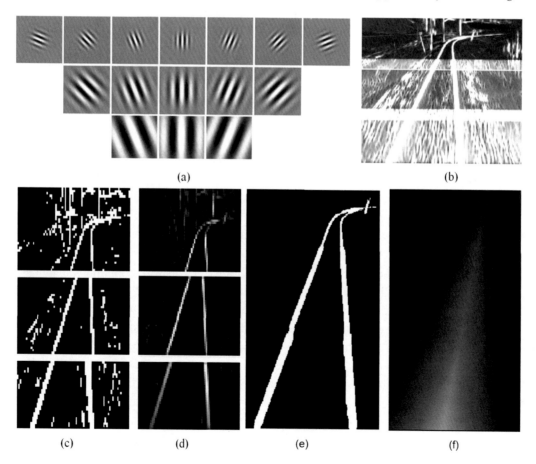

the coefficients are kept (Figure 2.c). After that, small disconnected clusters are eliminated with erosion (Figure 2.d). Then, detection of the rails is done with morphological reconstruction, where the marker is created using intensity profile of the thresholded image for near sub-region and the markers for the remaining sub-regions are obtained from the overlapping parts of the adjacent sub-regions (Figure 2.e).

Considering the big data analysis strategy in real time, this multi-scale approach provides important advantages. First, the filters at all scales and orientations can be applied in parallel at the same time. By increasing computational power, all filter outputs can be obtained synchronously without any additional processing time. This is not only a great advantage in terms of applicability, but also allows the filter bank to expand where necessary. The orientation selection based on domain specific assumptions can provide significant reduction in data, where a dynamic ROI can be generated based for succeeding frames (Figure 2.f).

Rail Extraction Techniques and Geometric Modeling

The results of the reported strategies in the literature under above mentioned challenges show that the problem characteristics make it very hard to employ pixel-wise determination, where individual pixels are classified as rail or not. Instead, the knowledge about the geometry and possible patterns of the rails should be the corner stone for obtaining acceptable results at all conditions. Since employing image processing techniques can only partially solve the above-mentioned problems, they should be used as initial model of a fitting strategy, which should be based on domain-specific assumptions, rather than generating the final results. Based on the literature, which relies on observations and analysis on a huge number of videos, domain-specific assumptions can be described for two options: monocular vision and bird's eye view. In standard monocular cameras, the rails appear as a pair of long stripes starting from the bottom of the image. Despite being parallel to each other, the perspective effect of the camera makes the distance between the left and right rails inversely proportional to the distance from the camera, which result with an appearance that become closer as one move from bottom of the image to the top. Rails have smooth and slowly changing curvature and fortunately, this limits the amount of change in position and curvature of the rails between consecutive frames of a video. The appearance of the rails in the close proximity of the train varies to a limited degree and can be considered as linear. In addition to these assumptions, which are more appropriate for describing traditional steel rails (Nassu & Ukai, 2012), additional information is needed for extended transportation types such as rubber-tired metro, which is a rapid transportation system. Being a mix of road and rail technology, this vehicle has wheels which run on rolling pads inside guide bars for traction together with extra canals carrying communication or control structures (Espino & Stanciulescu, 2012). The bird's eye view strategies can acquire the scene directly using a camera, or by transforming the monocular cabin view using a perspective mapping (Wang et al., 2016). The aim is to obtain parallel stripes in the new domain, but the curves should be handled with care due to the distortions caused by the transformation.

To conclude, the geometry based strategies, where the rail shape is finally decided by a predefined template or a coefficient controlled polynomial not only improves the accuracy of intra-frame rail extraction process, but it can also be used to model inter-frame relations such that the overall tendency of change of the rails can be controlled. This would also enable finding solutions to the challenges, where the position of the rails cannot be clearly seen or temporarily vanish from sight.

In order to check the validity of these assumptions, Figure 3 presents the coefficients of linear and quadratic terms of six right and left turns, which are obtained by manual delineation of the rails fol-

Figure 3. Statistical analysis (Boxplot) of linear, quadratic, and third order coefficients for the turns of the same video

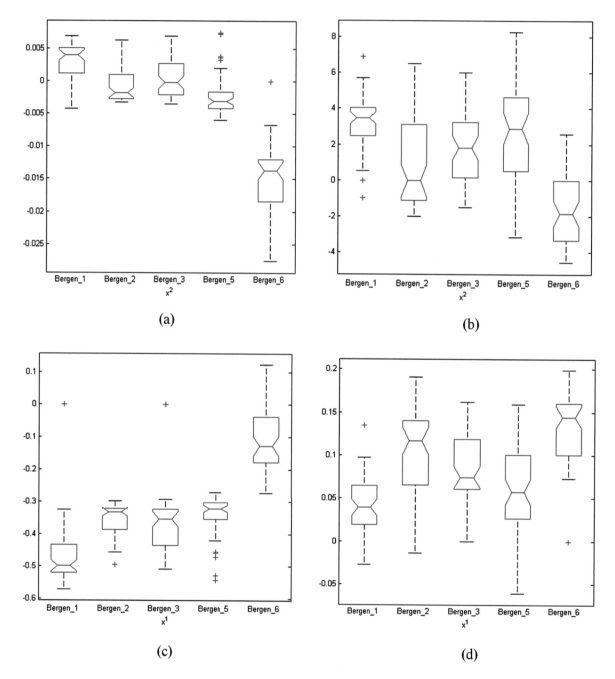

(a)

(b)

(c)

(d)

lowed by polynomial fitting. To observe the variations of coefficients of these polynomials, the central (red) line of the boxplot represents their median while top and bottom edges correspond to 75 and 25 percent confidence levels, respectively. The tail lines at the bottom and top of the boxes correspond to minimum and maximum observations, and the plus (+) shaped data points show the outliers. Based on these graphics, it can be concluded that the change of coefficients in different turns of a video is limited inside a certain margin and similar coefficients can be used to represent the rails.

This geometric knowledge is extensively used in literature. The sub-segments of the rails are linearly approximated and then merged for short distances in (Wohlfeil, 2011). This approach is extended to longer ranges using perspective mapping to obtain parallelism throughout the image in (Maire & Bigdeli, 2010). Under the influence of afore mentioned challenges, it is shown that the linear approximation can only have limited performance when the rails are highly curved in the short distance. This problem is partially solved by using a clothoid model for stereo vision systems (Ruder et al., 2003) or spline curves that are adjusted in every frame by a recursive estimation algorithm for monocular camera (Ross, 2012). Higher order polynomials are fitted to image processing results in (Selver et al., 2016), but no restriction is defined for polynomial coefficients such that impossible tracks are observed to be generated by this approach.

Dividing the rails into sub-segments and approximating different sections using different models can be considered as a multi-scale approach for solving the problem. This is used through the Hough transform in (Kaleli & Akgul, 2009), where vertical multi-sections are analyzed after inverse projective mapping. Still, the efforts were insufficient to represent the highly curved rails. Modeling each rail as a sequence of segments is proposed in (Nassu & Ukai, 2012), where multi section is defined as a single segment for the short range and multiple segments for the long range. The application represents superior performance compared to single parabola approaches by matching edge features to the candidate rail patterns, where patterns for the short range consists of almost parallel and straight line pairs but the patterns for the long range allows varying parabolas. Although the model allows fast and incremental extraction process and can represent the rail curvature better than sequences of straight segments, the patterns are limited to the template set and the wide acceptance and application of the algorithm requires many more field tests. It should also be noted that the similarity induced pattern matching would fail if the image processing results are poor.

When the effective ranges of the polynomial terms, such as the ones in Figure 3, are analyzed, it can be demonstrated that the variations of the coefficients in the corresponding range have almost no visual effect. Based on these analyses, it can be concluded that a predefined set of polynomial coefficients can be used to represent the rails due to the limited change of coefficients during a turn. This predefined set is created by manual delineation of 2185 frames, which are obtained from 29 left and 23 right turns belonging to 14 videos acquired during common public journeys, which include many of the challenging scenarios stated above. The results of image processing algorithms, particularly the employed multiscale filtering approach discussed in previous section, are modeled by this predefined set of coefficients in a least-squares sense. The obtained results using the proposed approach reveal that the performance of the developed method for coefficient prediction is very high. Moreover, the results are found to be visually indistinguishable from the ground truth.

Obstacle Detection

Once the rails are extracted, the obstacle detection problem can be reduced to a simpler domain, where only the predefined margins around the rails are analyzed. Considering the speed of the train, the algorithms can be divided into moving and still cases. At the latter case, the train is assumed to be still due to a waiting period at a station, railway crossing etc. The recognition of pedestrians and other objects passing through the railway before the train starts moving is an important subject, which is usually handled by background subtraction techniques (Mukojima et al., 2016). Figure 4.a illustrates such a case, where the train is waiting at a station and a motorcycle is crossing the railway. The yellow, orange and red zones indicate three alarm levels to warn the driver prior to departure. This system uses the practical application of MathWorks® ("Motion Based Multiple Object Tracking"), which detects multiple moving objects for a fixed camera. Therefore, the standing pedestrian on the right-hand side of the frame is not detected, while a remote object is recognized (See the second yellow box). This makes sense as still objects do not constitute an obstacle for the train unless they are in the middle of the rails or a predefined zone. Figure 4.b shows the same pedestrian running towards the train and recognized as an object.

The second case is the moving train scenario, where the main challenges of multiple object detection, tracking and identification occur. Depending on the application, the system should identify the obstacle type, such as pedestrian, vehicle or animal. Up to our research, there are not any studies, which consider the animals as specific obstacles and particularly focus on detecting them. On the other hand, pedestrian and vehicle detection are both exploited in detail from multiple perspectives, while the number of related papers in literature are significantly less for railway compared to self-driving cars. As expected, the detection of the obstacle type would bring additional computational complexity and burden, but in many cases, it provides vital information to the system. For instance, Figure 4.c shows a train approaching a station where passengers are waiting. Here, the detection and motion of pedestrians is of critical importance as many accidents have been reported.

Pedestrian detection is extensively studied in intelligent transportation society for autonomous cars (Ess, Leibe, & Gool, 2007; Dalal & Triggs, 2005; Gavrila & Munder, 2007) and a number of survey studies are also published. However, pedestrian detection for trains is rarely discussed (Geronimo, Lopez, Sappa, & Graff, 2010; Enzweiler & Gavrila, 2009; Paisitkriangkrai, Shen, & Zhang, 2008; Munder & Gavrila, 2006). Some of the studies focus on surveillance and the pedestrian detection techniques are divided into two as macroscopic and microscopic (Li, Yao, & Wang, 2012). Macroscopic detection is used to estimate crowd density for optimizing the traffic control, scheduling and emergency planning such as evacuation schemes without distinguishing each pedestrian, Microscopic detection focuses on recognition of individual pedestrians and has much wider application areas. These techniques can be grouped as model-based, feature-classifier-based and combined detection methods. Model-based detection relies on an exact definition of a pedestrian model. Then a matching process is applied to the candidate regions to measure the similarity. Models are based on shape, such as parametric contours (Lin & Davis, 2010). Their disadvantages in terms of big-data processing are the increased processing time when the number of candidate regions are high and computational burden to represent various postures. Feature-classifier based strategies rely on utilization of discriminative features, which can provide adequate representation of samples, and appropriate decision mechanisms, called classifiers, to isolate the objects of interest in the feature space. Most typical features used for this purpose are shape features, which represent the posture as a composition of lines and curves (i.e. edgelet) (Wu & Nevatia, 2005), gradients (i.e. shapelet) (Sabzmeydani & Mori, 2007), HOG or its extensions.

Although using all feature types together might be the most direct idea to obtain the most discriminative feature set, this approach causes the curse of dimensionality, which limits the generalization capacity of classifier. Although this effect can be reduced by using dimension reduction (e.g. Principle Component Analysis (Zeng & Ma, 2010), partial least squares (Schwartz, Kembhavi, Harwood, & Davis, 2009) etc.) or feature selection techniques (e.g. Minimum-redundancy-maximum-relevance (mRMR) (Peng, Long, & Ding, 2005) etc.), the extraction of each feature adds an extra time to the process and having too many features might prevent the real-time usability. Considering the classifiers, neural networks are preferred for their black box approach, while support vector machines (SVM) are also popular due to their robustness provided by the use of optimal hyperplane for decision. Combined techniques either collect model and feature information together or use additional properties to support them. For instance, shape features are combined with texture and color features, which are reported to increase the performance (Tuzel, Porikli, & Meer, 2008). Similar approaches use HOG with co-occurrence matrix (Schwartz et al., 2009), local receptive field (Walk, Majer, Schindler, & Schiele, 2010) and Local Binary Patterns (LBP) (Zeng & Ma, 2010). Combination can also be formulated for classifiers as fusion or multi-level schemes (Oliveira, Nunes, & Peixoto, 2010). The training and testing strategies for such combinations are discussed in detail while an optimal strategy, which is valid for all applications, for classifier ensembles has not been found yet (Duin, 2002; Kamel & Wanas, 2003; Dietrich, Palm, & Schwenker, 2003).

Similar to pedestrian detection, vehicle detection is an essential component of autonomous driving systems and many approaches have been developed for self-driving cars while none particularly focus on on-board railway systems. Only railway crossings are considered by fixed cameras, which can also be a part of driver support systems for trains if certain communication and warning technologies between a train and data-center are established. Recently, special interest is given to on-road vehicle detection using computer vision as cameras get cheaper in price, smaller in size and show great increase in quality. The vehicle detection also faces the same challenges with rail extraction and pedestrian detection. Due to space limitations of this paper, this topic is not discussed in detail here, but reader can access several survey papers about the topic (Siviraman & Trivedi, 2013). In a broad sense, the vehicle detection using monocular vision can be divided as appearance and motion based. Motion is a straight forward feature that can be calculated using background subtraction when the camera is still. For moving camera, a more complex analysis is required as the motion of the obstacle vehicle is a relative one compared to the train. Nevertheless, similar features are used for vehicle detection such as HOG, Haar-like, size, width, height, image intensity, texture and color. For decision making, also similar classifiers are employed including SVM, Kalman filtering, Markov Random Fields and Bayesian approach.

One of the important differences between pedestrian and vehicle detection research seems to be the availability of benchmark data sets. For instance, the wide variations of pedestrians in terms of appearance pose and scale are considered in Caltech data set (Dollár, Wojek, Schiele, & Perona, 2009). 250,000 frames (in 137 approximately minute long segments) for a total of 350,000 labeled bounding boxes and 2300 unique pedestrians are included in this extensive and challenging database. Several machine intelligence systems are built based on this data set and one of them ("Tracking Pedestrians from a Moving Car"), albeit being trained for moving cars, is applied directly to trains for demonstration. It is observed to produce successful results when approaching a station (Figure 4.c), while fails at typical railway scenarios such as level crossings (Figures 4.d-e) or workers on the track (Figures 4.f-g). The other data sets can be reviewed using the same paper (Dollár et al., 2009) and specific extensions, such as the one collected for cyclists (Li et al., 2016) can also be analyzed.

Future Trends for Big Data Analysis of Visual Support

The camera vision information constitutes one of the biggest sources of big data for railway driver support systems. Generating approximately 60 frames per second with three color channels at very high resolution and bit depth, this information requires utilization of carefully selected and designed processing steps, which preserve vital information and remove redundancies to enable robust real-time operations. Since monocular vision seems to dominate the related field, the rest of the discussions focus mainly on single

Figure 4. Object detection examples

(a)   (b)

(c)   (d)

(e)   (f)   (g)

camera cases. If multiple cameras are used, each one is assumed to be responsible for different part of the scene, such as the short distance with fixed and long distance with zoom cameras (Nassu & Ukai, 2011).

The first step of almost all applications is the rail extraction. Since the appearance of the rails are not parallel, two approaches seem to provide robust and computationally effective results for big data. The first one is handling different parts of the frames using different edge extractors. Here, different refers to scale and orientation variations to represent the varying characteristics of the tracks according to their distance to the camera(s) (Selver et al., 2016). Even when two cameras are used (i.e. standard + zoom) this strategy is shown to be effective (Nassu & Ukai, 2012). This method also enables the use of parallel programming, which can process these different parts at the same time and merge the results. The second approach aims to finalize the extraction strategy with an analytic representation of the rail track either with polynomials or other geometric shapes. This strategy is very useful both for representing the smooth characteristics of the rails and for compensating the faulty image processing results more effective than template matching strategies. Moreover, the polynomial or geometric definition of rail creates a parametric representation, which can be transformed to generate a dynamic ROI that can significantly reduce the search space for obstacle detection algorithms (Figure 4.a). This pre-processing step corresponds to data elimination and reduction that big-data analysis vitally need for real-time processing. An example is given in Figure 5, where the application runs real-time on C and handles the rail extraction problem in two zones as near and remote. The approach solely relies on edge detection and thresholding followed by polynomial fitting (Selver et al., 2016).

On the other hand, obstacle detection using monocular camera largely relies on a feature extraction-classification paradigm and based on machine learning. When considered as a classification problem, obstacle detection has two major components. These are the features, which represent the characteristic properties of an obstacle, and the classifiers, which are the decision mechanisms. The performances of the classifiers rely significantly on the representation capability of the features However, monocular images lack direct depth measurements and therefore multi-scale techniques are needed for this application too. In other words, each object should be handled based on its distance, position and orientation to the camera. Despite the fact that various features and multiple classifiers are proposed for obstacle detection problem, no optimal strategy, which can resolve all challenges, is found yet. Therefore, systems that adequately combine these features and classifiers are still needed. In a broad sense, two methodologies exist for combining diverse features. The first one is the use of a composite feature that is constructed by lumping diverse features together. However, as shown in the literature, using a composite feature has several disadvantages including computational complexity, curse of dimensionality, formation difficulty, increased processing time and redundancy. Thus, instead of using all features as a composite vector and giving it as an input to a single and essentially very complex classifier, a second approach can be used that is based on combining classifier subsets with feature subset vectors. Several studies in varying fields of applications present the advantages of this second approach. A successful example is the extension of HOG-LBP to multi-scale space for vehicle detection (Oliveira et al., 2010). This multi-scale analysis

Figure 5. Real time rail extraction of complete scene, near, and remote zones

(a)   (b)   (c)

can also be adopted to provide robustness on the ongoing challenges of the field such as the detection of partially-occluded obstacles by combining independent vehicle parts (Niknejad, Takeuchi, Mita, & McAllester, 2012) or shape based pedestrian detection by defining upper and lower body parts (Lin & Davis, 2010). Considering the decision makers, the ongoing trend for deep learning shows strong similarities with multi-scale approaches. For instance, a convolutional neural network for deep learning has many hidden layers while each of many neural networks in multi-scale model has single hidden layer. Nevertheless, deep learning can be considered as the inevitable classifier of the future as its learning schemes are very well adapted for big data processing.

At this point, the performance of existing approaches for obstacle detection methods are very hard to evaluate for railway applications because of the lack of datasets. It is well known that the public datasets have great contributions on the progress. Therefore, railway specific datasets, which can represent the challenges and real-life scenarios, are necessary to inspire new approaches as well as evaluating and comparing the existing ones. Introduction of such a data set is absolutely necessary to allow in depth analysis of existing challenges and possible solutions, to introduce performance metrics specific to these challenges, and to identify future research directions.

LIDAR BASED SYSTEMS

LIght Detection and Ranging (LIDAR) is an efficient tool for remote sensing and environment modeling (Lai, 2010; Li, Gong, & Zhou, 2007). It can be considered as an active sensor transmitting electromagnetic radiation and measuring back-scattered signals. By measuring the attenuation of the incident light pulse, LIDAR reflects the properties of the objects in its range. It is widely used in autonomous vehicles for generating an accurate map of the surroundings (Reitberger, Krzystek, &Utilla, 2008; Utkin, 2002). This allows recognition of the activities around a vehicle and plays a key role on the decisions shaping the trajectory and characteristics of the motion. Therefore, LIDAR based systems are widely applied for spatial data collection and support applications in many aspects. In recent years, they have been introduced to railway applications and greatly enhanced the spatial detail and efficiency in addition to traditional vision approaches. Nowadays, they are being used in applications such as rail track surveys, clearance measurements, infrastructure reconstruction and tunnel mapping (Morgan, 2009; Lesler, Perry, & McNease, 2010; Kremer & Grimm, 2012; Zhu & Hyypa, 2014). Some data centric examples for these applications are given in Figure 6, which are collected from publicly available videos.

Despite LIDAR's wide acceptance of use for obstacle detection in autonomous cars, the corresponding applications are still very limited for on-board driver support systems of trains. One of the reasons behind this is the fact that LIDARs, which are capable of representing obstacles at a meaningful range for trains, are not only rare, but also very expensive products ("RIEGL-Produkt Detail"). Considering the example on train speed and warning time at the introduction section, currently the products satisfying this condition are very limited, especially due to the exponential attenuation of the back-scattered signal by distance.

Challenges of LIDAR Data

LIDAR generates a point cloud by analyzing the echo of light pulses scattered from surrounding objects and provide a direct measure of change and field of view. However, the point cloud data produced by a

Figure 6. Frames of publicly available videos
From (a) (Kjell, 2014), (b) (Alastairfrance1989, 2011), (c) (RailwayTunnel Brockwille, 2013), (d) (SSIMichigan, 2013), (e) (EMC, INC., 2014).

(a)   (b)   (c)

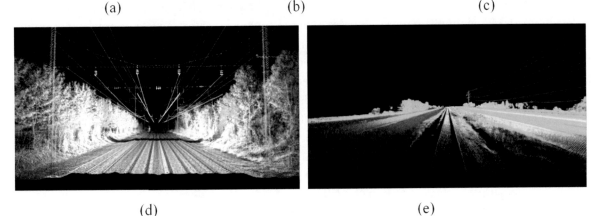

(d)   (e)

LIDAR has three drawbacks that limit its direct use on on-board driving assistance systems. First of all, a major challenge is increased data volume, which necessitates expansion of the software processing capabilities. Since the data size of a point cloud is very big; it should be transformed to a simpler form for more efficient processing without losing any characteristic features. To achieve this, specialized data formats are generated ("LASer (LAS) File Format Exchange Activities") and methods using planar, quadratic or higher order multi-scale (MSA) representations are developed (DeVore et al., 2013; Stelmaszczyk, 2000). Second, LIDAR data is affected significantly by noise, which deteriorates the signal to noise ratio (SNR). Although the noise is known to be correlated with the range of the measurement and range dependent noise is occasionally handled as non-Gaussian, its effects on backscattered signal are not well defined (Hu, 2010). If the obstacles were stationary, noise could be removed with a filter or by taking local averages of signal intensities over a selected neighborhood (Lerkvarnyu, Deijhan & Cheevasuvit, 1998). Unfortunately, the speed of the train together with the motion of the obstacles causes non-stationary behavior. Consequently, even the use of appropriate filters cannot eliminate noise while preserving characteristic information that is needed for identification of obstacles. Many approaches have been proposed for this problem using MSA analysis such as wavelets (H. Y. Zhang, Fan, T. H. Zhang, & Zheng, 2012), iterative machinery (Lai & Zheng, 2015), and optimization (Sun, Huang, & Fang, 2004). Finally, the third important drawback is the missing data in point clouds. In such cases, interpolation is required for correct representation of various structures such as poles, towers, and wires, which are essential for navigation. Thus, interpolating the point cloud to obtain the full-waveform not only enhance the intensity map but also increase the positioning accuracy and correct extraction of other useful parameters of the backscattered signal, such as pulse width, peak amplitude, and peak position. Similar to the previous drawbacks, again MSA methods can be utilized to overcome this limitation (Liu, 2011; Yang & Huang, 2005; Wagner, Ullrich, Ducic, Melzer, & Studnicka, 2006).

COMBINING CAMERA WITH LIDAR AND OTHER SENSORS

As discussed above, one of the primary functions of an on-board driver support system is to detect and classify the objects at a certain range to avoid collisions and to determine situations of risk during the navigation. Considering all sorts of risks and obstacles under given challenges, which make them hard to detect, it is highly unlikely to cover all cases using a single acquisition device or sensor. To capture all information ahead, combining the information provided by multiple sources is required. Using a set of sensors not only changes the way one should process the generated big data, but also carries feature and decision spaces to higher dimensions, where performing classification and/or situation assessment can be done at least in a more robust manner in expense of computational complexity.

The significant information increased due to utilization of multiple sensors can be considered as a field of real-time big data analysis. As being such, the complementary and redundant information should be identified to eliminate the latter. The complementary information should be properly explored to maximize the inference and confidence levels for obstacle detection and risk assessment. One of the most common combinations is the integration of a LIDAR sensor and a camera, which is extensively (Reina, Milella, Halft, & Worst, 2013; Jun, Wu, & Zheng, 2015; Veitch-Michaelis, Muller, Storey, Walton, & Foster, 2015; Brehar, Vancea, Marita, Giosan, & Nedevschi, 2015; Sock, Kim, Min, & Kwak, 2016; Oliveira & Nunes, 2013; Puttagunta, 2016) and comparatively (Premebida, Ludwig, & Nunes, 2009), studied by the intelligent vehicle, mobile robotics and autonomous transportation societies (Hung et al., 2015). This attention is mainly due to the complementary characteristics of these devices that allow improvements on system reliability and accuracy.

Elimination of Data as a Pre-Processing Step for Big Data Analysis

Elimination aims to improve the collected information quality by removing erroneous, inaccurate, incomplete, or unreasonable data. Considering the camera as the sensor of interest, some examples for acquisition of such data might be no information due to insufficient lighting or inverse illumination (i.e. unreasonable), extreme motion blur caused by the vibration (i.e. inaccurate), some kind of dirt, such as an insect, that stick to the lens during the journey (i.e. incomplete) and integrated circuit errors that cause dead pixel(s) or camera angle alterations due to changes at camera position or viewing angle (i.e. erroneous). Such data should be defined in the design, searched and identified during acquisition, corrected if possible or documented for fixing and removed before further processing, especially for real-time applications, since they will cause inconsistencies on system behavior.

Reduction mainly refers to unnecessary data resolution or quality and information repetition. Besides increasing the need for storage and transmission resources, it can reduce the analysis performance as well as creating computational complexity. Considering the camera again, the frame rates of the current devices and the visible area of the existing lenses are significantly higher than what is needed for rail extraction. Thus, instead of processing all frames, only some selected ones can be used and this selection may be automated with certain measures such as calculating the entropy differences between consecutive frames and requiring this difference to be greater than a certain threshold. However, elimination step should be developed with extreme care as it can result with loss of important information.

Finally, integration of the data after elimination and reduction should combine the data from different sensors in such a way that a composite form is created and provided to the system. For instance, cameras provide series of matrices while LIDAR generates unstructured point clouds. As the number of sensors increase, the level of heterogeneity is increased such that the acquired data format might even include semantics. Thus, the integration step should prepare the big data for computer analysis and/or intuitive user interpretation.

Applicability of Existing Obstacle Detection Approaches to Railways

Many important steps have to be properly addressed before a high-level combination can be achieved. Similar to other cases, several systems are proposed for autonomous cars, but only a few discussions are available about trains. Therefore, in this chapter, the applicability of existing studies to trains is discussed based on how those systems can reflect the challenges of railway systems. The first step of handling this bi-sensorial problem is determining ROIs in the image to perform vision-based classification. Considering pedestrian detection, a standard way is to use multi-scale feature extraction within a sliding-window, which has a fixed-size on several scales in horizontal and vertical directions such that all pedestrians located at varying distances and heading different orientations can be identified. This approach is reported to generate enormous number of candidate regions due to scale overlaps.

Taking the track of the rails into consideration, the importance of an object decreases as its distance from the railway increases. It is straightforward to notice that the ROI should cover a limited range to process on-the-fly and this can be fixed to a predefined range if the rails are extracted priory. This approach can be improved with the help of a LIDAR and vision registration procedure (Mašek, Kolarovksi, & Čamaj, 2016). If accomplished, LIDAR space can be exploited in order to avoid the rescaling process of regular sliding window method. The advantages of such a system is reported to be computational efficiency due to elimination of visual rescaling, implicit ROI generation by LIDAR range, decreased parameter dependency due to sliding window and direct obstacle range measurement.

Considering the features obtained from LIDAR and camera, (Premebida, Ludwig, & Nunes, 2009) surveys effective ones for both devices and also include some of the related works on pedestrian detection using multi-sensor data fusion (Gandhi & Trivedi, 2007). For ITS systems other than trains, most of the works that combine LIDAR and vision for object detection use LIDAR to generate object candidates, while final decision is given by vision. The alternatives of this cascade approach can be the fusion of features followed by a classifier (a.k.a. centralized) or obtaining a combination of classifier decisions for each sensor (a.k.a. decentralized). Regarding the application of this second approach to ITS, the biggest question is how to combine the results of different sensors? Experimental results showed that trainable fusion methods can outperform predefined rules and dimension reduction (such as mRMR) can increase the diversity of the classifiers and prevent redundancy. Still, predefined rules or weighting can be arranged based on the characteristics of the sensor at given conditions. For instance, LIDAR reliability decreases at long range and vision based classification are error-prone at low contrast. Accordingly, determining the operating condition of the sensor and using the learned weights after training for that condition would decrease the weights for the outputs of these two sensors when their reliability is low. Moreover, in terms of practical applications, since the fusion mechanisms do not depend entirely on a single sensor space, more robustness and safety can be achieved.

Combining Other Sensors With Camera and LIDAR

The combination of stereovision and LIDAR is also an emerging research area, where the focus is to match surface properties of LIDAR to dense 3D information of stereo camera system (Reina, Milella, Halft, & Worst, 2013, Veitch-Michaelis, Muller, Storey, Walton, & Foster, 2015). The challenges associated with cross calibration of camera parameters using the LIDAR and developing smart data selection methods, which would impose LIDAR data to regions with low image texture, constitute promising grounds for future studies.

Other multi-sensor combinations focus on a communication between a data center and the train (Govoni et al., 2015, Garcia et al., 2005). The most common example is the railway crossings, where very reliable systems with high confidence rates are needed. One of the very rare exceptions is stereovision combined with far-infrared system, which aligns spatio-temporal data between the two sensors by camera response timing model with grayscale intensity images captured by trigger-based cameras (Brehar et al., 2015).

Current research projects on railway industry are trying to integrate even more sources of information including but not limited to locomotive sensors, railway sensors, wearable sensors as well as geo-location information.

ACKNOWLEDGMENT

This study is conducted as a part of EUREKA-EURIPIDES project "ADORAS [Advanced Onboard Data Recording and Analysis System]" and supported by TUBITAK TEYDEB under grant 9150121, which is being conducted by Kentkart).

REFERENCES

Aguirre, E., Lopez-Iturri, P., Azpilicueta, L., Redondo, A., Astrain, J. J., Villadangos, J., & Falcone, F. et al. (2017). Design and implementation of context aware applications with wireless sensor network support in urban train transportation environments. *IEEE Sensors Journal, 17*(1), 169–178. doi:10.1109/JSEN.2016.2624739

Alastairfrance1989. (2011, May 26). *Railway Tunnel- LIDAR* [YouTube video]. Retrieved from https://www.youtube.com/watch?v=gJi69BTSbeQ

Amaral, V., Marques, F., Lourenço, A., Barata, J., & Santana, P. (2016). Laser-based obstacle detection at railway level crossings. *Journal of Sensors.*

Aminmansour, S., Maire, F., & Wullems, C. (2014, November). Near-miss event detection at railway level crossings. In *Proceedings of the 2014 International Conference on Digital Image Computing: Techniques and Applications (DICTA)* (pp. 1-8). IEEE. doi:10.1109/DICTA.2014.7008119

Bai, Z., & Jung, S. H. (2015). Image-based Subway Security System by Histogram Projection Technology. *Journal of Korea Multimedia Society, 18*(3), 287–297. doi:10.9717/kmms.2015.18.3.287

Berg, A., Öfjäll, K., Ahlberg, J., & Felsberg, M. (2015, June). Detecting rails and obstacles using a train-mounted thermal camera. In *Proceedings of the Scandinavian Conference on Image Analysis* (pp. 492-503). Springer International Publishing. doi:10.1007/978-3-319-19665-7_42

Brehar, R., Vancea, C., Marița, T., Giosan, I., & Nedevschi, S. (2015, September). Pedestrian detection in the context of multiple-sensor data alignment for far-infrared and stereo vision sensors. In *Proceedings of the 2015 IEEE International Conference on Intelligent Computer Communication and Processing (ICCP)* (pp. 385-392). IEEE. doi:10.1109/ICCP.2015.7312690

Buggy, S. J., James, S. W., Staines, S., Carroll, R., Kitson, P., Farrington, D., & Tatam, R. P. et al. (2016). Railway track component condition monitoring using optical fibre Bragg grating sensors. *Measurement Science & Technology, 27*(5), 055201. doi:10.1088/0957-0233/27/5/055201

Cañete, E., Chen, J., Díaz, M., Llopis, L., & Rubio, B. (2015). Sensor4PRI: A sensor platform for the protection of railway infrastructures. *Sensors (Basel, Switzerland), 15*(3), 4996–5019. doi:10.3390/s150304996 PMID:25734648

Chen, J., & Roberts, C. (2006, November). Effective condition monitoring of line side assets. In *Proceedings of the Institution of Engineering and Technology International Conference on Railway Condition Monitoring '06* (pp. 78-83). IET. doi:10.1049/ic:20060048

Chen, M., Mao, S., Zhang, Y., & Leung, V. C. (2014). *Big data: related technologies, challenges and future prospects.* Heidelberg: Springer. doi:10.1007/978-3-319-06245-7

Dalal, N., & Triggs, B. (2005, June). Histograms of oriented gradients for human detection. In *Proceedings of the 2005 IEEE Computer Society Conference on Computer Vision and Pattern Recognition (CVPR'05)* (Vol. 1, pp. 886-893). IEEE. doi:10.1109/CVPR.2005.177

DeVore, R., Petrova, G., Hielsberg, M., Owens, L., Clack, B., & Sood, A. (2013). Processing terrain point cloud data. *SIAM Journal on Imaging Sciences, 6*(1), 1–31. doi:10.1137/110856009

Dietrich, C., Palm, G., & Schwenker, F. (2003). Decision templates for the classification of bioacoustic time series. *Information Fusion, 4*(2), 101–109. doi:10.1016/S1566-2535(03)00017-4

Dollár, P., Wojek, C., Schiele, B., & Perona, P. (2009, June). Pedestrian detection: A benchmark. In *Proceedings of the IEEE Conference on Computer Vision and Pattern Recognition CVPR '09* (pp. 304-311). IEEE. doi:10.1109/CVPR.2009.5206631

Duin, R. P. (2002). The combining classifier: to train or not to train? In *Proceedings of the 16th International Conference on Pattern Recognition* (Vol. 2, pp. 765-770). IEEE. doi:10.1109/ICPR.2002.1048415

EMC, Inc. (2014, February 07). *EMC's 3D Mobile Lidar-Rail Road* [YouTube video]. Retrieved from https://www.youtube.com/watch?v=r2xlCwOLORc

Émilie Warden, P. (2011). *Big data glossary*. O'Reilly Media, Inc.

Enzweiler, M., & Gavrila, D. M. (2009). Monocular pedestrian detection: Survey and experiments. *IEEE Transactions on Pattern Analysis and Machine Intelligence, 31*(12), 2179–2195. doi:10.1109/TPAMI.2008.260 PMID:19834140

Espino, J. C., & Stanciulescu, B. (2012, September). Rail extraction technique using gradient information and a priori shape model. In *Proceedings of the 2012 15th International IEEE Conference on Intelligent Transportation Systems* (pp. 1132-1136). IEEE. doi:10.1109/ITSC.2012.6338870

Ess, A., Leibe, B., & Van Gool, L. (2007, October). Depth and appearance for mobile scene analysis. In *Proceedings of the 2007 IEEE 11th International Conference on Computer Vision* (pp. 1-8). IEEE. doi:10.1109/ICCV.2007.4409092

Fang, H. T., & Huang, D. S. (2004). Noise reduction in lidar signal based on discrete wavelet transform. *Optics Communications, 233*(1), 67–76. doi:10.1016/j.optcom.2004.01.017

Gandhi, T., & Trivedi, M. M. (2007). Pedestrian protection systems: Issues, survey, and challenges. *IEEE Transactions on Intelligent Transportation Systems, 8*(3), 413–430. doi:10.1109/TITS.2007.903444

Gavrila, D. M., & Munder, S. (2007). Multi-cue pedestrian detection and tracking from a moving vehicle. *International Journal of Computer Vision, 73*(1), 41–59. doi:10.1007/s11263-006-9038-7

Geronimo, D., Lopez, A. M., Sappa, A. D., & Graf, T. (2010). Survey of pedestrian detection for advanced driver assistance systems. *IEEE Transactions on Pattern Analysis and Machine Intelligence, 32*(7), 1239–1258. doi:10.1109/TPAMI.2009.122 PMID:20489227

Gerónimo, D., Sappa, A., López, A., & Ponsa, D. (2007, April). Adaptive image sampling and windows classification for on-board pedestrian detection. In *Proceedings of the International Conference on Computer Vision Systems*, Bielefeld, Germany (Vol. 39).

Govoni, M., Vitucci, E. M., Degli Esposti, V., Guidi, F., Tartarini, G., & Dardari, D. (2015, July). Study of a UWB multi-static radar for railroad crossing surveillance. In *Proceedings of the 2015 IEEE International Symposium on Antennas and Propagation & USNC/URSI National Radio Science Meeting* (pp. 516-517). IEEE. doi:10.1109/APS.2015.7304644

He, R., Ai, B., Wang, G., Guan, K., Zhong, Z., Molisch, A. F., ... & Oestges, C. P. (2016). High-Speed Railway Communications: From GSM-R to LTE-R. *IEEE vehicular technology magazine, 11*(3), 49-58.

Hodge, V. J., OKeefe, S., Weeks, M., & Moulds, A. (2015). Wireless sensor networks for condition monitoring in the railway industry: A survey. *IEEE Transactions on Intelligent Transportation Systems, 16*(3), 1088–1106. doi:10.1109/TITS.2014.2366512

Hu, J. (2010). Noise in laser. *Journal of Chifeng College, 26*(5), 112–113.

Hung, R., King, B., & Chen, W. (2015). Conceptual issues regarding the development of underground railway laser scanning systems. *ISPRS International journal of geo-information, 4*(1), 185-198.

Jun, W., Wu, T., & Zheng, Z. (2015, December). LIDAR and vision based pedestrian detection and tracking system. In *Proceedings of the 2015 IEEE International Conference on Progress in Informatics and Computing (PIC),* (pp. 118-122). IEEE.

Jwa, Y., & Sonh, G. (2015). Kalman filter based railway tracking from mobile lidar data. In *ISPRS Annals of Photogrammetry, Remote Sensing and Spatial Information Sciences* (pp. 159-164).

Kaleli, F., & Akgul, Y. S. (2009, October). Vision-based railroad track extraction using dynamic programming. In *Proceedings of the 2009 12th International IEEE Conference on Intelligent Transportation Systems* (pp. 1-6). IEEE. doi:10.1109/ITSC.2009.5309526

Kamel, M. S., & Wanas, N. M. (2003, June). Data dependence in combining classifiers. In *Proceedings of the International Workshop on Multiple Classifier Systems* (pp. 1-14). Springer Berlin Heidelberg.

Kastrinaki, V., Zervakis, M., & Kalaitzakis, K. (2003). A survey of video processing techniques for traffic applications. *Image and Vision Computing, 21*(4), 359–381. doi:10.1016/S0262-8856(03)00004-0

Kjell, T. (2014, March 11). *Vectorize rails wires and compute track geometry* [YouTube video]. Retrieved from https://www.youtube.com/watch?v=YeeLjN3viKQ

Kremer, J., & Grimm, A. (2012). The RailMapper—A dedicated mobile LiDAR mapping system for railway networks. *Int. Arch. Photogramm. Remote Sens. Spat. Inf. Sci,* 39-B5.

Lai, X., & Zheng, M. (2015). A Denoising Method for LiDAR Full-Waveform Data. *Mathematical Problems in Engineering.*

Lai, X. D. (2010). Airborne LiDAR Basic Principle and Application.

LASer (LAS) File Format Exchange Activities. (n. d.). Retrieved March 29, 2016, from https://www.asprs.org/committee-general/laser-las-file-format-exchange-activities.html

Lenior, D., Janssen, W., Neerincx, M., & Schreibers, K. (2006). Human-factors engineering for smart transport: Decision support for car drivers and train traffic controllers. *Applied Ergonomics, 37*(4), 479–490. doi:10.1016/j.apergo.2006.04.021 PMID:16765905

Lerkvarnyu, S., Deijhan, K., & Cheevasuvit, F. (1998). Moving average method for time series lidar data. Retrieved from http//www. gisdevelopment. net/aars/acrs/1998/ps3016. shtml

Lesler, M., Perry, G., & McNease, K. (2010, April). Using mobile LiDAR to survey a railway line for asset Inventory. In *Proceedings of the American Society for Photogrammetry and Remote Sensing (ASPRS) 2010 Annual Conference,* San Diego, CA.

Li, B., Yao, Q., & Wang, K. (2012, April). A review on vision-based pedestrian detection in intelligent transportation systems. In *Proceedings of the 2012 9th IEEE International Conference on Networking, Sensing and Control (ICNSC)* (pp. 393-398). IEEE. doi:10.1109/ICNSC.2012.6204951

Li, X., Flohr, F., Yang, Y., Xiong, H., Braun, M., Pan, S., & Gavrila, D. M. et al. (2016, June). A new benchmark for vision-based cyclist detection. In *Intelligent Vehicles Symposium (IV), 2016 IEEE* (pp. 1028-1033). IEEE.

Li, X., Gong, J. B., & Zhou, Z. W. (2007). Laser imaging radar waveform digitalize technology. *Hongwai Yu Jiguang Gongcheng*, (1), 474–477.

Lin, Z., & Davis, L. S. (2010). Shape-based human detection and segmentation via hierarchical part-template matching. *IEEE Transactions on Pattern Analysis and Machine Intelligence*, *32*(4), 606–618. PMID:20224118

Liu, L. L. (2011). *Decomposition of Airborne LiDAR Full-Waveform Data Based on LM Method*. Wuhan, China: Wuhan University.

Liu, P., Choo, K. K. R., Wang, L., & Huang, F. (2016). SVM or deep learning? A comparative study on remote sensing image classification. *Soft Computing*.

Maire, F. (2007, September). Vision based anti-collision system for rail track maintenance vehicles. In *Proceedings of the IEEE Conference on Advanced Video and Signal Based Surveillance AVSS '07* (pp. 170-175). IEEE. doi:10.1109/AVSS.2007.4425305

Maire, F., & Bigdeli, A. (2010, December). Obstacle-free range determination for rail track maintenance vehicles. In *Proceedings of the 2010 11th International Conference on Control Automation Robotics & Vision (ICARCV)* (pp. 2172-2178). IEEE. doi:10.1109/ICARCV.2010.5707923

Mancini, M., Costante, G., Valigi, P., & Ciarfuglia, T. A. (2016, October). Fast robust monocular depth estimation for Obstacle Detection with fully convolutional networks. In *Proceedings of the 2016 IEEE/RSJ International Conference on Intelligent Robots and Systems (IROS)* (pp. 4296-4303). IEEE. doi:10.1109/IROS.2016.7759632

Mašek, J., Kolarovszki, P., & Čamaj, J. (2016). Application of RFID Technology in Railway Transport Services and Logistics Chains. *Procedia Engineering*, *134*, 231–236. doi:10.1016/j.proeng.2016.01.064

Masson, É., & Berbineau, M. (2017). Railway Applications Requiring Broadband Wireless Communications. In *Broadband Wireless Communications for Railway Applications* (pp. 35–79). Springer International Publishing. doi:10.1007/978-3-319-47202-7_2

Möller, H., Hulin, B., Krötz, W., & Sarnes, B. (2001, November). Video based obstacle detection in catenaries of railways. In *Proceeding of 6th International Conference on Pattern Recognition and Information Processing* (Vol. 1, No. 7, pp. 275-287).

Morgan, D. Using mobile LiDAR to survey railway infrastructure. Lynx mobile mapper. In *Proceedings of the FIG Commissions 5(6) and SSGA Workshop*, Lake Baikal, Russia (pp. 32–40).

Motion-Based Multiple Object Tracking. (n. d.). Retrieved September 20, 2016, from https://www.mathworks.com/help/vision/examples/motion-based-multiple-object-tracking.html

Mukojima, H., Deguchi, D., Kawanishi, Y., Ide, I., Murase, H., Ukai, M., . . . Nakasone, R. (2016, September). Moving camera background-subtraction for obstacle detection on railway tracks. In *Proceedings of the 2016 IEEE International Conference on Image Processing (ICIP)* (pp. 3967-3971). IEEE. doi:10.1109/ICIP.2016.7533104

Munder, S., & Gavrila, D. M. (2006). An experimental study on pedestrian classification. *IEEE Transactions on Pattern Analysis and Machine Intelligence*, 28(11), 1863–1868. doi:10.1109/TPAMI.2006.217 PMID:17063690

Nassu, B. T., & Ukai, M. (2011, June). Rail extraction for driver support in railways. In *Proceedings of the Intelligent Vehicles Symposium (IV)* (pp. 83-88). IEEE. doi:10.1109/IVS.2011.5940410

Nassu, B. T., & Ukai, M. (2012). A Vision-Based Approach for Rail Extraction and its Application in a Camera Pan–Tilt Control System. *IEEE Transactions on Intelligent Transportation Systems*, 13(4), 1763–1771. doi:10.1109/TITS.2012.2204052

Niknejad, H. T., Takeuchi, A., Mita, S., & McAllester, D. (2012). On-road multivehicle tracking using deformable object model and particle filter with improved likelihood estimation. *IEEE Transactions on Intelligent Transportation Systems*, 13(2).

Ohta, M. (2005). Level crossings obstacle detection system using stereo cameras. *Quarterly Report of RTRI*, 46(2), 110–117. doi:10.2219/rtriqr.46.110

Oliveira, L., & Nunes, U. (2013, June). Pedestrian detection based on LIDAR-driven sliding window and relational parts-based detection. In *Proceedings of the Intelligent Vehicles Symposium (IV)* (pp. 328-333). IEEE. doi:10.1109/IVS.2013.6629490

Oliveira, L., Nunes, U., & Peixoto, P. (2010). On exploration of classifier ensemble synergism in pedestrian detection. *IEEE Transactions on Intelligent Transportation Systems*, 11(1), 16–27. doi:10.1109/TITS.2009.2026447

Paisitkriangkrai, S., Shen, C., & Zhang, J. (2008). Performance evaluation of local features in human classification and detection. *IET Computer Vision*, 2(4), 236–246. doi:10.1049/iet-cvi:20080026

Peng, H., Long, F., & Ding, C. (2005). Feature selection based on mutual information criteria of max-dependency, max-relevance, and min- redundancy. *IEEE Transactions on Pattern Analysis and Machine Intelligence*, 27(8), 1226–1238. doi:10.1109/TPAMI.2005.159 PMID:16119262

Premebida, C., Ludwig, O., & Nunes, U. (2009). LIDAR and vision-based pedestrian detection system. *Journal of Field Robotics*, 26(9), 696–711. doi:10.1002/rob.20312

Puttagunta, S. S., & Chraim, F. (2016). U.S. Patent No. 20,160,121,912. Washington, DC: U.S. Patent and Trademark Office.

Qi, Z., Tian, Y., & Shi, Y. (2013). Efficient railway tracks detection and turnouts recognition method using HOG features. *Neural Computing & Applications*, 23(1), 245–254. doi:10.1007/s00521-012-0846-0

RailwayTunnel Brockwille. (2013, January 11). *Lidar Scan of the Brockville Railway Tunnel* [YouTube video]. Retrieved from https://www.youtube.com/watch?v=oOGYwOeKJck

Reina, G., Milella, A., Halft, W., & Worst, R. (2013, October). LIDAR and stereo imagery integration for safe navigation in outdoor settings. In *Proceedings of the 2013 IEEE International Symposium on Safety, Security, and Rescue Robotics (SSRR)* (pp. 1-6). IEEE. doi:10.1109/SSRR.2013.6719333

Reitberger, J., Krzystek, P., & Stilla, U. (2008). Analysis of full waveform LIDAR data for the classification of deciduous and coniferous trees. *International Journal of Remote Sensing, 29*(5), 1407–1431. doi:10.1080/01431160701736448

Rezaei, M., & Sabzevari, R. (2009). *Multisensor data fusion strategies for advanced driver assistance systems*. Sensor and Data Fusion. doi:10.5772/6575

RIEGL. (n. d.). Produktdetail. Retrieved October 10, 2016, from http://www.riegl.com/nc/products/mobile-scanning/produktdetail/product/scannersystem/10/

Ross, R. (2012, September). Track and turnout detection in video-signals using probabilistic spline curves. In *Proceedings of the 2012 15th International IEEE Conference on Intelligent Transportation Systems* (pp. 294-299). IEEE. doi:10.1109/ITSC.2012.6338605

Ruder, M., Mohler, N., & Ahmed, F. (2003, June). An obstacle detection system for automated trains. In *Proceedings of the Intelligent Vehicles Symposium* (pp. 180-185). IEEE. doi:10.1109/IVS.2003.1212905

Sabzmeydani, P., & Mori, G. (2007, June). Detecting pedestrians by learning shapelet features. In *Proceedings of the 2007 IEEE Conference on Computer Vision and Pattern Recognition* (pp. 1-8). IEEE.

Schiavo, A. L. (2016). Fully Autonomous Wireless Sensor Network for Freight Wagon Monitoring. *IEEE Sensors Journal, 16*(24), 9053–9063. doi:10.1109/JSEN.2016.2620149

Schwartz, W. R., Kembhavi, A., Harwood, D., & Davis, L. S. (2009, September). Human detection using partial least squares analysis. In *Proceedings of the 2009 IEEE 12th international conference on computer vision* (pp. 24-31). IEEE. doi:10.1109/ICCV.2009.5459205

Selver, M. A., Er, E., Belenlioglu, B., & Soyaslan, Y. (2016, August). Camera based driver support system for rail extraction using 2-D Gabor wavelet decompositions and morphological analysis. In *Proceedings of the 2016 IEEE International Conference on Intelligent Rail Transportation (ICIRT)* (pp. 270-275). IEEE.

Sinha, D., & Feroz, F. (2016). Obstacle Detection on Railway Tracks Using Vibration Sensors and Signal Filtering Using Bayesian Analysis. *IEEE Sensors Journal, 16*(3), 642–649. doi:10.1109/JSEN.2015.2490247

Sivaraman, S., & Trivedi, M. M. (2013, June). A review of recent developments in vision-based vehicle detection. In *Proceedings of the Intelligent Vehicles Symposium* (pp. 310-315). doi:10.1109/IVS.2013.6629487

Sock, J., Kim, J., Min, J., & Kwak, K. (2016, May). Probabilistic traversability map generation using 3D-LIDAR and camera. In *Proceedings of the 2016 IEEE International Conference on Robotics and Automation (ICRA)* (pp. 5631-5637). IEEE.

SSIMichigan. (2013, June 26). *Mobile LiDAR Utilized on Rail Project-1* [YouTube video]. Retrieved from https://www.youtube.com/watch?v=hnig-Ldb-3s

Stelmaszczyk, K., Czyzewski, A., Szymanski, A., Pietruczuk, A., Chudzynski, S., Ernst, K., & Stacewicz, T. (2000). New method of elaboration of the lidar signal. *Applied Physics. B, Lasers and Optics, 70*(2), 295–299. doi:10.1007/s003400050048

Sun, B. Y., Huang, D. S., & Fang, H. T. (2005). Lidar signal denoising using least-squares support vector machine. *IEEE Signal Processing Letters*, *12*(2), 101–104. doi:10.1109/LSP.2004.836938

Teng, Z., Liu, F., & Zhang, B. (2016). Visual railway detection by superpixel based intracellular decisions. *Multimedia Tools and Applications*, *75*(5), 2473–2486. doi:10.1007/s11042-015-2654-x

Thaduri, A., Galar, D., & Kumar, U. (2015). Railway Assets: A Potential Domain for Big Data Analytics. *Procedia Computer Science*, *53*, 457–467. doi:10.1016/j.procs.2015.07.323

Tracking Pedestrians from a Moving Car (n. d.). Retrieved September 10, 2016, from https://www.mathworks.com/help/vision/examples/motion-based-multiple-object-tracking.html

Tuzel, O., Porikli, F., & Meer, P. (2008). Pedestrian detection via classification on riemannian manifolds. *IEEE Transactions on Pattern Analysis and Machine Intelligence*, *30*(10), 1713–1727. doi:10.1109/TPAMI.2008.75 PMID:18703826

Ultra Global Personal Rapid Transit Systems. (2011, September 07). Retrieved December 25, 2017, from http://www.ultraglobalprt.com/

Utkin, A. B., Lavrov, A. V., Costa, L., Simoes, F., & Vilar, R. (2002). Detection of small forest fires by lidar. *Applied Physics. B, Lasers and Optics*, *74*(1), 77–83. doi:10.1007/s003400100772

Veitch-Michaelis, J., Muller, J. P., Storey, J., Walton, D., & Foster, M. (2015). Data Fusion of LIDAR Into a Region Growing Stereo Algorithm. *The International Archives of Photogrammetry. Remote Sensing and Spatial Information Sciences*, *40*(4), 107.

Wagner, W., Ullrich, A., Ducic, V., Melzer, T., & Studnicka, N. (2006). Gaussian decomposition and calibration of a novel small-footprint full-waveform digitising airborne laser scanner. *ISPRS Journal of Photogrammetry and Remote Sensing*, *60*(2), 100–112. doi:10.1016/j.isprsjprs.2005.12.001

Walk, S., Majer, N., Schindler, K., & Schiele, B. (2010, June). New features and insights for pedestrian detection. In Proceedings of the 2010 IEEE conference on Computer vision and pattern recognition (CVPR) (pp. 1030-1037). IEEE. doi:10.1109/CVPR.2010.5540102

Wang, Z., Cai, B., Chunxiao, J., Tao, C., Zhang, Z., Wang, Y., . . . Zhang, F. (2016, June). Geometry constraints-based visual rail track extraction. In *Proceedings of the 2016 12th World Congress on Intelligent Control and Automation (WCICA)* (pp. 993-998). IEEE. doi:10.1109/WCICA.2016.7578298

Wang, Z., Wu, X., Yan, Y., Jia, C., Cai, B., Huang, Z., . . . Zhang, T. (2015, October). An inverse projective mapping-based approach for robust rail track extraction. In *Proceedings of the 2015 8th International Congress on Image and Signal Processing (CISP)* (pp. 888-893). IEEE. doi:10.1109/CISP.2015.7408003

Wohlfeil, J. (2011, June). Vision based rail track and switch recognition for self-localization of trains in a rail network. In *Proceedings of the Intelligent Vehicles Symposium (IV)* (pp. 1025-1030). IEEE. doi:10.1109/IVS.2011.5940466

Wu, B., & Nevatia, R. (2005, October). Detection of multiple, partially occluded humans in a single image by bayesian combination of edgelet part detectors. In *Proceedings of the Tenth IEEE International Conference on Computer Vision (ICCV'05)* (Vol. 1, pp. 90-97). IEEE.

Wu, X., Yuan, P., Peng, Q., Ngo, C. W., & He, J. Y. (2016). Detection of bird nests in overhead catenary system images for high-speed rail. *Pattern Recognition*, *51*, 242–254. doi:10.1016/j.patcog.2015.09.010

Yan, L., Fang, X., Li, H., & Li, C. (2016, May). An mmwave wireless communication and radar detection integrated network for railways. In *Proceedings of the 2016 IEEE 83rd Vehicular Technology Conference (VTC Spring)* (pp. 1-5). IEEE. doi:10.1109/VTCSpring.2016.7504133

Yang, G., & Huang, C. M. (2005). Decomposing algorithm of laser altimeter waveforms. *Chin J Space Sci*, *25*(2), 125–131.

Zeng, C., & Ma, H. (2010, August). Robust head-shoulder detection by pca-based multilevel hog-lbp detector for people counting. In *Proceedings of the 2010 20th International Conference on Pattern Recognition (ICPR)* (pp. 2069-2072). IEEE. doi:10.1109/ICPR.2010.509

Zhang, H. Y., Fan, G. H., Zhang, T. H., & Zheng, Y. H. (2012). Wavelet denoising study of laser radar waveform signal. *Research for Development*, *5*(31), 52–58.

Zhu, L., & Hyyppa, J. (2014). The use of airborne and mobile laser scanning for modeling railway environments in 3D. *Remote Sensing*, *6*(4), 3075–3100. doi:10.3390/rs6043075

Chapter 4
Wayside Train Monitoring Systems:
Origin and Application

Swastikaa Moudgil
Chandigarh College of Engineering and Technology, India

Ashim Bhasin
Chandigarh College of Engineering and Technology, India

Ankit Gupta
Chandigarh College of Engineering and Technology, India

ABSTRACT

The present competitive world of transport particularly the rail industry is driven by automation and centralization. New ways are being devised each day by the operators and managers to improve efficiency, operational safety, and risk control. Big Data and its multiple applications play a significant role in developing ways of analyzing and evaluating the rail data gathered and using it to enhance the transport industry. Wayside train Monitoring System is a field that is slowly gaining popularity through the different methods it provides to handle the big Data of the transport industry. It can measure the operational performance of rolling stock and infrastructure assets as well as the direct surroundings. The chapter addresses the problem of overall safety and optimum cost of railways transportation. Consequently, the chapter aims to resolve the following issues: How can the rail industry leverage the enormous amount of data available? How can industry players benefit from the data and use it to understand the real needs of travelers?

INTRODUCTION

The discipline of data collection and analysis has undergone a drastic change in the last 10 years. Technological progress in industries such as sales, healthcare, road transport, aviation etc. has given birth to new opportunities. The big-data technology helps improving data collection and analysis by providing

DOI: 10.4018/978-1-5225-3176-0.ch004

sophisticated tools for data collection, analysis, and visualization. It plays a vital role in reducing the human intervention in the reporting systems. The public transport industry has been at the forefront of utilizing applications of this technology. The railway system can be categorized into two different principles. The first one, based on a functional approach and the second based on safety. These are the sub-systems of the railways that need immediate attention of the Big Data technology:

1. Infrastructure
2. Trackside control-command and signaling
3. On-board control-command and signaling
4. Energy
5. Rolling stock
6. Operation and traffic management
7. Maintenance

Among the multiple approaches available, Wayside Train Monitoring System (WTMS), if used to its full capacity, can prove to be highly significant. WTMS provides methods to improve the detection, reporting, and analysis of occurrences. The chapter aims to investigate the potential for Big-Data in the railway industry with an objective of improving the safety level of the Single European Railway Area and the efficiency of the occurrence reporting by reducing human interference in the reporting process.

BACKGROUND

In today's world, there are many opportunities available to improve the productivity, reliability, velocity and safety of railroads. A major challenge in this field is the efficient utilization of 'Big Data' to improve these factors. Big Data is an all-encompassing term for any collection of data sets so large and complex that it becomes highly cumbersome to process them using traditional data processing approaches.

The 3 elements of Big Data are summarized using the 3 V's approach: Volume, Velocity, and Variety.

1. Volume is the size of the data sets: the magnitude order is from Terabyte to Petabyte;
2. Variety means that big-data can deal with data coming from multiple sources and having different structure;
3. Velocity can be understood as the capability to comprehend the vast input data and produce meaningful output.

Currently, railroads are dependent on sources like GPS, AEI readers, electronic data exchange, video inspections, hand-held field tables etc. to collect enormous quantities of data. The data is primarily divided into 3 categories: Fixed, Mobile and Organizational elements. The Fixed element comprises of the network, which is made of lines, stations, terminals, and all kinds of fixed equipment that ensures safe and continuous operation of the system. The Mobile Elements refers to all types of vehicles traveling on that network and lastly, the Organizational elements are the sub-systems that deal with the functioning of the fixed and mobile elements.

Therefore, the data from all the above sources and much more is growing both in quantity and quality and is getting more vast and frequent. The traditional approaches are not being fruitful to analyze such large sizes of data. So, this is where the big data technology comes into the picture. Fast methods requiring least human interference need to be developed to manage the humongous data. Wayside Train Monitoring System is playing a pivotal role in railway operation and vehicle maintenance. This novel concept of the European railways has various dimensions and tools that can be exploited to benefit the rail industry.

Two concepts currently at the leading edge of today's information technology revolution are Analytics and Big Data. The public transportation industry is utilizing and implementing Analytics and Big Data for a variety of purposes ranging from ridership forecasting to transit operations. Rail transit systems have been involved with these IT concepts because they are generally closed systems that involve sophisticated processing of large volumes of data.

FOCUS OF THE CHAPTER

The chapter provides a perfect amalgamation of the scope of Big Data in railways with WTMS. Since the time when the term was first coined in 2001, Big Data has found its application in fields ranging from sales to transport. The transport industry, particularly the railways, needs quick tactics to deal with the heterogeneous data in an optimized manner. Hence the technology of big data particularly Wayside Train Monitoring Systems is being exploited to its fullest. The key aspect of WTMS covered here is the safety approach. The railway system depends on the safety performance of the sub-systems and the way they are managed. The WTMS concept discussed in this chapter is an attempt to map the data available from variant sources and assort it to enhance the rail industry. WTMS and WIMS cover various tools including Train Conformity Check Systems, Weigh In Motion (WIM) (Indian Institute Of Technology Kanpur, n.d.) Wheel Impact Load Detector (WILD) etc. which have been discussed in detail in the later parts of the chapter. The chapter provides a vivid and a relative description of the Big Data in Railways, Origin of WTMS and a comparative study of the ARGOS approach. The world has recently witnessed some significant events including the WTMS Conference 2011 and the Intelligent Rail Summit 2016 that have contributed tremendously to this field. A deep insight into the Real Time Monitoring Systems has been done along with a parallel study of the Conventional Approach and the Big Data. The chapter also provides information on the novel idea of "IoT" (Internet of Trains) and illustrates the working of WTMS. The WTMS provides the uncompromising safety that has been justified effectively. The chapter highlights the most important features of WTMS and covers all the areas of study in Big Data including its relationship with the humans too.

BIG DATA IN THE TRANSPORT INDUSTRY

The prime reasons for implementing Big Data in the transport industry have been to monitor and improve the quality of service to the commuters and maintenance of assets to enhance the safety of the passengers. The scenario is not as simple as it seems. The transport industry accumulates different types of data that undergo heedful analysis to produce fruitful conclusions, which can then be used to improve the present condition of railways. After a deep analysis of the railway industry, it has been found that the complete rail data can be categorized as follows:

1. Data consolidated by the Infrastructure department that includes data describing:
   a. Track sleepers and their conditions of use
   b. Rail fastening systems and their conditions of use
   c. Rail conditions like temperature, track geometry, rail corrugation
2. Data based on the track-side control-command and signaling system:
   a. State of each signal of the infrastructure
   b. Availability of block sections
3. Data based on individual parameters like the contact force between wheel and rail which is used in Wayside Train Monitoring Systems:
   a. Actual weight of the rolling stock
   b. Load balance
   c. Geometry of the wheel
   d. Loading gauge (envelope)
   e. Temperature of axle boxes, wheels, and brake discs
   f. Pantograph (electrical trolley carried by collapsible frames)
4. Data required for the internal monitoring of the Safety Management Systems (SMS):
   a. CSIs, to be reported to comply with the EU legislation
   b. Indicators defined by the NOR, to be reported to comply with national legislation

The mostly widely used big-data implementation is in the private road transport. Private car drivers can easily rely on data available from the GPS applications as it provides real-time information on traffic, accidents, and disruptions. Applications like Google Maps, Apple Maps or Waze are well accustomed to deal with the data about the position of the users to calculate the average speed and to detect traffic jams.

The data from such applications is combined with the information provided automatically by the smart phones and is used to improve the quality of the information on traffic and itineraries. In public transport, the use of big-data is more oriented to manage the quality of the service. For instance, consider a company that manages public transport on light rail and buses in a European capital. The company relies on the data captured by contact-less readers (based on RFID technology) to detect the position of the passengers. After retrieving the data, the company can measure the number of passengers traveling on their train routes and their distribution in time. This conclusion can be used to deduce the rush hours and about the travel habits of the people. Tools of data mining like Weka can be used to support these conclusions through illustrations. Thus, the company can increase the number of trains or bogies on the given route for the specified time.

Big Data is an interesting tool that not only helps to manage the variant data but also to draw conclusions from the available data. Suppose the company is unable to know the passenger exit points from the sensors. In such conditions, some algorithms can be combined with the technology of Big Data to infer the exit point of the passengers by utilizing the passenger position and the bus position.

To prove the importance of Big-Data in the modern world, we present some statistics and graphs based on the data available on the UK Government's website. The UK Government conducts surveys twice every year to take feedback from its commuters. Figure 1 and 2 refer to two of the parameters covered in the survey from 2003-2015. One is the grade of cleanliness in the train and the second is the repairing and up keeping of the train. The commuters rated the parameters as very poor, fairly poor, fairly good, very good and none of the above. In Figure 1 and 2 Aut means autumn while Spr means Spring. (data.gov.UK, 2015)

Figure 1. Cleanliness on board

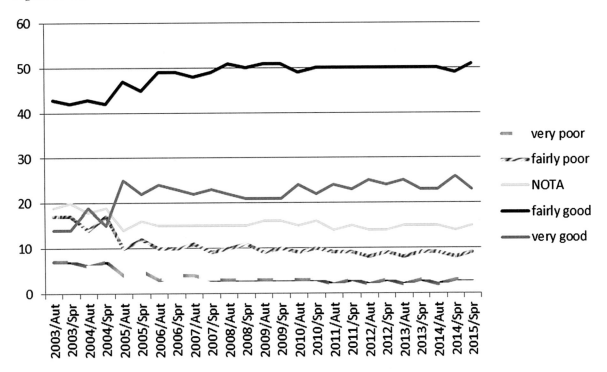

Figure 2. Up keep and repair of train

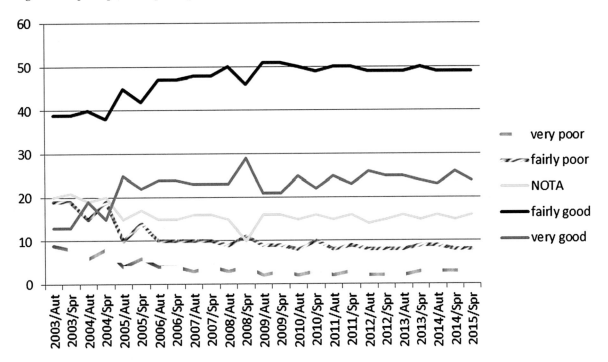

The number of commuters who were not satisfied with either of the two parameters reduced while the ones satisfied increased. This happened solely because the companies took care of the data collected and worked on the areas that needed attention. As a result, the level of cleanliness and up keeping improved. This shows how the analysis of Big-Data can be quite helpful to improve the quality of services to the railway users and helps companies increase their revenue through contented customer base.

BIG DATA IN RAILWAYS

The Big Data available in Railways can be broadly classified into three sub-categories:

- **Monitoring and Data Collection:** The monitoring phase of any management system is a 4-part process that includes- Planning, implementation, Checking, and Analysis. The monitoring of safety performance of railways at all levels, from operational to regulatory, is defined with the sole aim of continually improving the safety level of the railway system, when reasonably practicable. Unfortunately, the European Union Agency does not have a clear overview of the strength and quality of monitoring processes within sector companies. There is a divergence of opinion within the European states regarding the management monitoring systems. The UK approach sets a good reference in terms of safety management and consequently of data gathering and sharing across the whole industry in the whole country. The Safety bulletin is issued regularly by RSSB with the intention to inform the industry about safety performance and risk profiles.

However, in the rest of Europe, new companies are established with the purpose to support data sharing and cooperative safety management, but they are still in the primitive stages. This means that, in other European member states, data are collected and analyzed at a company level and shared with the National Safety Authority (NSA), only when it becomes strictly necessary or to fulfill legal requirements. The completeness of the internal monitoring process of each railway operator is linked to the collection of data.

Data collection is of 2 types: automatic and manual. It is automatic when the data acquisition is triggered by a specific event detected by sensors (such as trains traversing the route on a specific point) and then gathered and stored by means of technical equipment, without any human intervention. Manual reporting can be done using technical systems or IT equipment (tablets, mobile phones, etc.) but it is always done manually by humans. The decision to report is not triggered by sensors but is made by

Figure 3. Classification of Big Data in railways

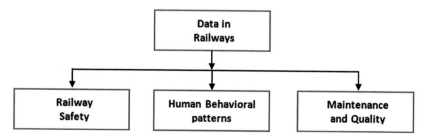

human beings according to their perception of reality. This introduces a subjective element. Automatic systems allow detection of issues which are not easily perceived by humans. For instance, the actual axle load of a freight wagon could be calculated by humans but it will require the use of a specific balance and then a reporting procedure. A WTMS makes its measurement and reporting much easier and reliable. The Artificial Intelligence industry has still not evolved enough to match the intelligence and flexibility of human beings so it is not possible to replace manual reporting made by humans with automatic reporting systems.

- **Instance of Implementation:** A Swedish train operator recently came into the spotlight because of a new algorithm able to forecast delays. According to the reports, the traffic controllers can be alerted of any possible delays, 2 hours before they occur. This predictive algorithm gives the traffic controller a chance to be proactive and manage the traffic to preserve the quality of the service. The algorithm is based on machine learning which uses historical data to identify events which led to train delays in the past. When the system detects the same type of pattern, an alert is raised to the traffic controller to make timely interventions.

This application of the technology is interesting because it not only makes use of historical data to detect unknown causes of delays (machine learning) but also because it allows the traffic controller to simulate the effectiveness of possible solutions.

- **Safety Mechanisms:** The concept of monitoring can easily be applied to railways safety too. The Railway Safety Directive (RSD) has given the responsibility to Infrastructure Managers, Railway Undertakings, and Entities in Charge of Maintenance to control risks arising from their operations. A proper Management System has been imposed to control the risks. A monitoring process is also required and a specific Common Safety Method (CSM) has been drafted by the European Union Agency. To ensure complete safety standards, the Management system covering all the departments of the railways must follow the given steps:
  - Submit all the strategies and plans involved in the monitoring.
  - Devise a system to collect all available data.
  - Plan a method to analyze the collected data and converting it into useful information.
  - Use the derived information to improve the processes and the management system.
- **Risk Models:** The European Union Agency identified the prevention of catastrophic accidents as a specific objective for the safety management data element of the Agency's Common Occurrence Reporting project. Catastrophic accidents are rare and are often attributed to a range of interrelated causes so they are difficult to simulate. In this case, the use of several data sets generated by different operators and NSAs for a complete safety analysis is useful. Developing and maintaining a risk model requires enough data, time and ample resources. Big Data technology has played an unparalleled role to support this process of developing risk models to project the right kind of information.

A team of data scientists and railway specialists having the capability to use different types of data sources as well as identifying new patterns and correlations in the data are appointed for the purpose. All this helps to identify additional and unknown hazards and to provide evidence to contradict safety

Figure 4. Big Data for risk model
Source: European Union Agency for Railways, n. d.

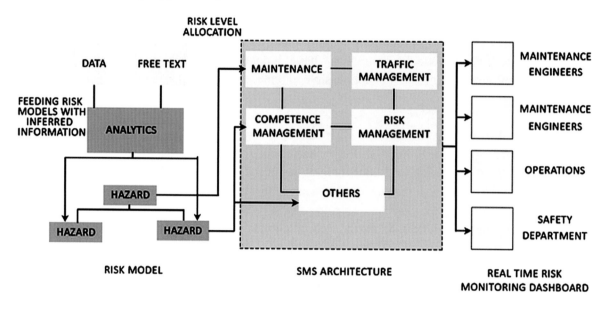

misconceptions. To build a risk model, it is necessary to check the availability of historical data in the industry along with the operational data, asset data, and safety records. Although new to railways, other sectors, including European and US aviation, are exploring and implementing this technology.

- **Big Data of Human Behaviour – OTRD:** As mentioned earlier the Big Data has 3 broad categories: variety, velocity, and volume. The increase in volume means more data is being collected but not analyzed as there is no capacity. Variety means that the humongous data available cannot be classified as there is no common structure. Velocity means the capability to collect, analyze and visualize more data in the same frame of reference (time). The Volume factor is extremely important in those branches of safety analysis where the description of the surrounding conditions is crucial to understand behaviors and causes. Even if the level of the data quality is held optimum, the data collection and description share a direct relation.

Monitoring human performance is a good example of tapping the full potential of Big Data. On Train Recording Device (OTRD) is a tool used to document human performance but it is too limited to describe the complexity of human performance and the relevant influencing factors. OTRD has clearly proved that changes in the vehicle affect the drivers' behavior too. This is not a direct observation but has been concluded from the understanding of the effects of noise and temperature on human performance. Using this model, it could be found that noisy locomotives generate delays because of the lower traction effort requested by the driver to minimize noise. The data to undertake this analysis comes from the OTRD complemented by other sources describing all the influencing factors. This analysis requires a massive amount of data to produce accurate results which justify that the Volume considered is an apt parameter of Big Data.

Automotive manufacturers are continuously conducting research to monitor and support car driver behavior, to prevent drivers sleeping. The addition of human observation in the OTRD system has increased an element of manual reporting thereby drastically increasing the complexity of the system. This is an example of the importance of using different and varied data sources i.e. Variety in Big Data. The Velocity factor is crucial in this scenario because all the data collected from the OTRD must be analyzed quickly and sent to the traffic control center of the organizations, which could take necessary steps on time to predict and prevent undesirable events.

CONVENTIONAL APPROACH VS. BIG DATA

The advent of Big Data technology has proved to be a boon for the IT world. So, the transport industry, particularly the railways, is gradually moving to this technology to meet the growing needs of its commuters. An organization cannot rely on real-time events to derive information about the system so it was necessary to discard the Conventional Approach to Data Analysis.

Unfortunately, typical "high information density" datasets needed for the conventional approach rarely exist in the present world so the data scientists have accepted Big-data and its multi-facet approach for resolving the issues. The need of the hour is to replace the traditional approach with the Big Data approach because data is a strategic asset that guides all business decisions.

INTRODUCTION TO WTMS

Wayside Train Monitoring Systems (WTMS) and Wayside Infrastructure Monitoring Systems (WIMS) are the subjects introduced in this section. WTMS was first used by the European Union Railways in countries like Switzerland and Finland as a means to improve safety, although the analysis of the data

Table 1.

Conventional Approach	Big Data
1. A collection of indicators that give specific details about real-time events forms the basis of Traditional Monitoring Systems.	1. Data need not necessarily be obtained from real-time events. Techniques like Machine Learning have helped to draw patterns and predict behavior.
2. Conventional Approach is highly dependent on "High-Density Information".	2. Big Data has the capability to elaborate big volumes of even "Low-Density Information".
3. The complete process of regression and data analysis is handled by human beings so the data schemes should be simple and self-explanatory.	3. Big Data has reduced the time taken for risk modeling because there are ideas like neural networks and machine learning to enable self- improvement.
4. This approach is dependent on highly explicit data with the prime focus on safety-related indicators (accidents and their precursors).	4. Big Data can infer information from the heterogeneous data and to reveal hidden information from the implicit data.
5. It only provides a limited, domain-specific data analysis.	5. It provides a cohesive monitoring that is essential to understand the reality and manage the business effectively.
6. The Conventional Approach only focused on regression of explicit data with a minimal focus on historic data.	6. Big Data has led to comprehensive monitoring that affects the decision making of traffic managers by depicting interrelations between different occurrences.

has been extended for maintenance purposes too. WTMS are technological systems installed at selected places along the track that perform measurements and checks on the moving rolling stock. Most tragedies, especially in freight traffic, are caused by defective wheel bearings and brakes, unbalanced loads, out of gauge devices, fire on board, etc. WTMS is very substantial in monitoring these parameters in real time, thus preventing accidents as often as possible. Therefore, this monitoring system is slowly garnering popularity to become the most competent tool to resolve the safety concerns of the railway's department. WTMS has always laid focus on achieving the following 3 targets:

1. Accident prevention.
2. Reduction of highly track-wearing rolling stock.
3. Supporting predictive maintenance of rolling stock and rail infrastructure.

COMPONENTS OF WTMS

The most well-known and important components of WTMS have been listed below:

1. **Train Conformity Check System (TCCS):** TCCS can detect and alert dispatchers about several dangerous or damaging defects on rolling stock caused by abnormal temperatures in the train surface and/or out of gauge transit. (Favo et al., 2010). This system is discussed in detail later in the chapter.
2. **Weigh in Motion (WIM):** This parameter weighs train wheels/wagons to detect wagon imbalances and overloads which might cause train derailment or overturning at sharp curves.
3. **Wheel Impact Load Detector (WILD):** Wheel failures account for 50% of all incidents of train derailments and are an outcome of severe rail deterioration which results in premature breaking of rails (Ansaldo, n. d.). Rail breaks prove to be dangerous and very expensive to repair. "Wheel Impact Load Detectors" (WILD) that are installed at strategic locations on the rail network produce data. WILD measures the vertical force or impact of each passing wheel on the rail.
4. **Hot Axle Bearing Detection/Hot Wheel Detection (HABD/HWD):** Another prominent cause of train derailments and long delays are burning off over-heated rail bearings. (Sneed & Smith, 1998). Infrared wayside bearing detectors have been used for the last four decades to notify train crews about the freight car bearings that may have reached burn-off temperature. (Cottrill & Derrible, 2015) Overheated bearings may be captured on infrared detectors if they happen to pass a wayside hot bearing detector (HBD) site.
5. **Pantograph Defect Detection:** (Aydin, Karakose & Akin, 2015; Massat, Laine & Bobillot, 2006). Most trains run on electricity and use pantograph that constantly remains in contact with the overhead electric lines to draw high voltage currents. Poor contact between the pantograph and the line may cause arcing and wearing of the contact strips. The breakdown of pantograph and catenary system causes great economic losses. Hence, companies have started monitoring the pantograph and catenary system to avoid huge economic losses.
6. **Wheel Measurement System (WMS):** (Yang, Chunsheng & Létourneau, 2005). This system uses techniques to monitors the parameters associated with the wheel status, mainly flats or non-uniform shape, for the worst values.

WORKING OF WTMS

1. The premier step is the detection of critical defects in rolling stock. There are multiple problems that are reported to the managers and need immediate attention. Some of them include:
    a. Bad track geometry (soft sub-structured/bad drainage, wrong stress-free temperature)
    b. Cracks and fatigue in rail (creep forces, bad wheel/rail interface)
    c. Rail corrugation and wear i.e. vehicle/track interaction
2. Secondly, WTMS receives alarms from these indicators and identifies the critical defects. These include Shifted load, Inadmissible Profile, Derailed Truck, load Unbalancing etc. WTMS further recognizes the possible events like Derailment, Inter Train Collision, train Infrastructure Collision etc. that may occur if necessary steps are not taken in time.
3. The next step is of Maintenance Optimization which means to plan for the losses that have or may occur in the near future. It includes indirect losses of bearings, track rupture or rolling stock repair.

Eventually, WTMS&WIMS issues notices and agendas proposing reformations steps in the areas where problems have been identified. This may include stopping of defective trains or rescheduling the timetable to reduce freight traffic and deploying workforce to repair the track.

SALIENT FEATURES OF WTMS

1. **Short Response Time:** Wayside Train Monitoring System ensures extensively automated surveillance of trains at normal line speed. This equipment allows detection of irregularities that can jeopardize rail operations before they cause a disruption. A Central Intervention Centre is networked with all the wayside train monitoring devices around the clock. Irregularities and nonconformities are reported in screen-based displays and alarms, analyzed by specialist and decisions are taken immediately.

Figure 5. Steps involved in working of WTMS

2. **Single Integrated System:** WTMS provides safety-relevant functions for loading-gauge and aerial detection, fire and chemical detection, hot box and brake-locking detection, detection of load displacement, overloading, wheel defects, and observation of natural hazards. WTMS provides tools for pantograph monitoring, interference measurements, and contact wire uplift measurements. All alarms and interventions are recorded in a database. This information is forwarded to all other railway companies that could work to optimize the maintenance of their rolling stocks. The various devices and techniques that are incorporated in the single integrated system of the Wayside Train Monitoring System are:

   a. **Wheel Load Checkpoints:** (Indian Institute Of Technology Kanpur, n. d.) These use strain gauges to measure maximum axle load, load displacement, and wheel defects. They help to avoid derailments and damage to rail infrastructure.

   b. **Fire and Chemical Detection:** Highly sensitive multi-component gas analyzers are installed along the network to measure the concentrations of gases such as CO, CO_2 and CH_4. Analysis of this data enables to draw conclusions regarding potential events, such as a possible fire if there is a rise in CO or CO_2 concentration.

   c. **Profile Clearance and Aerial Detection:** The aerial detection systems are equipped with laser scanners that provide a bird view of the rail track and the passing trains. These systems and their 3D displays can quickly reveal when the safety profile is violated to unsecured tarpaulins or protruding vehicle aerials and then corrective action can be taken.

   d. **Uplift Measurement and Pantograph Monitoring:** Contact wire uplift is measured using an electrically isolated potentiometer. Optical systems are to search for defects on pantographs.

   e. **Interference Measurement:** Interference measuring systems monitor electrical fields to prevent malfunction of track-release systems.

   f. **Natural Disaster Alarm Systems:** These systems are most common and yet effective to avert collisions with obstructions during natural hazards like a landslide, mudslide or avalanche. If an alarm is actuated, countermeasures can be quickly implemented, such as the closure of line sections, stopping trains and evacuation of trains.

TRAIN AND INFRASTRUCTURE MONITORING PLATFORM (T&IMP)

Train & Infrastructure Monitoring Platform (T&IMP) collects and delivers data coming from WTMS&WIMS and uses a common measuring and monitoring data representation to build finer data interpretation and foster the adoption of ever more effective intelligent maintenance[1] T&IMP Monitoring system authenticates operators by Username/Password. The main purpose of this platform is to retrieve data related to trains in transit and infrastructure apart from it some other functions include:

1. Monitoring the train in transit
2. Monitoring the infrastructure (rail, switches etc.) under supervision.
3. T&IMP can detect the defects
4. The system provides information/images that help take the appropriate decisions to avert accidents
5. T&IMP allows operators to get real-time status of the transit train to take appropriate measures in case of train failures.

Figure 6. T&IMP architecture

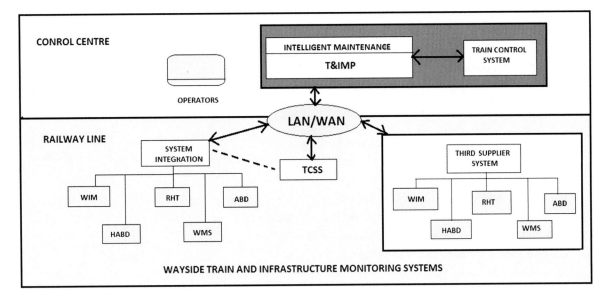

The integration of WTMS and WIMS with T&IMP offers the following advantages:

1. Consolidates the view of all the information in a unique Human Machine Interface.
2. Collects all the data, alarms and diagnostics coming from each wayside monitoring system so there is no scope for error.
3. The information of the wayside monitoring systems is associated with each train in transit and to each kind of infrastructure that provides T&IMP with a complete database of all the information.
4. T&IMP helps in intelligent maintenance through statistics and trend analysis.
5. Diagnostic of the state of the WTMS and WIMS.
6. Since T&IMP is a modular system, one wayside monitoring system can be added each time if required.

WORKING OF T&IMP

After the analysis of each train transit, the details are stored in the online database (Oracle) for statistical analysis that allows train maintenance optimization. Correlation filters are available to process and view the information. T&IMP has an important component called Human Machine Interface (HMI). T&IMP - HMI provides two levels of information management:

1. **Global Level:**
   a. At this level, the operator can monitor all WTMS and WIMS
   b. The installation sites are positioned in various points of the map
   c. Operator can choose a site and examine the generic information available about transits, infrastructures, alarms and alarm management

2. **Site Level:**
   a. Like the Global Level, the operator can manage the details for each site and for each WTMS and WIMS
   b. Examination of the monitoring data, images, alarms etc. can be done for each transit and infrastructure.

T&IMP HMI allow the operators the following benefits: (Ansaldo, n. d.)

1. To display the list of transits in all installation sites
2. They can create an alarm with visual and acoustic signals
3. To display alarm details
4. Manage data for each WTMS and WIMS
5. Power to activate/deactivate each WTMS and WIMS
6. Provides a View of the statistical data analysis and
7. Control measurement related to infrastructure

The Operator Interface (HMI) is a web service-based interface where the T&IMP server acts as a web server so any authorized operator can access it using a standard browser. The Operator Interface collects all information and diagnostics from the various WTMS and WIMS installed and displays them to Operator Interface HMIs at the Control Centre. All information provided to the Operator Interface HMIs is shown by train and by specific infrastructure.

REAL TIME SAFETY MONITORING WITH BIG DATA AND WTMS

The monitoring of specific occurrences in real time is a prevalent practice in some countries. For instance, in Switzerland or in Finland, there is a comprehensive Wayside Train Monitoring System already implemented and fully operational. WTMS is entirely based on real-time monitoring of different parameters like rail traffic, track temperature, bearing types etc. that are forwarded for detail analysis. As mentioned earlier, the railway's system is divided into three sub-systems with different components including infrastructure, track side signaling system, on board control command, rolling stock etc. These systems provide data on:

1. The contact force between wheel and rail, which comprises of the actual weight of rolling stock, load balance, the geometry of wheel etc.
2. Loading gauge (envelope)
3. The temperature of all possible components like wheels, axle boxes and brake discs and much more.

Apart from the above categorization, the data is also received from various departments including Safety Management System (SMS), Infrastructure and Rolling stock. Hence, modern and sophisticated tools are required for deep and careful analysis of the vast amount of data to produce optimal results. Big Data and WTMS are the answer to these problems. WTMS has an automatic reporting system that raises alarms for specific parameters of the rolling stock that enables traffic controllers to take timely action to avoid any calamity. This helps a great deal in avoiding accidents, improving the availability of the infrastructure and mitigating maintenance costs for both railway undertakings and infrastructure managers (IMs). Presently, the managers and the Railway Undertaking (RU's) collect data at an organizational level for their own purposes but a consolidated shared data and its national level analysis is a distant aim.

Big-data can be a big step in this direction. With this technology, it is possible to handle unstructured data from various input sources. For instance, data could be provided by sensors placed on the infrastructure (e.g. WTMS), traffic management systems or rolling stock. Our aim here is to answer the following question- How is "Big Data" handled and processed to provide real-time information on technical systems and organizations that run trains and manage the framework?

To answer this question, we suggest the reader go through the Components of WTMS as discussed in the previous sections of the Chapter before moving forward. The systems mentioned under the section provide data that can be sent to the concerned Railway Managers and Undertakings for processing. Some of the parameters are stored for later purposes while some are screened in real time for abnormal or unexpected behavior. Any deviation from the standard values raises an alarm to warn the system and the authorities about the observed anomaly which could possibly lead to a disaster or infrastructure degradation. The system may also suggest steps to avoid the possible events. Then it's the responsibility of the company to ensure that the data is properly handled and suggestions are implemented based on careful study of the data. This is where the human intervention comes into the picture.

Thus, real-time monitoring of organizations is another important task. Monitoring the implementation of internal processes in real-time is quite challenging. The usual internal monitoring methods based on audits and inspections along with manual reporting do not always generate enough data and intelligence to support proactive interventions. Hence it becomes necessary to draw inferences from the limited information that is available from the maintenance operations.

Following points could be considered while adopting Big Data to resolve safety issues brought up by the Wayside Train Monitoring System (WTMS):

1. Huge chunks of data that is collected can be analyzed effectively using big-data techniques such as data mining, regression, data cleaning etc.
2. Open text reports must be analyzed using text mining software.
3. Extraction of information and patterns from the data set by expert systems or data scientists, to be fed to the risk models n (see figure 4).
4. Modeling of Enterprise Architecture for the SMS of the operators. This means that the SMS is mapped and the responsibility of the risk control measures is allocated in the organization. Each person is allotted a dashboard with the list of the controlled and uncontrolled risks.

Consequently, the combination of big-data analytics, risk models and enterprise architecture to map the Safety Management Systems with the due support of the WTMS allows organizations to monitor their risks in real time and take actions accordingly.

INTERNET OF TRAINS (IoT): NEED OF THE HOUR

Introduction

With global passenger traffic expected to double by 2020, the railway industry is expected to face immense pressure to improve the passenger experience. The improvement could be in the form of better on-time performance, more onboard amenities, and more timely information. However, there are various factors like aging communication systems and slow adoption of automation that hamper this improvement in railways. The "Internet of Trains," assures that rail systems can resolve these issues and modernize rapidly. The Internet of Trains can be defined as the use of networks of intelligent onboard devices to connect to cloud-based applications that would enhance the communication and control systems. (Mittermayr, Stephanides & Maicz, 2011). The same network that strengthens safety through WTMS can also deliver data that helps reduce costs and improve operations. IoT solutions and dimensions are yet to be accepted and adapted by the industry completely. Apart from safety IoT offers dozens of other opportunities. Operators can drive costs down while using real-time data to elevate the passenger experience through better performance. Railway operators can rapidly accelerate implementation of the Internet of Trains by working with partners that provide solutions to system level challenges.

Features

1. Safety is the primary requirement of IoT applications. IoT has special systems that have been developed to display train velocity and report speeds back to central control systems. Interconnection of onboard monitoring systems with wayside signaling systems can regulate train speeds or even command trains to stop based on track conditions, the positions of switches and other factors.
2. By transmitting real-time system-wide location data to control centers, onboard systems help operators optimize the deployment of equipment and allocation of track capacity to avoid congestion. The train data can be used by Metro and commuter trains to reschedule the time table and is enabled to send information to customers via mobile apps.
3. IoT maintains the reliability of the equipment to maximize time on the tracks with preventive maintenance. Onboard sensors monitor equipment for signs of wear and alert operators when critical parts need repair. These onboard monitors are useful as they cut costs and help optimize asset utilization by reducing the need to take trains out of service for routine inspections or for long duration repairs.
4. More than operations and maintenance IoT has the potential to alter the prevailing business models that rail system operators and their suppliers have always run on. IoT has provided an indirect source of revenue to manufacturers as they can lease the devices based on usage metrics that remote sensors can track.

Issues of IoT

1. The Internet of Trains has proved to be a little problematic for operators who invested in independent legacy systems and equipment. Such equipment was not designed for connectivity so the challenge for developers of IoT solutions was to find ways to connect these previously unconnected systems

so that operators do not have to rip out and replace their entire infrastructure in order to realize the benefits of IoT.

2. The railways rely on wireless connectivity that makes them vulnerable to outside interference. Since rail traffic and various parameters related to it have become more complex a small glitch could cause suffering to many which can be avoided by IoT.

3. IoT calls for innovative thinking and an end-to-end vision ranging from the smart devices on trains that generate data to the gateways that aggregate it on the cloud.

Projects Based on IoT

1. **Wind River Helix:** Wind River Helix is a comprehensive portfolio of software, technologies, tools, and services for addressing the system-level challenges created by IoT. It collaborates with its partners and clients to work towards the holistic vision. It encompasses everything from the embedded software running edge devices to the systems using those devices. By using Wind River pre-validated components together, developers of IoT solutions can significantly accentuate the development process while complying with the rail industry's stern safety certifications. The goal of Helix is to enable developers to deliver high-quality, secure, and reliable solutions more quickly to a market that demands the best.

2. **VxWorks:** This industry-leading real-time operating system delivers intelligence at the device level. It has proven to be reliable in billions of smart devices and has been optimized for safety-critical functions. Safety Profile adds advanced time partitioning (application scheduling) to the space partitioning in the core VxWorks platform. Virtualization Profile integrates a real-time embedded hypervisor into the core of VxWorks that consolidates multiple stand-alone hardware platforms onto a single multi-core platform. VxWorks is also designed with multiple layers of improved security functionality to detect and prevent intrusions.

3. **Wind River Tie-Up With Intel:** This tie-up has led to the evolution of gateways that connect data and perform intelligent functions. Wind River Intelligent Device Platform XT is a customizable middleware development environment that provides security, rich networking varieties, and device management. Working together under the Helix umbrella, the combination of components enables developers to skip the tedious process of building their own infrastructure and customized software, and to focus their resources on perfecting the solutions. These benefits both the developers and the customers and speeds the delivery of solutions to make others realize the benefits of IoT.

SIGFNIFICANT COMPONENT OF WTMS: TRAIN CONFORMITY CHECK SYSTEM (TCCS)

Train Conformity Check System, first implemented in July 2009 by the Italian Railways Network (commonly known as the RFI) is an effective system to check the condition of the trains with respect to the prescribed standards for detection of defects that could possibly lead to loss of human life and rail infrastructure. TCCS makes use of highly sophisticated electro-optical cameras and sensors to capture information about the geometrical and thermal scanning of trains. This information is then stored and analyzed for possible defects in rolling stock in real time.

It is primarily used to report and reduce risks for rail line sections and to identify lower severity defects to help in maintenance optimization and reduction in track wear. It currently provides two subsystems: to detect 3-D profile defects (e.g. Open doors, shifted loads etc.) and abnormal overheating of parts throughout the surface of the rolling stock (e.g. Compartment fires, heating of electrical components etc.). The present TCCS configuration can be implemented to double-track rail lines and for rolling stocks with speeds up to 300km/h.

FUNCTIONS OF DIFFERENT MODULES OF TCCS

The whole TCCS structure can be divided typically into 4 modules for a better understanding approach. Each module covers a variety of functions that can be implemented using the available hardware and software implementations. The basic modules and functions include:

1. **Core Function Module:** The basic function of the core module is to calculate the train velocity by using sensors installed along a few meters of track length. The dataset is transmitted to the control centers for data retrieval. The automatic Unique Identification of the trains is done using the RFID (surfaced in Sweden and has since then been used all over Europe for train traffic management and individual train maintenance). Installed along with WTMS, RFID provides an effective tool for tracking trains across International borders and keeping a track of their service routine in order to extend the on-track life of the rolling stock. The core module also facilitates data storage, event logging, system diagnostics and Communication & Networking.

2. **3-D Profiling Module:** The accurate and detailed 3-D profile of rail vehicles is acquired using the sub-system. The information collected can be used to detect possible defects and conditions that could lead to train side collisions or load dropping from wagons. The sub-system makes use of four high-performance laser radars installed along both sides of the tracks. The laser scanners are placed in cabinets which are located above the maximum vehicle height. The raw data is mapped on 3-D Cartesian coordinates and the resultant images of the train surface are compared to the applicable limiting profiles to detect abnormal features. A very typical example of train accidents includes loading error or load displacements. Such accidents can be easily avoided using the 3-D profiling in comparison to the axle patterns.

3. **Thermo Graphic Scan Module:** Four high-speed linear thermographers are used to generate high definition thermographic maps of the entire body of the vehicle by recognizing the abnormal temperatures of the visible surfaces. A statistical analysis tool is available to facilitate setting off

Figure 7. Modularity in TCSS

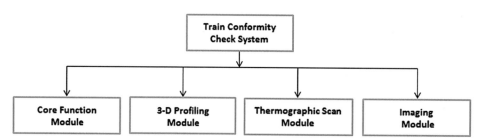

an alarm in case of faulty or extreme parameter values. The thermal images appear on the operator screen as pseudo-color maps or by overlaying the detected hot spots on the corresponding NIR (Near Infrared) images.

4. **Imaging Module:** Imaging of rolling stock is done using fast linear B/W Cameras with solid state NIR Illumination to avoid any disturbance to drivers. The images of the sides of the rolling stock can be obtained from cameras placed on the rolling stock plane level while the panoramic images can be obtained from cameras placed above the maximum height of rolling stocks. The panoramic images are preserved for future use while the side images can be used by OCR module to read the marking of the sides of the train or to identify the Unique Identification Number of the train.

Figure 8. Images from infrared sensors

Figure 9. Image of a bogie with hot spots on the NIR Image obtained from thermographic sensors

The Hardware and Software developments in the last decade have made it possible to use TCCS to avoid major train collisions and prevent trains from entering long tunnels when fire or other severe profile defects are detected. The latest version of TCCS provides a modular and flexible approach to answering questions regarding maintenance and safety of rolling stocks which can easily be implemented to the existing track lines across Europe. This version is also suitable for obtaining accurate measurements even in harsh environmental conditions.

ARGOS APPROACH TOWARDS WTMS

The inspection of the technical safety parameters was done manually till date. But with the advent of WTMS, completely automated inspection of these parameters has become possible. The parameters now measured are accurate and quantified. ARGOS is one of the primary systems which have revolutionized the measuring process. ARGOS came into limelight when it was installed by the Austrian Railways agencies and helped them understand the behavior of rolling stock and the railway tracks. This system focuses on providing services to reduce incidents of overload, unbalanced load, wheel damage and poor running performance among other irregularities of vehicles which reduce the life of both- the track and the rolling stock. The degradation of the condition of rolling stock doesn't occur continuously over time but usually occurs randomly, which poses a high danger by reducing the safety of vehicles in motion. ARGOS provides methods for measuring the vertical and horizontal forces of the rail using sensors. This data, together with other parameters, allows recognizing different patterns in vehicles.

Depending on the condition and types of the vehicles, the process can be divided into 3 levels:

1. **Derailment Detection (Level-1):** This system is capable of detecting already derailed trains or almost derailed ones. It raises an alarm as soon as it encounters wheels running narrowly over the screws and the clamps of the rail. Added to this ability, it can also detect 'jumping wheels' which can cause serious trouble at high speeds. The hardware used is simple force transducers that are cased in metal plate bodies.

Figure 10. Levels in ARGOS measurement

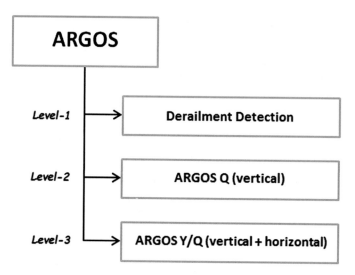

2. **ARGOS Q (Level-2):** This sub-system measures the vertical component (Q) of stress and strain on the rails using vignol rail and sleepers. An example is a system assembled by Hottinger Baldwin Messtechnik (HBM) which can be directly installed at the site. This system collects information through sensors along the track and loads it into software that provides a detailed analysis of the parameter values.

3. **ARGOS Q/Y (Level-3):** This is a variation to the ARGOS Q with the major addition that it can also calculate the horizontal component of the physical dimensions of stress and strain. They are represented as continuous time signals on a graph. The sensors also provide data about the rolling behavior, wheel overloading and the derailment coefficient Y/Q. The installation of this variation needs no specific changes in the existing infrastructure and can be connected to the existing rails within a day.

Thus, ARGOS has proven its worth by enhancing the reliability and safety of the railways over the last few years. It has helped researchers to get a deep insight into the complex behavior of the rolling stock and railway tracks. The information gathered by ARGOS can also be used by companies to reduce the costs and provide a good experience to their customers.

Unlike WTMS which covers a wide variety of parameters and aims at overall improvement of the railway industry, ARGOS is focused more on increasing the safety of the passengers and the train while in motion. ARGOS systems are mostly used for monitoring the rail-track contact and other parameters in real time which can be useful in stopping any disaster, moments before it is going to occur. While this data is stored for further periodic analysis of the infrastructure quality, it is also used by the Railway Authorities to measure the damage caused due to poor quality vehicles used by companies. This way, the data collected from ARGOS helps public sector corporations to regulate the charges for using the tracks based on the extent to which a company uses a resource (track in this case) and the damage caused by it's poor quality freight or wrong practices like increased train weight or increased number of bogies in a train. This data from ARGOS is then consolidated with data received from other sensors and detectors for further studies.

NOTABLE EVENTS IN FIELD OF WTMS

WTMS Conference 2011

The WTMS Conference was held in Lucrene, Switzerland in 2011 to draw inferences about the Wayside Train Monitoring Systems. The European Union Agency published documents that classified the railway accidents of the last twenty years that occurred across Europe. These documents were used as significant tools to understand the causes of the most important disasters that lead to great misery in Europe. The main dilemma was if the tragedies could have been averted by using WTMS. The conference, an eye-opener for many, covered all the vivid details of Wayside Train Monitoring Systems ranging from its features to potential. WTMS, namely the systems that check all possibly hazardous conditions of a running train, are made of different categories and technologies of sensors. WTMS includes all types of interactions like fire, chemical, mechanical, electrical etc. of a vehicle with the environment that cannot be made in a

Figure 11. (a) Lateral/Horizontal forces; (b) report on vertical forces
Source: Mittermayr, Stephanides & Maicz, 2011.

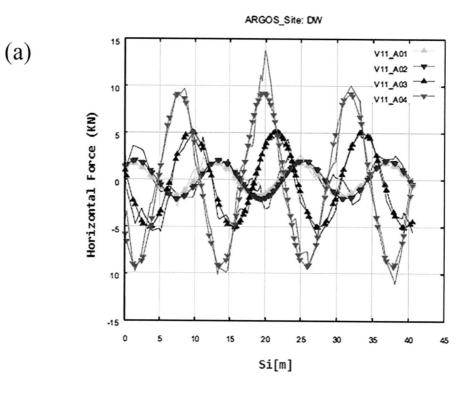

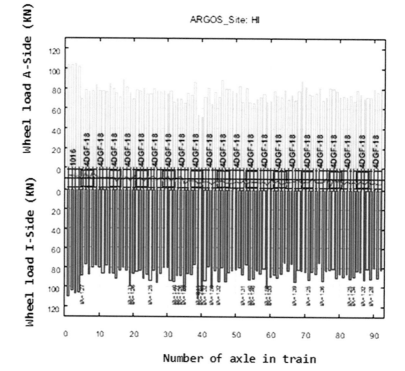

workshop. The speakers at the conference introduced the idea of WTMS to be two-dimensional, accident prevention and giving railway undertakings the opportunity to optimize maintenance. The conference concluded that the safety issues could be addressed by interfacing WTMS with the signaling equipment. The summary of the conclusions of the conference is as given below:

1. It would be profitable to integrate WTMS in the daily business of Infrastructure Managers and Railway Undertakings
2. The quality of live data can be improved by the cross-border data exchange between neighboring Infrastructure Managers. A set of laws should govern the data exchange process.
3. Data coming from WTMS should be used in the context of Safety Management Systems at Infrastructure Manager and Railway Undertakings
4. Maximize benefits by integrating physical quantities such as lateral forces and noise in a WTMS.
5. Reliable detection, monitoring of pantographs and measurement of interference currents to improve safety in tunnels, prevent damages to overhead lines and avoid faults.

Intelligent Rail Summit 2016

Another important event that took up challenges like recording, storing, transmitting, analyzing, visualization and distribution of data were the Intelligent Rail Summit. The data associated with the railways has recently been digitalized and covers different aspects ranging from infrastructure to rolling stock. (www.RailTech.com, 2016). With Big Data, one does not look at single values but only at dependencies and correlations. All such topics related to the data and its dependencies were taken up at the Intelligent Rail summit that was conducted at Naples, Italy on 24 November 2016. The seminars and presentations entailed issues of Big Data and WTMS alike. The seminar led to better understanding of the condition and the predictive behavior of assets especially rolling stock. The significant details of Train Conformity Check System (TCCS) given earlier were also spoken about by Nadia Mazzino, Vice President Innovation Projects "Ansaldo STS". TCCS has undergone vast expansion in all domains since its inception in 2009. It is no longer restricted to safety and maintenance solutions but is an interface between the Infrastructure managers with the real environment. The speakers also covered the issues related to the complexity of the ever increasing and how it is important to minimize the hardware needed to collect data and instead focus on upgrading and integrating software to reuse the available data. The data collected should not be used in a constrained manner but be free to be extracted by any department. This concept was also justified by Michael Osterkamp during the summit. Some specific case studies like the Swedish Transport Administration's use of RFID to identify vehicles were also presented. This technique has been incorporated with the WTMS sensors in Sweden, Finland, Denmark and many other European states to follow WTMS measurements over time for a particular component. Some light was also thrown upon the researches that are currently being undertaken in Sweden, specifically to guarantee if the varied data form wheel bearings, hot box can be used to predict damages. All this discussion was covered by Karl Akerlund who is a Detector system specialist at Trafikverket (Swedish Transport Administration). The issues of Pantograph monitoring which forms an inseparable part of WTMS was also raised upon during the summit by Arjan Rodenburg. The most fascinating part of the entire summit was the introduction to some new techniques that have been introduced like Automatic Pantograph Monitoring System (APMS) to deal with the limitations of Pantograph Monitoring Systems.

FUTURE RESEARCH DIRECTIONS

The digitalization of the railways led to the advent of Big Data technology in this sector. Various approaches and strategies are being adopted to uplift the railway's industry among them is WTMS covered in detail in this chapter. Big-Data is the first step of WTMS in which it feeds indicators foreseen in the reporting scheme. Various products like ORBIFLO are being introduced to enhance the operational efficiency and to unlock the full potential of the railway fleet. FleetWise® is an innovative, cost-effective data-management system designed to help transit authorities remotely collect and analyze operational and maintenance data and access a unified view to achieve superior fleet performance. Big data is also expected to transform various fields by working on different parameters including business performance, operationalization, integration and cultural shifts, i.e. Data analytics enabled decision making. Organizations like Railtech are organizing conferences to spread the word about Big data and Railways.

CONCLUSION

Since its introduction, Big Data technology has witnessed a plethora of applications in different fields but the most diverse and complex have been in the transport industry. The indicators fed by WTMS help the railway operators to make their reporting process more efficient and effective. The chapter provided an insight into the railway sub-systems, their interaction and affects. It has become necessary to replace the conventional approach with Big Data as it offers better and comfortable features with minimum human interference. The world witnessed notable summits and conferences that lead to popularity and close scrutiny of WTMS. Internet Of Trains (IoT) is a comprehensive term that promotes the novel idea of integrating rail data with cloud-based architecture. WTMS has different components and salient features that have been vividly discussed in the chapter. It is possible to conclude that manual reporting of operational occurrence can successfully be replaced by technical systems which can be used to investigate the most potential application of big-data techniques to manage railway safety.

Moreover, a long history of investigation can help in defining functional models and occurrence models that can be strengthened using big data techniques.

The European Union Agency still lacks a clear view of the current state of data collection and analytics and the difference between operators in terms of operations, size, budget, etc. A deep analysis of this could lead to improved monitoring and analysis that produce better and faster results. The WTMS and Big Data can work in parallel if the following myths are clarified well in time:

1. Big-data will still require data scientist and railway experts, to validate models generate by machine learning applications.
2. Big-data will not convert manual reporting systems in automatic ones.
3. Big-data cannot create information without meaningful data.

REFERENCES

Thaduri, A., Galar, D., & Kumar, U. (2015). Railway assets: A potential domain for big data analytics. *Procedia Computer Science*, *53*, 457–467. doi:10.1016/j.procs.2015.07.323

Mazzino, N., Cabeza-Lopez, P., Toapanta, W., & Lancia, A. (2013). Reducing costs through the integration of wayside train and infrastructure monitoring systems. In Proceedings of AusRAIL PLUS 2013, Canberra, ACT, Australia. .

Favo, F., Bocchetti, G., Mazzino, N., & Lancia, A. (2010). Train Conformity Check System; Technology and current operation experience. In Proceedings of the Electrical Systems for Aircraft, Railway and Ship Propulsion (ESARS). IEEE.

HBM. (2012). *ARGOS-a high accurate Wayside Train Monitoring System* Retrieved from https://www.unece.org/fileadmin/DAM/trans/main/temtermp/2012_2nd_Expert_Group_Meeting_Ankara/TEM_March_2012_Hbm_Argos_Ankara.pdf

Mittermayr, P., Stephanides, J., and Maicz, D. (2011). Argos-a decade of operational experience in wayside train monitoring.

Mitrovic, S. M. S. V. B., & Marton, Z. D. P. (2015). A site selection model for wayside train monitoring systems at Serbian railways. In *Re-Aggregation Heuristics For The Large Location Problems With Lexicographic Minimax Objective* (p. 49).

Maly, T., & Schöbel, A. (2010). Cost effectiveness of wayside derailment detection.

Schöbel, A., Stoytechva, N., Bakalski, I. & Karner, J. (2012). Results from first Bulgarian wayside train monitoring systems at Zimnitsa.

Bracciali, A. (2012). Wayside train monitoring systems: A state-of-the-art and running safety implications. In *Proceedings if the First International Conference on Railway Technology: research, Development and Maintenance*, LasPalmas de Gran Canaria, Spain. doi:10.4203/ijrt.1.1.11

Sneed, W. H., & Smith, R. L. (1998). On-board real-time railroad bearing defect detection and monitoring. In *Proceedings of the 1998 ASME/IEEE Joint Railroad Conference*. IEEE. doi:10.1109/RRCON.1998.668098

European Union Agency for Railways. (2016). *Big Data In Railways Common occurrence Reporting Programme*. Retrieved from http://www.era.europa.eu/Document-Register/Pages/Big-data-in-railways.aspx

Li, H., Parikh, D., He, Q., Qian, B., Li, Z., Fang, D., & Hampapur, A. (2014). Improving rail network velocity: A machine learning approach to predictive maintenance. *Transportation Research Part C, Emerging Technologies*, *45*, 17–26. doi:10.1016/j.trc.2014.04.013

Aydin, I., Karakose, M., & Akin, E. (2015). Anomaly detection using a modified kernel-based tracking in the pantograph–catenary system. *Expert Systems with Applications*, *42*(2), 938–948. doi:10.1016/j.eswa.2014.08.026

Stratman, B., Liu, Y., & Mahadevan, S. (2007). Structural health monitoring of railroad wheels using wheel impact load detectors. *Journal of Failure Analysis and Prevention*, *7*(3), 218–225. doi:10.1007/s11668-007-9043-3

Indian Institute of Technology Kanpur & Research Designs and Standards Organization Lucknow. (n. d.). *Wheel Impact Load Detection System(WILD)* Retrieved from http://home.iitk.ac.in/~vyas/pdf/WILD_Final.pdf

Cottrill, C. D., & Derrible, S. (2015). Leveraging big data for the development of transport sustainability indicators. *Journal of Urban Technology*, 22(1), 45–64. doi:10.1080/10630732.2014.942094

Ansaldo STS-A Hitachi Group Company. (n. d.). *Weigh In Motion(WIM)Wheel Impact Load Detector(WILD)* Retrieved from http://www.ansaldo-sts.com/sites/ansaldosts.message-asp.com/files/imce/asts_hitachi_wim_wild_lr.pdf

Massat, J.P., Laine, J.P., & Bobillot, A. (2006). Pantograph–catenary dynamics simulation. *Vehicle System Dynamics, 44*(Sup. 1), 551-559.

RailTech.com. (2016). *Wayside Train Monitoring Systems Intelligent Rail Summit.* Retrieved from http://www.railtech.com/intelligent-rail-summit-2016/wayside-train-monitoring-systems/

Song, B. Y., Zhong, Y., Liu, R. K., & Wang, F. T. (2014). Railway maintenance analysis based on big data and condition classification. In *Advanced Materials Research* (Vol. 919, pp. 1134–1138). Trans Tech Publications. doi:10.4028/www.scientific.net/AMR.919-921.1134

Teradata Corporation. (2015). *The Internet Of Trains Case Study/Transportation.* Retrieved from http://assets.teradata.com/resourceCenter/downloads/CaseStudies/EB8903.pdf

Yang, C., & Létourneau, S. (2005). Learning to predict train wheel failures. In *Proceedings of the eleventh ACM SIGKDD international conference on Knowledge discovery in data mining* (pp. 516-525). ACM, . doi:10.1145/1081870.1081929

Bocciolone, M., Caprioli, A., Cigada, A., & Collina, A. (2007). A measurement system for quick rail inspection and effective track maintenance strategy. *Mechanical Systems and Signal Processing, 21*(3), 1242–1254. doi:10.1016/j.ymssp.2006.02.007

Data.Gov.UK. (2015). *National Rail Passenger Survey* (csv data file). Retrieved from https://data.gov.uk/dataset/national-rail-passenger-survey

European Union Agency for Railways. (n. d.). Big data in railways. Retrieved from http://www.era.europa.eu/Document-Register/Documents/COR%20-%20Big%20Data.pdf

KEY TERMS AND DEFINITIONS

AEI Reader: Stands for Automatic Equipment Identification Reader. Used to identify the rolling stock using passive tags stuck on the side of the rail vehicles.

CSI: Stands for Common Safety Indicators. It is a set of rail safety data collected by the European Union and then used to improve the rail safety after assessments.

Loading Gauge (Envelope): Defines the maximum height and width of the rail vehicles and loads they carry to ensure safe travel through bridges and tunnels.

Pantograph: Apparatus mounted on the top of an electric train or tram and used to collect power by contacting an overhead cable.

Rail Corrugation: A frequently occurring rail wear pattern along the curves and tangential tracks.

RFID Technology: Stands for Radio Frequency Identification that uses electronic fields to identify the tags on RFID objects (scanned to retrieve the electronically stored information).

Rolling Stock: Equipment used in the railways including engines and carriages. They may be self-propelled (such as trains, locomotives) or pulled (such as coaches).

Thermographers: Devices used to measure heat variations across different regions of the rail vehicle and convert to visible signals.

ENDNOTE

[1]   http://www.ansaldo-sts.com/sites/ansaldosts.message_asp.com/files/imce/asts_hitachi_wim_wild_lr.pdf

Section 2
Innovations and Technologies

Chapter 5

Scalable Software Framework for Real-Time Data Processing in the Railway Environment

Stijn Verstichel
Ghent University, Belgium

Wannes Kerckhove
Ghent University, Belgium

Thomas Dupont
Ghent University, Belgium

Jabran Bhatti
Televic Rail NV, Belgium

Dirk Van Den Wouwer
Televic Rail NV, Belgium

Filip De Turck
Ghent University, Belgium

Bruno Volckaert
Ghent University, Belgium

ABSTRACT

To this day, railway actors obtain information by actively hunting for relevant data in various places. Despite the availability of a variety of travel-related data sources, accurate delivery of relevant, timely information to these railway actors is still inadequate. In this chapter, we present a solution in the form of a scalable software framework that can interface with almost any type of (open) data. The framework aggregates a variety of data sources to create tailor-made knowledge, personalised to the dynamic profiles of railway users. Core functionality, including predefined non-functional support, such as load balancing strategies, is implemented in the generic base layer, on top of which a use case specific layer – that can cope with the specifics of the railway environment – is built. Data entering the framework is intelligently processed and the results are made available to railway vehicles and personal mobile devices through REST endpoints.

DOI: 10.4018/978-1-5225-3176-0.ch005

INTRODUCTION

Today more than ever, public transportation operators are aware of the importance of investing in their passengers. Moreover, meeting passengers' public transportation needs, in addition to important environmental aspects (Hua, 2016, Pålsson & Kovács, 2014, Guerra et al., 2016) is acknowledged as a central goal in the European Commission's transport strategy roadmap (European Commission, 2011). In this roadmap, it is shown that acting on issues important to passengers, such as reducing noise in a train or providing wireless connectivity, enriches the customer experience. At the same time, due to the current information-centric nature of society, passengers expect public transportation to be more and more augmented / personalised with information from different sources (e.g. social networks, multi-modal travel information) (Sierpiński, 2017, van Lier et al., 2014). Recent ICT developments present opportunities to meet passengers' rising expectations. As a result, the amount of available mobile travel applications offering travel information to passengers has grown exponentially (Gardner, Haeusler & Tomitsch, 2010). Contemporary mobile applications, such as the travel information apps provided by European railway companies e.g. NMBS, NS, Deutsche Bahn, National Rail and SNCF, mostly offer Real Time Train Information (RTTI) about arrival and departure times as well as mobile ticketing services. Many mobile RTTI applications are mostly context specific, single-purpose applications that provide a solution to a particular problem or requirement. However, according to ORR, the (British) Office of Rail and Road, passengers want to receive live information and they want it at their fingertips (Office of Rail Regulation, 2012). Since the initial publication of this report, where train operators are required to provide appropriate, accurate and timely information to enable (prospective) passengers to plan and make their journeys with a reasonable degree of assurance, including in times of disruption, the ORR has elaborated on this key requirement. The ORR requires from a train operating company to publish a code on practice setting out how it will ensure compliance with this directive. In 2014, further studies and surveys were conducted to see whether passengers had noticed tangible improvements. The conclusions highlighted some improvements, but also raised several areas where special attention was needed. Because of this, the ORR published a new regulatory guidance, in collaboration with the industry (Rail Delivery Group, 2016) which issued 50 recommendations, in 2016 (Office of Rail and Road, 2016).

According to the Danish Rail operator DSB for instance, a delay is often not experienced as being problematic, as long as passengers are assisted and know how long they will have to wait, how they could move on from the next station, whether there is still time to grab a coffee, etc. Access to RTTI positively changes passengers' perception and experience of the quality of the public transportation service. Unfortunately, RTTI as it is currently offered to passengers is still mostly passive (passengers must actively search for the information they need), based on a single source (i.e. the database of the train operator) and largely not tailored to the (dynamic) personal needs of the individual passenger, making it difficult to find relevant information when needed. As such, passengers expect travel information to become more context-aware and more personalised. Another fundamental, yet often unapparent, requirement of RTTI is its reliability for the public to be able to confidently use the information available. The full potential of (open) data for railway travel has clearly not been materialized yet.

The problems related to RTTI discussed above, together with changing passenger expectations form an interesting gap in the passenger experience that the software framework presented in this chapter aims to tackle. This software framework was developed in the Flemish iMinds ICON research project TraPIST (acronym for Train Passenger Interfaces for Smart Travel). The approach taken differs from existing travel applications in many ways. First, passengers do not need to actively search for the information they need. Instead, personalised up-to-date information is sent to them during their travels. Second, the information that they need is offered to them when they need it (e.g. information about alternative connecting trains only become relevant when a passenger is likely to miss his/her intended connecting train). Third, the way the information is offered is highly personal and adapted to the context of the passenger (e.g. his / her travel goal, destination, activities or company). The proposed solution also differs from existing travel applications due to being built to easily and reliably connect to a multitude of data sources. Practical travel information (e.g. from the train operator's database) is not the only information that is relevant for passengers, but instead a combination of several data sources can offer passengers the most interesting and relevant information (e.g. tourist event information for leisure travelers, weather information, safety travel tips for the visited area), including publicly available open data sources.

Capturing the requirements and needs from the end-users has been executed in a multi-disciplinary approach, where the needs were extracted using novel user experience techniques. Although not the main topic of this chapter, we refer the interested reader to (Slegers et al., 2015).

The remainder of this chapter is structured as follows. The next section presents the background motivation for the research and development of the LimeDS framework, as well as introducing several relevant related works, both in the context of provisioning platforms as well as in the context of Semantic Web technologies. Subsequently, the challenges and issues motivating the design of the framework, exemplary railway related use cases and corresponding requirements are detailed, followed by an extensive presentation of the architectural design and internal details. Two Proof-of-Concept demonstrators are illustrated in the second-to-last part of this chapter. Finally, to conclude, several performance metrics were evaluated and are presented together with the envisaged future research directions.

BACKGROUND

Given these basic first requirements, in addition to the more elaborate listing later in this chapter, a highly scalable and customisable (micro service based) framework imposes itself, allowing to tie together different data sources, apply application logic to this data and deal with non-functional issues such as reliability and robustness (highly important in the case of the harsh railway environment), performance, caching, etc.

The framework allows application developers to focus on improving the Quality of Life (QoL) of passengers instead of having to focus on the technical aspects. A visual approach to the construction and adaptation of services is an added nice-to-have and aids in rapid construction of new applications and realisation of new ideas. In other words, the technology should help developers realising their ideas w.r.t. innovative data-driven applications, rather than having to focus on the low-level technical iterative wiring.

Next to the traditional non-functional support such as caching and load balancing, the presented framework also allows semantic processing of and reasoning on the data passing through, allowing e.g. highly personalised data relationships to be extracted.

In the following subsections, an overview is presented of the two most important aspects of the proposed approach, namely the facilitating service platform and the support for semantic technologies. The presented LimeDS framework has historically grown out of research into railway data provisioning systems. It must be noted however, that the framework is applicable to other domains as well. The challenges defined by means of the railway use cases have led to the definition of several general requirements.

Related Work on Service Provisioning Platforms

LimeDS (Lightweight modular environment for Data-oriented Services) is an open source toolkit for building JVM-based Web applications with a strong focus on developer productivity and interoperability with other services and devices. It allows developers to immediately focus on the use-case specific implementation by drastically reducing typical boiler-plate code for setting up HTTP endpoints, managing dependencies, configuring services, etc. This is made possible thanks to a visual editor used to connect (micro) service components (= Segments) together to form modular logical units (= Slices), that then can be deployed to any LimeDS runtime. This is illustrated in Figure 1. The individual blocks represent the Segments. All such Segment instances together form a Slice. For more advanced users, a Java API is provided that allows more complex modules to be created. Below we compare LimeDS with a number of related platforms and technologies.

Java API for Restful Web Services (JAX-RS) (Burke, 2009, Burke, 2013) is the Java standard specification for a Java API that allows implementing REST-based applications. It relies on annotations added as meta-data on classes to transform these into REST resources that are exposed as HTTP-endpoints. Various implementations of this standard exist ranging from Jersey (Oracle Corporation, 2015), to Resteasy (RedHat, 2015) and Apache Wink (Apache Software Foundation, 2015). LimeDS uses Apache Wink as a base layer and thus offers support for JAX-RS resources. On top of this, the Data Flow mechanism allows developers to build a Web API with integrated support for reliability, scalability and security with a minimal amount of code that can easily be modified at-runtime.

Figure 1. Segments and slices in LimeDS

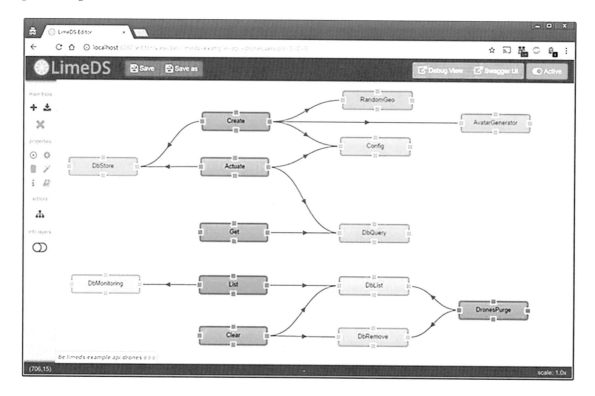

Dropwizard (Dallas, 2014) is an open-source Java project that integrates a number of mature libraries into a light-weight ecosystem targeted at developing REST-based applications. This is done by allowing JAX-RS resources to be wired with various support services, ranging from logging, to storage and authentication / authorisation. The goal of Dropwizard is similar to that of LimeDS, but the focus and scope differs. While Dropwizard is a very powerful framework to build high-performance REST-based applications that are easy to monitor and maintain, LimeDS provides a more dynamic environment where changes can be made on-the-fly while the application is running. Dropwizard also focuses on a single-node setup, while LimeDS can be configured to run as a cluster with load balancing.

OSGi (OSGi Alliance, 2003) is a proven standard that specifies a modular middleware framework for Java. OSGi implementations such as Apache Felix or Eclipse Equinox (The Eclipse Foundation, 2015) provide an execution environment where software modules (bundles) can be installed at-runtime and communicate safely in highly dynamic circumstances. While a lot of applications could benefit from the (at-runtime) modularity and loose coupling of the OSGi framework, a lot of developers struggle to unlock its true potential because of the steep learning curve. LimeDS is built on top of OSGi and can offer developers OSGi features such as dynamic reconfiguration of dependencies and at-runtime addition of new functionalities in a much easier to use package - albeit for a more restricted set of REST-based applications.

The Data Flow mechanism of LimeDS is loosely based on principles of Business Process Management (BPM) solutions, such as JBoss BPM Suite (RedHat, 2015), where interactions between components can also be modelled as a visual process. The difference is in the scale of the application domain. While BPM is typically used to implement the complex orchestration of distributed software systems, LimeDS will model interaction patterns of micro-services which are primarily found on the same system, although LimeDS Data Flow components can depend on external remote data sources and can be distributed over multiple systems, e.g. for load balancing purposes. A BPM instantiation could however integrate a LimeDS-based service to implement a certain process on a higher level. As a result, LimeDS can be a much more lightweight option in comparison with traditional BPM solutions, depending on the scope of the problem.

Vert.x (Clement Escoffier, 2015) is a Java-based framework that allows developers to build `reactive' applications by setting up modular components called Verticles and by routing data between these components using a distributed event bus. The 'reactive' keyword refers to the framework using event-driven, non-blocking calls and the fact that it is designed from the ground up to support high availability. Some of the additional services provided by Vert.x are: (i) the ability to use multiple programming languages (Java, JavaScript, Groovy and Ruby), (ii) integration of storage solutions (MongoDB, SQL and Redis), (iii) support for clustering, advanced capturing of metrics on a per-component basis and (iv) built-in support for authentication and authorisation. Vert.x and LimeDS overlap in some features, but the latter focuses on HTTP/JSON-based applications with a clear choice to build upon the services model of OSGi, while Vert.x offers a more generic approach. When developing those type of applications, LimeDS has an edge as there is no need for boilerplate code in setting up the HTTP endpoints.

Additionally, LimeDS has built-in support for semantic reasoning. Arguably the most important concept in the Semantic Web is the use of ontologies. They describe in a formal and well-defined way the concepts and relationships between these concepts in a particular system, often referred to as the domain. Apart from the fact that OWL is a well-defined vocabulary for describing a domain, because of its foundation in Description Logics, the model described in this formalism can be used as input for a reasoner to check consistency of the model and infer extra knowledge out of the model. Relevant related work on this last topic is presented separately in the next section.

Related Work on a Number of Relevant Semantic Web Technologies

A short, but comprehensive definition of an ontology, based on the definition by Gruber in (Gruber, 1993) is: "An ontology is a formal specification of an agreed conceptualisation of a domain in the context of knowledge description." Accordingly, an ontology describes in a formal manner the concepts and relationships, existing in a particular domain or system and using a machine-processable common vocabulary within a computerised system. It can also contain classification rules. This standardised representation of the semantics of a domain can then be used to exchange data and its attached domain model. This way an ontology encourages re-use, communication, collaboration and integration (Fernández-López, Gómez-Pérez & Juristo, 1997). By managing the data about the current context in an ontology, intelligent algorithms can be more easily defined that take advantage of this information to optimize and personalize applications.

OWL has different levels of expressive power, each of them varying in their trade-off between expressiveness and inferential complexity. They are, in order of increasing expressiveness: (i) OWL Lite: supports classification hierarchies and simple constraint features, (ii) OWL DL: OWL Description Logics, a subset providing great expressiveness without losing computational completeness and decidability and (iii) OWL Full: supports maximum expressiveness and syntactic freedom, however without computational guarantees. Using one of the three sub-language flavours of OWL, one can easily adapt to the required expressiveness. Arguably, the most interesting sublanguage for many application domains is OWL DL, balancing great expressiveness with inferential efficiency. Due to its foundation in description logics, OWL DL is also very flexible and computationally complete. The constraints imposed by the adoption of the DL formalism assure that a decidable reasoning implementation can be achieved. OWL can be seen as the evolution of several previous WorldWide Web Consortium (W3C) recommendations, being XML, XML Schema, Resource Description Framework (RDF) and RDF Schema. In this view, each step introduces more functionality, i.e. XML introduces a common syntax, XML Schema introduces data types and structure, RDF focuses on meta-data, allowing to say anything about anything, RDF Schema introduces RDF resource types and finally OWL specifically supports the construction of vocabularies and shared meanings.

Ontologies are considered as dynamic and evolving in time and are also tailored towards the distributed nature of the Web. Some of the serialisation formats of OWL are based on eXtensible Markup Language (XML), namely RDF/XML (Beckett and McBride, 2004) or OWL/XML (Hori et. al, 2004), others being Turtle (Beckett et. al, 2008) or Manchester Syntax (Horridge et. al, 2006). Serialisation is the process of converting an in-memory object or data structure into a format that can be persisted on disk or transmitted by some communication medium. Each of those potential serialisations serve different purposes. An elaborate discussion can be found in (Hitzler et. al, 2012).

In recent years, research and standardisation efforts have taken OWL into a next level, namely OWL 2. In contrast to the earlier decomposition of the description logics in OWL Light, OWL DL and OWL

Full, OWL 2 (World Wide Web Consortium, 2012) specifies three new types of sublanguages, called profiles, which have favourable computational properties and are easier to implement, namely OWL 2 EL (Existential quantification Logic): useful in applications employing ontologies that contain very large numbers of properties and/or classes, OWL 2 QL (Query Language): aimed at applications using very large volumes of instance data, and where query answering is the most important reasoning task and OWL 2 RL (Rule Language): used for applications which require scalable reasoning without sacrificing too much expressive power. The profiles are designed for increased efficiency of reasoning for specific types of applications.

JSON-LD (World Wide Web Consortium, 2014) is a JSON-based format to serialise and message data captured in an ontology. The syntax is designed to easily integrate into deployed systems that already use JSON, and provides a smooth upgrade path from JSON to JSON-LD. OWL can be easily integrated with various rule platforms. This is demonstrated by the Semantic Web Rule Language (SWRL) W3C Submission (Horrocks et al., 2004).

In description logic terminology, the T-Box contains the axioms defining the concepts and relations in an ontology, while the A-Box contains the assertions about the individuals in that domain (Carroll et al., 2004). OWL, however, does not explicitly make this distinction because model and data can be mixed in the same description, but for clarification purposes it is still beneficial to make this distinction. An example to illustrate the difference between T-Box and A-Box concerns a simplified description of my Personal Computer (PC). The T-Box description of a Dell Latitude E5400 laptop (concept) states that this type of computer has one serial number and an Intel(R) Core 2 DUO P8600 Central Processing Unit (CPU) (concept). The processor concept also has one serial number. A corresponding A-Box instantiation could be that the Dell Latitude E5400 with serial number 53-373-312-19 has the specific Intel(R) Core(TM)2 DUO P8600, with serial number 6.1.7600.16385.

The main reason for creating an ontology of all the concepts within a domain, such as the previous computer example, is that logical connections and relationships can be described between the concepts in the domain. This allows for inference to be applied to the ontology. The concepts in the domain need to be described, as well as the relationships and constraints that define the concepts. Once the ontology is constructed, inference rules can be declared about the concepts and their properties within the ontology.

A semantic reasoner is a piece of generic software, able to infer logical consequences, i.e., new knowledge, out of the information captured in an ontology. A wide range of mature reasoners exist today, e.g., Pellet (Sirin, et al., 2007), Hermit (Glimm et al., 2014) and Fact++ (Tsarkov & Horrocks, 2006). SPARQL (Prud'hommeaux & Seaborne, 2008) can be used to query data captured by an ontology. The leading language for encoding ontologies is OWL (McGuinness & Van Harmelen, 2004).

Three generally accepted conceptual phases can be distinguished in an inference process. These are: (i) Consistency checking and satisfiability: analyses the ontology model to find any contradicting axioms. For satisfiability, this conforms to determining whether a concept can have individuals. In case a concept is unsatisfiable but does have individuals defined, the ontology is inconsistent; (ii) Classification: depending on the definitions of all named concepts in the ontology, this process completes the already existing asserted concept hierarchy with the inferred one; and (iii) Realisation: since it is possible for a given individual to belong to more than one concept, this phase calculates the set of concepts to which each of the individuals can belong, taking into account the complete inferred concept hierarchy.

MAIN FOCUS OF THE CHAPTER

Challenges

Interoperability

Interoperability can be defined as the ability of a system or different systems to operate successfully by communicating and exchanging information with other external systems written and run by external parties. The LimeDS framework requires support for interoperability with both a wide range of different data sources or services and with various passenger applications that will depend on the framework to receive filtered, enriched and up-to-date information.

Nowadays, every passenger has his / her own device, but it does not stop there, there are a lot of different public displays both in stations and within the trains themselves, all with different form factors and capabilities, each conveying different information. This means LimeDS must be designed with this variety in mind. The public transport scene is a very dynamic environment. Dependent on the time of day, passenger needs can vary enormously, timetables can change dynamically and passengers must be informed as soon as possible at all times. The framework must make sure that it can withstand the quickly changing requirements that such an environment implies. To illustrate this with an example: new public data may become available, able to enhance a service that is being delivered to clients. We want the framework to help in quickly integrating this new data, without large developer effort.

Extensibility

Extensibility can be defined as the ability of a system to incorporate future growth on a functional level. Extensible systems are designed to support the addition of new features or modifications while minimizing the impact of these changes on existing parts of the system. A high level of extensibility is required to be successful:

Figure 2. Interoperability is a key feature of the LimeDS framework

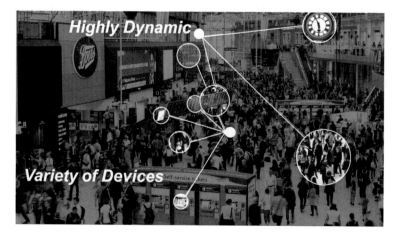

1. The more data sources that can be supported, the more added-value information can potentially be provided to the end-user.
2. When more data sources become available over time, it is only natural that the reasoning logic that processes this data will need to be extended as well.
3. For some aspects, the framework must rely on modules developed by third party developers. The framework will have to provide so-called service hooks where this applies, in order to give those third-party developers the tools to extend upon existing functionality without compromising the overall system operations.

Scalability

Scalability is the ability of a system to either handle increases in load with little to no impact on the performance of the system, or the ability to be readily enlarged. The framework must be able to support a large amount of data sources while still being able to process this input in a relatively small time period. There is also the implicit user load that the framework needs to consider. While we expect the framework to serve a whole range of information consumer applications or services, the potential user base for each of these consumers can be very large and the framework must support large numbers of users concurrently requesting information. On the other hand, this also suggests the framework must be able to withstand traffic peeks, since use of the different services is likely to fluctuate greatly throughout the day.

Usability

The usability of a system is determined by how easy it is for users to interact with it to achieve the desired goals. While the focus of the framework is on interoperability, extensibility and scalability, easy-of-use for applications developers has been considered.

Intermittent Connectivity

Another challenge is the harsh environment in which public transport sometimes operates. Software must be robust, since maintenance crews cannot always intervene in a timely manner. Communication to and from the train is not always guaranteed. The on-board systems need to be operational even when no new information from the wayside can be received. For instance: A train driving through a large barren area, without data-coverage, should still be able to display and show information on-board for its passengers. The same holds true for areas which do have data coverage. LimeDS looks at every connection as being unreliable and tries to cope with this, e.g. if a train enters a long tunnel through a mountain, the framework should somehow detect this, and fall back to a local mode, so that it can still inform the passengers as much and as accurate as possible. This can be done by storing data ahead of time, and providing a fall back mode to presenting this cached data while the main service cannot be reached.

Framework Use Cases

The goal of the software framework is to provide an end-to-end solution for processing data from multiple sources into useful information that can be provided to a wide range of passenger applications. Figure 4 shows an overview of how this framework is envisioned conceptually.

Figure 3. Although the always-connected paradigm is paramount, supporting this is not always straight-forward

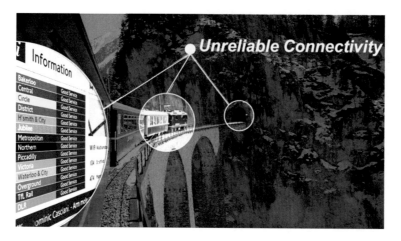

Figure 4. LimeDS framework conceptual design

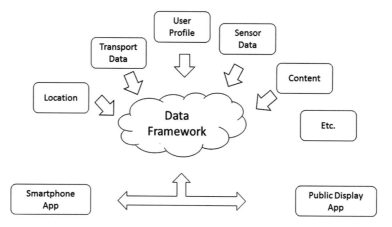

High volumes of heterogeneous data are transformed by the framework into (digested) information by passing data through several reasoning / processing components involved with near real-time data consolidation and dynamic profiling of passengers. In the following subsections, we describe in more detail a number of use cases for the software framework that are essential in order to achieve this. For the sake of clarity and ease of reference, the use cases are split up according to the involved actors: content providers, developers, system administrators, devices running the LimeDS framework and finally information consumers. Note that the presented use cases are not intended as a complete definition of features supported by LimeDS, but rather as a set of scenarios by which the resulting Proof-of-Concept can be evaluated.

Content Provider

A content provider can be any instance that provides data to the system, either actively or passively. This can be an external instance (e.g. the framework using the news feed of a newspaper) or an internal instance (e.g. a train equipped with the framework posting its GPS data to all participating devices). Two of the use cases apply to a content provider.

1. **Provide Access to Data:** A content provider makes a data source available to the framework and supplies (developers with the necessary information to implement) a module that allows the framework to extract data from this source.
2. **Push New Data:** A content provider actively pushes new data into the system using the framework API.

Developer and System Administrator

In the context of LimeDS, developers can expand upon the original system, offering additional functionality in packaged modules to the framework. The administrator role extends from the typical responsibilities such as managing the users and devices, to deciding which of the provided modules are actively deployed in the framework. This level of control is required as third-party developers can also provide modules, but their contributions need to be validated before they are put into use. For a developer, we define the following use cases:

1. **Add Input Controllers:** Developers can implement additional input controller modules which allow the framework to extract data from new data source types. This use case is closely related with "Provide access to data" in the Section 'Content Provider'.
2. **Add Reasoning Components:** Developers can implement additional reasoning component modules or incorporate new knowledge descriptions (e.g. in the form of rules) which enable the framework to make new conclusions based on the input data to extract new information.
3. **Add Information Consumers:** Developers can implement information consumers which can be distributed and deployed by the framework. Information consumers can be any software component that uses the framework to enhance the experience of the passengers, crew, etc. Typically, this will be a mobile application or an application driving public displays on board a train or in stations.

For an administrator, we define the following use cases:

1. **Manage Devices:** Administrators are responsible for setting up new framework devices and to review the status of existing ones. Registered devices can run the reasoning modules available in the framework. The framework must facilitate administrators in performing these tasks.
2. **Manage Modules:** Administrators must authorise modules before they can be deployed and installed. They also need to be able to revoke this authorisation at a later time.
3. **Manage Users:** Administrators are responsible for the management of users and roles and the assignation of the required user rights.

System Device and Information Consumer

A system device in this context is defined as any device that is equipped with the LimeDS framework. An information consumer is a piece of software that is dependent on the LimeDS framework; this can include Android or iPhone apps running on the passenger's phone or native applications that drive the content being displayed on the train screens. Figure 5 shows the use cases that apply to a system device and how these are related to those of the information consumer.

For the system device, we define the following use cases:

1. **Accept Input:** Each system device must be able to accept input data in a uniform way, either through an API or by using input modules that can actively fetch data from a source.
2. **Host Reasoning Modules:** Additional modules added by developers (such as reasoning components and on-board passenger service applications) and greenlighted by an administrator can be hosted on each of the system devices.
3. **Provide Information:** Each system device must support a mechanism allowing clients to retrieve information. Clients can be passenger applications, but can also be other system devices that require information from their peers.

For information consumers, we define the following use cases:

1. **Receive Information:** An information consumer must be able to receive/retrieve the required information in a uniform way. The application or services are dependent on a connected system device to support this use case, and LimeDS must support developers in interfacing with the device API.
2. **Generate Data:** An information consumer can also produce data that can be relevant to the operation of the framework, such as user preferences and user feedback. This data can enter the framework through any of the available system devices. Note that the inner workings and logic performed by an information consumer application or service is out of the scope of the framework.

Framework Requirements

Based on the use cases identified in the previous section we identified several requirements, which can be split into two categories: functional requirements and non-functional requirements. The latter are also commonly referred to as the so-called quality attributes of the system.

Generic Data Input Module

The framework will interface with a wide range of data sources, some of these will be periodically queried for new information by the framework itself, while other sources will want to actively push new

Figure 5. System device and information consumer

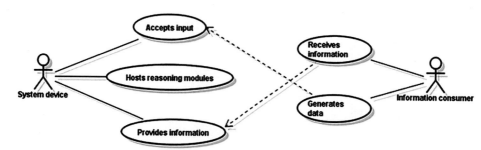

information to the framework using its API. A generic data input module is thus required that offers an elegant solution to both handle taking input from any potential data source as well as converting this data into an internal format the framework can easily work with. This is commonly referred to as the "Data Integration" challenge. Since we want to expose rich information to the passengers, it is important to be able to quickly and easily integrate different kinds of data sources that are available. Easy integration of web-based data sources via the framework is equally important (especially given that open data initiatives are more and more gaining momentum worldwide). Not all data is available as an accessible structured service however, more than often the data source is a regular file or webpage. Therefore, a flexible interface integration mechanism is to be provided and considered to be a key aspect of the framework.

These requirements are very important in our design, since devices and applications that use the LimeDS framework should be able to present accurate and clear data to the passengers at all times. In general, the richer the data we want to show, the more (heterogeneous) data sources should be used. For instance: a geographical map provider, location-based advertising, location-based weather information, upcoming public transportation connections, etc.

Modular Reasoning Engine

Many datasets will be available to the framework at any time, so some kind of reasoning is required to extract valuable information from this data. However, as reasoning will be performed for topics that can vary in scope, the decision was made that multiple modules, each performing a certain aspect of reasoning, will be needed. Some of these reasoning modules will make decisions in near real-time based on up-to-date data that is being streamed to the framework, while other modules will periodically generate new information based on historical data. This modular approach also allows us to easily add new functionality when the need arises. A modular reasoning engine thus enables us to partition the reasoning aspect of the framework and will coordinate routing the data between the various modules. Finally, the engine must support running third party reasoning components without putting the framework's core operations at risk, e.g. ensuring that the failure of one component can be contained so that other applications are not influenced by this failure, or can fall back on a degraded mode of operation.

Information Service

Data is made available to the system and several reasoning modules will be in place to extract valuable information from this data. After all, data are the individual facts where information can be derived

Figure 6. The possibilities are endless, and in practice the information is very varied in representation format

Figure 7. Support for a modular and tuneable reasoning algorithm

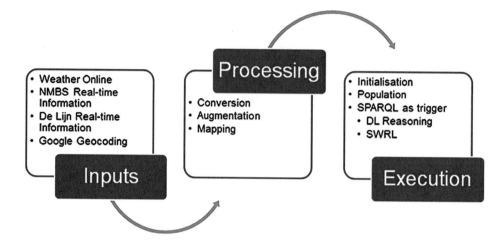

from. As such, for data to become information context should be included as well. It is essential that the framework can expose this generated information to interested parties (e.g. passenger applications) in different ways:

1. Querying model for historic information and on a need to know basis, i.e. just in time. In this case, interested services or passenger applications will look for the required information themselves by actively querying our framework API.
2. Notification / pub-sub mechanism for near real-time information. A mechanism is required that allows for services or passenger applications to express the topics they are interested in to the framework. This allows the framework to notify the necessary services or applications whenever new information becomes available that matches their field-of-interest.

Architectural Design

Having defined the scope and general technical requirements for the framework, the architecture of the system can be elaborated.

Framework Layers

The high-level architecture of the LimeDS system is shown in Figure 8. First, an abstraction layer is built on top of the operating system of the device on which the framework will be running. The goal of this module is to hide all the operating system specific details from the other framework modules, allowing these to run unmodified on all devices for which the abstraction layer can be implemented. As the framework is implemented in the Java programming language, system-independent development is achieved by using the Java Virtual Machine as abstraction layer.

On top of the abstraction layer the core platform is built, consisting of a number of utility components that facilitate the development of the actual LimeDS modules, namely the input adapters and functional components. Input adapters are needed that can convert data from multiple sources into a format that is

Figure 8. The high-level architecture of the LimeDS ecosystem

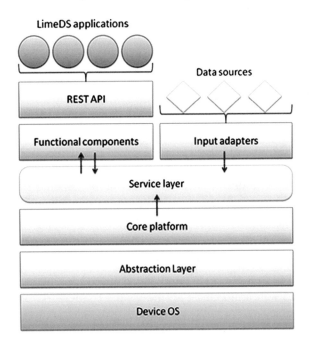

compatible with the internal representation used by the framework. A distinction can be made between data sources that will autonomously push new data into the framework (usually real-time data, e.g. GPS coordinates posted by a moving train) and data sources that will be queried by the framework itself (e.g. a Web Service that can be used to retrieve route information). The functional components are features responsible for implementing the actual logic that will result in the end-user services/applications targeted at providing a better travelling experience. Each such feature can be represented by a functional component that uses various input adapters, core platform components or even other functional components to transform unstructured, loose bits of data into useful information for the passenger. The functional components can also deploy endpoints to a REST API using the service layer, allowing applications (on mobile devices, public screens, etc.) to communicate with the framework.

Detailed Architecture Overview

From the requirements discussed in the previous sections, the framework architecture should support a wide range of use cases. The framework can only succeed in such a context when its design incorporates the aspects described in the subsections below.

Data Representation

The data representation used by the framework must be highly flexible to support a wide range of use cases, while retaining good developer usability and interoperability with existing solutions that produce data. The corresponding data model should not be fixed to a predefined schema, as this limits the capability to be extended in an intuitive manner. In its role as native object model for the dynamic scripting language JavaScript, JSON (Crockford, 2006) matches the requirement for a highly flexible representation. Additionally, thanks to its wide adoption in web technologies, JSON has good compatibility with all major programming languages. To model the JSON format internally LimeDS uses the Jackson JSON processor library (FasterXML, 2009).

Dynamic Module System

As the framework has been designed for modifiability, it should support changes to be made at runtime, in order to avoid any unnecessary downtime. For this reason, a dynamic module system has been introduced that can be used in combination with the service layer to implement a highly adaptable system. The dynamic module system for LimeDS has been based on the existing standard specification OSGi. This modular system design has other advantages as well. All modules conform to a certain contract (an interface). This means that new modules can be added in or swapped in, if they just adhere to the specifications of the contract. This leads to easy extensibility of the framework. This also leads to re-usability, since after a while an elaborate collection of modules becomes available.

Since communication between modules is restricted to the contracts, these contracts are an explicit description of the dependencies of a module. This allows the framework to define what should happen when a dependency is not available (for each module). Thanks to this, instead of crashing, the system will allow a module to execute an alternative scenario whenever the dependencies change at runtime.

Service System

The OSGi specification consists of a service model that provides a very good match with the envisioned LimeDS service layer. The service layer is one of the most important systems of the framework as it allows modules to communicate while retaining loose coupling, enabling functionality to be extended or replaced at runtime. It also provides the foundation for the dataflow system that is explained in the next section.

Dataflow System

The dataflow system is an abstraction on top of the service layer that facilitates developers in implementing data oriented processes, which are at the core of the different use cases that must be supported. Figure 9 shows the three interfaces that define the components from which entire dataflow processes can be built:

1. A producer specifies the generic interface for components that can make data available. It represents a pull-mechanism of communication in which the producer is queried whenever the data it provides is required in some part of the data flow.
2. A consumer specifies the generic interface for components that can consume data. It represents a push-mechanism of communication in which the consumer can be actively called whenever up-to-date content is available.
3. Connectors are the links between producers and consumers in the data flow model. Each connector defines which producer and consumer instances will participate in the connection and provides the logic that allows the data to be captured from the producer-side and transformed into appropriate output that can be delivered to the target instances on the consumer-side.

Figure 9. LimeDS models everything as a simple function call that takes input and produces output

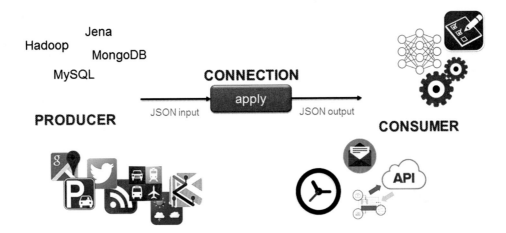

Components of the connector-type can be activated periodically to perform certain tasks, e.g. a connector that enriches all stored places of interest with up-to-date weather information can be activated hourly. To support these connectors, the framework must integrate a scheduler. We employ the Quartz library (Cavaness, 2006) to trigger the recurring tasks while a Connector Scheduler is responsible for the synchronization of schedulable connectors available from the service registry with the triggers that are enabled within the Quartz scheduler.

Once a dataflow component is defined and all its properties are set, the framework needs to take this definition and translate it to an active instance of the component that can participate in the various dataflow chains. This process is called the materialization of the component, i.e. the necessary components need to be deployed in the framework and corresponding interface wiring needs to be properly activated.

To illustrate the above theoretical presentation, an example is detailed below. The example concerns the tracking of a journey by a user and providing personalised travel information to that user.

Figure 10. A hypothetical example, illustrating how to combine multiple data flows to create a new passenger information service

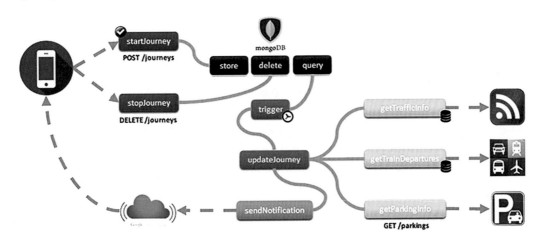

The entry-point for this flow is a function startJourney() that will initialise a new travel route. We use a MongoDB database to persist the journey data. The MongoDB instance is integrated with LimeDS, by providing three functions: store(), delete() and query(). We connect the startJourney()block to the store function to store the incoming requested travel route.

To be able to generate updates for the chosen journey, we introduce a trigger function that will be scheduled to execute periodically. Each time this function is executed, we use the database query function to retrieve the relevant route information. This data is then sent to an updateJourney() function that will check for route updates. This can be done by using three data sources:

1.   An RSS news feed that lists traffic updates.
2.   A Web Service that provides real-time information concerning train departures.
3.   A CSV file that contains parking information for which a new dump is generated every 15 minutes.

To integrate these three data sources in the dataflow, a function is made for each source that can connect to the original data source and transform the data into a compatible format. Once all the data is processed, the updateJourney() function can send an update to the user (if necessary) using the sendNotification() function, which uses the Google Cloud Messaging service to send the update to the phone of the user. The dataflow can be completed by adding a stopJourney() function that enables the user's travel assistant app to stop or cancel the journey. To do this, we rely on the database delete() function. LimeDS allows any function to be exposed over HTTP as a Web Service. We do this for the startJourney() and stopJourney() functions, so these operations can be called from the personal travel assistant mobile application. In addition we also expose the getParkingInfo() function.

Features which are inherently provided by the framework are data validation for any function (checking whether the data is consistent with a specific model or within specific constraints), e.g. it allows validating the journey information that is sent by the mobile client before initializing the update process. The framework also allows to add caching to any function. In the dataflow example above a remote call is made each time the traffic RSS feed and real-time train info Web Services are called. This can take a while to complete, and the number of allowed requests for these external sources could be limited. However, by adding a cache, we can circumvent these problems without writing any additional lines of code. Now the results will be cached locally and the amount of remote calls will be greatly reduced (based on tunable cache parameters).

Storage System

The framework storage system fully embraces the data representation as discussed in the Subsection 'Data Representation' by using subtypes of JsonNode as the main argument and return types. For the Proof-of-Concept, detailed later in this chapter, we chose to implement the storage service using MongoDB (Chodorow, 2013) as this technology uses a binary variant of JSON, both for storing data and as a query format for retrieving data. However, this implementation can easily be replaced by other NoSQL type of databases as the JSON representation can be mapped to any hierarchical key-value store.

Communication System

The LimeDS framework supports the standard specification JAX-RS (Hadley & Sandoz, 2009), allowing automated generation of REST Web Services based on annotated tools that are available in the framework. The principle is very similar to how data flows can be specified: JAX-RS annotated services are added to the service registry. The annotations contain information about the REST service path and the available HTTP methods. A JAX-RS Bridge module connects with the service registry and is continuously scanning for new annotated services. The JAX-RS Bridge then calls Apache Wink (Apache Software Foundation, 2015) for each discovered service. Wink is a library that translates the annotated resources to HTTP servlets, which can be hosted in a servlet container.

To facilitate calling the services provided in this way (or external REST services), a client utility library is provided by the framework that can be used to easily call REST services using a minimal amount of code. The client implementation is registered as a service with the service registry, allowing it to be accessed from any module. The client API allows expressing REST calls in a rather natural way, e.g. to post a JSON object to an example service, one can write the following statement:

```
JsonNode jsonObject = Json.from("\"{ \"example\": \"Hello world!\" }");
client.target("http://example.com/API/example")
.post(jsonObject).returnNoResult();
```

With both a way to easily expose REST services (server side) and a way to fluently call and make use of these services, the framework provides all the features that are required of a communication system.

Load Manager System

The framework further provides a load manager system which facilitates dataflow component developers in adding robustness and scalability to their services, allowing use cases to be implemented without introducing a lot of development overhead. For each registered service, the load manager will generate a proxy service that transparently captures all requests sent to the original service and redirects it to the service instance (running locally or remote) that is currently best suited to answer the request. This decision can be based on the number of requests for each instance, the mean response times, etc.

The framework can cope with situations that are a result of unreliability by providing a system that makes it possible to monitor the availability of external systems. Under normal circumstances, a train that loses its network connectivity would not be able to refresh its data. When employing LimeDS however, we see that train-deployed applications will autonomously query the availability of the external system / service / data source on the wayside. If this system is periodically inaccessible, LimeDS will notice this unavailability and act by transparently redirecting data calls to local storage / cached data until the external services are reachable again, at which point the original dataflow is restored.

Scalable Services

The final aspect to be presented is the scalability of the system. Because of the highly dynamic transportation context and the potentially high (and fluctuating) number of clients, the framework must be able to scale based on the number of users and connected devices. Two cases in particular are of importance.

Figure 11. LimeDS functions are designed to be robust

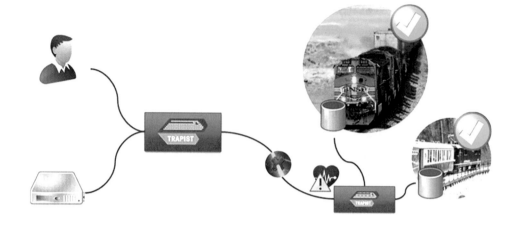

In the first case, imagine a large number of requests happening at about the same time. All these requests will start remote connections to external data sources via the framework. This will obviously generate a lot of remote requests, which may get blocked by the external services in question, because their allowed request quota was reached. This first case can be solved by using a caching mechanism. The framework allows to easily utilise caches that will store the results of certain requests within the configured timeframe. This will not only greatly reduce the load on the external services and thus attempt to stay below the allowed limits. It will also greatly reduce response times, since no more remote requests are needed if there is a cached answer available in the LimeDS framework.

Secondly, imagine if all requests would be tunnelled through a single LimeDS instance. This would put a lot of load on this server. The framework is however inherently able to balance the load between multiple instances that are setup in a cluster, each employing their own caches. This approach is based on the mechanism proposed in (Burns, et al, 2016).

Figure 12. Scalability as a native, inherent built-in feature

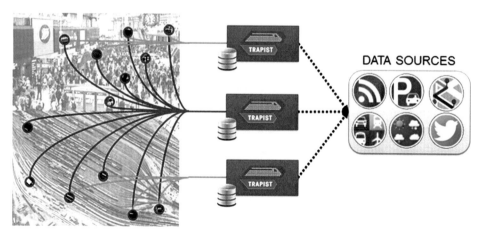

SOLUTIONS AND RECOMMENDATIONS

Two Proof-of-Concept demonstrator implementations, using the LimeDS framework as described in the previous section, have been successfully deployed. We succeeded in building a robust and modifiable framework, facilitating the addition of new functionality at any time (i.e. even at runtime when the system is in operation) and allowing various layers of robustness to be added to the system through the introduction of the concept of service dynamics. This implies that components are no longer statically bound, but rather rely on independent services executing the defined behaviour in case of service failure (e.g. in the event of system or network failures.

On-Board Passenger Information Display

Figure 13 shows a screenshot of an on-board display application powered by the LimeDS framework. The application depicts context-aware travel connections for passengers on board the train, i.e. relevant information about multi-modal connecting services at the next calling point of the train. To obtain this information, a dataflow was implemented on the LimeDS framework. A conceptual overview of this dataflow is drawn in Figure 14.

Figure 13. Context-aware travel connections on-board public display, powered by LimeDS

Bus connections in Brussel-Zuid

Destination	Due	Status	Platform	Feasibility	
				🚶	♿
BOCKSTAEL	12:55	On time	49	✗	✗
BOCKSTAEL	12:56	On time	49	◉	✗
BOCKSTAEL	12:58	On time	49	✓	◉
LOT STATION	13:01	On time	50	✓	✓

Figure 14. Conceptual view of the context-aware connections data flow

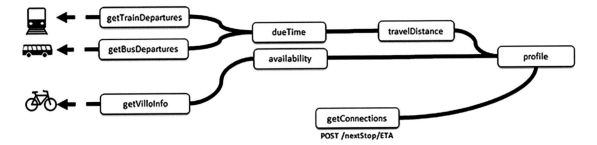

The dataflow is triggered when the client application (i.e., the on-board display application) sends a REST request to the framework URL of the getConnections() component. The next stop of the train and its Expected Time of Arrival (ETA) at the next stop are passed as arguments. This activates the input adapters developed to access real-time train (getTrainDepartures()) and bus (getBusDepartures()) information as well as information from a bike-sharing scheme (getVilloInfo()) through REST calls. Train and bus connections are next filtered on due time (dueTime-connector) and travel distance towards the platform of the connection to mark services that will already have left (by the time passengers from the requesting train arrive) as not feasible. Similarly, only operational bike-sharing stands near the next stop are passed through the availability connector. The profile filter further categorises the connections based on two profiles, namely, passengers with or without mobility impairment where the filter considers longer walking distances for the former. As such, the resulting departing services are marked as:

1. **Feasible:** When there is sufficient time to board, the service takes into account the real-time arrival time of the requesting train and the travel distance towards the platform of this service.
2. **Tight:** When the service is feasible but the margin is less than 60 seconds.
3. **Not Feasible:** When the service will no longer be available when the passenger arrives.

The on-board public display application extracts the resulting information from the REST response and properly displays it to train passengers as demonstrated in Figure 13. As such, train passengers are provided with timely, relevant information that is the result of combining multiple journey-related data sources.

Personalised Travel Connections

The second PoC concerns the personalisation of feasible connections at interchange stations in an off-board situation, enabled through a Semantic Web approach. The steps executed to create such an application using the LimeDS framework are presented in this section.

In general, we will use an ontology both to describe public transport related concepts as well as to support classification using a combination of OWL DL and SWRL based reasoning. The LimeDS framework can then be used to compose the data flows for specific applications, allowing to connect a variety of data producers (e.g. railway timetable information providers) with reasoning modules drawing conclusions based on the currently available information and context, and exposing these reasoning results as REST endpoints for visualisation by (mobile) client applications.

An important aspect of a satisfactory travel experience for all travelers is the fact that transportation information should be correct and accurate at all times, and preferably tuned for the specific situation or context of the person at hand. Let us clarify this with an example: a connecting public transportation option may not be feasible to catch for every type of person if only five minutes are scheduled between arriving at a station and boarding that scheduled connection leaving from a different platform, as there is a need to disembark, orient yourself and find / make your way to the other platform and finally board the connecting transport. In other words, the time a traveler requires to transfer between platforms can be dependent on the context (e.g. a first time visit versus daily use / knowledge of the station layout) and physical limitations of that person (e.g. people with physical disabilities or in wheelchairs, elderly, people using a child carrier or heavy travelling luggage). To come up with a true personalised travel guidance system, this contextual information needs to be captured and considered before presenting travelling guidance to the user. Another example of taking context into account when presenting personalised travel information is when delays are occurring: public transport connections that under normal circumstances are not considered because there is too little platform transfer time according to the regular (non-delayed) timetable, may become a valid transportation option in case the connection is delayed, and can therefore exceptionally be presented to the user as a viable alternative, allowing that person to potentially reach their destination quicker.

Ontology Engineering

In support of this scenario an ontology has been created extending two existing ontologies:

1. **Transit (Davis, 2011; Kaufman, 2014; Schaefer, 2014)**: A vocabulary for describing transit systems and routes, and
2. **Weather (Gajderowicz, 2011):** Based on the ontology created by Aaron Elkiss (Elkiss, 2011).

Starting from the *Transit* and *Weather* ontologies an extension has been modelled, representing the railway timetable from the Belgian National Railway Operator (NMBS/SNCB) at several Belgian railway stations. This represents the railway schedule as it should be if everything runs according to plan. The main new OWL class has been named *Connection*. Individuals of these *Connection*s represent the actual running of that service on a specific date and are used at runtime to determine which of the *Connection*s at any given railway station can be caught for the given traveler's profile. To perform the classification, a combination of OWL DL as well as SWRL reasoning is adopted. A number of illustrative axioms are presented in the following paragraphs.

For a *Connection* to be classified as suitable for travelers with a mobility impairment, the OWL definition is given below, based on the terms available in the *Transit* vocabulary. It specifies that the *Connection* should be on a route which has a pre-arrangement for mobility impaired passenger, this arrangement should have been confirmed by the operator and the *Connection* should depart from a platform at ground level:

```
MobilityImpairmentSuitableConnection
<=>
(route some owl:Thing)
and (hasAccessArrangement value prearranged)
and (platform some xsd:int[> "-1"^^xsd:int])
and (isArrangementOK value true)
```

It should be clear that for other situations or other transport modes, such as a bus, taxi or cycle hire, other definitions can be specified in the domain ontology, used for that specific operator deployment. However, thanks to the generic notion of a *MobilityImpairmentSuitableConnection*, the UI visualising this information does not need to be aware of the specific definitions in place for that specific situation. The reasoner performs the job of filtering and classification. At first, the use of as much DL-based axioms as possible has been pursued, for the reason of genericness and to support the ability to exchange multiple OWL DL enabled reasoner implementations. However, sometimes it might not be possible to purely rely on OWL DL. To facilitate those more complex situations, support for SWRL rules has been included as well. An example of using SWRL to support complex rules and to take the real-time running information of the *Connection* into account, is given below:

```
MobilityImpairmentSuitableConnection(?connection),
currentTime(Now, ?ct),
departureTime(?connection, ?departuretime),
hasDelay(?connection, ?delay),
add(?earliestdeparturetime, ?ct, 900000),
add(?realdeparturetime,
?departuretime, ?delay),
greaterThan(?realdeparturetime, ?earliestdeparturetime)
->
MobilityImpairmentTimedSuitableConnection(?connection)
```

This SWRL rule specifies that, for a *Connection* to be classified as a *MobilityImpairment**Timed**-SuitableConnection*, it should already have been classified as a *MobilityImpairmentSuitableConnection* and in addition its actual departure time should be at least 15 minutes in the future.

Other definitions have been included for other categories of passengers as well, such as *HearingImpairmentSuitableConnection* or *VisualImpairmentSuitableConnection* in case of *Connections* with specific requirements for an on-board Passenger Information System or considering the earlier introduced *Weather* ontology. Examples include a *FrostSuitableConnection*, *SnowSuitableConnection* or *BicycleSuitableConnection*.

LimeDS Dataflow

Once the ontology and its defining axioms have been agreed upon, the implementation within the LimeDS framework can start. For this, the integrated flow builder can be used. For the scenario presented in this section, the dataflow as modelled using the LimeDS Flow Builder is illustrated in Figure 15.

The main Flow Function is illustrated in the middle of the figure. This represents the configuration of the reasoner. In addition, the configuration also allows to specify the endpoint which should be exposed and used by client applications to trigger this data flow, as well as non-functional properties for caching, load-balancing and authentication/authorisation characteristics, and this in a user-friendly manner without the need to write any boilerplate code.

Finally, on the left-hand side in Figure 15, several input components (data producers) can be seen. These ensure that the correct information is: (i) fetched from the online data sources (e.g. for retrieving the at-runtime information of the railway operations, the weather at a certain location and optionally geocoding that location), and (ii) converted into JSON-LD ready for processing by the reasoner component, illustrated in the middle of the figure. On the right-hand side, components are linked to the reasoner for persistency functionality. As indicated earlier, built-in support for persistency by means of MongoDB is provided by the framework.

Figure 15. Data Flow to classify the personalised connections

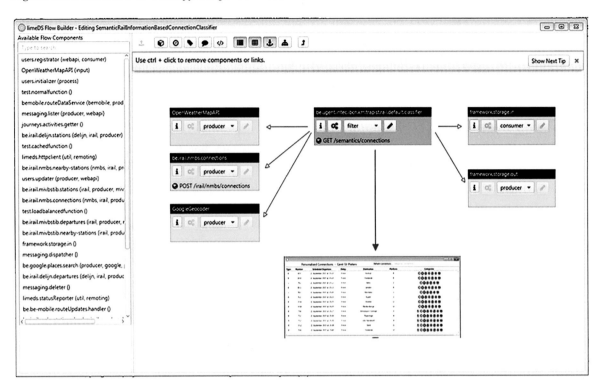

Figure 16. Based on the semantic model and at-runtime information, connections are classified in 10 categories

1 Advised for mobility impaired
2 Advised for bicycles
3 Advised for frosty weather
4 Advised for snowy weather
5 Generally feasible
6 Advised for hearing impaired
7 Advised for visual impaired
8 Environmental friendly
9 Petrol head friendly
10 Railway geek friendly

Evaluation

The LimeDS platform was evaluated during the TraPIST project for different scenarios on a low-resource server instance (2 cores, Intel Xenon CPU E5-2630 @ 2.3 GHz, 2GB RAM). In a first scenario, we subjected the host machine to an increasing number of requests per second. This was done for four different server implementations: a pure Jetty (8.1.14) servlet-based implementation (The Eclipse Foundation, 2011), a LimeDS (limeDS.0.1.0-pre-alpha) Java implementation, a LimeDS (limeDS.0.1.0-pre-alpha) JavaScript implementation and a Node-RED (0.13.3) implementation (JS Foundation, 2015). It should be noted that the purpose of this test was to find a scaling breaking point (in part the reason why modest hardware resources were used). Also, note that the Servlet (Jetty, version 8.1.14) measurement can be considered a performance baseline, but offers none of the high-level features of LimeDS. The test was executed until the server crashed or timeouts started to occur on the client. The Jetty implementation could maintain good response times before crashing at > 260 RPS. The LimeDS Java implementation can almost match the servlet implementation up until 200 RPS, before failing at > 220 RPS. The JavaScript variant performs slightly worse and fails earlier at > 200 RPS. Node-RED stopped working at > 180 RPS. The results are graphically presented in Figure 17.

In a second scenario, illustrated in Figure 18, we tested the data processing capabilities of LimeDS, opposed to an equivalent Jetty servlet implementation by sending data that contained extensive profile information of users. We see similar response times and a linear increase in processing time for all implementations. Large requests up to 30 MB can be processed under 2 seconds. 30 MB requests are huge, given the nature of typical Web Service requests. Note that a default configured Node-RED setup is incapable of processing requests this large and responds with an error message when passing an array of 100 user records.

The third scenario evaluates the impact of the dataflow size/complexity on the response time of the functions calls (implemented in JavaScript). The highest curve in Figure 19 shows the average response

Figure 17. High load response times

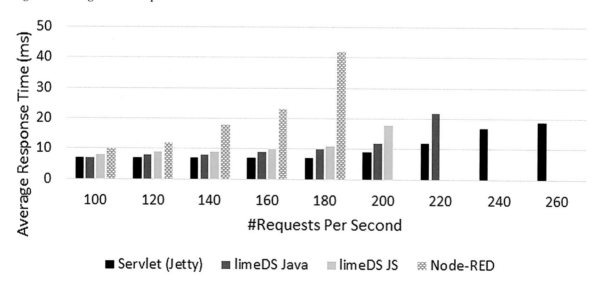

Figure 18. Data processing

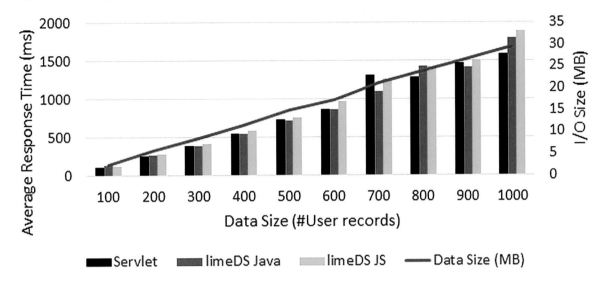

Figure 19. Effect of dataflow size on function calls

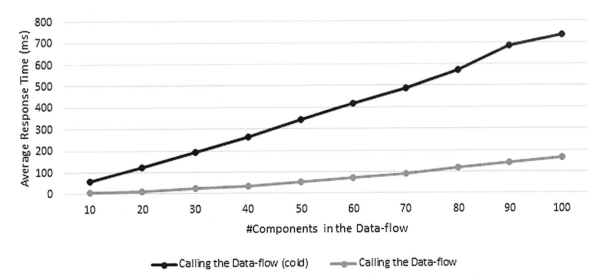

time when the dataflow is called for the first time, while the lowest curve shows the average response time for all subsequent calls. This warm-up phenomenon that can be witnessed is to do with the way our JavaScript engine is initialised.

Related to the previous scenario, we also tested the deployment and undeployment time required for increasingly larger/more complex dataflows. As expected, the deployment time increases for larger dataflows, but remains linear. Undeployment remains practically constant.

Figure 20. Effect of dataflow size on (un)deployment process

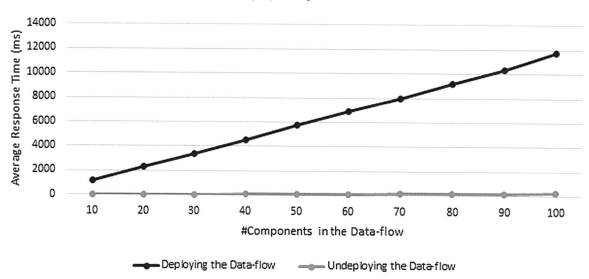

FUTURE RESEARCH DIRECTIONS

The presented framework rapidly grew from an OSGi abstraction layer and library in Java for internal use, to a full-featured development platform with a visual (JavaScript-based) editor. After several successful collaborative research projects with industrial partners, it was decided to share the platform with the open-source community as an Apache License, version 2.0 software package, available at http://www.limeds.be. Future research will continue to expand the LimeDS feature set and improve upon the runtime engine to evolve the platform into a general purpose, reliable and easy-to-use service development framework. Ideally, it will allow developers to setup a cluster of LimeDS instances in the Cloud and immediately start designing logical data flows on top of these instances, by connecting readily available modules. Aspects such as deployment and configuration are taken care of by the framework, while the uploaded flows are executed by our runtime engine. Future research directions include:

1. **Profiling Support:** With the current release, it can be difficult to detect certain kinds of bugs. A LimeDS *Aspect* can easily be introduced that maintains statistics for each *Segment* and reports back issues to a central monitoring system. The challenge is to integrate this information with the visual editor to allow quick troubleshooting.
2. **Enhanced Processing Engine:** Although LimeDS is built with scalability in mind from the start, there is always room for improvement. LimeDS's current thread per request model is eventually limited in terms of scalability by the maximum amount of allowed threads. We are evaluating asynchronous programming tools to improve the framework in this aspect. The benefit of LimeDS is that we can update the processing engine transparently, without needing to change modules written for LimeDS.
3. **Support for Popular Technologies Out-of-the-Box:** The success of a framework like LimeDS relies on the presence of a rich eco-system. It is made relatively easy to create and distribute share-

able modules and several adapters and connectors (that can be used straight from the visual editor) for popular technologies are made available, allowing users to dispose of a set building blocks for their applications. Future connectors include: Twitter & Slack integration, modules to interact with the underlying OS, Big Data and storage technologies, etc.

CONCLUSION

In this chapter, we presented a multi-source, data processing software framework suitable for the railway transport sector, allowing for agile development of data processing applications which rely on a multitude of heterogeneous open data and knowledge sources. A real-time data consolidation mechanism has been implemented on top of the service layer of the OSGi-based platform. This abstraction allows to provide robustness, easy configurability and extensibility. The LimeDS framework embraces HTTP(S) and other proven web technologies for transferring data between nodes running on different host machines as well as client applications that make use of the enriched information offered by these nodes. Two Proof-of-Concept demonstrator using the framework were developed and integrated with a passenger information system that visualises real-time information on on-board public train and station displays. These demonstrators have a focus on offering personalised and context-filtered information to the end-user, allowing that end-user to be presented with information tailored to his or her needs and (physical) disabilities. LimeDS can deal with sudden unavailability of select data sources and offers a developer-friendly way of reasoning over this data. Furthermore, it can (visually) aid with the construction of data processing/reasoning workflows and provides inherent configurable support for scaling, resilience and fall back scenarios.

REFERENCES

Apache Software Foundation. (2015). *Apache Wink – a simple yet solid framework for building RESTful Web Services*. Retrieved January 17, 2017, from https://wink.apache.org/

Beckett, D., Berners-Lee, T., & Prud'hommeaux, E. (2008). Turtle-terse RDF triple language. *W3C Team Submission, 14*(7). Retrieved April 13, 2017, from https://www.w3.org/TeamSubmission/turtle/

Beckett, D., & McBride, B. (2004). RDF/XML syntax specification (revised). *W3C recommendation, 10*. Retrieved April 13, 2017, from http://www.w3.org/TR/rdf-syntax-grammar

Burke, B. (2009). *RESTful Java with JaX-RS*. O'Reilly Media, Inc.

Burke, B. (2013). *RESTful Java with Jax-RS 2.0*. O'Reilly Media, Inc.

Burns, B., Grant, B., Oppenheimer, D., Brewer, E., & Wilkes, J. (2016). Borg, omega, and kubernetes. *Communications of the ACM, 59*(5), 50–57. doi:10.1145/2890784

Carroll, J. J., Dickinson, I., Dollin, C., Reynolds, D., Seaborne, A., & Wilkinson, K. (2004, May). Jena: implementing the semantic web recommendations. In *Proceedings of the 13th international World Wide Web conference on Alternate track papers & posters* (pp. 74-83). ACM. doi:10.1145/1013367.1013381

Cavaness, C. (2006). *Quartz Job Scheduling Framework: Building Open Source Enterprise Applications*. Pearson Education.

Chodorow, K. (2013). *MongoDB: the definitive guide*. O'Reilly Media, Inc.

Clement Escoffier, M. K. (2015). *Vert.x – a toolkit for building reactive applications on the JVM*. Retrieved January 17, 2017, from http://vertx.io/

Dallas, A. (2014). *RESTful Web Services with Dropwizard*. Packt Publishing Ltd.

Davis, I. (2011). *TRANSIT: A vocabulary for describing transit systems and routes*. Retrieved January 23, 2017, from http://vocab.org/transit/terms.html

Elkiss, A. (2011). *A weather ontology*. Retrieved January 23, 2017, from http://www.csd.abdn.ac.uk/˜ggrimnes/AgentCities/WeatherAgent/weather-ont.daml

European Commission. (2011). *Roadmap to a Single European Transport Area – Towards a competitive and resource efficient transport system*. Retrieved January 17, 2017 from http://eur-lex.europa.eu/legal-content/EN/TXT/PDF/?uri=CELEX:52011DC0144&from=EN

Faster XML, LLC. (2009) *Jackson JSON Processor Wiki*. Retrieved February 03, 2017 from http://wiki.fasterxml.com/JacksonHome

Fernández-López, M., Gómez-Pérez, A., & Juristo, N. (1997). Methontology: from ontological art towards ontological engineering.

Foundation, J. S. (2015). *Node-RED – A visual tool for wiring the Internet of Things*. Retrieved February 3, 2017, from http://nodered.org/

Gajderowicz, B. (2011). *Using decision trees for inductively driven semantic integration and ontology matching* [Doctoral dissertation]. Ryerson University, Program of Computer Science.

Gardner, N., Haeusler, M. H., & Tomitsch, M. (2010). *Infostructure: A Transport Research Project*. Freerange Press.

Glimm, B., Horrocks, I., Motik, B., Stoilos, G., & Wang, Z. (2014). HermiT: An OWL 2 reasoner. *Journal of Automated Reasoning, 53*(3), 245–269. doi:10.1007/s10817-014-9305-1

Gruber, T. R. (1993). A translation approach to portable ontology specifications. *Knowledge Acquisition, 5*(2), 199–220. doi:10.1006/knac.1993.1008

Guerra, C. F., García-Ródenas, R., Sánchez-Herrera, E. A., Rayo, D. V., & Clemente-Jul, C. (2016). Modeling of the behavior of alternative fuel vehicle buyers. A model for the location of alternative refueling stations. *International Journal of Hydrogen Energy, 41*(42), 19312–19319. doi:10.1016/j.ijhydene.2016.07.165

Hadley, M., & Sandoz, P. (2009). JAX-RS: Java™ API for RESTful Web Services. *Java Specification Request, 311*. Retrieved January, 2017, from http://java.net/nonav/projects/jsr311/sources/svn/content/trunk/www/drafts/spec20080827.pdf

Hitzler, P., Krötzsch, M., Parsia, B., Patel-Schneider, P. F., & Rudolph, S. (2009). OWL 2 web ontology language primer. *W3C recommendation, 27*(1), 123. Retrieved April 13, 2017, from https://www.w3.org/TR/owl-primer/

Hori, M., Euzenat, J., & Patel-Schneider, P. (2003). OWL Web ontology language XML presentation syntax.*W3C Technical Report*. Retrieved April 13, 2017, from http://www.w3.org/TR/owl-xmlsyntax/

Horridge, M., Drummond, N., Goodwin, J., Rector, A. L., Stevens, R., & Wang, H. (2006, November). The Manchester OWL Syntax. In OWLed (Vol. 216).

Hua, G.B. (2016). *Smart Cities as a Solution for Reducing Urban Waste and Pollution.*

Kaufmann, S. (2014). *Opening public transit data in Germany.* Doctoral dissertation, University of Ulm.

McGuinness, D. L., & Van Harmelen, F. (2004). OWL web ontology language overview. *W3C recommendation, 10*(10). Retrieved January 23, 2017, from https://www.w3.org/TR/owl-features/

Office of Rail and Road. (2016). *Information for passengers.* Retrieved April 13, 2017, from http://orr.gov.uk/__data/assets/pdf_file/0015/4353/information-for-passengers-guidance-on-meeting-the-licence-condition.pdf

Office of Rail Regulation. (2012, December). *Passenger Information.* Retrieved January 17, 2017, from http://orr.gov.uk/__data/assets/pdf_file/0014/4352/Passenger-information.pdf

Oracle Corporation. (2015). *Jersey – RESTfulWeb Services in Java.* Retrieved January 17, 2017, from https://jersey.java.net/

OSGi Alliance. (2003). *OSGi Service Platform, Release 3.* IOS Press, Inc.

Pålsson, H., & Kovács, G. (2014). Reducing transportation emissions: A reaction to stakeholder pressure or a strategy to increase competitive advantage. *International Journal of Physical Distribution & Logistics Management, 44*(4), 283–304. doi:10.1108/IJPDLM-09-2012-0293

Prud'hommeaux, E., & Seaborne, A. (2008, January). SPARQL Query Language for RDF. In *Proceedings of the World Wide Web Consortium, Recommendation REC.* Retrieved January 23, 2017, from http://www.w3.org/TR/rdf-sparql-query/

Rail Delivery Group. (2016). *Approved Code of Practice - Provision of Customer Information.* Retrieved April 13, 2017, from http://www.raildeliverygroup.com/about-us/publications.html?task=file.download&id=469771025

RedHat. (2015). *RestEASY – Distributed peace of mind.* Retrieved January 17, 2017, from http://resteasy.jboss.org/

RedHat. (2015). *Red Hat JBoss BPM Suite -- the JBoss platform for Business Process Management (BPM).* Retrieved January 17, 2017, from http://resteasy.jboss.org/

Schäfer, P. (2014). *Offline-Reiseplaner für Bahnverbindungen* [Bachelor's thesis].

Sierpiński, G. (2017). Technologically advanced and responsible travel planning assisted by GT Planner. In *Contemporary Challenges of Transport Systems and Traffic Engineering* (pp. 65–77). Springer International Publishing. doi:10.1007/978-3-319-43985-3_6

Sirin, E., Parsia, B., Grau, B. C., Kalyanpur, A., & Katz, Y. (2007). Pellet: A practical owl-dl reasoner. *Web Semantics: Science, Services, and Agents on the World Wide Web*, 5(2), 51–53. doi:10.1016/j.websem.2007.03.004

Slegers, K., Ruelens, S., Vissers, J., & Duysburgh, P. (2015, April). Using game principles in ux research: A board game for eliciting future user needs. In *Proceedings of the 33rd Annual ACM Conference on Human Factors in Computing Systems* (pp. 1225-1228). ACM. doi:10.1145/2702123.2702166

The Eclipse Foundation. (2011). *Jetty - a Web server and javax.servlet container*. Retrieved February 3, 2017, from https://eclipse.org/jetty/

The Eclipse Foundation. (2015). *Equinox – an implementation of the OSGi core framework specification*. Retrieved January 17, 2017, from http://www.eclipse.org/equinox/

Tsarkov, D., & Horrocks, I. (2006, August). FaCT++ description logic reasoner: System description. In *Proceedings of the International Joint Conference on Automated Reasoning* (pp. 292-297). Springer Berlin Heidelberg. doi:10.1007/11814771_26

van Lier, T., De Witte, A., Mairesse, O., Hollevoet, J., Kavadias, D., & Macharis, C. (2014). Assessing the social relevance of school transport in Flanders (Belgium). *International Journal of Social Economics*, 41(2), 162–179. doi:10.1108/IJSE-01-2012-0167

World Wide Web Consortium. (2012). OWL 2 web ontology language document overview. Retrieved January 23, 2017, from https://www.w3.org/TR/owl2-overview/

World Wide Web Consortium. (2014). JSON-LD 1.0: a JSON-based serialization for linked data. Retrieved January 23, 2017, from http://www.w3.org/TR/json-ld/

Chapter 6
Predicting Behavior of Passengers Using Data Collected Through Smart Cards

Gaurav Ahlawat
Panjab University, India

Ankit Gupta
Chandigarh College of Engineering and Technology, India

Avimanyou K Vatsa
University of Missouri, USA

ABSTRACT

Many attempts have been made to derive insights and any useful information about the behavior of the passengers traveling using different data analytics approaches and techniques. The different ways the researchers have tried to model the travel behavior and also their attempt to measure the behavioral changes at an individual level will be discussed in this chapter. The insights derived using these methods can help policy makers and the authorities to make necessary and important changes to the railways. The transit systems of the Railways provide us with the data, which is analysed using different techniques and methodologies and derived insights from.

INTRODUCTION

Big Data is the new frontier, the frontier which encompasses the leading technologies for collecting and then analyzing data. This analyzed data is then turned into usable information which the management of an organization can use to take decisive actions. Big Data is the result of the continuous evolution of data analytic techniques which have been in existence for decades but were not of practical use due to lack of computational power. With the increased computational power, reduced prices for storing data and huge amounts of data available and collected from all the devices and the progress in the technological sector, the use of these analytic techniques has become practical.

DOI: 10.4018/978-1-5225-3176-0.ch006

Big Data is any data or technique which can be associated with the 4 V's, which are Volume, Variety, Velocity and Value. It can be defined as a combination of software and hardware which are able to handle input data, which can be structured, semi-structured or un-structured into an algorithm or a model at high speed and be able to derive useful information from it in a timely manner (Hilbert & Martin 2015).

The Data Acquisition is governed by the 4 V's and can be understood as the process of not only collection of data, but also filtering and cleaning or that data before it is stored and is the first and the most important part of Big Data (Lyko & Klaus, 2016). It doesn't matter how much data you have collected, how many different sources you have used for collecting data or over how long a period if the quality of data is poor, all algorithms and models will also output poor results. Many researchers have stated in their literary works of how the poor data quality has a significant negative impact on any organization's efficiency and that good quality data plays a part in the success of companies (Madnick et al., 2004; Haug et al., 2009; Even & Shankaranarayanan, 2009). In this chapter smartcards used in railway systems will be discussed as a source of collecting good quality and accurate data regarding the passengers as compared to surveys.

Since the turn of the century, our ability to produce data has increased exponentially. More and more people have access to the internet, new innovations in the field of communication, smart phones, Internet of Technology (IOT) have all contributed substantially to the huge amounts of data that are being generated on a daily basis in the form of health records of patients, transactional data present with the banks, digital prints of people surfing on the internet. But the evolution in the technologies of computation and data storage, which have enabled the computer scientists and statisticians alike, are the reason that they are able to make sense from these huge amounts of data. This Data and the increased computational capabilities have helped doctors make strides in the field of treatment of diseases like Cancer, study the Human genome, reduce the timeline for development of and for testing of new drugs. Big data has helped the banks around the world to detect and/ or avert frauds, money laundering and make banking safer. It has played an important role in reducing the cost of numerous companies around the world and made their processes more efficient and hence more profitable. It has helped companies like Amazon, Google and Netflix know what their customers like and predict their preferences and what to suggest to their customers. Big Data now has started having a huge impact on how we travel using the public transportation systems like Railways and Airlines (https://hortonworks.com/blog/big-data-public-transportation/). Big Data and how it is affecting Railways and its interaction with its passengers will be specifically discussed in this paper.

Big Data and its analytics techniques can be and need to be applied to huge amounts of data which is being produced by the various aspects and elements of Railways including the millions of people who are travelling long distances, ticket reservations being made, locomotives and freight cars, vendor management, dealing with the goods and freights being loaded, dispatched and unloaded and the thousands of staff working around the country in this sector (Jose, 2016).

Millions of people interact with the Railways and its services on a daily basis. It is not possible to cater to the needs and problems of every passenger on an individual level. So, the problem the planners in government agencies are facing is how to change prevalent policies and services and devise new ones to provide a better experience to the passengers? Big Data is the answer to these problems. Big Data can help group Railway passengers at a lower level into different target groups and help modify policies and services to better the experience of people who fall under different target groups and then monitor and study the effect these policies and services had on them.

This chapter is divided into the following parts. The first part introduces Longitudinal Panel Surveys and other ways of collecting data from which behavioral patterns of the passengers can be analyzed. The 2nd part discusses Smart Cards and how they are used in the transit systems for fare collection and how data is collected using them. In the 3rd part Mining of the Smartcard data is explained and a fusion approach for mining smartcard data is discussed in the 4th part. The 5th part discusses the various validation methods for verifying the results and the 6th part discusses London Underground metro system as a case study. The chapter is concluded in the 7th part.

Longitudinal Panel Surveys

The first approach (or technique) that will be discussed is the Longitudinal Panel Surveys, which were used for measuring the behavioral changes in the passengers at an individual level.

Longitudinal panel surveys "collect information on the same set of variables from the same sample members at two or more points in time" (Tourangeau et al., 1997). These surveys are very useful for understanding and getting insights about the trends in the behavior of the travelers and can be used to assess what effect a service or policy change had on the behavior of travelers.

But they are not very popular, despite all their potential and researchers have moved on from them to use other approaches for modelling the traveler's behavior. The main reason for this is the level of difficulty associated with carrying out the surveys. The traditional data collection methods have relied on memory and reporting, which are often restricted by the precision of data, time-in-sample effect, seam effect. (Tourangeau et al., 1997)

Alternates to the Survey

With the advancements made in the field of GPS and mobile technologies, a number of avenues have been opened which have been used by researchers to study the travel behavior. One of them was, using GPS to collect data as for data loggers to replace the diaries that were maintained for collecting data related to travelers and travel (Wolf, 2000).

Recently GPS-enabled smartphones and other wearable gadgets have been used to collect multi-variable travel data. This multi-variable data which is collected over a long span of time for a set sample is similar to and can be effectively a panel survey.

The approach or technology that has been the focal point of interest for the researchers is the Smart Cards. Public transit-focused data streams from the Smart Cards used in the automatic fare collection (AFC) systems have become or are in the process of becoming common among transit agencies around the world and many have proposed the Smart Cards as an alternative to the travel surveys which is easier to deal with, provides with accurate and precise data and can help model and study the travel behavior of passengers and use them to make policies, optimize the resources and the planning (Strambi et al., 2009; Chu and Chapleau, 2013, Morency, 2013).

Now, the different studies and works done by researchers around the world for studying the Travel Behavior analysis using Smart Cards will be discussed.

What Are Smart Cards?

Smart Cards are the pocket-sized cards that have embedded integrated circuits and can be used to provide authentication and personnel access to its users. It is increasingly being used in the systems installed at the transit systems in the huge number of railways stations and bus stations around the world in place of paper tickets and tokens to provide the passengers access to the public transport. The smart card systems are used to collect the fare for the public transport. Now in this chapter, we are going to see how exactly these systems can help us in finding and predicting the behavior of the travelers.

The Smart card systems automatically and continuously collect the traveler's data in the form of data, which can be the ID of the card and record the ID, which will contain the personal information of the traveler, the starting point of their journey, that is the station they boarded the train from and at what time exactly they entered the station, the destination of their journey which Is the station at which they make the exit and at exactly what time and the amount they paid. Now all this data is collected by the systems through the Smart Cards every time they are used at the transit systems to enter or exit the station. So they are continuously able to gather all this data, the data which then can be used to analyze the patterns of the travelers which might include the individual's frequency of use of the transport system on any particular day, the stations they travel from and to on any particular day of the week or month or a period and the trip sequences (Utsunomiya et al., 2006).

SMART CARDS

The authors of "Smart Card Data use in public transit: A Literature Review" (Pelletier et al., 2011), have provided the description of what Smart Card is, issues surrounding it, the different international standards, which are all discussed below.

Smart Cards are the portable cards of the size of credit cards which are designed to store and sometimes process data. With the portability and the durability that is associated with Smart Cards, they are very suitable for use in identifying, authorizing and making payments.

Additional Features which can be associated with Smart Cards:

- The card can be equipped with only a memory card for storage of data or with memory and a small processor for both the storage and processing of the data.
- Can be a contact card or a contactless card, that is, the card can be made which needs to be in contact with a machine for the purpose of payment or authorization or the card can work similarly to RFID tags and will communicate without the need of making any physical contact.
- The information and data present on the data may be encrypted or unencrypted depending on the purpose.
- The size of memory present in the cards can vary, which was about 2 to 4 Kb only earlier, which was used to store important personal and transactional data, but over the years this size has increased, with up to 64Kbs now available.
- In the case of Railways or other transport systems with installed transit systems for payment, a contact smart card with a low amount of memory is required, with a chip embedded inside the plastic card. The card is brought into contact with the chip reader present in the transit system for the payment purposes or recognition purposes.

Types of Smart Cards

- **Contact:** In the contact smart cards, the card consists of contact pads which provide the electrical connectivity when the card is placed on the card reader. These pads act as the medium of communication between the smart card's information and the host or the reader. These types of smart cards do not contain any battery and all the power needed for the identification and other purposes are provided by the reader or the host. Example: MetroCard used in the New York City (Rizai & Atefeh, 1999)
- **Contactless:** In this type of smart cards the card doesn't need to be in physical contact with the reader or the host for the transfer of data for the identification and other purposes. In these cards communicate with the reader and also receive power from the reader or the host through the RF induction. The cards don't contain batteries and only have an inductor which uses the RF technology to power the card. Example: Octopus Smartcard in Hong Kong and Oyster Smartcard in London, UK.

The Hybrid, Dual Interface and the USB type smart cards are variations of the two main categories of the smart cards, that is the contact and the contactless cards.

Standards

The Smart Card hardware must be compatible with international standards, which in the case of contact-based smart cards is covered by ISO/IEC7816. Under this standard, the layout of the contact plate and usage (PART 1 AND 2 OF ISO7816), the electrical interface of the card (Part 3) and the selections of applications (PART 4) are covered. The contactless Smart cards have a separate international standard. The public transit systems are usually closed, which means the operators have their own separate cards for the transaction and can only be used for that system. More information about the standards is provided in the following table (McDonald, 2000) in Figure 2.

Figure 1. Types of smart cards

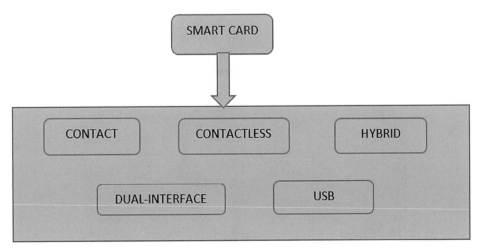

Figure 2. Technologies used in contactless cards
Source: McDonald 2000.

Technology used	Frequency	Data Transmission Rate	Applications
ISO/IEC 14443	13.56 MHz	106Kbps	Transport, physical access control
ISO/IEC 15693	13.56 MHz	26Kbps	Physical Access control, parking
Felica ISO/IEC 15408	13.56MHz	212Kbps	Transport, identification
NFC ISO/IEC 18092	13.56MHz	212Kbps	Payment
EZ-PASS	902, 928, 5900	N/A	Toll booths, drive throughs

Concerns About What Data Is Being Collected by the Smartcards?

Over the years the amount and the nature of data stored on the smart cards are rising and subsequently causing concerns about the privacy of the data associated with them. People are concerned about the security of their data present in the cards because of the larger issue of how secure the transit systems are to both the inner and outer threats of theft of data. There have been many studies which have debated the privacy concerns associated with the Smart Cards. Figure 3 consists of the elements which have an impact on the privacy.

Clarke (2001) reported in his study how the concerns related with Smart Card usage are almost similar to the concerns associated with credit cards, cell phones and tracking technologies. The very nature of Smart cards not only makes it vulnerable to identity theft but also with misuse of behavioral information. In another study (Reid, 2007), it is pointed out how the vulnerability is not present at the point where the cards and terminal interact as they are normally encrypted, but at the centralized database of storage

Figure 3. Concerns associated with the smart cards and their use

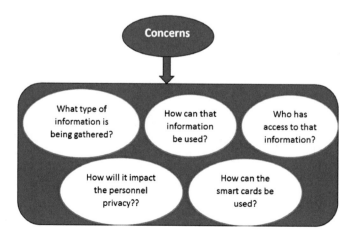

where all the information gathered from the transactions is stored. A study (Cottrill, 2009) also pointed at how the linking of an individual's demographic and socioeconomic information with their smart card use will not be acceptable to the users.

Public Transit Implementation

Different sectors have different international standards for the implementation of Smart Cards. The most popular standard in public transit is the ITSO (International Transport Smartcard Organization, 2009) and the Calypso network of associations (Smart Card Alliance, 2009). These standards provide specifications which cover the cards, the information systems and the format protocols of the data

Different Levels of Studies on Smartcard Data

The studies on Smartcards can be divided into 3 categories based on their level of research:

- **Strategic Level Studies:** The studies which are related to the long-term network planning or the analysis of the customer behavior or the demand forecasting are classified as Strategic level studies. Example: (Agard et al., 2006) and (Bagchi and White, 2005) state how smart card data can be used to better understand passenger behavior.

Figure 4. Advantages of smart cards

ADVANTAGES OF SMART CARDS
User Role in data collection minimized compared to ways and process of past
The combining of personal data with the travel data and other information helps increase the quality of the data and the ultimate results being derived from that data
Cost reduction
Improvement in the service being provided to the public
The fare policies can be implemented in a flexible manner
The improvement in the payment mechanism and the control on information flow
The increased reliability and the durability of the cards

Figure 5. Disadvantages of smart cards

DISADVANTES OF SMART CARDS
The feedback of the passenger cannot be collected
The trip purpose information can be provided by the smart card
The development cost is high and so is the cost associated with research on it
High risk
High implementation cost associated with the Smart Cards
Issues associated with market penetration

- **Tactical Level Studies:** In these studies, the prime focus is on the longitudinal and individual trip patterns and the schedule adjustment. Example: Trépanier et al. (2007) describe how the problem of service adjustment should be tackled on a route to route basis.
- **Operational Level Studies:** Supply and demand management and operations of smart card system are the focus of these studies. Example: Trépanier et al. (2009) discuss how the smart card systems can be used for calculating the performance parameters of the transit network.

Are Smart Cards a Better Option for Data Collection?

The assumption on which all the work in the field of Smart Cards depends on and the work was done by researchers in the field of behavioral analysis of passengers depends on, is that the data which the Smart Cards collect is useful and can give results which are significant enough both statistically and in practice to be used by policy makers and the researchers to use them in making important decisions. This assumption was debated and came out strong in the following discussion.

In Diamond (2009), the reason and the need for the continuous data collection are debated. The argument and the discussion surrounding it are based on the idea whether this continuous data collection even fit for the purpose of modelling the behavior of the travels and identifying the change in the behavior of passengers over the time.

According to the study, large-scale mobility surveys at city, regional or national level are justified and are needed for providing information and data which are used for proposing and building travel models and evaluate planning, policy or infrastructure options. For feeding information to these models, multi-variable data including travel modes, purpose, time of day, origin, destination and cost are required and a multitude of other variables about the socio-demographics are required for studying travel behavior.

Smart cards, therefore, are viable options for collecting all the data mentioned above and therefore are fit for the purpose. Therefore, the scale and nature of continuously monitoring and collecting all this data through the Smart cards meet the need for current and detailed data on travel behavior. According to the study, a continuous survey approach is needed for better monitoring of the changes in behavior, for which we think Smart Cards fits the bill perfectly.

Now, the Smart Cards provide us with the data about the passengers over a long period of time, without any disruption and this data can be used to analyze the passenger behavior on a day to day basis, the difference in weekly, monthly or yearly travel patterns. This feature of Smart Cards is also of huge advantage because as stated in their study that the intra-personnel variability in travel is considerable over a course of a week, which is not identified in the traditional surveys and also leads to a poorer modeling of travel behavior, which is avoided in the case of Smart Cards (Stopher, Kockelman, Greaves and Clifford, 2008).

The data collected by the smartcards is consistent of good quality and does not suffer from poor quality or any discrepancy which is many times an issue in the case of periodical surveys due to human errors. Smart cards are also able to track the travel behavior at different stages in the economic cycles, unlike the surveys which are affected by all the external and physical factors and therefore are very less likely to be able to properly monitor and better understand the travel behavior of people.

Smart cards, therefore, represent an important and much-needed move away from the traditional periodical data collection through surveys, panel data and from single-day observations to the continuous collection of multi-variable data over a huge span of time for observing the travel behavior. As the transit systems around the world are developed and the Smart Cards are about to be used at all these transit points and become more accessible, more and more longitudinal observations are available for extractions from the collected data for the behavior analysis of passengers.

Different Smart Cards

Some of the Smart cards which are used in the transit systems around the world and used to collect the data on which Big Data is applied to derive useful information have been listed in Table 1.

MINING THE DATA OF SMART CARDS FOR USEFUL INFORMATION

For improving the overall performance of the transit systems, while retaining the loyal customers and for the formation of marketing strategies, a better understanding of passengers and their travel patterns

Table 1. Different Smartcards used in different countries

Name	Oyster Card	MetroCard	Octopus Card	EZ Link Card	Suica
Place	Greater London, UK	New York, US	Hong Kong	Singapore	Kanto area, Japan
Travel Modes	London Underground, buses, trams	NYC Subway, NYC buses	All public transport in Hong Kong and in convenience stores and restaurants, vending machines	Singapore mass and light rapid transit and buses and Sentosa Express	Transport Services
Technology	Contactless Smart Card, RFID	Magnetic Strip based	Contactless Smart card	CEPAS (Contactless e-purse)	RFID technology
First Used	Jul-03	1993-1994	1997	2002	2001
Chips based on	MIFARE DESFire EV1 chips	-	Sony 13.56 MHz FeliCa radio frequency identification (RFID) chip	Sony Felica	FeliCa
Compatible Technology	ISO/IEC 14443 types A and B	-	ISO/IEC 14443	ISO/IEC 14443	ISO/IEC 14443
Security Features	accessible using secret codes and that also through permitted devices	-	Encryption and three pass mutual authentication protocol	Triple DES algorithm for security	-
Data Stored	Personnel information and journey transaction	Personal data is collected and stored in AFC (Automated fare collection) database centrally	Minimum collection principle is followed according to which least amount of personnel information is collected	Personnel information	-
Big Data application	Origin-Destination Matrices for London Underground, Modelling and analysis of TfL-wide fare policy changes	Using big data for genetic mapping of the transit system, devise fare strategies	-	Greater understanding of commuter patterns, peak periods during day, passenger behavior and to increase the efficiency of the organization	-

is very important. This study was done on passengers using Bus Transit systems but can be generalized for users of any transport transit system.

But the identification of travel patterns of passengers at an individual level is very difficult and challenging to carry out. An effective and efficient data mining procedure that predicted and modelled the travel patterns of users of transit system was introduced by Ma et al. (2013). This new method modelled the travel patterns of users of the transit system in Beijing, China. Temporal and Spatial characteristics of the smart card transactional data of travelers are used to identify the transit riders' trip chains. The useful information that can be extracted from the data can be in the form of groups of or clusters of passengers who have shown similar or homogenous travel patterns, the focus of the study was twofold, one being the individual travel pattern recognition and the other one being the travel regularity mining.

For the purpose of predicting and modelling a transit rider's travel patterns on an individual level from their historical travel data and trip chains, the DBSCAN (Density-based Spatial Clustering of Applications with Noise) algorithm is used. The DBSCAN algorithm is a density-based algorithm, which groups together the points which are densely packed, where the low-density markings are the outliers. Then the K-means++ algorithms and rough set theory are used for the classification and clustering of pattern recognition of traveler's travel behavior.

In Figure 6 it is shown how the Transit Smartcard database is used to first generate the Trip Chains, which are then used to model the travel patterns of individual passengers using their travel history and also use the trip chains for Regularity clustering, from which rules are extracted.

Figure 6. Different focuses for data mining
Source: Ma et al., 2013

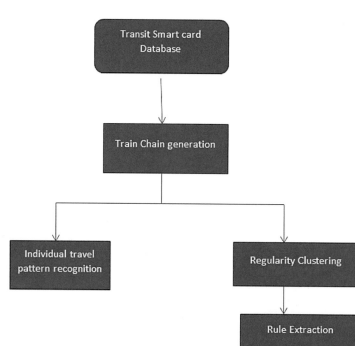

Data Description

The data used in the study was collected from the AFC (Automatic Fare Collection) systems of Beijing transit systems for buses and subways. The dataset is composed of transaction data from 3,845,444 smart cards over a period of a travel week (in this particular case it was from Monday, July 5th to Friday 9th, 2010). The smart card system collected and stored information regarding the boarding location (only in case of distance based fares), alighting location, transaction time, smartcard ID, remaining balance, transaction amount, boarding and alighting stop. Of the total transaction data collected from the smart cards, about 58%, that is 2,225,298 of the smart cards contained two transactions for all five weekdays. The weekly temporal distribution of smart card holders with two transactions is shown in Figure 7.

Trip Chain Generation

The first thing to do in this study is the generation of Trip Chains. Without the trip chain information, the Spatial and temporal patterns of individual transit riders cannot be examined. A trip chain is defined as a series of trips made by a traveler on a daily basis and is considered a useful way to demonstrate travelers' behaviors (McGuckin & Nakamoto, 2004).

In this particular study, for the generation of trip chains, Markovic chain based Bayesian decision tree algorithm by (Ma et al., 2012) was used in conjunction on with speed profiles from GPS data which can lead to more than 90% of the smart card data to be accurately assigned.

Individual Travel Pattern Recognition

For investigating into the individual travel patterns of each transit rider after the construction of the trip chains, clustering algorithms are used. Now, this was shown in the table of trip chains earlier, which

Figure 7. Weekly temporal distribution for smart card holders with two transactions
Source: Ma et al., 2013.

		Last Transaction Time of the Day											
		0-2	2-4	4-6	6-8	8-10	10-12	12-14	14-16	16-18	18-20	20-22	22-24
First Transaction Time of the day	0 to 2		1	1	28	23	14	39	71	81	62	64	5
	2 to 4			1	18	13	25	18	90	332	308	35	5
	4 to 6				564	912	1035	1988	5667	17344	10162	1725	181
	6 to 8				604	7944	14218	19078	48595	450200	463309	63897	7249
	8 to 10					657	18638	25097	37577	203237	480059	104944	22082
	10 to 12						339	10141	17948	20899	23422	19500	6724
	12 to 14							497	9369	19540	11447	11644	7996
	14 to 16								531	10767	9123	6733	4924
	16 to 18									431	5802	8721	1709
	18 to 20										303	6367	1777
	20 to 22											110	375
	22 to 24												2

showed that an individual traveler is more likely to show a certain travel pattern over a multi-day period. In this study, DBSCAN algorithm is used for retrieving the travel patterns.

One of the examples from the trip chain table, DBSCAN can infer several patterns like the ones discussed below:

- The first trip of the transit rider is around 7 AM and last at around 6 PM.
- Repetition of the routes takes place on weekdays and anything else might be flagged as noise.
- The transit rider may be taking different routes to the same location.

Regularity Clustering

Clustering algorithms have been used for investigating customer royalty in industries like shopping. This same approach can be applied for clustering the transit riders. This clustering can be based on the similarity of travel patterns, which can be used to place or segregate them into different regularity levels based depending on temporal and spatial characteristics. For this purpose, K means++ algorithms are used. More can be read about this algorithm in Arthur and Vassilvitskii (2007).

Using Rough Set Theory for Performance Enhancement

The reason for using the rough set theory for improving the clustering performance instead of Fuzzy theory and Bayesian prior probability in the Naïve Bayes classifier because it does not need any prior information about the data. The rough set theory can deal with both the continuous and the discrete input data and deals with missing and incomplete information very well.

Comparing Different Classification Techniques

Comparison of the rough set algorithm and several other classification algorithms used in research of transportation engineering, like Naive Bayes Classifier, C4.5 Decision tree, K-nearest neighbor and three hidden layers Neural Network is done on the basis of accuracy and efficiency.

The total sample size for this is 37001, with 33% of the data for training and the rest 67% data considered as test data, with each algorithm executed for 10 iterations.

The results of the evaluations showed that the proposed rough set based algorithm outperforms the other algorithm in terms of efficiency. But the proposed algorithm underperformed as compared to the C4.5 decision tree algorithm in terms of accuracy, but the proposed algorithm was two times faster than the decision tree algorithm, Figure 8 models the results of these algorithms based on their performance.

Summarizing the Study

This study proposed series of efficient and effective data mining approaches with the aim of predicting and modelling the travelling patterns of the transit passengers using the data collected by the Smart Cards. DBSCAN is used for detection of individual transit riders historical travel pattern based on their trip chains. Then the K-Means++ algorithm and rough set theory are used in conjunction for classification of travel pattern regularities. Then the performance of proposed algorithm is compared with other

Figure 8. Performance comparison of two algorithms on different parameters
Source: Ma et al., 2013.

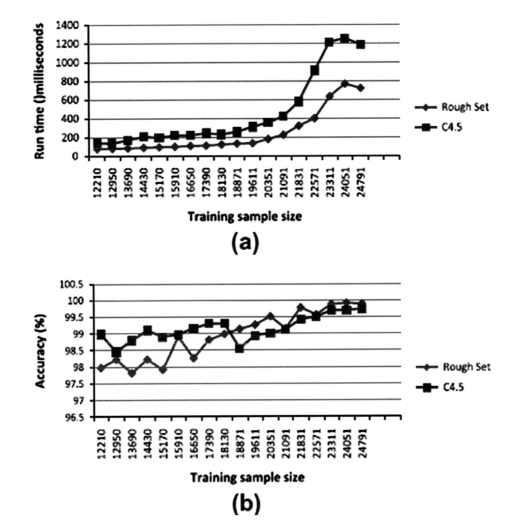

classification algorithms, which indicated that it outperformed all the other data mining algorithms in terms of both accuracy and efficiency.

Application of insights from the study: The travel patterns of transit passengers as a population and also on an individual level can be derived from the Smart Card Data using the approach mentioned in this study. This can help the Railways and other transportation systems to better optimize their service so as to be able to better serve the travelers. The Smart Card Data can be used to divide the people into different target groups based on their individual travel patterns and learn their travelling habits.

MINING BEHAVIORAL PATTERNS

The aim of Kusakabe et al., (2014) is to estimate the behavioral attributes of travelers through data fusion methodology applied to the data collected through the Smart Cards and to observe the changes over a period of time in the trip attributes. This study uses person trip survey data with the Naïve Bayes probabilistic model for filling the absence of certain data attributes that the Smart Cards do not collect. With this model, the trip purpose can be estimated using the data fusion methodology and the survey data. The proposed method successfully predicted the trip purposes about 86.2% of the validation data.

As seen in Figure 9, the person trip survey data is used in this study to complement the different variables of data that is calculated using the Smart Cards. As you can see the ID numbers are not the same in the two datasets. That is why the boarding and alighting stations are used for combining or merging the two datasets together.

Figure 10 is the flow chart which pictures the proposed data fusion method used in this study. The data fusion concept is used for the estimation of the elements of Smart Card data and the person trip survey data, which complement each other. Now, the 'c' variable used in the flow chart is the behavioral attributes only present in the person trip survey data such as the trip purpose, origin and destination of the traveler. The attributes contained in the 'F' variable are the behavioral attributes present in both the datasets, such as the boarding times and the stations. The 'g' variable used in the flow chart contains the attributes only present in the dataset of Smart Cards, such as the trip frequency of the travelers.

The proposed method provides us with the relationship between the attributes in 'c' and 'g', which otherwise cannot be obtained if the two datasets are observed as a single dataset. The main assumption made in this study is that the conditional probability of the trips observed in the Smart Card dataset is the same as the trips that are recorded in the person trip survey data, which is $p(c|F)$. The $p(c|F)$ is the distribution which represents the probability of a traveler with 'c' behavioral attributes at the gate of a station when the traveler has the 'F' attribute.

Figure 9. Schema of the two types of data used in this proposed method
Source: Kusakabe et al., 2014.

PERSON TRIP SURVEY DATA										
Personal ID	Trip ID	Zone of Origin	Zone of Destination	Departure Time	Arrival Time	Trip Purpose	Destination Station	Time at departure station	Arrival Station	Time at arrival station
PT92133	1	A	B	10:50	11:30	Leisure	A	11:05	C	11:23
PT92133	2	B	A	14:20	15:10	Return Home	C	14:25	A	15:05
PT95664	1	K	C	7:10	8:00	Commuting	M	7:25	B	7:50

SMART CARD DATA					
Date	Departure Station	Time at Departure Station	Arrival Station	Time at Arrival Station	Smart Card ID
13/10/2007	A	7:10	C	7:23	A257DK
13/10/2007	A	7:12	C	7:24	B68DS
13/10/2007	A	7:11	B	7:18	B672RR

Figure 10. Overview of the methodology used
Source: Kusakabe et al., 2014.

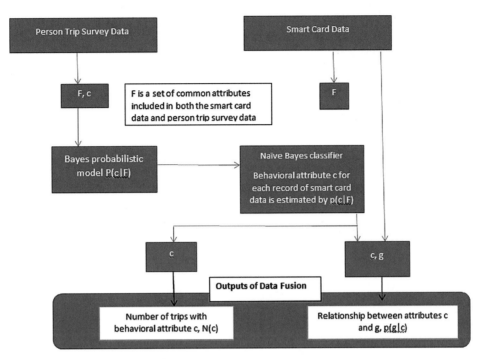

Data Description

The study is based on two different datasets, Person Trip Survey Dataset and the Smart Card Dataset. The person trip survey dataset consists of Personal ID, trip ID, origin, destination, departure and arrival time, trip purpose, boarding and alighting stations and times. The Smartcard dataset consists of Smartcard ID, boarding and alighting stations and times. The two datasets do not have any common ID's and are obtained separately but have common boarding stations, alighting stations and boarding and alighting times although they are not exactly same due to different precision level. The Person trip survey data was obtained in 2002 from the 'the 4th Kei-had-shin Metropolitan Area Person Trip Survey', from a major station in Osaka, Japan, which consisted of 1586 trips made by 1576 travelers. The Smartcard data consist of actual data collected by the smart cards, which covers 7,074,786 trips made by 553,259 passengers over a period of 20 months through Oct 2007 to May 2009.

Formation of the Naïve Bayes Probabilistic Model

The main requirement of the data fusion method of the Smart card data with the person trip survey is that the of the low calculation load. The reason for this is that the Smart card's data grows very large over a period of time. This study uses the Naïve Bayes Classifier for the data fusion methodology, which is a classification method which accounts for the missing or absent attributes by use of the naïve Bayes probabilistic model. This probabilistic model treats all the variables to be discrete variables to avoid the presuming the p(c|F) distribution form and for the ease of treating the originally discrete variables. But due to the treatment of the variables discretely, the small amount of data present in the person trip survey data becomes a problem. To reduce the minimum required amount of data, the naïve Bayes classifier makes the assumption of each element of F being conditionally independent of each and every other element of F when 'c' is given.

Now the mathematics behind this model will be discussed.

$$p\left(c|F\right) = \frac{1}{p\left(F\right)} p\left(c\right) \prod_{k=1}^{K} p\left(f_k \mid c\right) \tag{1}$$

This equation 1 is described using the Bayes' theorem, where the p(c), p(F) and p(f$_k$|c) are the probability distributions of the person trip survey data. The f$_k$ is one instance behavioral attributes of the vector F.

The equation of the classifier used is:

$$\hat{c}\left(F\right) = \arg\max_{c \in C} p\left(c \mid F\right) \tag{2}$$

where the C consists of all the possible values of 'c'.

Now, the equation 2 is used to calculate the number of trips with the behavioral attribute c using the following equation 3:

$$N\left(c\right) = \sum_{F \in S} \delta\left(c, F\right) N_s\left(F\right)$$

where

$$\delta\left(c, F\right) = \begin{cases} 1 & if \ \hat{c}\left(F\right) = v \\ 0 & otherwise \end{cases} \tag{3}$$

After this, the trip purpose is estimated. The trip purpose can be thought of a key attribute in the context of the behavior of the travelers. But this cannot be observed in the smart card data and for the purpose of doing so the person trip survey data is used, where it is defined as:

{ 'commuting to work', 'commuting to school', 'leisure', 'business', 'returning home' }

In this study, the attribute 'g', which is the trip frequency representing the trip pattern as recorded by the Smart data, is a very useful in analyzing the changes in the travel demand as the total number of trips is affected by both the number of travelers and the number of trips by each traveler.

The two tables in Figure 11, which contains the estimated values of conditional probability for the different trip purposes, were estimated using the 1095 trips of the person trip survey data, representing the values of duration of stay and arriving time at the station for corresponding trip purposes. The tables showed that the trips of travelers commuting to work and school showed relatively similar trends. The patterns which were clear from the study of the tables are as stated below:

Figure 11. Estimated values of conditional probability
Source: Kusakabe et al., 2014.

Estimated values of $p(f_s|c)$ from person trip survey data at the target station.

f_s (h)	c				
	Commuting to work	Commuting to school	Leisure	Business	Return to home
0	0.000	0.000	0.021	0.000	0.000
1	0.002	0.000	0.075	0.088	0.000
2	0.002	0.014	0.103	0.027	0.000
3	0.000	0.000	0.133	0.083	0.000
4	0.000	0.040	0.120	0.014	0.000
5	0.010	0.051	0.073	0.018	0.000
6	0.014	0.071	0.036	0.020	0.000
7	0.014	0.125	0.038	0.000	0.000
8	0.030	0.269	0.014	0.023	0.000
9	0.132	0.151	0.035	0.000	0.000
10	0.225	0.131	0.005	0.014	0.000
11	0.165	0.050	0.015	0.076	0.000
12	0.123	0.023	0.013	0.038	0.000
13	0.093	0.013	0.000	0.025	0.000
14 and above	0.111	0.025	0.000	0.000	0.000
No return trip	0.079	0.036	0.319	0.574	1.000

Estimated values of $p(f_a|c)$ from person trip survey data at the target station.

f_a (h)	c				
	Commuting to work	Commuting to school	Leisure	Business	Return to home
5–6	0.032	0.011	0.006	0.051	0.000
7–8	0.781	0.611	0.067	0.115	0.000
9–10	0.152	0.253	0.224	0.214	0.004
11–12	0.017	0.097	0.207	0.158	0.000
13–14	0.010	0.028	0.196	0.163	0.031
15–16	0.003	0.000	0.137	0.191	0.166
17–18	0.004	0.000	0.140	0.094	0.391
19–20	0.002	0.000	0.022	0.014	0.287
21–22	0.000	0.000	0.000	0.000	0.113
23–24	0.000	0.000	0.000	0.000	0.009

- The commuters to work and school arrived in the morning and had a longer duration of stay as compared to the travelers on leisure and business trips.
- Commuting trips to work and school were completed before the 11 am were 98.2% and 97.2% respectively.
- The trips of travelers commuting to work had the longer duration of stay as compared to that of travelers commuting to schools.
- Leisure and business trips were taken during the daytime, but the duration of stay was different.
- One way business trips occupied about 57.4% that is those travelers did not go to the station on the same day, while those on leisure trips were only about 31.9%.
- Trips recorded in the Smart cards and also the person trip surveys indicated that the trips for returning home increased after 3 pm and most of them being one-way trips and that 80% of the total trips after 5 pm are returning home trips.

Figure 12 shows the estimated results of the trip purposes using the equations stated earlier. In total 76.8% trips were correctly estimated. But only a few commutes to school and business trips were correctly estimated, which was 37.5% for school and none at all for the business trips. One reason for this might

Figure 12. Number of trips at targeted station correctly estimated by trip purposes
Source: Kusakabe et al., 2014.

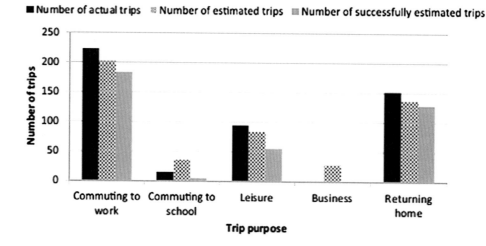

be a low number of these trips as observed and another reason might be the similarity in the duration of stay and arrival characteristics with other trips.

The Figure 13 shows the number of trips correctly estimated using the redefined trip purpose as stated:

{ 'commuting to school or work', 'leisure or business', 'returning home' }

With this change, the number of successfully estimated trips increased, with about 86.2% of the trips correctly predicted. These results showcased that the organization of the trip purposes using the similarity of trip characteristics increased the estimation results.

Application of insights from this study: This study uses an approach which helps us estimate the behavioral attributes of the travelers and estimate the trip purposes of the travelers based on the changes

Figure 13. Number of trips at the target station correctly estimated when trip purposes were reorganized
Source: Kusakabe et al., 2014.

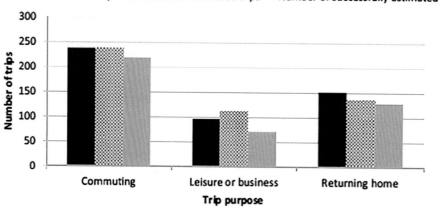

in their trip attributes over a period of time. Therefore, this approach can help the rail authorities to learn about the trip purposes of the travelers based on the data collected from the Smart Cards and classify the travelers based on their trip purposes. This insight can help them draw up the schedule of the railways and decide upon their running frequency based on the demographic of the travelers.

METHODS FOR VALIDATION OF THE FINDINGS

There are different methods for validation of the results and the findings made from the data mining techniques. Munizaga et al. (2014) try to verify the assumptions and results made in different methods for estimation of travel behavior which is used for the management and planning. For this the study takes into account the three sources of information which are:

- The same databases which were used for making the estimation.
- OD (Origin-Destination) survey in which the card numbers of a group of users has been recorded.
- Sample of volunteers.

According to the study, the use of rule-based learning for driving OD matrices has been a recurrent practice over the years. Many researchers have done work on it, like Barry et al. (2002), who estimate station to station OD flows for travelers of New York metro through the data collected through Metro-Card, Zhao et al. (2007), infer rail passenger trip OD matrices from origin only automatic fare collection system and many more.

In most of these cases, the reliability of the results, which are the estimation of travel behavior and the OD matrices and the alighting stops, relies heavily on the many assumptions made to obtain the results. Many researchers believe that these assumptions need to be validated and a few attempts have been made to do so, like, Barry et al. (2009) proposed for compression of different sources of information for the validation of the data obtained from the Smart Cards, but the unavailability of additional information on every occasion and the quality and coverage of the data makes this approach not a viable option for the validation of data.

Therefore, to address this problem of validation of data, this study proposed a series of methods for the validation of assumptions made in the methodologies used in recording data about the boarding positions, alighting stops, and routes chosen by travelers, the purpose of travel and more.

Now first of all the methodology we are going to validate is by Munizaga and Palma (2012). This method proposed a method for observation of card transactions in the transit system of public transport systems and the estimation of travel sequences using the information collection from those transaction sequences. In this method, only the boarding transactions are used as the alighting stops information is not collected. This methodology made some assumptions which are:

The trip stage begins at the time and the location when and where the validations occur.

The end of the trip stage can be found at the station most convenient to reach the next boarding location.

Trips are defined as sequences of trip stages with less than minutes between the end of one stage and between the beginnings of the next stage.

With the assumptions made above, the estimation for over 80% alighting stops was made of the boarding transactions and OD matrices were made from it. But they recognized the need for more sophisticated methods for the identification of trips and its stages.

Devillaine et al. (2012) used the results from the above study for the estimation of location, duration and purpose of the trips. Some assumptions are made for the validation of this study as well, like using the elapsed time for estimation of the purpose of the trips.

Now, this study analyzes the above-mentioned methodologies with the validation of the assumptions the focus. For this first of all the use of endogenous validation is taken into consideration. In the endogenous validation, the data is analyzed to verify the assumptions made and for the detection of any anomalous behavior, with the improvements in the methodology the ultimate aim.

Endogenous Validation

Assumption 1: Proposed use of 1km as a limit for walking distance, that is, searching for a position time alighting estimate was conducted within the threshold.
Validation: See Figure 14.

This Figure 14 shows the spatial distribution of alighting estimation failures due to this assumption. It is also found that such an assumption is not reasonable due to varying distributions and concentration of the connections in different parts of one city only. Therefore, a reliable and large exogenous database required to analyze the phenomenon in greater detail.

Assumption 2: Estimation of alighting stops for the last boarding using the first transaction, with the assumption that there is a cycle that begins and ends at the same time, which is at 0:00 and 23:59.
Validation: See Figure 15.

Figure 14. Spatial distribution of alighting estimation
Source: Munizaga et al., 2014

Figure 15. Distribution of tractions according to time
Source: Munizaga et al., 2014.

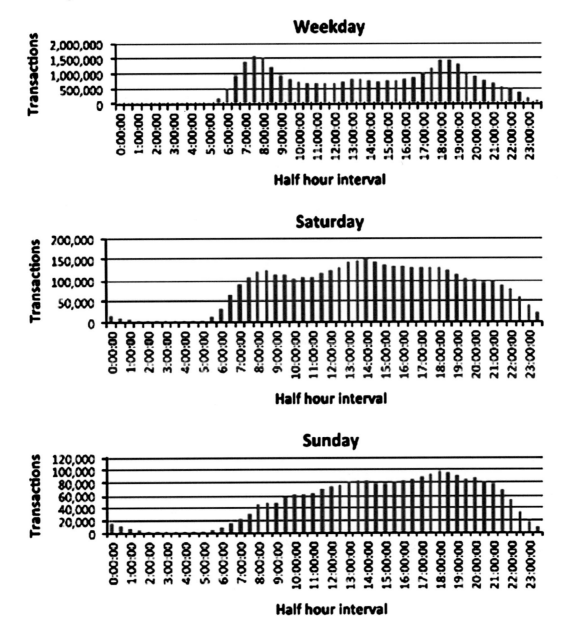

From the Figure 15, it is clear that there is some activity just before and after midnight. Therefore because of this, the assumption will fail because the first/last trips of the day will not be correctly identified. The suggestion made in the study is for changing the transition period from midnight to the period of the day with the lowest observed activity, which in this case is 4:00 am.

Other assumptions: Some other assumptions which are validated in this study include the study of the cause of failure of estimation method for alighting, which is about 5% of the total transactions.

However, in this study with the help of the distributions of single transactions, estimation for about 7% of the total transactions was possible and other assumptions like the trip stage identification were also considered in this endogenous study.

Exogenous Validation Using OD Metro Surveys

- **Sample Distribution:** This study used the data collected from the surveys conducted in the Metro de Santiago for the validation of the assumptions and methods used in the studies we mentioned. The data included in the survey included the time and place where the survey was taken, user type, origin, ID, the mode used to come to the station, destination, purpose and the income. After crossing this data from the survey with the one from the transactions, there were 684 cards which could be used for the validation purposes, with the final number dropping to 601, due to some missing data. During the validation of the data and assumptions, it appears that the percentage of success in alighting is better than the figures reported in Munizaga and Palma (2012) in the entire database, with the reason being that the database most likely not a representative of the sample.
- **Validation of Boarding Stop:** Boarding location was validated using the comparison between the location mentioned in the survey and the location estimated in the Munizaga and Palma (2012). The study did not expect any kind of difference to be present in this case and the coincidence was also 100%. But there were some errors made for complex bus stations in the study with the GPS data as there were some problems in the underground bus stations, with the overall correct estimation percentage dropping to 98.9%.
- **Validation of Alighting Stop:** The alighting stop needs to be validated as it is crucial for the proposed method as the methodology relied on the correct estimation of the alighting stops. In the validation with the survey, 84.2% of the times, the method estimated the alighting stops correctly, with the main source of error was the use of non-integrated methods like taxi or car or fare evasion.
- **Validation of Route Choices:** Metro OD survey contains information regarding the route choice within the metro network. Munizaga and Palma (2012) assumed a deterministic minimum cost choice for assigning route choices. From the available information, the study believes that a decision can be made to whether it is reasonable and correct to assume the deterministic choice or go with the stochastic model.

Three different cases were observed in route choice in OD pairs in which routes were chosen:

- OD pairs when all users in the sample chose the same route (67%)
- OD pairs in which one route was dominant over the others (18%)
- OD pairs in which users chose more than one route (15%)

From the above findings, it is clear that there are significant numbers of instances of the 3rd case, where the current approach is not sufficient and therefore a stochastic route choice model needs to be implemented.

Exogenous Validation With the Volunteers

In this study, 53 volunteers were recruited for the completion of the validation. They were shown the estimations of the method for a particular period of time which was 1 week, prior to the interview and were also given information from the database from their personal smartcard use. Then the volunteers were asked to validate the results of the model used. The total numbers of transactions made by them were 885, with 586 corresponding trips.

The validation of the trip stage identification by the volunteers shoed correct identification in 90.0%(527 trips) of the cases. The alighting stop of 448 trips out of the 527 correctly identified trips, with the correct estimation of the purpose of the trip for 352 trips.

Now the reasons for the failure of stage identification in Volunteer exogenous validation are as stated in Figure 16.

Now, the reasons for the failure of purpose assignment method are as stated in Figure 17.

Therefore, from all these validations, we can calibrate the different parameters for minimizing the errors and improve the results by implementing the methodological modifications as suggested in the study.

Application of insights from this study: The rail authorities around the world can use different approaches to the data collected using the Smart Cards. Smart Card data can be used to better understand the behavior of the travelers, their travelling habits and the purpose of their trips or their final destination based on their historical data. This study provides the different methods that can be used to validate and verify the assumptions that were made on the Smart Card data and the results of the different methods

Figure 16. Causes of failure in trip/trip stage identification procedure
Source: Munizaga et al., 2014

Due to passenger and bus crowding at the bus stop, the user boarded the 4th bus after arrival. The method used a threshold of 3 buses of the same route while the passenger is waiting at the stop	12
An intermediate trip stage did not have an alighting estimation, therefore, it was automatically coded as a trip stage	9
Incorrect cut due to distance relation criteria	8
Extremely short activity, impossible to detect	8
Error propagation because a previous trip was not correctly identified	8
Implementation errors	7
Waiting time over 30 min due to a large interval between buses or overcrowded buses that could not be bounded	4

Figure 17. Causes of failure in purpose assignment method
Source: Munizaga et al., 2014

"Other" activity with a duration of over 2 h	26
Stop-by at the house between trips)coded as "Other" instead of "Home"	16
Work activity with a duration of less than 2 h (typically work trips rather than trips to work)	14
Work activity of a student card holder	12
Study activity with a duration of less than 2 h (weekly)	10
"Other" activity conducted at the end of the day	7
Student activity using a regular card	5
Study activity conducted at the end of the day	3
Student activity with a duration of less than 5 h(weekend day)	1
Trip to home at 2 AM coded as work	1
Single trip (in a particular day) coded as "Home"	1

that were applied on that data to estimate travel behavior. It is really important that the assumptions and results made on the basis of the data collected from the Smart Cards are accurate because they are used to management and planning railway network.

CASE STUDY: TRANSPORT FOR LONDON (TfL)

Here we are going to discuss the Transport for London (TfL) as a case study to see whether the smart card used in London's transit systems of TfL have had any effect on the people's travel behavior or helped the authorities to better understand the behaviors of the passengers.

TfL is a local government's body which is responsible for the transport system in London and is composed of the London Underground, London Overground, Docklands Light Railways and TfL Rail, buses and trams. More than 8 million trips are made on the tubes, heavy railways and buses across the city of London and all these trips are a source of data which is being collected by the smart cards used by passengers for travelling on the public transport system. The smart card used in London for travelling on the tube or the buses is the Oyster Smartcard, as we mentioned earlier in the table.

Oyster Smartcard is one of the largest and more complex Automatic Fare Collection (AFC) projects in the world. Oyster has over the years surpassed the estimated made by its manufacturers, who earlier thought 3 million cards will be sufficient for catering to the needs of the public in London, but more than 10 million cards have already been issued and more than 5 million of those cards are in regular use on the network. We have discussed the technology being used in this Smartcard earlier in the table only.

Now how the data collected by this smart card has been used by researchers to better understand the passengers' behavior and plan policies using the data and also make data-driven decisions for implementing those policies. Some of the instances where Big Data has been used and helped both the TfL and also benefited the passengers are as discussed below:

- **Open Data:** TfL provides open data collected from different sources, like Oyster Smart Card and others, for developers from around the world to work and engage on and help innovate the public transport system. More than 8500 developers are registered for the Open Data of TfL, who are using its API and static data and feeds to power more than 500 travel apps. These applications are being used by travelers to get information regarding the mode of transport they should be using for which part of the journey and whether there are any delays or changes made to the schedule of the running of trains or buses.
- **Customized Customer Travel Info:** The TfL operates an Email service which is used to provide the travelers with important information. But instead of bombarding the travelers with tones of information about a delay occurring on a particular route on which they are not travelling on or have never used, it uses Big Data to customize and tailor the information every Oyster Smartcard holder receives. Using the data collected from the Oyster Smartcard, the TfL gets the information of the routes different travelers use during which part of the day and other travel patterns. Based on this data, it tailors the information it sends to the passengers and provides only relevant information which will be more helpful for them.
- **Origin-Destination Matrix:** Oyster Smartcard data can be used to estimate Origin-Destination (OD) flow matrix which can be used to reflect the current demand. OD matrix also deals with rail service reliability metrics which can capture excess journey time and also the variation in the time. The above-mentioned applications of the OD matrix can be used for representing both the rail demand in conjunction with service performance at the lowest level of any time period on any specific day of the week. The OD matrix provides the planners with a tool using which, they can easily monitor if there are any changes in the travel patterns over a period of time and thus can make data-driven and informed decisions to make any changes to the services.

There are numerous benefits of OD estimates at the time period level, some of which are listed below:

- Improved service planning
- Improved customer segmentation
- Improved assessment of system performance measurement
- Informed decisions can be made regarding fare policy

In addition to all its benefits, the OD matrix can also be used in enhancing the different components of Service planning which are mentioned in Figure 18.

System performance monitoring can be enhanced with the help of OD matrix in the following ways:

Estimates of Volume carried on the system and passenger-miles carried help in quantifying the transit system's performance in terms of cost per passenger and cost per passenger mile. These metrics are the performance metrics on which often considered as inputs for future funding provisions.

Figure 18. Different components of service planning

Component of Service Planning	Role of OD matrix
Network and Route design	Important input for calculating demand models which can be used for evaluating alternative network and route designs
Separate Weekday and Weekend travel pattern estimates	AFC systems like Oyster Smartcard make the data available for constricting OD matrix for weekends also without any additional cost
Frequency setting	OD matrix can also help with setting service frequency and dealing with dwelling and boarding time
Special Event Planning	Easy to update OD matrix helps better understand needs of public transport for passengers during special events and also help observe the travel patterns before and after the events.

OD flow matrices are used by planners for estimation of passenger loads on different line segments during different times of the day. Crowding levels can be therefore calculated for different segments of the line and therefore helping to make sure they have sufficient capacity so as to allow most passengers to board the first train.

Customer focused performance measures derived from OD flow matrix can be used for capturing the experience of the passengers in the transit system. For example, it is more desirable to incorporate passenger demand during a period of time so that any service delay which affects a number of travelers is more heavily weighed than the one affecting a smaller number of travelers.

Two areas which affect the interaction of passengers with the transit system and which can be improved with the help of OD matrix are as below:

- **Capital Investment and Demand Management:** Based on the OD matrix assigned using the path choice model, planners can get information regarding the volumes of transfer at major interchange stations. Using this information, the planners can decide on and also justify whether the station requires improvements. This can also be used to decide whether to increase the frequency of services on particular lines and stations depending on the calculation of the demand. Planners can also help the passengers by providing information regarding congestion and delay on particular lines and suggestion them alternative paths which are faster and less crowded.
- **Fare Policy and Monitoring:** TfL use fare policy to try to monitor and also change the number of people travelling on the tube. Like the fare of Oyster Smartcard using the pay-as-you-go option will have to pay more to travel using the tube during the peak hours of the day as compared to the passengers who are using the travel card option of the Oyster Smartcard. The TfL therefore can use OD matrices to see if there are any visible and significant changes in the travel patterns

of the people due to changes in the fare policy or not and whether this can be used strategically to divert the direction of movement of people towards other paths or modes of transport in order to de-congest one route or line and direct people towards a line which is less crowded and offers a faster path.

- **Customer Segmentation:** TfL has been using the data collected from Oyster Smartcards for segmenting its passenger base into different clusters. This helps them to better understand different segments of its customer base and better address the groups and their needs individually better which otherwise would not have been addressed, like offering different ticket plans for different segments or groups and other commercial offerings for those segments of customers. One of the most basic levels of cluster segmentation used by TfL is the clustering on the basis of the frequency of use of the public transport.

CONCLUSION

Big Data has disrupted the fields like healthcare and finance, revolutionizing the way things are done in them. It has also helped the manufacturing sector to be more efficient and to better the quality of the manufactured products. Now Railways and other public transportation systems have started to see the effect Big Data can have. Railways, in particular, is set to benefit from the use of Big Data due to the huge amounts of data it can potentially collect from the passengers, from the sensors on the Railway structures like railway engines, bridges and rail cars, stations. Technological advancements are being made in the field of Big Data almost every day. New methodologies, algorithms and analytic software are coming into the market. The branch of Big Data with a lot of promise for railways is Real Time Analytics.

Smart Cards coupled with the different types of sensors and GPS units can form an IOT (Internet of Things) ecosystem and provide the real-time data to the systems which analyzes and output results and insights in Real Time. This way the decision makers can have the information they need in time, to make a decision and have an effect on an event.

Smart Cards have been used in different railway networks around the world to better understand the travelers and use that knowledge in forming future policies regarding the pricing of the network, the traffic on particular routes and the schedule and frequency of rails during different periods of the day. This is possible because the Smart Cards provide the authorities with the data and this data is being stored in the servers and present in the form of relational databases of the organization which is assigned with the work of deriving insights from the huge amounts of data. But this data can be years old, or months, or weeks old. So these organizations are looking in the past see if there is any measurable change in the way the travelers are interacting with the railway network to predict the future. So, what can be done to make decisions immediately if there is any visible change? Real Time Analytics.

Real Time Analytics is the way to go for the Railways around the world to become dynamic and drive business innovation by making quicker and better business decisions based on Real Time data which keeps on filtering through.

Smart Cards are one of the easiest ways of setting up a system of Real Time Analytics. At every station, there are entry and exit gates which collect information from your smart cards when you enter or exit the stations. There are multiple ways in which the Real-time Analytics on this data collected at the gates can be utilized by the railway authorities, out of a couple have been discussed below:

Optimization: Real-Time Analytics in conjunction with simple Analytics can help see if there are any changes over the smallest periods of time and make decisions based on those changes which are visible using the Smart Card data and help optimize the system for better operational efficiency by increasing the network capacity and throughput capacity of the railway network.

Traffic Management: If the authorities can in real time see which route has what number of passengers going in one way, then the schedule of running trains can be changed in a metro railway system in real time to increase the frequency of trains running on that route and reducing it on another.

Rerouting trains in case of any problem on any railway track: The Real Time Analytics can help the authorities by rerouting trains if there are any problems on any railway track or platform, without causing a shutdown on a whole route or a jam of rails on that route for hours.

Big Data collected from Smart cards and IOT sensors can have a real impact on the way the Railways function. Therefore, it is up to the Railway departments, planning agencies and the developers around the world to use this opportunity to help and disrupt this mode of public transport and make it more efficient and more passenger friendly.

REFERENCES

Agard, B., Morency, C., & Trépanier, M. (2006, May 17–19). Mining public transport user behavior from smart card data. In *Proceedings of the 12th IFAC Symposium on Information Control Problems in Manufacturing INCOM '06*, Saint-Etienne, France.

Arthur, D., & Vassilvitskii, S. (2007). K-means++: the advantages of careful seeding. In *Proceedings of the Eighteenth Annual ACM-SIAM Symposium on Discrete Algorithms* (pp. 1027–1035).

Bagchi, M., & White, P. R. (2005). The potential of public transport smart card data. *Transport Policy, 12*(5), 464–474. doi:10.1016/j.tranpol.2005.06.008

Barry, J., Freiner, R., & Slavin, H. (2009). Use of entry-only automatic fare collection data to estimate linked transit trips in New York City. *Transportation Research Record, 2112*, 53–61. doi:10.3141/2112-07

Barry, J. J., Newhouser, R., Rahbee, A., & Sayeda, S. (2002). Origin and destination estimation in New York City with automated fare system data. *Transportation Research Record, 1817*, 183–187. doi:10.3141/1817-24

Chu, K. K., & Chapleau, R. (2013). Smart card validation data as multi-day transit panel survey to investigate individual and aggregate variation in travel behavior. In J. Zmud, M. Lee-Gosselin, M. Munizaga, & J. A. Carasco (Eds.), *Transport survey methods: Best practice for decision making* (pp. 649–671). Bingley: Emerald. doi:10.1108/9781781902882-036

Devillaine, F., Munizaga, M. A., & Trepanier, M. (2012). Detection activities of public transport users by analyzing smart card data. *Transportation Research Record, 2276*, 48–55. doi:10.3141/2276-06

Even, A., & Shankaranarayanan, G. (2009). Utility cost perspectives in data quality management. *Journal of Computer Information Systems, 50*(2), 127–135.

Haug, A., Pedersen, A., & Arlbjørn, J. S. (2009). A classification model of ERP system data quality. *Industrial Management & Data Systems, 109*(8), 1053–1068. doi:10.1108/02635570910991292

Hilbert, M. (2016). Big Data for Development: A Review of Promises and Challenges. *Development Policy Review*, *34*(1), 135-174.

Jose, S. (2016, April 06). Data analytics for smart railways. *The Hindu Business Line*. Retrieved from http://www.thehindubusinessline.com/opinion/data-analytics-for-smart-railways/article8442289.ece

Kusakabe, T., & Asakura, Y. (2014). Behavioral data mining of transit smart card data: A data fusion approach. *Transportation Research Part C, Emerging Technologies*, *46*, 179–191. doi:10.1016/j.trc.2014.05.012

Lathia, N., & Capra, L. (2011). How smart is your smartcard?: measuring travel behaviors, perceptions, and incentives. In *Proceedings of the 13th international conference on Ubiquitous computing*. ACM. doi:10.1145/2030112.2030152

Lyko, K., Nitzschke, M., & Ngomo, A.-C. N. (2016). *Big data acquisition. In New Horizons for a Data-Driven Economy* (pp. 39–61). Springer International Publishing. doi:10.1007/978-3-319-21569-3_4

Ma, X., Wang, Y., Feng, C., & Liu, J. (2012). Transit smart card data mining for passenger origin information extraction. *Journal of Zhejiang University. Science*, *C13*(10), 750–760. doi:10.1631/jzus.C12a0049

Ma, X., Wu, Y. J., Wang, Y., Chen, F., & Liu, J. (2013). Mining smart card data for transit riders travel patterns. *Transportation Research Part C, Emerging Technologies*, *36*, 1–12. doi:10.1016/j.trc.2013.07.010

Madnick, S., Wang, R., & Xian, X. (2004). The design and implementation of a corporate householding knowledge processor to improve data quality. *Journal of Management Information Systems*, *20*(1), 41–49.

McDonald, N. (2000). Multipurpose Smart Cards in Transportation: Benefits and Barriers to Use (Research Paper # 630). University of California Transportation Center.

McGuckin, N., & Nakamoto, Y. (2004, November 1–2). Trips, chains, and tours: using an operational definition. *Presented at: Understanding Our Nation's Travel: National Household Travel Survey Conference*, Washington DC.

Morency, C. (2013). Workshop synthesis: exploiting and merging passive public transportation data streams. In J. Zmud, M. Lee-Gosselin, M. Munizaga, & J. A. Carasco (Eds.), *Transport survey methods: Best practice for decision making* (pp. 711–720). Bingley: Emerald. doi:10.1108/9781781902882-039

Munizaga, M., Devillaine, F., Navarrete, C., & Silva, D. (2014). Validating travel behavior estimated from smartcard data. *Transportation Research Part C, Emerging Technologies*, *44*, 70–79. doi:10.1016/j.trc.2014.03.008

Munizaga, M. A., & Palma, C. (2012). Estimation of a disaggregate multimodal public transport origin-destination matrix from passive Smart card data from Santiago, Chile. *Transportation Research*, *24C*(12), 9–18. doi:10.1016/j.trc.2012.01.007

Pelletier, M. P., Trépanier, M., & Morency, C. (2011). Smart card data use in public transit: A literature review. *Transportation Research Part C, Emerging Technologies*, *19*(4), 557–568. doi:10.1016/j.trc.2010.12.003

Raimond, T. 2009. Moving towards continuous collection of large-scale mobility surveys: are the recompelling reasons? A discussant response. In P. Bonnel, M. Lee-Gosselin, J. Zmud et al. (Eds.), Transport Survey Methods: Keeping Up with a Changing World (pp. 541–548). Bingley: Emerald Group Publishing Ltd.

Riazi, A. (1999, March 21–25). MetroCard: Automating New York City's Public Transit System. In *Proceedings of the First International Conference on Urban Transportation Systems*, American Society of Civil Engineers, Miami, FL.

Strambi, O., Trépanier, M., & Cherrington, L. (2009). Data for public transit planning, marketing and model development: synthesis of a workshop. In P. Bonnel, M. Lee-Gosselin, J. Zmud et al. (Eds.), Transport Survey Methods: Keeping Up with a Changing World (pp. 349–357). Bingley: Emerald Group Publishing Ltd. doi:10.1108/9781848558458-020

Tourangeau R., Zimowski, M., Ghadialy, R. (1997). An introduction to panel surveys in transportation studies. Report prepared for the Federal Highway Administration.

Trépanier, M., Chapleau, R., & Tranchant, N. (2007). Individual trip destination estimation in transit smart card automated fare collection system. *Journal of Intelligent Transportation Systems: Technology, Planning, and Operations, 11*(1), 1–15. doi:10.1080/15472450601122256

Trépanier, M., Morency, C., & Blanchette, C. 2009. Enhancing Household Travel Surveys Using Smart Card Data? In *Proceedings of the 88th Annual Meeting of the Transportation Research Board.*

Utsunomiya, M., Attanucci, J., & Wilson, N. (2006). Potential uses of transit smart card registration and transaction data to improve transit planning. *Transportation Research Record: Journal of the Transportation Research Board, 1971*, 119–126. doi:10.3141/1971-16

Weinstein, L.S. (2015, November). Innovations in London's transport: Big Data for a better customer experience. *Transport for London.*

Zhao, J., Rahbee, A., & Wilson, N. (2007). Estimating a rail passenger trip origin-destination matrix using automatic data collection systems. *Computer-Aided Civil and Infrastructure Engineering, 22*(5), 376–387. doi:10.1111/j.1467-8667.2007.00494.x

Chapter 7
Dynamic Behavior Analysis of Railway Passengers

Myneni Madhu Bala
Institute of Aeronautical Engineering, India

Venkata Krishnaiah Ravilla
Institute of Aeronautical Engineering, India

Kamakshi Prasad V
JNTUH, India

Akhil Dandamudi
NIIT University, India

ABSTRACT

This chapter discusses mainly on dynamic behavior of railway passengers by using twitter data during regular and emergency situations. Social network data is providing dynamic and realistic data in various fields. As per the current chapter theme, if the twitter data of railway field is considered then it can be used for enhancement of railway services. Using this data, a comprehensive framework for modeling passenger tweets data which incorporates passenger opinions towards facilities provided by railways are discussed. The major issues elaborated regarding dynamic data extraction, preparation of twitter text content and text processing for finding sentiment levels is presented by two case studies; which are sentiment analysis on passenger's opinions about quality of railway services and identification of passenger travel demands using geotagged twitter data. The sentiment analysis ascertains passenger opinions towards facilities provided by railways either positive or negative based on their journey experiences.

INTRODUCTION

Considering the advancement in technology by 2050 the railway industry would be able to address competitive pricing, passenger desirable time slots, excellent customer service, and effective emergency services using a dynamic behavior analysis. The railway industry is often thought as conservative; it is necessary to proceed with the foresight to hold creative thinking beyond projecting the present into

DOI: 10.4018/978-1-5225-3176-0.ch007

the future. This thought piece focuses on the passenger experiences, which are anticipated here and are designed to generate a discussion about the future. It provides a big picture in taking dynamic decisions by the rail industry and governments.

Passengers are increasingly able to access data from anywhere through smart devices and cloud applications. As a result, faster access to data will influence passenger relationship with transportation, as well as their decision-making process. Passengers will expect the services certainty in terms of time, so reliable and accurate real-time information will be a key issue. Customer centric services will be based on a wealth of information about the individual passenger and their needs at that moment. These require a detailed understanding and analysis of the passenger experience measures and their satisfaction with key elements of their journey. This analysis would be used to identify satisfaction or dissatisfaction, to provide the feedback with guidance on those areas of improvement.

National Rail Passenger Survey (NRPS) enables rail operators to compare their service with others and to identify the areas of improvement. The department of transport uses this information to evaluate Train Operating Companies (TOCS), which is an official statistic on operator's service. Along with this statistic, big data analysis would play a vital role in the processing of the data collected from social networks. Twitter is one of the primary sources of informal data repository. While considering the previous survey reports there has been a long-term downward trend in the overall complaints rate through traditional channels. It has been attributed to passengers moving towards social media to complain about their train operators relatively than using more traditional methods. Due to the differences in approach to social media, recording complaints through this are not possible at present but should be considered as a long-term goal. The size of the customer base that interacts with the train operators through social media means that their feedback is a very rich source of information to be recorded. By working with train operators and social media analysts we can explore suitable measures that record categorization or sentiment of feedback through social media. The purpose of this analysis would be to identify the data which would help in gauging how train operators approach social media for passenger engagement and complaints perspective. Many have been working with the train operators to learn more about their approach to social media, which has opened opportunities in several different areas. Including time and resource dedicated to social media, the level of engagement, recording feedback. Based on the survey results, the report focus is on any commonality in train operator's approach to social media and it is feasible to record complaints through this channel, observing some of the major challenges in finding a reliable measure, including passenger behavior towards social media and assessing sentiment of feedback.

The main objective of this chapter is to understand the passenger behavior dynamically by using twitter data. This chapter mainly concentrates on extraction of dynamic data from social media, identification of the relevant hashtags of railway passengers, preprocessing on twitter data to remove unwanted text and symbols, identification of list of task-relevant words that define positive as well as negative opinion, preparation of word plots to find major discussions and sentiment analysis on passenger's opinion.

BACKGROUND

An explanatory study to investigate the use of text mining and sentiment analysis for railway services enhancement on relevant content extracted from twitter for exploring different applications. Due to the complexity of information extraction from social media for focused tasks like passenger complaints, trips planning, understanding passenger behavior at city visits and sentiment analysis on events. At present, Indian railways' current practice on performance survey is relying on multiple sources such as SMS, web feedback, and twitter hashtags.

TRADITIONAL COMPUTING

The traditional computing methods are accurate but these are not appropriate under uncertain situations. Soft computing is a collection of the early methods such as Fuzzy Logic, Neural Network, and later methods such as Genetic Algorithm, Rough Theory. (Denai, 2007) used computational intelligence to deal with uncertainty in data. The current research of behavior problems using soft computing methods is at the practice stage. (Avineri, 2004) has built the model on the passenger travel choices. (Qiang, 2008) have made a comparative analysis of support vector machine model and multilayer feedforward neural network. (Jin, 2008) has built a prediction model for passenger travel problems by using applied radial basis function neural network and regression neural network. (Ma, 2007) has given a solution for traffic and travel by combining neural network in the nonlinear relationship and Back Propagation neural network. (Qiu, 2008) worked on the prediction of resident's travel choice by using the probabilistic neural network on survey data of residents in Fangshan district of Beijing. Above said methods and models does not reveal passenger travel choice problems because of multiple starting points and important soft factors like comfort, punctuality, safety etc.

PASSENGER COMPLAINTS ON TWITTER

According to present surveys, the major concentration is on punctuality and reliability of services. One of the background survey, "social media: how to tweet your customers' right" done on 2015 in the UK. The main purposes of this survey were social media compliant content, passenger behavior in social media and capturing the sentiment of passenger's feedback. In this report, the major complaints on train service performance are of punctuality and reliability. It remains the main source of complaints at 34.7% in the 3rd quarter of 2014-15, with punctuality and cancellation measures deteriorating in the past year, but expected complaints in this area are to rise though the share of total complaints has fallen from 41.2% to 34.7%. The downtrend of complaints rate in the traditional channel has reduced; now taking to social media as a means of expressing their dissatisfaction. Presently, railways are exempted from social media data complaints. The latest statistics that showed complaints on passenger tweets make up 4.5% of all complaints in 2014-15 3rdquarter, down from 6% in 2010-11, possibly the outcome of the positive work of train operators are doing in with their customers on social media. Taking these into consideration, we have two scenarios; social media is the new vehicle for complaints and the focus is on twitter data in capturing feedback. There were few train operators on twitter 24 by 7 a week while others are on duty during business hours. In this scenario, over 90% of train operator's drive out a combination of proactive and reactive tweets. However, the scope of their commitment differs markedly. Consider a case, where the number of proactive tweets sent ranged from 500 to 33,000 at the same time as the volume of reactive tweets ranges from 10,000 to 126,000.

MODELING TRAVEL SURVEY

(Alireza, 2015) Traveling behavior of individual passenger based on twitter data is considered for modeling travel survey. In their research, four modeling approaches are discussed. Firstly, a trip based then tour-based models which consider individual travel information data; later evolved to activity-based models which consider the individual or household level travel attributes and to another travel demand models which are essential to policymakers for assessment of long-term travel needs. The advances in travel demand modeling for analyzing the people's day to day travel behavior which changes the need of socio-demographic databases and people economic attributes.

(Alireza, 2015) The individual traveling behavior of the passenger's based twitter data is considered for modeling travel survey. In their research, the four modeling approaches are discussed. Firstly, trip based then tour-based models which consider individual travel information data; later evolved to activity-based models which consider the individual or household level travel attributes; Next travel demand models are essential to policymakers for assessment of long-term travel needs. The advances in travel demand modeling for analyzing the people day to day travel behavior which changes the need of socio-demographic databases and people economic attributes. They proposed a framework for further applications of twitter passenger data for transport planning and management. They developed three components for tourism development on longitudinal data obtained from twitter. Finally, from this analysis, every passenger is automatically identified as visitor or residents of Sydney city.

PASSENGER ACTIVITY PURPOSE

The purpose of a passenger activity is analyzed with each tweet by using advanced text mining technique. The activities would be categorized as shopping, eating, entertainment, work. A study using text classification techniques. Latent Dirichlet Allocation (LDA) is a hierarchical Bayesian-based approach for finding similarities among categorical variables (Blei, 2003). The similar studies focused on the content of tweets rather than check-in data (Gao, 2012), geo-tagged data (Hasan, 2014) or sentiment analyses (Fu, 2015). This analysis is useful for finding the behavior of tourists at their attracting cities. One possible measure may be indistinguishable to record, the proportion of positive or negative feedback we receive via twitter. However, this requires other train operators that do not currently collect that data to adapt their processes to capture it.

MAIN FOCUS OF THE CHAPTER

The chapter focuses on the following issues:

- The impact of social network data and issues in data processing, in the field of railway service enhancement.
- A comprehensive framework for modeling social media data.
- Discussion on process of data extraction, preparation and processing techniques.
- A detailed discussion about passenger dynamic behavior.

- Sentiment analysis on passenger's positive and negative opinions not only on railways facilities but also on responses for regular and emergency situations.
- Identification of passenger travel demands using geotagged twitter data.

All these analyses would be useful for railways sector to identify and plan demand locations of tourists. According to the extracted knowledge, railways could take decision on allocating more number of coaches to specific tourist places in crowd time, to take decisions based on passenger feedback about facilities provided and complaints, to assess the reasons for damage in emergency situations.

ISSUES, CONTROVERSIES, PROBLEMS

Social Network Dynamic Data Sources

Nowadays, many people relate to social media to obtain effective feedback on policies, comforts, and security. Due to this the analysis would do justice to people's time, effort and expertise, and act on the ideas and feedback received. Table 1 shows a list of data sources where data is collected for different purposes such as feedback on service quality, security in the journey, passenger opinion on new services and schemes and detection of abnormal or undesirable events occurred in overall journey period for analysis. It is potentially a challenge for understanding passenger's opinion, as people don't have a prior idea of how the social media data would be implemented and the analysis is not totally open to innovative ideas or diverse opinions.

In this scenario, how to bring all these ideas into a whole or which idea to favor and to be able to explain to the public how the decision was made by authorities. Table 2 lists the issues in data processing in a traditional and social media data.

The use of social media in government services has been reported many times, with key aspect being citizen participation and transparency of government. Even though it is in infancy stage, more dynamic and huge data is available.

In developing a methodology to explore the potential of social media data for understanding passenger's behavior, three questions need to be addressed:

Q1: To what extent the passengers involved for sharing their opinion?
Q2: How can the value of such information be evaluated?
Q3: Can such data be practically extracted either automatically or semi-automatically?

Table 1. List of data sources

S. No.	Data Purpose	Traditional	Social Media (SM)
1	Service quality and security	Questionnaires	SM text
2	Passengers opinion on new schemes or services	Focus groups, committees, consultation meetings, Household questionnaires	SM text
3	Detection of the abnormal or undesirable event.	Physical devices e.g.: cc camera footage	SM text

Table 2. Issues in Data Processing

S. No.	Data Purpose	Traditional	Social Media
1	Service quality and security	Data Issues	Analysis of text content is effective in gathering service quality data.
2	Passengers opinion on new schemes or services	**Group and meetings:** • Resource intensive • Limited data sample • Sources of bias Household questionnaires. • Resource intensive • Some biases e.g: response rates.	Analysis of text content is effective in supplementing or replacing public opinion data sources.
3	Detection of abnormal or undesirable event	**Physical devices:** • Continuous monitoring • Level of accuracy is sufficient • High coverage is costly. **Management / operational / control systems** • Systems often belong to private operators and quality of data sharing is often a challenging issue. o Such systems don't enable real-time data processing, which is required for event detection.	• Low cost for authority • Even a small no. of similar reports constitutes a solid basis for verifying the event. • Many types of events can be detected. • Depends on human reporting. • Time constraints require the use of very efficient text mining techniques.

The first is tantamount to quantify the data with facts. While the second can be achieved with an assessment of model and the third requires a high-quality extraction methodologies that are critical to realizing the quality and scope of data.

The current approach is an ongoing analysis of social media information to reveal changes in trends concerning the level of satisfaction with service provided. If a positive trend is revealed, then it can be inferred that analysis on the information and acting in response to the content is an effective tool to address traveler's needs.

Q3 must be approached with the characteristics of unstructured text data within social media, where syntax-rules are often overlooked two-way and the use of local slang is rude.

Two criteria are commonly used to test hypotheses of this type by involving automatic text processing:

1. The information automatically extracted should be highly relevant. Domain experts are used to measuring the relevance of each item of information extracted. The precision rate is calculated i.e. the ratio of the correctly extracted items to the total no. of extracted items.
2. The extracted information should be complete. Domain experts identify the pertinent information within a finite set of text sources. The ratio of the relevant information found by automatic text mining the total number of the relevant information items can be calculated i.e. recall.

The searching goals can be defined in three characteristics of social media context, reflect its nature and the examples of its use in various domains:

• Social media data created by an individual, who refers to a specific experienced event or action plans to perform
• The event or action the individual comments on occurs either before or after the time point at which the content is achieved.
• The issue raised by the individual creating the content is personally important.

Twitter Data

Twitter is asserted to have, 500 million tweets per day, 288 million monthly active users with 80% of active users using mobile phones. This set up a wonderful opportunity for the public and private sector to benefit from the amount of freely available data provided online and improves their services. Crowd-sourcing social media for disaster or emergency management (Madhubala, 2017) is one of the examples to facilitate response and relief operations by emergency teams by using twitter data. Among the different approaches, some develop tools to track the information provided by social media to predict a likely event.

Tag Words Related to Railways

The government of India, the ministry of railways launched an official account with a tag word on twitter as #railminindia for all complaints, suggestions to be marked to concern General Managers (GM), Divisional Railway Managers (DRM) for appropriate action. Another Indian railway tag word in twitter is #indianrailway and #railways. Geo-tagged tweets of twitter data are used to develop location-based analysis on passenger behavior for identification of visiting plans including duration and place of visit. From this analysis, the general pattern on passenger trips as short or long is identified.

PROBLEMS

Extracting named travel and land use attributes information from hashtag data is a challenging issue in this analysis. Data mining is required to determine the activity location that is related to a tweet. This analysis is used in developing several advanced components of behavioral modeling frameworks such as tour based and activity based (Mojtaba, 2015). Travel attributes considered in these modeling frameworks are the trip purpose, departure time, mode of transport, activity duration, activity location, travel route, party composition and traffic condition. This analysis focuses on how twitter data can be used to facilitate and improve railways decisions on the enhancement of facilities, passenger safety and several couches.

SOLUTIONS AND RECOMMENDATIONS

For above-discussed problems, the solutions can be found from advanced text mining processes to address the dynamic data. An effective framework is needed to address multiple problems. An effective preprocess is one of the critical steps on social media data.

TEXT MINING PROCESS

Text mining is used to identify the passenger behavior in sentiment analysis. This process includes data extraction, preparation, and processing. The sentiment analysis on passenger opinions towards facilities provided by railways as a positive or negative, passengers response on regular and emergency situations. The activity purpose associated with in a tweet, it's determined by using an advanced text mining technique, Latent Dirichlet Allocation (LDA) (Blei, 2003). It is hierarchical Bayesian approach highly suitable for analyzing tweets data and finding similarity between categorical attributes. LDA is used to identify the correlations among words in twitter corpus, to find different hidden topics (discussions) and further classifying the text accordingly. Figure 1 is an overview of text mining process for sentiment analysis. It includes extraction of relevant messages, pre-process on extracted tweets, semantic process based on classification or sentiment analysis and summarization and visualization output inferences.

Extraction of Trip Purpose From Twitter Data Using LDA

The data considered for finding trip purpose is the content of tweets (text) rather than check-in data (Gao, 2012), geo-tagged data (Hasan, 2014) or sentiment analyses (Fu, 2015). In this analysis, they used unique word dictionary as 'Sydney_Resident_DB'. The pre-process on tweets is performed by removing unwanted content as prepositions and symbols. Now based on frequent words, around 400 unique words are identified with a minimum frequency of 20. In this work, words like "I'm", "Sydney" and "restaurant" were respectively used 3009, 1215 and 233 times in the text that was selected for further analysis. Nearly 17,000 words were not included in the analysis because they were slang expressions, prepositions and symbols had been repeated fewer than 20 times in the database. LDA was applied on identified 400 words to cluster the data and found 100-word clusters. From each cluster, the top 3 highest frequency words. Find the correlation between top 3 words and remaining words within the same cluster. An activity tag was assigned to each cluster by considering the top 3 words in each cluster and other correlations among words. The identified activity tags are named as Shopping, Entertainment, Eating,

Figure 1. Overview of text mining process

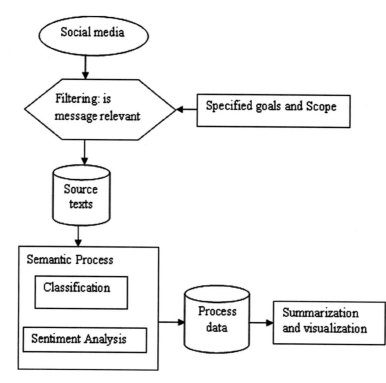

Work, Social, Study. Finally, each tweet was assigned with one of the cluster activity tags by checking against all the clusters and if there was an appropriate level of similarity. This finding on twitter data is helpful in analyzing the behavior of tourists.

Identification of Keywords

Automatic identification of meaningful keywords and their use in training classifiers is one of the important tasks in twitter analysis. To automatically identify relevant content from streams of text, text mining techniques have been used with considerable success. These practices with social media help to gain knowledge and understanding of public opinion across several social sciences (e.g.: Politics, entertainment, and business). For example, Twitter messages have been analyzed as an alternate to presidential approval rating data and presidential polls, where results show high correlation with these polls. Figure 2 is an example of Sample tweets and replies from railway officials. The sample tweets show complaints from passengers, consideration of social media data as the complaint by railway ministry and forwarded to concerned officials of Indian railways for further action.

The infinite nature of the message stream in social media is challenging from multiple perspectives. From a performance perspective, as the content posted on social media changes rapidly over time, periodic monitoring and possibly re-tuning of the system is required. Text mining is a means for automatic identifications of relevant messages in a stream of incoming messages. Specific remain and solutions are needed where the user must be in the loop for periodic monitoring and enhancement of the system.

CASE STUDY 1: SENTIMENT ANALYSIS ON PASSENGERS OPINIONS

Sentiment analysis is the process of identifying and extracting opinions from a given text. Sentiment analysis of social media has been used to estimate public mood (Johan, 2011), trends such as stock market behavior (Johan, 2011) and political election results (Jessica, 2011). Sentiment analysis is important to address some of the information needs of (railway/transport) policy makers. In the transport sector, the twitter as an information source for evaluating transit rider satisfaction (Collins, 2013). A case study of the Chicago Transit Authority, a correlation was found between irregular events (e.g. delays) and the

Figure 2. Sample tweets and replies from railway officials

volume of postings expressing negative sentiment. This correlation supports the notion that twitter is a valid source of dynamic information for inferring transport-related sentiments.

A survey on the role of negation in sentiment analysis depends on the construction of bag of negative words. In this process, the first challenge is the construction of common linguistic, which is highly relevant for sentiment analysis. The effective negation model includes common negation words and other lexical units about text classification type, the level of text granularity, target domain, and language used etc. Sentiment analysis makes use of a dedicated lexicon of words marked with their prior polarity as negative or positive (Michael, 2010). The matching of a given text with the lexicon to analyze emotions in the text is another approach for sentiment analysis (Sanjay, 2007).

The Indian railways have active involvement at social media on twitter passenger opinions. Figure 3 is an example of sample Tweets of Indian railway passengers on #swatchRailSwatchBharat and response of railway minister. It shows the response of passengers on event Swatch Bharat announced by the government of India. On this passenger opinion tweet, the response is given by concern minister.

EXPRESSIONS OF NEGATIVE/POSITIVE SENTIMENT

The natural languages are highly context dependent (Michael, 2010). For example, 'busy' word is described as positive in some context e.g. "the road is busy and should qualify for upgrade" but negative in others 'the road is busy and unsuited for further housing development'. The texts say the sentiment as positive: For "terribly good" and negative is "not at all desirable". Analysis of transport sentiment data has illustrated the difficulty with service quality related text. For example, the text like "train service is just fantastic" needs the surrounding context for interpretation. In this case is the preceding text related to late running trains may indicate whether it is genuine or sarcastic. The inferring sentiment is posed

Figure 3. Sample Tweets of Indian railway passengers on #swatchRailSwatchBharat and response of railway minister

Suresh Prabhu ☉ *(@sureshpprabhu)* Sep 18
Idea to internalise& institutionalise the //SwatchRailSwatchBharat,make it part of daily life,culture @narendramodi

Western Railway *(@WesternRly)*
Onlookers voluntarily taking cleanliness oath during a street play at station @sureshpprabhu @RailMinIndia

↩ 9   ⇄ 32   ♥ 121   •••

Sweta_Entomon *(@SwetapadmaDash)* Oct 2
Just beautifull Bhubaneswar Rail Stn, stark clean n nice thematic paints! Thks @sureshpprabhu Sir it feels really //SwatchRailSwatchBharat

as a text classification task (Johan, 2011), enabling the consideration of contextual. Classes to identifying sentiment are elaborated (Sanjay, 2007). The learned models should be trained using labeled data within the interested domain.

The sentiment analysis can be performed in the following steps:

Step 1: Data Extraction from twitter API
Step 2: Data Preprocess
Step 3: Identification of frequent words
Step 4: Calculation of polarity scores
Step 5: Sentiment Analysis

1. Data Extraction

Twitter is one of the social networking and microblogging services that allow users to post real-time messages, called tweets. Tweets are short text messages, limited to 140 characters in length. Due to the nature of this microblogging service (quick and short messages), people use acronyms, make spelling mistakes, use emoticons and other characters that express special meanings. Following are brief terminology associated with tweets.

- **Emoticons:** These are facial expressions pictorially represented enclosed with punctuation and letters; It expresses the user's mood.
- **Target:** The "@" symbol is used to refer to other users on the microblog like twitter. Referring other users in this manner automatically alerts them.
- **Hashtags:** Users usually use hashtags to mark topics. This is primarily done to increase the visibility of their tweets.

Figure 4 is an example of Indian railways #tagword on twitter. These are the familiar #tagwords, where the passengers are actively involving for sharing their opinions on services, security, complaints and tatkal services. Table 3 contains statistics on railways related tag word based tweets in twitter per day declared by Indian railways. In this case study, a sample of 1000 tweets is extracted by using #RailMinIndia hashtag from twitter API.

2. Data Pre-Processing

The extracted tweets text contains emoticon symbols, acronyms, symbols, URLs and highlights with quotes. Now the data must be done on pre-process to make data ready to analyze.

The following are the novel resources for pre-processing twitter data:

1. Emoticon dictionary
2. Acronym dictionary
3. List of stop words
4. Patterns of URLs
5. List of highlight symbols

Figure 4. Indian railways #tagword on twitter

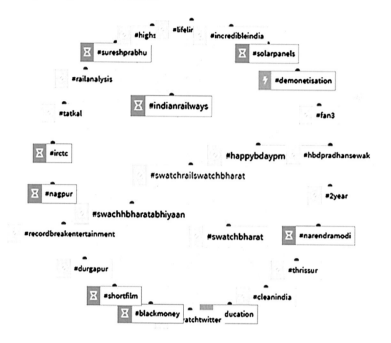

Emoticon Dictionary

The emoticon dictionary is prepared by labeling 170 emoticons listed on Wikipedia1 with their emotional state. Table 4 gives a part of emoticons dictionary. For example, ":)" symbol is labeled as positive and the ": =(" symbol is labeled as negative. We assign each emoticon a label from the following set of labels: Extremely-positive, Extremely-negative, Positive, Negative, and Neutral.

Acronym Dictionary

The acronym dictionary is prepared with translations for 5,184 acronyms. Table 5 gives the Sample Acronym Dictionary. For example, lol is translated to laugh out loud.

Table 3. General statistics on railways related tagword based Tweets

#Tagword	No. of Tweets
Indian railways	816
rail analysis	213
arctic	166
tatkal	135
train	131
railways	128

Table 4. Part of the Emoticons Dictionary

Emoticon	Polarity
:-):):o):]:3:c)	Positive
Emoticon	Positive
:D C	Positive
:-(:(:c:[	Negative
D8 D; D= DX	Negative
: j	Neutral

Table 5. Sample acronym dictionary

Acronym	English Expansion
gr8, gr8t	great
lol	laughing out loud
of	rolling on the floor
off	best friend forever

List of Stop Words

The Stanford tokenizer is used to tokenize the tweets (Klein and Manning, 2003). The stop word dictionary is used to identify stop words. All the other words which are found in WordNet are counted as English words. The stop words are filtered words used to save the disk space or speed up the text mining process. Stop words removal play an important role in reducing the length of documents in sentiment analysis. It is the process of filtering words which are of little help in processing the documents. Some words like articles, pronouns, etc., are prevalent in all the documents. These words don't determine the sentiment of a document. For example, words like „the", „a", "these", etc., are of no use in sentiment analysis and hence it can be removed. Country names, date of travel, numerical value baggage weight, etc., are also removed in our work. Table 6 shows the sample stop word list collected from http://www.webconfs.com/stop-words.php. Below is a comprehensive list of stop words ignored by Search Engines:

Patterns of URLs

The tweets text contains URLs data to share about relevant links. But for text analysis, there is no significance for URLs. All these links need to be removed from the text before processing. The general pattern for finding URLs is "http[[:album:]]".

Table 6. Sample stop word dictionary

able
about
above
abroad
according
accordingly
across
actually
adj
after

List of Highlight Symbols

The text contains highlighted part in the middle with special symbols as quotations, @, tab space or white spaces etc. All these also need to identify and removed from the text before processing.

The pre-processing of tweets includes the following steps:

Step 1: Replace all the emoticons with their sentiment polarity by looking up the emoticon dictionary
Step 2: Replace all URLs with a tag ||U||
Step 3: Replaces targets (e.g. "@John") with tag T||
Step 4: Replace all negations (e.g. not, no, never, not, cannot) by tag "NOT"
Step 5: Replace a sequence of repeated characters by three characters, for example, convert cooooooool to coool.

3. Identification of Frequent Words

After pre-process, now the tweets text contains meaning full text, emoticons, and acronyms. From the text content, the word list is prepared based on fixed word length. Now word frequency is computed for each word. Figure 5 is an example of sample word cloud of #RailMinIndia and #indianrailways. It shows the passenger major discussions such as Indian railways, online services and about the staff and train timings.

Figure 5. Sample word cloud of #RailMinIndia and #indianrailways

4. Polarity Scores

Polarity approximates the sentiment (polarity) of text by grouping variable(s) as positive, negative and neutral. Polarity score is calculated based on the impact of positive and negative words in the tweets text content. The equation employed to assign the value to a polarity of each sentence fist utilizes the sentiment dictionary to tag polarized words. A context cluster (x_i^T) of words is pulled from around this polarized word. In general default, 4 words before and two words after are to be considered as valence shifters.

The words in this context cluster are tagged as:

- **Neutral:** Neutral words hold no value in the equation but do affect word count (n).

$$x\_i^{\hat{}0}$$

- **Negator:** A character vector of terms reversing the intent of a positive or negative word.

$$x\_i^{\hat{}N}$$

- **Amplifier:** A character vector of terms that increase the intensity of a positive or negative word.

$$x\_i^{\hat{}a}$$

- **De-Amplifier:** A character vector of terms that decrease the intensity of a positive or negative word.

$$x\_i^{\hat{}d}$$

Table 7 shows a Sample Positive and Negative words identified from training data of passenger tweets. These words are identified as positive and negative based on the conversation about services provided by Indian railways.

Each polarized word is weighted as w based on the weights from the polarity. The weight c is utilized with amplifiers or de-amplifiers. In general, the default case is 8 and deamplifier weight is constrained to -1 as lower bound value. The context cluster (x_i^T) are summed and divided by the square root of the word count $\sqrt{(n)}$ by an unbounded polarity score (C). The context clusters consider the words found after the comma.

$$C = \frac{x\_i^{\hat{}2}}{\sqrt{n}}$$

where:

Table 7. Sample Positive and Negative words

Negative Words	Positive Words
refund	Ready
delay	Sold
poor	Change
not	Coaches
worst	Selling
useless	Travels
late	Lifeline
action	Light
waiting	Response
broken	Soon
pathetic	Food
unauthorized	Help

$$x\_i^{\hat{T}} = \sum \left(\left(1 + c * \left(x_i^{\hat{A}} - x\_i^{\hat{D}} \right) \right) * w \left(-1 \right)^\wedge \left(\sum x\_i^{\hat{N}} \right) \right)$$

$$x\_i^{\hat{A}} = \sum \left(w\_{neg} * x\_i^{\hat{a}} \right)$$

$$x\_i^{\hat{D}} = \max \left(x\_i^{\hat{D'}}, -1 \right)$$

$$x\_i^{\hat{D'}} = \sum \left(-W\_neg * x\_i^{\hat{a}} + x\_i^{\hat{d}} \right)$$

$$w\_neg = \left(\sum x\_i^{\hat{N}} \right) \bmod 2$$

Table 8 shows the polarity score of sample tweets. It gives the statistics of polarity scores in terms of total sentences taken, several words considered after pre-process, the average polarity score of words and other mean and standard polarity of sample twitter data.

Table 8. Polarity score of sample Tweets

	Polarity
Total sentences	113
Total words	1168
Average polarity	-0.035
Standard Polarity	0.21
Mean Polarity	-0.168

A data structure of polarity score contains:

- **Total Sentences:** Total sentences spoken.
- **Total Words:** Total words used.
- **Ave Polarity:** The sum of all polarity scores for that group divided by a number of sentences spoken.
- **Sd Polarity:** The standard deviation of that group's sentence level polarity scores.
- **Stan Mean Polarity:** A standardized polarity score calculated by taking the average polarity score for a group divided by the standard deviation.

Figure 6 is an example of Polarity Plot to Show the Sentiment of railway passengers twitter data. It varied between -0.5 to 0.5. This is the indication of positive and negative response to opinions. From this plot, we can conclude that the neutral sentiment is showing by passengers.

ANALYSIS OF LOCATION DATA

The railway system contains both upstream and downstream transport activity relevant to a geographic location. The authorities of sections of railways together form as closed networks.

For example, connections between intercity and local services may be posted on the website but are of interest to local providers seeking to improve connection services. Therefore, it is necessary to identify those messages pertinent to the location or specific transport services for the task. Two approaches to identifying the location from social network data are either:

1. To identify the current location of the person posting the message or
2. To identify the message content.

Figure 7 shows analysis of geotagged twitter data in railways. It outlines the process involved, for an example of public transport messages analysis based on the fusion of information either in the message or attached to it.

Figure 6. Example of polarity plot

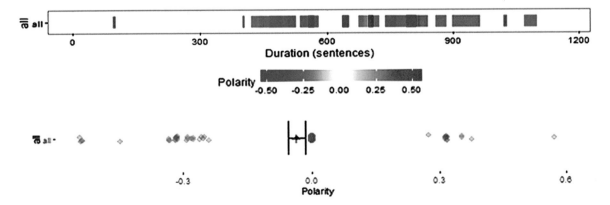

Figure 7. Analysis of geotagged Twitter data in railways

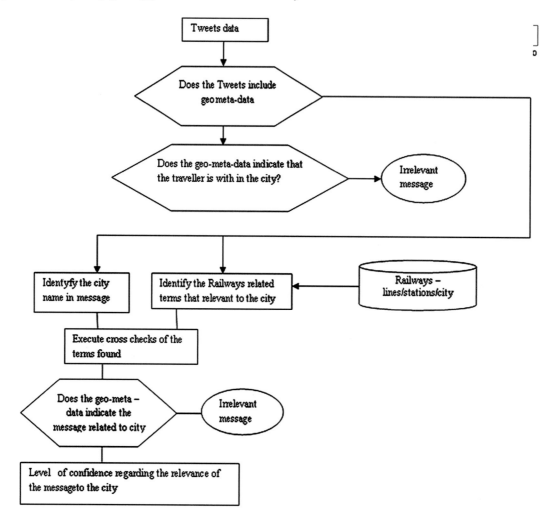

1. Message Text

A primary source of information on the location of the person posting the text message is voluntarily posted geo metadata associated with social media user account.

Limitations in Data

1. The message may link to transport in locations distinct from the user's home town while traveling.
2. Mobile Device GPS coordinates meta-data indicate the user's location, but this functionality is the user consent.

The limitations in this meta-data have been reviewed for potential location inference (Leetaru, 2013 and Andreas, 2010). Social network structures can be used for this purpose as users tend to live in close geographic proximity to their peers. And an estimate of user location may be inferred founded on the message content (Reid, 2014).

The second approach to identifying location data is taken from the contents of the message text. This task is a challenging when considering extreme ambiguity of place names. For example, "Liverpool" is the name of a UK city, a London rail station (Liveable Street), a city in the USA and an Australian suburb.

Several approaches haven proposed for identifying geolocation based on message content. Named entity recognition techniques can automatically annotate the text with mentions of entity names. Extracted location names are needed to align the inferred location with any other contextual information, in conjunction with relevant sources of location names.

The two types of social media observed were Facebook and twitter. These media functions in such a way as to assist in this and being the possibility of two-way exchanges the main advantage over standard websites. The stakeholders (authorities, ministers etc.) involve dynamic interaction with the public for example in providing a timely response to the passenger's feedback.

2. Different Modes of Use of The Media

The following are the different modes to access multimedia channels:

1. The public was strongly invited to engage with either Facebook or twitter within a section of the company website and the use of the media was purposeful.
2. The public is invited to engage with welcoming messages, the purpose of use in general or multifunctional.
3. Links to social media were given on the main website page but were small and the invitation to engage in generic
4. Logos were in website or links to twitter stream.

Now a day's most organizations had a Facebook page and twitter line that was focused on their core business. Some web pages gave links to Facebook/Twitter that was shared between organizations. One advantage of dedicated social media line or page would be an improved ability to conduct further analysis on public postings, e.g trends in sentiments or information requests.

3. Main Functions of Social Media in Railways

The main functions of social media data regarding railways are as follows:

1. **Information or Updates About Services on the Main Website:** This is one of the common types of message on Facebook from railways. This type of message was mainly one-directional i.e the main web page would not be adverse of changes to Facebook.
2. **Advising the Public on Travel Disruption:** This function is very much part of the core business survey, particularly those concerned with scheduling, timetable and ticket status.
3. **Handling Travel Queries and Complaints:** The stream of interaction between officers and the passengers is in two ways. Table 9 shows the questionnaires on different issues posted by railway passengers. Passengers show the different approaches used to deal with either straight forward or ordinary questions, personal queries or complaints.

Table 9. Questionnaires on different issues

Questionnaires Regarding Travel Booking	Responded Online
Specific Bookings	Advice to contact offline using individual personal Facebook Account
Complaints about travel	Organizations generally offered public apology offers to speak offline individually either by phone or email.

4. **Responding to Queries Around Use of Social Media:** Some of the public commented on the way in which the organization was using social media. This includes positive messages concerning the speed of responses as well as negative messages on non-response or unwanted presence on the users own social media.

5. **Seasonal Goodwill Message:** This was consistently informal in nature and aimed at promoting the concept of timelines, community, and friendly service.

CASE STUDY 2: IDENTIFICATION OF TRAVEL DEMANDS USING GEOTAGGED TWITTER DATA

From geotagged tweets, the location is identified and cross-checked with content referred locations. Figure 8 is an example of message text referred locations. This plot gives statistics as from India 268 tweets are posted out of 1000 tweets and the active locations on the social network are Delhi, Mumbai, Bengaluru, Karnataka, Hyderabad etc.

Table 10 shows statistics of location wise tweets. The geotagged locations and contents referred locations are considered as words list for finding the relevance of locations. So, these locations are considered as words set.

Figure 8. Message text referred locations

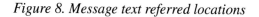

Table 10. Statistics of location wise tweets

India	Delhi	Mumbai	Bengaluru	Karnataka	Hyderabad
268	170	46	39	29	27

Text Content With Location

Figure 9 is an example of geotagged twitter data polarity plot of location based tweets. It shows the polarity score of locations found in the text.

From this plot, the average polarity is .33 from new Delhi location, neutral polarity from Pune and Lucknow cities and negative polarity from Mumbai and other places from India. Table 11 lists the polarity score on sample data of railway passenger tweets.

From the polarity score of the involvement in the social network at overall India, the level is neutral, from capital New Delhi is positive and other crowd places like Mumbai and Pune is negative.

UNDERSTANDING PASSENGER BEHAVIOUR

A key goal for all providers of rail services into London is to make sure that commuters have a safe and enjoyable journey. Yet whether the issue is delays, overcrowding or crime, rail journeys are frequently the cause of negative twitter sentiment and are frequently subject to complaints from passengers.

Our analysis of key negative language wording includes terms like "profit", "fault" and "greedy", emotional terms like "angry" and "frustrated" and more colorful phrases. We identified that there were in total an incredible 473,661 tweets using negative language between 1st April 2014 to 31st March 2015 leads to the worrying phase of rail providers who are looking forward to gaining the trust of passengers.

Figure 9. Geotagged Twitter data polarity plot

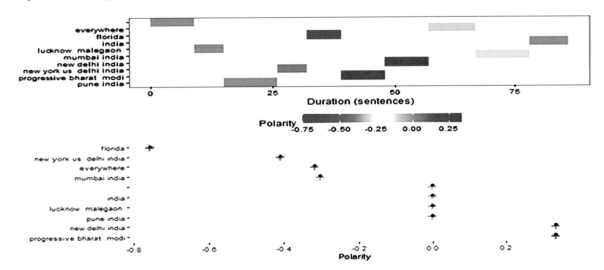

Table 11. Polarity score on sample data

Total Sentences	Total Words	Average Polarity
874	8649	-0.016

Regardless of the strength of incidents which leads the negative sentiment, it is in the interest of rail providers and the public that the negative impacts are reduced as soon as possible and in the most effective way. This may include using social media Twitter to answer criticisms, improve the handling of disturbance, share advice and reassure daily passengers that problems are being dealt when they occur.

SOLUTIONS AND RECOMMENDATIONS

The following are the solutions for different problems faced while their journey in rail from railway passenger posted tweets.

1. **Address Security Issues:** Using social media analysis, the keywords for these issues like "pickpocket", "thieves", "fight" and "drunk" are used to understand passenger difficulties in security satisfactions of their journey. The findings, displayed in the table below, show that there were 7,408 tweets using crime language during the last year. Whilst the volume of social media references to incidents of crime do not necessarily mean that crime is worse on a service. Rail providers should use this data to assess the incidence of reported crime and bridge with the relevant authorities to tackle it. For example, during periods of heavy commuter traffic, or major public events like football matches, social media analysis can play a key role in indicating incident locations, with images, videos and witness evidence being collated.

2. **Address the Services Provided by Railways:**
   a. **Hot and Cool Conditions:** Frequent customer's complaints on cool and hot extreme conditions due to improper service. During the spring and summer is the provision of adequate cooling systems. A particularly hot period, such as the summer of 2014, inevitably raises questions for rail providers in terms of effective air conditioning and cooling systems. In the summer sun and overcrowding causing daily travelers to overheat, some cases faint, ensuring properly regulated heating and cooling during different seasons is of paramount importance. A powerful mix of delays, crowding and heat creates some more uncomfortable situations for passengers, often creating strong reactions about services and these are reflected through Twitter. Using sentiment analysis keywords, we can examine the terms such as "too hot", "sauna" and "air con" measure the number of tweets issued by users on each individual rail service regarding hot and cool conditions in trains.

During the autumn and winter seasons, we examined sentiment around routine passengers complaining about poorly heated carriages on Twitter. With the varied temperatures as dropping to below freezing levels, comfort levels on poorly heated trains or long waits on windy platforms are most identified regular complaints by rail passengers. To analyze the twitter sentiment on this topic the positive words like "sub-zero", "freezer" and "icicles" are used. In this category, 12,076 tweets directed at rail operators complaining about being 'too cold' due to poor heating systems or long, cold waits.

Train providers should already be acting to improve passenger comfort, even before these statistics have been revealed. However, social media analysis can help to identify times and train services on maintenance of upgrading air conditioning or heating systems. It can be used to identify how such improvements positively impact passenger sentiment and provides operators a wonderful opportunity to share openly what measures they are taking to address this common complaint, such as the number of incidents identified, investigated and solved.

b. **Passenger Feelings About Their Rail Journey:** How customers describe situations that make them feel uncomfortable, anxious or lead to accidents are analyzed with words such as "slip", "injured", "panic" and "first aid". In an industry that prides itself on a strong safety record, looking after the wellbeing of its customers is key. Twitter provides a reliable source of data, provided by the crowd, to identify possible hazards, from narrow and slippery platforms and expired first aid boxes on trains, also to understand those conditions that cause the unhappy of passengers. As with all these areas, the key point is to encourage the passengers to contribute this data willingly and constructively for understanding and the evidence of action being taken to all concerns.

FUTURE RESEARCH DIRECTIONS

In future, passengers will increasingly be able to access data from anywhere through smart devices and cloud applications. Faster access to data will influence passenger relationship with transportation, as well as their decision making process. Passengers will expect the services certainty in terms of time, so reliable and accurate real-time information will be a key issue. Customer centric services will be based on a wealth of information about the individual passenger and their needs at that moment. These require a detailed understanding and analysis of the passenger experience measures and their satisfaction with key elements of their rail journey. This analysis is used to identify satisfaction or dissatisfaction to provide the feedback with guidance on those areas of improvement.

To improve this feedback mechanism dynamically and effectively it addresses the future of railway systems. For achieving this the future research contribution in a new framework with advanced data server as Social Internet of Things (SIoT). It includes the need of distributed environment for computing crowd dynamic data according to multiple themes like complaints on services, suggestions for improvement of service, swach Bharath (cleanliness) and security issues.

Propagation of research on Social Media through new advanced environments and effective advanced big data algorithms are needed for quick and effective processing. The theme of this book is served by this chapter to show the future needs of the railways for better decision making, monitoring of existing services and enhancements according to passenger needs. After the elaborated discussion, it directs the future research as a need of the expert system for automation of feedback process on the passenger's opinions in any of the form (SMS, web feedback, tweets in twitter etc.) with quick response for the betterment of railways.

CONCLUSION

This chapter highlights the extent to which rail passengers express their negative and positive opinions of rail services on Twitter as one of big data application. There can be many reasons for passengers choosing social media as a platform to criticize services, including the fact that it's convenient and instant. The rail industry should recognize that social media analysis can guide to improve services, by spotting the worst affected services and take meaningful action, as soon as possible.

Recommendation One

Rail providers should use their social media channels to turn around passenger's complaints and reduce negative sentiment. Too often, unsympathetic responses are given to problems reported, from delays to hot trains and batted away with the operational logic that creates a more bad feeling. Evidence, the action is being taken and a few goodwill gestures can go a long way to restoring consumer confidence.

Sites like Twitter are being used by passengers to report incidents such as a fight and alert the necessary authorities to act. They can achieve this by developing a quicker online relationship with respective officers, to gather confirmation and close incidents.

Recommendation Two

The temperature conditions of rail journeys are essential not only to the comfort of passengers also to their health and well-being. The few of the train satisfaction survey for 2015 listed "condition of the train" as key factors. This highlights the importance of passenger experience. Twitter provides to rail providers with a perpetual source of real-time dynamic information about rail services. Therefore, when looking to improve services, social media analysis should be an effective tool to pinpointing particularly challenging services and act to improve them.

Recommendation Three

The relationship between passengers and rail providers simply must develop, and the astonishing 473,661 tweets using negative language indicates that there is still abundant room for improvement. This association needs to be concentrate by rail providers trying to engage the public with regular updates online, which is moving beyond timetable and departure updates to provide evidence that passenger reported issues, ranging from comforts to costs of antisocial behavior are being addressed.

ACKNOWLEDGMENT

This research was supported by the Institute of Aeronautical Engineering under the research grant founded by Department of Science and Technology [grant number: File No. DST/TSG/AMT/2015/202/G dated 11.05.2016].

REFERENCES

Abbasi, A., Rashidi, T. H., Maghrebi, M., & Waller, S. T. (2015). Utilizing Location Based Social Media in Travel Survey Methods: bringing Twitter data into the play. In *Proceedings of the 8th ACM SIGSPATIAL International Workshop on Location-Based Social Networks*. ACM.

Avineri, E. (2004). A Cumulative Prospect Theory Approach to Passengers Behavior Modeling: Waiting Time Paradox Revisited. *Journal of Intelligent Transportation Systems, 8*(4), 195–204. doi:10.1080/15472450490523856

Blei, D. M., Ng, A. Y., & Jordan, M. I. (2003). Latent Dirichlet Allocation. *Journal of Machine Learning Research, 3*, 993–1022.

Bollen, J., Mao, H., & Pepe, A. (2011). Modeling Public Mood and Emotion: Twitter Sentiment and Socio-Economic Phenomena. In *Proceedings of the Fifth International AAAI Conference on Weblogs and Social Media.*

Bollen, J., Mao, H., & Zeng, X.-J. (2011). Twitter mood predicts the stock market. *Journal of computer science, 2*(1), 21-28.

Chung, J., & Mustafaraj, E. (2011). Can Collective Sentiment Expressed on Twitter Predict Political Elections? In *Proceedings of the 25th AAAI Conference on Artificial Intelligence*, San Francisco, CA (pp 1770-1771).

Collins, C., Hasan, S., & Ukkusuri, S. V. (2013). A novel transit rider satisfaction metric: Rider sentiments measured from online social media data. *Journal of Public Transportation, 16*(2), 21–45. doi:10.5038/2375-0901.16.2.2

Dan, K., & Manning, C. D. (2003). Accurate unlexicalized parsing. In *Proceedings of the 41st Meeting of the Association for Computational Linguistics* (pp 423 – 430).

Denai, M. A., Palis, F., & Zeghbib, A. (2007). Modeling and control of nonlinear systems using soft computing techniques. *Applied Soft Computing, 7*(3), 728–738. doi:10.1016/j.asoc.2005.12.005

Fu, K., Nune, R., & Tao, J. X. (2015). Social Media Data Analysis for Traffic Incident Detection and Management. In *Proceedings of the Transportation Research Board 94th Annual Meeting.*

Gao, H., Tang, J., & Liu, H. (2012). *Exploring Social-Historical Ties on Location-Based Social Networks.*

Grant-Muller, S. M., Gal-Tzur, A., Minkov, E., Kuflik, T., Nocera, S., & Shoor, I. (2016). Transport Policy: Social Media and User-Generated Content in a Changing Information Paradigm. In *Social media for government services* (pp. 325–366). Springer International Publishing.

Hasan, S., & Ukkusuri, S. V. (2014). Social contagion process in informal warning networks to understand evacuation timing behavior. *Journal of Public Health Management and Practice, 19*, S68–S69. doi:10.1097/PHH.0b013e31828f1a19 PMID:23529072

Hasan, S., & Ukkusuri, S. V. (2015). Urban activity pattern classification using topic models from online geo-location data. *Transportation Research Part C, Emerging Technologies, 44*, 363–381. doi:10.1016/j.trc.2014.04.003

Jin, X., & Jia, W. (2008). *Review of Researches on Artificial Neural Network* (pp. 65–66).

Jin, X., & Jia, W. (2008). *Review of Researches on Artificial Neural Network* (pp. 65–66).

Kaigo, M. (2012). Social media usage during disasters and social capital: Twitter and the Great East Japan earthquake. *Keio Communication Review, 34*, 19–35.

Kaplan, A. M., & Haenlein, M. (2010). Users of the world, unite! The challenges and opportunities of Social Media. *Business Horizons*, *53*(1), 59–68. doi:10.1016/j.bushor.2009.09.003

Lee, J. H. et al.. (2015). Can Twitter data be used to validate travel demand models*?* In *Proceedings of the 14th International Conference on Travel Behaviour Research*, Windsor, UK.

Lee, J. H., Davis, A. W., & Goulias, K. G. (2016). Activity Space Estimation with Longitudinal Observations of Social Media Data. In *Proceedings of the 95th Annual Meeting of the Transportation Research Board*.

Leetaru, K., Wang, S., Cao, G., Padmanabhan, A., & Shook, E. (2013). Mapping the global Twitter heartbeat: The geography of Twitter. *First Monday*, *18*(5). doi:10.5210/fm.v18i5.4366

Madhubala, M., & Narasimha Prasad, L. V. (2017). Automatic Assessment of Floods Impact Using Twitter Data. *International Journal of Civil Engineering and Technology*, *8*(5), 1228–1238.

Social Media: How to tweet your customers' right. (n. d.).

Nepal, S., Paris, C., & Georgakopoulos, D. (Eds.). (2015). *Social Media for Government Services*. Springer International Publishing.

Priedhorsky, R., Culotta, A., & Del, S. Y. (2014). Inferring the origin locations of tweets with quantitative confidence. In *Proceeding CSCW '14* (pp 1523-1536). doi:10.1145/2531602.2531607

Qiang, Z., Bin, W., Rui, Z., & Xia, X.C. (2008). Genetic Algorithm-Based Design for DNA Sequences Sets. *Chinese Journal of Computers*, *31*(12), 2193-2199.

Qiu, S., & Wang, Q. (2009). Freeway traffic incident detection based on BP neural network. In *China Measurement & Test* (pp. 48-52).

Rashidi, T., Auld, J., & Mohammadian, A. (2013). The effectiveness of Bayesian Updating Attributes in Data Transferability Applications: Transportation Research Record. *Journal of the Transportation Research Board*, *2344*, 1–9. doi:10.3141/2344-01

Schweitzer, L. (2012). How are we doing? opinion mining customer sentiment in us transit agencies and airlines via twitter. In *Proceedings of the Transportation Research Board 91st Annual Meeting*.

Sood, S., & Owsley, S. Kristian J Hammond & Larry Birnbaum. (2007). Reasoning through Search: A Novel Approach to Sentiment Classification. In *Proceedings of WWW '07 conference*.

Steiger, E., Ellersiek, T., & Zipf, A. (2014). Explorative public transport flow analysis from uncertain social media data. In *Proceedings of the 3rd ACM SIGSPATIAL International Workshop on Crowdsourced and Volunteered Geographic Information*, 1-7.

Steur, R. (2015). *Twitter as a spatiotemporal source for incident management* [Master thesis]. Utrecht University, Netherlands.

Wiegand, M., Balahur, A., Roth, B., Klakow, D., & Montoya, A. (2010). A Survey on the Role of Negation in Sentiment Analysis. In *Proceedings of the Workshop on NeSp-NLP '10*.

Chapter 8
Intelligent Transport Systems Services in VANETs and Case Study in Urban Environment

Hamid Barkouk
Abdelmalek Essaâdi University, Morocco

El Mokhtar En-Naimi
Abdelmalek Essaâdi University, Morocco

ABSTRACT

The VANET (Vehicular Ad hoc Network) is a collection of mobile nodes forming a temporary network on variable topology, operating without base station and without centralized administration. Communication is possible between vehicles within each other's radio range as well as with fixed components on road side infrastructure. The characteristics of VANET network that distinguishes it from other ad hoc networks, such as high mobility and communication with the infrastructure to support security or comfort applications, have prompted researchers to develop models and mobility specific protocols. The main goal of this chapter is firstly to compare the performance of three Ad hoc routing protocols: OLSR, AODV and DSDV, and secondly to examine the impact of varying mobility, density and pause time on the functionality of these protocols. The results of this chapter demonstrate that AODV have better performance in terms of Throughput and Packets Delivery Rate (PDR), whereas OLSR have best performance in terms of Packet Delivery Time (Delay).

INTRODUCTION

The integration of wireless communications technology between vehicles has begun some years ago and has led to Vehicular AdHoc Network (VANET). This technology is derived from mobile ad hoc networks (MANET), which also gave birth to the Wireless Sensor Networks (WSN). Thus, the practicality of MANETs is applied in WSNs and VANETs. If WSNs are spatially distributed to monitor physical or environmental conditions, such as temperature, sound, pressure, etc. VANETs are used in intelligent transport systems (ITS). ITSs are designed to offer to passengers and vehicles, road safety services (ac-

DOI: 10.4018/978-1-5225-3176-0.ch008

cident alert, driver assistance, traffic flow optimization, congestion reduction, etc.) and comfort services (Internet access, games, etc.) (Singh & Verma, 2013). One of the challenges of VANET networks is the efficient and timely dissemination of information with reasonable use of resources. Road safety applications are the main motivation of vehicle networks and have two major requirements, speed and reliability. Multi-hop communication is an important component of these applications.

In VANETs environment, a few issues and requirements are imposed, such as driver's behavior, different road topology, size of the network, multi-path and roadside obstacles, trip models, mobility and varying vehicular speed, etc. For these various reasons, Deploying and testing VANETs involves high cost, intensive labor and security constraints in real world, so simulation is a useful alternative in research prior to real implementation.

Figure 1 shows a part of VANET networks constraint.

Simulating a VANET involves two different aspects, the First, is related to the communication among vehicles and the second is related to the mobility of the VANET nodes. To achieve author's simulation objective, we have chosen three widely used simulators, NS-2.34 as network simulator and Move-2.92 and Sumo-0.12.3 as mobility simulator.

The routing process in the VANTE networks is an important issue that requires a thorough study before network deployment, the data packets are routed from the source node to the destination node using the vehicles available as relays, the large number of Vehicles, high dynamic and frequent change in vehicle density increase the challenge of the routing process.

Traffic lights and vehicle movement conditions cause frequent partitions in VANET networks and make routing a more difficult process. In our chapter, we will proceed to comparative study of two types of routing protocols belonging to topology based routing protocol class, proactive and reactive protocols.

The remainder of the chapter is organized as follows: Section III briefly discusses the ITS for Rail. Section IV discusses the ITS for VANET and precisely, the processes and constraints of routing in VANET, classification of different VANET routing protocols and an overview of the three routing protocols AODV, DSDV and OLSR. The section V shows the simulation results and performance comparison of the three above said routing protocols.

Figure 1. Future of Intelligent Transport Systems (ITS)
Future of Intelligent Transport Systems, 2011.

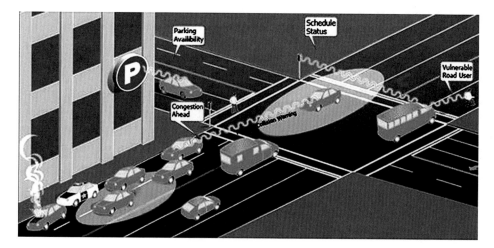

BACKGROUND

Since routing process is critical and important to achieve the objectives designed for VANETs networks, the study of various existing protocols and the designing of more advanced protocols is very challenging. In this context, this research chapter is designed to enrich the various existing research related to performance evaluation of VANET routing protocols. The majority of researches that have studied VANET routing protocols have used Random way point mobility model (Rajeshkumar & Sivakumar, 2013; Wasiq, Arshad, Javaid, & Bibi, 2011; Mohapatra & Kanungo, 2011; Kumar & Hans, 2015; Vats, Sachdeva, Saluja & Rathee, 2012). or manual mobility schema of nodes (Singh & Verma. 2013). In this chapter, the authors have user two network schemas, the first one is created manually and the second is a real schema provided by google Openstreetmap service. To do so, the authors used different simulation parameters and the most used tools to generate the results closer to reality.

INTELLIGENT TRANSPORT SYSTEM FOR RAIL

Cars of the future will be smarter and communicate with each other and with the surrounding infrastructure. The technology behind it is called V2X (Vehicle To Infrastructure) which will make traffic more efficient and will meet the growing needs for more road safety and comfort. Several scientific researches are already being carried out to apply the V2X technology in the field of communication between rail and road. This technology is suitable to be used for road-rail interactive uses cases (e.g. level crossings) as well as for pure railway use cases (e.g. information at platforms). Nevertheless, the automation and protection systems of the Road2Rail or Rail2Rail need to ensure the safety and performance of the operation.

1. **Positive Train Control:** Positive Train Control (PTC) refers to communication-based/processor-based train control technology designed to control train movements with safety, security, precision, and efficiency. The benefits of PTC system are (RTD integrates Positive Train Control into commuter rail lines) and (Hartong, Goel, Farkas, & Wijesekera, 2007):

   a. Prevent Train-to-train collisions.
   b. Prevents unsafe speeds on train track.
   c. Prevent Incursions into established work zone limits.
   d. Keeps trains from unsafely crossing rail switches (rail redirects).

   PTC is an overlay technology on existing reactive train control systems such as Automatic Train Control (ATC) and Automatic Train Stop (ATS) which would not prevent collisions under all circumstances. PTC is based on robust, predictive technology that detects upcoming conditions and takes control of the train when needed. A signal to stop the train will be send to the operators in case of over-speed, another train is stopped on the tracks ahead or maintenance crews are out working on the alignment. If the operator does not respond within eight seconds, the train will automatically slow to a stop.
   Figure 2 illustrates PTC infrastructure and slowing or stopping a train before an accident.

2. **Railway Collision Avoidance System (RCAS):** The implementation of safety-of-life services in transportation systems, e.g. for applications like collision avoidance of trains, requires reliable and

Figure 2. PTC infrastructure and functionalities
D. Scaper.

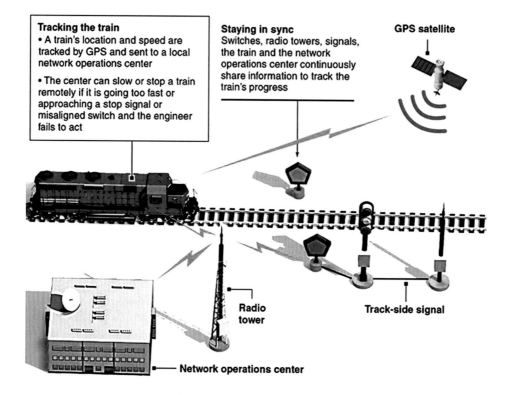

instantaneous information exchange. The german aerospace center Deutsches Zentrum für Luft- und Raumfahrt (DLR) is developing a Railway Collision Avoidance System (RCAS). a 'safety overlay' system which can be deployed on top of any existing safety infrastructure in train networks. RCAS will allow a train driver to have an up-to-date accurate knowledge of the traffic situation in the vicinity, and act in consequence (Strang, Hörste, & Gu, 2006; Rico-Garcia, Lehner, Strang, & Rockl, 2007; Lehner, Rico-García & Strang, 2011).

The idea of the Railway Collision Avoidance System (RCAS) is similar to the airborne Traffic Alert and Collision Avoidance System / Automatic Dependent Surveillance-Broadcast (TCAS/ADS-B) and the maritime Automatic Identification System (AIS). RCAS calculate the own position and movement vector and broadcast this information as well as additional data such as vehicle dimensions to all other trains in the area which is only limited by the range of the RCAS-sender. The train driver's cabin is equipped with a display showing the position of the other vehicles in the region. The RCAS-units analyse the received information, and compare position and movement vector with the own one to detect possible collisions, at this case an alert is displayed and the driver is advised of the most appropriate strategy to follow in order to avoid the danger (Rico-García, Strang, & Lehner, 2008).

Figure 3 illustrates the RCAS infrastructure.

Figure 3. RCAS infrastructure
Source: www.hbl.in/publicimages.png

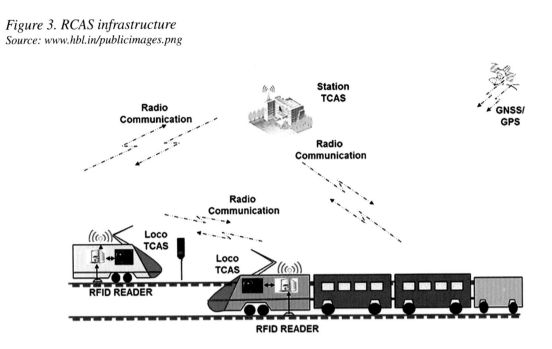

INTELLIGENT TRANSPORT SYSTEM FOR VANET

Processes and Constraints of VANET Routing

Due to the special characteristics of VANETs (Guizani, 2012), the routing process is a significant problem that needs advanced study before the effective deployment of the network. The data packets are send from the source node to the destination node by using vehicles available as a relay, the large number of vehicles, high mobility and the frequent change of vehicle density increase the challenge of the routing process. Cross the traffic lights, high mobility, rapid topology changing and vehicle traffic conditions, cause frequent disconnections and networks partitioning in VANETs that will make the routing process more difficult (Hartenstein & Laberteaux, 2010).

VANET Routing Protocols Classification

The VANET routing protocols fall into two major categories of topology-based and geographic based routing. In topology-based routing, each node should be aware of the network layout, also should able to forward packets using information about available nodes and links in the network. In contrast, geographic based routing should be aware of the nodes locations in the packet forwarding. The two classes are shown in Figure 2. (Kumar & Tyagi, 2014; Dhankhar & Agrawal, 2014; Beydoun, 2009).

Topology Based Routing Protocols

Due to their functionality, the topology based Routing protocols are classified into three types such as Reactive, Proactive and Hybrid protocols (Anggoro, Kitasuka, Nakamura, & Aritsugi, 2012; Beydoun, 2009).

Proactive Protocols

This type of protocol is proactive because, without requesting it, it receives information on the topology, which is constantly updated by the regular exchange of packets of the topology of Network between the nodes of the same network. Each node stores in its memory an absolute image of the network until it receives a new one. This recent network information therefore allows a minimum waiting time for determining the route to be taken, which is particularly important for the critical traffic time.

When routing information becomes unnecessary, quickly, many short routes are available to them. These, determined previously and remain unused, must be used before becoming invalid. These unused roads cause another inconvenience resulting from mobility: the large amount of over-traffic (Traffic Overhead) or waste of bandwidth generated when evaluating these unnecessary routes.

Unnecessary overhead directly influences network performance when the number of vehicles becomes large, resulting generation of a large number of packets, containing update information, which may congest the network.

Proactive protocols work best for networks that have low node mobility. Here are some types of these protocols:

- Optimized Link State Routing (OLSR)
- Fish-Eye State Routing (FSR)
- Destination-Sequenced Distance Vector (DSDV)
- Cluster-head Gateway Switch Routing Protocol (CGSR)

Figure 4. Schema of various routing protocols in VANET

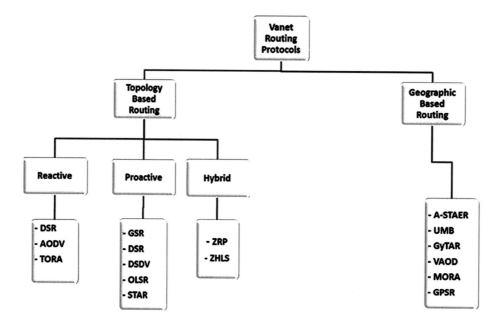

Reactive Protocols

The reactive protocols also known as on demand routing protocolsare based on the principle that there is no information on the topology of the network, since the network is in constant evolution. Therefore, whenever a node requires information about a route for a given target, it initiates a route discovery process.

The reactive protocols therefore update the roads on request. These protocols attempt to establish a route when a node requests to initiate communication with a node for which there is no route. This type of protocol is usually based on flooding of the network with Route Request (RREQ) messages and Route Reply (RREP) messages.

RREQ messages let you discover the route from the source to the target node. When the target node receives an RREQ message, it sends a RREP message to confirm that the route has been established and that it has transmitted the information. These RREQ and RREP messages are very important for updating the different routes (destinations).

This type of routing protocol is very effective for single-Hop networks because it typically minimizes the number of hops for the selected path and saves bandwidth.

Here are some types of these protocols:

- Ad hoc On Demand Distance Vector (AODV)
- Dynamic Source routing protocol (DSR)
- Temporarily ordered routing algorithm (TORA)
- Associativity Based routing (ABR)
- Signal Stability-Based Adaptive Routing (SSA)
- Location-Aided Routing Protocol (LAR

Table 1 shows comparison between reactive and proactive routing protocols.

Hybrid Protocols

Hybrid protocols simultaneously implement proactive routing and reactive routing. They use a proactive technique in a small area around the source where the number of hops is relatively small (Exp. three to four hops), and use reactive technique for the most distant nodes. The ZRP and CBRP protocols belong to this category. ZRP is essentially based on an area concept. A zone regroups the set of nodes at a maximum distance of X-hops from the reference node. Routing within a routing (intra-zone) zone is done proactively using a link state protocol. The routing to nodes outside this routing zone (interzone) is car-

Table 1. Advantages and disadvantages of reactive and proactive routing protocols

Topology-Based Routing Protocols	Reactive Routing Protocols (On-Demand)	Proactive Routing Protocols (Table-Driven)
Advantages	1. On-demand flooding of the network occurs to update the routing table. 2. Saves bandwidth as these protocols are beaconless	1. Route discovery is not required. 2. Real-time application latency is low.
Disadvantages	Have high route determining latency. 2. High flooding in the network causes disturbance in node communication.	Required part of the available bandwidth is occupied by unused path

Source: (Dhankhar & Agrawal, 2014).

ried out in a reactive manner. We distinguish two procedures: IARP and IERP respectively for intrazone and interzone routings. A second example of hybrid routing is the CBRP protocol. In this protocol, the network is decomposed into clusters. Each cluster consists of clusterheads, gateways (or routing nodes) as well as basic nodes. The role of clusterheads is first to discover the routing paths, then to retransmit the packets to the destination, and finally to maintain the routing paths. Gateway nodes have

Their neighborhood two or more clusterheads. When two clusterheads want to communicate, the gateway nodes act as a relay node to ensure the retransmission of packets between the clusterheads. The reactive aspect of the CBRP protocol appears when a node wishes to send data to a destination node; It then dispatches a request for a path request only to the representatives of the groups, in other words, to the clusterheads. The representative of the group when it receives the request, checks if the destination node is in the group, otherwise it retransmits the request to the representatives of the neighboring groups (Atéchian, 2010) and (Beydoun, 2009).

The advantage of hybrid protocols is that they are better suited to large size networks. However, this type of protocol combines the disadvantages of the proactive protocols and those of reactive protocols, such as exchange of regular control packets and flooding the whole network to seek a route to a remote node.

Geographical Routing Protocols

The routing protocols based on the position, also known as geographic protocols, require a location service such as GPS, for routing packets in the network. However, most of these protocols generate a lot of control packets that cause network congestion (Dhankhar & Agrawal, 2014; Rajeshkumar & Sivakumar, 2013).

Geographic routing protocols are the most suitable for ad hoc vehicle networks, since the routing mechanism is based on the geographical data of the nodes. In these protocols, the destination is represented by a specified region, also called a target region. Any node, within the target region, receives the packet when it is broadcast. The geographic routing protocols involve two steps: the first step is to retransmit the packet on a routing path constructed within a given area, known as the Forwarding Zone. The second step is to distribute the packet to the nodes within the target region (Geocast Region). The major difference between the different protocols of routing appears especially in the mechanism of retransmission of the packets (Atéchian, 2010; Salameh, 2011).

Example: GPSR, GyTAR.

Table 2 shows comparison between geographical topology-based routing protocols.

Optimized Link State Routing (OLSR)

OLSR is a routing protocol for ad-hoc networks based on the link state algorithm and is proactive because it uses periodic message exchanges to maintain information on the network topology at each node.

OLSR tries to limit the number of control messages by optimizing their number and distribution across the entire network. To do this, it relies on the election of multipoint relays (or Multi-Point Relays, MPRs) among the neighbors of each of the nodes of the network that will be the only ones to relay the messages of control of their voters (called multipoint relay selectors).

Table 2. Difference between topology-based and position-based routing protocols

VANET Routing Protocols	Topology-Based Routing Protocols	Position-Based Routing Protocols
Methodology	1. Use shortest path algorithms. 2. Packet forwarding is done based on link information stored in routing table.	1. Position determining service is used. 2. Vehicle position is required to forward data packets.
Benefits/ Strength	1. Route discovery is required to search best possible shortest route between source node and destination node. 2. Beaconless. 3. Suitable for unicast, multicast and broadcast routing.	1. Route discovery and maintaining protocol routes is not required. 2. Beaconing 3. Support high mobile environment.
Limitations	1. Use more overhead. 2. Route discovery and delay constraint maintenance. 3. Failure in discovering complete path due to frequent network changes.	1. Give least overhead. 2. Position finding services. 3. Deadlock may occur in location server.
Remarks	1. Basically proposed for MANETs. 2. Give less overhead and suitable for small networks.	1. Suitable for large networks such as VANETs. 2. Research is in progress for control congestion and small networks.

Source: (Dhankhar & Agrawal, 2014).

The way in which the MPRs are chosen makes possible to have optimized distribution of the control information over the whole network, by minimizing the overhead (in particular by avoiding during broadcasts that a node receives the same message from different Sources).

Moreover, the election of this sub-graph of the network makes it possible to ensure a limitation of the number of messages and links announced. In the standard configuration of OLSR, only the MPRs announce their links with their voters. This information is sufficient to determine a route from one point to another of the network (Clausen et al., 2003; Clausen & Jacquet, 2003; El Ali, 2012; Spaho, Ikeda, Barolli, & Xhafa, 2013).

Figure 5. Schema of OLSR network schema

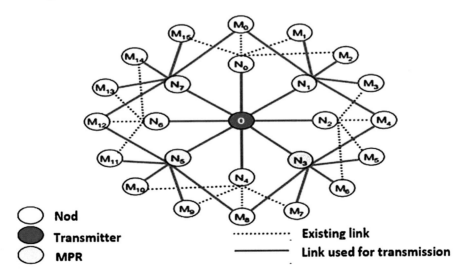

Ad Hoc On-Demand Distance Vector (AODV)

AODV "Ad hoc On Demand Distance Vector" Represents essentially an improvement of the DSDV algorithm. The AODV protocol reduces the number of message broadcasts and creates routes if necessary. The AODV is based on the use of the two mechanisms "Road Discovery" and "Road Maintenance" (used by the DSR), in addition to node-to-node routing, sequence number principle and exchange periodic.

The AODV uses the principles of sequence numbers to maintain the consistency of the routing information. Because of the mobility of the nodes in the ad hoc networks, the roads change frequently so that the roads maintained by certain nodes become invalid. The sequence numbers allow you to use the most recent routes.

In the same way, as in the DSR, the AODV uses a route request in order to create a path to a certain destination. However, the AODV maintains the paths in a distributed way by keeping a routing table at each node of transit belonging to the path sought. An entry in the routing table contains essentially:

1. The address of the destination
2. The next node
3. Distance in number of nodes (i.e. the number of nodes necessary to reach the destination)
4. The destination sequence number
5. The expiration time of the table entry

When a (intermediate) transit node sends the request packet to a neighbor, it also saves the identifier of the node from which the first copy of the request is received. This information is used to construct the reverse path, which will be traversed by the packet (route response) (this means that the AODV only supports symmetric links). Since the packet (route response) will be sent to the source, the nodes belonging to the return path will modify their routing tables along the path contained in the response packet. A node broadcasts a route request (RREQ: Route REQuest), in case it needs to know a route to a certain destination and such route is unavailable or the path to that destination has expired.

The destination sequence number field of the RREQ packet contains the last known value of the sequence number associated with the destination node. This value is copied from the routing table. If the sequence number is not known, the null value will be taken by default. The source sequence number of the RREQ packet contains the value of the sequence number of the source node.

The AODV routing protocol is designed for the mobile ad hoc networks with populations of tens to thousands of the mobile nodes. AODV can handle low, moderate and relatively high mobility rates, as well as a variety of data traffic levels. AODV has been designed to reduce dissemination of control traffic and eliminate overhead on data traffic, in order to improve scalability and performance (Anggoro, Kitasuka, Nakamura, & Aritsugi, 2012), (Manvi & Kakkasageri, 2009) and (Spaho, Ikeda, Barolli, & Xhafa, 2013).

Destination-Sequenced Distance-Vector (DSDV)

Bellman and Ford designed a centralized algorithm to compute shortest paths in weighted graphs. Bertsekas and Gallager designed it to be executed in a distributed fashion, which is called Distributed Bellman–Ford (DBF) algorithm (Singh & Verma. 2013) and (Wasiq, Arshad, Javaid, & Bibi, 2011). In

Figure 6. Route discovery in AODV

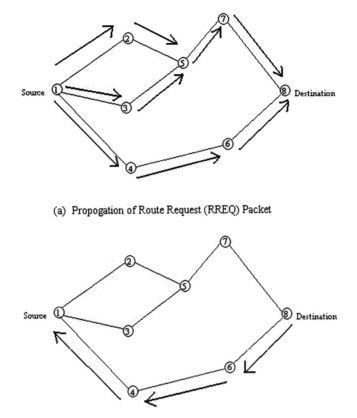

(a) Propogation of Route Request (RREQ) Packet

(b) Path taken by the Route Reply (RREP) Packet

distributed Bellman-Ford (DBF), each and every node maintains a cost to reach to every known destination. Thus, the routing table consists of entries. In the beginning, all the routing tables are empty and each node starts issuing periodic broadcast messages to its 1-hop neighborhood. Main disadvantage of DBF is that it suffers from a bouncing problem that leads to the count-to-infinity and looping issues. Loops can appear if out-of-date information is used to compute the shortest path. The main objective behind the designing of DSDV is to maintain simplicity and to avoid loop formation. In DSDV, to communicate with each other, each node refers its routing tables that are stored at each node of the network. Each routing table at each of the node has information regarding all available destinations and the number of hops to reach. To maintain consistency in dynamically varying topology, each node shares its routing entries with its neighbor either periodically or immediately when significant new information is available (Spaho, Ikeda, Barolli, & Xhafa, 2013). Each mobile node has its new sequence number and the following information for each new route:

- The destination's IP address.
- The number of hops required to reach the destination.
- The sequence number of the information received regarding that destination as originally marked by the destination.

Figure 7.

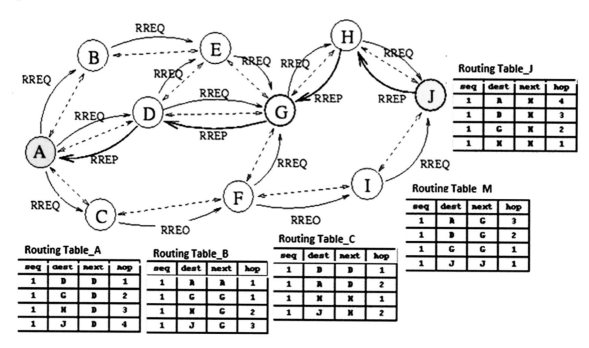

SIMULATIONS

1. **Simulation Objectives:** The main objective of the simulation is the comparison between the tree protocols, Optimized Link State Routing (OLSR) and Destination-Sequenced Distance Vector (DSDV) as proactive routing protocol and Ad-hoc On-Demand Distance Vector (AODV) reactive routing protocol, to measure their performance parameters (Packet Delivery Rate (PDR), Throughput, Average Time Delivery of Packets) by varying some network properties such as Mobility, Density and the Pause Time of nodes.

2. **Performance Metrics:** For network simulation, there are several performance metrics which is used to evaluate the performance. In this chapter, the authors has considered three performance metrics, the packet delivery rate (PDR), Average End-to-End Delay and throughput (Anggoro, Kitasuka, Nakamura, & Aritsugi, 2012). All metrics are measured as described below (Balandin, Andreev, & Koucheryavy, 2015) and (Salameh, 2011).

   a. **Throughput:** Is the average transfer rate of data between two end nodes in a network.

The highest flow identifies better performance of the routing protocol. It's calculated as follows:

$$Throughput\left(Kbits\right) = \frac{\Sigma SRP}{\left(SST - EST\right)}$$

SRP: Size of Received Packets
SST: Start Simulation Time

EST: End Simulation Time

b. **Packets Delivery rates (PDR):** Is the ratio between the number of packets received and the number of packets sent. It is calculated as follows:

$$Packets\ Delivery\ rates \left(\%\right) = \frac{\Sigma RP}{\Sigma SP}$$

RP: Received Packet
SP: Send Packet

c. **Average End-to-End Delay:** The average time that a packet takes to travel the network from a source to its destination. This is the time from the generation of the packet in the sender up to its reception at the destination (successfully delivered messages).

The average of the lowest end-to-end shows the best performance of the routing protocol. It is calculated as follows:

$$Average\ End-to-End\ Delay \left(ms\right) = \frac{\Sigma \left(PRT - PTT\right)}{\Sigma RP} * 1000$$

PRT: Packet Reception Time
PTT: Packet Transmission Time
RP: Received Packets

3. **Simulation Tools:** Performance evaluation was carried out for OLSR, AODV and DSDV routing protocols under the operating system Ubuntu 10.04 by using SUMO0.12.3 and MOVE-2.92 as generators of mobility and NS2 version 34 as network simulator.
   a. **SUMO (Simulation of Urban Mobility):** SUMO is a free and open source traffic simulation suite, implemented in 2001, portable and simulates road mobility designed to manage major road networks. It's mainly developed by employees of the Institute of Transportation Systems at the German Aerospace Centre. Some important features of SUMO are: Support for different types of vehicles, multi-lane roads with lane change, the rules of priority at intersections, supporting a graphical user interface, dynamic routing of vehicles and can use different formats to generate its output files (SUMO) and (Basagni, Ivan Stojmenovic & Giordano, 2012).
   b. **MOVE (Mobility Model Generation for Vehicular Networks):** MOVE is another open-source tool built on top of SUMO, which generates files traces of mobility used by NS-2 and QualNet. One of its characteristics is the set of GUIs (Graphical User Interfaces) that allow users to generate easily and faster mobility scenarios. Moreover, using these graphical interfaces, users can avoid having to write scripts from the beginning to describe scenarios of motion simulation and they do not need to know details of sub mobility simulator used (e.g. SUMO) and (Pathan, Monowar, & Khan, 2014) (Basagni, Ivan Stojmenovic, & Giordano, 2012).

Figure 8. Manual schema

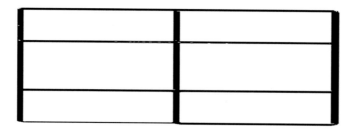

c.   **NS2 (Network Simulator):** NS2 is an open source emulator designed specifically for research in computer communication networks. Since its inception in 1989, NS2 has continuously generated considerable interest from industry, academia and government. NS2 now contains modules for many network components, such as the routing, transport layer protocol, application, etc. To examine network performance, NS-2 was originally intended for simulation of TCP, routing, and multicast protocols over wired and wireless networks. To increase the effectiveness of treatment, the primary driver of NS-2 is written in C + + programming language that defines the operations of the various objects that make up a network. Some examples of network objects are the nodes, links, agents and protocols such as routing, transport and application protocols (Network Simulator ns-2), (Salameh, 2011) and (Basagni, Stojmenovic, & Giordano, 2012).

4.   **Simulation Scenarios:**

a.   **Network Schema:** The authors have used both MOVE and SUMO tools to create the two network schemas below, the first is created manually and the second is based on "open street map" service. The first schema is the basis of our simulation.

i.   Manual Schema;

ii.   Real Schema Based on "Open Street Map" Service (Boulevard Pasteur – Tangier-Morocco).

b.   **Simulation Parameters:** In this simulation, we used environment size 650 m x 750 m, node density 10 to 100 nodes, variable speed 5 to 80 m/s and variable pause time 0 to 120 s. The network parameters we have used for our simulation purpose are shown in Table 3 (Pathan, Monowar, & Khan, 2014).

c.   **Simulation Steps:** The steps of the simulation are the following:

i.   Generate roads network diagram: Use MOVE for manual schema; Use the Open-Street-Map service for real schema.

ii.   Generate TCL file

iii. Generate the trace file

Figure 9. View of a cross in the manual schema

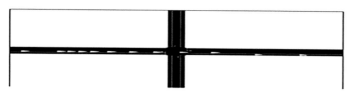

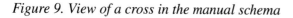

Figure 10. Boulevard Pasteur-Tangier-Morocco

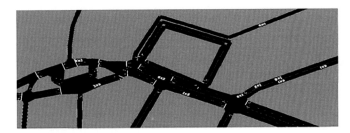

Figure 11. View of a cross in "Boulevard Pasteur"

Table 3. Simulation parameters

Parameter	Value
Topology Area	650m*750 m
Protocol	OLSR & AODV & DSDV
Simulation Time (s)	200 s
Mobile Nodes	10, 20, 40, 80,100
Nodes Speed (m/s)	5, 10, 20,40,80 m/s
Pause Time	0,30,60,90,120 s
Traffic Type	CBR/UDP
Mobility model	Urban scenarios, Created on Move-2.92 et Sumo-0.12.3
Network simulator	NS-2.34
Packet size	512 Bytes

    iv.   Analyze the results of trace files using AWK (language for processing text files).

    v.   Visualize the results using MS-Excel, Xgraph, Gnuplot, etc.

Figure 12 illustrates the details of the simulation steps (Salameh, 2011).

SIMULATION RESULTS AND ANALYSIS

Case 1

Effect of varying nodes Mobility on the Delay, PDR and the Throughput of AODV, OLSR and DSDV

Figure 12. VLAN simulation steps for manual schema

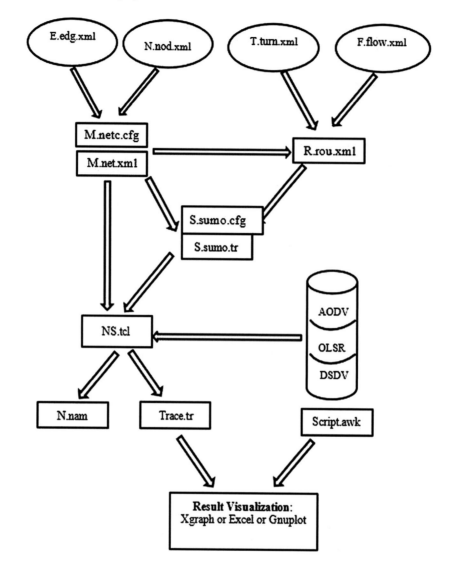

In this case, we analyze the effect of varying the nodes speed on the Average End-to-End Delay, the packet delivery rate and on the throughput for the three protocols, AODV, OLSR and DSDV.

We kept some parameters constant: Simulation time is 200 seconds and the number of vehicles is 40. As shown in Figure 13-15, we conclude the following results.

Result 1

The Figure 13 shows that:

- The delay of OLSR is the Lowest relative to DSDV and AODV.
- The delay of DSDV is lower than AODV.

Figure 13. Varying speed vs. delay (ms)

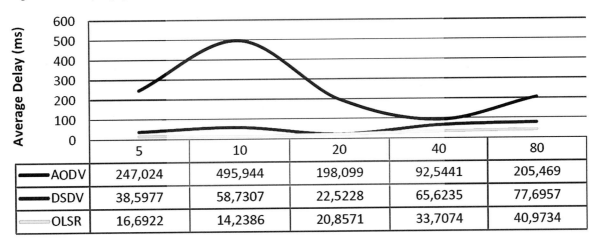

	5	10	20	40	80
AODV	247,024	495,944	198,099	92,5441	205,469
DSDV	38,5977	58,7307	22,5228	65,6235	77,6957
OLSR	16,6922	14,2386	20,8571	33,7074	40,9734

Figure 14. Varying speed vs. PDR (%)

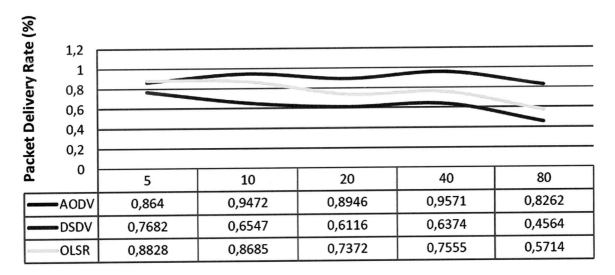

	5	10	20	40	80
AODV	0,864	0,9472	0,8946	0,9571	0,8262
DSDV	0,7682	0,6547	0,6116	0,6374	0,4564
OLSR	0,8828	0,8685	0,7372	0,7555	0,5714

Result 2

The Figure 14 shows that:

- The packets delivery rate of AODV is significantly higher than that of OLSR and DSDV. We recorded consistent packets delivery fraction values of AODV in different speed value.
- OLSR achieved higher value of packets delivery rate in different speed value than DSDV.

Result 3

The Figure 15 shows that:

Figure 15. Varying speed vs. throughput (Kbits)

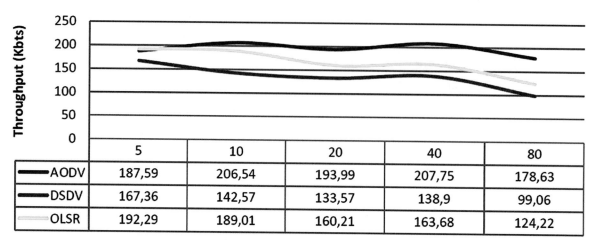

	5	10	20	40	80
AODV	187,59	206,54	193,99	207,75	178,63
DSDV	167,36	142,57	133,57	138,9	99,06
OLSR	192,29	189,01	160,21	163,68	124,22

- AODV has recorded higher throughput values in high and low mobility. In this case, AODV is the most efficient compared to DSDV and OLSR protocols.
- OLSR has recorded better Throughput value than DSDV.

Case 2

Effect of varying nodes density on the Delay, PDR and the Throughput of AODV, OLSR and DSDV.

In this study, we analyze the effect of varying the number of nodes (density) on the Average End-to-End Delay, the packet delivery rate and on the throughput for the three protocols, AODV, OLSR and DSDV.

We kept some parameters constant: Simulation time is 200 seconds and the speed of vehicles is 20 m/s. As shown in Figure 16-18, we conclude the following results.

Result 1

The Figure 16 shows that:

- The delay of OLSR is the Lowest relative to DSDV and AODV.
- The delay of DSDV is lower than AODV.

Result 2

The Figure 17 shows that:

- The number of packets delivered to the destination by AODV is more than 90% regardless of network density.
- OLSR has better performance compared to DSDV, with a higher PDR.

Figure 16. Varying density vs. average delay (ms)

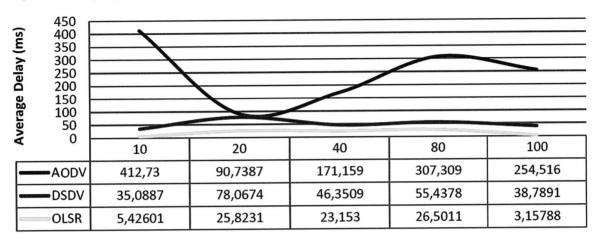

	10	20	40	80	100
AODV	412,73	90,7387	171,159	307,309	254,516
DSDV	35,0887	78,0674	46,3509	55,4378	38,7891
OLSR	5,42601	25,8231	23,153	26,5011	3,15788

Figure 17. Density vs PDR (%)

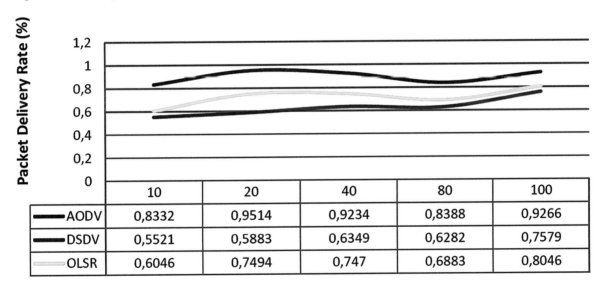

	10	20	40	80	100
AODV	0,8332	0,9514	0,9234	0,8388	0,9266
DSDV	0,5521	0,5883	0,6349	0,6282	0,7579
OLSR	0,6046	0,7494	0,747	0,6883	0,8046

Result 3

The Figure 18 shows that:

- AODV has recorded higher throughput values regardless of network density. In this case, AODV is the most efficient compared to DSDV and OLSR protocols.
- OLSR has recorded higher throughput compared to DSDV.

Figure 18. Varying density vs. throughput (Kbts)

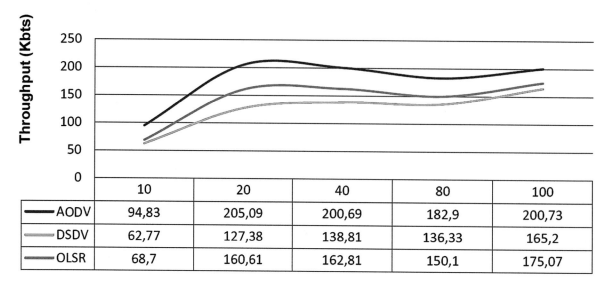

	10	20	40	80	100
AODV	94,83	205,09	200,69	182,9	200,73
DSDV	62,77	127,38	138,81	136,33	165,2
OLSR	68,7	160,61	162,81	150,1	175,07

Case 3: Effect of the varying Pause Time on the Delay, PDR, and the Throughput of AODV, OLSR, and DSDV

In this Case, we analyze the effect of varying the Pause Time on the Average End-to-End Delay, the packet delivery rate and on the throughput for the three protocols, AODV, OLSR and DSDV.

We kept some parameters constant: Simulation time is 200 seconds, the speed of vehicles is 50 m/s and the number of vehicles is 40.

As shown in Figure 19-21, we conclude the following results.

Result 1

The Figure 19 shows that:

Figure 19. Varying pause time vs average delay (ms)

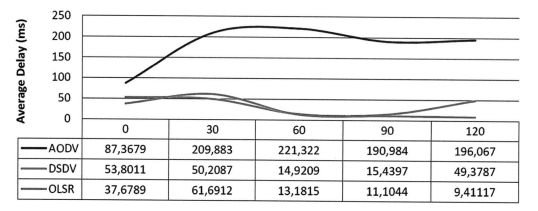

	0	30	60	90	120
AODV	87,3679	209,883	221,322	190,984	196,067
DSDV	53,8011	50,2087	14,9209	15,4397	49,3787
OLSR	37,6789	61,6912	13,1815	11,1044	9,41117

- OLSR have better performance than AODV and DSDV in terms of Average End-to-End Delay, regardless of pause time value (High pause time value →Low mobility, Low pause time value → High mobility).
- In most situations, DSDV have better performance than AODV in terms of Average End-to-End Delay.

Result 2

The Figure 20 shows that:

- AODV have better performance than OLSR and DSDV in terms of packet delivery rate regardless of pause time value.
- OLSR have better performance than DSDV in terms of average packet delivery rate.

Figure 20. Varying pause time vs PDR (%)

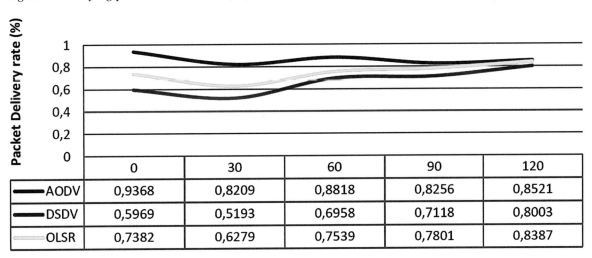

	0	30	60	90	120
AODV	0,9368	0,8209	0,8818	0,8256	0,8521
DSDV	0,5969	0,5193	0,6958	0,7118	0,8003
OLSR	0,7382	0,6279	0,7539	0,7801	0,8387

Figure 21. Varying pause time vs. throughput (Kbts)

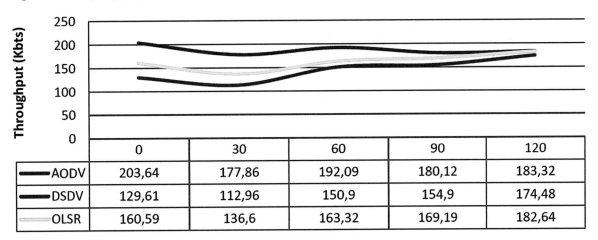

	0	30	60	90	120
AODV	203,64	177,86	192,09	180,12	183,32
DSDV	129,61	112,96	150,9	154,9	174,48
OLSR	160,59	136,6	163,32	169,19	182,64

Result 3

The Figure 21 shows that:

- AODV have high throughput values than OLSR and DSDV regardless of pause time value.
- OLSR have high throughput values than DSDV regardless of pause time value.

CONCLUSION

In this chapter, the authors have analyzed the performance of OLSR, ODV and DSDV protocols in a VANET network. Based on the different results in each case as indicated above, it can be concluded that the VANET protocols depend on a set of variables that make up the simulation environment such as mobility, density, network size, etc. The simulation environment does not really reflect a real case; we tried to approach the maximum possible of a real scenario.

By studying the three routing protocols, AODV, DSDV and OLSR in VANET, the authors have noticed that further performance evaluation is required to verify performance of a routing protocol with other routing protocols based on various traffic scenarios. The objects of our next research work will be focused on the comparison of different VANET protocols features to enhance existing protocols and design a new for VANET; on other hand, we will study the interoperability between Train Collision Avoidance systems and VANET.

REFERENCES

Anggoro, R., Kitasuka, T., Nakamura, R., & Aritsugi, M. (2012). Performance Evaluation of AODV and AOMDV with Probabilistic Relay in VANET Environments. In *Proceedings of the Third International Conference on Networking and Computing*. doi:10.1109/ICNC.2012.47

Atéchian, T. (2010). Protocole de routage géo-multipoint hybride et mécanisme d'acheminement de données pour les réseaux ad hoc de véhicules (VANETs).Thesis Institut National des Sciences Appliquées de Lyon.

Badreddine, G. (2012). Algorithme De Clusterisation Et Protocoles De Routage Dans Les Réseaux Ad Hoc [Thèse de doctorat]. de l'université de Technologie de Belfort-Montbéliard Tunisie.

Balandin, S., Andreev, S., & Koucheryavy, Y. (2015). *Internet of Things, Smart Spaces, and Next Generation Networks and Systems. Ebook*. Springer. doi:10.1007/978-3-319-23126-6

Basagni, S., Marco, C. I. S., & Giordano, S. (2012). Ad Hoc networking [eBook]. IEEE Press.

Clausen & P. Jacquet. Optimized Link State Routing Protocol (OLSR). (2003). RFC3626 T.

Dhankhar, S. & Agrawal, S. (2014). VANETs: A Survey on Routing Protocols and Issues. *International Journal of Innovative Research in Science, Engineering and Technology, 3*(6).

El Ali, F. (2012). *Communication unicast dans les réseaux mobiles dynamiques*. Université de Technologie de Compiègne.

Future of ITS. (2011). Website. Retrieved from https://mubbisherahmed.wordpress.com/2011/11/29/the-future-of-intelligent-transport-systems-its/

Garc'ıa, C. R., Lehner, A., Strang, T., & Röckl, M. (2007). Comparison of Collision Avoidance Systemsand Applicability to Rail Transport. In *Proceedings of the 7th International Conference on ITS ITST '07*.

García, C. R., Strang, T., & Lehner, A. (2008, July 22-24). A Broadcast Vehicle to Vehicle Communication System in Railway Environments. In *Proceedings of the ISVCS '08*, Dublin, Ireland. doi:10.4108/ICST.ISVCS2008.3805

Hartenstein, H., & Laberteaux, K. (2010). VANET Vehicular Applications and Inter-Networking Technologies [eBook]. Wiley.

Hartong, M., Goel, R., Farkas, C., & Wijesekera, D. (2007). PTC-VANET Interactions to Prevent Highway Rail Intersection Crossing Accidents. In *Proceedings of the IEEE 65th Vehicular Technology Conference VTC '07* (pp. 2550-2554). IEEE.

HBL. (n. d.). RCAS infrastructure. Retrieved from http://www.hbl.in/publicimages/hbl-product3571TCAS%20Deployment%20Diagram.png

Beydoun, K. (2009). Conception d'un protocole de routage hierarchique pour les réseaux de capteurs [Thesis]. L'U.F.R des sciances et technique de l'université de Franche-Comte.

Kumar, A., & Hans, R. (2015). Performance Analysis of DSDV, I-DSDV, OLSR, ZRP Proactive Routing Protocol in Mobile Ad Hoc Networks in IPv6. *International Journal of Advanced Science and Technology*, *77*, 25–36. doi:10.14257/ijast.2015.77.03

Kumar, A., & Tyagi, M. (2014). Geographical Topologies of Routing Protocols in Vehicular Ad hoc Networks – A Survey. *International Journal of Computer Science and Information Technologies*, *5*(3), 3062-3065.

Lehner, A., Rico-García, C., & Strang, T. (2011). A multi-broadcast communication system for high dynamic vehicular ad-hoc networks. Vehicle Information and Communication Systems, 2(3/4).

Manvi, S. S., Kakkasageri, M. S., & Mahapurush, C. V. (2009). Performance Analysis of AODV, DSR, and Swarm Intelligence Routing Protocols In Vehicular Ad hoc Network Environment. In *Proceedings of the Conference on Future Computer and Communication*. IEEE. doi:10.1109/ICFCC.2009.122

Mohapatra, S., & Kanungo, P. (2011). Performance analysis of AODV, DSR, OLSR and DSDV Routing Protocols using NS2 Simulator. In *Proceedings of the International Conference on Communication Technology and System Design*.

Network Simulator ns-2. Website. Retrieved from http://www.isi.edu/nsnam/ns

Pathan, A.-S. K., Monowar, M. M., & Khan, S. (2014). *Simulation Technologies in Networking and Communications*. CRC Press. doi:10.1201/b17650

Rajeshkumar, V., & Sivakumar, P. (2013). Comparative Study of AODV, DSDV and DSR Routing Protocols in MANET Using Network Simulator-2. International Journal of Advanced Research in Computer and Communication Engineering, 2(12).

Schaper, D2015). Red Tape Slows Control System That Could Have Saved Speeding Train. *NPR*. Retrieved from www.npr.org/2015/05/16/407127497/red-tape-slows-control-system-that-could-have-saved-speeding-train.jpg

RTD Fastracks. (n. d.). RTD integrates Positive Train Control into commuter rail lines. Retrieved from http://www.rtd-fastracks.com/ep3_149

Salameh, N. (2011). Conception d'un système d'alerte embarqué basé sur les communications entre véhicules [Thesis]. Institut National des Sciences Appliquées de Rouen.

Singh, A., & Verma, A.K. (2013) Simulation and Analysis of AODV, DSDV, ZRP IN VANET. *International Journal in Foundations of Computer Science and Technology*, *3*(5).

Spaho, E., Ikeda, M., Barolli, L., & Xhafa, F. (2013). Performance Evaluation of OLSR and AODV Protocols in a VANET Crossroad Scenario. In *Proceedings of the IEEE International Conference on Advanced Information Networking and Applications (AINA)* (pp. 577-582). doi:10.1109/AINA.2013.111

Strang, T., Meyer zu Hörste, M., & Gu, X. (2006). A rail collision avoidance system exploiting Ad-Hoc inter-vehicle communication and Galileo. In *Proceedings of the 13th World Congress and Exhibition on Intelligent Transportation Systems and Services*.

SUMO. (n. d.). Retrieved from http://www.dlr.de/ts/en/desktopdefault.aspx/tabid-9883/16931_read-41000/

Thomas, C., & Philippe, J. (2003). Optimized Link State Routing (OLSR RFC 3626).

Vats, K., Sachdeva, M., Saluja, K., & Rathee, A. (2012). Simulation and Performance Analysis of OLSRRouting Protocol Using OPNET. *International Journal of Advanced Research inComputer Science and Software Engineering*, *2*.

Wasiq, S., Arshad, W., Javaid, N., & Bibi, A. (2011). Performance Evaluation of DSDV, OLSR and DYMO using 802.11 and 802.11 p MAC-Protocols. In *Proceedings of the 2011 IEEE 14th International Multitopic Conference (INMIC)*. IEEE.

KEY TERMS AND DEFINITIONS

AWK: The name AWK comes from the names of the three creators, Alfred Aho, Peter Weinberger and Brian Kernighan. It is a scripting and line processing language integrated into most UNIX systems since 1979.

GPSR (Greedy Perimeter Stateless Routing): GPSR is a geographic routing protocol that has been designed and adapted for mobile ad hoc networks. GPSR uses the position of the current node, that of its neighbors and the location of the destination to make a routing decision.

GyTAR (Greedy Traffic Aware Routing Protocol): GyTAR is a geographic routing protocol. The source node is supposed to know its position and that of the recipient to be able to make routing decisions; this information is given by a location service such as GLS (Grid Location Service).

MANET (Mobile Ad-Hoc Network): MANETs networks are ad hoc networks, without fixed infrastructure and composed of mobile entities called nodes.

TCL (Tool Command Language): TCL is a simple programming language that was designed in 1988 by John Ousterhout and is divided into two parts, language and library.

WSN (Wireless Sensor Networks): WSn is a collection of wireless nodes deployed for monitoring certain phenomena of interest and transmitting collected data to one or more collection points, in an autonomous manner.

Xgraph: A UNIX-based tool that plots curves and is particularly useful in shell scripts.

Section 3
Big Data and Text Mining

Chapter 9

Study and Analysis of Delay Factors of Delhi Metro Using Data Sciences and Social Media:
Automatic Delay Prediction System for Delhi Metro

Arun Solanki
Gautam Buddha University, India

Ela Kumar
Indira Gandhi Delhi Technical University for Women, India

ABSTRACT

Delhi Metro passengers had a difficult time mostly on Monday morning as trains on the busy corridors are delayed due to technical problems or track circuit failure. This study found different factors like power failure, weather, rider load, festive season, etc. which are responsible for the delay of Delhi Metro. Due to these factors, Metro got delayed and run at a reduced speed causing much inconvenience to the people, who are hoping to reach their offices on time. Delhi Metro data are received from different sources which may be structured (timings, speed, traffic), semi-structured (images and video) and unstructured (maintenance records) form. So, there is heterogeneity in data. Except for this data, the feedback or suggestion of a rider is vital to the system. Nowadays riders are using social media like Facebook and Twitter very frequently. Three-tier architecture is proposed for the delay analysis of Delhi Metro. Different implementation techniques are studied and proposed for the social media module and delay prediction modules for the proposed system.

INTRODUCTION

The Delhi Metro, an intra-city electric rail system serving the National Capital Region (NCR), has been operational since December 2002. Metro services did not stop entirely due to the faults; it delayed for more than an average time. It has also watched in working hours that Metro is not on its schedule. As,

DOI: 10.4018/978-1-5225-3176-0.ch009

Delhi Metro trains run on automatic signaling system, and if a problem occurs, it operates on a manual signaling system. So, there is an acute need for study and analysis of this problem and to develop a system as a solution. The related data is collected from different types of databases like the Relational database, Transactional database, Multimedia database, spatial database, Time-series database, World Wide Web, etc.

The riders are the most important part of the Metro, and Whenever a passenger stuck in the metro due to delay, rider updated a Facebook status or tweets about the issue. A real-time data is generated and may be captured for analysis the problem. As this data may be big data; Hadoop or Map Reduce, which are advanced tools of data science used for sentimental analysis of tweets or Facebook updates. Data mining is done on both types of data i.e. operational data and rider social media data. The first and essential step of data mining is preprocessing which is applied for data cleaning, data integration, data transformation and data reduction. These steps of preprocessing filter the data from errors and noise and further used. This architecture has Data Acquisition, Data Processing, and Disruption Analysis & Results components. Data acquisition contains the data received from social media and operational data of Delhi Metro. These data may be in structured or unstructured form. Data Processing has three modules named Master Data, Integrated Data and Internal Analytics Aggregation. Disruption Analysis & Results contains the trends, application, and impact of disruption of Delhi Metro.

To handle big data problem Data science is used. Data science is also known as data-driven science which is an interdisciplinary field the scientific methods, processes and systems to extract knowledge or insights from data in various forms, either structured or unstructured, similar to Knowledge Discovery in Databases (KDD). Ali et al. (2016) discuss in their work that Data Science looks to create models that capture the underlying patterns of complex systems and codify those models into working applications while Big Data seems to collect and manage large amounts of various data to serve large-scale web applications and vast sensor networks. There are more than 40 data science techniques like clustering, search engine, deep learning, neural networks, Hadoop, etc. which can be used for analysis of delay factors which impacts the Delhi Metro. A predictive model is generated using multiple regressions to predict delay in Delhi Metro. In next section delay factors which mainly affect the Delhi Metro are discussed

DELAY FACTORS IN DELHI METRO

Identification of the delay factors and their reasons helps the future planning of service, and it can be used for traffic forecast. The delay factors can be broadly divided into two parts:

1. **Operational Side:** Fan and Weston (2012) discuss operational side algorithms like brute force, first-come-first-served, Tabu search, simulated annealing, genetic algorithms, ant colony optimization, dynamic programming and decision tree based elimination are already examined
2. **Passenger Side:** Nagy and Csiszar (2014) in their work discuss the specified factors (weather conditions, lines, service type, etc.) and the punctuality of vehicles (departure and arrival time) is predictable. These values can be used for passenger information on stations as well as on personalized travel information applications like journey planners.

As a rider, it has been watched many times that Delhi Metro is not on the schedule. Factors like power, weather, rider load, network congestion, festive seasons, speed and others are responsible for the delay. At that time trains are inducted into passenger services in a phased manner. At that point stations become overcrowded. If one train delayed, then another train of another phase also delays and become a chain. It takes more than 4-5 hours to overcome this problem. Following are main problems which affect the services of Metro.

1. **Power Failure:** Due to power failure, the trains ran at slow speed and stopped longer than normal at various stations.
2. **Weather:** The hot summer; the bone-chilling cold in the winter; and the patchy but intruding rain during Monsoon, every season impact rider in Delhi Metro. Delhi is one of the polluted city in the world, so all the dust which is in the Delhi's air pollution crisis during summer transforms to dirt during monsoon. There are different types of dust in Delhi Metro like chunky dirt, the wet dirt, and of course the brittle, sticky soil. All forms of dirt enter Delhi Metro wagons during Monsoon. The floor, which usually goes unnoticed, is dotted with dirt during Monsoon; responsible for a delay in Delhi Metro.
3. **Rider Load:** The Delhi Metro Rail Corporation (DMRC) has a network of 190km and still expanding with near 151 stations. But even as the Metro network is growing, rider load is increasing day by day. In the past; when 8.5km Metro line between Shahdara (Metro station) and Tis Hazari (Metro Station) was inaugurated to make travel smoother and faster, the ticketing system collapsed as the line was crowded four times its capacity. The situation has come back to haunt the system with most tracks packed beyond capacity during peak hours.
4. **Festive Season:** Each and every festival in India is celebrated with joy and happiness. Peoples go to each other place to celebrate the festival. Metro rider in Delhi has to face a harrowing time when they are left stranded on different lines, with hundreds of them waiting at a single station for about more than 40 minutes. The Delhi Metro has to run 106 extra train trips on the eve of Raksha Bandhan (a Hindu festival), i.e., 17th August 2016, and on 'Raksha Bandhan,' i.e. 18th August 2016 as the need arises.

DATA MINING PROCESS

Data is used to reflect information and rules describing the data must be used to interpret it. The most obvious one explains the meaning of the numbers, letters, etc. It answers the questions: What was measured, where, when and on what scale? This kind of information is essential for using the Delhi Metro data. A less obvious kind of information describing the data collected is its accuracy or validity. Raw data rarely provide this. One reason for this is the specification/legend of the data; made before the process of collection. The errors in the dataset are generated unintentionally during the process. The purpose of the data collected is to reflect a part of reality. It can be too optimistic to expect the data to have a "one to one" correlation with this part of reality.

Data mining is not specific to one type of data received from various recourses of Delhi Metro. Data mining applies to different kind of data collected from many resources. Different algorithms and approaches may differ when diverse types of data are obtained. Indeed, the challenges presented by various types of data vary significantly. To analyze Delhi Metro delay factors, different databases like object-relational databases, relational databases, object-oriented databases, transactional databases, unstructured and semi-structured repositories like World Wide Web; spatial databases, multimedia databases, time-series databases and textual databases which come under advanced database are studied. Here are some examples in more detail:

- **Relational Databases:** A relational database consists of tables which contain either value of entity attributes or values of attributes from entity relationships. In relational Databases tables, rows and columns are known relation, tuples, and attributes respectively. The most commonly used query language for the relational database is SQL, which allows retrieval and manipulation of the data stored in the relations. Data mining can benefit for data selection, transformation, and consolidation in comparison to SQL.

- **Transaction Databases:** A transaction database represents transactions as a set of records, each with a time stamp, an identifier and a set of items. Delhi Metro timetable is registered in transactional databases. One typical data mining analysis on such data is the called market basket analysis or association rules in which associations between items occurring together or in the sequence are studied.

- **Multimedia Databases:** Multimedia databases include video, images, audio and text media which are responsible for the delay in Delhi Metro. Relational databases are not capable of storing multimedia so it may be retained on extended object-relational or object-oriented databases, or simply on a file system. Data mining from multimedia repositories may require computer vision, computer graphics, image interpretation, and natural language processing methodologies.

- **Spatial Databases:** Spatial databases are databases that, in addition to general data, store geographical information like maps, and global or regional positioning where a delay occurs. Such spatial databases present new challenges to data mining algorithms.

- **Time-Series Databases:** Time-series databases contain time-related data such arrival and departure of trains, the exact time of delay, etc. These databases usually have a continuous flow of new information coming in, which sometimes causes the need for a challenging real-time analysis. Data mining in such databases commonly includes the study of trends and correlations between evolutions of different variables, as well as the prediction of trends and movements of the variables in time.

- **World Wide Web:** The World Wide Web is the great diversity of data mainly heterogeneous. A vast number of users are accessing its resources daily. Data on the World Wide Web is organized in interconnected documents. These documents can be text, audio, video, raw data, and even applications. Conceptually, the World Wide Web is comprised of three major components: The content of the Web, which encompasses documents available; the structure of the Web, which covers the hyperlinks and the relationships between documents; and the usage of the web, describing how and when the resources are accessed. A fourth dimension can be added relating the dynamic nature or evolution of the documents. Data mining in the World Wide Web, or web mining, tries to address all these issues and is often divided into web content mining, web structure mining and web usage mining.

To analyze the different types of data which are discussed above, data mining is the best technique. Data preprocessing is the first and essential step of Data Mining. So, the objective of data preprocessing completes the following task:

- Find a structured method to filter data from errors and noise.
- Present the methods of filtering, so that they can be implemented in an arbitrary language and applied to filter general data.
- Find and present a universal method for evaluation of the performance of one filter or for comparing the performance of one filter to another.

Raw data which is received initially; may be processed or no need to process, but may show homogeneity with other acquired data. So there is a need to make all data in same structure and processing consists of data filtration and data integration stages. As the data collected in stage one is not suitable for analysis due to the inclusion of unwanted information, further processing is required to perform on captured data to eliminate redundancy. Metro raw data is highly noisy, having missed or unknown values, impure and inconsistent. This data affects the system and data mining results. To improve the quality of the data and proposed the system and, consequently, of the mining results and system results; raw data is pre-processed using different tools and techniques. This processed data improves the efficiency and ease of the mining process. Data preprocessing is one of the most critical steps in a system development process which deals with the preparation and transformation of the initial dataset.

Data preprocessing for Delhi Metro raw data may be completed using following steps:

DATA CLEANING

Real-world mostly is incomplete, noisy, and inconsistent. Data cleaning (or data cleansing) routines attempt to fill in missing values, smooth out noise while identifying outliers, and correct inconsistencies in the data.

- **Missing Values:** The most important process of data cleaning is missing values. It consists of following methods:
- **Ignore the Tuple:** This is usually done when the class label is missing (assuming the mining task involves classification). This method is not very efficient unless the tuple contains several attributes with missing values. It is especially poor when the percentage of missing values per attribute varies considerably.
- **Fill in the Missing Value Manually:** In this approach, data is filled manually but, this approach is time-consuming and may not be feasible given a large data set with many missing values.
- **Use a Global Constant to Fill in the Missing Value:** Replace all missing attribute values by the same constant, such as a label like "Unknown" or NULL. If missing values are replaced by, say, "Unknown," then the mining program may mistakenly think that they form an interesting concept, since they all have a value in common-that of "Unknown." Hence, although this method is simple, it is not fool proof.
- **Use the Attribute Mean to Fill in the Missing Value:** For example, suppose that the delay means time of all trains 600 sec. Use this value to replace the missing value for the delay time.
- **Noisy Data:** Noise is a random error or variance in a measured variable. The following data smoothing techniques can be used to remove noise of Delhi Metro data:

- **Binning:** Binning methods smooth a sorted data value by consulting its "neighborhood," that is, the values around it. The sorted values are distributed into some "buckets," or bins. Because binning methods consult the neighborhood of values, they perform local smoothing. In smoothing by bin boundaries, the minimum and maximum values in a given bin are identified as the bin boundaries. The closest boundary value then replaces each bin value. In general, the larger the width, the greater the effect of the smoothing. Alternatively, bins may be equal-width, where the interval range of values in each bin is constant. Binning is also used as a discretization technique.
- **Regression:** Data can be smoothed by fitting the data to a function, such as with regression. Linear regression involves finding the "best" line to fit two attributes (or variables) so that one attribute can be used to predict the other. Multiple linear regression is an extension of linear regression, where more than two attributes are involved, and the data are fit to a multidimensional surface.
- **Clustering:** Outliers may be detected by clustering, where similar values are organized into groups, or "clusters." Intuitively, values that fall outside of the set of clusters may be considered outlier analysis.

DATA INTEGRATION

Data integration involves combining data from several diverse sources, which are stored using various technologies and provide a unified view of the data. Data integration may include inconsistent data and therefore needs data cleaning too. Data integration becomes increasingly important in cases of merging delay factors which are coming from different reasons. The most well-known implementation of data integration is building a data warehouse which contains a decade data related to delay factors of Delhi Metro. The benefit of a data warehouse enables to perform analyses based on the data in the data warehouse. This is not possible to do on the data available only in the current source system. The reason is that the source systems may not contain corresponding data, even though the data are identically named, they may refer to different entities. Data Integration can be physical or virtual

- **Physical:** Coping the data to warehouse
- **Virtual:** Keep the data only at the sources

DATA TRANSFORMATION

In this step of preprocessing data is converted into a set of data values from the source data format to the data format of a destination source. It is often used in a data warehouse system. Data transformation process involves two steps. In the first step, data mapping maps data elements from the source data system to the destination data system and captures any transformation that must occur. In second step code generation that creates the actual transformation program. Data element to data element mapping is frequently complicated by complex transformations that require one-to-many and many-to-one transformation rules. In short, in data transformation data is transformed or consolidated into forms appropriate for mining, by performing summary or aggregation operations.

DATA REDUCTION

Data reduction obtains a compressed representation of the data set that is much smaller in volume. The reduced data sets produce the more or less same analytical results as that of the original volume. There are some strategies for data reduction.

- **Data Aggregation and Attribute Subset Selection:** This is removable of irrelevant attributes through correlation analysis and one of the strategies for data reduction.
- **Dimensionality Reduction:** This is the reduction of the dimension of sets (e.g., using encoding schemes such as minimum length encoding or wavelets).
- **Numerosity Reduction:** This is known as "replacing" the data by alternative, smaller representations such as clusters or parametric models and it are considered to be the data reduction techniques. Generalizations with the use of concept hierarchies are one of the data reduction approaches by organizing the thoughts into varying levels of abstraction. Data discretization is very useful for the automatic generation of concept hierarchies from numerical data.

SOCIAL MEDIA AS TOOL FOR DELAY ANALYSIS

In India, the Delhi Metro, an intra-city electric rail system serving the National Capital Region (NCR), has been operational since December 2002. Delhi Metro inspection practices should be intended to find delay factors before it impacts the Metro. If delay factors are prior identified, then it improves the schedule of Delhi Metro and could enhance network productivity, capacity, and reliability. Now a day's every second is precious for the rider. Most of the rider uses the social media like Facebook or Twitter to share their current status. This real-time data may be used to analysis the factors which are affecting the schedule of Delhi Metro. Every day around 1.05 billion Facebook statuses are updated, and around 500 million messages are tweeted (as of the end of 2014) on every possible topic. Any trending event like sports, election, terrorist attack, etc. directly affects the volume of these posts and tweets. Due to its real-time, free availability, high visibility and global nature many people use it as a medium to report their problems, in addition to sharing daily life activities, thoughts, and emotions. Recently, city traffic authorities have also started feeding real-time traffic movements in the form of text, image and video form into their Facebook or Twitter pages for its commuters. Even the residents are using these social pages to report their problems and complaints directly to the authorities. However, the scattered nature of this humongous volume of data in the social network makes this information and challenges trying to track for both the authorities and the residents, and these data get buried under the ever-inflowing new feeds after a period. Moreover, it is impossible to put filters on these feeds so as to view the problems only for a particular road or locality on a given date and time. We propose a system to provide real-time traffic statuses and problems in a city from the data available on the social networks. The system crawls data from Facebook and Twitter continuously, mines them to extract information about traffic and track issues in real-time and shows them in an intuitive way in a dashboard. Although mining static documents are well studied in the literature, in this context there are new factors like social network language styles, ambiguous nature due to the varied length of feeds, high volume of noisy feeds, real-time data processing aspect, etc. that makes this problem challenging.

So, there is need of a system which provides real-time Delhi Metro statuses and difficulties in Delhi Metro from the data available on the social networks. The system crawls data from Facebook and Twitter continuously, mines them to extract information about traffic and track issues in real-time and shows them in an intuitive way in a dashboard.

FEASIBILITY STUDY

Is it feasible to develop a system which uses social media and data science? This is the first question which arises in a researcher mind. The answer to this question is the feasibility study of the domain. A feasibility study covers the study of rider behavior and information's, Delivery system; which would include e.g. data collection, processing and possible ways of receiving the useful information from passengers. Identification of candidate data sources that is used for the methodology establishment; and design of methods for data collection (where appropriate) Survey and analysis of where past incidents and risky behavior frequently occurred. Review of statistical, machine learning techniques and analytical methods employed in various domains, such as physics, psychology, sociology, bioinformatics, healthcare, etc.

ARCHITECTURE OF PROPOSED SYSTEM

The timetable or schedule of a Metro is set in this way that it always be conflict-free. Delhi Metro on its railway network are moved according to its timetable, However, in general, not all Metro trains run according to the timetable, due to delays such as excessive dwell times at stations, infrastructure and train faults, and the late arrival of the crew. When Metro does not operate according to the timetable, even by only a few seconds, there is an increased likelihood that they conflict with other trains, resulting in those trains also being delayed.

Metro operators, therefore, attempt to run trains to the timetable, or failing this, they try to minimize the cost of delays. The proposed analytical model as shown in figure 1 which consists of three stages, data inception, data processing and data analytics will serve as a base model for the analysis of delay factors in Delhi Metro.

Figure 1. Architecture of proposed system

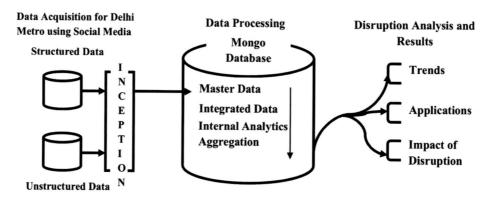

Data Acquisition

In data acquisition stage, real time data feeds of Delhi Metro feeds and timetable, customer feeds from Twitter, Metro rider who use Facebook, are streamed and stored in MongoDB. Delhi Metro feeds contain structured data whereas the customer feeds are semi-structured data. Digital images, audio, video, and social media posts are the examples of unstructured data and organizations store it all. Ideally, all of this information is converted into structured data, however; this is costly and time-consuming. Also, not all types of unstructured data can easily be transformed into a formal model. Different feeds need to be individually stored in three different collections in Mongo database for processing.

Data Processing

In the data processing stage, the captured master data from the first stage are processed for analysis. At this juncture, the additional data are filtered out from the captured feeds and delivered in a format suitable for analysis, in other words, enablers that are helpful to support decision-making process are identified. The identified key variables such as disruption data, rag, etc. are extracted from master data, integrated and stored in MongoDB for analysis.

Master Data

Fixing poor data quality at its source and managing constant change is what Master

Data Management is all about. The amount of data produces by the rider, and Delhi Metro is collected and using a Master Data Management (MDM), it's collected in a centralized repository. This master data allows the fast and efficient access, which is kept reliable, consistent, and accessible to those who need it and when they need it.

Integrated Data

For a system which uses social media data, sensor data and other real-time big data to drive business performance, MongoDB integration of data can prove a remarkably helpful tool. As a leading NoSQL database, MongoDB delivers the agility and scalability need to manage massive data sets. MongoDB Integration operations help speed the processing of big data while simplifying application code and limiting resource requirements. With MongoDB Integration data tools, researchers can more easily manipulate big data to get the answers.

Internal Analytics Aggregation

MongoDB's analytics aggregation is modeled on the concept of data processing pipelines. Documents enter a multi-stage pipeline that transforms the documents into an aggregated result. The most basic pipeline stages provide filters that operate like queries and document transformations that modify the form of the output document. Other pipeline operations provide tools for grouping and sorting documents by particular field or fields as well as tools for aggregating the contents of arrays, including arrays of documents. Also, pipeline stages can use operators for tasks such as calculating the average or concatenating a string. The pipeline provides efficient data aggregation using native operations within MongoDB and is the preferred method for data collection in MongoDB. The aggregation pipeline can operate on a shared collection.

Disruption Analysis and Results

Disruption is a loss of productivity, disturbance, hindrance or interruption to Delhi Metro schedule, resulting in lower efficiency. In the construction context, disrupted work is work that is carried out less efficiently than it would have been, had it not been for the cause of the disruption. If caused by different delay factor as discussed in the first section. In this stage, aggregation is performed by Mongo query on the stored data in the database by grouping values from multiple collections together and computes the results in representable format. Rider sentiments and trends are analyzed to find the delay factors and its impact on the schedule of Delhi Metro.

PROPOSED RESEARCH METHODOLOGY

In this section, different types/methods of data collection are discussed. Rider feedback data is collected from the various routes of Delhi Metro with the help of a well-drafted Questionnaire. Further, within these routes, non-probabilistic convenience sampling is followed, as it is appropriate for exploratory studies. Further convenience sampling method is used for two reasons firstly respondents are selected because they happen to be in the right place at the right time and secondly, convenience sampling technique is not recommended for detailed or casual research, but they can be in exploratory research for generating ideas. According to the chosen methodological research approach, the quantitative data is analyzed by using Factor Analysis by using SPSS or R or any other Software. The proposed system requires storing massive real-time data for analysis. When Big data is in the scenario, so there is a need for a scalable database which can accommodate big data. MongoDB is a NoSQL scalable database and is capable of storing significant amounts of data without complications. This database can accept the real-time data and may be used to accelerate the knowledge. The database is ideal for storing Delhi Metro live data feeds, easy to scale-up and provides various options to handle data consistency. In MongoDB, data are called documents which are stored in binary JSON (BSON) format and documents can be put in collections. There can be n number of groups depending on the usage. 'Big Data' means data sets are large, complex and so they impractical to manage with conventional databases like SQL. In recent years, big data technology is gaining popularity among large organizations as they deal with extensive data. For the chapter, the data sets can become a big data at some point in time, and this big data can provide a valuable in-depth analysis, and MongoDB can well accommodate this scalable data with no restrictions. These chapters discuss the implementation of a system in cloud environment provided by a cloud infrastructure provider. A standalone computer as a server or different small servers can be used for live data processing. Cloud computing concept provides a high reliable, secure environment for data storage and ease of use. Cloud computing will provide reliable services for next generation data centers which are built using virtualized compute and storage technologies. The idea of using the cloud as Infrastructure-as-a-Service (IaaS) is to provide users on-demand computing resources (servers, storage, and networking) and they offer flexibility in scalability. Python programming may be used for coding.

Python is widely used dynamic programming language for data analysis tasks. It emphasizes code readability, easy debugging and useful tool to implement algorithms. The Pymongo may be utilized for an interacting tool to communicate with MongoDB database from Python.

The evolution of proposed system may be divided into following stages:

1. Data Acquisition Stage
2. Data Representation
3. Design and Implementation of proposed system

Data Acquisition Stage

The first phase of implementation is data acquisition which is crucial for receiving valid and accurate data for further processing and analysis. The data are gathered in parallel in real time from multiple data sources which include riders and Delhi Metro. It is important to collect all data with necessary time stamping between all acquired data are valid data. The process of obtaining data feeds may be implemented using Python programming. Pymongo is an interactive tool and is used to interact with Mongo server. The Python program may be utilized for acquiring Delhi Metro data.

- Questionnaires may be a useful tool for knowledge acquisition when conducting a ("findings of", 2013) survey or ("Delhi Metro", 2011, 2014) customer satisfaction survey in Delhi Metro. Questionnaires are cheaper than personal interviewing of riders and also quicker as the sample size is large and widely dispersed in Metro. An appropriate time is to be given to riders to return the questionnaires. Due to the lack of personal contact between the respondent and the researcher, the design and layout of the questionnaire are all important. In general, surveys tend to have lower response rates than face-to-face or telephone interviews. However, questionnaires given to most riders may provide very high response rates. The main drawback of this approach is that riders may in some way be biased. Many pre-existing questionnaires are covering a broad range of delay conditions and rider satisfaction measures.
- Social Media like twitters provide ("Twitter Developer", 2017) Application Program Interfaces (API) to download the tweets on specific topics. These allow the researcher to access their data by hashtag, keywords, and locations. They also allow accessing social graph and Twitter stream.
- Delhi Metro Operational Data may be acquired from DMRC. This data will contain information about the departure and arrival time, delay, no of riders from each station and other raw information. The analysis of this data will play a significant role to develop proposed system. This data can be cross verified by the data which is collected from social media.
- Detailed List of Delay Event of Delhi Metro is available for each line in .xls format. Different groups based on weather condition, the crowd at stations, etc. may be created and classified for analysis purpose. An example of weather classification has been determined with consideration to the temperature and the precipitation:
  - Cold, dry weather (temperature between -5° C and +2° C).
  - Cold, wet weather (temperature between +3° C and +15° C, medium).
  - Moderate, dry weather (temperature around 15° C -28 ° C).
  - Moderate, wet weather (temperature around 15° C -28° C, medium, intense rain).

- ○ Hot, dry weather (temperature around 35-46° C).
- ○ Hot, wet weather (temperature between +30-40° C, medium, intense rain).
- ○ Weather conditions do not affect traffic: this code has been assigned to the delay events that could not have been classified into those as mentioned earlier.

Except for weather information, rider information on each station will be collected by the stations and stored in a central database. The Excel sheets contained the data of vehicle identification, service type, delay (in minutes), situation and timestamp of delay and cause of the delay. The sheets contain raw data as well which may or may not be used for analysis.

- • Code Tables for Delays with exploratory reason is available at each station; may be collected and used for further delay analysis.

According to (Koetse and Rietveld, 2009) and (Tsapakis, 2013), Weather Data supplies the main delay factors to Delhi Metro's infrastructure. It impacts the significant travel amount. According to some studies, the effect of rain depends on their intensity. The total travel time increases due to all mild, moderate and heavy rain. The weather data may be collected and used for data analysis.

Data Representation

Data representation stage consists of two major portions, such as aggregation/ compilation and results storage in a representable format that is helpful in analysis. The processed data are aggregated using mongo query by grouping matching data and delay results for that particular location are stored in MongoDB for decision making. The delay can be represented in the percentage format.

("What is MongoDB," 2017) MongoDB is an open-source document database and leading NoSQL database. MongoDB is written in C++. Any relational database has a typical schema design that shows many tables and the relationship between these tables. While in MongoDB, there is no concept of relationship.

MongoDB Storage Engine

With MongoDB, Delhi Metro can address diverse application needs, hardware resources, and deployment designs with a single database technology. Through the use of a pluggable storage architecture as shown in Figure 2, MongoDB can be extended with new capabilities and configured for optimal use of specific hardware architectures. Users can leverage the same MongoDB query language, data model, scaling, security and operational tooling across different applications, each powered by different pluggable MongoDB storage engines.

Advantages of MongoDB Over RDBMS

1. MongoDB is Schema-less i.e. it is a document database in which one collection holds different documents. Some fields, content, and size of the document can differ from one document to another.
2. The structure of a single object is clear.
3. No complex joins.

Figure 2. MongoDB storage architecture

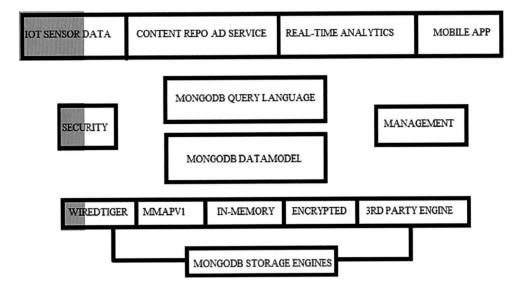

4. MongoDB has deep query-ability i.e. it supports dynamic queries on documents using a document-based query language that's nearly as powerful as SQL.
5. MongoDB is easy to scale.
6. Conversion/mapping of application objects to database objects not needed.
7. Uses internal memory for storing the (windowed) working set, enabling faster access to data.

Some Considerations While Designing Schema in MongoDB

1. Design schema according to preprocessed data.
2. Combine different objects into one document.
3. Delhi Metro data may be duplicated as space is cheap.
4. Do joins while writing, not on reading.
5. Optimize Schema for most frequent use cases in Delhi Metro scenario.
6. Do complex aggregation in the schema.

Design and Implementation of Proposed System

From analyzed data, an improved delay algorithm can be proposed and implemented. The data from various sources are continuously polled and after data mining and stage 4.1 and 4.2. It is used for implementation of the system.

According to (Bregman and Watkins, 2014) and (Limsopatham et al., 2015) for Social Media Module implementation a Support Vector Machine (SVM) can be applied intelligently to identify non-relevant tweet considering the problem as a two-class classification problem. A preprocessed tweet is classified as relevant tweet or noise. The relevant tweets are further classified as slow traffic, smooth traffic or moderate traffic using Multi-class Decision Jungle. Finally, Named Entity Recognition is applied to get the location information from these relevant tweets.

According to authors (Dahl et al., 2014), (Baker and Nied, 2013), ("Fujitsu Begins,"2016),(" Japan Trialing," 2016) and (Woollaston, 2015) Delay prediction can be completed using two approaches. The first approach contains the historical data, and it identifies the late train arrivals like seismograph which identifies the earthquake. This algorithm uses previous historical data to forecast the probable status of the Delhi Metro. Different machine learning algorithm like Kalman filtering, k-Nearest Neighbor, Artificial Neural Network, and Support Vector Regression may be used to develop this type of system. In the second approach, According to ("Maryland," 2016) and ("Metronotify App," 2017) whenever metro delays, the station master send a message to next station station-master with the approximate delay time in advance; this message transfers in real time and doesn't impact to other processes.

CONCLUSION

This chapter starts with the main factors which affect the Delhi Metro schedule. This study finds the main factors which influence the schedule of Delhi Metro is power, weather, rider load, network congestion, festive seasons, speed and others. So, there was an acute need to analyze and find the existing tools and techniques which can be helpful to overcome these factors. To investigate these factors, this study also discovered the types of data which is available with the Delhi Metro. The different type data which is stored in various databases like object-relational databases, relational databases, object-oriented databases, transactional databases, unstructured and semi-structured repositories like World Wide Web; spatial databases, multimedia databases, time-series databases and textual databases which come under advanced database are studied. This study finds that data mining process which includes data preprocessing technique is helpful to consider the real delay factors and its effect on Delhi Metro. A 3-tier Architecture having data acquisitions, data processing, and Disruption analysis & results are proposed and discussed. Different data may be acquired using Questionnaires, Social Media, Operational Data, Detailed List of Delay Event, Code Tables for Delays and Weather reports, for the purpose of analysis. This study found that data may be stored in MongoDB because it's a schema-less and NoSQL database. Social media as a tool and data science techniques which may be used for delay prediction in Delhi Metro are also studied in this chapter.

REFERENCES

Ali, A., Qadir, J., Rasool, R. U., Sathiaseelan, A., & Zwitter, A. (n. d.). Big Data for Development: Applications and Techniques. National University of Science and Technology, Pakistan. Retrieved from https://arxiv.org/pdf/1602.07810.pdf

Bregman, S., & Watkins, K. E. (2013, Oct 2). Best Practices for Transportation Agency Use of Social Media. Retrieved from https://books.google.co.in/books?id=TFzSBQAAQBAJ&dq=train+delay+prediction+using+social+media

Catherine, M. B., & Alexander, C. N. (n. d.). Predicting Bus Arrivals Using One Bus Away Real-Time Data. University of Washington, Seattle, WA. Retrieved from https://homes.cs.washington.edu/~anied/papers/AConradNied_OneBusAway_Writeup_20131209.pdf

Delhi Metro Rail Corporation Limited. (2013, July). Findings of Customer Satisfaction Survey conducted by DMRC. Retrieved from http://www.delhimetrorail.com/whatnew_details.aspx?id=KvlaOU2MsdElld

Delhi Metro Rail Corporation Limited. (2014). Delhi Metro to conduct online Customer satisfaction survey. Retrieved from http://www.delhimetrorail.com/whatnew_details.aspx?id=KvlaOU2MsdElld

Fan, B., Clive, R., & Weston, P. (2012). A comparison of algorithms for minimizing delay costs in disturbed railway traffic scenarios. *Journal of Rail Transport Planning & Management*, 2(1-2), 22–33. doi:10.1016/j.jrtpm.2012.09.002

Fujitsu Limited. (2016, July 19). Fujitsu Begins Field Trial for AI-Based Train Delay Prediction. Retrieved from http://www.fujitsu.com/global/about/resources/news/press-releases/2016/0719-02.html

India Today. (2011, April 18). Delhi Metro survey says it's a happy ride for all, India Today. Retrieved from http://indiatoday.intoday.in/story/survey-shows-commuters-travelling-on-delhi-metro-satisfied/1/135553.html

Japan Trialing Machine Learning on Railways to Predict Delays. (2016, July 22). Retrieved from http://aibusiness.org/japan-trialing-machine-learning-on-railways-to-predict-delays/

Koetse, M. P., & Rietveld, P. (2009). The impact of climate change and weather on transport: An overview of empirical findings. *Transportation Research Part D*, 14(3), 205–221. doi:10.1016/j.trd.2008.12.004

Limsopatham, N., Albakour, M. D., Macdonald, C., & Ounis, I. (n. d.). Tweeting Behavior during Train Disruptions within a City. School of Computing Science University of Glasgow. Retrieved from http://terrierteam.dcs.gla.ac.uk/publications/limsopatham2015icwsm.pdf

Maryland Transit Administrator. (n. d.). MARCTracker Live GPS Train Locations Retrieved from http://www.marctracker.com/PublicView/status.jsp

Metrotrains. (n. d.). METRONOTIFY APP. Retrieved from www.metrotrains.com.au/metronotify/

MongoDB. (n. d.). MongoDB Architecture. Retrieved from https://www.mongodb.com/mongodb-architecture

Nagy, E., & Csiszár, C. (2015). Analysis of Delay Causes in Railway Passenger Transportation. *Periodica Polytechnica Transportation Engineering*, 43(2), 73–80. doi:10.3311/PPtr.7539

Sjafjell, A. A., Dahl, E., & Skogen, S. (2014, June). On Implementations of Bus Travel Time Prediction Utilizing Methods in Artificial Intelligence. Norwegian University of Science and Technology. Retrieved from www.diva-portal.org/smash/get/diva2:751710/FULLTEXT01.pdf

Twitter. (n. d.). The Search API. Twitter Developer Documentation. Retrieved from https://dev.twitter.com/rest/public/search

Tsapakis, L., Cheng, T., & Bolbol, A. (2013). Impact of weather conditions on macroscopic urban travel times. *Journal of Transport Geography*, 28, 204–211. doi:10.1016/j.jtrangeo.2012.11.003

Woollaston, V. (2015, September 10). No more delays! Computer predicts when transport will be disrupted TWO hours before it happens… and sends in extra trains. *Dailymail*. Retrieved from http://www.dailymail.co.uk/sciencetech/article-3229123/No-delays-Computer-predicts-transport-disrupted-TWO-hours-happens-sends-extra-trains.html

Chapter 10
Social Media as a Tool to Understand Behaviour on the Railways

David Golightly
University of Nottingham, UK

Robert J. Houghton
University of Nottingham, UK

ABSTRACT

Social media plays an increasing role in how passengers communicate to, and about, train operators. In response, train operators and other rail stakeholders are adopting social media to contact their users. There are a number of opportunities for tapping this big data information stream through the overt use of technology to analyse, filter and present social media, including filtering for operational staff, or sentiment mapping for strategy. However, this analysis is predicated on a number of assumptions regarding the manner in which social media is currently being used within a railway context. In the following chapter, we present data from studies of rail social media that shed light on how big data analysis of social media exchange can support the passenger. These studies highlight important factors such as the broad range of issues covered by social media (not just disruption), the idiosyncrasies of individual train operators that need to be taken into account within social media analysis, and the time critical nature of information during disruption.

INTRODUCTION

Rail travel offers ample opportunity to fill `dead' time with transient activities (Jain and Lyons, 2008). The introduction of data networks and wi-fi across the railways, coupled with widespread smartphone adoption, allows many people to use social media while on the move. Passengers wish to communicate about their experience, either directly to transport operators in the form of query or comments, or to communicate with their social network about their travel experience. In response, transport operators

DOI: 10.4018/978-1-5225-3176-0.ch010

are seeking ways to utilise the opportunity of social media to improve passenger experience, particularly during disruption, and predominantly through Twitter (Pender et al., 2013, 2014; Liu et al., 2016).

There is interest in how technology can support the effective utilisation of social media. This might be with a view to extracting more information from social media to give transport operators faster intelligence on events occurring in and around their network (Periera at al., 2014; Mai & Hranac, 2012), or to understand attitudes of passengers. However, there may be other applications related to social media, such as tools to allow rapid response to tweets in times of disruption, Twitter dashboards for rail managers, and channels to repurpose social media to a wider set of users than just a rail operator's own followers, for example through customer information screens on stations (Golightly and Durk, 2016).

These kinds of 'big data' applications could be a vital tool for the rail industry and passengers, but are reliant on technologies such as natural language processing of tweets and sentiment analysis of incoming social media messages. The viability of such applications is based upon assumptions surrounding the nature of social media traffic, such as there being sufficient volume and content on any given channel to support meaningful analysis. Therefore, it is vital to underpin the development and deployment of such technology with a knowledge of which platforms are most relevant to rail communications, what situations or events are most likely to generate social media traffic, whether the use of social media is consistent and what the expectations of rail operators are in this arena.

The following chapter summarises a number of dedicated studies to understand the usage patterns inherent in how social media is used on the railways by both passengers and the rail stakeholders trying to communicate with them. By doing so, we identify a number of use cases, as well as some of the constraints around usage patterns that would need to be taken into account when developing applications (both passenger facing, and more 'back office' for rail operators) that draw on social media analytics. This chapter is intended to be most useful to those designing or procuring social media platforms and analysis technologies for the railways, as well as those involved in policy, such as those who may be including social media within the provisions of passenger information as part of a franchising agreement, or those looking to monitor passenger experience across the railways.

BACKGROUND

As recently as the beginning of this decade (Houghton and Golightly, 2011) few passengers, and fewer operators, actively used social media for anything other than marketing. Since then the landscape has changed dramatically, with many transport operators worldwide using social media as a means to communicate with their passengers. In a global survey of social media use in transport operations in 2013, 86% of operators preferred to use Twitter, 33% use Facebook, and only 12% of the operators not using any form of social media (Pender et al., 2013). More recent work with public transit (i.e. not just rail) in the US reports adoption rates by transport operators of 100% for Twitter (Liu et al., 2016). In Great Britain, all major train operating companies have active accounts, as does the main train information service channel (National Rail Enquiries), the infrastructure manager (Network Rail), as well as major stations and British Transport Police (Golightly and Durk, 2016).

The adoption of this innovative form of communication coincides with a period of unprecedented change for transport operations. Expanding cities and mobile lifestyles put greater demands on transport providers to keep stretched networks running with increased capacity (EU, 2011) in the face of emerging disruptive forces such as climate change (Koetse and Reitveld, 2009) and security threats (Gov. of India,

2013). Therefore, social media is set to play a vital role in the perception and operation of transport networks both tactically and strategically. This use of social media is anticipated to be most relevant during times of disruption and particularly through the use of Twitter where short messages can be rapidly disseminated to passengers informing them of service conditions and changes to timetables (Pender et al., 2014). As well as providing an information channel, organisational crisis communication through social media has been demonstrated to limit the impact of negative reactions (negative word of mouth; boycott) in comparison with other forms of media (Schultz et al., 2011).

While much of the communication by rail operators is still a manual process (Golightly and Durk, 2016) of replying to passenger comments, or broadcasting messages, there is much promise offered by technology. The internet generally, and social media in particular, can provide crucial context when trying to determine the causes of an unexpected event. This is particularly relevant when the event is caused "off the network" (e.g., a spike in passenger numbers due to a late running sporting event) or in the context of large events (Cottrill et al., 2017). The insight gathered through social media can help transport operators in predicting near-term non-recurrent supply changes allowing operators to plan accordingly (Periera at al., 2014; Mai & Hranac, 2012). This follows more general interest in the area of data mining, analysis and intelligence gathering through social media as part of broader emergency management scenarios (Sutton et al., 2008; Palen et al., 2010).

The volume of communications that might be generated by passengers on a transport network can be huge – each train operator in Great Britain regularly receives hundreds of tweets per hour as queries or comments that need to be reviewed and addressed. Figure 1 presents a model of the types of information that flow via Twitter between passengers and railway operators.

Preparing accurate, useful and tactful responses to these queries, with or without disruption, is a full-time job (Golightly and Durk, 2016) and tools to manage this communication, such as filtering based on Natural Language Processing (Yin et al., 2012) can streamline that process. There is also the potential for information mined through social media to be personalised and presented directly back to the passenger (Corsar et al., 2014), or to be coupled with other data sources to present very detailed information regarding service status (Rahman et al., 2015).

Figure 1. Information flow between passengers and operators

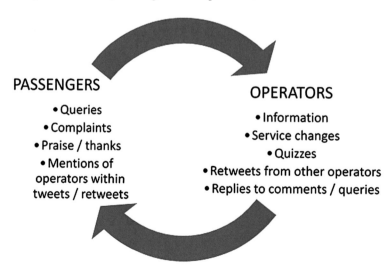

PASSENGERS
- Queries
- Complaints
- Praise / thanks
- Mentions of operators within tweets / retweets

OPERATORS
- Information
- Service changes
- Quizzes
- Retweets from other operators
- Replies to comments / queries

Therefore, if technologies based on big data analyses of social media are to be effective, it is critical to understand the constraints and characteristics of the content of social media that might shape the interpretation of results. This is most acute when considering the application of Twitter analytics in an area such as disruption management. The control and dissemination of information during disruption is a complex activity requiring multiple roles coordinating multiple (sometimes conflicting) information, with competing demands (Golightly et al., 2013). Often the windows of opportunity for action are brief, and the degrees of freedom in which to act are limited. Any delay in sensing or responding to the initial phases of an incident can exacerbate the situation rapidly (Belmonte et al., 2011). Therefore, the delivery of intelligence based on social media needs to be accurate, fast and deployed in a user-centred manner that compliments and enhances operational processes (Houghton and Golightly, 2011).

A scenario can help to illustrate. While major disruption events will be known to operational staff, a minor event, such as a peak of demand due to an overrunning concert, could be identified through social media. This might be through social media regarding the concert itself, but also through comments relating to crowding on the station. Social media tools, based on natural language processing and an ontology based around station names, can filter out this information, alerting social media managers through a dedicated social media dashboard, to manage customer expectation, or even advising of alternatives. Additionally, the dashboard could alert operational controllers who act to manage passenger levels (e.g. by warning train crew to anticipate high passenger levels).

Disruption is not a unitary phenomenon (Golightly et al., 2013, 2016) and varies by cause, location, duration etc. This can affect the trajectory of the disruption, which has a bearing on the kind of information that passengers need to know. Business reputation and social media are now explicit factors in real-time operational decision making during disruption (Golightly and Dadashi, 2016).

Understanding how the characteristics of disruption might correlate with Twitter useage could help to inform the design of technology as well as processes, for example, in the Passenger Information During Disruption (PIDD) code of practice used in Great Britain (ATOC, 2012). Additionally, there is evidence that transport operators vary in their social media strategy. While some choose to proactively distribute information, others are more reactive, replying to individual queries as they come in. In a study of transit services in the Strathclyde area of Scotland, this was due to local transport network constraints reducing the relevance of broadcast information (not all issues were believed to impact all people), though it may also have been through a desire not to generate negative perceptions of service quality (Gault et al., 2014). Therefore, technologies described in the scenario above need to reflect the specific nature of the type of disruption and potentially the style of operator in how they communicate.

The rest of this chapter considers potential applications, and some of the factors that need to be considered, regarding rail social media analytics and big data analysis. It opens by pulling out use cases from interviews conducted with rail stakeholders, transportation subject matter experts and, in particular, rail social media team managers and staff. It also highlights -- from an operational perspective -- some of the considerations relevant to rail social media analytics. A series of studies are then presented that examine how rail social media is used, examining which social media plaform (Facebook or Twitter) is most commonly used in the rail setting, and then investigating factors relating to operational characteristics and Train Operating Company (TOC) utilisation of social media that might influence the kind of data that is generated and how it should be analysed.

USE CASES

Two separate studies have been conducted with rail stakeholders to understand use cases for how social media, and social media analysis, can be applied to a railway context. The first of these studies (Houghton and Golightly, 2011) spoke to strategic management and the rail industry supply chain to understand, at that time, the potential of social media within a rail context. The second study (Golightly and Durk, 2016) was conducted more recently with rail social media managers and staff to understand how they were utilising social media, and their vision for how it could be used in the future. From both of these studies, use cases included:

- **Unstaffed Stations:** Many stations have either no staffing, or staffing at limited times. The opportunity to get additional data on station conditions would be useful. This might include factors such as ice on the platforms, or other forms of poor weather, but also information relating to crime and vandalism, or issues with assets such as ticketing machines.
- **Passenger Experience Issues:** Social media users commonly report issues with rolling stock particularly in relation to heating / air conditioning, Wi-Fi availability, which can be relayed to train maintenance crews. Additionally, passengers focus on factors such as crowding or lack of catering, which can also be fed back and rectified ideally in real time.
- **Public Order Issues:** The volume of people being transported by rail means that it is can be a potential flashpoint for violence, particularly taking into account the high number of football supporters that travel using rail to matches (British Transport Police, n. d.). Also, trains run late into the night, with increased risk of drink-related offences and accidents, occurring in and around the railway network.
- **Off-Network Events:** Events may take place away from the rail network itself but may have an impact on the service. For example, a concert or sport event may run late, meaning that a peak is passengers occurs later than expected at stations, which may need additional staffing or re-planning of services.
- **Understanding (and Managing) Misinformation:** One of the major concerns with social media, and of communication between transport users generally, was how misunderstandings and misinformation develops during incidents. At the early stages of an incident, in particular, transport users may start to communicate about potential causes and consequences of disruption, (for example, when a delay due to a minor derailment becomes exaggerated through word of mouth to be a major accident). Understanding when these misconceptions are occurring, and being able to correct them was considered to be more than just impression management, but also critical to ensuring that transport users had accurate information on which to re-plan journeys or expect the normal service to resume.
- **Managing Volume:** The sheer volume of tweets that social media account managers face is a significant challenge in its own right. Simply sorting through and responding to the number of messages is difficult given that it is still mostly a manual task. Tools to help sort incoming queries and comment and generate automatic responses could help account manager's loads, though there are concerns that humour and sarcasm, as well as passengers conveying all relevant information about their query in a single tweet, makes it difficult to automate the process.

- **Service Disruption Dashboards:** The nature and volume of social media content is already used a strong indicator of the effectiveness of disruption management strategy. For example, managers will look to check that the volume of negative tweets is decreasing, or that tweets with praise from passengers is increasing, during disruption as an indicator in real-time that a disruption management strategy is having a positive effect on passenger experience.

All of these use cases point to the viability and value of big data analysis of railway information, not just hypothetically, but as described by stakeholders themselves. The next question for a developer of such tools is to understand what is the landscape of content and usage of social media on the railways. In the next section, we consider some of the characteristics of rail social media behaviour.

CHARACTERISTICS OF SOCIAL MEDIA BEHAVIOUR

One key question to determine the nature of social media communications is to understand the kind of material that is available for analysis. The following section presents a series of studies of social media data in conjunction with the railways. These vary from macro-scale questions regarding which form of social media (Twitter or Facebook) is most relevant, through to questions of numbers of users in relation to train operator characteristics, including operational performance. We then present more detailed analysis of specific train operators in terms of the types of message they generate, and offer a specific example of how communications proceed within a given incident.

Which Social Media Platform?

The first question to answer is which social media platform is most commonly used on the railways. Apart from a small number of train operator Instagram accounts, the main channels for social media communication on the railways are Twitter and Facebook. Within that, global surveys of public transit operators (Pender et al., 2013; Liu et al., 2016) and interviews with GB rail stakeholders (Golightly and Durk, 2016) suggests that an overwhelming preference for Twitter over Facebook, despite Facebook penetration being double that of Twitter, both in the UK and globally (List of Popular Social Networks, n. d.). To confirm which platform is currently the most useful and popular for rail social media analysis, a comparison was made of the number of Facebook and Twitter 'followers' of the accounts of major Great Britain train operating companies.

The Office of Road and Rail National Rail Trends (ORR NRT) Data Portal lists passenger km (in millions) for all rail franchises in Great Britain. The criterion was applied that to be considered in the analysis, a franchise had to have a minimum of 5 million passenger Km per year. This criterion allowed us to exclude small and open access train operators that were atypical of the majority of rail operators, with a very limited social media presence and left a sample of 18 TOCs covering all major intercity, regional and London / South East based services.

A search was conducted for each TOC's Facebook page, which presents the number of user followers. A search was conducted for each TOC's Twitter profile. This gives a number of account followers. All 18 TOCs included in the analysis had a Twitter profile. Only 16 of the 18 had a Facebook profile. The mean number of Twitter followers for the TOCs was approximately 162,000, ranging between 35,600 and 650,000. The mean number of Facebook followers was approximately 25,000, ranging between 2,500 and 125,000.

Overall, the ratio of average Twitter followers to average Facebook followers is approximately 6.7:1, despite the overall UK social media statistics suggesting there are twice as many Facebook users to Twitter users. Also, a review of the content of these profiles confirms that most Twitter accounts are active with updates every day, if not every hour and in some cases almost every minute, on topics including service information, responses to queries and updates on delay or disruption. On the other hand, Facebook posts tend to be sporadic, often only every few days, and covering marketing information such as promotions, or notifications of major planned disruption (e.g. industrial action). In conclusion, and supporting previous studies and interview evidence, Twitter is by far the preferred platform for real time social media communications between passengers and operators.

Characteristics of Twitter Followers

Having established Twitter as the most useful source of information, a further question is what might be driving Twitter traffic. Previous work (Liu et al., 2016; Gault et al., 2014) from general public transit domains suggest that this is not just a question of the number of passengers, but may be down to more complex factors such as the style and preference of the operator, and the level of engagement with its followers.

To test this, a number of Twitter related characteristics for each TOC was correlated with a number of operational and service characteristics from each TOC.

Twitter characteristics, accessed via each TOC's Twitter profile page, included:

- Number of followers
- Number of tweets (including replies)
- Average tweets per day (by sampling at number of Tweets at two different dates and working out an average)

TOC operational characteristics, access via the ORR NRT portal, included:

- Number of passenger km operated per year (in million km)
- Number of train services operated per year (in thousands)
- A measure of performance – the ORR NRT gives a measure of Cancelled and Severely Late trains (CaSL), per TOC. CaSL is defined as the percentage of passenger trains cancelled in part or full, or that arrive at their final destination 30 or more minutes later than the time shown in the public timetable. As Cancelled and Severely Late trains would presumably generate tweets from operators, or require responses to passenger queries, CaSL is an appropriate performance measure. To give an absolute number of affected services that takes into account the size of operation of a TOC, CaSL has been multiplied by train services operated by a TOC per year.

Means and standard deviations for each variable are shown in Table 1. Correlations were performed using Pearson's r, shown in Table 2. Significant values (two tailed, $p < 0.05$, $df = 16$, $r > 0.44$) are marked in bold.

Table 1. Means and standard deviations for Twitter useage, operational and performance variables

	Followers (Thousands)	Tweets (Thousands)	Tweets Per Day (Thousands)	Passenger km (Millions)	Number of Services (Thousands)	Total CaSL Services (Thousands)
Average	167.39	301.79	0.21	7.03	399.36	12.3
St Dev	161.72	223.14	0.16	3.77	317.48	13.4

Table 2. Correlations of Twitter usage, operational and performance variables

	Followers	Tweets	Tweets per Day	Passenger km	Number of Services	Total CaSL
Followers	1.00	**0.52**	0.36	0.35	0.23	0.17
Tweets		1.00	**0.86**	**0.67**	0.44	**0.47**
Tweets Per day			1.00	**0.71**	0.41	0.43
Passenger Km				1.00	**0.75**	**0.72**
Number of services					1.00	**0.87**
Total CaSL						1.00

Taking each of the three Twitter related variables in turn, the number of followers is not significantly correlated with passenger km, number of trains or total number of CaSL. Bigger TOCs, even though they have a larger passenger base or number of services, do not necessarily have bigger sets of users following them. Indeed, inspection of the data suggests that some of the smaller, long distance TOCs have very high numbers of followers. This analysis backs up the reports of rail social media managers (Golightly and Durk, 2016) that strategy is an important factor in growing and maintaining a Twitter following.

The correlations suggest a link between number of tweets generated by the TOC, and operational and performance characteristics. Both passenger KM and CaSL were significant, suggesting that both numbers of people and number of delayed services will lead to a higher number of tweets from the TOC. Also, tweets per day suggests a similar though weaker pattern. More passenger km will lead to more tweets per day. However, the correlation between tweets per day and CaSL is not significant, suggesting that factors other than delay may generate the volume of tweets of a daily basis.

Content Analyses of Twitter Usage Patterns

While Twitter is shown to be most common social media communication channel, and higher service numbers generally leads to higher number of tweets from a TOC, there would seem to be factors other than sheer passenger numbers that influences the number of followers. This is important as those TOCs with high passengers are may not achieve the same level of penetration as other TOCs.

One of the limitations of the analysis above is that it does not differentiate between tweets that are broadcasts to all users, and tweets that are responses to specific queries. This is important as the design of the Twitter platform means that all followers do not automatically see exchanges directed to and from a user, unless they are also following both users in the exchange. Therefore, useful information flowing between TOCs and users will not always be seen by all Twitter followers of that TOC.

To test what type of information is being conveyed in Twitter exchanges with a TOC, five TOCs were followed for an extended period of two weeks and outgoing tweets were captured. Tweets were captured using NVivo with the NCapture plugin, and were filtered and categorised in Microsoft Excel according to the following scheme.

- **TOC Broadcast (TOCB):** A Tweet sent by the TOC to all its followers. This might be disruption information, a salutation at the start of the day, or marketing information.
- **TOC Directed Tweet (TOCDT):** A Tweet directed to a specific recipient (the tweet starts with the intended users name. In the case of a TOC this is usually a reply to a comment or query from a passenger) NB this is not to be confused with a Twitter Direct Message (DM).
- **TOC Retweet (TOCRT):** A recirculation by the TOC of a Tweet to all of its followers. In the case of the TOC this might be recirculating a tweet sent in by a passenger asking if anyone has found a lost personal item on a train.

Table 3 shows the breakdown of outgoing tweets from the five TOCs. Also, to gauge how much traffic might be generated by disruption events, the Network Rail Control Centre Incident Log, and National Rail Enquiries service update website, were monitored to identify potential disruption during the data captured period. The numbers of disruption events are also presented in Table 3.

Several points emerge. First, TOCs are variable in how they choose to communicate via Twitter, particularly with regards how they choose to broadcast information. Some TOCs (e.g. TOC3,5) will generate many broadcast messages, while others are far less likely to do so (e.g. TOC1). This is despite TOCs experiencing a similar numbers of disruption events over the analysis period. Therefore, TOC style is a critical factor to take into account when analysing the nature of exchange between TOC and passenger.

Second, in some cases the numbers of outgoing TOC tweets are extremely high, with TOC2 generating over 600 Tweets per day. Given that most of these TOCs have limited response out of hours (00:00-06:00) this means in some cases a response rate during operational hours is in the region of a tweet almost every minute.

Third, the large majority (72%) of tweets are not broadcasts of information, but are instead typically responses to incoming tweets. All TOCs to some extent, and some (e.g. TOC2) to a greater extent prefer to reply to issues rather than broadcast information. The implication is that information transmitted as replies are very unlikely to be seen by any user other than the recipient, or by actively searching within the TOCs timeline. Therefore, potentially useful information will not be seen by all followers of a TOC account.

Table 3. Outgoing tweets from the TOC

	TOC1	**TOC2**	**TOC3**	**TOC4**	**TOC5**
TOCBs	140	62	426	114	1476
TOCDTs	1695	8896	2181	7802	3952
TOCRTs	31	32	32	75	61
Total outgoing	1866	8990	2639	7991	5489
Average per day	133.3	642.1	188.5	570.8	392.1
Disruption events	32	27	31	18	29

Figure 2. Distribution of Tweet types by TOC; Y-axis is number of tweets.

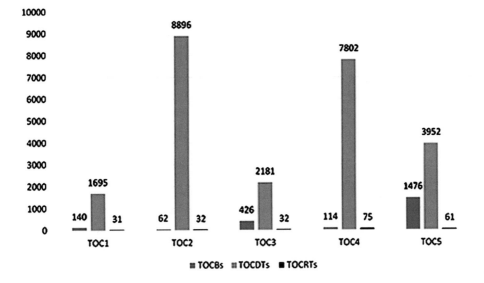

In terms of the content of tweets, Table 4 gives an example timeline of how TOCs use broadcasts during disruption. This is for a landslip blocking the line the in Banbury area of Great Britain. Out of the 142 tweets that were broadcasted by the TOC from the afternoon to evening on the day of the disruption, 123 of these tweets were replies to users, making it 86.6% as replies to users. The example also

Table 4. Timeline of broadcasts associated with major disruption event

14:52	Initial broadcast notifying all about incident occurrence and introduction of hashtag to categorise tweets *"Due to a landslip, all lines are currently blocked between #LeamingtonSpa & #Banbury. Delays, alterations & cancellations are expected."*
15:10	Notification of alternative means of transport with another TOC via a Retweet *"RT @SW_Trains: We're accepting @crosscountryuk tickets via any reasonable route following a landslip between Banbury & Leamington Spa"*
15:19	Update of incident to now inform commuters about rail replacement buses *"Due to a landslip, rail replacement buses are in operation in both directions between #LeamingtonSpa & #Banbury ran by @ chilternrailway ."*
15:30	Update to combine the separate hashtags into one for easier classification *"UPDATE: Our further tweets in regards the landslip disruption between #LeamingtonSpa & #Banbury will be under the hashtag #Harburylandslip"*
15:32	Notification of more alternative transport with other TOCs *"#Harburylandslip: Ticket acceptance is in place with @VirginTrains @SW_Trains @chilternrailway @LondonMidland @ FGW @eastcoastuk @TfL tube."*
16:35	Introduction of replacement bus service *"#Harburylandslip: There will soon be a limited coach service between LeamingtonSpa/Banbury and Oxford in both directions."*
17:40	Introduction of new service to cope with demand *"#Harburylandslip: There will be a service at xx:55 southbound from Banbury - Bournemouth/Southampton Central until the end of service today."*
18:10	Notification of cancelled route affected by incident *"#Harburylandslip: The 19:45 Bournemouth - Birmingham New Street is cancelled throughout."*
21:59	End of Twitter Operating hours, along with reminder of delay compensation *"We'll be back tomorrow at 8am. Further updates will be provided in regards to the #Harburylandslip. Please claim Delay Repay if affected 1/2"*

highlights the use of hashtags to allow passengers to follow an event over time, and to search. This is also supports coordination with other stakeholders who need to offer alternative services or might be affected. The mention of other TOCs in the timeline (15:32), and the retweet of another TOCs message of ticket acceptance (15:10), reinforces the idea of multiple stakeholders bringing each other in to the stream of information associated with an event. This is a powerful capability of Twitter. Finally, the management of the incident concludes for that day with information about how passengers can claim compensation (21:59).

IMPLICATIONS

A number of specific findings and implications for designers emerge from the analysis presented here. First, a number of use cases have been highlighted that would benefit from big data analysis. These typically regard intelligence regarding conditions in and around the railways, and is mostly concerned with real-time or near real-time intelligence. This is critical given the time responsive nature of the railways, particularly during disruption (Belmondo et al., 2011) and the increased emphasis on reputation and information management (Golightly and Dadashi, 2016). Some of the applications however are more about 'back office' services to support social media teams – generating automated answers, filtering queries and presenting dashboards, to help an operator understand its performance. The implication is that both of these areas, real time intelligence, and supporting social media teams, are fruitful areas for future development of rail social media big data analyses.

Second, this work has confirmed other studies that Twitter is the most important information channel for social media exchange on the railways (Pender et al., 2013; Liu et al., 2016). This is partly likely to be derived from functional aspects – the ability to post short messages to followers, and the conversational nature of the interface, and the way it readily lends itself to mobile devices – and partially because of attitudes around it being more for practical use rather than for communicating with a person's own social network as per Facebook (Passengerfocus, 2013). The overriding implication is that social media analysis for the railways should have Twitter at its core.

Third, while the volume of Twitter traffic has some relation with operational factors such as number of passengers and services, or experienced delay, this is not a simple relationship. In particular, the number of followers of a TOC account is determined by factors other than sheer size of the TOCs operations. Reinforcing other studies (Gault et al., 2014; Golightly and Durk, 2016), TOC style plays a significant role in shaping how a TOC uses Twitter and it how looks to communicate with its followers. Furthermore, by looking at the breakdown of type of message (broadcast, reply, retweet) this difference between TOC becomes more apparent. Some TOCs are highly reactive in how they tweet, replying mostly to queries and with little use of broadcast. Others are more proactive. The implication here for big data analysis are that: (1) TOCs use different strategies, with different styles of communication. This must be taken into account when designing algorithms and ontologies to process the content of tweets and (2) this will affect the kind of response and volume of response that a TOC can expect to generate. Some TOCs will generate more conversations with their passengers that are amenable to analysis, and this is not just determined by TOC size. Also, if a TOC wants to use its Twitter feed as a source of intelligence, it should actively look to grow its follower base.

Fourth, disruption and non-disruption are both encountered in the Twitter data. Indeed, one comment from social media managers is that many diverse non-disruption queries such as lost luggage, ticketing queries, and specific complaints, take up more time than disruption which can be communicated uniformly across all passengers. The implications for big data analysis are therefore (1) support is needed just as much for non-disruption as it is for disruption (2) when a disruption is occurring, there is a clear narrative, as well as use of pointer such as hashtags of locations (see Table 4) that can help with the interpretation of events. These narratives vary for different types of event (Golightly and Dadashi, 2016) and can be used to form ontologies, specific to each type of disruption, that can be embedded within analytical tools. As an illustration, coupling general language about delay (e.g. 'delay, 'disruption') with specific language regarding the type of disruption (e.g. 'train failure', blocked line'), with terminology specific to an operator geography (e.g. locations and stations for that operator), as well as general levels of interaction between the operator and passenger, which indicates volume of Twitter traffic, can provide a targeted data pre-processing ontology. This pre-processing ontology would, in turn, facilitate faster analysis of incoming tweets, prioritisation, dashboards for internal operational staff, and potentially a means to filter and re-publish particularly useful tweets to passengers through other channels such as other forms of social media, websites or even on-platform / in-station displays.

Fifth and finally, a methodological point arises from the correlations between Twitter and ORR data sets in Table 2 and 3. Twitter does not have to be the only dataset. Even with the relatively simple combination of Twitter data with open operational and performance data it has been possible to identify some relationships between social media and train operators. The implication is that there are many ways Twitter could be augmented with information from other data sets within big data analyses. Also, the focus of this paper has been analyses using social media as the major data source, there is potential for analyses on other data sets, where Twitter could play a more supplementary role (Rahman et al., 2015), for example by having condition monitoring data as the primary analysis, but supplementing that with comments on Twitter about ride quality and comfort.

Figure 3 represents the typology of passenger and social media users relevant to the railways. At the core, there are 'active users' – they generate tweets and retweets and thus generate both traffic and intelligence about activity on the railways. Second, there are 'passive followers' of railway Twitter ac-

Figure 3. Typology of passenger usage of Twitter and Twitter-based information

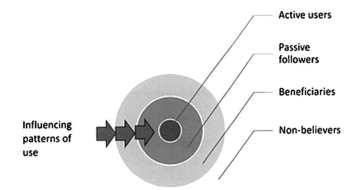

counts. They do not necessarily generate data, but they could view broadcasts and information on Twitter. Importantly, from this analysis, passive followers will benefit to varying degrees depending on whether a TOC broadcasts their messages or not. Third, there are potential 'beneficiaries'. These may not follow social media, but could benefit from filtered views of Twitter-based information. This might be through sentiment analytics, or for example through the presentation of a sub-set of most valuable tweets through disruption pages on operator websites (some TOCs and National Rail Enquiries already have a simplified version of this) or even on station information screens. Finally, there are 'non-believers' – passengers who have no interest in Twitter-based information. Key to the ongoing success of Twitter is to maintain the active user base, and to move more passengers from the outer circles to the inner stages of adoption and engagement with Twitter-based information. This typology is useful in that it allows developers and designers to have a clear idea of who is generating and using Twitter-based information.

CONCLUSION

Social media has been proposed as a potential target for big data analysis. This chapter has outlined some of the ways in which social media could be used, both for intelligence in and around the railways and to support in the management of social media accounts. Much of this is still manual and therefore opportunity exists. For new tools or analyses to be successful they must, however, take into account how passengers use rail social media and how operators control the railway. Following prior work (Pender et al., 2013; Liu et al., 2016) which looked at transport systems generally, analyses here demonstrate that Twitter is the predominant form of social media on the railways. Usage does not map completely to the size of train operator and factors such as strategy play an important role in the type of communication generated. Disruption is important, but equally non-disruption and more general passenger experience factors are communicated through Twitter and these are usually queries between passenger and train operator that will not necessarily be seen by all followers.

While we have outlined a number of implications for developers of big data analysis, the variation between TOCs indicates a policy implication. Not all TOCs are standard in their use of Twitter. The type of content that two TOCs will generate or will elicit from its passengers may vary because of strategy, not because of any operational concerns. Also, a TOC may appear to be performing less effectively on social media because it elects to broadcast information and invite comment. Therefore, the use of tools to present metrics, such as dashboards, that present data on both volume and content (i.e. sentiment) of tweets should only be used for comparison across TOCs, for example to study performance, with great caution.

Taking into account the opportunity and characteristics for rail social media, there is both a scope and need for developments in this area. Future work should look on one hand to develop tools that can filter queries with a high level of accuracy. As mentioned above, initial work in generally defining disruption characteristics (Golightly and Dadashi, 2016) could be used to inform specific disruption-related ontologies. Also, models of non-disruption, more general passenger experience (e.g. Stanton et al., 2013) could be used as the basis of ontologies for analysis. Finally, it is critical that any tool that is developed takes into accounts the needs of its users, particularly when embedded within an operational context (Houghton and Golightly, 2011).

ACKNOWLEDGMENT

The first author was funded by the Impetus partnership between Universities of Nottingham and Leicester, and the Transport Systems Catapult. We are also grateful for the input and support of the Rail Delivery Group and Jason Durk, at Govia Thameslink Railway, for invaluable access to industry experts and data.

REFERENCES

ATOC (Association of Train Operating Companies). (2012). Approved Code of Practice – Passenger Information During Disruption. Retrieved 05/11/14 from http://www.atoc.org/clientfiles/files/ACOP015v3%20-%20PIDD%20(2).pdf

Belmonte, F., Schön, W., Heurley, L., & Capel, R. (2011). Interdisciplinary safety analysis of complex socio-technological systems based on the functional resonance accident model: An application to railway traffic supervision. *Reliability Engineering & System Safety*, *96*(2), 237–249. doi:10.1016/j.ress.2010.09.006

British Transport Police. (n. d.). Football policing. Retrieved from http://www.btp.police.uk/advice_and_info/how_we_tackle_crime/football_policing.aspx

Corsar, D., Markovic, M., Gault, P. E., Mehdi, M., Edwards, P., Nelson, J. D., & Sripada, S. et al. (2015). TravelBot: Journey Disruption Alerts Utilising Social Media and Linked Data. In *Proceedings of the Posters and Demonstrations Track of the 14th International Semantic Web Conference (ISWC '15)*.

Cottrill, C., Gault, P., Yeboah, G., Nelson, J. D., Anable, J., & Budd, T. (2017). Tweeting Transit: An examination of social media strategies for transport information management during a large event. *Transportation Research Part C, Emerging Technologies*, *77*, 421–432. doi:10.1016/j.trc.2017.02.008

European Commission. (2011). Roadmap to a single European transport area—Towards a competitive and resource-efficient transport system (White Paper on transport). Luxembourg, Publications Office of the European Union.

Gault, P., Corsar, D., Edwards, P., Nelson, J. D., & Cottrill, C. (2014). You'll Never Ride Alone: The Role of Social Media in Supporting the Bus Passenger Experience. In *Proceedings of the Ethnographic Praxis in Industry Conference* (Vol. 2014, No. 1, pp. 199-212).

Golightly, D., & Dadashi, N. (2016). The characteristics of railway service disruption: Implications for disruption management. *Ergonomics*. PMID:27215348

Golightly, D., Dadashi, N., Sharples, S., & Dasigi, M. (2013). Disruption management processes during emergencies on the railways. *International Journal of Human Factors and Ergonomics*, *2*(2), 175–195. doi:10.1504/IJHFE.2013.057619

Golightly, D., & Durk, J. (2016). Twitter as part of operational practice and passenger experience on the railways. In P.E. Waterson, E. Hubbard & R. Sims (Eds.), *Proceedings of EHF2016. Contemporary Ergonomics and Human Factors 2016*. Loughborough: CIEHF.

Government of India (Railway Board). (2014) Disaster management plan Retrieved 05/11/14 from http://www.indianrailways.gov.in/railwayboard/uploads/directorate/safety/pdf/2014/DM_Plan_2014.pdf

Houghton, R. J., & Golightly, D. (2011). Should a signaller look at twitter? The value of user data to transport control. Retrieved from http://de2011.computing.dundee.ac.uk

Jain, J., & Lyons, G. (2008). The gift of travel time. *Journal of Transport Geography, 16*(2), 81–89. doi:10.1016/j.jtrangeo.2007.05.001

Koetse, M. J., & Rietveld, P. (2009). The impact of climate change and weather on transport: An overview of empirical findings. *Transportation Research Part D, Transport and Environment, 14*(3), 205–221. doi:10.1016/j.trd.2008.12.004

Liu, J. H., Shi, W., Elrahman, O.S., Ban, X.J., & Reilly, J.M. (2016). Understanding social media program usage in public transit agencies. *International Journal of Transportation Science and Technology, 5*(2), 83–92. doi:10.1016/j.ijtst.2016.09.005

Mai, E., & Hranac, R. (2013, January). Twitter interactions as a data source for transportation incidents. In *Proc. Transportation Research Board 92nd Ann. Meeting (No. 13-1636)*.

Palen, L., Starbird, K., Vieweg, S., & Hughes, A. (2010). twitter-based information distribution during the 2009 Red River Valley flood threat. *Bulletin of the American Society for Information Science and Technology, 36*(5), 13–17. doi:10.1002/bult.2010.1720360505

Passenger Focus. (2013) Short and Tweet: How passengers want social media during disruption. Retrieved April 8, 2013 from http://www.transportfocus.org.uk/research-publications/publications/short-and-tweet-how-passengers-want-social-media-during-disruption/

Pender, B., Currie, G., Delbosc, A., & Shiwakoti, N. (2013, October). Social Media Utilisation during Unplanned Passenger Rail Disruption What's Not to Like? In *Proc. Australasian Transport Research Forum 2013*.

Pender, B., Currie, G., Delbosc, A., & Shiwakoti, N. (2014). Social Media Use in Unplanned Passenger Rail Disruptions – An International Study. In *Transportation Research Board 93rd Annual Meeting Compendium of Papers*.

Pereira, F. C., Bazzan, A. L., & Ben-Akiva, M. (2014). The role of context in transport prediction. *IEEE Intelligent Systems, 29*(1), 76–80. doi:10.1109/MIS.2014.14

Rahman, S. S., Easton, J. M., & Roberts, C. (2015, August). Mining open and crowdsourced data to improve situational awareness for railway. In *Proceedings of the 2015 IEEE/ACM International Conference on Advances in Social Networks Analysis and Mining (ASONAM)* (pp. 1240-1243). IEEE. doi:10.1145/2808797.2809369

Schultz, F., Utz, S., & Göritz, A. (2011). Is the medium the message? Perceptions of and reactions to crisis communication via Twitter, blogs and traditional media. *Public Relations Review, 37*(1), 20–27. doi:10.1016/j.pubrev.2010.12.001

Social Media Ltd. (n. d.). *List of Popular Social Network*s. Retrieved from https://social-media.co.uk/list-popular-social-networking-websites

Sutton, J., Palen, L., & Shklovski, I. (2008, May). Backchannels on the front lines: Emergent uses of social media in the 2007 southern California wildfires. In *Proceedings of the 5th International ISCRAM Conference,* Washington, DC (pp. 624-632).

Yin, J., Lampert, A., Cameron, M., Robinson, B., & Power, R. (2012). Using social media to enhance emergency situation awareness. *IEEE Intelligent Systems, 27*(6), 52–59. doi:10.1109/MIS.2012.6

Chapter 11
Big Data and Natural Language Processing for Analysing Railway Safety:
Analysis of Railway Incident Reports

Kanza Noor Syeda
Lancaster University, UK

Syed Noorulhassan Shirazi
Lancaster University, UK

Syed Asad Ali Naqvi
Lancaster University, UK

Howard J Parkinson
Digital Rail Limited, UK

Gary Bamford
Digital Rail Limited, UK

ABSTRACT

Due to modern powerful computing and the explosion in data availability and advanced analytics, there should be opportunities to use a Big Data approach to proactively identify high risk scenarios on the railway. In this chapter, we comprehend the need for developing machine intelligence to identify heightened risk on the railway. In doing so, we have explained a potential for a new data driven approach in the railway, we then focus the rest of the chapter on Natural Language Processing (NLP) and its potential for analysing accident data. We review and analyse investigation reports of railway accidents in the UK, published by the Rail Accident Investigation Branch (RAIB), aiming to reveal the presence of entities which are informative of causes and failures such as human, technical and external. We give an overview of a framework based on NLP and machine learning to analyse the raw text from RAIB reports which would assist the risk and incident analysis experts to study causal relationship between causes and failures towards the overall safety in the rail industry.

DOI: 10.4018/978-1-5225-3176-0.ch011

INTRODUCTION

In this chapter, we describe the research we have been undertaking to understand Big Data (BD) and its application to management of safety in the railway. We undertook the journey described in this chapter because we realised that many of the traditional safety management approaches do not deal very well with the complex socio-technological systems we are increasingly facing in the railway environment. We notice that we are in a new paradigm when it comes to BD, Internet of Things (IoT), computing power and intelligent algorithms. There is a vast potential to take a data driven approach to safety and systems engineering with decisions being based on real data and not just engineering judgments. Our aim is to help in the construction of a suite of BD risk assessment and development tools for reducing safety risk in railway projects and operations. In the first part of the chapter we present a summary of our previous works (Angelov, Manolopoulos, Iliadis et al., 2016; Parkinson & Bamford, 2016; Parkinson, Bamford, & Kandola, 2016; Parkinson & Bamford, 2017) in which we set out to develop an understanding of BD as it applies to railway safety management. It also helps set the scene for the NLP research which is the main focus of the rest of this chapter.

In order to understand what was meant by BD and its application in railway safety, we undertook an initial phase of research. This research involved an investigation into various railway accident to explore accident causation and assess if the available data could have provided a prior warning of the catastrophe. This research also included evaluating whether the assessment could be classified as a BD approach or simply business as usual (BAU). We proposed a new mechanism for identifying and mitigating heightened risk called ELBowTie[1] (Parkinson et al., 2016). The next stage of our research was to go into a deeper analysis of the Grayrigg Accident (Branch, 2011). We analysed the engineering and management failures associated with Grayrigg using a bowtie risk assessment approach. We investigated the type of Big Data Analytics (BDA), available, that could potentially have been used to identify hazardous conditions prior to the accident. We then undertook meta-analysis conducted in previous research in order to develop an understanding of the wider state of play of intelligent analytics in current railway research and development. We finally move on the main focus of the chapter which describes on-going work being undertaken to employ machine learning and Natural Language Processing (NLP) to predict railway heightened risk.

The field of incident analysis consists of number of methods. Certain methods are based on accumulated expert knowledge with prescribed models and/or procedures. Although, these methods differ amongst themselves in terms of their level of detail, methodology, presumptions, aspects of focus, etc.; most prescribe certain basic Entities of Interest (EOI) that maybe common within several methods. We define EOI as factors that represent categories of information that may help explain an incident in terms of cause-effect relationships. Furthermore, due to the heterogeneous nature of each incident, a lot of relevant information is recorded in loose text instead of constrained value fields. Such text components enclose considerable richness that is invaluable for incident analysis and prediction. However, there is only limited work available aimed at applying text analysis to incident investigation. This is, primarily due to the difficulty and challenges related to interpretation of such data.

Natural Language Processing (NLP) represents a set of techniques that can computationally extract useful conceptual information from text. Our goal in this study is to assess the usefulness of NLP to the field of incident analysis in terms of identifying EOI from incident analysis reports. More specifically, based on that understanding, we want to ascertain the usefulness of NLP approaches to examine the presence of significant entities which are based on expert knowledge and presence of relationships among those entities. This work draws attention to the opportunities available by exploiting these technologies to enhance railway safety. The final part of the chapter contains a review of the wider opportunities for the rail industry in the digital era, especially regarding safety, where we describe a virtuous circle of railway digitisation.

BIG DATA AND RAILWAY SAFETY

In (Parkinson & Bamford, 2017) we set out to develop an understanding of BD as it applies to railway safety management. A literature review was undertaken of BD in general and in the railway domain. The 5V model i.e., Volume, Velocity, Variety, Veracity and Value, (Hilbert, 2015) was adopted to define BD. An Enterprise Data Taxonomy (EDT) was derived for railway data which was as comprehensive as possible at this early stage.

Three major accidents were reviewed and assessed to understand what the high-level accident causation was due to. The accidents reviewed were the Hatfield Accident in 2001, Platja de Castelldefels in Spain in 2010, and Santiago de Compostela also in Spain in 2013. Once identified, each of the causes was linked, using the EDT, to sources of data that may have highlighted the risk of the hazard together with its potential to propagate into a railway accident.

The data sources were evaluated according to the 5V model and assessed for their respective 'BDness' or BD quotient to provide a score that can then be interpreted as the potential for BDA. This BD Quotient is shown in Figure 1 along with an indication of where the respective accidents sit on this BD Quotient view. Clearly some data associated with railway accidents, especially ones with mainly technical causes are probably more BAU than BD.

The analysis of the accidents has shown that BD could potentially help in mitigating accidents where the causes are systemic and complex in nature. In (Parkinson & Bamford, 2016) we go on to introduce an enhanced ELBowTie methodology, illustrated in Figure 2, to provide a mechanism for feeding BD

Figure 1. Big data quotient
Source: Parkinson & Bamford, 2017.

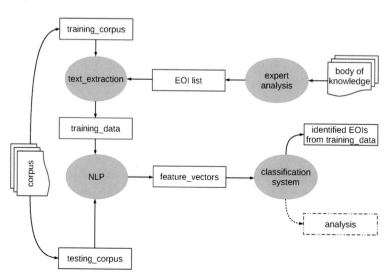

Figure 2. ElBowTie
Source: Parkinson & Bamford, 2017.

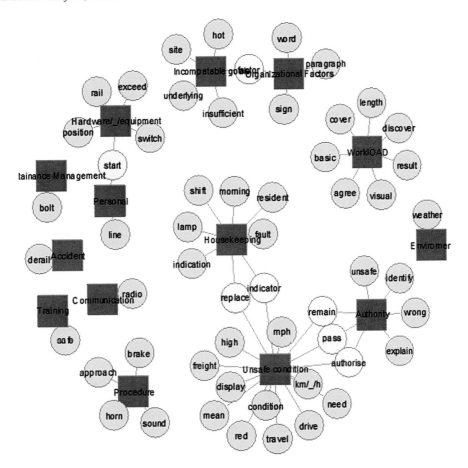

into safety risk assessments. During the research, we noticed that the visualisation of risks and associated data was a critical element of the analysis. We therefore developed the ELBowTie model which provides a means of linking to real-time data updates, enabling a 'live' risk dashboard to be envisaged. The results from this research lead to a greater understanding of BD and how it could be applied to improve railway safety.

The Grayrigg Accident

The work in (Parkinson et al., 2016) aimed to investigate the challenges encountered in safety assessments around the use of multiple data sources and analytics. Specifically, the research objectives included are: how to represent the details of the accident, how to link to the associated data sources to this representation and how to evaluate the analytical approaches that are available for analysing this data? This allowed us to define the types of algorithm needed to extract enhanced safety knowledge out of the data sources.

The current state of play in machine learning was explored and an overview of all the available analytical approaches was presented. A way forward on the application of the various analytical approaches was outlined to determine the data attributes and requirements to improve the identification of unsafe conditions. There are only 5 types of analytics. These are used for either standalone analysis or in combinations for more detailed assessments. These types are as follows:

1. **Bayesian Analytics:** Probabilistic inference algorithms
2. **Analogy Analytics:** Inference algorithms
3. **Symbolist Analytics:** Inverse deduction algorithms
4. **Evolution Analytics:** Genetic algorithms
5. **Connectionist Analytics:** Back propagation algorithms

We assessed these BASEC approaches in terms of the Grayrigg data for use in the ELBowTie. The objective was to investigate how this information could be applied to develop a prototype machine learning algorithm as depicted in Figure 3. The overall aim was to evaluate how the BASEC algorithms could be trained to recognise heightened risk situations on the rail infrastructure. The EDT, described

Figure 3. Proposed structure for combining BASEC
Source: Parkinson & Bamford, 2017.

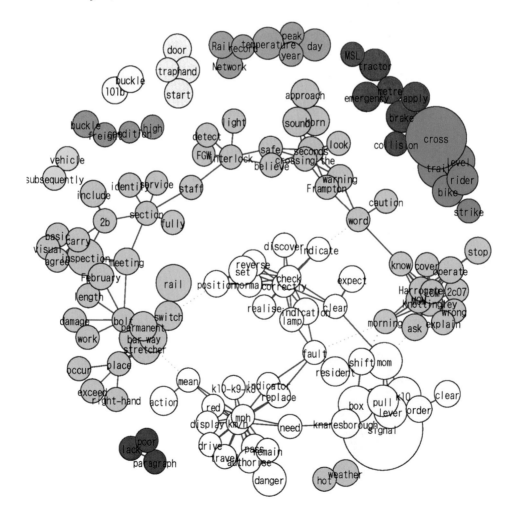

previously, comprises the entirety of data shown in Figure 3 on the left of the diagram which covers, for example, CCTV images, textual information, weather data etc.

We are currently working on some of these data streams, in particular, Neural Networks for monitoring wheel rail interface forces using deep learning, and autonomous platform train interface monitoring to increase passenger safety and reduce dwell time. These analyses in and of themselves may result in a trigger to warn of danger; however, often it is the complex relationships between these conditions that can provide important indicators to major accidents.

Meta-Analysis of Big Data Analytics at Two Major Railway Conferences

Next, we wanted to understand what analytical techniques are currently being used in the rail industry to see if there was opportunity for reuse. The work in (Parkinson, 2017) contains a review of available analytics approaches together with an evaluation of the analytical content of the work discussed earlier (Parkinson & Bamford, 2016; Parkinson et al., 2016). A review of 343 papers was undertaken, the focus being to establish algorithmic content of each paper. An evaluation was then made as to whether the algorithms identified could have been applied to the Grayrigg accident. Seven papers were identified as containing algorithms applicable to the identification of safety issues, these are listed in Table 1.

Part of the objective of the Grayrigg analysis was to identify particular analytics from the BASEC tribes to potentially indicate heightened risk. Table 2 contains the results of this analysis for the seven papers identified in Table 1. The analysis involved selecting only papers that contained 1st order algorithms that were directly applicable to Grayrigg and could form the basis of ELBowTie analytics. Other 2nd order algorithms which have a more tenuous connection, not targeted specifically at Grayrigg assets but could potentially be used in a wider analysis are contained in existing literature. These could be looked into further to include e.g. genetic algorithms in design, timetable heuristics, and supply chain game theory.

Table 1 and Table 2 illustrate that although these work present state of the art for rail technology, the impact of machine learning and data analytics is not advanced. Much work is taking place in generating technical data but the use of that data for system wide optimisation is still in its early stages. There, therefore, appears to be limited use of complex analytics within the current research and technical activity in the rail industry.

Table 1. Papers with analytics applicable to Grayrigg

Technique Category	Total Number of Papers in Category	Number Applicable to Grayrigg	Paper Reference and Comment
Performance	52	1	118 (reliability - FMEA to predict failures and plan maintenance)
Design	52	2	125 (bogie design to limit force on switches),240 (simulation of joint failure)
Remote Monitoring	45	2	170 (vibration to detect defects) + vision paper from Brussels
Whole System	31	2	248 whole system - -application of BD analytics + semantic paper from Brussels

Table 2. BASEC analytics against paper classification

Type of Analytics	Performance (1)	Design (2)	Remote Monitoring (2)	Whole System (2)
B	X		X	
A		X	X	
S				
E				
C		X		XX

NLP for Railway Incident Analysis

Incident analysis reports usually comprise of an assorted set of information from incident description to legal obligations, to policies, procedures, and description of various components. Much of the information in these reports represents tangential issues with less relevance to incident factors.

Further, information related to incident factors may be scattered across the documentation. In this context NLP approaches need to be honed towards the identification of relevant information -- incident factors and their relationships. What is needed is a point of reference for the NLP approaches to conduct their search. This point of reference was provided through a set of general concepts that are relevant to incident analysis. We have termed these concepts as Entities of Interest (EOI). EOIs (see Table 3) are abstract concepts that represent different types of faults and causal factors in incident analysis. In deriving EOIs our goal was to cover a broad spectrum of incident relevant concepts. The broader the spectrum of EOIs, the lower the probability that NLP analyses based on these EOIs will miss any relevant incident factors.

EOI Extraction

To derive the list of EOIs we turned to the literature on incident analysis (Gano, 2011; Harms-Ringdahl, 2013; Hollnagel & Speziali, 2008; Johnson, 2003; Latino, Latino, & Latino, 2016; Livingston, Jackson, & Priestley, 2001; Sklet, 2002; Woloshynowych, Rogers, Taylor-Adams, & Vincent, 2005; Ziedelis & Noel, 2011). Many mature incident analysis methods express reality by means of a limited number of prescriptive models, artefacts, and taxonomies. These prescriptive models and artefacts represent element of accumulated expert knowledge and experience. These methods explain incidents through various abstract incident types and causes, for example, the list of general failure types in *Tripod*, analysis tree in *MORT*, and *SORTM* in *HPIP* (see Table 3). We identified several significant incident analysis methods within this category and used their models, artefacts, and taxonomies to inform the derivation of our EOIs. Our criteria for selecting these incident analysis methods were a) they had to be generalised (not domain specific) in their application, and b) they had to be significant in the field. Significance means that the method should have been used in multiple studies by different authors, or that it is widely used in industry for incident analysis. The EOIs in relation to the incident analysis methods are shown in Table 3 and the Appendix.

Moreover, the work intends to inform and advance railway incident analysis efforts by illustrating how these novel technologies, together with expert knowledge, can be leveraged to improve railway safety. More specifically, we are interested in extracting entities of interest from textual report describing incidents. In doing so, we hope to reveal causes of accidents, catalogue potential safety measures, and show how to better leverage technologies to improve the safety. The work mainly involves, but is not limited to the following:

- Review state-of-the-art incident analysis techniques with respect to railway safety.
- Understanding various NLP techniques for named entity recognition.
- Classification and prediction approaches based on machine learning to establish correlation between causes and failures.
- Design and build tool chain using Python and Perl scripts to provide implementation of our model.

The structure of the remainder of this paper is: The following background section presents a brief overview of incident analysis domain by providing a purpose and benefits of incident analysis. The method section discusses the method and details overview of the involved process. In analysis section, we present our analysis and finally conclusion section concludes the paper.

BACKGROUND

This section provides purpose and benefits of incident analysis and multi-incident analysis domain from the perspective of railway safety.

Incident Analysis

Accidents, and incidents of faults and failures are an unavoidable reality for even moderately complex systems. Accidents, though unfortunate events, also provide an opportunity to uncover vulnerabilities and latent errors in systems. In this vein, accident and incident analysis plays an important role in improving system dependability and robustness. The purpose and benefit of an incident analysis is realised when it can explain the dynamics of "how" and "why" an incident happened in terms of its root causes and other relevant incident factors. Root causes are those entrenched systemic risk factors within an enterprise, environment, or domain that may have either caused or contributed to several latent and active failures. The work by (Reason, 1990) states that accidents happen when latent and active failures converge under the right circumstances. Therefore, unless the root causes are identified and their effects mitigated, the risk of accidents in a domain will persist as before. Conversely, the identification and mitigation of the root causes will contribute towards the avoidance of incidents in the future. We define incident factors as all relevant factors related to an incident, which may include causal factors, performance shaping factors, post-event factors, and other matters concerning safety.

Multi-Incident Analysis

Incidents when analysed individually often seem to be caused by isolated reasons such as equipment failure, mishap, or negligence. However, when incidents are analysed in the context of other incidents in the broader domain then patterns begin to emerge between them. These patterns may indicate basic and underlying reasons for incidents – the root causes. The practice of analysing several incidents together is called multi-incident analysis. It provides the analyst with a broader view of the hazard space in a domain, which leads to lessons-learned that contribute towards improving the state of the art for the whole domain.

For the purposes of learning from and preventing future safety incidents, many fields have developed domain specific multi-incident analysis approaches. For example, the DATIX incident reporting system is used by the NHS in the UK for incident reporting and learning (Alrwisan, Ross, & Williams, 2011); the Australian Incident Monitoring System (AIMS) is an incident reporting and analysis system for the health care sector in Australia (Beckmann, Baldwin, Hart, & Runciman, 1996) ; AERO, AQD, BASIS, HeliStat, AirFASE, PEAT, QUORUM Perilog, Aviation Safety Data Mining Workbench are all multi-incident analysis and reporting system developed in the aviation industry (Gain Working Group B, 2003).

The rail industry in Great Britain suffers around 75,000 safety related mainline railway incidents. To learn from these incidents, they are recorded in a database called the Safety Management Information System (SMIS). These events that cover everything from derailments and signals passed at danger to passenger slips, trips and falls and operating irregularities, are classified through the Incident Factor Classification System (IFCS) (Board, 2013; Dadashi, Scott, Wilson, & Mills, 2013).

Table 3. Comparison of incident analysis methods

EOI	Description	Tripod	Fishbone	TOR	HPIP	CREAM	MORT
EF	Equipment Failure (Hardware)	Hardware	Machines	Property Loss (breakage or damage)	--	Equipment Failure	
MP	Maintenance Problem	Maintenance Management	Measurements	Supervision (unsafe acts, initiative)	--	--	Maintenance
DP	Design Problem	Design	Material	--	--	--	Design
OP	Operational Procedures	Operating Procedures	Methods	Operational (job procedures)	Procedures	--	Procedures
VC	Violation Conditions	Violation including Conditions	Environment	--	--	--	--
--	--	House Keeping	--	--	Human Engineering (Bad lights, errors not detectable)		
--	Incompatible Goals	--	--	--	--	--	--
CF	Communication Factors	--	Authority (bypassing, conflicting orders)	Communication		Communication	
OF	Organizational Factors	Organization	--	Management (policy, goals)	Organization Factors	Management Problems	Management
TF	Training Factors	Organization	--	Coaching (unusual situation, training)	Training	Lack of knowledge	Training
--	Defence Planning				Inadequate Plan		
HF	Human Factors		People	Personal Traits			Human Factors

Most multi-incident analysis methods, including the preceding, are quantitative in nature. Generally, these methods collect data about incidents into a database through an incident reporting system.

Then use statistical analysis to find interesting correlations between various factors, fields, and characteristics of the data. However, there are several inherent problems in this type of analysis which may make it difficult to discover root causes, these include:

- **Inappropriate Abstraction:** The attributes used to describe an incident would have to be reasonably generic to accommodate many incidents. Consequently, the distinct details of each incident are abstracted away due to this generic representation.
- **Irrelevance:** Generally, the choice of attributes is not specifically to support root cause analysis, but may be influenced by regulatory requirements, statistical reporting requirements, and the convenience and objectivity with which an attribute may be measured.
- **Semantic Differences:** The changing definitions of attributes across time and space and due to the different purposes of the data and collection methods used, may create data integration and normalization problems for statistical analysis.

Further, the data points or incident factors being recorded in the database are chosen by the creators of the database as per their accumulated insights or domain knowledge at the time. As the domain evolves some new incident factors may become relevant, and some old ones may become irrelevant. Therefore, there is a need to periodically update the domain knowledge and the incident factors, so that the multi-incident database remains relevant and useful. Domain knowledge about the dynamics of incidents and accidents is implicit within incident analyses reports. These reports can, therefore, be used as source material for updating the multi-incident database.

In our work, we have used various Natural Language Processing (NLP) techniques to jointly analyse incident analyses reports from the domain of Railway Incident Analysis, to identify interesting patterns of incident factors and the relationships between them.

Method

To this end we focus on the domain of Railway Incident Analysis, and propose a framework that can bridge the gap between text analysis and incident analysis. The following are the key steps involved as shown in Figure 4:

Step 1: Obtain several railway incident analysis reports as raw corpus - this is done through custom crawler scripts that extracts summary of 298 reports from RAIB[2].

Step 2: The corpus is divided into sets of trainings and testing textual data for subsequent phases of the process.

Step 3: Produce a list of appropriate EOI from existing incident analysis approaches literature, such as Tripod, MORT, etc. (see Table 31).

Step 4: The EOI list will be used to manually extract relevant text representing each EOI from several incident analysis reports from the railway incident domain.

Step 5: The text thus extracted are processed using textual analysis and NLP and transformed into representative vectors.

Figure 4. Overview of proposed framework

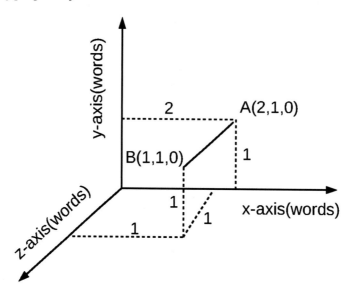

Step 6: These feature vectors are fed as input to a machine learning based classification system, for training purpose.

Step 7: The testing textual data is also processed using NLP and supplied to the trained classification system that identifies EOI within the testing data.

Step 8: The output of the classification system may be used in subsequent analyses such as visualization, clustering, co-occurrence and correspondence etc.

Data

The investigation reports of railway accidents in the UK published by the Rail Accident Investigation Branch (RAIB), the independent railway accident investigation organization for the UK, from 2008 to 2010. These reports are quite comprehensive and provides information related to an incident in detail, such as sequence of events preceding, during, and following the accident; the immediate cause, causal factors, and other factors contributed to the accident. Furthermore, it provides recommendations to address the causal and contributory factors.

Analysis

Traditional text analysis approaches are based on using a structure and language consistent with first-order predicate logic where data is represented in terms of tuples and grouped into relations (Codd, 1970). A problem arises when such approaches are used to analyse the incident analysis reports because mostly these reports include textual data that is impossible to analyse with the traditional approaches such as relational databases. In particular, when it comes to identify the patterns and define sub categories that would enable incident analysts and experts to categories the entities meaningfully. Below we discuss text analysis approaches which potentially can be useful for domain of railway incident analysis.

Topic Modeling

Topic modeling is a text analysis technique which enables the discovery of the main themes that pervade a large and otherwise unstructured collection of textual data. It can organize the collection according to the discovered themes and can be adapted to many kinds of data - such as extracting information from incident reports (Blei, 2012). This technique has previously been applied successfully in order to estimate the expected duration of the incidents i.e., defined as a period that spans from incident occurrence to clearance (Noland & Polak, 2002) (Ozbay et al., 2009) (Pereira, Rodrigues, & Ben-Akiva, 2013). This period allows the experts to plan and execute a response strategy. We believe this can still be very much relevant to railway incident analysis. However, our aim in this work is to analyse the text from existing reports to reveal the key entities of interest and possibly understand the relationship between those entities through quantified means. Such quantified relationship between entities can provide guidance to incident experts when they perform post event analysis.

Here, we analyse a subset of our main corpus consisting of six incident reports and using a topic modeling technique to infer the hidden topic structure. We then computed the inferred topic distribution (see Table 4), the distribution over topics that best describes its collection of words.

Our results show the most probable entities/topics which can be useful to build the causation model by mapping each entity against cause and effect category. Therefore, these interpretable entities arise by computing the hidden structure that most likely generated the observed collection of incident reports. For example, Table 5 lists topics discovered from underlying reports (i.e., subset of corpus).

The usefulness of topic models for railway incident analysis is due to the fact, that the inferred hidden structure resembles the thematic structure of the collection which annotates each document in the collection. This could be taxing to perform manually during incident analysis process. Further, these annotations can be used to aid subsequent stages of incident analysis process like information retrieval, classification and corpus exploration (Blei, 2012; Wallach, 2006).

For this task, we use topicmodels[3] package in R[4] which provides implementation of *Latent Dirichlet Allocation (LDA)* technique (Page). LDA facilitates the automatic identification of entities from corpus. The aim is to infer the latent structure of entities given the words and documents. The way LDA works is that for each topic (number of topics are predefined - 5 in our study) two actions are performed. First, it computes the proportion of words in document d that are currently assigned to topic t, and secondly, the proportion of assignments to topic t over all documents that come from this word w. It then reassigns w a new topic based on generative model which is essentially the probability that topic t generated word w, so it makes sense that we re-sample the current word's topic with this probability. The process is repeated until it reaches a steady state where all assignments are good.

Table 4. Topic probabilities

Report ID	Topic 1	Topic 2	Topic 3	Topic 4	Topic 5
1	**0.2039801**	0.07462687	0.08955224	0.09950249	**0.53233831**
2	**0.28823529**	0.11176471	0.10588235	0.13529412	**0.35882353**
3	**0.2056962**	**0.48417722**	0.11708861	0.09493671	0.09810127
4	0.41441441	0.12612613	0.16216216	0.11711712	0.18018018
5	0.13846154	0.13846154	**0.49230769**	0.07179487	0.15897436
6	0.11911357	0.09695291	0.09418283	**0.65096953**	0.03878116

Table 5. List of top 5 entities per document

Report ID	Topic 1	Topic 2	Topic 3	Topic 4	Topic 5
1	Train	rail	track	signal	crossing
2	driver	inspection	buckle	points	trail
3	accident	bar	reported	signaler	around
4	switch	stretcher	temperature	mom	level
5	brake	work	day	box	tractor
6	door	permanent	derailed	danger	approaching

However, an important step in text analysis is preprocessing and we perform this preliminary step to transform the corpus for analysis. The tm package is used to perform clean up (removing hyphens and colons etc.), remove punctuation, convert to lower case, remove common words (such as articles, conjunction and common verbs etc.), stemming[5] and lemmatization[6]. The latter is needed to take grammatical context into account. The Table 4 and Table 5 list topic probabilities and the top terms in topics 1 through 5 respectively. The highest probabilities are shown in bold.

The quick analysis of the two tables shows that the technique has performed well. For instance, topic 5 is about level crossing that caused that accident. Similarly, the report 6 is about derailment. The highest probability in each row is in bold. By looking at these results, it seems that incident expert can use such a technique to perform unsupervised classification of corpus of documents which can assist in subsequent incident analysis process. However, it is important to examine the results carefully to check the validity before the inferring analysis.

Cluster Analysis

Generally, the problem incident that the analyst face is how to catgorise large collection of documents in some meaningful way. The problem is due to the fact that, such reports generally do not have pre-defined classification schemes that are known to fit the collection. Therefore, techniques like clustering analysis can also be useful to analyse these reports automatically based on their structure and content. It is worth mentioning here that clustering results depend rather critically on the underlying algorithm that is employed (Diday & Simon, 1980). For cluster analysis, we use main dataset (corpus294 - i.e. summary of 298 RAIB reports) and subset of it with 6 reports (corpus6 - containing text against entities of interest) and load into an object that can be manipulated by tm package. After the preprocessing steps as explained in previous topic modelling section, we create a Document Term Matrix (DTM)- i.e., a matrix in which the documents are represented as rows and words as columns. For corpus6 there are six documents and nearly 2000 words which can be mathematically represented as 2000 dimensional space in which each of the word representing a coordinate axis and each document is represented as a point that space (illustration is shown in Figure 5).

We employ hierarchical clustering using Ward's method (Ward Jr, 1963) to compute distance between these documents. The visualization of these grouping for both corpora (corpus298 and corpus6) are shown in Figure 6 and Figure 7 respectively. Each branch of dendrogram represents a distance at which a cluster merge occurred.

Figure 5. Illustration of document vectorization in 3-word space

Clearly, the close branches mean high similarity. From an incident analysis point of view, we can obtain how closely two reports are similar thus potentially be indication of similar incidents. This could also mean the flow of events between those two incidents is highly correlated. Such an information can be useful for incident experts when complementing evidence is obtained by quantifying similarity of incident reports. Similarly, we plot the clusters in Figure 8 for both corpora and, the intuition behind these plot is to apply dimensionality reduction technique for ease of visualization.

The dimensionality reductions capture the variability between the cluster and plot first two components - which in our case explains 70% variability for corpus298 and over 13% corpus6. However, the results do not have straightforward interpretation when it comes to analysing incident reports. However, there are many text mining techniques that perform better in grouping based on entities rather than word frequencies.

Figure 6. Cluster grouping: dendrogram for corpus298

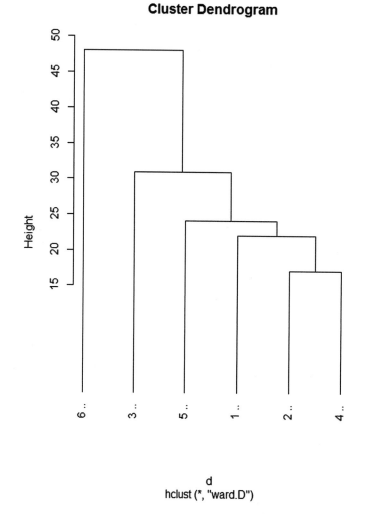

Natural Language Processing

To support the incident analysis, we investigated the natural language processing techniques to get an insight by converting the text into spatial representation of network of words and entities. These graphs of entities visually express the relationship between words and entities of interest which can provide an understanding of how the entities influences safety on railways. In this work, we were focused on visual representation of the key entities and their relationships. Mainly there are three main approaches when it comes to extraction of information from text: thematic, networks and semantic (Popping, 2000). The topic modeling approach presented earlier is a kind of thematic approach since it is based on the frequency of concepts that allows classification of the topics of text. On the other hand, semantic analysis also considers the relationships among concepts using semantic grammar, while network analysis is based on network text analysis to obtain semantically linked concepts. Like this approach the authors in (Figueres-Esteban, Hughes, & Van Gulijk, 2015) analyse Close Call Records[7] to get insight into rail-

Figure 7. Cluster grouping: dendrogram for corpus6

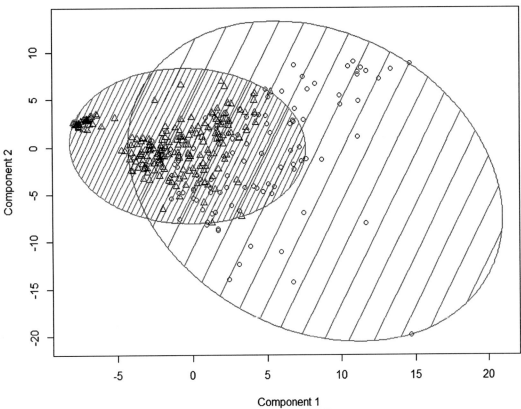

ways safety. To test value of NLP we preprocess the dataset, corpus6 through tagging and tokenization process as explained in (Hughes, Figueres-Esteban, & Van Gulijk, 2016). We perform this analysis using KHCoder[8] which is a free software for quantitative analysis and computational linguistics.

The main objective of using a NLP approach for incident analysis in this work is the matching of entireties of interests which are specified using rich linguistics patterns that incorporates as fundamental the notion of embedding of patterns and various linguistic predicates. Further, this would help to analyse the structure of words, phrases and sentences (making use of linguistic rules).

To meet this objective, we segment the extracted text file related to each EOI into words using, stemming, lemmatization and Part of Speech (POS) tagging. The later divides the data into the simples POS such as verbs, and nouns and includes conjugated forms as distinct entities. The descriptive statistics including term frequencies and document frequency distribution are plotted. These statistics visually represents the number of documents that contains each term and to evaluate the correlation between term frequency, the number of occurrences of each term in the data, and document frequency, the number of documents in which each term is used (see Figure 9 and Figure 10 which visually represents descriptive statistics for corpus6).

Figure 8. Variation explained by principal components for corpus298 and corpus6

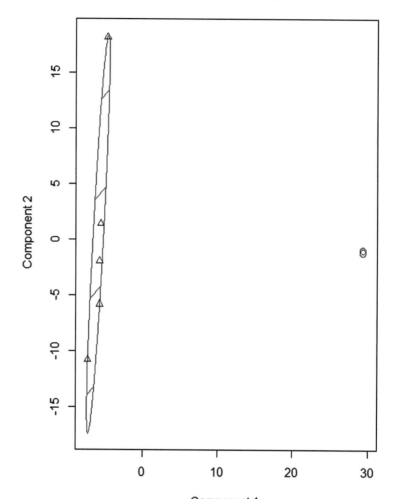

CLUSPLOT(d)

Component 1
These two components explain 70.11 % of the point variability.

In order to find the words that are closely associated with the entities of interests, we perform word association by making estimations from data using conditional probability calculations. For example, which words closely related to the entity like Human Factor or Technical Factor. The Figure 11 shows a correspondence analysis on extracted words to explore what kinds of word have a similar appearance pattern. The top right shows the words related to EOI of Hardware/Equipment failures. Such an information can help analyst to build the causation model by identifying causes and failures through related terms.

Similarly, the various co-occurrence network diagrams are shown in Figure 12, Figure 13 and Figure 14. These graphs show the words with similar appearance patterns i.e., with high degree of co-occurrence, connected by edges. This helps to understand the co-occurrence structure of words. In addition, the entities to text mapping is also shown which represents the association between entities and words. For instance,

Figure 9. Term frequency distribution

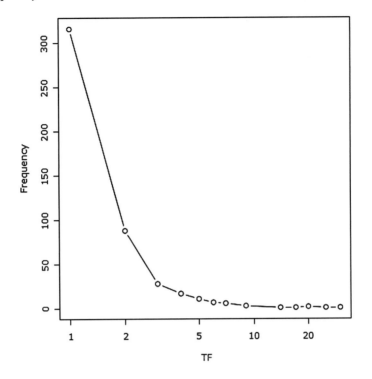

Figure 10. Term frequency-document frequency plot

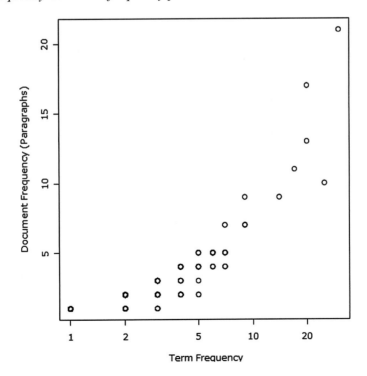

Figure 11. Results of a correspondence analysis

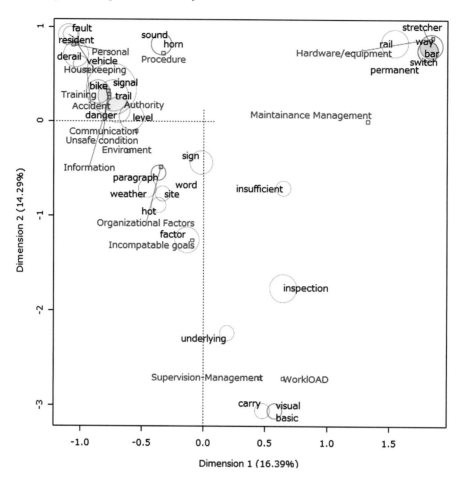

the sequence of events such as a passenger hand being trapped in the door interlocking mechanisms, highlighted in red. The correspondence and association analysis is solely drawn from a text file which contains the representative text of against each EOI from six incident reports.

BASELINING THE SYSTEM

One of our biggest problems was knowing how to start training a system that could flag up heightened railway risk. Structured data sources are relatively easy to analyse, however, unstructured data source (e.g. Word files, Excel sheets, images) are much more difficult. Multiple data sources are even more so, hence the need for a machine learning approach to the analysis. It became apparent that to try to undertake predictions we had first to understand past performance and thoroughly represent accident causation and that was the intention of the previous section. In relation to first part of chapter related to BDA, Figure 15, illustrates the proposed approach we are exploring. First of all, it is necessary for railway technology and safety experts to tag objects of interest in the accident and incident reports using the railway

Figure 12. Network: words graph network

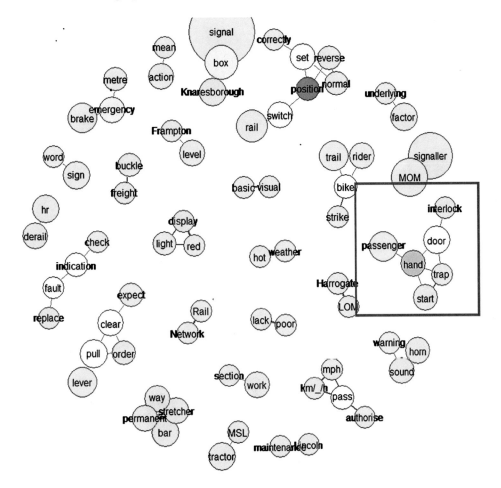

accident causation taxonomy we are developing. NLP and statistical analysis of the complete accident records are then studied and clusters and correlation between accident causation factors are established.

This causation clustering and correlation gives a statistical relationship of the important causes in situations that led to accidents. The theory is that if we can identify when these complex conditions are in place, there is a heightened chance that a serious accident could happen. Having trained our system to look for heightened risk we then stream the analytics engine with the railway data, real time and historical, structured and unstructured, let us call it operational data. Because of our previous work we have established that data is available to flag up heightened risk and it can be linked to accident causation. The data is used as a proxy for the causation analysis as these are linked from the data to the accident causes via the ELBowTie.

The analysed operational data is compared with the data derived from the accident and incident records. If there is a similarity, a flag is raised. The system is interrogated to determine whether we have met a false positive or false negative or if we have indeed averted a potential accident. In simple terms, if the output of each stage is similar, then there is likely to be a heightened risk. The system will learn

Figure 13. Network graph: words mapping to EOI

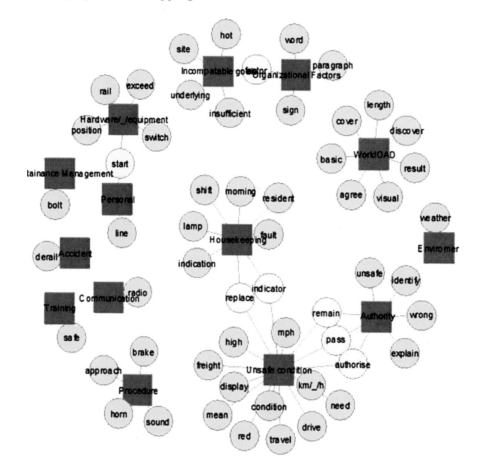

from accidents and incidents on an ongoing basis and become more accurate as it gets feedback and increasing data. Clearly to begin with this type of system would have to be run in parallel with existing safety management system until sufficient confidence is built up.

CONCLUSION

In this paper, we have presented our journey into railway digitisation, largely involving the analysis of railway accidents in terms of their causation and the data that can be used to proactively indicate heightened risk. Current safety management approaches are struggling to come to terms with the complex socio-technical systems we are now developing in the rail industry. Our journey was mainly driven by the need to understand how best to deal with these changes.

Our future activities will include working to build targeted algorithms and applications to aid analysis of an increasing proportion of the enterprise data taxonomy. We will analyse the full accident record from RAIB using Natural Language Processing to build up a comprehensive cluster model of accident

Figure 14. Network graph: modularity co-occurrence

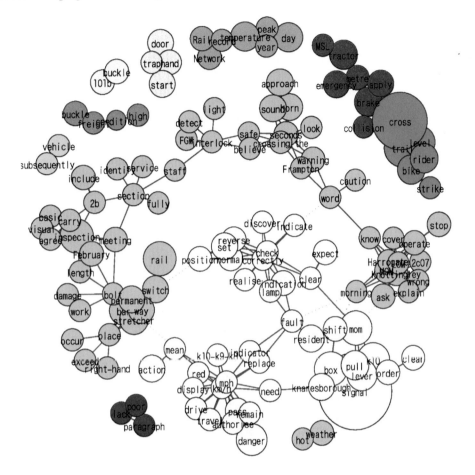

causation which will be linked to the enterprise data taxonomy. Building on that, the aim is to set up a suite of analytical tools to assess the enterprise data. This will start with the most critical areas, especially unstructured data, including safety requirements, hazard records, and vision systems. We will test the analytics using simulated and real data from the operational railway starting with simple accident and incident scenarios. The increasing use of machine learning will help to reduce safety risk on the railway and will also have the potential to facilitate cost reduction and increased accuracy during railway system development.

This paper describes systems that combines Natural Language Processing (NLP) to obtain the capability to gain insight into railway accident reports by unleashing previously unknown patterns of interests for railway safety. We show that it is possible to gain high value by using text analysis to map different sequences of language text to the concepts and entities in incident domains. The frequency, distribution and co-occurrence of these entities form patterns that can provide useful indicators for investigations, and assist incident experts in establishing root cause analysis using relevant supporting information.

Figure 15. Proposed analytics and training approach

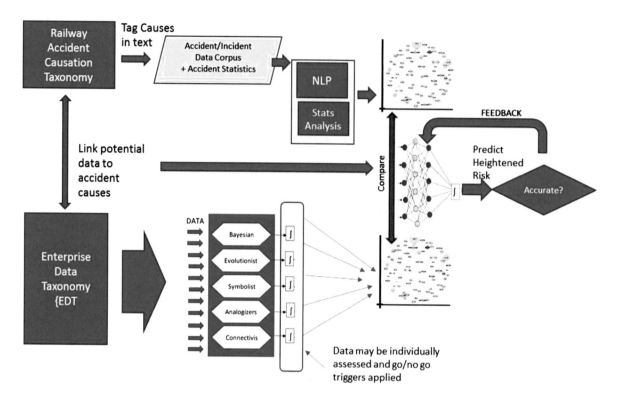

Further, such a process can be enriched, and when more data is available, by applying additional machine learning approaches. The enriched data such as investigation reports not only contains part of speech information, but also a rich lexicon, and a great deal of domain knowledge embodied on concepts and entities. This knowledge can be fed into machine learning to effectively provide means to express concepts and entities for advances of safety in railways.

AVAILABILITY

This raw dataset and our custom scripts on which this work is based, is available online[9].

ACKNOWLEDGMENT

This work is sponsored by Santander Universities program and Digital Rail. We are also thankful to RAIB for providing the railway accident investigation reports on which this work is based. We are also grateful to RSSB for providing insightful comments and input to the use of incident classification system. We are also thankful to Paul Rayson and Stephen Wattam for useful discussion on Natural Language Processing approaches.

REFERENCES

Alrwisan, A., Ross, J., & Williams, D. (2011). Medication incidents reported to an online incident reporting system. *European Journal of Clinical Pharmacology, 67*(5), 527–532. doi:10.1007/s00228-010-0986-z PMID:21240481

Angelov, P., Manolopoulos, Y., Iliadis, L., Roy, A., & Vellasco, M. (2016). Advances in Big Data. Springer.

Beckmann, U., Baldwin, I., Hart, G., & Runciman, W. (1996). The Australian Incident Monitoring Study in Intensive Care: AIMS-ICU. An analysis of the first year of reporting.

Blei, D. M. (2012). Probabilistic topic models. *Communications of the ACM, 55*(4), 77–84. doi:10.1145/2133806.2133826

RAI Branch. (2011). Rail accident report: Derailment at Grayrigg 23 February 2007 (Report 20(2008), v5).

Codd, E. F. (1970). A relational model of data for large shared data banks. *Communications of the ACM, 13*(6), 377–387. doi:10.1145/362384.362685

Dadashi, N., Scott, A., Wilson, J. R., & Mills, A. (2013). *Rail Human Factors: Supporting reliability, safety and cost reduction*. CRC Press. doi:10.1201/b13827

Diday, E., & Simon, J. (1980). *Clustering analysis Digital pattern recognition* (pp. 47–94). Springer. doi:10.1007/978-3-642-67740-3_3

Figueres-Esteban, M., Hughes, P., & Van Gulijk, C. (2015). The role of data visualization in railway big data risk analysis. *Paper presented at the European Safety and Reliability Conference*. doi:10.1201/b19094-377

Gain Working Group B. (2003). *Guide to Methods and Tools for Airline Flight Safety Analysis*.

Gano, D. L. (2011). *Reality Charting: Seven Steps to Effective Problem-solving and Strategies for Personal Success*. Apollonian Publications.

Harms-Ringdahl, L. (2013). *Guide to safety analysis for accident prevention*. IRS Riskhantering.

Hilbert, M. (2015). Big Data for Development: A Review of Promises and Challenges. Development Policy Review. *martinhilbert.net*.

Hollnagel, E., & Speziali, J. (2008). *Study on Developments in Accident Investigation Methods: A Survey of the State-of-the-Art*.

Hughes, P., Figueres-Esteban, M., & Van Gulijk, C. (2016). Learning from text-based close call data. *Paper presented at the Safety and Reliability*. doi:10.1080/09617353.2016.1252083

Johnson, C. (2003). *A Handbook of Incident and Accident Reporting*. Glasgow University Press.

Latino, R. J., Latino, K. C., & Latino, M. A. (2016). *Root cause analysis: improving performance for bottom-line results*. CRC press.

Livingston, A., Jackson, G., & Priestley, K. (2001). Root causes analysis: Literature review. *HSE Contract Research Report*.

Noland, R. B., & Polak, J. W. (2002). Travel time variability: A review of theoretical and empirical issues. *Transport Reviews*, 22(1), 39–54. doi:10.1080/01441640010022456

Ozbay, K. M., Xiao, W., Jaiswal, G., Bartin, B., Kachroo, P., & Baykal-Gursoy, M. (2009). Evaluation of incident management strategies and technologies using an integrated traffic/incident management simulation. *World Review of Intermodal Transportation Research*, 2(2-3), 155–186. doi:10.1504/WRITR.2009.023305

Page, L. W. Latent Dirichlet allocation. Retrieved from https://en.wikipedia.org/wiki/Latent_Dirichlet_allocation

Parkinson, H., & Bamford, G. (2016). The potential for using big data analytics to predict safety risks by analyzing rail accidents. *Paper presented at the 3rd International Conference on Railway Technology: Research, Development and Maintenance*, Cagliari, Sardinia, Italy.

Parkinson H J, a. B. G. (2017). Big Data in Railway Accident Prediction Including a Review of Current Analytical Methods. *International Journal of Railway Technology (IJRT)*.

Parkinson, H. J., Bamford, G., & Kandola, B. (2016). The Development of an Enhanced Bowtie Railway Safety Assessment Tool using a Big Data Analytics Approach. In *IET Conference Proceedings*. Retrieved from http://digital-library.theiet.org/content/conferences/10.1049/cp.2016.0510

Parkinson, H. J., & Bamford, G. J. (2017). Big Data and the Virtuous Circle of Railway Digitization. In P. Angelov, Y. Manolopoulos, L. Iliadis, A. Roy, & M. Vellasco (Eds.), *Advances in Big Data: Proceedings of the 2nd INNS Conference on Big Data, October 23-25, 2016, Thessaloniki, Greece* (pp. 314-322). Cham: Springer International Publishing. doi:10.1007/978-3-319-47898-2_32

Pereira, F. C., Rodrigues, F., & Ben-Akiva, M. (2013). Text analysis in incident duration prediction. *Transportation Research Part C, Emerging Technologies*, 37, 177–192. doi:10.1016/j.trc.2013.10.002

Popping, R. (2000). Computer-assisted text analysis. *Sage (Atlanta, Ga.)*.

Reason, J. (1990). *Human error*. Cambridge university press. doi:10.1017/CBO9781139062367

RSS Board. (2013). Development of the Incident Factor Classification System. Retrieved from https://www.rssb.co.uk/improving-industry-performance/human-factors/human-factors-case-studies/developing-the-incident-factor-classification-system

Sklet, S. (2002). *Methods for accident investigation*. Trondheim: Gnist Tapir.

Wallach, H. M. (2006). Topic modeling: beyond bag-of-words. *Paper presented at the Proceedings of the 23rd international conference on Machine learning*.

Ward, J. H. Jr. (1963). Hierarchical grouping to optimize an objective function. *Journal of the American Statistical Association*, 58(301), 236–244. doi:10.1080/01621459.1963.10500845

Woloshynowych, M., Rogers, S., Taylor-Adams, S., & Vincent, C. (2005). The investigation and analysis of critical incidents and adverse events in healthcare.

Ziedelis, S., & Noel, M. (2011). Comparative analysis of nuclear event investigation methods, tools and techniques. *European Commission, Joint Research Center*.

KEY TERMS AND DEFINITIONS

Entities of Interests (EOI): The factors that represent categories of information that may help explain an incident in terms of cause effect relationships.

Incident: An incident is an unexpected, unplanned event, in a sequence of events that occurs through a combination of causes; it results in physical harm - injury or disease - to an individual, damage to property, a near miss, a loss or any combination of these effects.

Incident Analysis: The incident analysis is a structured process for identifying what happened, how and why it happened, what can be done to reduce the risk of recurrence and make care safer, and what was learned.

Multi-Incident Analysis: The practice of analysing a number of incidents together is called Multi-incident analysis.

Natural Language Processing (NLP): Represents a set of techniques that can computationally extract useful conceptual information from text.

Root Causes: Those entrenched systemic risk factors within an enterprise, environment, or domain that may have either caused or contributed to a number of latent and active failures.

Topic Modelling (TM): The topic modeling is a text analysis technique which enables the discovery of the main themes that pervade a large and otherwise unstructured collection of textual data.

ENDNOTES

1   http://www.digitalrail.co.uk/elbowtie/
2   https://www.gov.uk/raib-reports?report_type\%5B\%5D=investigation-report
3   https://cran.r-project.org/web/packages/topicmodels/topicmodels.pdf
4   https://www.r-project.org/about.htm
5   https://en.wikipedia.org/wiki/Stemming
6   https://en.wikipedia.org/wiki/Lemmatisation
7   https://www.rssb.co.uk/risk-analysis-and-safety-reporting/reporting-systems/close-call-system
8   http://khc.sourceforge.net/en/
9   https://github.com/kanzanoor/nlp-paper-digitalrail.git

APPENDIX

Table 6. Description of EOI for incident analysis methods

Model	EOI	Abbreviation	Description
Tripod	Hardware	HW	Inadequate supply and function of equipment and materials.
Tripod	Maintenance management	MM	A necessary maintenance activity was delayed or postponed.
Tripod	Design	DE	An inherent design problem in a device that may cause the device to function in an unexpected manner.
Tripod	Procedures	PR	Procedures may be ambiguous, incorrect, or inappropriate.
Tripod	Violation Inducing Conditions	VC	Conditions that pressure the workers to violate procedures.
Tripod	Housekeeping	HK	Conditions and violations that are known, but have not been fixed over a certain period of a time.
Tripod	Incompatible Goals	IG	Organisational and individual goals that conflict with safety requirements.
Tripod	Communication	CO	A message could not be sent, sent to the wrong recipient, or misinterpreted by the recipient.
Tripod	Organisation	OR	Organisational structures may hinder the prevention or mitigation of incidents.
Tripod	Training	TR	Lack of competent workers due to inadequate training.
Tripod	Defence Planning	DP	Deficiencies in the planning of detection and response procedures for incidents.
Fishbone	People	PE	Anyone involved in the incident.
Fishbone	Methods	MD	The processes including policies, procedures, rules, regulations and laws.
Fishbone	Machines	MC	Any equipment, computers, tools, etc.
Fishbone	Materials	MT	Raw materials, parts, pens, paper, etc.
Fishbone	Measurements	MS	Data used in the process.
Fishbone	Environment	EN	Conditions, such as location, time, temperature, and culture.
TOR	Unusual Situation	US	Failure to coach (New employee, tool, equipment, process and material).
TOR	Training	TR	Not formulated or need not foreseen.
TOR	Conflicting Goals	CG	Duties and goals are not clear.
TOR	Authority	AU	Authority inadequate to cope the situation.
TOR	Co-operation	CO	Failure to plan (co-operation).
TOR	Supervision	SP	Failure to see problems, observe and correct.
TOR	Property Loss	PL	Accidental breakage or damage.
TOR	Unsafe Conditions	UC	Inefficient or unsafe conditions.
TOR	Personal Traits	PT	Physical condition, impairment, alcohol, personality, work habits and work assignment.
HPIP	Procedures	PR	Formal written guidance provided to workers or supervisors.
HPIP	Training	TR	Training indicated as if an individual failed to perform.

continued on following page

Table 6. Continued

Model	EOI	Abbreviation	Description
HPIP	Organisational Factors	OF	Factors that influence human performance reliability and enhance organizational effectiveness.
HPIP	Work Environment	WE	Housekeeping, bad lights, cold/hot, noisy.
HPIP	Human Engineering	HE	Reliable human performance (Human-machine interface, complex systems, non-fault tolerance system).
HPIP	Supervision	SP	Inadequacies in task planning and follow-up contributed to an event.
HPIP	Communication	CO	Misunderstood, late communication, no communication.
IFCS	Practice and Processes	PP	The rules, standards, processes and methods of working.
IFCS	Communication	CO	How we relay information to each other in the context of safety critical information.
IFCS	Information	IN	Information is used to support an activity.
IFCS	Workload	WL	Workload is about understanding the demand created by activities.
IFCS	Equipment	EQ	Faulty, design not compatible with its use.
IFCS	Knowledge, Skills and Experience	KE	Appropriate knowledge, familiar with the circumstances.
IFCS	Supervision Management	SM	Decisions about resources, budgets, work allocation and planning.
IFCS	Work Environment	WE	Lighting levels, noise, temperature and vibrations.
IFCS	Personal	PE	A collection of influences that may affect the individual (fatigue, physical and mental well-being).
IFCS	Team Work	TW	How to work together and coordinate to achieve safe performance.
CREAM	Working Conditions	WC	--
CREAM	Operational Support	OS	Support provided by specially designed decision aids.
CREAM	Procedures	PR	Formally dene patterns of response, heuristics, or routines to be used.
CREAM	Available Time	AT	Time to deal with the situation.
CREAM	Training and Experience	TE	Operational experience, training, or familiarization.
CREAM	Collaboration Quality	CQ	Social climate among the workers.
MORT	Communication	CO	--
MORT	Maintenance	MM	--
MORT	Design	DE	--
MORT	Operability	OP	--
MORT	Training	TR	--
MORT	Procedure	PR	--
MORT	Time	TI	--
MORT	Knowledge	KN	--
MORT	Worker Problem	WP	--
MORT	Technical Information System	TI	--

Section 4
Applications and Use Cases

Chapter 12
Evolution of Indian Railways Through IoT

Shaik Rasool
MJCET, India

Uma Dulhare
MJCET, India

ABSTRACT

Indian Railways is the largest rail network in the world, can be plays an essential role in the development of infrastructure areas such as coal, electric power, steel, concrete and other critical industries. Indian government has started concentrating on the modernization of the railways through huge investment. Internet of Things(IoT) is vital attention to expansion and excellence. The chapter will commence with the past history of rail transport in India Further section will support the IoT which is another great trend in technology. The later section of the chapter will give attention to how Internet of things could expertise the railroad industry, introducing a remedy which will be made to modernize aging sites at railroads, improve basic safety. The railway can help the passenger to utilize fewer interruptions in the event that's what they need. There's a large number of things that require to be watched and the railway can run as a completely digital service, without having to have people walking the tracks, it brings cost benefits and increased safety for the workforce.

INTRODUCTION

A brief history of rail transport in India commenced in the mid-nineteenth century. The key of the pressure for building Railways in India came from London. In 1848, there was not a single kilometer of railway line in India. The country's first train, built by the fantastic Indian Peninsula Railway (GIPR), opened up in 1853, between Bombay and Thane. The East Indian Train Company was established one particular June 1845 in Greater London with a deed of settlement with a capital of? 4, 000, 1000, largely raised in Greater London. The Great Southern India Railway Co. was founded in Britain in 1853 and registered in 1859. Construction of track in Madras Presidency commenced in 1859 and the 80-mile link from Trichinopoly to Negapatam was opened in 1861. The Carnatic Train founded in 1864, opened

DOI: 10.4018/978-1-5225-3176-0.ch012

up a Madras-Arakkonam-Kancheepuram line in 1865. The Great Lower India Railway Company was subsequently merged with the Carnatic Railway Company in 1874 to create the South Indian Railway Business.

A British engineer, Robert Maitland Brereton, was accountable for the expansion of the railways from 1857 onwards. The Allahabad-Jabalpur branch brand of the East Indian Train had been opened in June 1867. Brereton was accountable for linking this with the GIPR, resulting in a combined network of 6, 400 km (4, 000 mi). Hence it became possible to travel straight from Bombay to Calcutta. This route was officially opened on six March 1870 and it was area of the inspiration for French writer Jules Verne's book All over the world in 80 Days. In the opening wedding ceremony, the Viceroy Lord Mayonaise concluded that "it was thought desirable that, if possible, at the first possible moment, the entire country should be protected with a network of lines within an even system" (History of rail transport in India, 2017).

By 1875, about? 95 million were used by British companies in India. By 1880 the network had a way mileage of about 18, 500 km (9, 1000 mi), mostly radiating back to the inside from the three major port cities of Bombay, Madras and Calcutta. Simply by 1895, India had begun building its locomotives, and in 1896, sent technicians and locomotives to help build the Uganda Railways.

In 1900, the GIPR became a government possessed company. The network distributed to the modern-day states of Assam, Rajputhana and Madras Presidency and soon various autonomous kingdoms started to have their own rail systems. In 1905, an early Train Board was constituted, but the powers were technically vested under Lord Curzon. It served under the Department of Commerce and Industry and had a government railway official offering as chairman, and a railway manager from The United Kingdom and an agent of one of the company railways as the other two members. The first time in its history, the Railways commenced to make a profit.

In 1907 almost all the rail companies were taken over by the government. The subsequent year, the first electric locomotive made its appearance. With the arrival of World War 1, the railways were used to meet the needs of the British outside India. With the finish of the war, the railways were in a situation of disrepair and break. Large scale corruption by British officials involved in the running of such railways companies was rampant. Income were never reinvested in the development of British Isles colonial India. In 1920, with the network having expanded to 61, two hundred and twenty km (38, 040 mi), a purpose for main management was mooted by Sir William Acworth. Structured on the East India Railway Committee chaired by Acworth, the government went ahead of the management of the Railways and detached the finances of the Railways from other governmental profits.

The time between 1920 and 1929 was a period of financial rate of growth; there were 41, 1000 mi (66, 000 km) of railway lines portion the; the railways displayed a capital value of some 687 million pristine; and in addition, they carried over 620 million passengers and roughly 90 million tons of goods annually. Following the Great Depression, the railways suffered economically for the next eight years. The Second World War significantly crippled the railways. Beginning in 1939, about forty percent of the rolling stock including locomotives and trainers was taken to the center East. The railways workshops were converted to ammunitions workshops and many railway tracks were disassembled to ensure that the Allies in the conflict. By 1946, all train systems had been used over by the authorities.

The first railway on Indian sub-continent ran over a stretch of 21 years old miles from Bombay to Thane. The idea of a railway to hook up Bombay with Thane, Kalyan and with the Thal and Bhore Ghats hillsides first occurred to Mister. George Clark, the Main Engineer of the Bombay Government, during a visit to Bhandup in 1843.

The conventional inauguration wedding was performed on sixteenth April 1853, when 13 railway carriages carrying about 400 guests left BoriBunder at 3. 30 private message: "...amidst the loud applause of a vast bunch and the salute of 21 guns." The first passenger train steamed out of Howrah train station destined for Hooghly, a distance of 24 kilometers, on 15th August, 1854. Thus, the first part of the East Indian Train was opened to open public traffic, inaugurating the starting of railway transport on the Eastern side of the sub-continent in Figure 1.

In south the first series was opened on Istauch, July, 1856, by the Madras Railway Company. That ran between Vyasarpadi Jeeva Nilayam (Veyasarpandy) and Walajah Road (Arcot), a distance of 63 miles. In the North, a length of 119 miles of line was laid from Allahabad to Kanpur on 3rd Drive 1859. The first section from Hathras Road to Mathura Cantonment was exposed to traffic on the nineteenth of October, 1875.

These were the small beginnings which is due course developed into a network of railway lines all over the country. By 1880 the Indian Railway system a new route distance of about 9000 a long way. INDIAN

RAILWAYS, the top transport organization of the country is the most significant rail network in Okazaki, japan and the world's second most significant under one management in Figure 2.

Indian Railways is the lifeline of area in Table 1. It traverses the size and breadth of the country providing the required connectivity and integration for balanced regional development. The system never rests; it is often up and working unceasingly for the last several decades. Costly integral part of every Indian's being. It is one of the pillars of area. In an earlier age, the Indian Railways have been described as "imperium in imperio", a disposition within an empire. The size and scale is gigantic. The United Claims, China and Russia are the only countries which may have longer railway lengths, scored in kilometers. The railways have played a major role in catalyzing the speed of economic development and continue to be a fundamental factor of the growth engine of the. Indian Railways has recently been attempting to reform itself by making use of many commissions and committees from time to time unabatedly. Indeed, average person and appreciated customers want with the achievements in regard to Organizational Traditions

Figure 1. First passenger train service

Figure 2. Organization structure

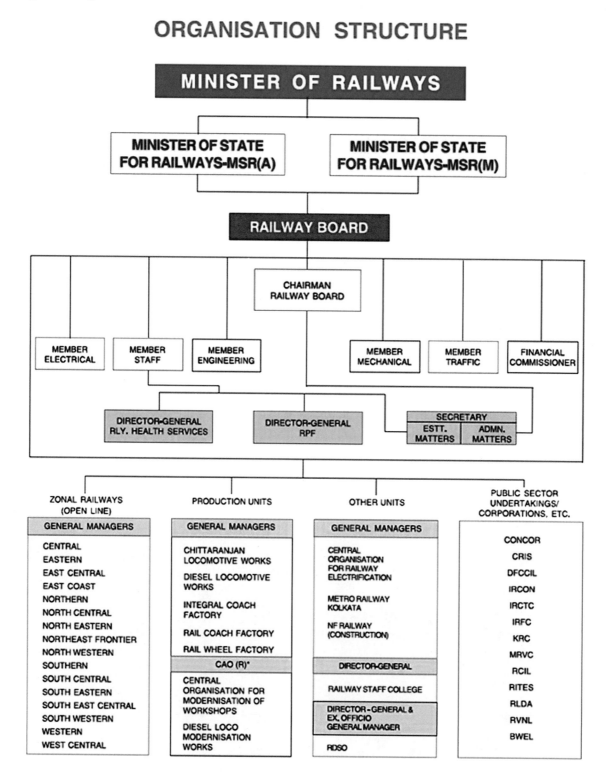

Table 1. Indian Railways is a multi-gauge, multi-traction system

	Broad Gauge (1676 mm)	**Meter Gauge (1000 mm)**	**Narrow Gauge (762/610 mm)**	**Total**
Track Kilometers	86,526	18,529	3,651	108,706
Route Kilometers	**Electrified**	**Total**		
	16,001	63,028		

and Company Development or improved entire organization. The services provided by the railways have changed substantially over the past years. Indian govt has begun concentrating on the modernization of the railways through huge investment. Ministry of Railways have signed Memorandum of Understandings with the international countries like China, Portugal and so on. for technical Cooperation in Train Sector wherein Train stop Development is one of the cooperation areas. Modernization is a continuous and ongoing process on Indian Railways. IOT is important to deliver ability for secure, safe and productive freight and passenger train locomotives with a target progress and excellence.

INDIAN RAILWAYS AND SAFETY

Present Perspective Indian

Railways are the world's second-largest railway, with 6, 853 stations, 63, 028 mls of track, 37, 840 passenger coaches and 222, 147 freight cars. Yearly it carries some 4. 83 billion passengers and 492 million plenty of shipment cars. of the 10 million passengers who rise aboard one of almost 8, 520 trains every day, about 550,000 have hold d accommodations. Safe transport of passengers is key business objective of any vehicles system. Railways are known as the safest function of mass transportation and Safety has been named the key issue for the railways and one of its special qualities. All business strategies exhale from this theme and then try to achieve Accident Free Program. Safety is, therefore, the real key performance index which the top managements need to monitor and take preventative steps based on styles of accidents which are the manifestations of a few of the unsafe practices on the system (Sambamurthy & HasaneAhamma, 2013).

Collisions

Collisions are the most dreaded accidents. That is very difficult to stop such collisions because of speed of moving trains, which desire a business lead distance to stop. Accidents happen due to human being errors and/or faulty equipment.

Head-On and Rear-End-Collisions

A head-on collision is one where the front ends of two ships, trains, airplanes or vehicles hit each other, as opposed to aside-collision or rear-end crash. With rail, a head-on collision often implies a collision on a one line railway in Figure 3 and Figure 4.

Figure 3. Head-on collision

Figure 4. Rear-end collision

Current Technologies Used

The Anti-Collision Device (ACD) is a self-acting microprocessor-based data communication device designed and developed by Kankan Railway. The system contains Loco ACD with a console (message display) for the new driver (in each Loco Engine), Guard ACD with remote control (fitted in Guard Van), Station ACD with gaming system (fitted in Station Masters' Cabin), Manned and Unmanned Gates ACD with hooters and flashers (in each location) and Repeater ACDs (fitted at locations having obstructions in radio communication such as hilly areas) which work in live concert to prevent this sorts of collisions and mishaps like-Head on collisions, Rear end collisions, Collisions thanks to derailment, Collisions at the level crossing entrance..

NEW STEPS TOWARDS SAFETY AND SECURITY

Security of 13 million travelers that Indian Railways provide every day features extremely important importance to the machine. More than the years, apart from the regular safety rules followed, the network has taken a number of steps through ground breaking use of technology and got up training to it is manpower to enhance security standards. Constitution of Rs. 17, 000 crore non-lapsable Special Railway Safety Account (SRSF) to replace the arrears of aging resources of Railways over the next six years has been a historical move in this effort. A number of distressed connections, old tracks, signaling system and other safety development devices will be substituted during this period. As much as budget allocation for basic safety is concerned, Rs. you, 400 crore was allotted in the revised estimation for the year 2001-02 and Rs. 2, 210 crore for the yr 2002-2003. Extensive field studies of the Anti-Collision Unit (ACD), indigenously produced by Konkan Railway, is going as well as once implemented across the Zonal Railways, this progressive technology will help railways reduce injuries due to collision between trains (Safety Measures by Indian Railways, n. d.).

Security of train passengers is at present a shared responsibility of the Railway Protection Power (RPF) and the Authorities Reserve Police (GRP). Initiatives are on to change the Railway Act to provide more powers to the RPF in ensuring security of passengers on teaches and within Railway areas. Deployment of women court Force has been made for security and assistance of women passengers.

HONORS AND AWARDS

Indian Railways achieved several recognitions and awards in sports activities, tourism sector and for excellence in operational concerns. Inside the Common Prosperity Games in Manchester, the Indian teams record performance has been mainly credited to Railway team's superiority in sports. Except one member the complete women's Tennis team which bagged the gold medal belonged to Railways. Mohd Ali Qamar of Indian Railways has bagged gold medal for boxing and other individuals from Railways helped India win medals in many a team events. A number of sportspersons from Railways were conferred with the desirable Arjuna Awards and other major sports awards (Indianrailways.gov., n. d.).

MANAGEMENT OF INDIAN RAILWAYS

Indian Railway is a department of Government and the Ministry of Railways functions under the rules of Minister for Railways assisted by Minister of State for Railways. The policy formation and management of Indian Railway Table consists of Chairman and half a dozen functional members. Wide powers are vested in the Board to effectively regulate the running of 18 zonal railways, metro train Organizational Structure (Calcutta), development units, construction organization and other rail establishments. These kinds of are generally headed by General Managers. Nine part organizations under the Ministry of Railways viz. IRCON, RITES, CONCOR, RCIL, RVNL, MRVC, IRFC, and KRCL undertake specialized jobs adding to Indian Railways' development and progress. RITES and IRCON have their business abroad also (Railways, 2013).

CHALLENGES

The greatest challenge facing Indian Railways today is it is inability to meet the demands of its customers, both freight and traveling. Apart from the segment of investment, quality of delivery is also a problem. Cleanliness, punctuality of services, safety, quality of ports, capacity of trains, quality of food, security of passengers and ease of booking tickets are issues that need urgent attention. Indian Railways has endured from chronic and significant under-investment because of this which the network expansion and modernization has not happened at the requisite pace resulting in an erosion of the share in national shipment and passenger traffic. There is also a clear recognition of the fact that for providing as the lifeline of the nation and making a contribution to the country's growth (Indian Railways Lifeline of the nation, 2015).

Indian Railways is striving to boost its market share and increase the service quality to be able to ensure that also is an experience beyond other modes of travel. This is achieved by eliminating capacity bottlenecks which constrain development, improve productivity of possessions and efficiency of businesses and optimal employment of its resources including human being capital. The high occurrence networks of the Indian Railways are facing severe capacity constraints coupled with a low-passenger prices thereby leading to raises in freight tariffs to cross subsidize passenger profits. Nevertheless, that only permits recovery of costs and does not leave enough resources for investment in network expansion and substitute of assets. e operationally and financially sound.

Because the growth throughout the economy picks up in the years to come, IR will have a challenging task ahead because of line and airport capacity constraints in moving the increment a traffic. Therefore, there is requirement of significant investment in the network, especially the HDN routes and its feeder and other important ways. This would include prioritized capacity enhancement works such as doubling/ tripling/quadrupling and traffic facility works like Second time beginners Block Sections, bypasses, for a longer time loops for running long haul trains. The Items sheds along these paths would also need to be strengthened. The capacity of Workshops needs to be increased to serve to larger volume of maintenance of wagons and coaches. Similarly, prioritized electrification and signaling & phone system works are also well worth addressing for reasons of safety and efficiency. Right now, there is a sizable shelf of pending projects which is estimated at Rs. 4, 91, 510 crore on the basis of at first estimated costs Of these, fund requirement of the prioritized works such as doubling, new lines, see conversion, traffic facilities, sign & telecom works, training courses and electrification is believed at Rs 2, '08, 054 crore. Such prioritization of works as every developmental requirement can ensure a sustained flow of funds for such assignments and focused attention can be given for early on completion and commissioning of these works. These will have an immediate mechanical bearing on the line capacity which will ensure higher earnings and optimal use of assets. installment obligations on your 6 Even more, there are regular requirements for new lines. Via the point of view of remote area on-line and meeting the requirements of all for gain access to also, construction of newlines also assumes importance. However, all these demands do not lead to feasible projects from the point of view of Railways. Hence, a huge range of socially desirable projects have recently been sanctioned in the previous creating huge throw-forward responsibility and thin spread of funds. In many situations, IR carries the duty of losses from functions in case such projects are undertaken. To give push to execution of these socially desirable projects, alliance with State Governments would be the way in advance Projects have been languishing for years on consideration of absence of certain funding. Delay in setup of projects causes time overruns and cost overruns. This has an impact on the viability of the projects once they are completed. The available resources are normally share thinly over all endorsed projects. In the current year, projects have recently been prioritized and funding guaranteed for all the jobs that could be taken up for early completion.

RAILWAY TECHNOLOGY INNOVATION

India became the first developing country and the 5th country in the world to roll out the first indigenously built "state-of-the-art" high hp three phase electric locomotive when the first such loco was flagged faraway from Chittranjan Locomotive Gets results (CLW). CLW has recently been obtaining progressive indigenization and the expense of locomotives has come down to the amount of Rs. 13. 65 crore (Shristi, 2016).

Large horse power Electric Locos, Diesel Locos and Superior technology LHB type instructors have been introduced on the Indian Railways. The technology to produce such locos and coaches has also been adopted on Indian Railways as one step towards technological upgradation. Also, high-speed goods carriages are being introduced to upgrade the products trains for high speed. The Indian Railways have completed the first phase of the computerized Freight Operation Info System to permit online tracking of cargo. The second phase of the project covering Terminal Administration System would be completed in 2004-05 and would increase the quality of services substantially. The increased use of IT by Indian Railways would lead to optimal utilization of the existing infrastructure, rolling stock and man-power and, in the process, not only increase earnings from gets traffic but also impact substantial reduction in in business cost. During the X-Plan period, an endeavor to upgrade technology in every sphere with the objectives of bettering reliability, reduce maintenance requirement, increase client satisfaction and reduce cost of procedure has been made. The technology initiatives include the following:

- **Track:** Higher Axle Load & Speeds, mechanized maintenance, advancements in welding technology and better methods of diagnosis rail flaws.
- **Chariot:** Improvement in axle tons, speeds, pay load to tare ratio and advantages of self-steering bogies.
- **Operation of High Speed Freight Trains on Indian Railways:** Till lately, the Indian railways got been operating freight locomotives with a maximum rate of 75 /80 kph. A modified type of Casunub bogie fitted to air brake pedal wagons has enabled carriages to be run at a maximum speed of 100 kph.

While increasing the maximum speed potential of freight trains causes improvement in utilization of carriages and locomotives, it also reduces the speed differential box between passenger trains and freight trains. This would augment the section volumes, particularly on those parts working to saturation or near-saturation levels.

- **Trainers and EMUs:** Introduction of stainless-steel coaches to reduce maintenance requirements, use of air springs in EMUs to boost riding comfort, and so on.
- **Computer Based Central Traffic Control System:** Endeavours has been taken to introduce Computer based Central Traffic Control system on Ghaziabad - Kanpur section under modernization of Signaling and Telecommunication system on this system.

Opportunity for IT Firms

The National Democratic Alliance (NDA) government's first railway budget, which envisages implementing Net connectivity at stations and trains, digitizing land documents, integrating all its personal computers and attaining a paperless office in five years, has thrown up a billion dollar opportunity for technology organizations in India (Srivastava, 2014).

Union train minister Sadananda Gowda said the Indian Railways will opt for an organization resource planning (ERP) solution, which is typically used to integrate freight, voyager, human resources and management functions across the country. The railways have recently been toying with the idea of implementing an ENTERPRISE RESOURCE PLANNING solution for almost a decade but they have done it in chances and ends during the United Progressive Alliance's (UPA's) tenure.

For instance, on 26 June, 2007, Mint had reported that the railways was planning to implement an ERP solution that was compatible with the Freight Operations Info System (FOIS). In 2006-07, India's most significant IT services provider, Tata Consultancy Providers Ltd (TCS) designed the ERP for the Indian Railway Catering and Tourism Corp. Ltd (IRCTC). About 6 June 2010, the Business Standard reported that L&T Infotech Ltd acquired won two turnkey ENTERPRISE RESOURCE PLANNING projects that were considered and tendered by the Centre for Railway Info System (CRIS), the THAT arm of the Indian Railways.

SAP is managing ERP for subsidiaries of the Indian Railways (these include locomotive factories, instructor factories, etc.). Until recently, L&T Infotech was one of the sellers handling ERP implementation for Indian Railways. In an emailed reaction to a query, L&T Infotech said the company is not managing the ERP setup for railways anymore. TCS didn't respond to an email seeking comment.

Gowda said the Indian Railways plans to revamp the ticket reservation system to support online sale for 7, 200 tickets each minute as against the current limit of 2, 000, that Wi-Fi services will be made available in select trains as well as major channels and that it will have digitization and GIS (geographic information system) mapping of land assets for better management and usage. Similar press releases, with these specific figures, had been made through the 2013-14 railway budget provided by the UPA authorities.

Gowda said there will end up being a provision for real-time monitoring of locomotives, mobile-based wake up call for passengers and vacation spot arrival alerts, and stop navigation information system. This kind of is in addition to the pilot project of providing paid workstations in select trains for people who do buiness holidaymakers, which will be launched in 2015.

Industry experts say these measures can have a transformational impact on domestic IT industry.

"It [the railway budget] reinforces some of the key global trends such as mobility, social mass media and digitization. In present world, the things that can win or lose an organization are speed and adaptability. Moving on to a mobile system will help delivering on these trends," said Sanjoy Sen, senior overseer, Deloitte Touche Tohmatsu India Pvt. Ltd. "Traditionally, THAT and ITeS companies in India earn majority of the income from outside the house. Nonetheless, as India sees these key global tendencies institutionalized through government's procedures, it is good media for IT industry, inches he said.

Sector's home income was pegged at Relating to software lobby body Nasscom, the IT Rs. 1. 15 trillion in fiscal 2014 and it is expected to range between Rs. 1. 25 trillion and Rs. 1. 289 trillion in fiscal 2015. Relating to R. Chandrashekhar, director of Nasscom, "providing Wi fi services, next-gen e-ticketing system, GIS mapping and digitization of records will allow the Indian Railways in its overall growth goals. "

Dinesh Malkani, president-sales, India and Saarc, of Cisco Systems Inc., said the technology-led initiatives released in the railway budget "are definitely a step the right way, both for the citizens and the IT industry". "We see a huge prospect of the IT industry to leverage existing strengths in cloud, mobility and IoT (Internet of Things) strategies to deliver impressive solutions around paperless and digitized office buildings, technology-based safety solutions as well as truly linked operations".

SanchitVirGogia, chief analyst of Greyhound Research, too, believes this is "transformational... especially from the mobility stand point. Mobility is going to drive a lot of consumption and will also be needing a lot of investment".

Big Indian software services businesses, which consider digital business and mobility to become key income growth motorists in the next few years, will be fighting for their share in the opportunity. For illustration, TCS expects its digital business to generate $3-5 billion of revenues over the next few years. HCL Technologies Ltd too said its digital system integration (DSI), providing services to companies that are going digital, is the new generation proposition and one of the key growth areas for the company.

"Global enterprises today view digitalization as a route to business model transformation. Indian Railways' digitalization efforts signify a major shift towards onboarding what HCL calls Gen 2 propositions, which in change lead to creation of sustainable competitive advantage, inches said Sanjeev Nikore, leader, APMEA (Asia Pacific/Middle East/Africa), India Business and Tactical Engagements, HCL Technologies.

IOT AND INDIA

Internet of Things (IoT) is famous by most as the next great innovation in technology as shown in Figure 5. A new where every object we use has a sensor, enabling it to hook up to the internet so it can contact your lover and the user is a global that seems like something out of science fiction. Together with the Net of Issues fast drawing near, that world could turn into a truth very soon. Specialists suppose the IoT market could be worth just as much as $1. 7 trillion by 2020, with more than 62 billion devices connecting to the IoT by that time. But where will much of that improvement come from? The Scenario. S. is always near by the forefront of scientific improvements, and China is in the middle of a tremendous economic expansion, but some say India will be the location to find IoT progress, even becoming the major consumer of IoT devices in five years. When some challenge the says, it's clear the near future is bright for the IoT in India. Area of the push to increase the potential of the web of Things in India is coming from the countrywide government. Collaboration between the Department of Consumer gadgets and Information Technology and the Ministry of Down-town Development has resulted in an emphasis in programs designed to expand the sizes of the country in using the IoT. A lot of these endeavors will be the support of smart towns, cities (or cities that use IoT devices to deal with traffic, resources, and other aspects), health care IoT receptors for monitoring health, and Indian Railways. In the Indian Railways example, IoT devices on the locomotives communicate through the cloud to suggest fuel ingestion. This information can be used to increase efficiency on India's railroads. These sorts of projects make the perfect indication showing how important India's government views the IoT, but several of obstacles remain in existence which may prevent the country from becoming the biggest customer of IoT devices

Figure 5. IoT devices

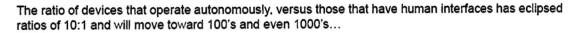

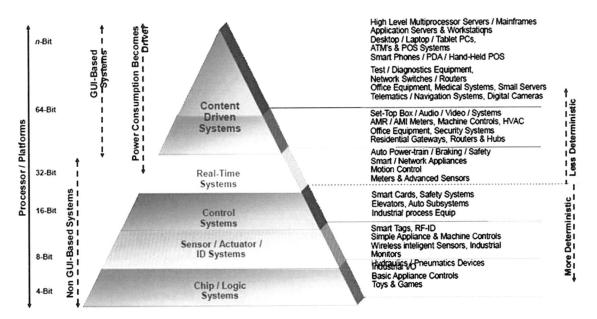

as predicted. Probably, the most solid challenge is internet ease of access among the list of basic human population.

Several startup companies have arisen in India aiming to harness the potential of the IoT. One company called CarIQ manufactures a device that turns normal cars into smart vehicles. This IoT device information and assesses data like mileage and speed while also considering driving behaviors, all while contacting other cars. The device of Life Plot is like the Indian government's healthcare initiative, in which the linked device can track record medical data about a patient, providing remote analysis with little training needed. These are simply a few good examples of companies totally utilizing the potential of the Internet of Items (Arsene, 2016).

Nevertheless, challenges continue to be, the future of the IoT in India is a great one. The government is fully support the work to develop better structure, companies are coming away with innovative products, and industries be aware of benefits the Internet of Things provides. With more time and resources, IoT progress could prove to be impressive on a huge size. In case that improvement continues, the prediction about IoT utilization in India may come true ultimately.

IOT AND RAILWAYS

This give attention to how Internet of things could expertise the railroad industry, introducing a simple solution that will be designed to modernize aging networks at railroads, improve safety, drive down expenses and present passengers an improved linked experience. The solution may be offered to cover all aspects of the train system, from the teaches themselves to areas. It comes each time when railways are coping with range of challenges, from ageing systems to difficult environmental situations to new federal government safety requirements. IOT will have four lines, such as Connected Stop. The component takes the various disparate parts of traditional in-station networks and marketing and sales communications systems and brings them together into a standards-based IP network. The network includes many methods from routers and switches to security cameras, digital signs and video storage. Info around location can easier permit railway officials in order to traffic and alert passengers when there is a plan hold off, while video cameras will permit railway representatives to monitor what's heading on in their channels and more quickly package with issues of security and scheduling. Connected Teach ensures a rider experience that features on-board services like Wi-Fi as well as video surveillance and set operations. Passengers are able to use the Wi-Fi network to do such tasks as pay fares, keep monitor of the train routine, browse the Web and work. The railway will become more efficient that help the passenger to work with fewer disturbances if that's what they want.

IOT Based Train Control Technology

Linked Trackside offers a ruggedized IP structure that hooks up the coach to a mobile to Multiprotocol Sticker Switching (MPLS) backhaul network and then the data center. This sort of part of the overall solutions features a fühler network that offers processing power at the edge--a process. Train operators can more quickly learn when there is a concern on the tracks--when the data returning from the edge will not fit the norm--and the computers on the advantage can examine the data they are getting, make a decision what data to dispose of and what things send again to the info centre, which can help save the railway networking and storage costs. This IOT based Train Control technology combines with products from various OEMs to create a communications system that will reduce rail accidents--such as train collisions and derailments--and comply with steadily strict governmental regulations. Former reducing the likelihood of major incidents on the railways, the IoT will also improve the passenger experience in more mundane ways. Pattern Recognition technology will generate a sequence of images as trains move over the tracks, adding nourishment to visual and statistical techniques into asset and keep track of maintenance systems, monitoring the status of the keep track of, level-crossings, adjustment switches, imperfections and joints in real time. Connected devices will interact independently with sensors on the network to measure things such as water table levels, which can impact railway embankments should the ground become water logged. Meanwhile, in-ground detectors will discover landslides or possibly the potential for them. Best suited now there is many things that need to be observed and the railway can run as a totally digital service, and not have to have people walking the tracks, it brings cost savings and increased safety for the staff.

Intelligent Identification System of Railway Logistics

The intelligent identification system of railway logistics by means of IOT may be used to timely track, effective control and manage various areas of train logistics. The intelligent recognition system of railway strategies by means of IOT is a whole system with blend of hardware and software using computer as the core (Guoa, Zhanga, & Lib, 2012).

The Composition of the System

The intelligent identification system of railway logistics by means of IOT is made to address issues of the railway logistics in information collection, transmission, processing and sharing. Based on electronic digital identification technology, the system aims to achieve the collection of information, units up information system by modern information network technology, and connects operating areas and business network with information technology and network platform, which achieves the management of scientific, organized, and digital, to be able to track and monitor item in entire procedure. The intelligent identification system of railway logistics by means of IOT is comprised of the goods electric tag, reader, handheld target audience, repeater, host, tag rewritable devices and data indication channel.

The Rules of the Program

The cellular signal with character of goods identity is received by the reader which is sent by tags, and then sent to the central computer from the repeater. The central computer receives the protected signal of goods from these readers, creates various documents by analysis and processing so that professionals can access a variety of information in time. To be able to ensure the accuracy and reliability of information, portable reader which is applied in department for goods loading and storage works as the other identification. Found in addition, tag rewritable devices are designed to ensure the re-use of digital tags.

Educate Management Systems

The planet's aging transportation infrastructure is slowly but surely being replaced by train management systems (TMS). Within a TMS, train locomotives become interconnected communication hubs, transmitting data among themselves and network control centers, and acquiring instructions from the control centers. Machine-to-machine communication, centrally managed in a cloud-based architecture, permits operators to apply equipment, monitors, and stations more proficiently while drastically reducing protection risks. Safety is the primary requirement of IoT applications and solutions for a TMS. For example, one critical application is on-board train location and detection systems that permit trains to be "aware" of the positions of other trains. This reduces the chance of accident while enabling trains to operate safely in close proximity to each other, thus making more efficient use of track capacity. Rate monitoring and control is yet another important protection application. Software has recently been developed that can show coach velocity for drivers and report speeds to central control systems. Once onboard monitoring systems are interconnected with wayside signaling systems, they can control train speeds or even command trains to stop depending on track conditions, the positions of switches, the occurrence of other locomotives on the track, and elements (The Internet of Trains, 2016).

Setting up Safer, More Efficient Highspeed Trains

A lot of passengers count on railways every day. To keep trains jogging smoothly and safely, employees need continuous, real-time information about authorized speed, signaling points, safe distance between trains, vehicle businesses and environment, and more. Yet yesterday's railway communications systems often can't keep speed with modern demands.

Today, GSM for Railways (GSM-R) cellular technologies provides a single, reliable communication system for critical railway systems. And 3G/4G broadband connection can permit more effective teach solutions for drivers and more enjoyable journeys for passengers.

With the everywhere reach, proven reliability and strong security inherent in commercial cellular networks, train operators can deliver a variety of Internet of Things (IoT) applications that boost efficiency and deliver an improved voyager experience.

- Rolling stock navy management can lower functioning and maintenance costs, help train operators optimize generating behaviour and reduce energy consumption
- Passenger Wi-Fi can hook up passengers to the Internet, link rail employees to their customers and convey travel information
- Real-time passenger infotainment systems provide real-time journey status, notify passengers of any interruptions, and display entertainment and advertising
- Real-time CCTV can improve management of security events and monitoring of the interior and exterior train environment
- Automated traveling counting can track teach load dynamically for individuals and businesses centres.

Wireless Monitoring Railway Vehicles

There is practically one particular. 5 million railroad autos in the United Declares alone, and railroad companies would prefer to know the dimensions of the location and current position of every single one of them. Would be the hatches open or closed? Are actually the handbrakes on or off? Are wheel bearings overheating and calling for preventative maintenance? Are the internal temperatures appropriate for the onboard cargos?

Present a few decades before, railroads could only answer these questions by having train crews and backyard clerks physically inspect the trains. Therefore, it is no shock that railroads have recently been eager to adopt helpful technologies when they emerged out. Tracking car locations became easier with introduction of programmed equipment id (AEI) systems, which use wayside scanners to read transponders mounted on spending rail cars. Preventative maintenance was improved with the extra of wayside code readers that measure wheel temps and broadcast alerts when a high temperature conditions are detected.

But one railroad wanted more. That they wanted to be able to track as many parameters as possible, and be able to get all of the data in real time, at a single location.

A web-affiliated asset monitoring provider resolved the challenge using B+B's Wzzard Sensor platform. They linked the sensors in the railcars to wireless, battery-powered Wzzard Intelligent Edge Nodes as shown in Figure 6. Wzzard Intelligent Edge Nodes form a self-healing woven network that reports the sensor data to the Wzzard Network Gateway, which offers Ethernet connectivity via either cellular or wired contacts. The provider also prepared each railcar with a GPS tracker. Like the edge nodes, the GPS UNIT device reported to the network gateway. And thanks a lot to the cellular sites, all of this real time data could now be monitored at the central control office.

Figure 6. Wireless monitoring of rail cars

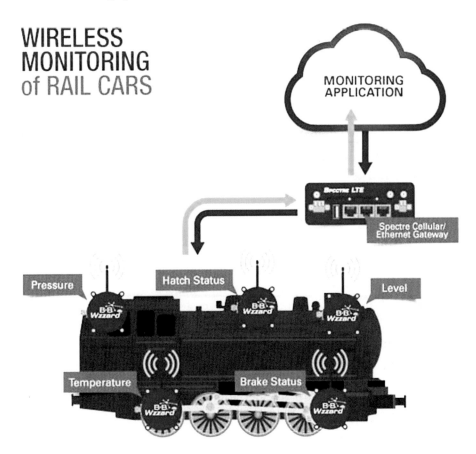

Standardized M2M (Machine-to-Machine) Protocols

IoT puts "sensors on all manner of machines to acquire data, linking them over born and wireless networks, and then applying data stats to determine when a train's wheel needs upgrading, an engine power needs fixing, a soybean field needs watering, or a patient needs reviving, very well. Standardized M2M (machine-to-machine) protocols are in the works to facilitate communications, but developers aren't waiting to see what happens. The automotive industry has recently been quick on the subscriber base, driven by to be able to improve vehicle safety. Ann Arbor, Michigan's 2800 vehicle basic safety pilot is testing the technology and the expense of vehicle-to-vehicle communications. In commercial aviation, London City Airport terminal is testing ways to get rid of the nuisances of flying... delayed flights, absent baggage, even getting a taxi (Taberner, 2015).

How about the railways? Change may seem to be slow as trains have much longer lives than many methods of transportation. Yet, as The Economist reports, there is no shortage of new ideas, from brake to route-planning to moving platforms.

Union Pacific has already deployed sensors to predict and prevent derailments. Infrared sensors are located every 20 miles on the tracks to take about 20 million temperatures readings, looking for overheating. Trackside microphones listen for a change in the sound of bearings, suggesting impending failure. They use ultrasound imaging to look for flaws inside of wheels.

The ability to improve businesses and traveling service is a key benefit for IoT / M2M. Rail passengers have recently been surfing the web on locomotives using wi-fi networks. In respect to EURAIL magazine, M2M networks are now implemented to create a more reliable and robust service using more and more high quality, resistant connections. In the UK, under the Disability Elegance Act, station entrances must provide a Customer Data System (CIS) screen. M2M over 3G is providing a quick, economical alternative to cabled systems.

There are a number of technology challenges to be conquer as IoT and M2M technologies proliferate across the rails: Universal cell coverage is needed along monitors to transmit precise locations; battery-powered sensors must previous on a railcar for five to seven years without replacement; and standardization is required for receptors, networks, and messaging.

PDS_busbars Development continues as railroad companies turn to key technologies to increase efficiency, safety, trustworthiness, and supply an improved passenger experience.

- Laminated multilayer busbars provide efficient and small connections for propulsion, additional, and other IGBT primarily based converters.
- High consistency circuit materials offer the performance needed by M2M receptors, wireless base stations, dish antennas, and network machines and storage.
- Superior temperature silicone materials are ideal as gaskets and seals, cushions, and cold weather and acoustic insulation in demanding conditions.
- Cellular and specialty silicones help manage vibration for quiet interior cabins.

OVERCOMING CHALLENGES

Clearly, the Internet of Trains creates a variety of opportunities. A barrier for several operators, however, is that they have a substantive investment in legacy systems and equipment which may have performed independently and are not suitable for connectivity. While operators may be keen to obtain the economies, efficiencies, and opportunities that IoT pledges, they also have an understandable interest in guarding that investment. The problem for developers of IoT solutions is to find techniques to hook up these previously unconnected systems so that operators do not have to rip away and replace their whole infrastructure in order to realize the great things about IoT. Interrelated with the issues of safety and on-line is the matter of security. As rail systems rely more on cordless connectivity, they become more vulnerable to outside distraction and intrusion. The implications of even a tiny interruption become particularly severe as trains become more powerful, carry more passengers, and travel faster. Systems that are critical for safe procedure can be affected with a simple electric device, a cellular phone, or a tiny piece of malicious code downloaded from the Net. When passenger safety and life is at risk, strong security turns into a fundamental requirement.

Prevention of Train Accidents Using Wireless Sensor Networks

In these times train accidents are most common and destruction scheduled to these accidents are definitely more severe and takes many lives of passengers hence to reduce the car accident rate due to impact and breakage of track can be reduced to maximum by the means of designing a system that makes use of network to a limited area (using a Zig-Bee module), microcontroller for monitoring the Zig-Bee module, educate motor, LCD display, devices, and an integral part of internal memory space for dumping the mandatory program (in Keil). The look cost is low and the designed system reduces impact between opposite trains about the same train and even when the train is moving over between two tracks. Every train contains a solitary system or a free one. The Zig-Bee component is described below:

Zig-Bee is a specification for a suite of high level communication protocols used to produce personal area systems made from small, low-power digital radios. Zig-Bee is based on an IEEE 802. 15 standard. Nevertheless low-powered, Zig-Bee devices often transmit data over much longer distances by passing data through intermediate devices to succeed in more distant ones, building a mesh network; i. electronic., a network with no centralized control or high-power transmitter/receiver able to reach all of the network devices. The decentralized mother nature of such wireless adhoc networks make them well suited for applications where a central node cannot be relied after. Zig-Bee can be used in applications that require a low data rate, long electric battery life, and secure marketing. Zig-Bee has an identified rate of 250 kbit/s, best suited for routine or intermittent data or a single signal transmitting from a sensor or input device. Applications include wireless light switches, electric meters with in-home-displays, traffic management systems, and other consumer and professional equipment that will need short-range wireless copy of information at relatively low rates. The technology defined by the Zig-Bee specification will likely be simpler and less expensive than any other WPANs, such as Bluetooth or Wi-Fi. Zig-Bee networks are secured by 128-bit symmetric security keys. In home software applications, transmission distances range from 10 to 90 meters line-of-sight, depending on power output and environmental characteristics. Zig-Bee uses the direct-sequence spread spectrum (DSSS) is a modulation strategy. As with other divide spectrum technologies, the sent signal takes up more bandwidth than the information signal that modulates the carrier or broadcast consistency. The name 'spread spectrum' originates from the truth that the carrier indicators occur over the full bandwidth (spectrum) of a device's transmitting frequency. Direct-sequence spread-spectrum transmissions multiply the data being transmitted by a "noise" signal. This kind of noise signal is a pseudorandom sequence of just one and -1 ideals, at a frequency much higher than that of the original signal. The resulting signal resembles white-noise, like a music saving of "static". However, this noise-like signal can be used to exactly restore the original data at the obtaining end, by multiplying it by the same pseudorandom sequence (because $1 \times 1 = 1$, and $-1 \times -1 = 1$). This kind of process, known as "de-spreading", mathematically produces a correlation of the transmitted PN pattern with the PN collection that the receiver thinks the transmitter is using. The resulting effect of boosting signal to sound ratio on the funnel is called process gain. This effect can be produced larger by employing a longer PN sequence and more chips per little, but physical devices used to generate the PN sequence impose practical boundaries on attainable processing gain. If an undesired transmission device transmits on the same channel but with another type of PN sequence (or no sequence at all), the de-spreading process results in no processing gain for that signal. This result is the foundation for the code division multiple access (CDMA) property of DSSS, which allows multiple transmitters to share the same channel within the limits of the cross-correlation properties with their PN.

Integrated Management of Urban Railway Crossing Areas

Railway level crossings have high impact on urban mobility, both so that regards safety of passengers and citizens and for the complex relationships with car related and congestions. Indeed, rail crossings can be a web host to numerous and severe accidents, having causes varying from faults in buffer closing to incorrect conduct of pedestrians and individuals, who can get stuck in the crossing area. Indeed, accidents at level crossing in Indian railways are accounting for 49% of total fatalities in railway transport over the last decade. In downtown scenarios, traffic congestions in the nearby road network is also correlated with train crossing accidents; indeed, the occurrence of any queue often prevents careless drivers to leave the crossing area in time when limitations are closing, thus blockage train transit. Additionally, changes in closure times (due e. g. to teach delay) might bring about unforeseen effects on normal highway traffic flows that can propagate from the bridging zone to local areas and, even, to other geographically distant parts of the city (Magrini, 2015).

These concerns show that railway crossings are complex entities in whose optimal management cannot be addressed unless with the aid of an intelligent transportation system able of integrating both the railway and road views. The proposed infrastructure, called SIMPLE (Railway Safety and Infrastructure for Mobility applied at level crossings), consists of several innovation points. First of all, SIMPLE employs state-of-the-art M2M communication paradigms. This shows the applicability of such protocols to the IT IS domain; in particular STRAIGHT FORWARD devices talk natively with a M2M Gateway, while legacy systems may easily be integrated by providing suitable adapters. Secondly, BASIC leverages on progressive stuck vision technologies; specially designed sensor nodes are being used to build a Smart Camera Network (SCN) devoted to traffic assessment in areas critical for railways crossings. Third, a new danger zone sensor is integrated for providing superior safety in railway crossing by uncovering possible obstacles between the barriers of the traversing. Last, all such components of the working platform have been analyzed and validated during an intensive test exercise kept in the mid-sized town of Montecatini, Italy. The experimental activities showed the effective impact of the aforementioned technologies in the ITS domain.

Infrastructure Architecture

SIMPLE is composed by several choices, each of which deploys specific functionalities. It has then been decided to organize the overall in a modular architecture that contain subsystems with well-defined tasks and interfaces. This is advantageous for what take care extensibility, adaptability and configurability of the full program. Figure 7 shows the key building blocks of BASIC infrastructure. Starting from the bottom, the two subsystem for in situ data collection are reported, particularly the Road Monitoring Program (RMS) and the Bridging Level Monitoring System (CLMS). In such systems, besides conventional COTS sensors, we use specially designed palpeur sensors to find and early notify obstacles on the level crossing area as well as a network of pervasive smart cameras based on Net of Things (IoT) paradigms for assessing traffic levels on roads around the city.

More in details, in the RMS a specially designed device known as M2M Gateway (GW) is in charge of orchestrating the communications. Indeed, the RMS represents an example of M2M Area Network, since inside this area the communications protocols between each component and the GW are ETSI M2M standard compliant. The RMS is composed by t Smart Camera Network (SCN) and commercial sensors (COTS sensors). In addition, the Variable Message Signs (VMS) are within the RMS with the aim of providing information to users about the railway crossing status and a forecast about the time of closing of level crossing barriers. The CLMS is within charge rather than the monitoring the genuine crossing level area. This includes a radar fühler for obstacle detection as well as a system for detecting the limitations status. Besides being linked to all of those other SIMPLE system, the CMLS is connected to the railway signaling system for safety-critical communication of anomalous events.

With the medium level, a do it yourself and standard-based Service Control Unit (SCU) integrates data collected in situ along with other information obtained through the text to third get together services e. g. to railway operator for timely train traffic data. The SCU also provides data to users by a web

Figure 7. Architecture of SIMPLE

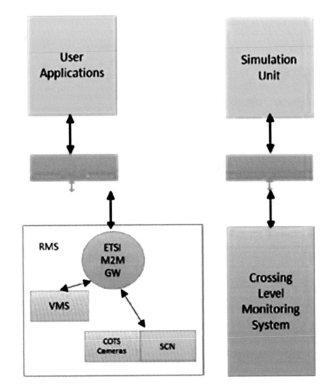

user interface. Certainly, User Applications might be implemented on top of the services provided by the SCU. Furthermore, a Simulation Unit in included in the architecture. Many of these unit is in fee of instantiating forecasting model based on the data provided by the SCU, in order to approximate traffic and barrier seal times.

Crossing Level Monitoring System

The traversing level monitoring product is a modular system you can use to control multiple railway crossings distributed around a metropolitan center in order to find obstacles and particular in their actual traversing areas. The system is made up in a couple of networked danger zone sensors, having both realizing and on-board processing features, linked to a so called Remote Station that is in charge of conversing with the SCU. In addition, radar sensors are linked directly to the railway signaling system to promptly notify the occurrence of obstacles.

Radar has been chosen as a dependable solution for this protection critical component with esteem to optical or ultrasound sensors, since it is less sensitive to climate (such as rain, are and snow) as well as strong sun glares and environmental noises and vibrations. Both radar range and azimuth resolutions have been chosen matching typical vehicles and obstacles proportions, in order to boost SNR, also to avoid fake alarms due to vehicles and folks moving outside the level crossing barriers.

A great on-board system for concentrate on detection has been developed. Instead of by using a traditional DSP architecture for the signal processing algorithm execution, all the processing string has been implemented within a single FPGA which furthermore manages the low level HW interfaces of the device. This HW solution was preferred to a possible software solution due to real-time constraints together with the huge amount of calculations required by some processing algorithms such as FFT.

Whenever an barrier is detected by the radar system and the barriers of the bridging are closed, a concept is delivered to the train signaling system to stop train circulation. Similarly, such information is delivered to the Remote Station, which, in turn, make available to the SCU all the information of interest.

High-Speed Train Data Stream Using Class-Based Delta-Encoding

Railway transportation plays an important role in both economic and social development. The requirements of the railway traffic increase in recent decades. In order to meet the growing demand, a new generation control system of railway transportation emerges. It consists of collection, transmission, analysis and scheduling module. In such a context, an information transmission system is built to connect trains and scheduling center. However, the infrastructure of the railway system cannot provide enough bandwidth for such amount of data. As a result, the efficiency of data transmission cannot be ensured. In this paper, we focus on the compression algorithm that reduce the amount of transmitted data and improve the system performance. Based on the analysis of the common algorithms, an efficient compression algorithm, named delta-encoding, is proposed (Lin & Wang, 2015).

It consists of two steps: preprocessing and compression.

Delta-encoding utilizes a class-based difference model, which reduces the data redundancy, to realize a preprocessing algorithm. With the combination of preprocessing algorithm and a regular compression algorithm, delta-encoding has better performance on compression ratio, and becomes a universal hybrid algorithm for structured data in IoT system rather than a specific algorithm in high-speed train system. Delta-encoding have advantages in both compression ratio and compression time.

The high-speed train data stream consists of structural operational records, and control/scheduling commands. They represent the train status and the message between train and railway-side devices, such as balise and track circuit. In order to provide real-time information for the scheduling center, trains have to upload their status in a short period. However, trains stay in a stable status in most of their running time. Short upload period will lead to uploading more redundant information. Although the commonly used data compression algorithms can help reducing the bandwidth, they are not designed for specific data structure so that they cannot minimize the compressed size. With the combination of preprocessing algorithm and a regular compression algorithm, delta-encoding has better performance, and becomes a universal hybrid algorithm for structured data in IoT system rather than a specific algorithm in high-speed train system. The approach is as follows:

- First, based on difference algorithm and the characteristic of high-speed train data stream, a class-based difference model for data compression is proposed.
- Next, a compression algorithm is designed with the difference model, and has a better efficiency than common algorithms for high-speed train data stream.
- Finally, based on the class-based difference model, a universal hybrid algorithm is proposed for structured data in IoT system.

Delta-encoding has various application scenarios, there are still some problems need to be solve. In the classification process, it is easy for some well-defined data format to locate its feature (such as FID) from specific position. However, in other situations, due to the restriction of the protocol, some classification message could be filtered out. Without detailed description, manual classification in advance will not work well. Therefore, a machine learning algorithm is needed to replace the manual approach. It will capture the feature from the whole content of each piece of data but not from specific position. This simplify the work of manual definition, and it becomes the next step of research.

CONCLUSION

Indian Railways can have exceptional improvement in asset management using IoT for Running Stock like Coaches, Chariot and Locomotives. The optimum use of assets can be facilitated once their exact location is known in real time. Keep track of maintenance can become better and manpower can be effectively utilized. The great pressure that railways is facing as a result of whopping income bill as well as severe critique by experts can be eased after the handheld devices can permit management to optimally deploy staff for maintenance works. The property will have sensors describing the with use of intelligent monitoring systems, they will reach the right location at the right time. IR today relies heavily on resource chain partners. Lot of time and effort is wasted in pursuing the supplies, gaining access to information of vendor. Almost all this can be programmed using IoT. The role of purchase department can be limited only to give the purchase order, the balance work can be handled by intelligent systems when the network has information on consignments, stock position etc. IoT is the future, and it includes already arrived.

REFERENCES

CodrinArsene. (2016, July). IoT ideas that will soon revolutionize our world in 8 ways. Media Labs. Retrieved from https://www.ymedialabs.com/internet-of-things-ideas/

https://en.wikipedia.org/wiki/Multiprotocol_Label_Switching

Government of India Ministry of Railways. (2015, February). Indian Railways Lifeline of the nation (white paper).

Guo, Z., Zhang, Z., & Li, W. (2012). Establishment of Intelligent Identification Management Platform in Railway Logistics System by Means of the Internet of Things, Establishment of Intelligent Identification Management Platform in Railway Logistics System by Means of the Internet of Things. *Procedia Engineering*, *29*, 726–730. doi:10.1016/j.proeng.2012.01.031

Indian Railways. (n. d.). Evolution (printable section). Retrieved from http://www.indianrailways.gov.in/railwayboard/print_section.jsp?lang=0&id=0%2C1%2C261

Lin, Y., & Wang, P. (December 2015), Class-Based Delta-Encoding for High-Speed Train Data Stream. In *Proceedings of the 2015 IEEE 34th International Performance on Computing and Communications Conference (IPCCC)*.

Magrini, M. (2015). An Infrastructure for Integrated Management of Urban Railway Crossing Area. In *Proceedings of the 2015 IEEE 18th International Conference on Intelligent Transportation Systems*.

Ministry of Railways, New Delhi. (2013). Investment Promotion and Infrastructure Development Cell.

Management Paradise. (n. d.). Safety measures by Indian Railways. Retrieved from http://www.managementparadise.com/forums/service-sector-management-s-s-m/201685-safety-measures-indian-railways.html

Sambamurthy, N., & Ahammad, S. H. (2013). Prevention of Train Accidents Using Wireless Sensor Networks. *International Journal of Engineering Research and Applications*, *3*(6).

Shristi, (September 2016) The Theory of Everything: Indian Railways. Retrieved from https://gradeup.co/the-theory-of-everything-indian-railways-i-8d46521a-7e69-11e6-995d-fccaa0f5d0cc

Srivastava, M. (July 2014), Tech push by railways a billion dollar opportunity for IT firms. Livemint. Retrieved from http://www.livemint.com/Politics/VrfxsV8tsaLVEqF46ATvaO/Tech-push-by-railways-a-billion-dollar-opportunity-for-IT-fi.html

Taberner, T. (2015). How the Internet of Things will change the way we monitor the Railways (White Paper). Eurotech UK.

The Internet of Trains. (2016). Wind (White Paper).

Wikipedia. (2017, June 06). History of rail transport in India. Retrieved from https://en.wikipedia.org/wiki/History_of_rail_transport_in_India

Chapter 13

Application of Big Data Technologies for Quantifying the Key Factors Impacting Passenger Journey in a Multi-Modal Transportation Environment

Shruti Kohli
University of Birmingham, UK

Shanthini Muthusamy
University of Birmingham, UK

ABSTRACT

Transportation systems are designed to run in normal conditions. The occurrence of planned works, unscheduled major events or disturbances can affect the transportation services that intended to provide and as a result, the disruptive nature may have a significant impact on the operation of the transport modes. This chapter focuses on the impact of disruptions in the multimodal transportation using the available open data. The enablers (key variables) of the datasets are taken into account to evaluate the service performance of each transport mode and its influence on other transport modes in case of disturbances. The high-volume, streaming data collected for a long time is a good potential use case for applying text mining techniques on big data. This chapter provides an insight into research being carried out for developing capabilities to store and analyze multi-modal data feeds for predictive analysis.

DOI: 10.4018/978-1-5225-3176-0.ch013

INTRODUCTION

In recent years, transport industry has seen tremendous growth that's proportionate to urbanization and increase in population. Multimodal systems have evolved as an important player and have been recognized as the most promising area for research in recent years. According to Lyons (2002), the public relies on multiple transport system to reach their destination. Catapult Transport System (2011) states that the multimodal transport network has drawn attention in the emerging intelligent mobility market and contributes highly to the efficient movement of people and goods around the world. The European Commission have started funding more multimodal transportation projects in recent years, e.g. Link (2010) paper encourages multimodal travel across European countries. To attain sustainable multi-modal transport systems in the urban area, it is vital to develop and maintain a smooth flow of traffic across all transportation modes which is not often the case due to scheduled and unscheduled major events or disturbances taking place. These factors not only lead to disruptions but also affect the normal working behavior of the transport systems. These disruptions are further seen to be influenced by a number of factors including weather, holidays, events, signaling problems, strike, wear-and-tear, engineering works etc. that definitely affects the performance of transport network. A comprehensive approach is required to analyzing disruptions in such multi-modal environment. Open-sharing of transport data by public transportation agencies like Transport for London(TFL), Network Rail, National Rail etc. is significant in the study of multimodal analysis. This has led to the improvement and innovation of transport services to the public. Opening up TfL data has been valued at £15-58 million per year and has resulted in over 200 travel apps being developed by private companies. The Government is supporting the UK's data infrastructure, most recently with £14 million to make data routinely collected by business and local government accessible for researches, including for transport research at Leeds and Glasgow Universities. Opening up transport datasets will improve public services and re-use of these datasets will generate economic benefits. In future, transport data can be integrated with other sector's data to attain efficient sustainable transport networks (Catapult Transport System, 2011).

The emphasis on multi modal transportation has not captured only recent attention. Following the publication of the Integrated Transport White Paper – A New Deal for Transport in July 1998, a number of multi-modal studies were announced (Booz Allen, 2012). These studies provide insights into the total demand for travel over a comparatively long time period and facilitate to establish a framework that would provide for an integrated transport system covering all modes, including the more sustainable means of travel such as walking and cycling. They are not perfect substitutes; as each is most appropriate for some specific users and purpose. Multi-modal transport planning requires tools for evaluating the quality of each mode, such as Level-of-Service standards which can be used to indicate problems and ways to improve each mode. It is no doubt complicated because modes differ in various ways, including their availability, speed, density, costs, limitations, and most appropriate uses. The planning aspect has been further discussed in the section below.

UNDERSTANDING MULTI-MODAL TRANSPORT SYSTEM

The report, Integrating Australia's Transport Systems: A Strategy For An Efficient Transport Future (Booz Allen, 2012) gives a brief description of various cities with integrated transport planning. Table 1 list some of the popular cities having integrated transport services (Booz Allen, 2012). Focusing on London,

Table 1. Integrated transport services in different cities

Examples of Integrated Transport Services Type	London	Hong Kong	Singapore
Physical	Extensive network of modes (walking, cycling, taxi, bus, rail, ferry, and airports) with well-designed stations and terminals	Well-designed intermodal stations integrated into neighborhoods.	Transit stations are designed to integrate multiple modes and local development
Fare	Oyster card can be used for most urban transport services.	Octopus Card introduced in 1997 useable on most transport services.	EZ Card usable on all public transport modes, parking, and small retail purchases.
information	London has led the way in public transport signage.	Good signage	TransitLink Guide and extensive signage provide comprehensive information on all aspects of traveling.
Institutional	The City of London manages all aspects of transport planning and operations.	Single governing authority helps to implement integration	TransLink multi-modal agency established in 1989. Provides strategic planning and integrated services.

its overall public transport network is characterized by a well-established rail network complemented by an extensive bus network and a ferry network. All these networks are integrated by multi-modal stations that are designed for ease of interchange for high volumes of passengers. At major train stations, built bus interchanges have been developed which are in walking distance of the railway and tube stations

Much research had been going on to identify the best practice of developing multi-modal transportation. Some of the key points of developed comprehensive guidelines (Litman, 2011) are:

- Multi-modal transportation planning should have integrated institutions, networks, stations, user information, and fare payment systems.
- Consider a variety of transportation improvement options, including improvements to various modes, and mobility management strategies such as pricing reforms and smart growth land use policies. Consider various combinations of these options, such as public transport improvements plus supportive mobility management strategies.
- Consider all significant impacts, including long-term, indirect and non-market impacts such as equity and land use changes. This should at least include:
  - Congestion
  - Roadway costs
  - Parking costs
  - Consumer costs
  - Traffic accidents
  - Energy consumption
  - Pollution emissions
  - Equity impacts
  - Land use development impacts
  - Community livability
- Impacts that cannot be quantified and monetized (measured in monetary values) should be described.

- Multi-modal comparisons should be comprehensive and marginal and should account for factors such as transit system economies of scale and scope.

- Special consideration should be given to transport system connectivity, particular connections between modes, such as the quality of pedestrian and cycling access to transit stops and stations.

- Special consideration should be given to the quality of mobility options available to people who are physically or economically disadvantaged, taking into account universal design (the ability of transport systems to accommodate people with special needs such as wheelchair users and people with wheeled luggage) and affordability.

- Indicate impacts with regard to strategic objectives, such as long-range land use and economic development.

- Use comprehensive transportation models that consider multiple modes, generated traffic impacts (the additional vehicle traffic caused by expansion of congested roadways), and the effects of various mobility management strategies such as price changes, public transit service quality improvements and land use changes.

- People involved in transportation decision-making (public officials, planning professionals, and community members) should live without using a personal automobile for at least two typical weeks each year that involve normal travel activities (commuting, shopping, social events, etc.) in order to experience the non-automobile transportation system.

BACKGROUND

Various literature studies carried out on the multimodal transportation paved way for the improvement of the performance of the overall transport system. However, Liu (2011) mentioned the lack of sufficient datasets makes harder to achieve the desired multimodal network. Modeling and analyzing a multimodal transportation is a big challenge in terms of limited availability of quality data sets. Also, Jäppinen (2013) emphasized open data approach to analyze sustainable urban mobility in the multimodal network. When designing a multimodal transport network using open source, the challenge lies in dealing with different data formats obtained from different service providers. Lyons (2002), stated that the British transport industry is complex and emphasized the importance of standardizing data to enable transfer of information between heterogeneous systems in their research paper. Modeling a multimodal network involves the integration of various modes which in turn increases the complexity of merging different datasets from different sources and is not a straight forward process (Chen, 2011).

The literature on the analysis of disruptions mainly involved building a mathematical model for the single mode of transport (Scott, 2006; Unnikrishnan, 2011; Rodríguez-Núñez, 2014. These models are analyzed based on critical links, inbound and outbound travel. The concept of analyzing multimodal network is gaining importance in recent years due to the expansion of transport industry, population growth and to provide efficient travel services. Burgholzer (2013) simulated a model to analyze disruptions in intermodal transport based on available real-time data and identify the critical links that are affecting the network as a whole. The proposed model analyses the impact of disruption across multimodal transport system. In this analytical investigation of three transport models (train, tube, and bus), the focus is to analyze how the disturbance on one transport model affecting the other transport models based on captured data. The analysis results will help to plan future transport network model with respect to new infrastructure requirements, optimized and sustainable transport system. This will also help to keep the cost minimum and value for money to stakeholders.

The most common technique used in modeling multimodal transportation systems is Geographic Information Systems technology (Liu, 2011; Thrill, 2000; Mandloi, 2010), for geospatial data management. Some of the research studies based on network performance indicators such as critical links (Burgholzer, 2013) and open data (Hielkema, 2013). The study on open data is considerably less when compared to other techniques in use.

The aim of the chapter is to set up a framework for analyzing disruption patterns in the multi-modal environment. The chapter provides details of multi-model feeds and provides comprehensive details of big data technologies that can be used to store and mine public data feeds. It describes a system framework that is being developed to process the live remote feeds from multiple transport networks and to analyze the processed real-time feeds to detect and determine the runtime service conflict between multiple modes. The study area used to analyze the impact of disruptions in multimodal systems is London. The city's major stations are analyzed for disruptions where multimodal transport access is prevalent, particularly, with a focus on three modes of public transports: Train, Bus, and Tube in real time. Nevertheless, the prototype model can be applicable to other stations in London. The proposed model is implemented using Python programming and Mongo database. The heterogeneous data sets (train, bus, and tube) are collected from open data sources such as TFL and Network Rail are processed and stored in MongoDB, a scalable database. The system will then be queried upon to calculate the disruption rate in bus and tube by taking train feed as decisive feed and presents the final outcome in a percentage format. Also, various disruptions are analyzed individually across multiple modes. MongoDB is used in this chapter as it is scalable, high performance and NoSQL database to accommodate big data for future data analytics. The endeavor is to use big data technologies to store and mine public data feeds to reduce delays in a multi-modal environment.

OPEN DATA FEEDS FOR VARIOUS MODES OF TRANSPORTATION

The use of open data in transportation will benefit the passengers for optimized travel, improve transport services, easy system administration, and historic/predictive analysis purposes. However, there are challenges in accessing those data due to its nature of complexity, uneven availability and poor quality. According to (Jäppinen,2013), the benefits of open data are highlighted to achieve sustainable urban mobility pattern. Based on the Catapults Transport systems report (2011), only very little real-time data related to transport are available and some of the valuable datasets (aggregated format) are owned by the private data service providers requires paid access. Also, unavailability of standard global format for datasets poses even more challenging task for developers to benefit the usage of datasets. The Government outlines the summary of various datasets and links to all UK open datasets.

1. **Darwin Data Feeds:** Darwin feeds live train information to station screens and online channels, including the National Rail app, providing real-time arrival and departure predictions, platform numbers, delay estimates, schedule changes and cancellations. Darwin takes feeds directly from every train operator's customer information system, combining it with train location data provided by the infrastructure manager, Network Rail (NR). This ensures that passengers see the same live information whether they choose to look for it on station screens, on the internet, via an app, or by

asking station staff. All of Britain's train operating companies and NR have been involved in Darwin, which was funded by the national station's improvement program to provide real-time information, clearer way-finding, better accessibility, and improved waiting areas for passengers. National Rail Enquiries (NRE) support the principle of transparency and contribute to the wider industry agenda by making data openly available in the public domain. NRE have a selection of APIs and XML feeds that are available for use by third-party developers to create their own applications.

2. **Transport of London Unified Data Feeds:** TFL has recently launched unified data feeds encouraging unification of the data for modes of transport into a common format and structure (common canonical data model). The majority of the transport data provided by each mode of transport is semantically similar. Historically, the data for each mode has been shared with you in different formats and structures. This makes the development of multi-mode applications difficult as you will need to write code for each mode of transport. The core identifiers for all stations and platforms have been normalized to the national NaPTAN standard. This standard is an identification scheme that is supported by the DfT nationally, allowing the API to integrate data from transport authorities outside of London. The complexity of mapping between multiple identification systems used within TfL has been hidden from consumers of the API. The unified API is designed for applications to use in real time and at high volume. Previously the data has been provided in a variety of ways from flat file to streams. The new API has been designed to allow you to query in real-time and on demand, so that end customers always have the latest information. Some of the multi-modal core datasets included and available to developers are (TFL,2017):

   a. Journey Planning (current and future)
   b. Status (current and future)
   c. Disruptions (current) and Planned works (future)
   d. Arrival/departure predictions (instant and web sockets)
   e. Timetables
   f. Embarkation points and facilities
   g. Routes and lines (topology and geographical)
   h. Fares

OVERCOMING CHALLENGES OF THE OPEN DATA FEEDS

Extraction of open data feeds from multiple sources is one of the key challenges in mulita modal transportation environment. The main challenging task is to capture the heterogeneous datasets from various service providers. Based on the key findings of Transport Data Revolution report by Catapult Transport Systems(2011), there are 11 obvious transport related data gaps where some of the datasets do not exist at all in the UK and while others exist in 'silos' or not openly or freely available. There is no standardized data format available which increases the complexity in capturing the data feeds. Dealing with real-time and dynamic datasets is another challenge. Limited availability of real-time data makes it harder for developers to build an efficient system. Some of the dynamic feeds are not constantly updated. Unavailability of quality datasets will comprise the quality of system performance. Lack of integration and communication between the multimodal transport services is another key challenge that is hard to address. Manipulations of heterogeneous data from multi-sources are highly complex as they need better interaction and communication between various datasets. Analyze and manage the compiled big data sets. The three big challenges in dealing with big datasets are storage, processing and data management. New techniques, skills, and tools are needed to manage and analyze big datasets.

- Low latency has also been identified as an ever-prevailing challenge. Some data sets are time-sensitive; in particular bus and rail arrivals can be out of date within the 30s. The unified API supports the latest technologies to deliver this information at the lowest possible latencies (web sockets) in ways that scale to meet high volumes. This capability is delivered by rail and buses even though the source data systems use differing paradigms behind the scenes (bus Countdown uses streams).
- Minimizing structural and operational complexity is another such identified problem. Much of TfL's source data is provided from back-office operational systems. The data is rich, but in many places, it is over-complicated for most consumer applications. The unified API is designed for customer-facing applications in mind and the data that is output is designed to be easily understandable, and supportive of common customer-facing application use cases.
- **Support of Common Web and Data Formats:** The unified API supports output in both XML and JSON format. JSON is quickly becoming the de facto data format for the web and mobile applications, due to its ease of integration into browser technologies and server technologies that support Javascript. XML is also widely used as the data interchange format for data-rich applications. JSON also allows easier integration with web-based mapping technologies such as Google Maps and Open Street map.
- **Supportive of Future Change Whilst Minimizing User Impact:** The unified API acts as a mediator and façade between the users of the API and changes to the core source systems that provide the data. This shields user of the API from changes to those source systems as the API can implement logic to maintain the structures and methods that applications have been developed. Despite various challenges, there had been a number of projects based on an open Data feed, Table 2. The details regarding the same are available at Rail Delivery Group website.

BIG DATA TECHNOLOGIES FOR MULTI-MODAL TRANSPORTATION

Railways have been at the forefront in utilizing and implementing analytics and big data, from ridership forecasting to transit operations rail transit systems have been especially involved with these it concepts, and tend to be especially amenable to the advantages of analytics and big data because they are generally closed systems that involve sophisticated processing of large volumes of data. The more that public transportation professionals and decision makers understand the role of analytics and big data in their industry in perspective, the more effectively they will be able to utilize its promise (Gokasar et al., 2014). Using big data, several key indicators for transport was demonstrated to measure performance of cities (Wang et al., 2014) and for sustainability (Cottrill et al., 2015). Big data processing and data mining has been used to develop architecture for traffic cloud data mining and optimization of strategies and related data processing and network optimization methods (Xu et al., 2014). There are other case studies such as big data analytics for safety management, (Otero et al., 2014), crowdsourcing for intelligent transport system (Hielkema, 2013), crowd sourcing geo-social network (Yan et al., 2013), intelligent transport system for predicting driver behavior (Van et al., 2014). Several opportunities in public transport and processing techniques and their challengers were described in transport domain (Chandio et al., 2015).

Table 2. Rail projects based on open data feeds

Team Name	Theme	Summary
Disruption Feed	Disruption Information	Provides a basic prototype visualization tool (route map). It displays the disruption affected locations based on the output from the data produced using the new form.
Trainilicious	Passenger Loading	This project used a feed from the existing on-train CCTV for counting passengers in carriages in real-time. They deployed face and body recognition software in conjunction with the CCTV feed and used this data output to provide the information through a customer app.
Good things *(come to those who wait)*	Passenger Loading	The project was to build an app to influence the behavior of customers by incentivising to take a different (less crowded) train. Incentives included ideas like free coffee.
Taxi	Social – Taxi Sharing	Integrated taxi sharing. It worked on concept of connecting customers on board in a train, with others who want to share a taxi to the same destination
Plan-A-Roo	Dynamic Rerouting	Dynamic rerouting in the event of disruption
Ugo	Ticket Validity	The project enabled hardware and software solution for stations. Customers need to scan tickets using a reader in the digital box. Information about that ticket, station and how to find the train is also displayed.
WaveRoll	Passenger Loading / Passenger Data Collection	The project used beacons to count a number of mobile signals in a carriage to give a real-time loading value for each carriage.
RICCS	Disruption Support Tool	Control room decision support tool for analysis of disruption and fastest route to restoring service.
Journey	Ticket Choices	It facilitated tool for enabling customers to determine the ticket selection based on time vs price, rather than only fastest / most direct.
Rail Assist	Passenger Assist	It provided API linked to the 'Disabled Passengers' database that enabled early notification of platform numbers to disabled people and connects assisted travellers with staff on the station.
Train Guard	Disruption Alerting	It provided tool for telling customers about issues that might affect their journey before they travel - like concerts, social events

Source: McClair, n.d.

There are endless possibilities of big data analytics in the multi modal transportation environment and one of the main areas is to look into disruption analyzing for maximizing customer experience.

AVAILABLE TOOS FOR BIG DATA ANALYSIS

There are many Big Data tools available in the market. According to Forbes(Forbes,2016), 10 hottest big data technologies based on Forrester's analysis are:

1. **Predictive Analytics:** This includes software and/or hardware solutions that allow firms to discover, evaluate, optimize, and deploy predictive models to improve business performance or mitigate risk.
2. **NoSQL Databases:** These data bases are different from a relational database and include key-value, document, and graph databases.
3. **Search and Knowledge Discovery:** This includes tools and technologies that support self-service extraction of information and new insights from large repositories of unstructured and structured

data which may reside in multiple sources such as file systems, databases, streams, APIs, and other platforms and applications.

4. **Stream Analytics:** Stream analytics can be understood as software that can filter, aggregate, enrich, and analyze a high throughput of data from multiple disparate live data sources and in any data format.
5. **In-Memory Data Fabric:** In-memory data fabric provides low-latency access and processing of large quantities of data by distributing data across distributed computer systems.
6. **Distributed File Stores:** It includes any computer network where data is stored on more than one node, often in a replicated fashion, for redundancy and performance.
7. **Data Virtualization:** Data virtualization implies technology that delivers information from various data sources, including big data sources such as Hadoop and distributed data stores in real-time.
8. **Data Integration:** Tools for data integration across solutions such as Amazon Elastic MapReduce (EMR), Apache Hive, Apache Pig, Apache Spark, MapReduce, Couchbase, Hadoop, and MongoDB.
9. **Data Preparation:** It refers to software that eases the burden of sourcing, shaping, cleansing, and sharing diverse and messy data sets to accelerate data's usefulness for analytics.
10. **Data Quality:** Data Quality products conduct data cleansing and enrichment on large, high-velocity data sets, using parallel operations on distributed data stores and databases.

The one being used for developing the current big data capability at the center have been described below:

MongoDB and Big Data

MongoDB (2017) is free and open-source, published under the GNU Affero General Public License It is a distributed database at its core, so high availability, horizontal scaling, and geographic distribution are built in and easy to use. It is a document database that stores data in flexible, JSON-like documents, meaning fields can vary from document to document and data structure can be changed over time. The document model maps to the objects in application code, making data easy to work with Ad hoc queries, indexing, and real-time aggregation provide powerful ways to access and analyze data. Whether document, graph, key-value, or wide-column, all of them offer a flexible data model, making it easy to store and combine data of any structure and allow dynamic modification of the schema without downtime or performance impact. The prominent features of Mongo DB that make it most suitable for storing streaming, heterogeneous data have been listed in Table 3.

*   **Mongodb Compass:** MongoDB Compass analyzes documents and displays rich structures within your collections through an intuitive GUI. It allows you to quickly visualize and explore schema to understand the frequency, types, and ranges of fields in your data set. Get immediate insight into server status and query performance. Real-time server statistics let you view key server metrics and database operations. Drill down into database operations easily and understand your most active collections. Visualize, understand, and work with your geospatial data.
*   **Hadoop Framework:** Hadoop (2017) is a framework written in Java for running applications on large clusters of commodity hardware and incorporates features similar to those of the Google File System (GFS) and of the MapReduce computing paradigm. Hadoop's HDFS is a highly fault-tolerant distributed file system and, like Hadoop in general, designed to be deployed on low-cost

Table 3. Features of MongoDB

Fast, Iterative Development. A flexible data model coupled with dynamic schema and idiomatic drivers make it fast for developers to build and evolve applications. Automated provisioning and management enable continuous integration and highly productive operations. Contrast this against static relational schemas and complex operations that have hindered in the past.
Flexible Data Model. MongoDB's document data model makes it easy to store and combine data of any structure, without giving up sophisticated validation rules, data access and rich indexing functionality. You can dynamically modify the schema without downtime. It reduces time to prepare data for the database and provides more time tp put data to work.
Multi-Datacenter Scalability. MongoDB can be scaled within and across geographically distributed data centers, providing new levels of availability and scalability. As your deployments grow in terms of data volume and throughput, MongoDB scales easily with no downtime, and without changing your application. And as your availability and recovery goals evolve, MongoDB lets you adapt flexibly, across data centers, with tunable consistency.
Integrated Feature Set. Analytics and data visualization, text search, graph processing, geospatial, in-memory performance and global replication allow you to deliver a wide variety of real-time applications on one technology, reliably and securely. RDBMS systems require additional, complex technologies demanding separate integration overhead and expense to do this well.
Complex Query handling: MongoDB is not limited to simple Key-Value operations. Developers can build rich applications using complex queries, aggregations and secondary indexes that unlock the value in structured, semi-structured and unstructured data. A key element of this flexibility is MongoDB's support for many types of queries. A query may return a document, a subset of specific fields within the document or complex aggregations and transformation of many documents.

Figure 1. Working with MongoDB
Source: MongoDB Architecture, n.d.

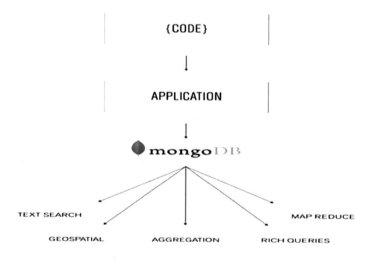

hardware. It provides high throughput access to application data and is suitable for applications that have large data sets. Hadoop 2.7 is comprised of four main layers:

- ○ Hadoop Common is the collection of utilities and libraries that support other Hadoop modules.
- ○ HDFS, which stands for Hadoop Distributed File System, is responsible for persisting data to disk.
- ○ YARN, short for Yet Another Resource Negotiator, is the "operating system" for HDFS.
- ○ MapReduce is the original processing model for Hadoop clusters. It distributes work within the cluster or map, then organizes and reduces the results from the nodes into a response to a query. Many other processing models are available for the 2.x version of Hadoop.

Hadoop clusters are relatively complex to set up, so the project includes a stand-alone mode which is suitable for learning about Hadoop, performing simple operations, and debugging. An Ubuntu 14.04 server with a non-root user with Sudo privileges with JAVA is required to run and store data in HDFS.

- **SPARK:** Apache Spark is an open-source big data processing framework built around speed, ease of use, and sophisticated analytics. Spark provides a comprehensive, unified framework to manage big data processing requirements with a variety of data sets that are diverse in nature (text data, graph data, etc.) as well as the source of data (batch v. real-time streaming data). It comes with a built-in set of over 80 high-level operators. In addition to Map and Reduce operations, it supports SQL queries, streaming data, machine learning and graph data processing. Resilient Distributed Dataset(RDD) is the core concept in Spark framework. It is just like a table in a database which can hold any type of data. Spark stores data in RDD on different partitions to rearrange computations and optimize data processing (Spark,2017).
- **Ubuntu Server:** Feeds were stored from TFL, National Rail Data Feeds, Network Rail data feed in Ubuntu server to collect live feeds for data processing. The idea of using ubuntu is to provide users dedicated computing resources (servers, storage, and networking) and they offer flexibility in scalability.
- **Python and PyMongo:** Python programming is used to coding. Python is widely used dynamic programming language for data analysis tasks. It emphasizes code readability, easy debugging and a good tool to implement algorithms. The Pymongo is an interacting tool to communicate with MongoDB database from Python. The Pymongo package is a native driver for MongoDB. Pymongo 3.3 supports MongoDB 2.4, 2.6, 3.0 and 3.2.

BIG DATA AND TEXT MINING

The disruption feeds include lots of unstructured information in form of human-generated reasons for the delay. So, it was important to identify ways of mining unstructured data. Mining unstructured data is an eminent research being carried out at various research centers in the world. If we say structured data is big, then unstructured data is huge. The generally accepted maxim is that structured data represents only 20% of the information available to an organization. That means that 80% of all the data is in unstructured form. If businesses are gaining value from analyzing only 20% of their data, then there is a massive potential waiting to be leveraged in the analysis of unstructured data. Unlocking this potential represents the next Big Data challenge. And for the text portion of unstructured data, the solution is text analytics. Also known as text mining or natural language processing, text analytics is the science of turning unstructured text into structured data. It has moved from university research into real-world products that can be used by any business.

Text analytics is focused on extracting key pieces of information from conversations. By understanding the language, the context, and how language is used in everyday conversations, text analytics uncovers the "who," "where," and "when" of the conversation, the "what" or the "buzz" of the conversation, "how" people are feeling and "why" the conversation is happening. Conversations are categorized and topics of discussion are identified. Given the complexity and actual distribution of data over many sources or sites, managing and mining big data are non-trivial yet very attractive tasks (Wu et al., 2014). While the notion of big data primarily concerns about data volumes, however (Wu et al., 2014) argue that size is not the main characteristic or challenge of big data. They also discuss the technical challenges related to data samples, structures, heterogeneity of sources, mining models and algorithms, and systems infrastructures that would support data analytics. In addition, (Wu et al., 2014) proposed the HACE theory, in which they explained the characteristics of big data through being (i) huge with Heterogeneous and various data sources, (ii) Autonomous with dispersed and decentralized control, (iii) Complicated and Evolving in data and knowledge associations. They conclude that in order to create value through big data analytics, high-performance computing platforms are required and a standardized and reliable information sharing protocol is needed. In addition, there is a need to design global models that are able to fuse and form a unified view of data from multiple sources. Also, there is a persistent need for carefully designed data mining algorithms that are able to analyze model correlations between scattered sites, and are able to fuse decisions from multiple sources to gain the best value of the big data (Wu et al., 2014). Figure 2 depicts various stages of a text mining process.

Figure 2 depicts a text mining process. Tokenization transforms each and every word or character in documents' text into a token. Tokenization itself is a complex process. It includes sub-processes such as:

1. **Change Case:** Change case transforms the case of all the tokens to uppercase or lower case to avoid treating them like two tokens;
2. **N-Grams:** Once tokens have the same case, then n-grams operator takes place and this operator merges different tokens together to form structures that have a meaning. To illustrate, assumingly To illustrate, assumingly we have 2 tokens: Big and Data. The n-gram operator will fuse them into "Track derailment" and that normally improves accuracy of later classification

Figure 2. Understanding text mining process

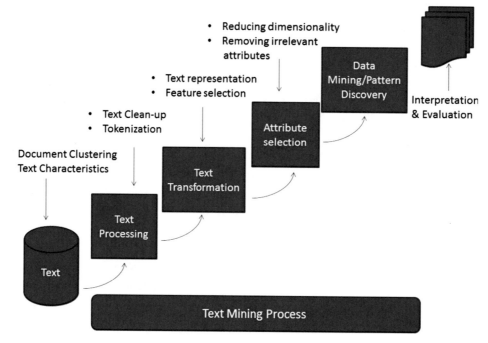

3. **Stemming:** The process of stemming brings the word to its stem. That is, to make sure that the same words, which have various tenses, adjectives, nouns, etc. are considered the same. Also, this enhance classification accuracy;

4. **Filter Stopwords:** The filter stop words operator removes stop words e.g., an, a, or, etc. This ensures that the words being matched together will be keywords, not just simple stopwords;

5. **Filter Tokens:** The filter tokens operator takes the minimum and maximum length as a parameter.

Once the document is pre-processed it's ready for applying unsupervised clustering technique like clustering to understand patterns in data. Clustering can be understood as a grouping of similar records into separate, or overlapping, clusters are one of the fundamental tasks in data mining. So basically clustering is classifying unclassified data. Depending on the type of observations, or cases, clustering can be executed using central or pairwise techniques. Central clustering minimizes the average distance between an observation and its cluster center. Thus, clustering solution can be described by means of cluster centroids. Clustering can be used to achieve both objectives; description and prediction. Clustering is used in information retrieval systems to enhance the efficiency and effectiveness of the retrieval process. Clustering is achieved by partitioning the documents in a collection into classes such that documents that are associated with each other are assigned to the same cluster. This association is generally determined by examining the index term representation of documents or by capturing user feedback on queries on the system. In cluster-oriented systems, the retrieval process can be enhanced by employing characterization of clusters. Usage of various text mining techniques to analyze public transport feeds has been explored in this chapter.

WORKING WITH PUBLIC TRANSPORT DATA FEEDS

To identify the disruption actors in the multi-modal environment it was planned to download feeds from different modes of transportation simultaneously and store them in MongoDB. Figure 3 shows the architecture diagram of the system model. The proposed analytical model consists of three stages, data inception, data processing, and data analytics. In data acquisition stage, real time data feeds of the bus, tube and train are streamed and stored in MongoDB. Bus and tube feed from Transport for London contains structured data whereas the train feeds from Network Rail contain semi-structured data. Three feeds (bus, tube, and train) are individually stored in three different collections in Mongo database for processing. In the data processing stage, the captured master data from the first stage are processed for analysis. At this stage, the unnecessary data are filtered out from the captured feeds and delivered in a format suitable for analysis, in other words, enablers that are helpful to support decision making process are identified. The identified key variables such as disruption data, RAG (Railway Action Group) specifications etc. are extracted from master data, integrated and stored in MongoDB for analysis. In the analytics stage, aggregation is performed by mongo query on the stored data in the database by grouping values from multiple collections (train, bus, and tube) together and computes the results in representable format. Proposed system architecture has been presented in Figure 3.

Figure 3. System architecture

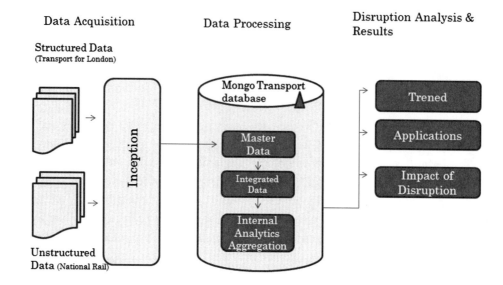

System Requirements

To analyze the impact of disruptions, the timely update of multimodal transport information by data providers are necessary for the evaluation of results. The area of interest in this chapter is London. The reason behind choosing the area is multimodal accessibility; it includes some areas where passengers are enduring the worst delays in the country due to delays in journey lines and frequent occurrences of strikes in recent months. London has been identified to have long average commute time. London's overall public transport network is characterized by an extensive network of modes (cycling, underground, DLR, ferry, bus, taxi, air and walking). Department for transport released transport statistics for Great Britain 2015, where it states that people working in London have the longest average commute (Transport Statistics,2016). Also, the Transport statistics report discloses that the half of all passenger journeys involved with bus transport and unveils the percentage share of journeys and kilometers by public transport modes. Multimodal transportation analysis will need integration of data from multiple sources and there are some limitations exist such as data gaps. Major stations were selected on the basis of multimodal network infrastructure. According to London travel demand survey report (2005/06 - 2013/14), Trips to or from central London have a high public transport mode share (TFL survey,2014). Almost 50 percent of trips between central London and inner London are made by National Rail and Underground/DLR, and a further 23 per cent are made by bus. Trips between central and outer London are dominated by rail, with 80 percent of trips made by National Rail or Underground. For trips between inner and outer London, approximately 45 percent are made by public transport. Transport for London's transfer plan identifies. After identifying the location to be analyzed it's important to segregate the feeds and store in the system and for these system requirements need to be analyzed. System requirements have been identified as functional and non-functional requirements.

Functional Requirements

Functional Requirements can be classified as Input and Output as follows:

- **Input:** The availability and accessibility of real-time transport data from data sources such as TFL (Transport for London), Network Rail have been identified. The real-time data are captured using Python and serve as inputs to the system. The data retrieved using python is in JSON format and stored in MongoDB. Among the various sources of Open Data Feeds (list available in Appendix I) following data sources have been identified and used for research purpose:
- **Transport for London:** TFL's open data micro-site, TFL (2017), provides metadata that highlights the key components of various transport datasets. For instance, data refresh rates, maximum time permitted between capturing and displaying the feed, maximum time the information can be displayed before being updated. TFL's Unified API *requires* authentication to access datasets across all modes of transport (London over-ground, tube, bus, rail, tram and DLR) and outputs data in both XML and JSON format (schema-less standard). This single Restful API is designed to query data in real time and at high volume for the latest information. Based on Catapult transport Systems report (2011), TFL has acknowledged that some leading software developers found the data being complex to work with. This is because the data are created by a wide range of systems, and TFL's adherence to UK transport data standards along with their custom data protocols. However, TFL also states that for creating multi-modal applications using new API is less challenging rather than the old API. The following data feeds from TFL are taken into consideration for analysis:
  - **Bus Feed:** This API provides real-time bus arrival information across all TfL bus stops and piers. Instant requests give a snapshot of the data with live bus arrival information valid at that point in time. The refresh rate of the bus data feed is every 30 seconds.
  - **Tube Feed:** This API provides real-time tube data across all TfL tube station including line, station status, and prediction services. The refresh rate of tube feed is every 30 seconds.
  - **Network Rail:** Network Rail (2017) provides six various data feeds, TD (train describer), VSTP (very short time planning), Train movements, RTPPM (real time public performance measure), schedule and TSR (temporary speed restriction). The data feeds are delivered as messages using STOMP (simple text-oriented messaging protocol). The real-time feeds need a subscription to specific ACTIVEMQ Topic (for example, RTPPM_ALL) and can be accessed using STOMP connection. The RTPPM data feed is taken as part of chapter analysis. RTPPM data shows the performance of trains (Urban) against the timetable in terms of percentage of the train arriving at destination on time and is updated every minute. The disturbances of Network Rail are compared with tube and bus feeds of TFL to compute the analysis results.
- **Output:** Multimodal disturbances and behavior of the transport system are analyzed using live and stored processed data feeds in MongoDB.
- **Integration:** Once feeds are downloaded it needs to be integrated. Data feeds contain enormous information about various locations so it is important to identify the transfer points. Transfer points are a very important concept in multimodal transportation which provides connectivity between two modes, Wang (2009). As Tolley (2014) stated "points on a network where several routes converge and often act as the focus of transport services or for the exchange of traffic be-

tween two modes of transport". People coming to London by urban train may have to take another mode of transport to reach their destination. The intuition is that there may be possible interdependency between various modes of transport operating in major stations in London. In the proposed model, the station acts as a transfer point between two modes and helpful to analyze the impact of one mode having on the other in case of disturbances. The inputs stored in MongoDB needs to be mapped with various interaction points to get coverage of maximum delay/disruption factors.

- **Enablers:** Decision support key variables such as disruption, mode name, line statuses etc. to analyze the behavior of the system in case of disturbances.
- **Aggregation:** Grouping matched the set of variables from different modes in MongoDB are done by mongo query. The behavior of the system: Seamless acquisition of valid data and processing is vital for the system to calculate accurate disturbances on the multimodal transport system.

Non-Functional Requirements

Non-functional requirements are equally important as like any other operational functional of the system model. The following non-functional elements are required for sustainable transport in the multimodal network.

- **Scalability:** To scale-up for future big data analysis in MongoDB.
- **Interoperability:** Standardised data format for all transport modes are necessary for efficient communication between multiple modes.
- **Flexibility:** To extend the functionality of the system (historic/ predictive analysis).
- **Efficiency:** Efficient working system
- **Capacity, Current, and Forecast:** To store more data for current and future analysis to attain sustainable transport systems.

The use case diagram of the proposed model in Figure 4 depicts the system's behavior and interaction among various elements of the system. The system operates in the Hadoop environment to prevent data loss and gives better usage of storage. Once the key goals for the study were identified the study was divided into three key phases, Figure 5. Table 4 depicts functionalities being addressed in different phases.

First two phases were completed and results were stored in Mongo DB as a collection Disruption that included time-based feeds of rail, tube and bus disruption). The implementation of first two phases was completed as in following three stages.

1. **Data Acquisition:** The first stage of implementation is data acquisition which is crucial for receiving valid and accurate data for further processing and analysis. These data are gathered in parallel in real time from multiple data sources, Transport for London (TFL) and Network Rail. As the chapter deals with the multimodal network, three modes of transport (bus, tube, and train) are analyzed for disruptions. Bus and tube data are accessed from TFL and urban train data is accessed from Network Rail. TFL's pre-processed data feeds can be gathered using Unified API call and provides structured data in JSON format. Network Rail publishes real-time feeds as JSON messages on ACTIVE MQ Topics using STOMP connection. The RTPPM data feed of Network Rail gives real-time performance measure of all urban trains irrespective of different operators and is of semi-structure nature. It is important to gather all data with necessary time stamping between

Figure 4. Use case diagram

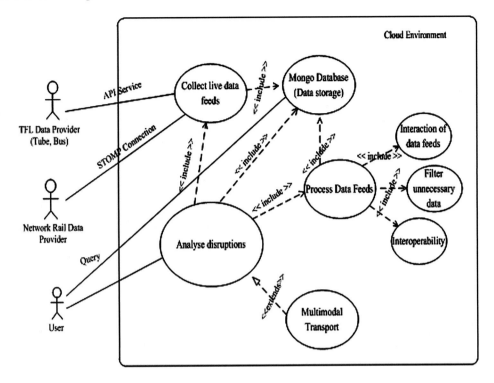

Figure 5. Various phases of multi-modal feed analysis

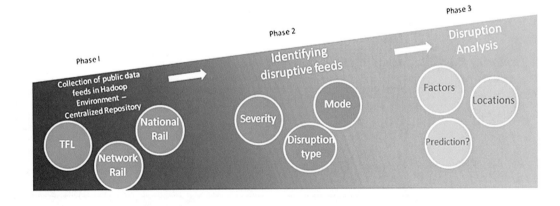

Table 4. Phases of feed analysis

Collection of Feeds	Disruption Identification	Multi-Modal Disruption Analysis
• Conversion to JSON • Storage in HDFS • Storage in MongoDB • Feed objects visualization with Mongo Compass • Identifying Transfer points	• Matching Time Stamps • Identifying high severity feeds • Collections disruption description in MongoDB	• Performing LDA to identify important topics discussed • K-Means clustering identify disruption factors • Need improvement with more data • Predicting future disruptions

all acquired data are valid data. The process of acquiring data feeds are implemented using Python programming. Pymongo is an interactive tool and is used to interact with Mongo server. The Python program is used for loading TfL bus and tube data starts with importing necessary libraries, JSON, MongoClient, Pymongo, requests to make API request. After import, relevant API call is made to load the response which is stored in MongoDB under individual collection names bus and tube. The RTPPM train feeds are loaded from Network Rail using imported libraries such as STOMP, JSON, and MongoClient. STOMP connection can be established using authentication keys and the feeds are delivered as messages which are pushed into MongoDB under collection name network rail. At this stage, the acquired big data contains a lot of information where some of them may not be useful for analysis. Data is stored in MongoDB and visualized using MongoDB compass. During the data acquisition phase work, it was identified that the data streams are downloadable at a very high speed and so high capacity framework is required to store the feeds and as well as mine the feeds using the spark.(specifically Pyspark). This work is being continued and improved. The work was started with a single cluster node and is being improved further. The figure below shows the draft framework of infrastructure being developed:

While exploring collected feeds it was identified that each feed included objects depicting the various aspect of train movement. The below table shows the available keys (or categories) on each bus, train and tube feeds and selection of specific keys identified for multimodal transport analysis.

2. **Data Processing:** The data processing stage consists of following steps: data filtration, data integration. As the data collected in stage one are not suitable for analysis due to the inclusion of unwanted information, further processing is required to perform on captured data to eliminate redundancy. In order to do that, decision support variables/ enablers in the currently captured data are identified and filtered. Enablers chosen for disruption analysis are highlighted in Table 1. From the table,

Figure 6. Exploring Big Data Technologies to store and mine Public Data feeds

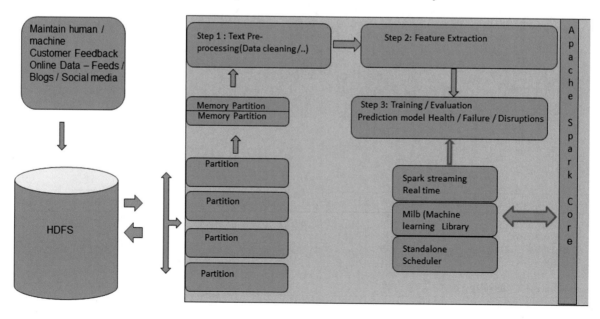

Table 5. Entities selected from various data feeds

Bus Data Feed	Train Data Feed	Tube Data Feed
Id	owner	Name
lineStatuses	timestamp	Id
Created	classification	Disruptions
Reason	schemaLocation	Created
lineId	Sender:	modeName
Disruption	application	Modified status Severity
validityPeriods	Publication:	serviceTypes
Type	TopicID	line Statuses
statusSeverity Description	RTPPMData:	Id
modeName	snapshotTStamp	statusSeverity Description
Created	SystemMsg	Created
Modified	RAGThresholds:	statusSeverity
Type	<threshold values>	lineId
Name	WebPPMLink	Type
affectedRoutes	PPT:	Reason
isWholeLine	Rag	Disruption
categoryDescription	ragDisplay Flag	Description
additionalInfo	text	categoryDescription
affectedStops	NationalPage:	isWholeLine
Created	WebDisplay Period	closureText
Description	WebFixedMsg1	affectedRoutes
Category	WebFixedMsg2	Category
Type	WebMsgOf Moment	Type
	StaleFlag	affectedStops

the most important key in tube and bus is disruption which gives the list of disruptions happening in that particular mode. In the RTPPM feed of Network Rail, there is no disruption key and deriving disruption details for trains is not a straightforward process. Based on the available keys, the keys such as RAG, text, and trends in are selected. They all provide the performance information for each train. After data filtration, the integration of filtered datasets is performed and processed. In the integration process, initialization of variables and global configuration parameters such as sector code (Network Rail) and area name (TFL bus and tube) are defined. The scale of 0.2 is chosen to summarize the list of disruptions happening in the system. As stated above, using the key parameters, bus and tube disruption information are derived and under the separate collection name, disruptions. For train, it is necessary to implement a logic to derive the disruption information from the available keys as it doesn't have a disruption key on its own.

3. **Data Representation:** Data representation stage consists of two major portions, such as aggregation/ compilation and results in storage in a representable format that will be helpful in analysis. The

processed data are aggregated using mongo query by grouping matching data and the disruption results for that particular location are stored for decision making. The disruptions can be represented in a percentage format. The percentage is calculated based on the received count of disruptions in the bus, train, and tube. Disruption percentage is calculated based on the following equation.

Disruption = (Number of disruptions in tube/train/bus)/ Total number of disturbances *100

Algorithm 1. Data Acquisition

Input: Live Data Feed from API, Stomp connection
Output: Data allocated into respective database and collections within MongoDB
Step 1: Establish API's and STOMP connections
Step 2: Retrieve live feeds from API's and Stomp connections
Step 3: Create database and collections and store live feeds

Algorithm 2.1. Data Filtration

Input: Live data feed process data set
Output: filtered data in fixed size block and send each block to processing stage
Step 1: Filter data with a parameter such Sector code, area name, rail disruption validity, and scale. All other unnecessary data will be discarded.
Step 2: Transmit the filtered data to the processing stage.

Algorithm 2.2. Processing and Calculation Algorithm

Input: Filtered Data
Output: Disruption data send back to MongoDB
Step 1: For Network Rail Operator Performance metrics taken to derive disturbance data
Step 2: Calculate the disruption data for Tube and Bus
Step 3: Transmit the disruption data to MongoDB

Algorithm 3. Multi-Modal Summarization Algorithm

Input: Disruption Data.
Output: Disruption summary (text data)
Step 1: Gather the disruption data from MongoDB server
Step 2: Apply Summarization for individual modal pie from the total disruption data capture.
Step 3: Disruption summary displayed by MongoDB query.

For the preliminary study, the algorithms were run on five major stations within London namely London Bridge, London Victoria, London Euston, Liverpool Street, Paddington. Each station is with the minimum accessibility of three transport system such as Network Rail, Tube, and Bus In all these stations, respective transport system disturbances are retrieved i.e. standalone disturbances from Tube, Bus and Network Rail and also disturbances on multimodal environment, i.e. impact of one transport system on other transport systems.

Table 6 indicates the disturbance details across three different transport systems for each major location. The count indicates the number of disturbances such as delay in departure/arrivals, service cancellations etc. received from three individual data feeds. Based on the retrieved data, disruptions are analyzed across the multimodal system. The table results show no impact on the tube from Network Rail disturbances in different scenarios. On contrary, it has an impact on the bus. Some of the following points are worth noting for the evaluation of the test results. They are i) during analysis period, tube disruptions were always minimal when compared to train and bus disruptions ii) the incomplete nature of data coverage at regular intervals iii) some datasets are not updated frequently and missing vital information regarding stops iv) Essential key variable is not available in Network Rail's real-time performance measure to calculate disruption to get accurate results. Data quality has a direct impact on the quality of the decisions made based on that data. In- depth analysis of data taken over a long period may give a detailed insight of the multimodal disruptions. Once the disruption factors were identified and stored in MongoDB. It was required to mine the disruption factors for identifying common elements of disruption in all available types of transportation. Hadoop HDFS system was used to store the MongoDB database extracted results and pyspark was used to deploy LDA and Clustering techniques on the disruption database.

Figure 7 provides a visualization of frame wok that is being developed to use big data technologies for storing the public data feeds and mining it for proactively identifying the disruptions in a multi-modal environment.

Table 6. Multimodal disturbance analysis on a single event

Station	Date of Data Capture and Analysis	Network Rail	Tube	Bus	Major Event/Incidents
London Bridge	20/Aug/2016	Count-69 Percentage-89.61%	No disturbance found	Count-8 Percentage- 10.39%	Major Engineering works at London Bridge
London Victoria	28/Aug/2016	Count-58 Percentage - 100%	No disturbance found	No disturbance found	Line Closure
Euston	28/Aug/2016	Count-70 Percentage - 100%	No disturbance found	No disturbance found	Reduced services
Liverpool Street	28/Aug/2016	Count-58 Percentage-62.36%	No disturbance found	Count-35 Percentage- 37.64%	TFLRail Track closure (No Tube involved)
Paddington	28/Aug/2016	Count-70 Percentage-97.22%	No disturbance found	Count-2 Percentage- 2.78%	Notting Hill Carnival

Figure 7. Big Data framework for multi-modal feed analysis

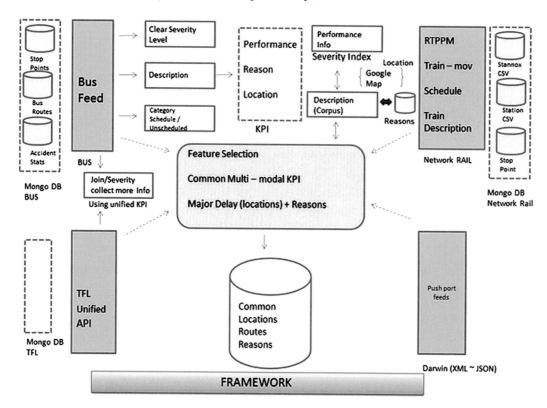

TEXT MINING ON MULTI-MODAL DISRUPTION DATA FEEDS

Once the disruption feeds for various transports were collected for the same time. The description field of disruption object provides a comprehensive detail of reason of delay. However, it was identified to be a free text field where the reason for the delay was written. It was identified to be a good candidate for text mining. LDA was identified to be an important technique to analyze important topics in delay descriptions. Bigrams were constructed followed by document matrix and application of LDA. In natural language processing, Latent Dirichlet allocation (LDA) is defined as a generative statistical model which allows sets of observations to be explained by unobserved groups that explain why some parts of the data are similar. E.g. if observations are words collected into documents, then each document is a mixture of a small number of topics and that each word's creation is attributable to one of the document's topics.

Initial LDA analysis provided some topics for disruption, however, the major topics were related to Bus and so the prototype needs to be improved with more data feeds to get a very good mix and match of multi-modal data feeds. This could result in the generation of interesting topics from the multi-modal analysis. As a final control application of our model, we now consider the identification of clusters in the network. Recall, clusters are a function of networks, bus routes, population movement, and demographic information. Clusters are important in this context and should be targeted to identify the root cause of the disruption. The information of clusters can be conveniently used for a number of control applications, and referring to network planning and city management, they can be also used to design transport routes within clusters, and to minimize the use of transport resources to connect the clusters. Such clusters if

Figure 8. Methodology for deploying text mining model on disruption descriptions

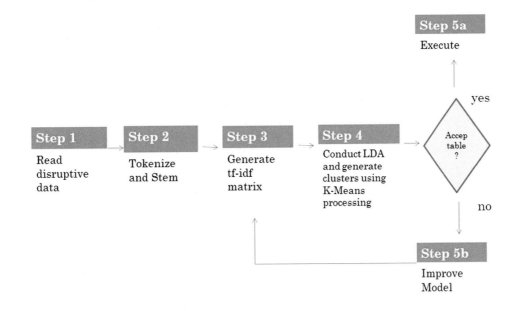

Algorithm 4. Text Mining Disruption Descriptions

Step 1: Gather the disruption data from MongoDB server
Step 2: Apply LDA to identify important topics in delay feeds
Step 3: K-Means to identify patterns of disruptions
Step 4: Analysing results to identify disruption factors

Figure 9. K-Means clustering on disruption feed

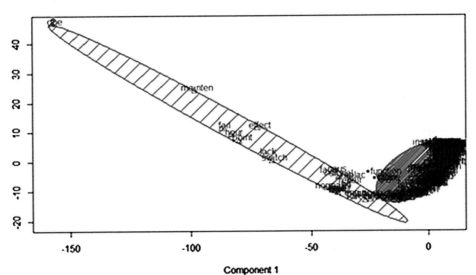

Component 1
These two components explain 97.28 % of the point variability.

Table 7. Initial results of LDA model

Topics in LDA model:
Topic #0:
road bridge bus closed works use 2017 place april friday stops diverted water january buses diversion line lane nan march
Topic #1:
nan way 2017 april bridge bus buses closed diversion diverted friday january lane line march monday works place returning road
Topic #2:
street diverted place works april routes 1800 diversion closed 2017 water january line buses monday stops route friday bridge station
Topic #3:
serving buses january stops 1800 monday stop serve friday bus bridge april line closed diversion diverted 2017 lane works march
Topic #4:
unable serve stop bus works march use diversion station 2017 stops buses street april lane bridge closed diverted friday january
Topic #5:
returning line diversion lane route bus works road water march friday 1800 street serve 2017 april bridge use buses closed
Topic #6:
stop closed use january stops bridge friday water monday station 2017 buses street lane diverted works diversion bus april nan
Topic #7:
road lane march diverted buses friday diversion routes station route stop water place works closed bus bridge april 2017 january
Topic #8:
route january road routes station monday stops water friday 1800 use april buses diverted serve unable bridge 2017 bus closed
Topic #9:
way monday 1800 march friday station bus april stops diversion route january use road line buses street bridge closed diverted

Table 8. Initial results of K-Means clustering

>>> >>> >>> ... ... Cluster 0: Words:
traffic via
westbound
closed
works
traffic
facilitate works place
westbound closed
place
closed facilitate
closed facilitate works
Cluster 1: Words:
via
diversion
due
route
line
line route
stop
via line
via line route
diversion via
Cluster 2: Words:
usual due
usual due major
disruption
due major disruption
due major
serving usual due
major disruption
serving usual
major
usual

improved could help in planning the maintenance work for minimum disruption and finally, the same information regarding clusters could be given to some interested service providers as a means to link clusters (e.g., taxi companies, car rental companies, advertising companies, etc.).

The figure above provides a glance of results achieved from clustering and LDA. It was observed that most high severity disruptions were related to buses and the key issue had been maintenance work. The severe weather conditions were one of the factors that had highly impacted all modes of transportation. It's too early to make some conclusions and therefore works are being carried to collect and my huge volume of data feeds and develop a KPI for multi-modal transportation in London.

FUTURE RESEARCH DIRECTIONS

This chapter provides a glimpse of work being done for mining streaming public data feeds. Work is being further developed into prototype system, that could identify and predict disturbances impacting multi-modal transportation. Definitely, the results will improve by increasing the amount of historical data and using more accurate robust machine learning models. Readers are encouraged to provide feedback and contribute in the area of multi-modal transportation

CONCLUSION

The chapter details the live streaming of available transport system data feeds into MongoDB for storing big data for future references and analysis. Along with living streaming of data into MongoDB, the disturbances occurred within the multimodal transport system are derived. The initial study [G1] indicates the level of disturbances between the transport system by any or all systems such as Network Rail, TFL's tube, and bus. The effort is being done to mine the disruption feeds further using various models of text mining as delay description is a free text field. This chapter provides brief about an initial study being done at the center. Although the live streaming of data feeds from TFL and Network Rail is possible without any issues such as speed and storage, one of the main concerns for future modeling would be reliable streaming from individual transport system and their availability. Each provider has their own time interval on updating their data system, there are chances that the modeling could produce less accurate results. However, this chapter set an example of live feeding into MongoDB means there are future scope for further development and make use of multimodal transport system with respect to the sustainable operating model.

REFERENCES

Apache. (2017). Hadoop. Retrieved from http://hadoop.apache.org/

Apache. (2017). Spark. Retrieved from http://spark.apache.org/

Buckley, S., & Lightman, D. (2015). Ready or not, big data is coming to a city (transportation agency) near you. In *Proceedings of the Transportation Research Board 94th Annual Meeting* (No. 15-5156).

Burgholzer, W., Bauer, G., Posset, M., & Jammernegg, W. (2013). Analyzing the impact of disruptions in intermodal transport networks: A micro simulation-based model. *Decision Support Systems*, *54*(4), 1580–1586. doi:10.1016/j.dss.2012.05.060

Chandio, A. A., Tziritas, N., & Xu, C. Z. (2015). Big-data processing techniques and their challenges in transport domain. *ZTE Communications*.

Chen, S., Tan, J., Claramunt, C., & Ray, C. (2011). Multi-scale and multi-modal GIS-T data model. *Journal of Transport Geography*, *19*(1), 147–161. doi:10.1016/j.jtrangeo.2009.09.006

Cottrill, C. D., & Derrible, S. (2015). Leveraging big data for the development of transport sustainability indicators. *Journal of Urban Technology*, *22*(1), 45–64. doi:10.1080/10630732.2014.942094

Deci, E. L., & Ryan, R. M. (1991). A motivational approach to self: Integration in personality. In *Proceedings of Nebraska Symposium on Motivation* (vol. 38, pp. 237-288). Lincoln, NE: University of Nebraska Press.

DfT. (2009), NATA (New Approach for Transport Appraisal) Refresh: Appraisal for a Sustainable Transport System, UK Department for Transport Retrieved from www.dft.gov.uk/pgr/economics/integratedtransporteconomics3026

Faizrahnemoon, M., Schlote, A., Maggi, L., Crisostomi, E., & Shorten, R. (2015). A big-data model for multi-modal public transportation with application to macroscopic control and optimisation. *International Journal of Control*, *88*(11), 2354–2368. doi:10.1080/00207179.2015.1043582

Fiosina, J., Fiosins, M., & Müller, J. (2013). Big Data Processing and Mining for the future ICT-based Smart Transportation Management System.

Gokasar, I., & Simsek, K. (2014). *Using "Big Data".* For Analysis and Improvement of Public Transportation Systems in Istanbul.

Hielkema, H., & Hongisto, P. (2013). Developing the Helsinki smart city: The role of competitions for open data applications. *Journal of the Knowledge Economy*, *4*(2), 190–204. doi:10.1007/s13132-012-0087-6

Lauriault, T. P., Craig, B. L., Taylor, D. F., & Pulsifer, P. L. (2007). Today's data are part of tomorrow's research: Archival issues in the sciences. *Archivaria*, *64*, 123–179.

Li, R., Kido, A., & Wang, S. (2015). Evaluation index development for the intelligent transportation system in smart community based on Big Data. *Advances in Mechanical Engineering*.

Litman, T. (2011). Introduction to multi-modal transportation planning. Victoria Transport Policy Institute.

Liu, L. (2011). Data model and algorithms for multimodal route planning with transportation networks [Doctoral dissertation]. München, Techn. Univ.

Lyons, G., & Harman, R. (2002). The UK public transport industry and provision of multi-modal traveller information. *International Journal of Transport Management*, *1*(1), 1–13. doi:10.1016/S1471-4051(01)00002-7

Mandloi, D., & Thill, J. C. (2010). Object-oriented data modeling of an indoor/outdoor urban transportation network and route planning analysis. In *Geospatial Analysis and Modelling of Urban Structure and Dynamics* (pp. 197–220). Springer Netherlands. doi:10.1007/978-90-481-8572-6_11

McClair, K. (2015). Retrieved from http://www.raildeliverygroup.com/media-centre/press-releases/2015/724-2015-12-14.html

Mohamed, A. Z. (2014). A review on crowd sourcing geo-social related big data approaches as a solution to the transportation problem. *Applied Mechanics of Materials*, *663*, 622–626. doi:10.4028/www.scientific.net/AMM.663.622

MongoDB. (2015). MongoDB on Gartner's Magic Quadrant for Operational Database Management Systems 2015. Retrieved from https://www.mongodb.com/collateral/gartner-mq-2015?jmp=homepage

MongoD.B. (n. d.). Architecture. Retrieved from https://www.mongodb.com/mongodb-architecture

Rockshore. (2017). Network Rail Feeds. http://nrodwiki.rockshore.net/index.php/About_the_Network_Rail_feeds

Otero, C. E., Rossi, M., Peter, A., & Haber, R. (2014, January). Determining the human-perceived level of safety in transportation systems using big data analytics. In *Proceedings of the International Conference on Internet Computing (ICOMP)*. The Steering Committee of The World Congress in Computer Science, Computer Engineering and Applied Computing (WorldComp).

Press, G. (2016). (2016). Top 10 hot big data technologies. Forbes. Retrieved from https://www.forbes.com/sites/gilpress/2016/03/14/top-10-hot-big-data-technologies/#7216f28865d7

Rodríguez-Núñez, E., & García-Palomares, J. C. (2014). Measuring the vulnerability of public transport networks. *Journal of Transport Geography*, *35*, 50–63. doi:10.1016/j.jtrangeo.2014.01.008

Scott, D. M., Novak, D. C., Aultman-Hall, L., & Guo, F. (2006). Network robustness index: A new method for identifying critical links and evaluating the performance of transportation networks. *Journal of Transport Geography*, *14*(3), 215–227. doi:10.1016/j.jtrangeo.2005.10.003

TFL Survey. (2014). Travel in London report. Retrieved from http://content.tfl.gov.uk/travel-in-london-report-7.pdf

TFL. (2017). Open data users. Retrieved from https://tfl.gov.uk/info-for/open-data-users/

Thill, J. C. (2000). Geographic information systems for transportation in perspective. *Transportation Research Part C, Emerging Technologies*, *8*(1), 3–12. doi:10.1016/S0968-090X(00)00029-2

Tolley, R., & Turton, B. J. (2014). *Transport systems, policy, and planning: a geographical approach*. Routledge.

Catapult Transport Systems. (2016). Transport Data Revolution. Retrieved from https://ts.catapult.org.uk/wp-content/uploads/2016/04/The-Transport-Data-Revolution.pdf

Transport for London | Every Journey Matters. (n.d.). Tube, Overground, TfL Rail, DLR & Tram status updates. Retrieved from https://tfl.gov.uk/tube-dlr-overground/status/

UK Governemnt. (2016). Transport Statistics. Retrieved from https://www.gov.uk/government/collections/transport-statistics-great-britain

Unnikrishnan, A., & Figliozzi, M. (2011). Online freight network assignment model with transportation disruptions and recourse. *Transportation Research Record: Journal of the Transportation Research Board*, (2224), 17-25.

Van Oort, N. (2014, February 18-20). Big data opportunities in public transport: Enhancing public transport by itcs. In Proceedings of IT-TRANS '14, Karlsruhe, Germany.

Wang, M., Wang, J., & Tian, F. (2014). City Intelligent Energy and Transportation Network Policy Based on the Big Data Analysis. *Procedia Computer Science*, *32*, 85–92. doi:10.1016/j.procs.2014.05.401

Wang, X. B., Zhang, G. J., Hong, Z., Guo, H. F., & Yu, L. (2009), December). Modeling and implementing research of multimodal transportation network. In Information Science and Engineering (ICISE), 2009 1st International Conference on (pp. 2100-2103). IEEE.

Xu, X., & Dou, W. (2014, November). An assistant decision-supporting method for urban transportation planning over big traffic data. In *Proceedings of the International Conference on Human Centered Computing* (pp. 251-264). Springer International Publishing.

Yan, K. F. (2013). Using crowdsourcing to establish the big data of the intelligent transportation system. In *Advanced Materials Research*, *791*, 2118–2121. doi:10.4028/www.scientific.net/AMR.791-793.2118

Yao, X., & Jiang, B. (2009). Geospatial modeling of urban environments. http://journals.sagepub.com/doi/pdf/10.1068/b3605ged

Zhang, J., Arentze, T. A., & Timmermans, H. J. (2012). A Multimodal Transport Network Model for Advanced Traveler Information System. *JUSPN*, *4*(1), 21–27. doi:10.5383/JUSPN.04.01.004

ADDITIONAL READING

BCMoT. (2008). 2008/09–2010/11 Service Plan, British Columbia Ministry of Transportation. Retrieved from www.bcbudget.gov.bc.ca/Annual_Reports/2007_2008/trans/trans.pdf

Cervero, R., & Arrington, G. B. (2008). Vehicle trip reduction impacts of transit-oriented housing. *Journal of Public Transportation*, *11*(3), 1–17. doi:10.5038/2375-0901.11.3.1

Dowling, R., McLeod, D., Guttenplan, M., & Zegeer, J. (2002). Multimodal corridor level-of-service analysis. *Transportation Research Record: Journal of the Transportation Research Board*, (1802), 1-6.

NATA Refresh. (2009). Appraisal for a sustainable transport system.

Schweppe, F. C., Merrill, H. M., & Burke, W. J. (1989). Least-cost planning: Issues and methods. *Proceedings of the IEEE*, *77*(6), 899–907. doi:10.1109/5.29330

Weinstein Agrawal, A., Schlossberg, M., & Irvin, K. (2008). How far, by which route and why? A spatial analysis of pedestrian preference. *Journal of Urban Design*, *13*(1), 81–98. doi:10.1080/13574800701804074

KEY TERMS AND DEFINITIONS

API: A belief that one's own culture is superior to other cultures.

Data Feed: Data feed is a mechanism for users to receive updated data from data sources.

ERRAC: European rail research Advisory Council.

K-Means: K-means clustering aims to partition n observations into k clusters in which each observation belongs to the cluster with the nearest mean, serving as a prototype of the cluster.

LDA: LDA stands for Latent Dirichlet allocation (LDA). It is a generative statistical model that allows sets of observations to be explained by unobserved groups to explain why some parts of the data are similar.

TFL: Transport of London.

Topic Modeling: Topic modeling is a frequently used text-mining tool for discovery of hidden semantic structures in a text body.

UITP: International Association of Public Transport.

Chapter 14

Big Data Analytics for Train Delay Prediction:
A Case Study in the Italian Railway Network

Emanuele Fumeo
University of Genoa, Italy

Luca Oneto
University of Genoa, Italy

Giorgio Clerico
University of Genoa, Italy

Renzo Canepa
Rete Ferroviaria Italiana S.P.A., Italy

Federico Papa
Ansaldo STS S.P.A., Italy

Carlo Dambra
Ansaldo STS S.P.A, Italy

Nadia Mazzino
Ansaldo STS S.P.A., Italy

Davida Anguita
University of Genoa, Italy

ABSTRACT

Current Train Delay Prediction Systems (TDPSs) do not take advantage of state-of-the-art tools and techniques for extracting useful insights from large amounts of historical data collected by the railway information systems. Instead, these systems rely on static rules, based on classical univariate statistic, built by experts of the railway infrastructure. The purpose of this book chapter is to build a data-driven TDPS for large-scale railway networks, which exploits the most recent big data technologies, learning algorithms, and statistical tools. In particular, we propose a fast learning algorithm for Shallow and Deep Extreme Learning Machines that fully exploits the recent in-memory large-scale data processing technologies for predicting train delays. Proposal has been compared with the current state-of-the-art TDPSs. Results on real world data coming from the Italian railway network show that our proposal is able to improve over the current state-of-the-art TDPSs.

DOI: 10.4018/978-1-5225-3176-0.ch014

INTRODUCTION

Big Data Analytics is one of the current trending research interests in the context of railway transportation systems. Indeed, many aspects of the railway world can greatly benefit from new technologies and methodologies able to collect, store, process, analyze and visualize large amounts of data (Paakkonen & Pakkala, 2015; Thaduri, Galar, & Kumar, 2015; Zarembski, 2014; Jina, Wah, Chenga et al., 2015; Wu & Chin, 2014; Schmidt, Chen, Matheson, & Ostrouchov, 2016) as well as new methodologies coming from machine learning, artificial intelligence, and computational intelligence to analyze that data in order to extract actionable information (Chen & An, 2016; Yu & Boyd, 2016; Aridhi & Nguifo, 2016; Colombo & Ferrari, 2015; Al-Jarrah, Yoo, Muhaidat, Karagiannidis, & Taha, 2015). Examples are: condition based maintenance of railway assets (Fumeo, Oneto, & Anguita, 2015; Li, Qian, Parikh, & Hampapur, 2013; Li et al., 2014; Núñez, Hendriks, Li et al., 2014), automatic visual inspection systems (Feng et al., 2014; Aytekin, Rezaeitabar, Dogru et al., 2015), risk analysis (Figueres-Esteban, Hughes, & Van Gulijk, 2015), network capacity estimation (Branishtov, Vershinin, Tumchenok et al., 2014), optimization for energy-efficient railway operations (Bai, Ho, Mao, Ding, & Chen, 2014), marketing analysis for rail freight transportation (Xueyan & Depeng, 2014), usage of ontologies and linked data in railways (Morris, Easton, & Roberts, 2014; Tutcher, 2014), big data for rail inspection systems (Li, Zhong, Liang et al., 2015), complex event processing over train data streams (Ma, Wang, Chu et al., 2015), fault diagnosis of vehicle on-board equipment for high speed railways (Wang, Xu, Zhao et al., 2015; Zhao, Xu, & Hai-feng, 2014; Noori & Jenab, 2013) and for conventional ones (Bin & Wensheng, 2015), research on storage and retrieval of large amounts of data for high-speed trains (Wang, Li, Hei et al., 2015), development of an online geospatial safety risk model for railway networks (Sadler et al., 2016), train marshalling optimization through genetic algorithms (Qingyang & Xiaoyun, 2015), research on new technologies for the railway ticketing systems (Zhu, Wang, Shan et al., 2014). The work described in this book chapter tackles the problem of predicting train delays using Big Data Analytics, aiming at improving traffic management and dispatching and at scaling to large railway networks at the same time. In particular, this work will focus on exploiting the large amount of historical train movements data collected by the railway information systems.

Delays can be due to various causes: disruptions in the operations flow, accidents, malfunctioning or damaged equipment, construction work, repair work, and severe weather conditions like snow and ice, floods, and landslides, to name a few. Although trains should respect a fixed schedule called Nominal Timetable (NT), Train Delays (TDs) occur daily and can affect negatively railway operations, causing service disruptions and losses in the worst cases. Rail Traffic Management Systems (TMSs) (Davey, 2012) have been developed to support the management of the inherent complexity of rail services and networks by providing an integrated and holistic view of operational performance, enabling high levels of rail operations efficiency. By supporting TMSs with an advanced TDPS able to provide accurate delay predictions, it is possible to improve traffic management and dispatching remarkably, for instance in terms of:

- Passenger information systems, increasing the perception of the reliability of railway passenger services and, in case of service disruptions, providing valid alternatives to passengers looking for the best train connections (Muller-Hannemann & Schnee, 2009; Dotoli, Epicoco, Falagario et al., 2016).

- Freight tracking systems, estimating time to arrival of goods correctly in order to improve customers' decision-making processes (Langer & Vaidyanathan, 2014).
- NT planning, providing the possibility of updating the train trip scheduling to cope with recurrent TDs (Cordeau, Toth, & Vigo, 1998).
- Delay management (rescheduling), allowing traffic managers to reroute trains in order to utilize the railway network in a better way (Dollevoet, Corman, D'Ariano et al., 2014; Li, Shou, & Ralescu, 2014).

Due to its key role, a TMS stores the information about every Train Movement (TM), i.e. every train arrival and departure timestamp at "checkpoints" (e.g. a station, a switch, etc.) monitored by signaling systems. Datasets composed by TM records have been used as fundamental data sources for every work addressing the problem of building a TDPS. For instance, Milinkovic et al. (Milinkovic, Markovic, Veskovic et al., 2013) developed a Fuzzy Petri Net model to estimate TDs based both on expert knowledge and on historical data. Berger et al. (Berger, Gebhardt, Müller- Hannemann et al., 2011) presented a stochastic model for TDs propagation and forecasts based on directed acyclic graphs. Pongnumkul et al. (Pongnumkul, Pechprasarn, Kunaseth et al., 2014) worked on data-driven models for TD predictions, treating the problem as a time series forecast one. Their system was based on autoregressive integrated moving average and nearest neighbor models, although applied over a limited set of data from a few trains. Finally, Kecman et al. (Goverde, 2010; Hansen, Goverde, & Van Der Meer, 2010; Kecman, 2014; Kecman & Goverde, 2015) developed an intensive research in the context of TD prediction and propagation by using process mining techniques based on innovative timed event graphs, on historical TM data, and on expert knowledge about railway infrastructure. However, these models are based on classical univariate statistics, while our solution integrates multivariate statistical concepts that allow our models to be extended in the future by including other kind of data (e.g. weather forecasts, passenger flows, etc.). Moreover, these models are not especially developed for Big Data technologies, possibly limiting their adoption for large scale networks.

For these reasons, this book chapter investigates the problem of predicting train delays for large scale railway networks by treating it as a time series forecast problem where every train movement represents an event in time, and by exploiting Big Data Analytics methodologies. Delay profiles for each train are used to build a set of data-driven models that, working together, make possible to perform a regression analysis on the past delay profiles and consequently to predict the future ones.

In the regression framework, and more in general in the supervised learning framework, Extreme Learning Machines (ELM) represent a state of the art tool (Huang, Zhou, Ding et al., 2012). ELM (Cambria & Huang, 2013; Huang, Huang, Song et al., 2015; Huang, Zhu, & Siew, 2006) were introduced to overcome problems posed by back-propagation training algorithm (Huang, 2014, 2015; Ridella, Rovetta, & Zunino, 1997; Rumelhart, Hinton, & Williams, 1988) potentially slow convergence rates, critical tuning of optimization parameters, and presence of local minima that call for multi-start and re-training strategies. The original ELM are also called "Shallow" ELM (SELM) because they have been developed for the single-hidden-layer feedforward neural networks (Huang, Li, Chen et al., 2008; Huang, Chen, & Siew, 2006; G. B. Huang, Zhu, & Siew, 2004), and they have been generalized in order to cope with cases where ELM are not neuron alike. SELM were later improved to cope with problems intractable by shallow architectures (Bengio, 2009; Bengio, Courville, & Vincent, 2013; Vincent, Larochelle, Bengio et al., 2008; Hinton, Osindero, & Teh, 2006; Zhou, Huang, Lin et al., 2015) by proposing various Deep

ELM (DELM) built upon a deep architecture (Kasun, Zhou, Huang et al., 2013; Tang, Deng, & Huang, 2016; Tissera & McDonnell, 2016), so to make possible to extract features by a multilayer feature representation framework.

This work considers both SELM and DELM for predicting TDs, and proposes an adaptation of their typical learning strategies to exploit Big Data parallel architectures in order to meet the high-demanding requirements of Dynamic Large-Scale Railway Networks. In particular, the proposed implementations fully exploit the recent Apache Spark (Zaharia et al., 2012; Meng et al., 2016) in-memory large-scale data processing technology upon a state-of-art Big Data architecture (Reyes- Ortiz, Oneto, & Anguita, 2015) (Apache Spark on Apache YARN (Dean & Ghemawat, 2008; White, 2012)) running on the Google Cloud infrastructure (Google, 2016).

The described approach and the prediction system performance have been validated based on the real historical data provided by Rete Ferroviaria Italiana (RFI), the Italian Infrastructure Manager (IM) that controls all the traffic of the Italian railway network (Rete Ferroviaria Italiana, 2016). For this purpose, a set of novel Key Performance Indicators (KPIs), agreed with RFI and based on the requirements of their systems, has been designed and used. Several months of TM records from the entire Italian railway network have been exploited, showing that the new proposed methodology outperforms the current technique used by RFI, which is largely based on the state-of-the-art approach of (Kecman & Goverde, 2015), to predict TDs in terms of overall accuracy.

Train Delay Prediction Problem: The Italian Case

A railway network can be considered as a graph where nodes represent a series of checkpoints consecutively connected. Any train that runs over the network follows an itinerary composed of n_c checkpoints $C = \left\{ C_0, C_1, C_2, \cdots, C_{n_c} \right\}$, which is characterized by a station of origin, a station of destination, some stops and some transits at checkpoints in between (see Figure 1). For any checkpoint C_i, a train should arrive at time $t_A^{C_i}$ and should depart at time $t_D^{C_i}$, defined in the NT. Usually time references included in the NT are approximated with a precision of 30 seconds or 1 minute. The actual arrival and departure times of a train are defined as $\hat{t}_A^{C_i}$ and $\hat{t}_D^{C_i}$. The difference between the time references included in the NT and the actual times, either of arrival $\left(\hat{t}_A^{C_i} - t_A^{C_i} \right)$ or of departure $\left(\hat{t}_D^{C_i} - t_D^{C_i} \right)$, is defined as TD. Moreover, if the TD is greater than 30 seconds or 1 minute, then a train is considered as a delayed train. Note that, for the origin station there is no arrival time, while for the destination station there is no departure time. A dwell time is defined as the difference between the departure time and the arrival time for a fixed checkpoint $\left(\hat{t}_D^{C_i} - \hat{t}_A^{C_i} \right)$, while a running time is defined as the amount of time needed to depart from the first of two subsequent checkpoints and to arrive to the second one $\left(\hat{t}_A^{C_{i+1}} - \hat{t}_D^{C_i} \right)$.

In order to tackle the problem of building a TDPS, the following solution is proposed. Taking into account the itinerary of a train, the goal is to be able to predict the TD that will affect that specific train for each subsequent checkpoint with respect to the last one on which the train has transited. To make it general, for each checkpoint C_i, where $i \in \left\{ 0, 1, \cdots, n_c \right\}$, the prediction system must be able to predict the TD for each subsequent checkpoint $\left\{ C_{i+1}, C_{i+2}, \cdots, C_{n_c} \right\}$. Note that C_0 is a virtual checkpoint that

Figure 1. A railway network depicted as a graph, including a train itinerary from checkpoint M to checkpoint Q

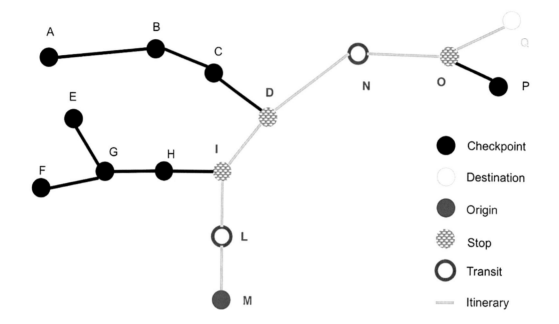

reproduces the condition of a train that still has to depart from its origin. In this solution, the TD prediction problem is treated as a time series forecast problem, where a set of predictive models perform a regression analysis over the TD profiles for each train, for each checkpoint C_i of the itineraries of these trains, and for each subsequent checkpoint C_j with $j \in \{i+1, i+2, \cdots, n_c\}$. Figure 2 shows the data needed to build forecasting models based on the railway network depicted in Figure 1. Basically, based on the state of the network between time $(t - \delta^-)$ and time t, the proposed system must be able to predict TD occurring from time t and $(t + \delta^+)$, and this is nothing but a classical regression problem.

Finally, it is worth noting that the intrinsic time varying nature of the delay phenomenon must be considered, which is due mainly to changes in the NT. This means that, in order to obtain good performances, the models should take into account only the amount of historical data representative of the actual distribution of the TD. For these reasons, considering a model built at day d_0 able to predict the TDs at day $(d_0 + 1)$, we have to rely on the historical data available between $(d_0 - \Delta^-)$ and d_0. Since Δ^- is a critical hyperparameter in the TD prediction problem, its value has been agreed with RFI experts.

To sum up, for each train characterized by a specific itinerary of n_c checkpoints, n_c models have to be built for C_0, $(n_c - 1)$ for C_1, and so on. Consequently, the total number of models to be built for each train can be calculated as

$$n_c + (n_c - 1) + \cdots + 1 = n_c (n_c - 1) / 2.$$

Figure 2. Data available for the TD prediction models for the network of Figure 1

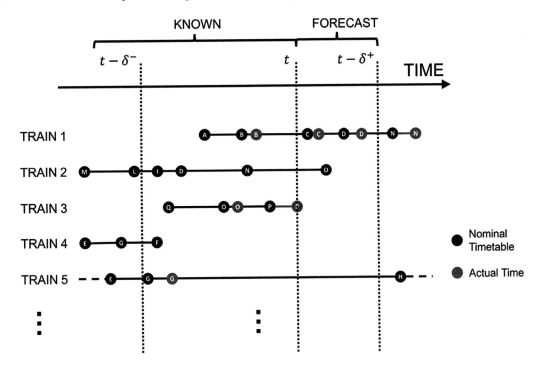

These models work together in order to make possible to estimate the TD of a particular train during its entire itinerary.

Considering the case of the Italian railway network, every day RFI controls approximately 10 thousand trains traveling along the national railway network. Every train is characterized by an itinerary composed of approximately $n_c \approx 12$ checkpoints, which means that the number of TMs is greater than or equal to 120 thousands per day. This results in roughly 1 message per second and more than 10 GB of messages per day to be stored. Note that every time that a complete set of TM records describing the entire planned itinerary of a particular train for one day is retrieved, the predictive models associated with that train must be retrained. The retraining phases can be performed at night, when only a few trains are traveling through the railway network and all the data of the just passed day is available, in order not to load the systems at daytime. Moreover, the continuous retraining of models allows both to cope with the intrinsic time dynamic nature of the system and to obtain the best possible performing model every new day. Since for each train at least $n_c \left(n_c - 1 \right) / 2 \approx 60$ models have to be built, the number of models that has to be retrained every day in the Italian case is greater than or equal to 600 thousand.

Train Delay Prediction Systems

This section deals with the problem of building a data-driven TDPS. In particular, focusing on the prediction of the TD profile of a single train, there is a variable of interest (i.e. the TD profile of a train along with its itinerary) and other possible correlated variables (e.g. information about other trains traveling on the network, day of the week, etc.). The goal is to predict the TD of that train at a particular time in the future $t = t + \delta^{+}$, i.e. at one of its following checkpoints. Due to the dynamic nature of the problem, only a part of the historical data have to be used (days in $\left[d_0 - \Delta^{-}, d_0 \right]$), namely the most recent ones, which represent the distribution under exam. Given the previous observations, the TD prediction problem can be mapped into a classical time varying multivariate regression problem (Takens, 1981; Packard, Crutchfield, Farmer, & Shaw, 1980).

In the conventional regression framework (Vapnik, 1998; Shawe-Taylor & Cristianini, 2004) a set of data $\mathcal{D}_n = \left\{ \left(\boldsymbol{x}_1, y_1 \right), \ldots, \left(\boldsymbol{x}_n, y_n \right) \right\}$, with $\boldsymbol{x}_i \in \mathcal{X} \in \mathbb{R}^d$ and $y_i \in \mathcal{Y} \in \mathbb{R}$, is available from the automation system. The goal of the authors is to identify the unknown model $\mathfrak{S} : \mathcal{X} \rightarrow \mathcal{Y}$ through a model $\mathfrak{M} : \mathcal{X} \rightarrow \mathcal{Y}$ chosen by an algorithm $\mathcal{A}_{\mathcal{H}}$ defined by its set of hyperparameters $\mathcal{H}$. The accuracy of the model $\mathfrak{M}$ in representing the unknown system $\mathfrak{S}$ can be evaluated with reference to different measures of accuracy (Elattar, Goulermas, & Wu, 2010; Ghelardoni, Ghio, & Anguita, 2013). In the case reported by this book chapter, they have been defined together with RFI experts.

In order to map the TD prediction problem into a dynamic multivariate regression model, let us consider the train of interest T_k, which is at checkpoint $C_i^{T_k}$ with $i \in \left\{ 0, 1, \cdots, n_c \right\}$ at time t_0. The goal is to predict the TD at one of its subsequent checkpoints $C_j^{T_k}$, with $j \in \left\{ i+1, i+2, \cdots, n_c \right\}$. Consequently, the input space $\mathcal{X}$ will be composed by:

- The current day of the week (Monday, Tuesday, etc.);
- A boolean value indicating whether the current day is a holiday or a working day;
- The TDs, the dwell times and the running times for T_k for $t \in \left[t_0 - \delta^{-}, t_0 \right]$;
- The TDs, the dwell times and the running times for all the other trains T_w with $w \neq k$ which were running over the same line of the railway network during the day for $t \in \left[t_0 - \delta^{-}, t_0 \right]$.

Concerning the output space $\mathcal{Y}$, it is composed by $C_j^{T_k}$ with $j \in \left\{ i+1, i+2, \cdots, n_c \right\}$ where $t_0 + \delta^{+}$ is equal to the NT of T_k for every $C_j^{T_k}$.

Figure 3 shows a graphical representation of the mapping of the TD prediction problem into a multivariate regression problem. For instance, in this representation, the variable of interest is represented by the delay profile of T_k. The other possible related variables are represented by the information regarding all the other trains traveling along the network simultaneously to T_k. An example of $\boldsymbol{x}_i \in \mathcal{X}$ is highlighted in red. Analogously, all the aforementioned elements of the regression problem are depicted in the figure under examination.

Finally, $\mathcal{D}_n$ has to be built by exploiting the historical dataset composed of all the information collected during the days in $\left[d_0 - \Delta^{-}, d_0 \right]$, so to cope with the dynamism of the problem.

Shallow Extreme Learning Machines (SELM)

SEL were originally developed for the single-hidden-layer feedforward neural networks

Figure 3. Mapping of the TD prediction problem into a multivariate regression problem

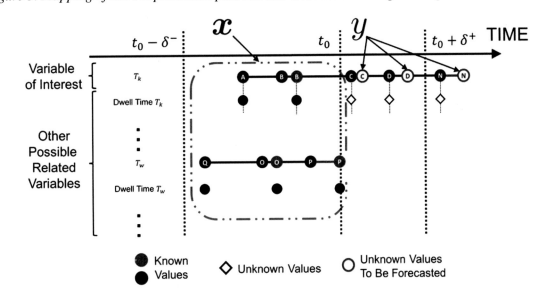

$$f\left(\boldsymbol{x}\right) = \sum_{i=1}^{h} w_i g_i\left(\boldsymbol{x}\right) \qquad (1)$$

where $g_i : \mathbb{R}^d \to \mathbb{R}, i \in \left\{1,\cdots,h\right\}$ is the hidden-layer output corresponding to the input sample $\boldsymbol{x} \in \mathbb{R}^d$, and $\boldsymbol{w} \in \mathbb{R}^h$ is the output weight vector between the hidden layer and the output layer.

In this case, the input layer has d neurons and connects to the hidden layer (having h neurons) through a set of weights $W \in \mathbb{R}^{h \times (0,\cdots,d)}$ and a nonlinear activation function $\varphi : \mathbb{R} \to \mathbb{R}$. Thus the i-th hidden neuron response to an input stimulus $\boldsymbol{x}$ is:

$$g_i\left(x\right) = \varphi\left(W_{i,0} + \sum_{j=1}^{d} W_{i,j} x_j\right) \qquad (2)$$

Note that Eq. (2) can be further generalized to include a wider class of functions (Bisio, Gastaldo, Zunino et al., 2015; Huang, Chen, & Siew, 2006; Huang et al., 2004); therefore, the response of a hidden neuron to an input stimulus $\boldsymbol{x}$ can be generically represented by any nonlinear piecewise continuous function characterized by a set of parameters. In SELM, the parameters W are set randomly. A vector of weighted links, $\boldsymbol{w} \in \mathbb{R}^h$, connects the hidden neurons to the output neuron without any bias. The overall output function of the network (see Figure 4) is:

$$f\left(x\right) = \sum_{i=1}^{h} w_i \varphi\left(W_{i,0} + \sum_{j=1}^{d} W_{i,j} x_j\right) = \sum_{i=1}^{h} w_i \varphi_i\left(x\right) \qquad (3)$$

Figure 4. SELM structure

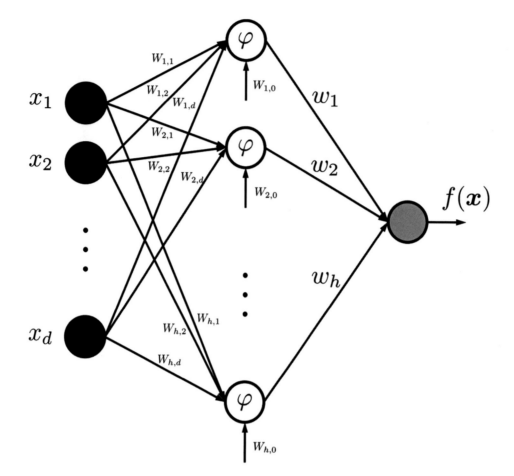

It is convenient to define an activation matrix, $A \in \mathbb{R}^{n \times h}$, such that the entry $A_{i,j}$ is the activation value of the j-th hidden neuron for the i-th input pattern. The A matrix is:

$$A = \begin{bmatrix} \varphi_1(\boldsymbol{x}_1) & \cdots & \varphi_h(\boldsymbol{x}_1) \\ \vdots & \ddots & \vdots \\ \varphi_1(\boldsymbol{x}_n) & \cdots & \varphi_h(\boldsymbol{x}_n) \end{bmatrix} \quad (4)$$

In the SELM model the weights W are set randomly and are not subject to any adjustment, and the quantity w in Eq. (3) is the only degree of freedom. Hence, the training problem reduces to minimization of the convex cost:

$$w^* = \arg\min_w \|Aw - y\|^2 \quad (5)$$

A matrix pseudo-inversion yields the unique L2 solution, as proven in (G. B. Huang, Chen, & Siew, 2006; G. B. Huang et al., 2012):

$$w^* = A^+ y \tag{6}$$

The simple, efficient procedure to train a SELM therefore involves the following steps: (I) Randomly generate hidden node parameters (in this case W); (II) Compute the activation matrix A (Eq. (4)); (III) Compute the output weights (Eq. (6)).

Despite the apparent simplicity of the SELM approach, the crucial result is that even random weights in the hidden layer endow a network with notable representation ability. Moreover, the theory derived in (G. B. Huang et al., 2012) proves that regularization strategies can further improve the approach's generalization performance. As a result, the cost function of Eq. (5) is augmented by a regularization factor (G. B. Huang et al., 2012). A common approach is then to use the L2 regularizer

$$\boldsymbol{w}^* = \arg \min_{\boldsymbol{w}} \left\| A\boldsymbol{w} - \boldsymbol{y} \right\|^2 + \lambda \left\| \boldsymbol{w} \right\|^2 \tag{7}$$

and consequently the vector of weights $\boldsymbol{w}^*$ is then obtained as follows:

$$\boldsymbol{w}^* = \left(A^T A + \lambda I \right)^{-1} A^T \boldsymbol{y} \tag{8}$$

where $I \in \mathbb{R}^{h \times h}$ is an identity matrix. Note that h, the number of hidden neurons, is an hyperparameter that needs to be tuned based on the problem under exam.

Based on these considerations, it is possible to detect two main problems that would limit the application of SELM for building a TDPS:

- The first issue is that finding the solution of Eq. (7) through the approach of Eq. (8) is not efficient if n or h are large;
- The second issue is that we have to explore all the historical information about the TMs looking for the right portion of data in order to build D_n. Scanning all the data for extracting the right one depending on T_k, δ^+, δ^-, and Δ^- must be as most efficient as possible.

These two issues can be solved by adopting a parallel optimization method for the solution of Eq. (7) and a state of the art technology for storing and processing large amount of data.

The first issue can be solved, by resorting to a Stochastic Gradient Descent (SGD) algorithm. The SGD algorithm is a very general optimization algorithm, which is able to solve a problem in the form of Eq. (8) efficiently (Meng et al., 2016). Algorithm 1 reports the SGD algorithm for solving Eq. (7), where τ and n_{iter} are parameters related with the speed of the optimization algorithms. Therefore, usually τ and n_{iter} are set based on the experience of the user. In any case τ and n_{iter} can be seen as other regularization terms as λ since they are connected with the early stopping regularization technique (Caruana, Lawrence, & Lee, 2001; Prechelt, 1998).

Algorithm 1. SGD for SELM

Input: $D_n, \lambda, \tau, n_{iter}$
Output: w

```
1 Read D_n ;
2 Compute A ;
3 w = 0 ;
4 for t ← 1 to n_iter do
```
$$5 \qquad w = w - \frac{\tau}{\sqrt{t}} \frac{\partial}{\partial w} \left[Aw - y^2 + \lambda w^2 \right] ;$$
```
6 return (w, b) ;
```

Note that Algorithm 1 it suitable for being implemented with the Apache Spark technology (Meng et al., 2016). Apache Spark is designed to efficiently deal with iterative computational procedures that recursively perform operations over the same data, such as in Algorithm 1. Moreover, one of the main ideas behind the Apache Spark technology (Meng et al., 2016; Zaharia et al., 2012) is to reduce the accesses to the disk as much as possible and instead to operate in memory. For this reason, Apache Spark is also useful for solving the second issue related to the application of SELM for building a DTDPS. Indeed, Spark allows to dramatically reduce the large number of disk accesses (necessary to build $\mathcal{D}_n$) by keeping, based on the available volatile memory, as much data as possible in memory, consequently speeding up the creation of different datasets $\mathcal{D}_n$ for different values of T_k, δ^+, δ^-, and Δ^-.

Algorithm 1 is well-suited for implementation in Spark and many of these tools are already available in MLlib (Meng et al., 2016). Basically, the implementation of Algorithm 1 reported in Algorithm 2 is an application of two functions: a map for the computation of the gradient and a reduction function for the sum of each single gradient.

Algorithm 2. SGD for SELM on Spark (d ≥ h)

Input: $D_n, \lambda, \tau, n_{iter}$
Output: w

```
1 Read D_n ;
2 Compute A ; /* Compute the projection ϕ
3 w = 0 ;
4 for t ← 1 to n_iter do
5     g = (A, y).map(Gradient())
          /* Compute the gradient for each sample
6     .reduce(Sum())
          /* Sum all the gradients of each sample
```

7 $\qquad w = w - \dfrac{\tau}{\sqrt{t_.}} g$;

8 `return` w ;

The main problem of Algorithm 2 is the computation and storage of A. If $h \ll d$ it means that $A \in \mathbb{R}^{n \times h}$ will be much smaller than the dataset which belongs to $\mathbb{R}^{n \times d}$. In this case, it is more appropriate to compute it before the SGD algorithms starts the iterative process and keep it in memory (note that the computation of A is fully parallel). In this way, all the data $\mathbb{R}^{n \times d}$ projected by ϕ into to matrix $A \in \mathbb{R}^{n \times h}$ can be largely kept in volatile memory (RAM) instead of reading from the disk. If instead $h \gg d$, employing Algorithm 2 we risk that $A \in \mathbb{R}^{n \times h}$ does not fit into the RAM, consequently making too many accesses to the disk. For this reason, we adopt two different strategies:

- If h is approximately the same magnitude or smaller than d, we use Algorithm 2 and we compute the matrix A at the beginning;
- If $h \gg d$, we adopt Algorithm 3 where $\phi\left(x_i\right)$ is computed online in order to avoid to read the data from the disk.

Quite obviously, the limit is given by the size of the RAM of each node and the number of nodes. Until the algorithm is able to keep most of the data in memory, it is better to use Algorithm 2. Algorithm 3 allows us to partially reduce the effect of having to access the data on the disk by paying the price of computing $\phi\left(x_i\right)$ online. In fact, Algorithm 3 does not precompute $A \in \mathbb{R}^{n \times h}$ at the beginning but it keeps the data $\mathcal{D}_n$ in memory and, at every iteration of the SGD algorithm, it computes online both the projection induced by ϕ and the gradient. Consequently, there is no need to store $A \in \mathbb{R}^{n \times h}$.

Algorithm 3. SGD for SELM on Spark (d ≤ h)

Input: $D_n, \lambda, \tau, n_{iter}$
Output: w

1 `Read` D_n ;

2 $w = 0$;

3 `for` $t \leftarrow 1$ `to` n_{iter} `do`

4 $\qquad g = D_n.map(\phi~\&Gradient())$

$\qquad$ `/* Compute both the projection` ϕ `and the gradient for each sample`

5 $\qquad .reduce(Sum())$

$\qquad$ `/* Sum all the gradients of each sample`

6 $\qquad w = w - \dfrac{\tau}{\sqrt{t}} g$;

7 `return` w ;

Deep Extreme Learning Machines (DELM)

Due to its shallow architecture, feature learning using SELM may not be effective even with a large number of hidden nodes. Since feature learning is often useful to improve the accuracy of the final model, multilayer (deep) solutions are usually needed. In (Kasun et al., 2013) a multilayer learning architecture is developed using ELM-based autoencoder (AE) as its building block, which results in a sort of "Deep" ELM (DELM). The original inputs are decomposed into l hidden layers, each one composed of $h_{i \in \{1, \cdots, l\}}$ hidden neurons, and the outputs of the previous layer are used as the inputs of the current one (see Figure 5). Basically, instead of having just one output, we have a series of outputs $\hat{x}_j$ with $j \in \{1, \cdots, d\}$ such that

$$\hat{x}_j = f_j(\boldsymbol{x}) = \sum_{i=1}^{h} w_{j,i} \varphi \left(W_{i,0} + \sum_{j=1}^{d} W_{i,j} x_j \right) = \sum_{i=1}^{h} w_{j,i} \varphi_i(\boldsymbol{x}) \qquad (9)$$

where $w_{j,i}$ with $j \in \{1, \cdots, d\}$ are found with the same random approach of SELM. Before the supervised regularized least mean square optimization, the encoded outputs are directly fed into the last layer for decision making, without random feature mapping.

Figure 5. DELM AE block

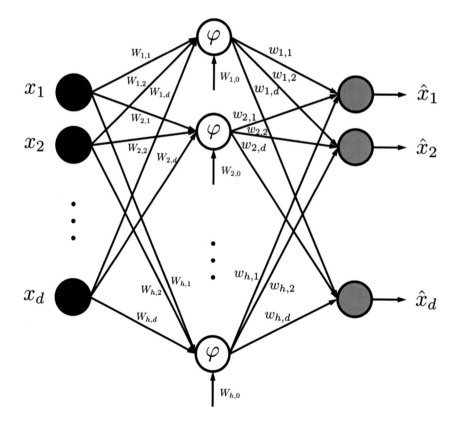

However, the approach developed in (Kasun et al., 2013) does not fully exploit the potential of a multilayer implementation of ELM. Indeed, a new more powerful architecture that exploits the potential of a DELM is presented in (Tang et al., 2016), which considers multilayer as a whole with unsupervised initialization like in the classical Deep Learning approaches. After the unsupervised initialization, the entire network is trained by back propagation, and all the layers are hard coded together (Bengio, 2009; Bengio et al., 2013). Note that, as for SELM, DELM do not require fine-tuning for the entire system, and consequently the training speed can be much faster than the traditional back propagation based Deep Learning.

Although the approach of (Tang et al., 2016) can be much more effective than the one of (Kasun et al., 2013), it requires more complex and time-consuming computations. Instead, the approach described in (Kasun et al., 2013) can produce improved results over the simple SELM since the number of hidden layers increases, and its implementation for big data problems can directly exploit the results of the previous section. Consequently, with reasonably small modifications, we are able to take advantage of a simple deep architecture by exploiting only the tools presented in the previous section.

MODEL SELECTION

Model Selection (MS) deals with the problem of optimizing the performance of a learning procedure by tuning the hyperparameters of any learning algorithm (Bartlett, Boucheron, & Lugosi, 2002; Anguita, Ghio, Oneto, & Ridella, 2012). Resampling techniques like hold out, cross validation and bootstrap (Anguita et al., 2012) are often used by practitioners because they work well in many situations. Nevertheless, other methods exist in literature: for example, (Vapnik, 1998) is the seminal work on Vapnik-Chervonenkis Dimension, which states the conditions under which a set of hypothesis is learnable. Later these results have been improved with the introduction of the Rademacher Complexity (Bartlett & Mendelson, 2002), together with its localized counterpart (Bartlett, Bousquet, & Mendelson, 2005). The theory of (Floyd & Warmuth, 1995), later extended by (Langford & McAllester, 2004), was another step forward in the direction of understanding the learning properties of an algorithm by tightly connecting compression to learning. A breakthrough was made with the Algorithmic Stability (Bousquet & Elisseeff, 2002; Poggio, Rifkin, Mukherjee et al., 2004; Oneto, Ghio, Ridella et al., 2015), which states the properties that a learning algorithm should fulfil in order to achieve good generalization performance. The PAC-Bayes theory represents another fundamental brick (Lever, Laviolette, & Shawe-Taylor, 2013; Tolstikhin & Seldin, 2013; Germain, Lacasse, Laviolette et al., 2015; Bégin, Germain, Laviolette et al., 2016) for MS, especially in the context of ensemble methods. Indeed, although it is well known that combining the outputs of a set of different learning procedures gives much better results than considering those learning procedures separately, it is hard to combine them appropriately in order to obtain satisfactory performances (Nitzan & Paroush, 1982; Catoni, 2007) and it is not trivial to assess the performance of the resulting learning procedure. Finally, Differential Privacy (DP) allowed reaching a milestone result by connecting the privacy preservation in data analysis and the generalization capability of a learning algorithm. From one hand, it proved that a learning algorithm that shows DP properties also generalizes (Dwork et al., 2014, 2015c). From the other hand, if an algorithm does not hold DP, it allows to state the conditions under which a hold-out set can be reused without risk of false discovery by means of a DP procedure called Thresholdout (Dwork et al., 2015a, 2015b, 2015d).

In this book chapter, we will use the 10-Fold Cross Validation (Kohavi, 1995; Anguita et al., 2012; Anguita, Ghio, Ridella et al., 2009; Arlot & Celisse, 2010) method in order to tune the hyperparameters of SELM and DELM. In particular, for SELM we have that $h \in \{1, 2, \cdots\}$, $\lambda \in [0, \infty)$, and $\Delta^- \in \{1, 2, \cdots\}$ days must be tuned, while for DELM we have to find the optimal values of $l \in \{1, 2, \cdots\}$, $h_{i \in \{1, \cdots, l\}} \in \{1, 2, \cdots\}$, $\lambda \in [0, \infty)$, and $\Delta^- \in \{1, 2, \cdots\}$ days. Since it is not possible to fully explore all the combinations of hyperparameters, a search for the best set of hyperparameters over a finite grid of points is performed. Since we are dealing with a large amount of data and a large number of models to train, this approach results computationally intractable. Consequently, the approach of (Bergstra & Bengio, 2012) has been selected, which consists in performing a random search by trying n_{MC} combinations of the hyperparameters. In (Bergstra & Bengio, 2012) it is also shown (both empirically and theoretically) that randomly chosen trials are more efficient than trials on a grid.

DESCRIPTION OF DATA AND CUSTOM KPIS

In order to validate the proposed methodology and to assess the performance of the new prediction system, a large number of experiments have been performed on the real data provided by RFI. The Italian IM owns records of the TM from the entire Italian railway network over several years. For the purpose of this work, RFI gave access to more than 1 year of data related to two main areas in Italy, including more than 1000 trains and several checkpoints.

Each record refers to a single TM, and is composed by the following information: Date, Train ID, Checkpoint ID, Checkpoint Name, Arrival Time, Arrival Delay, Departure Time, Departure Delay and Event Type. The last field, namely "Event Type", refers to the type of event that has been recorded with respect to the train itinerary. For instance, this field can assume four different values: Origin (O), Destination (D), Stop (F) and Transit (T). The Arrival (Departure) Time field reports the actual time of arrival (departure) of a train at a particular checkpoint. Combining this information with the value contained in the Arrival (Departure) Delay field, it is possible to retrieve the scheduled time of arrival (departure). Note that, although IMs usually own proprietary software solutions, this kind of data can be retrieved by any rail TMS, since systems of this kind store the same raw information but in different formats. For example, some systems provide the theoretical time and the TD of a train, while others provide the theoretical time and the actual time, making the two information sets exchangeable without any loss of information. Finally, note that the information has been anonymized for privacy and security concerns.

The approach used to perform the experiments consisted in (i) building the needed set of models based on SELM and DELM for each train in the dataset, (ii) simultaneously tuning the models' hyperparameters through suitable models selection methodologies, (iii) applying the models to the current state of the trains, and finally (iv) validating the models in terms of performance based on what had really happened at a future instant. Consequently, simulations have been performed for all the trains included in the dataset adopting an online-approach that updates predictive models every day, in order to take advantage of new information as soon as it becomes available.

The results of the simulations have been compared with the results of the current TD prediction system used by RFI. The RFI system is quite similar to the one described in (Kecman & Goverde, 2015), although the latter includes process mining refinements which potentially increase its performance.

In order to fairly assess the performance of the proposed prediction system, a set of novel KPIs agreed with RFI has been designed and used. Since the purpose of this work was to build predictive models able to forecast the TD, these KPIs represent different indicators of the quality of these predictive models. Note that the predictive models should be able to predict, for each train and at each checkpoint of its itinerary, the TD that the train will have in any of the successive checkpoints. Based on this consideration, three different indicators of the quality of predictive models have been used, which are also proposed in Figure 6 in a graphical fashion:

- **Average Accuracy at the i-th Following Checkpoint for Train j (AAiCj):** For a particular train j, the absolute value of the difference between the predicted delay and its actual delay is averaged, at the i-th following Checkpoint with respect to the actual Checkpoint.
- **AAiC:** The average over the different trains j of AAiCj.
- **Average Accuracy at Checkpoint-i for Train j (AACij):** For a particular train j, the average of the absolute value of the difference between the predicted delay and its actual delay, at the i-th checkpoint, is computed.
- **AACi:** The average over the different trains j of AACij.
- **Total Average Accuracy for Train j (TAAj):** The average over the different checkpoints i-th of AASij (or equiva- lently the average over the index i of AAiSj).
- **TAA:** The average over the different trains j of TAAj.

RESULTS

This section reports the results of the experiments exploiting the approaches described in the previous sections, benchmarked with the data and KPIs described above.

Figure 6. KPIs for the train and the itinerary of Figure 1

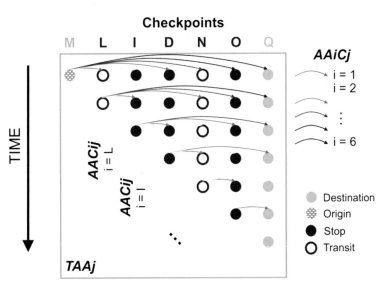

The performance of different methods for building a TDPS have been compared:

- **RFI:** the RFI system has been implemented, which is quite similar to the one described in (Kecman & Goverde, 2015). Note that, the RFI method has no hyperparameters to tune;
- **SELM:** SELM has been exploited, where the set of possible configurations of hyperparameters is searched in $h \in \{1, 2, \cdots, 10^4\}$ and $\lambda \in [10^{-6}, 10^4]$;
- **DELM:** DELM has been exploited, where the set of possible configurations of hyperparameters has been defined as $l \in \{1, 2, \cdots, 10\}$, $h_{i \in \{1, \cdots, l\}} \in \{1, 2, \cdots, 10^4\}$, and $\lambda \in [10^{-6}, 10^4]$;

Note that $d_0 - \Delta^-$ is set equal to the time of the last change in the NT, and $t_0 - \delta^-$ is set equal to the time, in the NT, of the origin of the train, as suggested by the RFI experts.

Finally, 10 Fold Cross Validation has been exploited in order to optimize the different hyperparameters of the learning algorithms. The random search in the space of the hyperparameters has been done by setting $n_{MC} = 300$.

Table 1, Table 2 and Table 3 report the KPIs of the different methods in the different scenarios. Note that these tables are not complete due to space constraints, and that the train and station IDs have been anonymized because of privacy issues. In particular, it is possible to draw up the following comments:

- Table 1 reports the AAiCj and AAiC. From Table 1 it is possible to observe that the DELM method is the best performing method, and it improves up to $\times 2$ the current RFI system. All the data-driven methods (both SELM and DELM) improve over the RFI system by a large amount. Finally, note that the accuracy decreases as j increases, since the forecasts refer to events that are further into the future. Moreover, since some trains have less checkpoints than the others, a symbol '-' has been placed for those checkpoints that are not included in the itinerary of the considered trains (see for example train $j = 14$, which only passes through two checkpoints).
- Table 2 reports the AACij and the AACi. From Table 2 it is possible to derive the same observations derived from Table 1. In this case, it is also important to underline that not all the trains run over all the checkpoints, and this is the reason why for some combinations of train j and station i there is a symbol '-'.
- Table 3 reports the TAAj and the TAA. The latter is more concise and underlines better the advantage, from a final performance perspective, of the DELM with respect to the actual RFI prediction system.

Finally, we compared the performance of a Matlab and Apache Spark implementations of the training phase of SELM and DELM. The first implementation run on a PC with 4 Intel Xeon CPU E5-4620@2.20GHz, 128 GB of RAM, 500 GB of SSD running Windows Server 2012 R2 and Matlab R2016a. The second one, instead, run over four n1-standard-16 machines of the Google Compute Engine, which include 60 GB of ram, 16 cores and 500 GB SSD disk each, allowing the deployment of a cluster with Apache Spark 1.6.2 on Apache Hadoop 2.6.4. In order to perform the experiments reported in the book chapter, the Matlab implementation did not finished neither 1% of the experiments after 1 months, while our spark implementation took approximately one day.

Table 1. *AAiCj & AAiC - ELM based and RFI prediction systems KPIs (in minutes)*

AAiCj j\i	1st			2nd			3rd			4th			5th		
	RFI	SELM	DELM	RFI	SELM	DELM	RFI	SELM	DELM	RFI	SELM	DELM	RFI	SELM	DELM
1	1.8±0.5	1.6±0.1	1.5±0.2	2.1±0.2	1.8±1.3	1.7±0.3	2.3±0.5	2.1±0.2	1.9±0.6	2.5±1.5	2.3±1.3	2.1±0.6	2.7±0.0	2.4±1.1	2.3±0.3
2	3.2±0.9	1.8±0.6	1.7±0.4	3.4±0.7	1.9±0.9	1.9±0.7	3.8±0.2	2.2±0.3	2.1±1.4	4.2±1.8	2.4±0.3	2.3±0.3	4.6±2.0	2.6±0.9	2.5±1.1
3	1.9±0.2	1.4±1.3	1.3±0.4	2.0±0.7	1.6±0.1	1.4±0.5	2.3±0.7	1.8±0.2	1.7±0.3	2.6±1.0	1.9±0.2	1.8±0.0	2.8±1.5	2.0±0.0	1.9±1.4
4	2.0±0.8	1.5±0.2	1.3±0.3	2.2±0.9	1.6±0.4	1.6±0.1	2.6±0.9	1.9±0.7	1.8±0.0	3.0±1.1	2.1±0.3	2.0±0.9	3.4±0.2	2.3±0.1	2.1±0.0
5	1.4±0.2	0.9±0.3	0.8±0.2	1.7±0.7	1.0±0.5	1.0±0.1	2.0±1.2	1.2±0.1	1.2±0.5	2.3±1.3	1.4±0.7	1.3±0.1	2.6±0.3	1.6±0.5	1.5±0.4
6	1.4±0.9	1.3±0.1	1.2±0.1	1.7±0.2	1.5±0.9	1.5±0.1	2.0±0.5	1.8±0.6	1.7±0.5	2.3±1.5	2.1±1.8	1.9±0.5	2.6±0.8	2.3±1.0	2.1±0.2
7	1.3±0.4	1.0±0.1	0.9±0.5	1.4±0.6	1.1±0.3	1.0±0.2	1.6±0.2	1.3±0.0	1.2±0.3	1.8±0.9	1.5±0.8	1.4±0.7	2.0±0.5	1.6±0.0	1.5±0.1
8	1.3±0.3	1.0±0.0	0.9±0.3	1.6±0.3	1.3±0.4	1.1±0.4	1.9±0.7	1.4±0.1	1.3±0.4	2.1±0.3	1.6±1.0	1.5±0.3	2.3±0.7	1.7±0.2	1.7±0.4
9	1.2±0.6	0.8±0.0	0.7±0.1	1.2±0.2	0.9±0.2	0.8±0.1	1.4±0.1	1.0±0.2	0.9±0.4	1.5±0.3	1.1±0.2	1.1±0.4	1.5±0.8	1.2±0.3	1.1±0.1
10	1.5±0.0	1.0±0.3	0.9±0.1	1.6±0.4	1.1±0.2	1.0±0.1	2.0±0.7	1.3±0.2	1.2±0.1	2.3±1.3	1.5±0.1	1.4±0.1	2.4±1.5	1.6±1.2	1.5±0.5
11	1.4±0.1	1.2±0.1	1.1±0.7	1.5±0.7	1.3±0.1	1.3±0.1	1.7±0.4	1.5±0.3	1.4±0.7	1.9±0.7	1.6±0.1	1.4±0.0	2.1±0.5	1.7±0.5	1.6±0.9
12	2.1±0.0	1.6±0.8	1.4±0.4	2.6±0.0	1.9±0.0	1.7±0.2	3.1±1.9	2.1±0.1	2.0±1.7	3.5±1.0	2.3±0.1	2.2±0.0	3.8±0.0	2.6±1.3	2.4±0.6
13	1.2±0.3	0.9±0.2	0.8±0.0	1.3±0.4	1.0±0.4	0.9±0.2	1.4±1.1	1.1±0.5	1.0±0.1	1.6±0.0	1.3±0.1	1.2±0.7	1.6±0.8	1.4±0.5	1.3±0.2
14	3.1±0.4	2.1±0.3	1.9±1.2	—	—	—	—	—	—	—	—	—	—	—	—
15	1.1±0.3	0.8±0.2	0.8±0.3	1.2±0.4	0.9±0.1	0.8±0.0	1.3±0.1	1.0±0.1	0.9±0.3	1.5±0.5	1.1±0.1	1.0±0.9	1.6±0.1	1.1±0.1	1.1±0.3
16	3.9±0.1	1.0±0.2	0.9±0.1	—	—	—	—	—	—	—	—	—	—	—	—
17	1.2±0.2	0.8±0.2	0.8±0.2	1.4±0.3	1.0±0.6	0.9±0.2	1.7±0.4	1.1±0.2	1.0±0.7	1.9±0.4	1.3±0.1	1.1±0.2	2.1±0.3	1.4±0.2	1.3±0.3
18	2.0±0.1	1.3±0.0	1.2±0.7	2.4±0.7	1.5±0.6	1.4±0.5	2.9±2.0	1.7±0.7	1.6±0.1	3.4±1.1	1.9±0.3	1.7±0.8	3.7±0.3	2.1±0.5	1.9±0.4
19	1.7±0.8	1.1±0.2	1.1±0.2	2.0±0.1	1.3±0.1	1.2±0.1	2.4±1.1	1.5±0.8	1.4±0.8	2.8±2.0	1.6±0.1	1.5±0.1	3.0±0.5	1.8±0.5	1.7±0.8
20	1.9±0.1	1.3±0.2	1.2±0.5	2.2±0.1	1.4±0.3	1.4±0.3	2.7±0.3	1.6±0.5	1.5±0.5	3.1±1.6	1.8±0.2	1.7±0.2	3.3±1.2	2.0±0.3	1.8±0.4
21	1.3±0.2	0.4±0.1	0.4±0.0	1.3±0.1	0.4±0.1	0.4±0.1	1.5±0.2	0.5±0.1	0.5±0.3	1.7±0.1	0.6±0.3	0.6±0.0	2.2±0.6	0.7±0.3	0.7±0.3
22	1.5±0.0	0.7±0.1	0.6±0.1	1.6±0.5	0.7±0.1	0.6±0.2	1.8±0.3	0.8±0.7	0.8±0.0	1.9±0.2	0.9±0.0	0.9±0.4	2.2±0.3	1.1±0.3	1.0±0.2
23	1.5±0.1	0.3±0.2	0.3±0.1	1.7±0.2	0.4±0.1	0.4±0.2	1.8±0.3	0.5±0.0	0.5±0.1	1.8±0.3	0.6±0.1	0.5±0.1	2.0±0.2	0.7±0.1	0.7±0.1
24	1.1±0.2	0.5±0.2	0.5±0.3	1.2±0.1	0.6±0.2	0.6±0.1	1.2±0.0	0.7±0.3	0.6±0.4	1.2±0.1	0.8±0.1	0.8±0.1	1.3±0.1	1.0±0.3	0.9±0.1
25	1.2±0.7	0.4±0.1	0.4±0.2	1.2±0.4	0.5±0.0	0.4±0.0	1.3±0.3	0.6±0.2	0.6±0.1	1.3±0.0	0.7±0.1	0.7±0.0	1.5±0.6	0.9±0.1	0.8±0.3

continued on following page

Table 1. Continued

AAiCj	RFI	SELM	DELM	RFI	SELM	DELM	RFI	SELM	DELM	RFI	SELM	DELM	RFI	SELM	DELM
j\i	1st			2nd			3rd			4th			5th		
26	1.9±0.0	0.7±0.0	0.6±0.1	2.0±0.5	0.8±0.4	0.8±0.4	2.4±0.2	1.0±0.0	0.9±0.5	2.6±0.5	1.1±0.1	1.0±0.5	3.1±1.0	1.1±0.0	1.0±0.3
27	1.0±0.8	0.4±0.0	0.4±0.0	1.1±0.0	0.5±0.2	0.5±0.0	1.1±0.7	0.6±0.1	0.6±0.2	1.1±0.1	0.7±0.1	0.7±0.2	1.1±0.1	0.8±0.4	0.8±0.1
28	1.0±0.2	0.4±0.1	0.3±0.0	1.1±0.2	0.4±0.0	0.4±0.1	1.2±0.4	0.5±0.3	0.5±0.3	1.1±0.1	0.6±0.1	0.6±0.0	1.2±0.6	0.8±0.2	0.7±0.2
29	1.9±0.5	0.7±0.0	0.6±0.1	2.0±1.3	0.8±0.1	0.7±0.2	2.3±1.0	0.9±0.6	0.8±0.3	2.6±0.2	1.0±0.3	0.9±0.1	3.0±2.0	1.0±0.3	0.9±0.0
30	1.0±0.3	0.4±0.2	0.3±0.0	1.1±0.1	0.4±0.2	0.4±0.0	1.2±0.2	0.5±0.1	0.5±0.2	1.1±0.1	0.7±0.2	0.6±0.1	1.2±0.3	0.8±0.1	0.7±0.1
AAiC	3.0±0.4	1.6±0.3	1.5±0.1	2.9±0.6	1.7±0.1	1.6±0.2	3.2±0.6	2.0±0.0	1.8±0.2	3.4±1.4	2.2±0.5	2.1±0.2	3.4±0.1	2.4±0.7	2.2±0.3

Table 2. AACij & AACi - ELM based and RFI prediction systems KPIs (in minutes)

AACij	RFI	SELM	DELM	RFI	SELM	DELM	RFI	SELM	DELM	RFI	SELM	DELM	RFI	SELM	DELM
j\i	1			2			3			4			5		
1	2.9±1.6	2.3±1.0	2.0±0.1	-	-	-	-	-	-	2.2±0.1	2.2±0.2	2.1±0.6	-	-	-
2	0.0±0.0	0.1±0.0	0.1±0.0	-	-	-	-	-	-	2.5±0.9	1.7±0.9	1.6±0.4	-	-	-
3	0.2±0.1	0.0±0.0	0.0±0.0	-	-	-	-	-	-	2.2±0.2	1.6±0.2	1.5±0.7	-	-	-
4	1.7±0.2	1.5±0.1	1.4±0.1	2.3±0.5	1.8±0.1	1.7±0.0	2.9±1.0	1.8±0.6	1.7±0.3	-	-	-	-	-	-
5	-	-	-	1.1±0.2	1.1±0.6	1.0±0.1	1.1±0.6	0.9±0.3	0.8±0.0	-	-	-	-	-	-
6	-	-	-	1.2±0.5	1.4±0.1	1.3±0.3	1.8±0.0	1.8±0.4	1.7±0.9	-	-	-	-	-	-
7	-	-	-	1.8±0.4	1.3±0.3	1.2±0.1	1.7±0.1	1.5±0.1	1.5±0.4	-	-	-	-	-	-
8	-	-	-	1.5±0.4	1.4±0.2	1.2±0.4	3.0±2.7	2.5±0.5	2.3±0.1	-	-	-	-	-	-
9	-	-	-	1.1±1.1	1.0±0.1	0.9±0.1	1.2±0.5	1.1±0.4	1.1±0.4	-	-	-	-	-	-

continued on following page

Table 2. Continued

AACij / j\i	1			2			3			...	4			5		
	RFI	SELM	DELM	RFI	SELM	DELM	RFI	SELM	DELM		RFI	SELM	DELM	RFI	SELM	DELM
10	-	-	-	1.9±0.0	1.2±0.4	1.1±0.4	1.8±0.2	1.4±0.5	1.2±0.1		-	-	-	-	-	-
11	1.3±0.0	1.1±0.3	1.1±0.4	1.8±1.3	1.1±0.2	1.0±0.4	1.2±0.1	1.1±0.0	1.0±0.0		-	-	-	-	-	-
12	-	-	-	-	-	-	-	-	-		3.9±0.0	1.0±0.3	0.9±0.1	-	-	-
13	-	-	-	-	-	-	-	-	-		5.8±2.9	2.7±0.5	2.6±0.5	-	-	-
14	-	-	-	-	-	-	-	-	-		6.7±0.6	4.3±0.6	4.1±0.6	-	-	-
15	-	-	-	-	-	-	-	-	-		3.8±0.3	1.0±0.3	0.9±0.0	-	-	-
16	-	-	-	-	-	-	-	-	-		3.7±2.4	1.0±0.1	0.9±0.2	-	-	-
17	-	-	-	-	-	-	-	-	-		5.9±2.6	2.4±0.1	2.2±0.0	-	-	-
18	-	-	-	1.3±0.3	0.9±0.1	0.9±0.4	-	-	-		-	-	-	1.6±0.3	1.9±0.9	1.8±0.3
19	-	-	-	2.5±1.4	1.4±0.5	1.3±0.6	-	-	-		-	-	-	1.1±0.3	1.1±0.1	1.0±0.3
20	-	-	-	1.6±0.1	1.3±0.1	1.2±0.1	-	-	-		-	-	-	2.5±0.4	2.3±0.8	2.1±0.6
21	-	-	-	1.2±0.6	0.9±0.0	0.8±0.1	-	-	-		-	-	-	1.3±0.2	1.3±0.5	1.2±0.3
22	-	-	-	1.5±0.3	1.1±0.2	1.0±0.1	-	-	-		-	-	-	2.5±0.4	2.3±1.2	2.2±0.7
23	-	-	-	1.3±0.4	1.1±0.2	1.1±0.8	-	-	-		-	-	-	2.4±0.4	2.2±0.8	1.9±0.3
24	-	-	-	-	-	-	1.2±0.0	0.8±0.1	0.7±0.2		-	-	-	-	-	-
25	-	-	-	-	-	-	1.9±0.5	0.5±0.5	0.8±0.1		-	-	-	-	-	-
26	-	-	-	-	-	-	1.6±0.7	1.1±0.2	1.0±0.4		-	-	-	-	-	-
27	-	-	-	-	-	-	1.3±0.1	1.1±0.1	1.0±0.2		-	-	-	-	-	-
28	-	-	-	-	-	-	1.7±0.7	0.9±0.0	0.8±0.1		-	-	-	-	-	-
29	-	-	-	-	-	-	1.4±0.5	1.2±0.2	1.1±0.1		-	-	-	-	-	-
30	-	-	-	2.5±0.5	2.1±0.4	2.0±0.4	2.1±1.0	1.8±0.5	1.7±0.2		-	-	-	-	-	-
AACi	3.3±0.1	1.5±0.3	1.4±0.4	3.1±1.6	1.5±0.0	1.3±0.3	3.3±0.5	1.4±0.0	1.3±0.4		4.2±0.6	2.2±0.8	2.1±0.3	6.2±2.4	4.2±1.6	3.9±1.6

Table 3. TAAj & TAA - ELM based and RFI prediction systems KPIs (in minutes)

j	TAAj		
	RFI	**SELM**	**DELM**
1	2.2±0.8	1.9±0.9	1.7±0.0
2	4.3±0.2	2.1±0.5	2.0±1.7
3	2.3±0.5	1.5±0.5	1.4±0.2
4	2.4±0.5	1.7±0.4	1.5±0.5
5	1.7±0.4	1.1±0.3	1.0±0.5
6	1.9±0.3	1.6±0.3	1.6±0.1
7	1.5±0.7	1.2±0.2	1.1±0.6
8	1.9±0.5	1.4±0.3	1.4±0.3
9	1.4±0.5	0.9±0.2	0.8±0.2
10	1.8±0.1	1.1±0.3	1.0±0.8
11	1.8±0.6	1.4±1.0	1.3±0.0
12	2.8±2.2	1.9±0.5	1.7±0.5
13	1.4±0.4	1.1±0.1	1.0±0.2
14	3.1±0.6	2.0±0.1	1.8±0.9
15	1.2±0.5	0.9±0.3	0.8±0.1
16	3.9±0.5	0.9±0.2	0.9±0.3
17	5.8±1.4	2.6±0.6	2.5±0.9
18	6.7±2.5	4.1±0.4	3.8±0.7
19	3.8±0.7	0.9±0.1	0.9±0.4
20	3.7±1.1	0.9±0.2	0.9±0.1
21	5.9±0.8	2.3±1.3	2.1±0.5
22	4.9±0.7	2.1±0.4	2.0±0.2
23	6.5±1.1	3.5±2.1	3.2±0.3
24	5.1±0.9	2.1±0.3	2.1±0.2
25	4.6±1.4	1.7±0.0	1.6±0.6
26	5.6±1.8	2.7±0.2	2.6±1.0
27	6.2±0.1	2.7±0.6	2.4±0.3
28	5.5±3.6	2.6±1.8	2.4±0.7
29	4.2±0.8	1.0±0.4	1.0±0.4
30	4.7±1.0	1.7±0.4	1.6±0.8
•••			
TAA	3.3±1.8	1.9±0.6	1.7±0.8

CONCLUSION

This book chapter deals with the problem of building a TDPS based on state-of-the-art tools and techniques able to rapidly grasp the knowledge hidden in historical data about TM. In particular, the proposed solution improves the state-of-the-art methodologies actually exploited from the IM like RFI.

Results on real world TM data provided by RFI show that advanced analytics approaches can perform up to twice better than current state-of- the-art methodologies. In particular, exploiting historical data about TM gives robust models with high performance with respect to the actual TD prediction system of RFI. We have also shown how to efficiently and effectively tune the hyperparameters involved in the learning algorithms. Finally, by exploiting the Apache Spark in memory technology, we have been able to build a system with high performance, also in terms of the required training time for building all the models needed for dealing with a large-scale Railway Network. Future works will take into account also exogenous information available from external sources, such as weather information, information about passenger flows by using touristic databases, about railway assets conditions, or any other source of data which may affect railway dispatching operations.

ACKNOWLEDGMENT

This research has been supported by the European Union through the projects Capacity for Rail - C4R (European Union's Seventh Framework Programme for research, technological development and demonstration under grant agreement 605650) and Innovative Intelligent Rail - In2Rail (European Union's Horizon 2020 research and innovation programme under grant agreement 635900).

REFERENCES

Al-Jarrah, A. Y., Yoo, P. D., Muhaidat, S., Karagiannidis, G. K., & Taha, K. (2015). Efficient machine learning for big data: A review. *Big Data Research*, 2(3), 87–93. doi:10.1016/j.bdr.2015.04.001

Anguita, D., Ghio, A., Oneto, L., & Ridella, S. (2012). In-sample and out-of-sample model selection and error estimation for support vector machines. *IEEE Transactions on Neural Networks and Learning Systems*, 23(9), 1390–1406. doi:10.1109/TNNLS.2012.2202401 PMID:24807923

Anguita, D., Ghio, A., Ridella, S., & Sterpi, D. (2009). K-fold cross validation for error rate estimate in support vector machines. In *Proceedings of the International conference on data mining*.

Aridhi, S., & Nguifo, E. M. (2016). Big graph mining: Frameworks and techniques. *Big Data Research*, 6, 1–10. doi:10.1016/j.bdr.2016.07.002

Arlot, S., & Celisse, A. (2010). A survey of cross-validation procedures for model selection. *Statistics Surveys*, 4(0), 40–79. doi:10.1214/09-SS054

Aytekin, C., Rezaeitabar, Y., Dogru, S., & Ulusoy, I. (2015). Railway fastener inspection by real-time machine vision. IEEE Transactions on Systems, Man, and Cybernetics. *Systems*, 45(7), 1101–1107.

Bai, Y., Ho, T. K., Mao, B., Ding, Y., & Chen, S. (2014). Energy-efficient locomotive operation for chinese mainline railways by fuzzy predictive control. *IEEE Transactions on Intelligent Transportation Systems*, 15(3), 938–948. doi:10.1109/TITS.2013.2292712

Bartlett, P. L., Boucheron, S., & Lugosi, G. (2002). Model selection and error estimation. *Machine Learning*, 48(1-3), 85–113. doi:10.1023/A:1013999503812

Bartlett, P. L., Bousquet, O., & Mendelson, S. (2005). Local rademacher complexities. *Annals of Statistics, 33*(4), 1497–1537. doi:10.1214/009053605000000282

Bartlett, P. L., & Mendelson, S. (2002). Rademacher and gaussian complexities: Risk bounds and structural results. *Journal of Machine Learning Research, 3*, 463–482.

B'egin, L., Germain, P., Laviolette, F., & Roy, J. F. (2016). Pac-bayesian bounds based on the r'enyi divergence. In *Proceedings of the International conference on artificial intelligence and statistics.*

Bengio, Y. (2009). Learning deep architectures for AI. *Foundations and trends in Machine Learning, 2*(1), 1-127.

Bengio, Y., Courville, A., & Vincent, P. (2013). Representation learning: A review and new perspectives. *IEEE Transactions on Pattern Analysis and Machine Intelligence, 35*(8), 1798–1828. doi:10.1109/TPAMI.2013.50 PMID:23787338

Berger, A., Gebhardt, A., Müller-Hannemann, M., & Ostrowski, M. (2011). Stochastic delay prediction in large train networks. Informatics.

Bergstra, J., & Bengio, Y. (2012). Random search for hyper-parameter optimization. *Journal of Machine Learning Research, 13*, 281–305.

Bin, Z., & Wensheng, X. (2015). An improved algorithm for high speed train's maintenance data mining based on mapreduce. In *Proceedings of the International conference on cloud computing and big data.* doi:10.1109/CCBD.2015.27

Bisio, F., Gastaldo, P., Zunino, R., & Cambria, E. (2015). A learning scheme based on similarity functions for affective common-sense reasoning. In *Proceedings of the International joint conference on neural networks.* doi:10.1109/IJCNN.2015.7280633

Bousquet, O., & Elisseeff, A. (2002). Stability and generalization. *Journal of Machine Learning Research, 2*, 499–526.

Branishtov, S. A., Vershinin, Y. A., Tumchenok, D. A., & Shirvanyan, A. M. (2014). Graph methods for estimation of railway capacity. In *Proceedings of the IEEE 17th international conference on intelligent transportation systems* (pp. 525-530). doi:10.1109/ITSC.2014.6957743

Cambria, E., Huang, G. B., Kasun, L. L. C., Zhou, H., Vong, C. M., Lin, J., & Liu, J. et al. (2013). Extreme learning machines. *IEEE Intelligent Systems, 28*(6), 30–59. doi:10.1109/MIS.2013.140

Caruana, R., Lawrence, S., & Lee, G. (2001). Overfitting in neural nets: Backpropagation, conjugate gradient, and early stopping. In Neural information processing systems.

Catoni, O. (2007). *Pac-bayesian supervised classification: The thermodynamics of statistical learning.* Institute of Mathematical Statistics.

Chen, Y., & An, A. (2016). Approximate parallel high utility itemset mining. *Big Data Research, 6*, 26–42. doi:10.1016/j.bdr.2016.07.001

Colombo, P., & Ferrari, E. (2015). Privacy aware access control for big data: A research roadmap. *Big Data Research, 2*(4), 145–154. doi:10.1016/j.bdr.2015.08.001

Cordeau, J. F., Toth, P., & Vigo, D. (1998). A survey of optimization models for train routing and scheduling. *Transportation Science, 32*(4), 380–404. doi:10.1287/trsc.32.4.380

Davey, E. (2012). Rail traffic management systems (TMS). In IET professional development course railway signalling and control systems.

Dean, J., & Ghemawat, S. (2008). Map-reduce: Simplified data processing on large clusters. *Communications of the ACM, 51*(1), 107–113. doi:10.1145/1327452.1327492

Dollevoet, T., Corman, F., DAriano, A., & Huisman, D. (2014). An iterative optimization framework for delay management and train scheduling. *Flexible Services and Manufacturing Journal, 26*(4), 490–515. doi:10.1007/s10696-013-9187-2

Dotoli, M., Epicoco, N., Falagario, M., Seatzu, C., & Turchiano, B. (2016). A decision support system for optimizing operations at intermodal railroad terminals. IEEE Transactions on Systems, Man, and Cybernetics: Systems, 47(3), 487-501.

Dwork, C., Feldman, V., Hardt, M., Pitassi, T., Reingold, O., & Roth, A. (2014). Preserving statistical validity in adaptive data analysis. arxiv:1411.2664(v3)

Dwork, C., Feldman, V., Hardt, M., Pitassi, T., Reingold, O., & Roth, A. (2015a). Generalization in adaptive data analysis and holdout reuse. arxiv:1506.02629(v2)

Dwork, C., Feldman, V., Hardt, M., Pitassi, T., Reingold, O., & Roth, A. (2015b). Generalization in adaptive data analysis and holdout reuse. In Neural information processing systems.

Dwork, C., Feldman, V., Hardt, M., Pitassi, T., Reingold, O., & Roth, A. (2015c). Preserving statistical validity in adaptive data analysis. In *Proceedings of the Annual ACM symposium on theory of computing*. doi:10.1145/2746539.2746580

Dwork, C., Feldman, V., Hardt, M., Pitassi, T., Reingold, O., & Roth, A. (2015d). The reusable holdout: Preserving validity in adaptive data analysis. *Science, 349*(6248), 636–638. doi:10.1126/science.aaa9375 PMID:26250683

Elattar, E. E., Goulermas, J., & Wu, Q. H. (2010). Electric load forecasting based on locally weighted support vector regression. *IEEE Transactions on Systems, Man and Cybernetics. Part C, Applications and Reviews, 40*(4), 438–447. doi:10.1109/TSMCC.2010.2040176

Feng, H., Jiang, Z., Xie, F., Yang, P., Shi, J., & Chen, L. (2014). Automatic fastener classification and defect detection in vision-based railway inspection systems. *IEEE Transactions on Instrumentation and Measurement, 63*(4), 877–888. doi:10.1109/TIM.2013.2283741

Figueres-Esteban, M., Hughes, P., & Van Gulijk, C. (2015). The role of data visualization in railway big data risk analysis. In *Proceedings of the European safety and reliability conference*. doi:10.1201/b19094-377

Floyd, S., & Warmuth, M. (1995). Sample compression, learnability, and the Vapnik-Chervonenkis dimension. *Machine Learning, 21*(3), 269–304. doi:10.1007/BF00993593

Fumeo, E., Oneto, L., & Anguita, D. (2015). Condition based maintenance in railway transportation systems based on big data streaming analysis. In Proceedings of the INNS big data conference. doi:10.1016/j.procs.2015.07.321

Germain, P., Lacasse, A., Laviolette, F., Marchand, M., & Roy, J. F. (2015). Risk bounds for the majority vote: From a pac-bayesian analysis to a learning algorithm. *The Journal of Machine Learning Research, 16*(4), 787-860.

Ghelardoni, L., Ghio, A., & Anguita, D. (2013). Energy load forecasting using empirical mode decomposition and support vector regression. *IEEE Transactions on Smart Grid, 4*(1), 549–556. doi:10.1109/TSG.2012.2235089

Google. (2016). Google Compute Engine. Retrieved from 3 May 2016 from https://cloud.google.com/compute/

Goverde, R. M. P. (2010). A delay propagation algorithm for large-scale railway traffic networks. *Transportation Research Part C, Emerging Technologies, 18*(3), 269–287. doi:10.1016/j.trc.2010.01.002

Hansen, I. A., Goverde, R. M. P., & Van Der Meer, D. J. (2010). Online train delay recognition and running time prediction. In Proceedings of the IEEE international conference on intelligent transportation systems. doi:10.1109/ITSC.2010.5625081

Hinton, G. E., Osindero, S., & Teh, Y. W. (2006). A fast learning algorithm for deep belief nets. *Neural Computation, 18*(7), 1527–1554. doi:10.1162/neco.2006.18.7.1527 PMID:16764513

Huang, G., Huang, G. B., Song, S., & You, K. (2015). Trends in extreme learning machines: A review. *Neural Networks, 61*, 32–48. doi:10.1016/j.neunet.2014.10.001 PMID:25462632

Huang, G. B. (2014). An insight into extreme learning machines: Random neurons, random features and kernels. *Cognitive Computation, 6*(3), 376–390. doi:10.1007/s12559-014-9255-2

Huang, G. B. (2015). What are extreme learning machines? Filling the gap between frank Rosenblatts dream and john von Neumanns puzzle. *Cognitive Computation, 7*(3), 263–278. doi:10.1007/s12559-015-9333-0

Huang, G. B., Chen, L., & Siew, C. K. (2006). Universal approximation using incremental constructive feedforward networks with random hidden nodes. *IEEE Transactions on Neural Networks, 17*(4), 879–892. doi:10.1109/TNN.2006.875977 PMID:16856652

Huang, G. B., Li, M. B., Chen, L., & Siew, C. K. (2008). Incremental extreme learning machine with fully complex hidden nodes. *Neurocomputing, 71*(4), 576–583. doi:10.1016/j.neucom.2007.07.025

Huang, G. B., Zhou, H., Ding, X., & Zhang, R. (2012). Extreme learning machine for regression and multiclass classification. *IEEE Transactions on Systems, Man, and Cybernetics. Part B, Cybernetics, 42*(2), 513–529. doi:10.1109/TSMCB.2011.2168604 PMID:21984515

Huang, G. B., Zhu, Q. Y., & Siew, C. K. (2004). Extreme learning machine: a new learning scheme of feedforward neural networks. In Proceedings of the IEEE international joint conference on neural networks.

Huang, G. B., Zhu, Q.-Y., & Siew, C.-K. (2006). Extreme learning machine: Theory and applications. *Neurocomputing*, *70*(1), 489–501. doi:10.1016/j.neucom.2005.12.126

Jina, X., Wah, B. W., Chenga, X., & Wanga, Y. (2015). Significance and challenges of big data research. *Big Data Research*, *2*(2), 59–64. doi:10.1016/j.bdr.2015.01.006

Kasun, L. L. C., Zhou, H., Huang, G. B., & Vong, C. M. (2013). Representational learning with elms for big data. *IEEE Intelligent Systems*, *28*(6), 31–34.

Kecman, P. (2014). Models for predictive railway traffic management (PhD thesis). TU Delft, Delft University of Technology.

Kecman, P., & Goverde, R. M. P. (2015). Online data-driven adaptive prediction of train event times. *IEEE Transactions on Intelligent Transportation Systems*, *16*(1), 465–474. doi:10.1109/TITS.2014.2347136

Kohavi, R. (1995). A study of cross-validation and bootstrap for accuracy estimation and model selection. In Proceedings of the International joint conference on artificial intelligence.

Langer, T., & Vaidyanathan, S. (2014). Smart Freight: Applications of Information and Communications Technologies to Freight System Efficiency (White Paper). ACEEE.

Langford, J., & McAllester, D. (2004). Computable shell decomposition bounds. *Journal of Machine Learning Research*, *5*, 529–547.

Lever, G., Laviolette, F., & Shawe-Taylor, F. (2013). Tighter pac-bayes bounds through distribution-dependent priors. *Theoretical Computer Science*, *473*, 4–28. doi:10.1016/j.tcs.2012.10.013

Li, H., Parikh, D., He, Q., Qian, B., Li, Z., Fang, D., & Hampapur, A. (2014). Improving rail network velocity: A machine learning approach to predictive maintenance. *Transportation Research Part C, Emerging Technologies*, *45*, 17–26. doi:10.1016/j.trc.2014.04.013

Li, H., Qian, B., Parikh, D., & Hampapur, A. (2013). Alarm prediction in large-scale sensor networks - a case study in railroad. In Proceedings of the IEEE international conference on big data.

Li, Q., Zhong, Z., Liang, Z., & Liang, Y. (2015). Rail inspection meets big data: Methods and trends. In 18th international conference on network-based information systems.

Li, X., Shou, B., & Ralescu, D. (2014). Train rescheduling with stochastic recovery time: A new track-backup approach. IEEE Transactions on Systems. *Man and Cybernetics: Systems*, *44*(9), 1216–1233.

Ma, M., Wang, P., Chu, C. H., & Liu, L. (2015). Efficient multipattern event processing over high-speed train data streams. *IEEE Internet of Things Journal*, *2*(4), 295–309. doi:10.1109/JIOT.2014.2387883

Meng, X., Bradley, J., Yavuz, B., Sparks, E., Venkataraman, S., & Liu, D., ... & Xin, D. (2016). MLlib: Machine Learning in Apache Spark. *Journal of Machine Learning Research*, *17*(34), 1–7.

Milinkovic, S., Markovic, M., Veskovic, S., Ivic, M., & Pavlovic, N. (2013). A fuzzy petri net model to estimate train delays. *Simulation Modelling Practice and Theory*, *33*, 144–157. doi:10.1016/j.simpat.2012.12.005

Morris, C., Easton, J., & Roberts, C. (2014). Applications of linked data in the rail domain. In Proceedings of the IEEE international conference on big data. doi:10.1109/BigData.2014.7004429

Muller-Hannemann, M., & Schnee, M. (2009). Efficient timetable information in the presence of delays. In Robust and online large-scale optimization. doi:10.1007/978-3-642-05465-5_10

Nitzan, S., & Paroush, J. (1982). Optimal decision rules in uncertain dichotomous choice situations. *International Economic Review*, *23*(2), 289–297. doi:10.2307/2526438

Noori, K., & Jenab, K. (2013). Fuzzy reliability-based traction control model for intelligent transportation systems. IEEE Transactions on Systems, Man, and Cybernetics. *Systems*, *43*(1), 229–234.

Nunez, A., Hendriks, J., Li, Z., De Schutter, B., & Dollevoet, R. (2014). Facilitating maintenance decisions on the Dutch railways using big data: The aba case study. In Proceedings of the IEEE international conference on big data.

Oneto, L., Ghio, A., Ridella, S., & Anguita, D. (2015). Fully empirical and data-dependent stability-based bounds. *IEEE transactions on cybernetics*, *45*(9), 1913-1926.

Paakkonen, P., & Pakkala, D. (2015). Reference architecture and classification of technologies, products and services for big data systems. *Big Data Research*, *2*(4), 166–186. doi:10.1016/j.bdr.2015.01.001

Packard, N. H., Crutchfield, J. P., Farmer, J. D., & Shaw, R. S. (1980). Geometry from a time series. *Physical Review Letters*, *45*(9), 712–716. doi:10.1103/PhysRevLett.45.712

Poggio, T., Rifkin, R., Mukherjee, S., & Niyogi, P. (2004). General conditions for predictivity in learning theory. *Nature*, *428*(6981), 419–422. doi:10.1038/nature02341 PMID:15042089

Pongnumkul, S., Pechprasarn, T., Kunaseth, N., & Chaipah, K. (2014). Improving arrival time prediction of thailand's passenger trains using historical travel times. In *Proceedings of the International joint conference on computer science and software engineering*. doi:10.1109/JCSSE.2014.6841886

Prechelt, L. (1998). Automatic early stopping using cross validation: Quantifying the criteria. *Neural Networks*, *11*(4), 761–767. doi:10.1016/S0893-6080(98)00010-0 PMID:12662814

Qingyang, Y., & Xiaoyun, Y. (2015). Scheduling optimization model and algorithm design for two-way marshalling train. In *Proceedings of the International conference on intelligent transportation, big data and smart city*. doi:10.1109/ICITBS.2015.178

Rete Ferroviaria Italiana. (2016). Gruppo Ferrovie Dello Stato Italiane. Retrieved 3 May 2016 from http://www.rfi.it/

Reyes-Ortiz, J. L., Oneto, L., & Anguita, D. (2015). Big data analytics in the cloud: Spark on Hadoop vs MPI/OpenMP on Beowulf. The *Proceedings of the INNS Big Data conference*.

Ridella, S., Rovetta, S., & Zunino, R. (1997). Circular backpropagation networks for classification. *IEEE Transactions on Neural Networks*, *8*(1), 84–97. doi:10.1109/72.554194 PMID:18255613

Rumelhart, D. E., Hinton, G. E., & Williams, R. J. (1988). Learning representations by back-propagating errors. *Cognitive modeling*, *5*(3).

Sadler, J., Griffin, D., Gilchrist, A., Austin, J., Kit, O., & Heavisides, J. (2016). Geosrm - online geospatial safety risk model for the gb rail network. *IET Intelligent Transport Systems, 10*(1), 17–24. doi:10.1049/iet-its.2015.0038

Schmidt, D., Chen, W. C., Matheson, M. A., & Ostrouchov, G. (2016). Programming with BIG data in r: Scaling analytics from one to thousands of nodes. *Big Data Research, 6*, 1–10.

Shawe-Taylor, J., & Cristianini, N. (2004). *Kernel methods for pattern analysis. Cambridge University Press.*

Takens, F. (1981). *Detecting strange attractors in turbulence.* Springer.

Tang, J., Deng, C., & Huang, G. B. (2016). Extreme learning machine for multilayer perceptron. *IEEE transactions on neural networks and learning systems, 27*(4), 809-821.

Thaduri, A., Galar, D., & Kumar, U. (2015). Railway assets: A potential domain for big data analytics. In Proceedings of the INNS big data conference. doi:10.1016/j.procs.2015.07.323

Tissera, M. D., & McDonnell, M. D. (2016). Deep extreme learning machines: Supervised autoencoding architecture for classification. *Neurocomputing, 174*, 42–49. doi:10.1016/j.neucom.2015.03.110

Tolstikhin, I. O., & Seldin, Y. (2013). Pac-bayes-empirical-Bernstein inequality. In Neural information processing systems.

Tutcher, J. (2014). Ontology-driven data integration for railway asset monitoring applications. In Proceedings of the IEEE international conference on big data. doi:10.1109/BigData.2014.7004436

Vapnik, V. N. (1998). *Statistical learning theory.* Wiley New York.

Vincent, P., Larochelle, H., Bengio, Y., & Manzagol, P. A. (2008). Extracting and composing robust features with denoising autoencoders. In *Proceedings of the International conference on machine learning.* doi:10.1145/1390156.1390294

Wang, B., Li, F., Hei, X., Ma, W., & Yu, L. (2015). Research on storage and retrieval method of mass data for high-speed train. In *Proceedings of the International conference on computational intelligence and security.* doi:10.1109/CIS.2015.120

Wang, F. h. Xu, T., Zhao, Y., & r. Huang, Y. (2015). Prior LDA and SVM based fault diagnosis of vehicle on-board equipment for high speed railway. In *Proceedings of the IEEE 18th international conference on intelligent transportation systems.*

White, T. (2012). *Hadoop: The definitive guide.* O'Reilly Media.

Wu, Z., & Chin, O. B. (2014). From big data to data science: A multi-disciplinary perspective. *Big Data Research, 1*, 1–10. doi:10.1016/j.bdr.2014.08.002

Xueyan, Z., & Depeng, G. (2014). Application of big data technology in marketing decisions for railway freight. In *Proceedings of the International Conference of Logistics Engineering and Management.*

Yu, C., & Boyd, J. (2016). Fb+-tree for big data management. *Big Data Research, 4*, 25–36. doi:10.1016/j.bdr.2015.11.003

Zaharia, M., Chowdhury, M., Das, T., Dave, A., Ma, J., McCauley, M., ... & Stoica, I. (2012). Resilient distributed datasets: A fault-tolerant abstraction for in-memory cluster computing. In Proceedings of the USENIX conference on networked systems design and implementation.

Zarembski, A. M. (2014). Some examples of big data in railroad engineering. In Proceedings of the IEEE international conference on big data. doi:10.1109/BigData.2014.7004437

Zhao, Y., Xu, T., & Hai-feng, W. (2014). Text mining based fault diagnosis of vehicle on-board equipment for high speed railway. In *Proceedings of the 17th IEEE international conference on intelligent transportation systems.*

Zhou, H., Huang, G. B., Lin, Z., Wang, H., & Soh, Y. C. (2015). Stacked extreme learning machines. *IEEE Transactions on Cybernetics, 45*(9), 2013–2025. doi:10.1109/TCYB.2014.2363492 PMID:25361517

Zhu, Y. T., Wang, F. Z., Shan, X. H., & Lv, X. Y. (2014). K-medoids clustering based on map-reduce and optimal search of medoids. In *Proceedings of the International conference on computer science education.*

Compilation of References

Abbasi, A., Rashidi, T. H., Maghrebi, M., & Waller, S. T. (2015). Utilizing Location Based Social Media in Travel Survey Methods: bringing Twitter data into the play. In Proceedings of the 8th ACM SIGSPATIAL International Workshop on Location-Based Social Networks. ACM.

Agard, B., Morency, C., & Trépanier, M. (2006, May 17–19). Mining public transport user behavior from smart card data. In *Proceedings of the 12th IFAC Symposium on Information Control Problems in Manufacturing INCOM '06*, Saint-Etienne, France.

Aguirre, E., Lopez-Iturri, P., Azpilicueta, L., Redondo, A., Astrain, J. J., Villadangos, J., & Falcone, F. et al. (2017). Design and implementation of context aware applications with wireless sensor network support in urban train transportation environments. *IEEE Sensors Journal*, 17(1), 169–178. doi:10.1109/JSEN.2016.2624739

Alastairfrance1989. (2011, May 26). *Railway Tunnel- LIDAR* [YouTube video]. Retrieved from https://www.youtube.com/watch?v=gJi69BTSbeQ

Albrecht, T., & Dasigi, M. (2016). ON-TIME: A Framework for Integrated Railway Network Operation Management. In *Traffic Management* (pp. 167–181). Hoboken, NJ, USA: John Wiley & Sons, Inc. doi:10.1002/9781119307822.ch12

Ali, A., Qadir, J., Rasool, R. U., Sathiaseelan, A., & Zwitter, A. (n. d.). Big Data for Development: Applications and Techniques. National University of Science and Technology, Pakistan. Retrieved from https://arxiv.org/pdf/1602.07810.pdf

Al-Jarrah, A. Y., Yoo, P. D., Muhaidat, S., Karagiannidis, G. K., & Taha, K. (2015). Efficient machine learning for big data: A review. *Big Data Research*, 2(3), 87–93. doi:10.1016/j.bdr.2015.04.001

Alrwisan, A., Ross, J., & Williams, D. (2011). Medication incidents reported to an online incident reporting system. *European Journal of Clinical Pharmacology*, 67(5), 527–532. doi:10.1007/s00228-010-0986-z PMID:21240481

Amadi-Echendu, J. E., Brown, K., Willett, R., & Mathew, J. (Eds.). (2010). Definitions, concepts and scope of engineering asset management. In Engineering Asset Management Review (Vol. 1). Springer. doi:10.1007/978-1-84996-178-3

Amaral, V., Marques, F., Lourenço, A., Barata, J., & Santana, P. (2016). Laser-based obstacle detection at railway level crossings. *Journal of Sensors*.

Aminmansour, S., Maire, F., & Wullems, C. (2014, November). Near-miss event detection at railway level crossings. In *Proceedings of the 2014 International Conference on Digital Image Computing: Techniques and Applications (DICTA)* (pp. 1-8). IEEE. doi:10.1109/DICTA.2014.7008119

Angelov, P., Manolopoulos, Y., Iliadis, L., Roy, A., & Vellasco, M. (2016). Advances in Big Data. Springer.

Anggoro, R., Kitasuka, T., Nakamura, R., & Aritsugi, M. (2012). Performance Evaluation of AODV and AOMDV with Probabilistic Relay in VANET Environments. In *Proceedings of the Third International Conference on Networking and Computing*. doi:10.1109/ICNC.2012.47

Anguita, D., Ghio, A., Ridella, S., & Sterpi, D. (2009). K-fold cross validation for error rate estimate in support vector machines. In *Proceedings of the International conference on data mining*.

Anguita, D., Ghio, A., Oneto, L., & Ridella, S. (2012). In-sample and out-of-sample model selection and error estimation for support vector machines. *IEEE Transactions on Neural Networks and Learning Systems*, *23*(9), 1390–1406. doi:10.1109/TNNLS.2012.2202401 PMID:24807923

Ansaldo STS-A Hitachi Group Company. (n. d.). *Weigh In Motion(WIM)Wheel Impact Load Detector(WILD)* Retrieved from http://www.ansaldo-sts.com/sites/ansaldosts.message-asp.com/files/imce/asts_hitachi_wim_wild_lr.pdf

Apache Software Foundation. (2015). *Apache Wink – a simple yet solid framework for building RESTful Web Services*. Retrieved January 17, 2017, from https://wink.apache.org/

Apache. (2017). Hadoop. Retrieved from http://hadoop.apache.org/

Apache. (2017). Spark. Retrieved from http://spark.apache.org/

Aridhi, S., & Nguifo, E. M. (2016). Big graph mining: Frameworks and techniques. *Big Data Research*, *6*, 1–10. doi:10.1016/j.bdr.2016.07.002

Arlot, S., & Celisse, A. (2010). A survey of cross-validation procedures for model selection. *Statistics Surveys*, *4*(0), 40–79. doi:10.1214/09-SS054

Arthur, D., & Vassilvitskii, S. (2007). K-means++: the advantages of careful seeding. In *Proceedings of the Eighteenth Annual ACM-SIAM Symposium on Discrete Algorithms* (pp. 1027–1035).

Atéchian, T. (2010). Protocole de routage géo-multipoint hybride et mécanisme d'acheminement de données pour les réseaux ad hoc de véhicules (VANETs).Thesis Institut National des Sciences Appliquées de Lyon.

ATOC (Association of Train Operating Companies). (2012). Approved Code of Practice – Passenger Information During Disruption. Retrieved 05/11/14 from http://www.atoc.org/clientfiles/files/ACOP015v3%20-%20PIDD%20(2).pdf

Avineri, E. (2004). A Cumulative Prospect Theory Approach to Passengers Behavior Modeling: Waiting Time Paradox Revisited. *Journal of Intelligent Transportation Systems*, *8*(4), 195–204. doi:10.1080/15472450490523856

Aydin, I., Karakose, M., & Akin, E. (2015). Anomaly detection using a modified kernel-based tracking in the pantograph–catenary system. *Expert Systems with Applications*, *42*(2), 938–948. doi:10.1016/j.eswa.2014.08.026

Aytekin, C., Rezaeitabar, Y., Dogru, S., & Ulusoy, I. (2015). Railway fastener inspection by real-time machine vision. IEEE Transactions on Systems, Man, and Cybernetics. *Systems*, *45*(7), 1101–1107.

Azaria, A., Ekblaw, A., Vieira, T., & Lippman, A. (2016). MedRec: Using Blockchain for Medical Data Access and Permission Management. In *2016 2nd International Conference on Open and Big Data (OBD)* (pp. 25–30). IEEE. doi:10.1109/OBD.2016.11

B'egin, L., Germain, P., Laviolette, F., & Roy, J. F. (2016). Pac-bayesian bounds based on the r'enyi divergence. In *Proceedings of the International conference on artificial intelligence and statistics*.

Badreddine, G. (2012). Algorithme De Clusterisation Et Protocoles De Routage Dans Les Réseaux Ad Hoc [Thèse de doctorat]. de l'université de Technologie de Belfort-Montbéliard Tunisie.

Bagchi, M., & White, P. R. (2005). The potential of public transport smart card data. *Transport Policy, 12*(5), 464–474. doi:10.1016/j.tranpol.2005.06.008

Baglee, D., & Marttonen, S. (2014, January). The need for Big Data collection and analyses to support the development of an advanced maintenance strategy. In *Proceedings of the International Conference on Data Mining (DMIN)* (p. 3). The Steering Committee of The World Congress in Computer Science, Computer Engineering and Applied Computing (WorldComp).

Bahga, A., & Madisetti, V. K. (2016). Blockchain Platform for Industrial Internet of Things. *Journal of Software Engineering and Applications, 9*(10), 533–546. doi:10.4236/jsea.2016.910036

Bai, Y., Ho, T. K., Mao, B., Ding, Y., & Chen, S. (2014). Energy-efficient locomotive operation for chinese mainline railways by fuzzy predictive control. *IEEE Transactions on Intelligent Transportation Systems, 15*(3), 938–948. doi:10.1109/TITS.2013.2292712

Bai, Z., & Jung, S. H. (2015). Image-based Subway Security System by Histogram Projection Technology. *Journal of Korea Multimedia Society, 18*(3), 287–297. doi:10.9717/kmms.2015.18.3.287

Balandin, S., Andreev, S., & Koucheryavy, Y. (2015). *Internet of Things, Smart Spaces, and Next Generation Networks and Systems. Ebook.* Springer. doi:10.1007/978-3-319-23126-6

Barry, J. J., Newhouser, R., Rahbee, A., & Sayeda, S. (2002). Origin and destination estimation in New York City with automated fare system data. *Transportation Research Record, 1817*, 183–187. doi:10.3141/1817-24

Barry, J., Freiner, R., & Slavin, H. (2009). Use of entry-only automatic fare collection data to estimate linked transit trips in New York City. *Transportation Research Record, 2112*, 53–61. doi:10.3141/2112-07

Bartlett, P. L., Boucheron, S., & Lugosi, G. (2002). Model selection and error estimation. *Machine Learning, 48*(1-3), 85–113. doi:10.1023/A:1013999503812

Bartlett, P. L., Bousquet, O., & Mendelson, S. (2005). Local rademacher complexities. *Annals of Statistics, 33*(4), 1497–1537. doi:10.1214/009053605000000282

Bartlett, P. L., & Mendelson, S. (2002). Rademacher and gaussian complexities: Risk bounds and structural results. *Journal of Machine Learning Research, 3*, 463–482.

Basagni, S., Marco, C. I. S., & Giordano, S. (2012). Ad Hoc networking [eBook]. IEEE Press.

Beckett, D., & McBride, B. (2004). RDF/XML syntax specification (revised). *W3C recommendation, 10.* Retrieved April 13, 2017, from http://www.w3.org/TR/rdf-syntax-grammar

Beckett, D., Berners-Lee, T., & Prud'hommeaux, E. (2008). Turtle-terse RDF triple language. *W3C Team Submission, 14*(7). Retrieved April 13, 2017, from https://www.w3.org/TeamSubmission/turtle/

Beckmann, U., Baldwin, I., Hart, G., & Runciman, W. (1996). The Australian Incident Monitoring Study in Intensive Care: AIMS-ICU. An analysis of the first year of reporting.

Belmonte, F., Schön, W., Heurley, L., & Capel, R. (2011). Interdisciplinary safety analysis of complex socio-technological systems based on the functional resonance accident model: An application to railway traffic supervision. *Reliability Engineering & System Safety, 96*(2), 237–249. doi:10.1016/j.ress.2010.09.006

Bengio, Y. (2009). Learning deep architectures for AI. *Foundations and trends in Machine Learning, 2*(1), 1-127.

Bengio, Y., Courville, A., & Vincent, P. (2013). Representation learning: A review and new perspectives. *IEEE Transactions on Pattern Analysis and Machine Intelligence, 35*(8), 1798–1828. doi:10.1109/TPAMI.2013.50 PMID:23787338

Berg, A., Öfjäll, K., Ahlberg, J., & Felsberg, M. (2015, June). Detecting rails and obstacles using a train-mounted thermal camera. In *Proceedings of the Scandinavian Conference on Image Analysis* (pp. 492-503). Springer International Publishing. doi:10.1007/978-3-319-19665-7_42

Berger, A., Gebhardt, A., Müller-Hannemann, M., & Ostrowski, M. (2011). Stochastic delay prediction in large train networks. Informatics.

Bergstra, J., & Bengio, Y. (2012). Random search for hyper-parameter optimization. *Journal of Machine Learning Research, 13*, 281–305.

Beydoun, K. (2009). Conception d'un protocole de routage hierarchique pour les réseaux de capteurs [Thesis]. L'U.F.R des sciances et technique de l'université de Franche-Comte.

Bin, Z., & Wensheng, X. (2015). An improved algorithm for high speed train's maintenance data mining based on mapreduce. In *Proceedings of the International conference on cloud computing and big data.* doi:10.1109/CCBD.2015.27

Bisio, F., Gastaldo, P., Zunino, R., & Cambria, E. (2015). A learning scheme based on similarity functions for affective common-sense reasoning. In *Proceedings of the International joint conference on neural networks.* doi:10.1109/IJCNN.2015.7280633

Biswas, K., & Muthukkumarasamy, V. (2016). Securing Smart Cities Using Blockchain Technology. In *Proceedings of the 2016 IEEE 18th International Conference on High Performance Computing and Communications; IEEE 14th International Conference on Smart City; IEEE 2nd International Conference on Data Science and Systems (HPCC/SmartCity/DSS)* (pp. 1392–1393). IEEE. doi:10.1109/HPCC-SmartCity-DSS.2016.0198

Blei, D. M. (2012). Probabilistic topic models. *Communications of the ACM, 55*(4), 77–84. doi:10.1145/2133806.2133826

Blei, D. M., Ng, A. Y., & Jordan, M. I. (2003). Latent Dirichlet Allocation. *Journal of Machine Learning Research, 3*, 993–1022.

Bocciolone, M., Caprioli, A., Cigada, A., & Collina, A. (2007). A measurement system for quick rail inspection and effective track maintenance strategy. *Mechanical Systems and Signal Processing, 21*(3), 1242–1254. doi:10.1016/j.ymssp.2006.02.007

Bollen, J., Mao, H., & Zeng, X.-J. (2011). Twitter mood predicts the stock market. Journal of computer science, 2(1), 21-28.

Bollen, J., Mao, H., & Pepe, A. (2011). Modeling Public Mood and Emotion: Twitter Sentiment and Socio-Economic Phenomena. In *Proceedings of the Fifth International AAAI Conference on Weblogs and Social Media.*

Bousquet, O., & Elisseeff, A. (2002). Stability and generalization. *Journal of Machine Learning Research, 2*, 499–526.

Bracciali, A. (2012). Wayside train monitoring systems: A state-of-the-art and running safety implications. In *Proceedings if the First International Conference on Railway Technology: research, Development and Maintenance*, LasPalmas de Gran Canaria, Spain. doi:10.4203/ijrt.1.1.11

Brandon, D. (2016). The Blockchain: the future of business information systems? *International Journal of the Academic Business World, 10*(2), 33–41.

Branishtov, S. A., Vershinin, Y. A., Tumchenok, D. A., & Shirvanyan, A. M. (2014). Graph methods for estimation of railway capacity. In *Proceedings of the IEEE 17th international conference on intelligent transportation systems* (pp. 525-530). doi:10.1109/ITSC.2014.6957743

Bregman, S., & Watkins, K. E. (2013, Oct 2). Best Practices for Transportation Agency Use of Social Media. Retrieved from https://books.google.co.in/books?id=TFzSBQAAQBAJ&dq=train+delay+prediction+using+social+media

Brehar, R., Vancea, C., Mariţa, T., Giosan, I., & Nedevschi, S. (2015, September). Pedestrian detection in the context of multiple-sensor data alignment for far-infrared and stereo vision sensors. In *Proceedings of the 2015 IEEE International Conference on Intelligent Computer Communication and Processing (ICCP)* (pp. 385-392). IEEE. doi:10.1109/ICCP.2015.7312690

Brewer, J. (2011). *National Information Systems Catalogue for Non-Network Rail Systems.* Retrieved from www.sparkrail.org

British Transport Police. (n. d.). Football policing. Retrieved from http://www.btp.police.uk/advice_and_info/how_we_tackle_crime/football_policing.aspx

Buckley, S., & Lightman, D. (2015). Ready or not, big data is coming to a city (transportation agency) near you. In *Proceedings of the Transportation Research Board 94th Annual Meeting* (No. 15-5156).

Buggy, S. J., James, S. W., Staines, S., Carroll, R., Kitson, P., Farrington, D., & Tatam, R. P. et al. (2016). Railway track component condition monitoring using optical fibre Bragg grating sensors. *Measurement Science & Technology, 27*(5), 055201. doi:10.1088/0957-0233/27/5/055201

Burgholzer, W., Bauer, G., Posset, M., & Jammernegg, W. (2013). Analyzing the impact of disruptions in intermodal transport networks: A micro simulation-based model. *Decision Support Systems, 54*(4), 1580–1586. doi:10.1016/j.dss.2012.05.060

Burke, B. (2009). *RESTful Java with JaX-RS.* O'Reilly Media, Inc.

Burke, B. (2013). *RESTful Java with Jax-RS 2.0.* O'Reilly Media, Inc.

Burns, B., Grant, B., Oppenheimer, D., Brewer, E., & Wilkes, J. (2016). Borg, omega, and kubernetes. *Communications of the ACM, 59*(5), 50–57. doi:10.1145/2890784

Cambria, E., Huang, G. B., Kasun, L. L. C., Zhou, H., Vong, C. M., Lin, J., & Liu, J. et al. (2013). Extreme learning machines. *IEEE Intelligent Systems, 28*(6), 30–59. doi:10.1109/MIS.2013.140

Cañete, E., Chen, J., Díaz, M., Llopis, L., & Rubio, B. (2015). Sensor4PRI: A sensor platform for the protection of railway infrastructures. *Sensors (Basel, Switzerland), 15*(3), 4996–5019. doi:10.3390/s150304996 PMID:25734648

Carroll, J. J., Dickinson, I., Dollin, C., Reynolds, D., Seaborne, A., & Wilkinson, K. (2004, May). Jena: implementing the semantic web recommendations. In *Proceedings of the 13th international World Wide Web conference on Alternate track papers & posters* (pp. 74-83). ACM. doi:10.1145/1013367.1013381

Caruana, R., Lawrence, S., & Lee, G. (2001). Overfitting in neural nets: Backpropagation, conjugate gradient, and early stopping. In Neural information processing systems.

Catapult Transport Systems. (2016). Transport Data Revolution. Retrieved from https://ts.catapult.org.uk/wp-content/uploads/2016/04/The-Transport-Data-Revolution.pdf

Catherine, M. B., & Alexander, C. N. (n. d.). Predicting Bus Arrivals Using One Bus Away Real-Time Data. University of Washington, Seattle, WA. Retrieved from https://homes.cs.washington.edu/~anied/papers/AConradNied_OneBusAway_Writeup_20131209.pdf

Catoni, O. (2007). *Pac-bayesian supervised classification: The thermodynamics of statistical learning.* Institute of Mathematical Statistics.

Cavaness, C. (2006). *Quartz Job Scheduling Framework: Building Open Source Enterprise Applications.* Pearson Education.

Chandio, A. A., Tziritas, N., & Xu, C. Z. (2015). Big-data processing techniques and their challenges in transport domain. *ZTE Communications.*

Chen, J., & Roberts, C. (2006, November). Effective condition monitoring of line side assets. In *Proceedings of the Institution of Engineering and Technology International Conference on Railway Condition Monitoring '06* (pp. 78-83). IET. doi:10.1049/ic:20060048

Chen, M., Mao, S., Zhang, Y., & Leung, V. C. (2014). *Big data: related technologies, challenges and future prospects.* Heidelberg: Springer. doi:10.1007/978-3-319-06245-7

Chen, S., Tan, J., Claramunt, C., & Ray, C. (2011). Multi-scale and multi-modal GIS-T data model. *Journal of Transport Geography, 19*(1), 147–161. doi:10.1016/j.jtrangeo.2009.09.006

Chen, Y., & An, A. (2016). Approximate parallel high utility itemset mining. *Big Data Research, 6,* 26–42. doi:10.1016/j.bdr.2016.07.001

Chodorow, K. (2013). *MongoDB: the definitive guide.* O'Reilly Media, Inc.

Christidis, K., & Devetsikiotis, M. (2016). Blockchains and Smart Contracts for the Internet of Things. *IEEE Access, 4,* 2292–2303. doi:10.1109/ACCESS.2016.2566339

Chu, K. K., & Chapleau, R. (2013). Smart card validation data as multi-day transit panel survey to investigate individual and aggregate variation in travel behavior. In J. Zmud, M. Lee-Gosselin, M. Munizaga, & J. A. Carasco (Eds.), *Transport survey methods: Best practice for decision making* (pp. 649–671). Bingley: Emerald. doi:10.1108/9781781902882-036

Chung, J., & Mustafaraj, E. (2011). Can Collective Sentiment Expressed on Twitter Predict Political Elections? In *Proceedings of the 25th AAAI Conference on Artificial Intelligence*, San Francisco, CA (pp 1770-1771).

Clausen & P. Jacquet. Optimized Link State Routing Protocol (OLSR). (2003). RFC3626 T.

Clement Escoffier, M. K. (2015). *Vert.x – a toolkit for building reactive applications on the JVM.* Retrieved January 17, 2017, from http://vertx.io/

Codd, E. F. (1970). A relational model of data for large shared data banks. *Communications of the ACM, 13*(6), 377–387. doi:10.1145/362384.362685

CodrinArsene. (2016, July). IoT ideas that will soon revolutionize our world in 8 ways. Media Labs. Retrieved from https://www.ymedialabs.com/internet-of-things-ideas/

Collins, C., Hasan, S., & Ukkusuri, S. V. (2013). A novel transit rider satisfaction metric: Rider sentiments measured from online social media data. *Journal of Public Transportation, 16*(2), 21–45. doi:10.5038/2375-0901.16.2.2

Collomb, A., & Sok, K. (2016). Blockchain / Distributed Ledger Technology (DLT): What Impact on the Financial Sector? *Communications & Stratégies,* (103), 93–111. Retrieved from https://search.proquest.com/docview/1841718518

Colombo, P., & Ferrari, E. (2015). Privacy aware access control for big data: A research roadmap. *Big Data Research, 2*(4), 145–154. doi:10.1016/j.bdr.2015.08.001

Cordeau, J. F., Toth, P., & Vigo, D. (1998). A survey of optimization models for train routing and scheduling. *Transportation Science, 32*(4), 380–404. doi:10.1287/trsc.32.4.380

Corsar, D., Markovic, M., Gault, P. E., Mehdi, M., Edwards, P., Nelson, J. D., & Sripada, S. et al. (2015). TravelBot: Journey Disruption Alerts Utilising Social Media and Linked Data. In *Proceedings of the Posters and Demonstrations Track of the 14th International Semantic Web Conference (ISWC '15).*

Cottrill, C. D., & Derrible, S. (2015). Leveraging big data for the development of transport sustainability indicators. *Journal of Urban Technology, 22*(1), 45–64. doi:10.1080/10630732.2014.942094

Cottrill, C., Gault, P., Yeboah, G., Nelson, J. D., Anable, J., & Budd, T. (2017). Tweeting Transit: An examination of social media strategies for transport information management during a large event. *Transportation Research Part C, Emerging Technologies*, 77, 421–432. doi:10.1016/j.trc.2017.02.008

Dadashi, N., Scott, A., Wilson, J. R., & Mills, A. (2013). *Rail Human Factors: Supporting reliability, safety and cost reduction*. CRC Press. doi:10.1201/b13827

Dalal, N., & Triggs, B. (2005, June). Histograms of oriented gradients for human detection. In *Proceedings of the 2005 IEEE Computer Society Conference on Computer Vision and Pattern Recognition (CVPR'05)* (Vol. 1, pp. 886-893). IEEE. doi:10.1109/CVPR.2005.177

Dallas, A. (2014). *RESTful Web Services with Dropwizard*. Packt Publishing Ltd.

Dan, K., & Manning, C. D. (2003). Accurate unlexicalized parsing. In *Proceedings of the 41st Meeting of the Association for Computational Linguistics* (pp 423 – 430).

Data.Gov.UK. (2015). *National Rail Passenger Survey* (csv data file). Retrieved from https://data.gov.uk/dataset/national-rail-passenger-survey

Davey, E. (2012). Rail traffic management systems (TMS). In IET professional development course railway signalling and control systems.

Davis, I. (2011). *TRANSIT: A vocabulary for describing transit systems and routes*. Retrieved January 23, 2017, from http://vocab.org/transit/terms.html

Dean, J., & Ghemawat, S. (2008). Map-reduce: Simplified data processing on large clusters. *Communications of the ACM*, 51(1), 107–113. doi:10.1145/1327452.1327492

Deci, E. L., & Ryan, R. M. (1991). A motivational approach to self: Integration in personality. In *Proceedings of Nebraska Symposium on Motivation* (vol. 38, pp. 237-288). Lincoln, NE: University of Nebraska Press.

Delhi Metro Rail Corporation Limited. (2013, July). Findings of Customer Satisfaction Survey conducted by DMRC. Retrieved from http://www.delhimetrorail.com/whatnew_details.aspx?id=KvlaOU2MsdElld

Delhi Metro Rail Corporation Limited. (2014). Delhi Metro to conduct online Customer satisfaction survey. Retrieved from http://www.delhimetrorail.com/whatnew_details.aspx?id=KvlaOU2MsdElld

Denai, M. A., Palis, F., & Zeghbib, A. (2007). Modeling and control of nonlinear systems using soft computing techniques. *Applied Soft Computing*, 7(3), 728–738. doi:10.1016/j.asoc.2005.12.005

Dennis, R., & Owen, G. (2015). Rep on the block: A next generation reputation system based on the blockchain. In *Proceedings of the 2015 10th International Conference for Internet Technology and Secured Transactions (ICITST)* (pp. 131–138). IEEE. doi:10.1109/ICITST.2015.7412073

Devillaine, F., Munizaga, M. A., & Trepanier, M. (2012). Detection activities of public transport users by analyzing smart card data. *Transportation Research Record*, 2276, 48–55. doi:10.3141/2276-06

DeVore, R., Petrova, G., Hielsberg, M., Owens, L., Clack, B., & Sood, A. (2013). Processing terrain point cloud data. *SIAM Journal on Imaging Sciences*, 6(1), 1–31. doi:10.1137/110856009

DfT. (2009), NATA (New Approach for Transport Appraisal) Refresh: Appraisal for a Sustainable Transport System, UK Department for Transport Retrieved from www.dft.gov.uk/pgr/economics/integratedtransporteconomics3026

Dhankhar, S. & Agrawal, S. (2014). VANETs: A Survey on Routing Protocols and Issues. *International Journal of Innovative Research in Science, Engineering and Technology*, 3(6).

Diday, E., & Simon, J. (1980). *Clustering analysis Digital pattern recognition* (pp. 47–94). Springer. doi:10.1007/978-3-642-67740-3_3

Dietrich, C., Palm, G., & Schwenker, F. (2003). Decision templates for the classification of bioacoustic time series. *Information Fusion, 4*(2), 101–109. doi:10.1016/S1566-2535(03)00017-4

Digital Railway. (2017). Digital Railway - Frequently Asked Questions. Retrieved from http://digitalrailway.co.uk/resources/

Dollár, P., Wojek, C., Schiele, B., & Perona, P. (2009, June). Pedestrian detection: A benchmark. In *Proceedings of the IEEE Conference on Computer Vision and Pattern Recognition CVPR '09* (pp. 304-311). IEEE. doi:10.1109/CVPR.2009.5206631

Dollevoet, T., Corman, F., DAriano, A., & Huisman, D. (2014). An iterative optimization framework for delay management and train scheduling. *Flexible Services and Manufacturing Journal, 26*(4), 490–515. doi:10.1007/s10696-013-9187-2

Dotoli, M., Epicoco, N., Falagario, M., Seatzu, C., & Turchiano, B. (2016). A decision support system for optimizing operations at intermodal railroad terminals. IEEE Transactions on Systems, Man, and Cybernetics: Systems, 47(3), 487-501.

Duin, R. P. (2002). The combining classifier: to train or not to train? In *Proceedings of the 16th International Conference on Pattern Recognition* (Vol. 2, pp. 765-770). IEEE. doi:10.1109/ICPR.2002.1048415

Dwork, C., Feldman, V., Hardt, M., Pitassi, T., Reingold, O., & Roth, A. (2014). Preserving statistical validity in adaptive data analysis. arxiv:1411.2664(v3)

Dwork, C., Feldman, V., Hardt, M., Pitassi, T., Reingold, O., & Roth, A. (2015a). Generalization in adaptive data analysis and holdout reuse. arxiv:1506.02629(v2)

Dwork, C., Feldman, V., Hardt, M., Pitassi, T., Reingold, O., & Roth, A. (2015b). Generalization in adaptive data analysis and holdout reuse. In Neural information processing systems.

Dwork, C., Feldman, V., Hardt, M., Pitassi, T., Reingold, O., & Roth, A. (2015c). Preserving statistical validity in adaptive data analysis. In *Proceedings of the Annual ACM symposium on theory of computing.* doi:10.1145/2746539.2746580

Dwork, C., Feldman, V., Hardt, M., Pitassi, T., Reingold, O., & Roth, A. (2015d). The reusable holdout: Preserving validity in adaptive data analysis. *Science, 349*(6248), 636–638. doi:10.1126/science.aaa9375 PMID:26250683

El Ali, F. (2012). *Communication unicast dans les réseaux mobiles dynamiques.* Université de Technologie de Compiègne.

Elattar, E. E., Goulermas, J., & Wu, Q. H. (2010). Electric load forecasting based on locally weighted support vector regression. *IEEE Transactions on Systems, Man and Cybernetics. Part C, Applications and Reviews, 40*(4), 438–447. doi:10.1109/TSMCC.2010.2040176

Elkiss, A. (2011). *A weather ontology.* Retrieved January 23, 2017, from http://www.csd.abdn.ac.uk/˜ggrimnes/AgentCities/WeatherAgent/weather-ont.daml

EMC, Inc. (2014, February 07). *EMC's 3D Mobile Lidar-Rail Road* [YouTube video]. Retrieved from https://www.youtube.com/watch?v=r2xlCwOLORc

Émilie Warden, P. (2011). *Big data glossary.* O'Reilly Media, Inc.

Enzweiler, M., & Gavrila, D. M. (2009). Monocular pedestrian detection: Survey and experiments. *IEEE Transactions on Pattern Analysis and Machine Intelligence, 31*(12), 2179–2195. doi:10.1109/TPAMI.2008.260 PMID:19834140

Espino, J. C., & Stanciulescu, B. (2012, September). Rail extraction technique using gradient information and a priori shape model. In *Proceedings of the 2012 15th International IEEE Conference on Intelligent Transportation Systems* (pp. 1132-1136). IEEE. doi:10.1109/ITSC.2012.6338870

Ess, A., Leibe, B., & Van Gool, L. (2007, October). Depth and appearance for mobile scene analysis. In *Proceedings of the 2007 IEEE 11th International Conference on Computer Vision* (pp. 1-8). IEEE. doi:10.1109/ICCV.2007.4409092

European Commission. (2011). *Roadmap to a Single European Transport Area – Towards a competitive and resource efficient transport system*. Retrieved January 17, 2017 from http://eur-lex.europa.eu/legal-content/EN/TXT/PDF/?uri=CELEX:52011DC0144&from=EN

European Commission. (2011). Roadmap to a single European transport area—Towards a competitive and resource-efficient transport system (White Paper on transport). Luxembourg, Publications Office of the European Union.

European Union Agency for Railways. (2016). *Big Data In Railways Common occurrence Reporting Programme*. Retrieved from http://www.era.europa.eu/Document-Register/Pages/Big-data-in-railways.aspx

European Union Agency for Railways. (n. d.). Big data in railways. Retrieved from http://www.era.europa.eu/Document-Register/Documents/COR%20-%20Big%20Data.pdf

Even, A., & Shankaranarayanan, G. (2009). Utility cost perspectives in data quality management. *Journal of Computer Information Systems*, *50*(2), 127–135.

Faizrahnemoon, M., Schlote, A., Maggi, L., Crisostomi, E., & Shorten, R. (2015). A big-data model for multi-modal public transportation with application to macroscopic control and optimisation. *International Journal of Control*, *88*(11), 2354–2368. doi:10.1080/00207179.2015.1043582

Fan, B., Clive, R., & Weston, P. (2012). A comparison of algorithms for minimizing delay costs in disturbed railway traffic scenarios. *Journal of Rail Transport Planning & Management*, *2*(1-2), 22–33. doi:10.1016/j.jrtpm.2012.09.002

Fang, H. T., & Huang, D. S. (2004). Noise reduction in lidar signal based on discrete wavelet transform. *Optics Communications*, *233*(1), 67–76. doi:10.1016/j.optcom.2004.01.017

Faster XML, LLC. (2009) *Jackson JSON Processor Wiki*. Retrieved February 03, 2017 from http://wiki.fasterxml.com/JacksonHome

Favo, F., Bocchetti, G., Mazzino, N., & Lancia, A. (2010). Train Conformity Check System; Technology and current operation experience. In Proceedings of the Electrical Systems for Aircraft, Railway and Ship Propulsion (ESARS). IEEE.

Feng, H., Jiang, Z., Xie, F., Yang, P., Shi, J., & Chen, L. (2014). Automatic fastener classification and defect detection in vision-based railway inspection systems. *IEEE Transactions on Instrumentation and Measurement*, *63*(4), 877–888. doi:10.1109/TIM.2013.2283741

Fernández-López, M., Gómez-Pérez, A., & Juristo, N. (1997). Methontology: from ontological art towards ontological engineering.

Figueres-Esteban, M., Hughes, P., & Van Gulijk, C. (2015). The role of data visualization in railway big data risk analysis. *Paper presented at the European Safety and Reliability Conference*. doi:10.1201/b19094-377

Fiosina, J., Fiosins, M., & Müller, J. (2013). Big Data Processing and Mining for the future ICT-based Smart Transportation Management System.

Floyd, S., & Warmuth, M. (1995). Sample compression, learnability, and the Vapnik-Chervonenkis dimension. *Machine Learning*, *21*(3), 269–304. doi:10.1007/BF00993593

Foundation, J. S. (2015). *Node-RED – A visual tool for wiring the Internet of Things*. Retrieved February 3, 2017, from http://nodered.org/

Fu, K., Nune, R., & Tao, J. X. (2015). Social Media Data Analysis for Traffic Incident Detection and Management. In *Proceedings of the Transportation Research Board 94th Annual Meeting*.

Fujitsu Limited. (2016, July 19). Fujitsu Begins Field Trial for AI-Based Train Delay Prediction. Retrieved from http://www.fujitsu.com/global/about/resources/news/press-releases/2016/0719-02.html

Fumeo, E., Oneto, L., & Anguita, D. (2015). Condition based maintenance in railway transportation systems based on big data streaming analysis. In Proceedings of the INNS big data conference. doi:10.1016/j.procs.2015.07.321

Future of ITS. (2011). Website. Retrieved from https://mubbisherahmed.wordpress.com/2011/11/29/the-future-of-intelligent-transport-systems-its/

Gain Working Group B. (2003). *Guide to Methods and Tools for Airline Flight Safety Analysis*.

Gajderowicz, B. (2011). *Using decision trees for inductively driven semantic integration and ontology matching* [Doctoral dissertation]. Ryerson University, Program of Computer Science.

Galar, D., Palo, M., Van Horenbeek, A., & Pintelon, L. (2012). Integration of disparate data sources to perform maintenance prognosis and optimal decision making. Insight-non-destructive testing and condition monitoring, 54(8), 440-445.

Galar, D., Kans, M., & Schmidt, B. (2016). Big Data in Asset Management: Knowledge Discovery in Asset Data by the Means of Data Mining. In *Proceedings of the 10th World Congress on Engineering Asset Management (WCEAM '15)* (pp. 161-171). Springer International Publishing. doi:10.1007/978-3-319-27064-7_16

Galar, D., Thaduri, A., Catelani, M., & Ciani, L. (2015). Context awareness for maintenance decision making: A diagnosis and prognosis approach. *Measurement*, *67*, 137–150. doi:10.1016/j.measurement.2015.01.015

Gallaher, M. P., O'Conor, A. C., Dettbarn, J. L., & Gilday, L. T. (2004). Cost Analysis of Inadequate Interoperability in the U.S. Capital Facilities Industry. *NIST*. doi:10.6028/NIST.GCR.04-867

Gandhi, T., & Trivedi, M. M. (2007). Pedestrian protection systems: Issues, survey, and challenges. *IEEE Transactions on Intelligent Transportation Systems*, *8*(3), 413–430. doi:10.1109/TITS.2007.903444

Gano, D. L. (2011). *Reality Charting: Seven Steps to Effective Problem-solving and Strategies for Personal Success*. Apollonian Publications.

Gao, H., Tang, J., & Liu, H. (2012). Exploring Social-Historical Ties on Location-Based Social Networks.

Garc'ıa, C. R., Lehner, A., Strang, T., & Röckl, M. (2007). Comparison of Collision Avoidance Systems and Applicability to Rail Transport. In *Proceedings of the 7th International Conference on ITS ITST '07*.

García, C. R., Strang, T., & Lehner, A. (2008, July 22-24). A Broadcast Vehicle to Vehicle Communication System in Railway Environments. In *Proceedings of the ISVCS '08*, Dublin, Ireland. doi:10.4108/ICST.ISVCS2008.3805

Gardner, N., Haeusler, M. H., & Tomitsch, M. (2010). *Infostructure: A Transport Research Project*. Freerange Press.

Gartner, Inc. (2016). Gartner's 2016 Hype Cycle for Emerging Technologies Identifies Three Key Trends That Organizations Must Track to Gain Competitive Advantage. Retrieved May 29, 2017, from http://www.gartner.com/newsroom/id/3412017

Gartner. (n. d.). Gartner IT Glossary. Retrieved from http://www.gartner.com/it-glossary/big-data/

Gault, P., Corsar, D., Edwards, P., Nelson, J. D., & Cottrill, C. (2014). You'll Never Ride Alone: The Role of Social Media in Supporting the Bus Passenger Experience. In *Proceedings of the Ethnographic Praxis in Industry Conference* (Vol. 2014, No. 1, pp. 199-212).

Gavrila, D. M., & Munder, S. (2007). Multi-cue pedestrian detection and tracking from a moving vehicle. *International Journal of Computer Vision, 73*(1), 41–59. doi:10.1007/s11263-006-9038-7

Germain, P., Lacasse, A., Laviolette, F., Marchand, M., & Roy, J. F. (2015). Risk bounds for the majority vote: From a pac-bayesian analysis to a learning algorithm. *The Journal of Machine Learning Research, 16*(4), 787-860.

Geronimo, D., Lopez, A. M., Sappa, A. D., & Graf, T. (2010). Survey of pedestrian detection for advanced driver assistance systems. *IEEE Transactions on Pattern Analysis and Machine Intelligence, 32*(7), 1239–1258. doi:10.1109/TPAMI.2009.122 PMID:20489227

Gerónimo, D., Sappa, A., López, A., & Ponsa, D. (2007, April). Adaptive image sampling and windows classification for on-board pedestrian detection. In *Proceedings of the International Conference on Computer Vision Systems*, Bielefeld, Germany (Vol. 39).

Ghelardoni, L., Ghio, A., & Anguita, D. (2013). Energy load forecasting using empirical mode decomposition and support vector regression. *IEEE Transactions on Smart Grid, 4*(1), 549–556. doi:10.1109/TSG.2012.2235089

Glimm, B., Horrocks, I., Motik, B., Stoilos, G., & Wang, Z. (2014). HermiT: An OWL 2 reasoner. *Journal of Automated Reasoning, 53*(3), 245–269. doi:10.1007/s10817-014-9305-1

Gokasar, I., & Simsek, K. (2014). *Using "Big Data"*. For Analysis and Improvement of Public Transportation Systems in Istanbul.

Golightly, D., & Durk, J. (2016). Twitter as part of operational practice and passenger experience on the railways. In P.E. Waterson, E. Hubbard & R. Sims (Eds.), *Proceedings of EHF2016. Contemporary Ergonomics and Human Factors 2016*. Loughborough: CIEHF.

Golightly, D., & Dadashi, N. (2016). The characteristics of railway service disruption: Implications for disruption management. *Ergonomics*. PMID:27215348

Golightly, D., Dadashi, N., Sharples, S., & Dasigi, M. (2013). Disruption management processes during emergencies on the railways. *International Journal of Human Factors and Ergonomics, 2*(2), 175–195. doi:10.1504/IJHFE.2013.057619

Google. (2016). Google Compute Engine. Retrieved from 3 May 2016 from https://cloud.google.com/compute/

Goverde, R. M. P. (2010). A delay propagation algorithm for large-scale railway traffic networks. *Transportation Research Part C, Emerging Technologies, 18*(3), 269–287. doi:10.1016/j.trc.2010.01.002

Government of India (Railway Board). (2014) Disaster management plan Retrieved 05/11/14 from http://www.indianrailways.gov.in/railwayboard/uploads/directorate/safety/pdf/2014/DM_Plan_2014.pdf

Government of India Ministry of Railways. (2015, February). Indian Railways Lifeline of the nation (white paper).

Govoni, M., Vitucci, E. M., Degli Esposti, V., Guidi, F., Tartarini, G., & Dardari, D. (2015, July). Study of a UWB multistatic radar for railroad crossing surveillance. In *Proceedings of the 2015 IEEE International Symposium on Antennas and Propagation & USNC/URSI National Radio Science Meeting* (pp. 516-517). IEEE. doi:10.1109/APS.2015.7304644

Grant-Muller, S. M., Gal-Tzur, A., Minkov, E., Kuflik, T., Nocera, S., & Shoor, I. (2016). Transport Policy: Social Media and User-Generated Content in a Changing Information Paradigm. In Social media for government services (pp. 325–366). Springer International Publishing.

Gruber, T. R. (1993). A translation approach to portable ontology specifications. *Knowledge Acquisition, 5*(2), 199–220. doi:10.1006/knac.1993.1008

Guerra, C. F., García-Ródenas, R., Sánchez-Herrera, E. A., Rayo, D. V., & Clemente-Jul, C. (2016). Modeling of the behavior of alternative fuel vehicle buyers. A model for the location of alternative refueling stations. *International Journal of Hydrogen Energy, 41*(42), 19312–19319. doi:10.1016/j.ijhydene.2016.07.165

Guo, Z., Zhang, Z., & Li, W. (2012). Establishment of Intelligent Identification Management Platform in Railway Logistics System by Means of the Internet of Things, Establishment of Intelligent Identification Management Platform in Railway Logistics System by Means of the Internet of Things. *Procedia Engineering, 29*, 726–730. doi:10.1016/j.proeng.2012.01.031

Hadley, M., & Sandoz, P. (2009). JAX-RS: Java™ API for RESTful Web Services. *Java Specification Request, 311*. Retrieved January, 2017, from http://java.net/nonav/projects/jsr311/sources/svn/content/trunk/www/drafts/spec20080827.pdf

Hansen, I. A., Goverde, R. M. P., & Van Der Meer, D. J. (2010). Online train delay recognition and running time prediction. In Proceedings of the IEEE international conference on intelligent transportation systems. doi:10.1109/ITSC.2010.5625081

Harms-Ringdahl, L. (2013). *Guide to safety analysis for accident prevention*. IRS Riskhantering.

Hartenstein, H., & Laberteaux, K. (2010). VANET Vehicular Applications and Inter-Networking Technologies [eBook]. Wiley.

Hartong, M., Goel, R., Farkas, C., & Wijesekera, D. (2007). PTC-VANET Interactions to Prevent Highway Rail Intersection Crossing Accidents. In *Proceedings of the IEEE 65th Vehicular Technology Conference VTC '07* (pp. 2550-2554). IEEE.

Hasan, S., & Ukkusuri, S. V. (2014). Social contagion process in informal warning networks to understand evacuation timing behavior. *Journal of Public Health Management and Practice, 19*, S68–S69. doi:10.1097/PHH.0b013e31828f1a19 PMID:23529072

Hasan, S., & Ukkusuri, S. V. (2015). Urban activity pattern classification using topic models from online geo-location data. *Transportation Research Part C, Emerging Technologies, 44*, 363–381. doi:10.1016/j.trc.2014.04.003

Haseloff, S. (2005). Context awareness in information logistics.

Haug, A., Pedersen, A., & Arlbjørn, J. S. (2009). A classification model of ERP system data quality. *Industrial Management & Data Systems, 109*(8), 1053–1068. doi:10.1108/02635570910991292

HBL. (n. d.). RCAS infrastructure. Retrieved from http://www.hbl.in/publicimages/hbl-product3571TCAS%20Deployment%20Diagram.png

HBM. (2012). *ARGOS-a high accurate Wayside Train Monitoring System* Retrieved from https://www.unece.org/fileadmin/DAM/trans/main/temtermp/2012_2nd_Expert_Group_Meeting_Ankara/TEM_March_2012_Hbm_Argos_Ankara.pdf

He, R., Ai, B., Wang, G., Guan, K., Zhong, Z., Molisch, A. F., ... & Oestges, C. P. (2016). High-Speed Railway Communications: From GSM-R to LTE-R. *IEEE vehicular technology magazine, 11*(3), 49-58.

Heuwinkel, K., Deiters, W., Konigsmann, T., & Loffeler, T. (2003, May). Information logistics and wearable computing. In *Proceedings of the 23rd International Conference on Distributed Computing Systems Workshops* (pp. 283-288). IEEE. doi:10.1109/ICDCSW.2003.1203568

Hielkema, H., & Hongisto, P. (2013). Developing the Helsinki smart city: The role of competitions for open data applications. *Journal of the Knowledge Economy, 4*(2), 190–204. doi:10.1007/s13132-012-0087-6

Hilbert, M. (2015). Big Data for Development: A Review of Promises and Challenges. Development Policy Review. *martinhilbert.net*.

Hilbert, M. (2016). Big Data for Development: A Review of Promises and Challenges. *Development Policy Review*, *34*(1), 135-174.

Hinton, G. E., Osindero, S., & Teh, Y. W. (2006). A fast learning algorithm for deep belief nets. *Neural Computation*, *18*(7), 1527–1554. doi:10.1162/neco.2006.18.7.1527 PMID:16764513

Hipkin, I. (2001). Knowledge and IS implementation: Case studies in physical asset management. *International Journal of Operations & Production Management*, *21*(10), 1358–1380. doi:10.1108/01443570110404763

Hirsch, M., Opresnik, D., Zanetti, C., & Taisch, M. (2013, September). Leveraging Assets as a Service for Business Intelligence in Manufacturing Service Ecosystems. In *Proceedings of the 2013 IEEE 10th International Conference on e-Business Engineering (ICEBE)* (pp. 162-167). IEEE. doi:10.1109/ICEBE.2013.25

Hitzler, P., Krötzsch, M., Parsia, B., Patel-Schneider, P. F., & Rudolph, S. (2009). OWL 2 web ontology language primer. *W3C recommendation, 27*(1), 123. Retrieved April 13, 2017, from https://www.w3.org/TR/owl-primer/

Hodge, V. J., OKeefe, S., Weeks, M., & Moulds, A. (2015). Wireless sensor networks for condition monitoring in the railway industry: A survey. *IEEE Transactions on Intelligent Transportation Systems*, *16*(3), 1088–1106. doi:10.1109/TITS.2014.2366512

Hollnagel, E., & Speziali, J. (2008). *Study on Developments in Accident Investigation Methods: A Survey of the State-of-the-Art.*

Hori, M., Euzenat, J., & Patel-Schneider, P. (2003). OWL Web ontology language XML presentation syntax. *W3C Technical Report*. Retrieved April 13, 2017, from http://www.w3.org/TR/owl-xmlsyntax/

Horridge, M., Drummond, N., Goodwin, J., Rector, A. L., Stevens, R., & Wang, H. (2006, November). The Manchester OWL Syntax. In OWLed (Vol. 216).

Houghton, R. J., & Golightly, D. (2011). Should a signaller look at twitter? The value of user data to transport control. Retrieved from http://de2011.computing.dundee.ac.uk

https://en.wikipedia.org/wiki/Multiprotocol_Label_Switching

Hua, G.B. (2016). *Smart Cities as a Solution for Reducing Urban Waste and Pollution.*

Huang, G. B., Zhu, Q. Y., & Siew, C. K. (2004). Extreme learning machine: a new learning scheme of feedforward neural networks. In Proceedings of the IEEE international joint conference on neural networks.

Huang, G. B. (2014). An insight into extreme learning machines: Random neurons, random features and kernels. *Cognitive Computation*, *6*(3), 376–390. doi:10.1007/s12559-014-9255-2

Huang, G. B. (2015). What are extreme learning machines? Filling the gap between frank Rosenblatts dream and john von Neumanns puzzle. *Cognitive Computation*, *7*(3), 263–278. doi:10.1007/s12559-015-9333-0

Huang, G. B., Chen, L., & Siew, C. K. (2006). Universal approximation using incremental constructive feedforward networks with random hidden nodes. *IEEE Transactions on Neural Networks*, *17*(4), 879–892. doi:10.1109/TNN.2006.875977 PMID:16856652

Huang, G. B., Li, M. B., Chen, L., & Siew, C. K. (2008). Incremental extreme learning machine with fully complex hidden nodes. *Neurocomputing*, *71*(4), 576–583. doi:10.1016/j.neucom.2007.07.025

Huang, G. B., Zhou, H., Ding, X., & Zhang, R. (2012). Extreme learning machine for regression and multiclass classification. *IEEE Transactions on Systems, Man, and Cybernetics. Part B, Cybernetics, 42*(2), 513–529. doi:10.1109/TSMCB.2011.2168604 PMID:21984515

Huang, G. B., Zhu, Q.-Y., & Siew, C.-K. (2006). Extreme learning machine: Theory and applications. *Neurocomputing, 70*(1), 489–501. doi:10.1016/j.neucom.2005.12.126

Huang, G., Huang, G. B., Song, S., & You, K. (2015). Trends in extreme learning machines: A review. *Neural Networks, 61*, 32–48. doi:10.1016/j.neunet.2014.10.001 PMID:25462632

Huckle, S., Bhattacharya, R., White, M., & Beloff, N. (2016). Internet of Things, Blockchain and Shared Economy Applications. *Procedia Computer Science, 98*, 461–466. https://doi.org/10.1016/j.procs.2016.09.074

Hughes, P., Figueres-Esteban, M., & Van Gulijk, C. (2016). Learning from text-based close call data. *Paper presented at the Safety and Reliability*. doi:10.1080/09617353.2016.1252083

Hu, J. (2010). Noise in laser. *Journal of Chifeng College, 26*(5), 112–113.

Hung, R., King, B., & Chen, W. (2015). Conceptual issues regarding the development of underground railway laser scanning systems. *ISPRS International journal of geo-information, 4*(1), 185-198.

India Today. (2011, April 18). Delhi Metro survey says it's a happy ride for all, India Today. Retrieved from http://indiatoday.intoday.in/story/survey-shows-commuters-travelling-on-delhi-metro-satisfied/1/135553.html

Indian Institute of Technology Kanpur & Research Designs and Standards Organization Lucknow. (n. d.). *Wheel Impact Load Detection System(WILD)* Retrieved from http://home.iitk.ac.in/~vyas/pdf/WILD_Final.pdf

Indian Railways. (n. d.). Evolution (printable section). Retrieved from http://www.indianrailways.gov.in/railwayboard/print_section.jsp?lang=0&id=0%2C1%2C261

Ingwald, A., & Kans, M. (2016). Service management models for railway infrastructure, an ecosystem perspective. In *Proceedings of the 10th World Congress on Engineering Asset Management (WCEAM '15)* (pp. 289-303). Springer International Publishing. doi:10.1007/978-3-319-27064-7_28

Irving, G., & Holden, J. (2016). How blockchain-timestamped protocols could improve the trustworthiness of medical science. *F1000 Research, 5*, 222. doi:10.12688/f1000research.8114.2 PMID:27239273

Jain, J., & Lyons, G. (2008). The gift of travel time. *Journal of Transport Geography, 16*(2), 81–89. doi:10.1016/j.jtrangeo.2007.05.001

Japan Trialing Machine Learning on Railways to Predict Delays. (2016, July 22). Retrieved from http://aibusiness.org/japan-trialing-machine-learning-on-railways-to-predict-delays/

Jina, X., Wah, B. W., Chenga, X., & Wanga, Y. (2015). Significance and challenges of big data research. *Big Data Research, 2*(2), 59–64. doi:10.1016/j.bdr.2015.01.006

Jin, X., & Jia, W. (2008). *Review of Researches on Artificial Neural Network* (pp. 65–66).

Johnson, C. (2003). *A Handbook of Incident and Accident Reporting*. Glasgow University Press.

Jose, S. (2016, April 06). Data analytics for smart railways. *The Hindu Business Line*. Retrieved from http://www.thehindubusinessline.com/opinion/data-analytics-for-smart-railways/article8442289.ece

Jun, W., Wu, T., & Zheng, Z. (2015, December). LIDAR and vision based pedestrian detection and tracking system. In *Proceedings of the 2015 IEEE International Conference on Progress in Informatics and Computing (PIC),* (pp. 118-122). IEEE.

Jwa, Y., & Sonh, G. (2015). Kalman filter based railway tracking from mobile lidar data. In *ISPRS Annals of Photogrammetry, Remote Sensing and Spatial Information Sciences* (pp. 159-164).

Kaigo, M. (2012). Social media usage during disasters and social capital: Twitter and the Great East Japan earthquake. *Keio Communication Review, 34,* 19–35.

Kaleli, F., & Akgul, Y. S. (2009, October). Vision-based railroad track extraction using dynamic programming. In *Proceedings of the 2009 12th International IEEE Conference on Intelligent Transportation Systems* (pp. 1-6). IEEE. doi:10.1109/ITSC.2009.5309526

Kamel, M. S., & Wanas, N. M. (2003, June). Data dependence in combining classifiers. In *Proceedings of the International Workshop on Multiple Classifier Systems* (pp. 1-14). Springer Berlin Heidelberg.

Kans, M., & Ingwald, A. (2016). Business Model Development Towards Service Management 4.0. Procedia CIRP, 47, 489-494.

Kaplan, A. M., & Haenlein, M. (2010). Users of the world, unite! The challenges and opportunities of Social Media. *Business Horizons, 53*(1), 59–68. doi:10.1016/j.bushor.2009.09.003

Karim, R., Westerberg, J., Galar, D., & Kumar, U. (2016). Maintenance Analytics–The New Know in Maintenance. *IFAC-PapersOnLine, 49*(28), 214-219. doi:10.1016/j.ifacol.2016.11.037

Kastrinaki, V., Zervakis, M., & Kalaitzakis, K. (2003). A survey of video processing techniques for traffic applications. *Image and Vision Computing, 21*(4), 359–381. doi:10.1016/S0262-8856(03)00004-0

Kasun, L. L. C., Zhou, H., Huang, G. B., & Vong, C. M. (2013). Representational learning with elms for big data. *IEEE Intelligent Systems, 28*(6), 31–34.

Kaufmann, S. (2014). *Opening public transit data in Germany.* Doctoral dissertation, University of Ulm.

Kecman, P. (2014). Models for predictive railway traffic management (PhD thesis). TU Delft, Delft University of Technology.

Kecman, P., & Goverde, R. M. P. (2015). Online data-driven adaptive prediction of train event times. *IEEE Transactions on Intelligent Transportation Systems, 16*(1), 465–474. doi:10.1109/TITS.2014.2347136

Khosrowshahi, F., Ghodous, P., & Sarshar, M. (2014). Visualization of the modeled degradation of building flooring systems in building maintenance. *Computer-Aided Civil and Infrastructure Engineering, 29*(1), 18–30. doi:10.1111/mice.12029

Kjell, T. (2014, March 11). *Vectorize rails wires and compute track geometry* [YouTube video]. Retrieved from https://www.youtube.com/watch?v=YeeLjN3viKQ

Koetse, M. P., & Rietveld, P. (2009). The impact of climate change and weather on transport: An overview of empirical findings. *Transportation Research Part D, 14*(3), 205–221. doi:10.1016/j.trd.2008.12.004

Kohavi, R. (1995). A study of cross-validation and bootstrap for accuracy estimation and model selection. In Proceedings of the International joint conference on artificial intelligence.

Kremer, J., & Grimm, A. (2012). The RailMapper—A dedicated mobile LiDAR mapping system for railway networks. *Int. Arch. Photogramm. Remote Sens. Spat. Inf. Sci, 39*-B5.

Kroll, B., Schaffranek, D., Schriegel, S., & Niggemann, O. (2014, September). System modeling based on machine learning for anomaly detection and predictive maintenance in industrial plants. In Proceedings of 2014 IEEE Emerging Technology and Factory Automation (ETFA) (pp. 1-7). IEEE doi:10.1109/ETFA.2014.7005202

Kumar, A., & Tyagi, M. (2014). Geographical Topologies of Routing Protocols in Vehicular Ad hoc Networks – A Survey. *International Journal of Computer Science and Information Technologies*, 5(3), 3062-3065.

Kumar, A., & Hans, R. (2015). Performance Analysis of DSDV, I-DSDV, OLSR, ZRP Proactive Routing Protocol in Mobile Ad Hoc Networks in IPv6. *International Journal of Advanced Science and Technology*, 77, 25–36. doi:10.14257/ijast.2015.77.03

Kusakabe, T., & Asakura, Y. (2014). Behavioral data mining of transit smart card data: A data fusion approach. *Transportation Research Part C, Emerging Technologies*, 46, 179–191. doi:10.1016/j.trc.2014.05.012

Lai, X. D. (2010). Airborne LiDAR Basic Principle and Application.

Lai, X., & Zheng, M. (2015). A Denoising Method for LiDAR Full-Waveform Data. *Mathematical Problems in Engineering*.

Landscheidt, S., & Kans, M. (2016). Method for Assessing the Total Cost of Ownership of Industrial Robots. *Procedia CIRP*, 57, 746–751. doi:10.1016/j.procir.2016.11.129

Langer, T., & Vaidyanathan, S. (2014). Smart Freight: Applications of Information and Communications Technologies to Freight System Efficiency (White Paper). ACEEE.

Langford, J., & McAllester, D. (2004). Computable shell decomposition bounds. *Journal of Machine Learning Research*, 5, 529–547.

LASer (LAS) File Format Exchange Activities. (n. d.). Retrieved March 29, 2016, from https://www.asprs.org/committee-general/laser-las-file-format-exchange-activities.html

Lathia, N., & Capra, L. (2011). How smart is your smartcard?: measuring travel behaviors, perceptions, and incentives. In *Proceedings of the 13th international conference on Ubiquitous computing*. ACM. doi:10.1145/2030112.2030152

Latino, R. J., Latino, K. C., & Latino, M. A. (2016). *Root cause analysis: improving performance for bottom-line results*. CRC press.

Lauriault, T. P., Craig, B. L., Taylor, D. F., & Pulsifer, P. L. (2007). Today's data are part of tomorrow's research: Archival issues in the sciences. *Archivaria*, 64, 123–179.

Lee, J. H., Davis, A. W., & Goulias, K. G. (2016). Activity Space Estimation with Longitudinal Observations of Social Media Data. In *Proceedings of the 95th Annual Meeting of the Transportation Research Board*.

Lee, J., Kao, H. A., & Yang, S. (2014). Service innovation and smart analytics for industry 4.0 and big data environment. Procedia CIRP, 16, 3-8.

Lee, B., & Lee, J.-H. (2017). Blockchain-based secure firmware update for embedded devices in an Internet of Things environment. *The Journal of Supercomputing*, 73(3), 1152–1167. doi:10.1007/s11227-016-1870-0

Lee, J. H. et al.. (2015). Can Twitter data be used to validate travel demand models? In *Proceedings of the 14th International Conference on Travel Behaviour Research*, Windsor, UK.

Leetaru, K., Wang, S., Cao, G., Padmanabhan, A., & Shook, E. (2013). Mapping the global Twitter heartbeat: The geography of Twitter. *First Monday*, 18(5). doi:10.5210/fm.v18i5.4366

Lehner, A., Rico-García, C., & Strang, T. (2011). A multi-broadcast communication system for high dynamic vehicular ad-hoc networks. Vehicle Information and Communication Systems, 2(3/4).

Lenior, D., Janssen, W., Neerincx, M., & Schreibers, K. (2006). Human-factors engineering for smart transport: Decision support for car drivers and train traffic controllers. *Applied Ergonomics, 37*(4), 479–490. doi:10.1016/j.apergo.2006.04.021 PMID:16765905

Lerkvarnyu, S., Deijhan, K., & Cheevasuvit, F. (1998). Moving average method for time series lidar data. Retrieved from http//www. gisdevelopment. net/aars/acrs/1998/ps3016. shtml

Lesler, M., Perry, G., & McNease, K. (2010, April). Using mobile LiDAR to survey a railway line for asset Inventory. In *Proceedings of the American Society for Photogrammetry and Remote Sensing (ASPRS) 2010 Annual Conference*, San Diego, CA.

Le, T., & Jeong, H. D. (2016). Interlinking life-cycle data spaces to support decision making in highway asset management. *Automation in Construction, 64*, 54–64. doi:10.1016/j.autcon.2015.12.016

Lever, G., Laviolette, F., & Shawe-Taylor, F. (2013). Tighter pac-bayes bounds through distribution-dependent priors. *Theoretical Computer Science, 473*, 4–28. doi:10.1016/j.tcs.2012.10.013

Li, B., Yao, Q., & Wang, K. (2012, April). A review on vision-based pedestrian detection in intelligent transportation systems. In *Proceedings of the 2012 9th IEEE International Conference on Networking, Sensing and Control (ICNSC)* (pp. 393-398). IEEE. doi:10.1109/ICNSC.2012.6204951

Li, H., Qian, B., Parikh, D., & Hampapur, A. (2013). Alarm prediction in large-scale sensor networks a case study in railroad. In Proceedings of the IEEE international conference on big data.

Li, Q., Zhong, Z., Liang, Z., & Liang, Y. (2015). Rail inspection meets big data: Methods and trends. In 18th international conference on network-based information systems.

Liggins, M. II, Hall, D., & Llinas, J. (Eds.). (2017). *Handbook of multisensor data fusion: theory and practice.* CRC press.

Li, H., Parikh, D., He, Q., Qian, B., Li, Z., Fang, D., & Hampapur, A. (2014). Improving rail network velocity: A machine learning approach to predictive maintenance. *Transportation Research Part C, Emerging Technologies, 45*, 17–26. doi:10.1016/j.trc.2014.04.013

Limsopatham, N., Albakour, M. D., Macdonald, C., & Ounis, I. (n. d.). Tweeting Behavior during Train Disruptions within a City. School of Computing Science University of Glasgow. Retrieved from http://terrierteam.dcs.gla.ac.uk/publications/limsopatham2015icwsm.pdf

Lin, Y., & Wang, P. (December 2015), Class-Based Delta-Encoding for High-Speed Train Data Stream. In *Proceedings of the 2015 IEEE 34th International Performance on Computing and Communications Conference (IPCCC)*.

Lin, Z., & Davis, L. S. (2010). Shape-based human detection and segmentation via hierarchical part-template matching. *IEEE Transactions on Pattern Analysis and Machine Intelligence, 32*(4), 606–618. PMID:20224118

Li, R., Kido, A., & Wang, S. (2015). Evaluation index development for the intelligent transportation system in smart community based on Big Data. *Advances in Mechanical Engineering*.

Litman, T. (2011). Introduction to multi-modal transportation planning. Victoria Transport Policy Institute.

Liu, L. (2011). Data model and algorithms for multimodal route planning with transportation networks [Doctoral dissertation]. München, Techn. Univ.

Liu, J. H., Shi, W., Elrahman, O.S., Ban, X.J., & Reilly, J.M. (2016). Understanding social media program usage in public transit agencies. *International Journal of Transportation Science and Technology, 5*(2), 83–92. doi:10.1016/j.ijtst.2016.09.005

Liu, L. L. (2011). *Decomposition of Airborne LiDAR Full-Waveform Data Based on LM Method.* Wuhan, China: Wuhan University.

Liu, P., Choo, K. K. R., Wang, L., & Huang, F. (2016). SVM or deep learning? A comparative study on remote sensing image classification. *Soft Computing.*

Livingston, A., Jackson, G., & Priestley, K. (2001). Root causes analysis: Literature review. *HSE Contract Research Report.*

Li, X., Flohr, F., Yang, Y., Xiong, H., Braun, M., Pan, S., & Gavrila, D. M. et al. (2016, June). A new benchmark for vision-based cyclist detection. In *Intelligent Vehicles Symposium (IV), 2016 IEEE* (pp. 1028-1033). IEEE.

Li, X., Gong, J. B., & Zhou, Z. W. (2007). Laser imaging radar waveform digitalize technology. *Hongwai Yu Jiguang Gongcheng,* (1), 474–477.

Li, X., Shou, B., & Ralescu, D. (2014). Train rescheduling with stochastic recovery time: A new track-backup approach. IEEE Transactions on Systems. *Man and Cybernetics: Systems, 44*(9), 1216–1233.

Lomotey, R. K., & Deters, R. (2014, April). Towards knowledge discovery in big data. In *Proceedings of the 2014 IEEE 8th International Symposium on Service Oriented System Engineering (SOSE)* (pp. 181-191). IEEE. doi:10.1109/SOSE.2014.25

Lutchman, R. (2006). Sustainable asset management: linking assets, people, and processes for results. DEStech Publications, Inc.

Lyko, K., Nitzschke, M., & Ngomo, A.-C. N. (2016). *Big data acquisition. In New Horizons for a Data-Driven Economy* (pp. 39–61). Springer International Publishing. doi:10.1007/978-3-319-21569-3_4

Lyons, G., & Harman, R. (2002). The UK public transport industry and provision of multi-modal traveller information. *International Journal of Transport Management, 1*(1), 1–13. doi:10.1016/S1471-4051(01)00002-7

Madhubala, M., & Narasimha Prasad, L. V. (2017). Automatic Assessment of Floods Impact Using Twitter Data. *International Journal of Civil Engineering and Technology, 8*(5), 1228–1238.

Madnick, S., Wang, R., & Xian, X. (2004). The design and implementation of a corporate householding knowledge processor to improve data quality. *Journal of Management Information Systems, 20*(1), 41–49.

Magrini, M. (2015). An Infrastructure for Integrated Management of Urban Railway Crossing Area. In *Proceedings of the 2015 IEEE 18th International Conference on Intelligent Transportation Systems.*

Mai, E., & Hranac, R. (2013, January). Twitter interactions as a data source for transportation incidents. In *Proc. Transportation Research Board 92nd Ann. Meeting (No. 13-1636).*

Maire, F. (2007, September). Vision based anti-collision system for rail track maintenance vehicles. In *Proceedings of the IEEE Conference on Advanced Video and Signal Based Surveillance AVSS '07* (pp. 170-175). IEEE. doi:10.1109/AVSS.2007.4425305

Maire, F., & Bigdeli, A. (2010, December). Obstacle-free range determination for rail track maintenance vehicles. In *Proceedings of the 2010 11th International Conference on Control Automation Robotics & Vision (ICARCV)* (pp. 2172-2178). IEEE. doi:10.1109/ICARCV.2010.5707923

Maly, T., & Schöbel, A. (2010). Cost effectiveness of wayside derailment detection.

Ma, M., Wang, P., Chu, C. H., & Liu, L. (2015). Efficient multipattern event processing over high-speed train data streams. *IEEE Internet of Things Journal, 2*(4), 295–309. doi:10.1109/JIOT.2014.2387883

Management Paradise. (n. d.). Safety measures by Indian Railways. Retrieved from http://www.managementparadise.com/forums/service-sector-management-s-s-m/201685-safety-measures-indian-railways.html

Mancini, M., Costante, G., Valigi, P., & Ciarfuglia, T. A. (2016, October). Fast robust monocular depth estimation for Obstacle Detection with fully convolutional networks. In *Proceedings of the 2016 IEEE/RSJ International Conference on Intelligent Robots and Systems (IROS)* (pp. 4296-4303). IEEE. doi:10.1109/IROS.2016.7759632

Mandloi, D., & Thill, J. C. (2010). Object-oriented data modeling of an indoor/outdoor urban transportation network and route planning analysis. In *Geospatial Analysis and Modelling of Urban Structure and Dynamics* (pp. 197–220). Springer Netherlands. doi:10.1007/978-90-481-8572-6_11

Manvi, S. S., Kakkasageri, M. S., & Mahapurush, C. V. (2009). Performance Analysis of AODV, DSR, and Swarm Intelligence Routing Protocols In Vehicular Ad hoc Network Environment. In *Proceedings of the Conference on Future Computer and Communication*. IEEE. doi:10.1109/ICFCC.2009.122

Maryland Transit Administrator. (n. d.). MARCTracker Live GPS Train Locations Retrieved from http://www.marc-tracker.com/PublicView/status.jsp

Mašek, J., Kolarovszki, P., & Čamaj, J. (2016). Application of RFID Technology in Railway Transport Services and Logistics Chains. *Procedia Engineering, 134*, 231–236. doi:10.1016/j.proeng.2016.01.064

Massat, J.P., Laine, J.P., & Bobillot, A. (2006). Pantograph–catenary dynamics simulation. *Vehicle System Dynamics, 44*(Sup. 1), 551-559.

Masson, É., & Berbineau, M. (2017). Railway Applications Requiring Broadband Wireless Communications. In *Broadband Wireless Communications for Railway Applications* (pp. 35–79). Springer International Publishing. doi:10.1007/978-3-319-47202-7_2

Matzutt, R., Hohlfeld, O., Henze, M., Rawiel, R., Ziegeldorf, J. H., & Wehrle, K. (2016). POSTER. In *Proceedings of the 2016 ACM SIGSAC Conference on Computer and Communications Security - CCS'16* (pp. 1769–1771). New York, New York, USA: ACM Press. doi:10.1145/2976749.2989059

Ma, X., Wang, Y., Feng, C., & Liu, J. (2012). Transit smart card data mining for passenger origin information extraction. *Journal of Zhejiang University. Science, C13*(10), 750–760. doi:10.1631/jzus.C12a0049

Ma, X., Wu, Y. J., Wang, Y., Chen, F., & Liu, J. (2013). Mining smart card data for transit riders travel patterns. *Transportation Research Part C, Emerging Technologies, 36*, 1–12. doi:10.1016/j.trc.2013.07.010

Mazzino, N., Cabeza-Lopez, P., Toapanta, W., & Lancia, A. (2013). Reducing costs through the integration of wayside train and infrastructure monitoring systems. In Proceedings of AusRAIL PLUS 2013, Canberra, ACT, Australia. .

McClair, K. (2015). Retrieved from http://www.raildeliverygroup.com/media-centre/press-releases/2015/724-2015-12-14.html

McDonald, N. (2000). Multipurpose Smart Cards in Transportation: Benefits and Barriers to Use (Research Paper # 630). University of California Transportation Center.

McGuckin, N., & Nakamoto, Y. (2004, November 1–2). Trips, chains, and tours: using an operational definition. *Presented at: Understanding Our Nation's Travel: National Household Travel Survey Conference*, Washington DC.

McGuinness, D. L., & Van Harmelen, F. (2004). OWL web ontology language overview. *W3C recommendation, 10*(10). Retrieved January 23, 2017, from https://www.w3.org/TR/owl-features/

McNulty, R. (2011). *Realising the Potential of GB Rail: Final Report of the Rail Value for Money Study : Detailed Report*. UK Department for Transport. Retrieved from http://assets.dft.gov.uk/publications/report-of-the-rail-vfm-study/realising-the-potential-of-gb-rail.pdf

Meier, H., Roy, R., & Seliger, G. (2010). Industrial product-service systems—IPS 2. *CIRP Annals-Manufacturing Technology, 59*(2), 607–627. doi:10.1016/j.cirp.2010.05.004

Meng, X., Bradley, J., Yavuz, B., Sparks, E., Venkataraman, S., & Liu, D., ... & Xin, D. (2016). MLlib: Machine Learning in Apache Spark. *Journal of Machine Learning Research, 17*(34), 1–7.

Metrotrains. (n. d.). METRONOTIFY APP. Retrieved from www.metrotrains.com.au/metronotify/

Michalos, G., Sipsas, P., Makris, S., & Chryssolouris, G. (2016). Decision making logic for flexible assembly lines reconfiguration. *Robotics and Computer-integrated Manufacturing, 37*, 233–250. doi:10.1016/j.rcim.2015.04.006

Milani, F., García-Bañuelos, L., & Dumas, M. (2016). *Blockchain and business process improvement*. Retrieved from http://www.bptrends.com/bpt/wp-content/uploads/10-04-2016-ART-Blockchain-and-Bus-Proc-Improvement-Milani-Garcia-Banuelos-Dumas.pdf

Milinkovic, S., Markovic, M., Veskovic, S., Ivic, M., & Pavlovic, N. (2013). A fuzzy petri net model to estimate train delays. *Simulation Modelling Practice and Theory, 33*, 144–157. doi:10.1016/j.simpat.2012.12.005

Ministry of Railways, New Delhi. (2013). Investment Promotion and Infrastructure Development Cell.

Mitrovic, S. M. S. V. B., & Marton, Z. D. P. (2015). A site selection model for wayside train monitoring systems at Serbian railways. In *Re-Aggregation Heuristics For The Large Location Problems With Lexicographic Minimax Objective* (p. 49).

Mittermayr, P., Stephanides, J., and Maicz, D. (2011). Argos-a decade of operational experience in wayside train monitoring.

Mohamed, A. Z. (2014). A review on crowd sourcing geo-social related big data approaches as a solution to the transportation problem. *Applied Mechanics of Materials, 663*, 622–626. doi:10.4028/www.scientific.net/AMM.663.622

Mohapatra, S., & Kanungo, P. (2011). Performance analysis of AODV, DSR, OLSR and DSDV Routing Protocols using NS2 Simulator. In *Proceedings of the International Conference on Communication Technology and System Design*.

Möller, H., Hulin, B., Krötz, W., & Sarnes, B. (2001, November). Video based obstacle detection in catenaries of railways. In *Proceeding of 6th International Conference on Pattern Recognition and Information Processing* (Vol. 1, No. 7, pp. 275-287).

MongoD.B. (n. d.). Architecture. Retrieved from https://www.mongodb.com/mongodb-architecture

MongoDB. (2015). MongoDB on Gartner's Magic Quadrant for Operational Database Management Systems 2015. Retrieved from https://www.mongodb.com/collateral/gartner-mq-2015?jmp=homepage

MongoDB. (n. d.). MongoDB Architecture. Retrieved from https://www.mongodb.com/mongodb-architecture

Moore, J. F. (1993). Predators and prey: A new ecology of competition. *Harvard Business Review, 71*(3), 75–83. PMID:10126156

Morency, C. (2013). Workshop synthesis: exploiting and merging passive public transportation data streams. In J. Zmud, M. Lee-Gosselin, M. Munizaga, & J. A. Carasco (Eds.), *Transport survey methods: Best practice for decision making* (pp. 711–720). Bingley: Emerald. doi:10.1108/9781781902882-039

Morgan, D. Using mobile LiDAR to survey railway infrastructure. Lynx mobile mapper. In *Proceedings of the FIG Commissions 5(6) and SSGA Workshop*, Lake Baikal, Russia (pp. 32–40).

Morris, C., Easton, J., & Roberts, C. (2014). Applications of linked data in the rail domain. In Proceedings of the IEEE international conference on big data. doi:10.1109/BigData.2014.7004429

Motion-Based Multiple Object Tracking. (n. d.). Retrieved September 20, 2016, from https://www.mathworks.com/help/vision/examples/motion-based-multiple-object-tracking.html

Mukojima, H., Deguchi, D., Kawanishi, Y., Ide, I., Murase, H., Ukai, M., . . . Nakasone, R. (2016, September). Moving camera background-subtraction for obstacle detection on railway tracks. In *Proceedings of the 2016 IEEE International Conference on Image Processing (ICIP)* (pp. 3967-3971). IEEE. doi:10.1109/ICIP.2016.7533104

Muller-Hannemann, M., & Schnee, M. (2009). Efficient timetable information in the presence of delays. In Robust and online large-scale optimization. doi:10.1007/978-3-642-05465-5_10

Munder, S., & Gavrila, D. M. (2006). An experimental study on pedestrian classification. *IEEE Transactions on Pattern Analysis and Machine Intelligence*, 28(11), 1863–1868. doi:10.1109/TPAMI.2006.217 PMID:17063690

Munizaga, M. A., & Palma, C. (2012). Estimation of a disaggregate multimodal public transport origin-destination matrix from passive Smart card data from Santiago, Chile. *Transportation Research*, 24C(12), 9–18. doi:10.1016/j.trc.2012.01.007

Munizaga, M., Devillaine, F., Navarrete, C., & Silva, D. (2014). Validating travel behavior estimated from smartcard data. *Transportation Research Part C, Emerging Technologies*, 44, 70–79. doi:10.1016/j.trc.2014.03.008

Nagy, E., & Csiszár, C. (2015). Analysis of Delay Causes in Railway Passenger Transportation. *Periodica Polytechnica Transportation Engineering*, 43(2), 73–80. doi:10.3311/PPtr.7539

Nakamoto, S. (2008). *Bitcoin: A Peer-to-Peer Electronic Cash System*. Retrieved from https://bitcoin.org/bitcoin.pdf

Nassu, B. T., & Ukai, M. (2011, June). Rail extraction for driver support in railways. In *Proceedings of the Intelligent Vehicles Symposium (IV)* (pp. 83-88). IEEE. doi:10.1109/IVS.2011.5940410

Nassu, B. T., & Ukai, M. (2012). A Vision-Based Approach for Rail Extraction and its Application in a Camera Pan–Tilt Control System. *IEEE Transactions on Intelligent Transportation Systems*, 13(4), 1763–1771. doi:10.1109/TITS.2012.2204052

Nepal, S., Paris, C., & Georgakopoulos, D. (Eds.). (2015). Social Media for Government Services. Springer International Publishing.

Network Rail Limited. (2013). *Network Rail Technical Strategy*.

Network Simulator ns-2. Website. Retrieved from http://www.isi.edu/nsnam/ns

Newcombe, S., & Tucker, G. (2016). Enabling greater use of cross-industry remote condition monitoring. In *Proceedings of the International Conference on Railway Engineering (ICRE 2016)*. Institution of Engineering and Technology. doi:10.1049/cp.2016.0520

Niekamp, S., Bharadwaj, U. R., Sadhukhan, J., & Chryssanthopoulos, M. K. (2015). A multi-criteria decision support framework for sustainable asset management and challenges in its application. *Journal of Industrial and Production Engineering*, 32(1), 23–36. doi:10.1080/21681015.2014.1000401

Niknejad, H. T., Takeuchi, A., Mita, S., & McAllester, D. (2012). On-road multivehicle tracking using deformable object model and particle filter with improved likelihood estimation. *IEEE Transactions on Intelligent Transportation Systems*, 13(2).

Nitzan, S., & Paroush, J. (1982). Optimal decision rules in uncertain dichotomous choice situations. *International Economic Review*, 23(2), 289–297. doi:10.2307/2526438

Noland, R. B., & Polak, J. W. (2002). Travel time variability: A review of theoretical and empirical issues. *Transport Reviews*, 22(1), 39–54. doi:10.1080/01441640010022456

Noori, K., & Jenab, K. (2013). Fuzzy reliability-based traction control model for intelligent transportation systems. IEEE Transactions on Systems, Man, and Cybernetics. *Systems*, 43(1), 229–234.

Nunez, A., Hendriks, J., Li, Z., De Schutter, B., & Dollevoet, R. (2014). Facilitating maintenance decisions on the Dutch railways using big data: The aba case study. In Proceedings of the IEEE international conference on big data.

Office of Rail and Road. (2016). *Information for passengers.* Retrieved April 13, 2017, from http://orr.gov.uk/__data/assets/pdf_file/0015/4353/information-for-passengers-guidance-on-meeting-the-licence-condition.pdf

Office of Rail Regulation. (2011). *National Rail Trends 2010 - 2011 Yearbook.* Retrieved from http://www.orr.gov.uk/__data/assets/pdf_file/0017/3482/nrt-yearbook-2010-11.pdf

Office of Rail Regulation. (2012, December). *Passenger Information.* Retrieved January 17, 2017, from http://orr.gov.uk/__data/assets/pdf_file/0014/4352/Passenger-information.pdf

Ohta, M. (2005). Level crossings obstacle detection system using stereo cameras. *Quarterly Report of RTRI*, 46(2), 110–117. doi:10.2219/rtriqr.46.110

Oliveira, L., & Nunes, U. (2013, June). Pedestrian detection based on LIDAR-driven sliding window and relational parts-based detection. In *Proceedings of the Intelligent Vehicles Symposium (IV)* (pp. 328-333). IEEE. doi:10.1109/IVS.2013.6629490

Oliveira, L., Nunes, U., & Peixoto, P. (2010). On exploration of classifier ensemble synergism in pedestrian detection. *IEEE Transactions on Intelligent Transportation Systems*, 11(1), 16–27. doi:10.1109/TITS.2009.2026447

Olsson, N. O., & Bull-Berg, H. (2015). Use of big data in project evaluations. *International Journal of Managing Projects in Business*, 8(3), 491–512. doi:10.1108/IJMPB-09-2014-0063

Oneto, L., Ghio, A., Ridella, S., & Anguita, D. (2015). Fully empirical and data-dependent stability-based bounds. *IEEE transactions on cybernetics*, 45(9), 1913-1926.

Oracle Corporation. (2015). *Jersey – RESTful Web Services in Java.* Retrieved January 17, 2017, from https://jersey.java.net/

OSGi Alliance. (2003). *OSGi Service Platform, Release 3.* IOS Press, Inc.

Otero, C. E., Rossi, M., Peter, A., & Haber, R. (2014, January). Determining the human-perceived level of safety in transportation systems using big data analytics. In *Proceedings of the International Conference on Internet Computing (ICOMP).* The Steering Committee of The World Congress in Computer Science, Computer Engineering and Applied Computing (WorldComp).

Ozbay, K. M., Xiao, W., Jaiswal, G., Bartin, B., Kachroo, P., & Baykal-Gursoy, M. (2009). Evaluation of incident management strategies and technologies using an integrated traffic/incident management simulation. *World Review of Intermodal Transportation Research*, 2(2-3), 155–186. doi:10.1504/WRITR.2009.023305

Paakkonen, P., & Pakkala, D. (2015). Reference architecture and classification of technologies, products and services for big data systems. *Big Data Research*, 2(4), 166–186. doi:10.1016/j.bdr.2015.01.001

Packard, N. H., Crutchfield, J. P., Farmer, J. D., & Shaw, R. S. (1980). Geometry from a time series. *Physical Review Letters*, 45(9), 712–716. doi:10.1103/PhysRevLett.45.712

Page, L. W. Latent Dirichlet allocation. Retrieved from https://en.wikipedia.org/wiki/Latent_Dirichlet_allocation

Paisitkriangkrai, S., Shen, C., & Zhang, J. (2008). Performance evaluation of local features in human classification and detection. *IET Computer Vision*, *2*(4), 236–246. doi:10.1049/iet-cvi:20080026

Palen, L., Starbird, K., Vieweg, S., & Hughes, A. (2010). twitter-based information distribution during the 2009 Red River Valley flood threat. *Bulletin of the American Society for Information Science and Technology*, *36*(5), 13–17. doi:10.1002/bult.2010.1720360505

Pålsson, H., & Kovács, G. (2014). Reducing transportation emissions: A reaction to stakeholder pressure or a strategy to increase competitive advantage. *International Journal of Physical Distribution & Logistics Management*, *44*(4), 283–304. doi:10.1108/IJPDLM-09-2012-0293

Parkinson H J, a. B. G. (2017). Big Data in Railway Accident Prediction Including a Review of Current Analytical Methods. *International Journal of Railway Technology (IJRT)*.

Parkinson, H. J., & Bamford, G. J. (2017). Big Data and the Virtuous Circle of Railway Digitization. In P. Angelov, Y. Manolopoulos, L. Iliadis, A. Roy, & M. Vellasco (Eds.), *Advances in Big Data: Proceedings of the 2nd INNS Conference on Big Data, October 23-25, 2016, Thessaloniki, Greece* (pp. 314-322). Cham: Springer International Publishing. doi:10.1007/978-3-319-47898-2_32

Parkinson, H. J., Bamford, G., & Kandola, B. (2016). The Development of an Enhanced Bowtie Railway Safety Assessment Tool using a Big Data Analytics Approach. In *IET Conference Proceedings*. Retrieved from http://digital-library.theiet.org/content/conferences/10.1049/cp.2016.0510

Parkinson, H., & Bamford, G. (2016). The potential for using big data analytics to predict safety risks by analyzing rail accidents. *Paper presented at the 3rd International Conference on Railway Technology: Research, Development and Maintenance*, Cagliari, Sardinia, Italy.

Park, S., Park, S. I., & Lee, S. H. (2016). Strategy on sustainable infrastructure asset management: Focus on Korea's future policy directivity. *Renewable & Sustainable Energy Reviews*, *62*, 710–722. doi:10.1016/j.rser.2016.04.073

Passenger Focus. (2013) Short and Tweet: How passengers want social media during disruption. Retrieved April 8, 2013 from http://www.transportfocus.org.uk/research-publications/publications/short-and-tweet-how-passengers-want-social-media-during-disruption/

Pathan, A.-S. K., Monowar, M. M., & Khan, S. (2014). *Simulation Technologies in Networking and Communications*. CRC Press. doi:10.1201/b17650

Pelletier, M. P., Trépanier, M., & Morency, C. (2011). Smart card data use in public transit: A literature review. *Transportation Research Part C, Emerging Technologies*, *19*(4), 557–568. doi:10.1016/j.trc.2010.12.003

Pender, B., Currie, G., Delbosc, A., & Shiwakoti, N. (2014). Social Media Use in Unplanned Passenger Rail Disruptions – An International Study. In *Transportation Research Board 93rd Annual Meeting Compendium of Papers*.

Pender, B., Currie, G., Delbosc, A., & Shiwakoti, N. (2013, October). Social Media Utilisation during Unplanned Passenger Rail Disruption What's Not to Like? In *Proc. Australasian Transport Research Forum 2013*.

Peng, H., Long, F., & Ding, C. (2005). Feature selection based on mutual information criteria of max-dependency, max-relevance, and min- redundancy. *IEEE Transactions on Pattern Analysis and Machine Intelligence*, *27*(8), 1226–1238. doi:10.1109/TPAMI.2005.159 PMID:16119262

Penna, R., Amaral, M., Espíndola, D., Botelho, S., Duarte, N., Pereira, C. E., . . . Frazzon, E. M. (2014, July). Visualization tool for cyber-physical maintenance systems. In *Proceedings of the 2014 12th IEEE International Conference on Industrial Informatics (INDIN)* (pp. 566-571). IEEE. doi:10.1109/INDIN.2014.6945575

Pereira, F. C., Bazzan, A. L., & Ben-Akiva, M. (2014). The role of context in transport prediction. *IEEE Intelligent Systems*, 29(1), 76–80. doi:10.1109/MIS.2014.14

Pereira, F. C., Rodrigues, F., & Ben-Akiva, M. (2013). Text analysis in incident duration prediction. *Transportation Research Part C, Emerging Technologies*, 37, 177–192. doi:10.1016/j.trc.2013.10.002

Perko, I., & Ototsky, P. (2016). Big Data for Business Ecosystem Players. *Naše gospodarstvo [Our economy]*, 62(2), 12-24.

Poggio, T., Rifkin, R., Mukherjee, S., & Niyogi, P. (2004). General conditions for predictivity in learning theory. *Nature*, 428(6981), 419–422. doi:10.1038/nature02341 PMID:15042089

Pongnumkul, S., Pechprasarn, T., Kunaseth, N., & Chaipah, K. (2014). Improving arrival time prediction of thailand's passenger trains using historical travel times. In *Proceedings of the International joint conference on computer science and software engineering*. doi:10.1109/JCSSE.2014.6841886

Popping, R. (2000). Computer-assisted text analysis. *Sage (Atlanta, Ga.).*

Prechelt, L. (1998). Automatic early stopping using cross validation: Quantifying the criteria. *Neural Networks*, 11(4), 761–767. doi:10.1016/S0893-6080(98)00010-0 PMID:12662814

Premebida, C., Ludwig, O., & Nunes, U. (2009). LIDAR and vision-based pedestrian detection system. *Journal of Field Robotics*, 26(9), 696–711. doi:10.1002/rob.20312

Press, G. (2016). (2016). Top 10 hot big data technologies. Forbes. Retrieved from https://www.forbes.com/sites/gilpress/2016/03/14/top-10-hot-big-data-technologies/#7216f28865d7

Priedhorsky, R., Culotta, A., & Del, S. Y. (2014). Inferring the origin locations of tweets with quantitative confidence. In *Proceeding CSCW '14* (pp 1523-1536). doi:10.1145/2531602.2531607

Prud'hommeaux, E., & Seaborne, A. (2008, January). SPARQL Query Language for RDF. In *Proceedings of the World Wide Web Consortium, Recommendation REC*. Retrieved January 23, 2017, from http://www.w3.org/TR/rdf-sparql-query/

Puttagunta, S. S., & Chraim, F. (2016). U.S. Patent No. 20,160,121,912. Washington, DC: U.S. Patent and Trademark Office.

Qiang, Z., Bin, W., Rui, Z., & Xia, X.C. (2008). Genetic Algorithm-Based Design for DNA Sequences Sets. *Chinese Journal of Computers*, 31(12), 2193-2199.

Qingyang, Y., & Xiaoyun, Y. (2015). Scheduling optimization model and algorithm design for two-way marshalling train. In *Proceedings of the International conference on intelligent transportation, big data and smart city*. doi:10.1109/ICITBS.2015.178

Qiu, S., & Wang, Q. (2009). Freeway traffic incident detection based on BP neural network. In *China Measurement & Test* (pp. 48-52).

Qi, Z., Tian, Y., & Shi, Y. (2013). Efficient railway tracks detection and turnouts recognition method using HOG features. *Neural Computing & Applications*, 23(1), 245–254. doi:10.1007/s00521-012-0846-0

Rahman, S. S., Easton, J. M., & Roberts, C. (2015, August). Mining open and crowdsourced data to improve situational awareness for railway. In *Proceedings of the 2015 IEEE/ACM International Conference on Advances in Social Networks Analysis and Mining (ASONAM)* (pp. 1240-1243). IEEE. doi:10.1145/2808797.2809369

RAI Branch. (2011). Rail accident report: Derailment at Grayrigg 23 February 2007 (Report 20(2008), v5).

Rail Delivery Group. (2016). *Approved Code of Practice - Provision of Customer Information.* Retrieved April 13, 2017, from http://www.raildeliverygroup.com/about-us/publications.html?task=file.download&id=469771025

RailTech.com. (2016). *Wayside Train Monitoring Systems Intelligent Rail Summit.* Retrieved from http://www.railtech.com/intelligent-rail-summit-2016/wayside-train-monitoring-systems/

RailwayTunnel Brockwille. (2013, January 11). *Lidar Scan of the Brockville Railway Tunnel* [YouTube video]. Retrieved from https://www.youtube.com/watch?v=oOGYwOeKJck

Raimond, T. 2009. Moving towards continuous collection of large-scale mobility surveys: are the recompelling reasons? A discussant response. In P. Bonnel, M. Lee-Gosselin, J. Zmud et al. (Eds.), Transport Survey Methods: Keeping Up with a Changing World (pp. 541–548). Bingley: Emerald Group Publishing Ltd.

Rajeshkumar, V., & Sivakumar, P. (2013). Comparative Study of AODV, DSDV and DSR Routing Protocols in MANET Using Network Simulator-2. International Journal of Advanced Research in Computer and Communication Engineering, 2(12).

Rashidi, T., Auld, J., & Mohammadian, A. (2013). The effectiveness of Bayesian Updating Attributes in Data Transferability Applications: Transportation Research Record. *Journal of the Transportation Research Board, 2344,* 1–9. doi:10.3141/2344-01

Reason, J. (1990). *Human error.* Cambridge university press. doi:10.1017/CBO9781139062367

RedHat. (2015). *Red Hat JBoss BPM Suite -- the JBoss platform for Business Process Management (BPM).* Retrieved January 17, 2017, from http://resteasy.jboss.org/

RedHat. (2015). *RestEASY – Distributed peace of mind.* Retrieved January 17, 2017, from http://resteasy.jboss.org/

Reina, G., Milella, A., Halft, W., & Worst, R. (2013, October). LIDAR and stereo imagery integration for safe navigation in outdoor settings. In *Proceedings of the 2013 IEEE International Symposium on Safety, Security, and Rescue Robotics (SSRR)* (pp. 1-6). IEEE. doi:10.1109/SSRR.2013.6719333

Reitberger, J., Krzystek, P., & Stilla, U. (2008). Analysis of full waveform LIDAR data for the classification of deciduous and coniferous trees. *International Journal of Remote Sensing, 29*(5), 1407–1431. doi:10.1080/01431160701736448

Rete Ferroviaria Italiana. (2016). Gruppo Ferrovie Dello Stato Italiane. Retrieved 3 May 2016 from http://www.rfi.it/

Reyes-Ortiz, J. L., Oneto, L., & Anguita, D. (2015). Big data analytics in the cloud: Spark on Hadoop vs MPI/OpenMP on Beowulf. The *Proceedings of the INNS Big Data conference.*

Rezaei, M., & Sabzevari, R. (2009). *Multisensor data fusion strategies for advanced driver assistance systems.* Sensor and Data Fusion. doi:10.5772/6575

Riazi, A. (1999, March 21–25). MetroCard: Automating New York City's Public Transit System. In *Proceedings of the First International Conference on Urban Transportation Systems,* American Society of Civil Engineers, Miami, FL.

Ridella, S., Rovetta, S., & Zunino, R. (1997). Circular backpropagation networks for classification. *IEEE Transactions on Neural Networks, 8*(1), 84–97. doi:10.1109/72.554194 PMID:18255613

RIEGL. (n. d.). Produktdetail. Retrieved October 10, 2016, from http://www.riegl.com/nc/products/mobile-scanning/produktdetail/product/scannersystem/10/

Robert, J., Kubler, S., & Le Traon, Y. (2016). Micro-billing Framework for IoT: Research & Technological Foundations. In *Proceedings of the 2016 IEEE 4th International Conference on Future Internet of Things and Cloud (FiCloud)* (pp. 301–308). IEEE. doi:10.1109/FiCloud.2016.50

Rockshore. (2017). Network Rail Feeds. http://nrodwiki.rockshore.net/index.php/About_the_Network_Rail_feeds

Rodríguez-Núñez, E., & García-Palomares, J. C. (2014). Measuring the vulnerability of public transport networks. *Journal of Transport Geography, 35,* 50–63. doi:10.1016/j.jtrangeo.2014.01.008

Rong, K., Hu, G., Lin, Y., Shi, Y., & Guo, L. (2015). Understanding business ecosystem using a 6C framework in Internet-of-Things-based sectors. *International Journal of Production Economics, 159,* 41–55. doi:10.1016/j.ijpe.2014.09.003

Ross, R. (2012, September). Track and turnout detection in video-signals using probabilistic spline curves. In *Proceedings of the 2012 15th International IEEE Conference on Intelligent Transportation Systems* (pp. 294-299). IEEE. doi:10.1109/ITSC.2012.6338605

RSS Board. (2013). Development of the Incident Factor Classification System. Retrieved from https://www.rssb.co.uk/improving-industry-performance/human-factors/human-factors-case-studies/developing-the-incident-factor-classification-system

RTD Fastracks. (n. d.). RTD integrates Positive Train Control into commuter rail lines. Retrieved from http://www.rtd-fastracks.com/ep3_149

Ruder, M., Mohler, N., & Ahmed, F. (2003, June). An obstacle detection system for automated trains. In *Proceedings of the Intelligent Vehicles Symposium* (pp. 180-185). IEEE. doi:10.1109/IVS.2003.1212905

Rumelhart, D. E., Hinton, G. E., & Williams, R. J. (1988). Learning representations by back-propagating errors. *Cognitive modeling, 5*(3).

Sabzmeydani, P., & Mori, G. (2007, June). Detecting pedestrians by learning shapelet features. In *Proceedings of the 2007 IEEE Conference on Computer Vision and Pattern Recognition* (pp. 1-8). IEEE.

Sadler, J., Griffin, D., Gilchrist, A., Austin, J., Kit, O., & Heavisides, J. (2016). Geosrm - online geospatial safety risk model for the gb rail network. *IET Intelligent Transport Systems, 10*(1), 17–24. doi:10.1049/iet-its.2015.0038

Salameh, N. (2011). Conception d'un système d'alerte embarqué basé sur les communications entre véhicules [Thesis]. Institut National des Sciences Appliquées de Rouen.

Sambamurthy, N., & Ahammad, S. H. (2013). Prevention of Train Accidents Using Wireless Sensor Networks. *International Journal of Engineering Research and Applications, 3*(6).

Sankavaram, C., Kodali, A., & Pattipati, K. (2013, January). An integrated health management process for automotive cyber-physical systems. In *Proceedings of the 2013 International Conference on Computing, Networking and Communications (ICNC)* (pp. 82-86). IEEE. doi:10.1109/ICCNC.2013.6504058

Schäfer, P. (2014). *Offline-Reiseplaner für Bahnverbindungen* [Bachelor's thesis].

Schaper, D2015). Red Tape Slows Control System That Could Have Saved Speeding Train. *NPR.* Retrieved from www.npr.org/2015/05/16/407127497/red-tape-slows-control-system-that-could-have-saved-speeding-train.jpg

Schiavo, A. L. (2016). Fully Autonomous Wireless Sensor Network for Freight Wagon Monitoring. *IEEE Sensors Journal, 16*(24), 9053–9063. doi:10.1109/JSEN.2016.2620149

Schmidt, D., Chen, W. C., Matheson, M. A., & Ostrouchov, G. (2016). Programming with BIG data in r: Scaling analytics from one to thousands of nodes. *Big Data Research, 6,* 1–10.

Schmitt, L., Létourneaux, F., De Keyzer, I., & Crompton, P. (2016). CAPACITY4RAIL: Toward a Resilient, Innovative and High-capacity European Railway System for 2030/2050. In *Materials and Infrastructures 2* (pp. 105–114). Hoboken, NJ, USA: John Wiley & Sons, Inc. doi:10.1002/9781119318613.ch8

Schöbel, A., Stoytechva, N., Bakalski, I. & Karner, J. (2012). Results from first Bulgarian wayside train monitoring systems at Zimnitsa.

Schultz, F., Utz, S., & Göritz, A. (2011). Is the medium the message? Perceptions of and reactions to crisis communication via Twitter, blogs and traditional media. *Public Relations Review, 37*(1), 20–27. doi:10.1016/j.pubrev.2010.12.001

Schwartz, W. R., Kembhavi, A., Harwood, D., & Davis, L. S. (2009, September). Human detection using partial least squares analysis. In *Proceedings of the 2009 IEEE 12th international conference on computer vision* (pp. 24-31). IEEE. doi:10.1109/ICCV.2009.5459205

Schweitzer, L. (2012). How are we doing? opinion mining customer sentiment in us transit agencies and airlines via twitter. In *Proceedings of the Transportation Research Board 91st Annual Meeting*.

Scott, D. M., Novak, D. C., Aultman-Hall, L., & Guo, F. (2006). Network robustness index: A new method for identifying critical links and evaluating the performance of transportation networks. *Journal of Transport Geography, 14*(3), 215–227. doi:10.1016/j.jtrangeo.2005.10.003

Selver, M. A., Er, E., Belenlioglu, B., & Soyaslan, Y. (2016, August). Camera based driver support system for rail extraction using 2-D Gabor wavelet decompositions and morphological analysis. In *Proceedings of the 2016 IEEE International Conference on Intelligent Rail Transportation (ICIRT)* (pp. 270-275). IEEE.

Shawe-Taylor, J., & Cristianini, N. (2004). *Kernel methods for pattern analysis. Cambridge University Press.*

Shingler, R., Fadin, G., & Umiliacchi, P. (2008). From RCM to predictive maintenance: the InteGRail approach. In *Proceedings of the 4th IET International Conference on Railway Condition Monitoring (RCM 2008)* (pp. 17–17). IEE. doi:10.1049/ic:20080324

Shristi, (September 2016) The Theory of Everything: Indian Railways. Retrieved from https://gradeup.co/the-theory-of-everything-indian-railways-i-8d46521a-7e69-11e6-995d-fccaa0f5d0cc

Sierpiński, G. (2017). Technologically advanced and responsible travel planning assisted by GT Planner. In *Contemporary Challenges of Transport Systems and Traffic Engineering* (pp. 65–77). Springer International Publishing. doi:10.1007/978-3-319-43985-3_6

Singh, A., & Verma, A.K. (2013) Simulation and Analysis of AODV, DSDV, ZRP IN VANET. *International Journal in Foundations of Computer Science and Technology, 3*(5).

Sinha, D., & Feroz, F. (2016). Obstacle Detection on Railway Tracks Using Vibration Sensors and Signal Filtering Using Bayesian Analysis. *IEEE Sensors Journal, 16*(3), 642–649. doi:10.1109/JSEN.2015.2490247

Sirin, E., Parsia, B., Grau, B. C., Kalyanpur, A., & Katz, Y. (2007). Pellet: A practical owl-dl reasoner. *Web Semantics: Science, Services, and Agents on the World Wide Web, 5*(2), 51–53. doi:10.1016/j.websem.2007.03.004

SIS, SS-ISO 55000:2014, Asset management – Overview, principles and terminology. (2014).

Sivaraman, S., & Trivedi, M. M. (2013, June). A review of recent developments in vision-based vehicle detection. In *Proceedings of the Intelligent Vehicles Symposium* (pp. 310-315). doi:10.1109/IVS.2013.6629487

Sjafjell, A. A., Dahl, E., & Skogen, S. (2014, June). On Implementations of Bus Travel Time Prediction Utilizing Methods in Artificial Intelligence. Norwegian University of Science and Technology. Retrieved from www.diva-portal.org/smash/get/diva2:751710/FULLTEXT01.pdf

Sklet, S. (2002). *Methods for accident investigation*. Trondheim: Gnist Tapir.

Slegers, K., Ruelens, S., Vissers, J., & Duysburgh, P. (2015, April). Using game principles in ux research: A board game for eliciting future user needs. In *Proceedings of the 33rd Annual ACM Conference on Human Factors in Computing Systems* (pp. 1225-1228). ACM. doi:10.1145/2702123.2702166

Sneed, W. H., & Smith, R. L. (1998). On-board real-time railroad bearing defect detection and monitoring. In *Proceedings of the 1998 ASME/IEEE Joint Railroad Conference*. IEEE. doi:10.1109/RRCON.1998.668098

Social Media Ltd. (n. d.). List of Popular Social Networks. Retrieved from https://social-media.co.uk/list-popular-social-networking-websites

Social Media: How to tweet your customers' right. (n. d.).

Sock, J., Kim, J., Min, J., & Kwak, K. (2016, May). Probabilistic traversability map generation using 3D-LIDAR and camera. In *Proceedings of the 2016 IEEE International Conference on Robotics and Automation (ICRA)* (pp. 5631-5637). IEEE.

Song, B. Y., Zhong, Y., Liu, R. K., & Wang, F. T. (2014). Railway maintenance analysis based on big data and condition classification. In *Advanced Materials Research* (Vol. 919, pp. 1134–1138). Trans Tech Publications. doi:10.4028/www.scientific.net/AMR.919-921.1134

Sood, S., & Owsley, S. Kristian J Hammond & Larry Birnbaum. (2007). Reasoning through Search: A Novel Approach to Sentiment Classification. In *Proceedings of WWW '07 conference.*

Spaho, E., Ikeda, M., Barolli, L., & Xhafa, F. (2013). Performance Evaluation of OLSR and AODV Protocols in a VANET Crossroad Scenario. In *Proceedings of the IEEE International Conference on Advanced Information Networking and Applications (AINA)* (pp. 577-582). doi:10.1109/AINA.2013.111

Srivastava, M. (July 2014), Tech push by railways a billion dollar opportunity for IT firms. Livemint. Retrieved from http://www.livemint.com/Politics/VrfxsV8tsaLVEqF46ATvaO/Tech-push-by-railways-a-billion-dollar-opportunity-for-IT-fi.html

SSIMichigan. (2013, June 26). *Mobile LiDAR Utilized on Rail Project-1* [YouTube video]. Retrieved from https://www.youtube.com/watch?v=hnig-Ldb-3s

Steiger, E., Ellersiek, T., & Zipf, A. (2014). Explorative public transport flow analysis from uncertain social media data. In *Proceedings of the 3rd ACM SIGSPATIAL International Workshop on Crowdsourced and Volunteered Geographic Information*, 1-7.

Stelmaszczyk, K., Czyzewski, A., Szymanski, A., Pietruczuk, A., Chudzynski, S., Ernst, K., & Stacewicz, T. (2000). New method of elaboration of the lidar signal. *Applied Physics. B, Lasers and Optics, 70*(2), 295–299. doi:10.1007/s003400050048

Steur, R. (2015). *Twitter as a spatiotemporal source for incident management* [Master thesis]. Utrecht University, Netherlands.

Stouffer, K., Pillitteri, V., Lightman, S., Abrams, M., & Hahn, A. (2015). *Guide to Industrial Control Systems (ICS) Security*. doi:10.6028/NIST.SP.800-82r2

Strambi, O., Trépanier, M., & Cherrington, L. (2009). Data for public transit planning, marketing and model development: synthesis of a workshop. In P. Bonnel, M. Lee-Gosselin, J. Zmud et al. (Eds.), Transport Survey Methods: Keeping Up with a Changing World (pp. 349–357). Bingley: Emerald Group Publishing Ltd. doi:10.1108/9781848558458-020

Strang, T., Meyer zu Hörste, M., & Gu, X. (2006). A rail collision avoidance system exploiting Ad-Hoc inter-vehicle communication and Galileo. In *Proceedings of the 13th World Congress and Exhibition on Intelligent Transportation Systems and Services.*

Stratman, B., Liu, Y., & Mahadevan, S. (2007). Structural health monitoring of railroad wheels using wheel impact load detectors. *Journal of Failure Analysis and Prevention, 7*(3), 218–225. doi:10.1007/s11668-007-9043-3

SUMO. (n. d.). Retrieved from http://www.dlr.de/ts/en/desktopdefault.aspx/tabid-9883/16931_read-41000/

Sun, J., Yan, J., & Zhang, K. Z. K. (2016). Blockchain-based sharing services: What blockchain technology can contribute to smart cities. *Financial Innovation, 2*(1), 26. doi:10.1186/s40854-016-0040-y

Sun, B. Y., Huang, D. S., & Fang, H. T. (2005). Lidar signal denoising using least-squares support vector machine. *IEEE Signal Processing Letters, 12*(2), 101–104. doi:10.1109/LSP.2004.836938

Sutton, J., Palen, L., & Shklovski, I. (2008, May). Backchannels on the front lines: Emergent uses of social media in the 2007 southern California wildfires. In *Proceedings of the 5th International ISCRAM Conference,* Washington, DC (pp. 624-632).

Syed, B., Pal, A., Srinivasarengan, K., & Balamuralidhar, P. (2012, December). A smart transport application of cyber-physical systems: Road surface monitoring with mobile devices. In *Proceedings of the 2012 Sixth International Conference on Sensing Technology (ICST)* (pp. 8-12). IEEE.

Taberner, T. (2015). How the Internet of Things will change the way we monitor the Railways (White Paper). Eurotech UK.

Takens, F. (1981). *Detecting strange attractors in turbulence.* Springer.

Taneja, J., Katz, R., & Culler, D. (2012, April). Defining cps challenges in a sustainable electricity grid. In *Proceedings of the 2012 IEEE/ACM Third International Conference on Cyber-Physical Systems (ICCPS)* (pp. 119-128). IEEE. doi:10.1109/ICCPS.2012.20

Tang, J., Deng, C., & Huang, G. B. (2016). Extreme learning machine for multilayer perceptron. *IEEE transactions on neural networks and learning systems, 27*(4), 809-821.

Teng, Z., Liu, F., & Zhang, B. (2016). Visual railway detection by superpixel based intracellular decisions. *Multimedia Tools and Applications, 75*(5), 2473–2486. doi:10.1007/s11042-015-2654-x

Teradata Corporation. (2015). *The Internet Of Trains Case Study/Transportation.* Retrieved from http://assets.teradata.com/resourceCenter/downloads/CaseStudies/EB8903.pdf

TFL Survey. (2014). Travel in London report. Retrieved from http://content.tfl.gov.uk/travel-in-london-report-7.pdf

TFL. (2017). Open data users. Retrieved from https://tfl.gov.uk/info-for/open-data-users/

Thaduri, A., Galar, D., & Kans, M. (2016). Maintenance 4.0 in Railway Transportation Industry. In *Proceedings of the 10th World Congress on Engineering Asset Management (WCEAM '15)* (pp. 317-331). Springer International Publishing.

Thaduri, A., Galar, D., & Kumar, U. (2015). Railway Assets: A Potential Domain for Big Data Analytics. *Procedia Computer Science, 53,* 457–467. doi:10.1016/j.procs.2015.07.323

The Eclipse Foundation. (2011). *Jetty - a Web server and javax.servlet container.* Retrieved February 3, 2017, from https://eclipse.org/jetty/

The Eclipse Foundation. (2015). *Equinox – an implementation of the OSGi core framework specification.* Retrieved January 17, 2017, from http://www.eclipse.org/equinox/

The Internet of Trains. (2016). Wind (White Paper).

Thill, J. C. (2000). Geographic information systems for transportation in perspective. *Transportation Research Part C, Emerging Technologies, 8*(1), 3–12. doi:10.1016/S0968-090X(00)00029-2

Thomas, C., & Philippe, J. (2003). Optimized Link State Routing (OLSR RFC 3626).

Tiddens, W. W., Braaksma, A. J. J., & Tinga, T. (2015). The adoption of prognostic technologies in maintenance decision making: A multiple case study. *Procedia CIRP, 38*, 171–176. doi:10.1016/j.procir.2015.08.028

Tissera, M. D., & McDonnell, M. D. (2016). Deep extreme learning machines: Supervised autoencoding architecture for classification. *Neurocomputing, 174*, 42–49. doi:10.1016/j.neucom.2015.03.110

Tolley, R., & Turton, B. J. (2014). *Transport systems, policy, and planning: a geographical approach.* Routledge.

Tolstikhin, I. O., & Seldin, Y. (2013). Pac-bayes-empirical-Bernstein inequality. In Neural information processing systems.

Tourangeau R., Zimowski, M., Ghadialy, R. (1997). An introduction to panel surveys in transportation studies. Report prepared for the Federal Highway Administration.

Tracking Pedestrians from a Moving Car (n. d.). Retrieved September 10, 2016, from https://www.mathworks.com/help/vision/examples/motion-based-multiple-object-tracking.html

Transport for London | Every Journey Matters. (n.d.). Tube, Overground, TfL Rail, DLR & Tram status updates. Retrieved from https://tfl.gov.uk/tube-dlr-overground/status/

Trépanier, M., Morency, C., & Blanchette, C. 2009. Enhancing Household Travel Surveys Using Smart Card Data? In *Proceedings of the 88th Annual Meeting of the Transportation Research Board.*

Trépanier, M., Chapleau, R., & Tranchant, N. (2007). Individual trip destination estimation in transit smart card automated fare collection system. *Journal of Intelligent Transportation Systems: Technology, Planning, and Operations, 11*(1), 1–15. doi:10.1080/15472450601122256

Tsapakis, L., Cheng, T., & Bolbol, A. (2013). Impact of weather conditions on macroscopic urban travel times. *Journal of Transport Geography, 28*, 204–211. doi:10.1016/j.jtrangeo.2012.11.003

Tsarkov, D., & Horrocks, I. (2006, August). FaCT++ description logic reasoner: System description. In *Proceedings of the International Joint Conference on Automated Reasoning* (pp. 292-297). Springer Berlin Heidelberg. doi:10.1007/11814771_26

TSLG. (2012). *The Rail Technical Strategy 2012.* Retrieved from https://www.rssb.co.uk/library/future railway/innovation-in-rail-rail-technical-strategy-2012.pdf

Tutcher, J. (2014). Ontology-driven data integration for railway asset monitoring applications. In Proceedings of the IEEE international conference on big data. doi:10.1109/BigData.2014.7004436

Tutcher, J., Easton, J. M., & Roberts, C. (2017). Enabling Data Integration in the Rail Industry Using RDF and OWL: The RaCoOn Ontology. *ASCE-ASME Journal of Risk and Uncertainty in Engineering Systems, Part A. Civil Engineering (New York, N.Y.), 3*(2). doi.org/10.1061/AJRUA6.0000859

Tuzel, O., Porikli, F., & Meer, P. (2008). Pedestrian detection via classification on riemannian manifolds. *IEEE Transactions on Pattern Analysis and Machine Intelligence*, *30*(10), 1713–1727. doi:10.1109/TPAMI.2008.75 PMID:18703826

Twitter. (n. d.). The Search API. Twitter Developer Documentation. Retrieved from https://dev.twitter.com/rest/public/search

UK Governemnt. (2016). Transport Statistics. Retrieved from https://www.gov.uk/government/collections/transport-statistics-great-britain

Ultra Global Personal Rapid Transit Systems. (2011, September 07). Retrieved December 25, 2017, from http://www.ultraglobalprt.com/

Unnikrishnan, A., & Figliozzi, M. (2011). Online freight network assignment model with transportation disruptions and recourse. *Transportation Research Record: Journal of the Transportation Research Board*, (2224), 17-25.

Utkin, A. B., Lavrov, A. V., Costa, L., Simoes, F., & Vilar, R. (2002). Detection of small forest fires by lidar. *Applied Physics. B, Lasers and Optics*, *74*(1), 77–83. doi:10.1007/s003400100772

Utsunomiya, M., Attanucci, J., & Wilson, N. (2006). Potential uses of transit smart card registration and transaction data to improve transit planning. *Transportation Research Record: Journal of the Transportation Research Board*, *1971*, 119–126. doi:10.3141/1971-16

van Lier, T., De Witte, A., Mairesse, O., Hollevoet, J., Kavadias, D., & Macharis, C. (2014). Assessing the social relevance of school transport in Flanders (Belgium). *International Journal of Social Economics*, *41*(2), 162–179. doi:10.1108/IJSE-01-2012-0167

Van Oort, N. (2014, February 18-20). Big data opportunities in public transport: Enhancing public transport by itcs. In *Proceedings of IT-TRANS '14, Karlsruhe, Germany*.

Vapnik, V. N. (1998). *Statistical learning theory*. Wiley New York.

Vats, K., Sachdeva, M., Saluja, K., & Rathee, A. (2012). Simulation and Performance Analysis of OLSRRouting Protocol Using OPNET. *International Journal of Advanced Research inComputer Science and Software Engineering*, *2*.

Veitch-Michaelis, J., Muller, J. P., Storey, J., Walton, D., & Foster, M. (2015). Data Fusion of LIDAR Into a Region Growing Stereo Algorithm. *The International Archives of Photogrammetry. Remote Sensing and Spatial Information Sciences*, *40*(4), 107.

Vincent, P., Larochelle, H., Bengio, Y., & Manzagol, P. A. (2008). Extracting and composing robust features with denoising autoencoders. In *Proceedings of the International conference on machine learning*. doi:10.1145/1390156.1390294

Wagner, W., Ullrich, A., Ducic, V., Melzer, T., & Studnicka, N. (2006). Gaussian decomposition and calibration of a novel small-footprint full-waveform digitising airborne laser scanner. *ISPRS Journal of Photogrammetry and Remote Sensing*, *60*(2), 100–112. doi:10.1016/j.isprsjprs.2005.12.001

Walk, S., Majer, N., Schindler, K., & Schiele, B. (2010, June). New features and insights for pedestrian detection. In *Proceedings of the 2010 IEEE conference on Computer vision and pattern recognition (CVPR)* (pp. 1030-1037). IEEE. doi:10.1109/CVPR.2010.5540102

Wallach, H. M. (2006). Topic modeling: beyond bag-of-words. *Paper presented at the Proceedings of the 23rd international conference on Machine learning*.

Wang, B., Li, F., Hei, X., Ma, W., & Yu, L. (2015). Research on storage and retrieval method of mass data for high-speed train. In *Proceedings of the International conference on computational intelligence and security*. doi:10.1109/CIS.2015.120

Wang, F. h. Xu, T., Zhao, Y., & r. Huang, Y. (2015). Prior LDA and SVM based fault diagnosis of vehicle on-board equipment for high speed railway. In *Proceedings of the IEEE 18th international conference on intelligent transportation systems.*

Wang, X. B., Zhang, G. J., Hong, Z., Guo, H. F., & Yu, L. (2009), December). Modeling and implementing research of multimodal transportation network. In Information Science and Engineering (ICISE), 2009 1st International Conference on (pp. 2100-2103). IEEE.

Wang, Z., Cai, B., Chunxiao, J., Tao, C., Zhang, Z., Wang, Y., . . . Zhang, F. (2016, June). Geometry constraints-based visual rail track extraction. In *Proceedings of the 2016 12th World Congress on Intelligent Control and Automation (WCICA)* (pp. 993-998). IEEE. doi:10.1109/WCICA.2016.7578298

Wang, Z., Wu, X., Yan, Y., Jia, C., Cai, B., Huang, Z., . . . Zhang, T. (2015, October). An inverse projective mapping-based approach for robust rail track extraction. In *Proceedings of the 2015 8th International Congress on Image and Signal Processing (CISP)* (pp. 888-893). IEEE. doi:10.1109/CISP.2015.7408003

Wang, G., Gunasekaran, A., Ngai, E. W., & Papadopoulos, T. (2016). Big data analytics in logistics and supply chain management: Certain investigations for research and applications. *International Journal of Production Economics, 176,* 98–110. doi:10.1016/j.ijpe.2016.03.014

Wang, M., Wang, J., & Tian, F. (2014). City Intelligent Energy and Transportation Network Policy Based on the Big Data Analysis. *Procedia Computer Science, 32,* 85–92. doi:10.1016/j.procs.2014.05.401

Ward, J. H. Jr. (1963). Hierarchical grouping to optimize an objective function. *Journal of the American Statistical Association, 58*(301), 236–244. doi:10.1080/01621459.1963.10500845

Wasiq, S., Arshad, W., Javaid, N., & Bibi, A. (2011). Performance Evaluation of DSDV, OLSR and DYMO using 802.11 and 802.11 p MAC-Protocols. In *Proceedings of the 2011 IEEE 14th International Multitopic Conference (INMIC).* IEEE.

Weinstein, L.S. (2015, November). Innovations in London's transport: Big Data for a better customer experience. *Transport for London.*

White, T. (2012). *Hadoop: The definitive guide.* O'Reilly Media.

Whyte, J., Stasis, A., & Lindkvist, C. (2016). Managing change in the delivery of complex projects: Configuration management, asset information and big data. *International Journal of Project Management, 34*(2), 339–351. doi:10.1016/j.ijproman.2015.02.006

Wiegand, M., Balahur, A., Roth, B., Klakow, D., & Montoya, A. (2010). A Survey on the Role of Negation in Sentiment Analysis. In *Proceedings of the Workshop on NeSp-NLP '10.*

Wikipedia. (2017, June 06). History of rail transport in India. Retrieved from https://en.wikipedia.org/wiki/History_of_rail_transport_in_India

Witte, J. H. (2016). The Blockchain: A Gentle Four Page Introduction. Retrieved from http://arxiv.org/abs/1612.06244

Wohlfeil, J. (2011, June). Vision based rail track and switch recognition for self-localization of trains in a rail network. In *Proceedings of the Intelligent Vehicles Symposium (IV)* (pp. 1025-1030). IEEE. doi:10.1109/IVS.2011.5940466

Woloshynowych, M., Rogers, S., Taylor-Adams, S., & Vincent, C. (2005). The investigation and analysis of critical incidents and adverse events in healthcare.

Woollaston, V. (2015, September 10). No more delays! Computer predicts when transport will be disrupted TWO hours before it happens… and sends in extra trains. *Dailymail*. Retrieved from http://www.dailymail.co.uk/sciencetech/article-3229123/No-delays-Computer-predicts-transport-disrupted-TWO-hours-happens-sends-extra-trains.html

World Wide Web Consortium. (2012). OWL 2 web ontology language document overview. Retrieved January 23, 2017, from https://www.w3.org/TR/owl2-overview/

World Wide Web Consortium. (2014). JSON-LD 1.0: a JSON-based serialization for linked data. Retrieved January 23, 2017, from http://www.w3.org/TR/json-ld/

Wörner, D., & von Bomhard, T. (2014). When your sensor earns money. In *Proceedings of the 2014 ACM International Joint Conference on Pervasive and Ubiquitous Computing Adjunct Publication - UbiComp '14 Adjunct* (pp. 295–298). New York, New York, USA: ACM Press. doi:10.1145/2638728.2638786

Wu, B., & Nevatia, R. (2005, October). Detection of multiple, partially occluded humans in a single image by bayesian combination of edgelet part detectors. In *Proceedings of the Tenth IEEE International Conference on Computer Vision (ICCV'05)* (Vol. 1, pp. 90-97). IEEE.

Wu, X., Yuan, P., Peng, Q., Ngo, C. W., & He, J. Y. (2016). Detection of bird nests in overhead catenary system images for high-speed rail. *Pattern Recognition*, *51*, 242–254. doi:10.1016/j.patcog.2015.09.010

Wu, Z., & Chin, O. B. (2014). From big data to data science: A multi-disciplinary perspective. *Big Data Research*, *1*, 1–10. doi:10.1016/j.bdr.2014.08.002

Xu, X., & Dou, W. (2014, November). An assistant decision-supporting method for urban transportation planning over big traffic data. In *Proceedings of the International Conference on Human Centered Computing* (pp. 251-264). Springer International Publishing.

Xueyan, Z., & Depeng, G. (2014). Application of big data technology in marketing decisions for railway freight. In *Proceedings of the International Conference of Logistics Engineering and Management*.

Yang, C., & Létourneau, S. (2005). Learning to predict train wheel failures. In *Proceedings of the eleventh ACM SIGKDD international conference on Knowledge discovery in data mining* (pp. 516-525). ACM, . doi:10.1145/1081870.1081929

Yang, G., & Huang, C. M. (2005). Decomposing algorithm of laser altimeter waveforms. *Chin J Space Sci*, *25*(2), 125–131.

Yan, K. F. (2013). Using crowdsourcing to establish the big data of the intelligent transportation system. In *Advanced Materials Research*, *791*, 2118–2121. doi:10.4028/www.scientific.net/AMR.791-793.2118

Yan, L., Fang, X., Li, H., & Li, C. (2016, May). An mmwave wireless communication and radar detection integrated network for railways. In *Proceedings of the 2016 IEEE 83rd Vehicular Technology Conference (VTC Spring)* (pp. 1-5). IEEE. doi:10.1109/VTCSpring.2016.7504133

Yao, X., & Jiang, B. (2009). Geospatial modeling of urban environments. http://journals.sagepub.com/doi/pdf/10.1068/b3605ged

Yin, J., Lampert, A., Cameron, M., Robinson, B., & Power, R. (2012). Using social media to enhance emergency situation awareness. *IEEE Intelligent Systems*, *27*(6), 52–59. doi:10.1109/MIS.2012.6

Yuan, Y., & Wang, F.-Y. (2016). Towards blockchain-based intelligent transportation systems. In *Proceedings of the 2016 IEEE 19th International Conference on Intelligent Transportation Systems (ITSC)* (pp. 2663–2668). IEEE. doi:10.1109/ITSC.2016.7795984

Yu, C., & Boyd, J. (2016). Fb+-tree for big data management. *Big Data Research*, *4*, 25–36. doi:10.1016/j.bdr.2015.11.003

Zaharia, M., Chowdhury, M., Das, T., Dave, A., Ma, J., McCauley, M., ... & Stoica, I. (2012). Resilient distributed datasets: A fault-tolerant abstraction for in-memory cluster computing. In Proceedings of the USENIX conference on networked systems design and implementation.

Zanella, G. L., & Pinasco, M. (2016). *Deliverable D8.1 Requirements for the Integration Layer*. Retrieved from http://www.in2rail.eu/download.aspx?id=9c5d1b91-17bc-4a17-8d0a-283332c96ab4

Zarembski, A. M. (2014). Some examples of big data in railroad engineering. In Proceedings of the IEEE international conference on big data. doi:10.1109/BigData.2014.7004437

Zeng, C., & Ma, H. (2010, August). Robust head-shoulder detection by pca-based multilevel hog-lbp detector for people counting. In *Proceedings of the 2010 20th International Conference on Pattern Recognition (ICPR)* (pp. 2069-2072). IEEE. doi:10.1109/ICPR.2010.509

Zhang, Y., & Wen, J. (2017). The IoT electric business model: Using blockchain technology for the internet of things. *Peer-to-Peer Networking and Applications, 10*(4), 983–994. doi:10.1007/s12083-016-0456-1

Zhang, H. Y., Fan, G. H., Zhang, T. H., & Zheng, Y. H. (2012). Wavelet denoising study of laser radar waveform signal. *Research for Development, 5*(31), 52–58.

Zhang, J., Arentze, T. A., & Timmermans, H. J. (2012). A Multimodal Transport Network Model for Advanced Traveler Information System. *JUSPN, 4*(1), 21–27. doi:10.5383/JUSPN.04.01.004

Zhao, Y., Xu, T., & Hai-feng, W. (2014). Text mining based fault diagnosis of vehicle on-board equipment for high speed railway. In *Proceedings of the 17th IEEE international conference on intelligent transportation systems.*

Zhao, J., Rahbee, A., & Wilson, N. (2007). Estimating a rail passenger trip origin-destination matrix using automatic data collection systems. *Computer-Aided Civil and Infrastructure Engineering, 22*(5), 376–387. doi:10.1111/j.1467-8667.2007.00494.x

Zhou, H., Huang, G. B., Lin, Z., Wang, H., & Soh, Y. C. (2015). Stacked extreme learning machines. *IEEE Transactions on Cybernetics, 45*(9), 2013–2025. doi:10.1109/TCYB.2014.2363492 PMID:25361517

Zhu, Y. T., Wang, F. Z., Shan, X. H., & Lv, X. Y. (2014). K-medoids clustering based on map-reduce and optimal search of medoids. In *Proceedings of the International conference on computer science education.*

Zhu, L., & Hyyppa, J. (2014). The use of airborne and mobile laser scanning for modeling railway environments in 3D. *Remote Sensing, 6*(4), 3075–3100. doi:10.3390/rs6043075

Ziedelis, S., & Noel, M. (2011). Comparative analysis of nuclear event investigation methods, tools and techniques. *European Commission, Joint Research Center.*

Zikopoulos, P., & Eaton, C. (2011). *Understanding big data: Analytics for enterprise class hadoop and streaming data.* McGraw-Hill Osborne Media.

About the Contributors

Shruti Kohli is working as a lead researcher in an area of Big Data Analytics, Birmingham Centre for Railway Research and Education. Her current research revolves around Big Data application and machine learning, working on IoT sensor data for mining health of rail assets. On Academics front, She holds Ph.D. in Technology and MPhil in Operational research, and has worked with India's leading Universities, BIT Mesra Deemed University, IP University, UPT University for 12+ years doing research and teaching in Computer Sciences. With two Ph.D. near submission, she has built a strong research base. She has a keen interest in an area of Information retrieval, Operational Research, Data Mining, Web Analytics, Simulation, and Modelling. She had been working with open crowd source data and is totally fascinated by the variety of user behavior patterns over the net and have the keen interest in web analytics. She has many publications in national and international journals and has presented the paper at international conferences

A. V. Senthil Kumar obtained his BSc Degree (Physics) in 1987, P.G. Diploma in Computer Applications in 1988, MCA in 1991 from Bharathiar University. He obtained his Master of Philosophy in Computer Science from Bharathidasan University, Trichy during 2005 and his Ph.D. in Computer Science from Vinayaka Missions University during 2009. To his credit he has industrial experience for five years as System Analyst in a Garment Export Company. Later he took up teaching and attached to CMS College of Science and Commerce, Coimbatore and now he is working as a Director & Professor in the Department of Research and PG in Computer Applications, Hindusthan College of Arts and Science, Coimbatore since 05/03/2010. He has to his credit 6 Book Chapters, 85 papers in International Journals, 2 papers in National Journals, 23 papers in International Conferences, 5 papers in National Conferences, and edited four books in Data Mining, Mobile Computing, Fuzzy Expert Systems and one more book in Web Usage Mining by process (IGI Global, USA).. Key Member for India, Machine Intelligence Research Lab (MIR Labs).

John Easton is a Lecturer currently working in the Birmingham Centre for Railway Research and Education at the University of Birmingham. His current research interests centre on methods for the storage, processing and display of railway related datasets; in particular data representation and exchange via ontologies and parallel, semi-autonomous processing by software agents. Selected work in this area has included the TRIME third-rail monitoring system, which in 2012 was the joint winner of the Stephenson Award for Engineering Innovation at the National Rail Awards, and a range of EU-funded projects including INTERAIL, AUTOMAIN, OnTime, Capacity4Rail, and In2Rail. On a day-to-day basis, John is heavily involved in the Centre's £1.65 million Strategic Partnership with Network Rail on the theme of data management and integration. John is the deputy chair of the IET's Railway Technical and Professional Network executive team, and from 2015 to 2017 acted as the IET representative on the NSAR-led Routes into Rail group. From July 2015 to March 2016 he worked with the network simulation team on the cross industry Digital Railway programme.

Clive Roberts is the Professor of Railway Systems at the University of Birmingham, and Director of the Birmingham Centre for Railway Research and Education. Over the last 20 years he has developed a broad portfolio of research aimed at improving the performance of railway systems. Clive leads a number of large EPSRC, European Commission and industry funded projects, and works extensively with the railway industry in Britain and overseas.

* * *

Gaurav Ahlawat is a Final year student, and starting his graduate studies at Rutgers University, New Jersey, in Fall 2017.

Davide Anguita received the Laurea degree in Electronic Engineering and a Ph.D. degree in Computer Science and Electronic Engineering from the University of Genoa, Genoa, Italy, in 1989 and 1993, respectively. After working as a Research Associate at the International Computer Science Institute, Berkeley, CA, on special-purpose processors for neurocomputing, he returned to the University of Genoa. He is currently Associate Professor of Computer Engineering with the Department of Informatics, BioEngineering, Robotics, and Systems Engineering (DIBRIS). His current research focuses on the theory and application of kernel methods and artificial neural networks.

Enes Ataç received the B.S. degree from Dokuz Eylül University, İzmir, Turkey, in 2016. He is research assistant at department of Electrical and Electronics Engineering with Izmir Institute of Technology, Izmir, Turkey. He has been also currently M.S. Student in Dokuz Eylül University, Izmir, Turkey. His research interests include image processing, adaptive filter theory, artificial neural networks and signal processing.

M. Madhu Bala obtained her Ph.D in Computer Science and Engineering, JNTUH for her research contribution on Feature extraction for image identification and content based image categorization with machine learning algorithms in image mining. Her post-graduation M.Tech (CSE) from JNTUH and Graduation B.Tech (ECE) are from JNTUK campus. She has several research publications in international journals like; IEEE, Elsevier, Springer, CSIC indexed in SCI, SJR, SCOPUS and Thomson & Reuters to her credit. She presented research papers in various international conferences organized by Geo Spatial World Forum, Indian unit of Pattern Recognition and Artificial Intelligence in India and abroad. She contributed a several research article and book chapters in Springer and Elsevier publications on Machine learning applications in computer vision and data analytics. She is certified in R Programming" from Johns Hopkins University, Maryland, USA, and also on "Big Data Analytics" from NASSCOM for associate analytics job role. She has teaching, industry and research experience for over 20 years. She has offered faculty services for finishing school training programs conducted at JNTUH and acted as resource person for FDPs' and workshops funded by Department of Science and Technology. Currently holding the Dean Research and Professor in CSE in Institute of Aeronautical Engineering. Dr. M. Madhu Bala contributions in research areas are Data Mining, Information Retrieval, Data Analytics, Data Process and Model Construction. She published her workouts in RPUBS cloud on text mining, social network data (twitter) analysis, Sentiment analysis, clustering and prediction models using machine learning algorithms and multiple visualization methods in R.

Gary Bamford's management and technical experience relates to evaluation of changes and risks when implementing new or improved systems designs and integration of new technologies into businesses. Primary skills and areas of expertise include: Data analytics; including real time data capture and analysis. Data management of large data sets and analysis of trends and signals related to complex systems. Expert in statistical analysis, particularly in situations where the data signal to noise ratio is small. Risk management, including business continuity planning, project/programme risk management and change management activities. Experience in the use of Active Risk Manager (ARM) software. System performance evaluations, involving cost benefit analyses and business impact assessments (e.g. Train Delay modelling, Communication System Outages). System engineering, including programme management, requirements management, systems modelling and development of safety and systems engineering plans. Software engineering, including the design and development of real time systems and assessment of reliability, safety and assurance issues related to their operation. Requirements management particularly related to managing computer systems and software requirements. Experienced in the use of the requirements capture tool DOORS. Business process outsourcing, including modelling of business processes/services and evaluation of the risks involved in outsourcing of these processes and services.

Hamid Barkouk is a PHD in Faculty of Sciences and Technologies of Tangier, LIST Laboratory (Laboratoire d'Informatique, Systèmes et Télécommunications). author of several research article.

Burak Belenlioglu was born in Izmir, Turkey. He graduated from Fırat University Software Engineering Department in 2015. He has been working at Kentkart since June, 2015. His current responsibilities include CCTV systems and image processing for embedded software systems. His research interests include Linux, embedded system, real time video and audio streaming, video and audio encoding, decoding, image processing, and parallel programming.

Ashim Bhasin is an undergraduate student in the Department of Computer Science and Engineering at Chandigarh College of Engineering and Technology (Degree Wing), Chandigarh, India. His research areas include Artificial Intelligence and Data Mining. He wants to pursue his career in Data Mining and Machine Learning.

Jabran Bhatti obtained his Master's degree in Electrical Engineering and the Ph.D. degree in Engineering Sciences from Ghent University, Ghent, Belgium in 2006 and 2012, respectively. Jabran's Ph.D. research focused on novel algorithms in the domain of wireless digital communications. He currently leads the research and innovation actions of Televic Rail N.V. and has over 10 years of experience in both European and nationally funded research projects.

Renzo Canepa received the Laurea degree in Electric Engineering from the University of Genoa in 1993. After the completion of its studies, he started working in the Italian Railway National Company (now RFI), in the Engineering Department. He is currently involved in the specification and implementation of signalling systems and command and control systems, including automatic route setting, both on the Italian High-Speed lines and on conventional lines. He is also involved in the technological upgrading of conventional lines. Previously, he has been involved in the specification and implementation of a national planning and supervision system for trains.

Giorgio Clerico was born in Ceva (CN), Italy in 1988. He received his BSc in Computer Engineering and his MSc in Electronic Engineering respectively in 2013 and 2016. He worked as Data Analyst Engineer for Smartware and Data Mining s.r.l. (Iso Sistemi group). He is actually working as a PostDoc at the University of Genoa with particular interest in Machine Learning and Data Mining techniques.

Carlo Dambra was born in Genova (Italy) on September 19, 1963. He received the PhD in Electronic Engineering and Information Technology in 1993 at the University of Genova, Dept. of Biophysical and Electronic Engineering. He has been invited as expert in the evaluation of EC project proposals in FP6 and FP7 in the IST, IST for SME specific measures, Integrated Applications for Digital Sites (IADS) for Telematics and IST High Performance Computing and Networking (HPCN) programmes. Recently he has been deputy coordinator of the PROTECTRAIL "The Railway-Industry Partnership for Integrated Security of Rail Transport" (GA 242270) project and project manager for the following projects: SECUR-ED "Secured Urban Transportation - A European Demonstrator" (GA 261605), "EXCROSS Exploiting safety results across transportation modes" (GA 284895), "DEMASST Demo for mass transportation security: roadmapping study" (GA 218264). He is currently involved in the IN2RAIL "Innovative Intelligent Rail'' (GA 635900) H2020 project as WP leader and in the Shift2Rail Joint Undertaking initiatives.

Akhil Dandamudi has an education as an engineering in the computer science field and is currently working for a software firm.

Sinan Dogan was born in Izmir, Turkey. He graduated from Ege University Computer Engineering Department in 2016. He has been working at Kentkart since August, 2016. His current responsibilities include CCTV systems and embedded software systems. His research interests include Linux, embedded systems, and analog camera systems.

Uma N. Dulhare received her Ph.D from Osmania University Hyderabad. She has more than 20 years of academic experience. Currently, she is working as a professor, Department of Computer Science & Engineering, MuffaKham Jah College of Engineering & Technology, Hyderabad. She has published more than 20 research papers in reputed National & International Journals. Her research interests include Data Warehouse and Data Mining, Intrusion Detection systems, Information Retrieval System, Big Data Analytics. She is the member of various professional bodies like ISTE, IAENG UCAEE, CSTA, ISRD. She is also a pride recipient of the "Best Computer Science Faculty 2013, Best Academic Researcher 2015" of ASDF Global Awards also recipient of "Outstanding Educator & Researcher 2016" NFED Award.

Thomas Dupont is a software engineer in the Department of Information Technology (INTEC) at Ghent University and a senior researcher at IMEC. In 2009, he obtained his Master of Science Computer Science Engineering, after which he immediately started working as a full-time researcher at the Faculty of Engineering and Architecture of Ghent University. His focus has been on designing and realizing distributed middleware architectures for multiple research areas like the railway industry, intelligent transportation systems and micro-service framework. More recently challenges in the IoT and Smart Cities domain (City-of-Things) are being tackled in the form of high performance software systems, dealing with big data and high throughput.

El Mokhtar En-Naimi is a Professor in Faculty of Sciences and Technologies of Tangier, Department of Computer Science. He is responsible for a Bachelor of Sciences and Technologies, BST Computer Engineering ("Licence LST-GI"), from January 2012 to October 2016. Actually, he is a Head of Computer Science Department, since October 2016. He is also a member of the LIST Laboratory (Laboratoire d'Informatique, Systèmes et Télécommunications), the University of Abdelmalek Essaâdi, FST of Tangier, Morocco. He is an Autor and/or Co-Autor of several Articles in Computer Science, in particular, in SMA, Cases Based Reasoning (CBR), eLearning, Big DATA, Datamining, Wireless sensor network, VANet, MANet, etc. In addition, he is an Associate Member of the ISCN - Institute of Complex Systems in Normandy, the University of the Havre, France, since 2009.

Emanuele Fumeo was born in Genoa, Italy in 1988. He is currently a PhD Student of the University of Genoa at the SmartLab laboratory. He received his Bachelor and Master degrees in Electronic Engineering at the University of Genoa in 2011 and 2014 respectively. His current research interests focus on the application of big data, machine learning and data mining methodologies to railway transportation systems. He is currently involved in the context of some EU-funded research projects (such as the In2Rail H2020 project).

Diego Galar is a Professor of Condition Monitoring in the Division of Operation and Maintenance Engineering at LTU, Luleå University of Technology where he is coordinating several H2020 projects related to different aspects of cyber physical systems, Industry 4.0, IoT or industrial Big Data. He was also involved in the SKF UTC centre located in Lulea focused on SMART bearings. He is also actively involved in national projects with the Swedish industry and also funded by Swedish national agencies like Vinnova. He is also principal researcher in Tecnalia (Spain), heading the Maintenance and Reliability research group. He has authored more than three hundred journal and conference papers, books and technical reports in the field of maintenance, working also as member of editorial boards, scientific committees and chairing international journals and conferences. In industry, he has been technological director and CBM manager of international companies, and actively participated in national and international committees for standardization and R&D in the topics of reliability and maintenance. In the international arena, he has been visiting Professor in the Polytechnic of Braganza (Portugal), University of Valencia and NIU (USA). Currently, he is visiting professor in University of Sunderland (UK) and University of Maryland (USA), also guest professor in the Pontificia Universidad Católica de Chile.

David Golightly is a Senior Research Fellow in the Human Factors Research Group, University of Nottingham. His background is in the study of learning, problem solving and expertise, particularly involving the use of ICT. He has worked on a number of rail-related projects including understanding situation awareness in rail traffic control, driver advisory for capacity management, evaluating the impact of procedural change on signalling workload and awareness, and on passenger and end-to-end journey experience to encourage modal shift.

Ankit Gupta is working as an Assistant Professor in the Department of Computer Science and Engineering at Chandigarh College of Engineering and Technology (Degree Wing), Chandigarh India. He received his BTech in Computer Science and Engineering in 2004 from Uttar Pradesh Technical University, Lucknow, India and MTech in Computer Science in 2012 from Birla Institute of Technology, Mesra, Ranchi, India. He is enrolled as a doctoral candidate with Department of Computer Science and Engineering, Birla Institute of Technology, Mesra, Ranchi, India. His research work focuses on information retrieval, web analytics and web mining. He is an active member of IEEE, and IAENG International Society for Engineers.

Robert J. Houghton is an Assistant Professor in Human Factors in the Department of Mechanical, Materials and Manufacturing Engineering at the University of Nottingham and a member of the Human Factors Research Group. Recent projects have involved the design of digital services, the internet of things (spanning both domestic applications and transport asset condition monitoring) and crowd sourcing across domains as diverse as assessing sanitation in the developing world, citizen journalism, and mapping the surface of Mars. More broadly, he is interested in the development of methods for the analysis and design of decision-making in networked systems of humans and machines.

Wannes Kerckhove is a software engineer in the Department of Information Technology (INTEC) at Ghent University and a senior researcher at IMEC. In 2009, he obtained his Master of Science Computer Science Engineering, after which he immediately started working as a full-time researcher at the Faculty of Engineering and Architecture of Ghent University. His research focuses on the design and implementation of robust and scalable software systems for a range of application domains (railway, smart cities, etc.).

Ela Kumar is working as head in IGDTUW, Delhi. Before this, she was an associate professor and dean in School of ICT, GBU, Greater Noida. She has published more than 10 books and 100 research papers in national and international journals.

Uday Kumar is the Chair Professor of Operation and Maintenance Engineering, and Director of Luleå Railway Research Center and Scientific Director of the Strategic Area of Research and Innovation—Sustainable Transport at Luleå University of Technology, Luleå, Sweden. Before joining Luleå University of Technology, Dr. Kumar was Professor of Offshore Technology (Operation and Maintenance Engineering) at University of Stavanger, Norway. Dr. Kumar has research interests in the subject area of reliability and maintainability engineering, maintenance modeling, condition monitoring, LCC and risk analysis, etc. Dr. Kumar has been a keynote and invited speaker at numerous congresses, conferences, seminars, industrial forums, workshops, and academic institutions. He is an elected member of the Swedish Royal Academy of Engineering Sciences (IVA).

Nadia Mazzino holds a Laurea degree in Math (1990) and she works in Ansaldo STS since 1993. From 1993 to 1998, she worked on the requirement definition to the delivery of a new traffic command and control system. From 1999 to 2006, she has been involved in a big project for Italian Railway: eight centres for command and control of traffic, PIS, D&M, Security. Since 2003 she has the responsibility of coordinating engineering department activities on all these systems. She was in a continuous empowering project to find out new solutions to make the product much more complete. From 2007 to nowadays, she works in a new area of the company (Innovation & Competitiveness) and she has the responsibility of the development of innovative projects and of the business for railway customers. The main projects are in the security area (development of a new Security Management System), risk reduction area (diagnostic wayside systems, level crossing protection).

Swastikaa Moudgil is an undergraduate student in the Department Of Computer Science and Engineering at Chandigarh College Of Engineering and Technology, Chandigarh, India. Her research areas include Programming in Core Python, Web Analytics and Artificial Intelligence. She wants to pursue her career as a Data Scientist with an aim to derive significant conclusions from real time data and use them to contribute for the welfare of society.

Syed Asad Ali Naqvi is a Research Associate in the School of Computing and Communications at Lancaster University. He acquired his PhD in Computer Science form Lancaster University in 2015. His research interests are Incident Analysis, Risk Analysis, Cyber Security, and Aspect Oriented Programming.

Luca Oneto was born in Rapallo, Italy in 1986. He received his BSc and MSc in Electronic Engineering at the University of Genoa, Italy respectively in 2008 and 2010. In 2014, he received his PhD from the same university in "School of Sciences and Technologies for Knowledge and Information Retrieval," with the thesis "Learning Based On Empirical Data." He is currently an Assistant Professor at University of Genoa with particular interests in Statistical Learning Theory, Machine Learning, and Data Mining.

Federico Papa holds a Laurea degree in Civil Engineering - Transportation Engineering and Logistics (2009), and received his PhD in Transportation and Logistics Engineering in 2013 from the University of Genoa, C.I.E.L.I. (Centro Italiano di Eccellenza per la Logistica Integrata). He has a six years' experience in the field of EU-funded projects, and from 2014 on he works in the Innovation Unit of Ansaldo STS, holding the position of Innovation & Competitiveness Engineer.

Howard J. Parkinson is a UK Chartered Engineer and a Member of the Institution of Railway Signal Engineers (IRSE) and a Fellow of the Institution of Mechanical Engineers (IMechE) with a PhD in Engineering from Manchester University. He is currently involved in training, consultancy and research. The research contributes to his publications, training and innovation. He regularly presents railway safety engineering seminars and also helps clients to get their products more widely recognised in the rail industry. Having been involved at senior level on many large railway projects for over 20 years; he has the experience to work effectively when under pressure in complex situations. Howard has been involved in the international railway industry working on infrastructure signaling ATP/ETCS, and railway systems integration projects at a senior level. Project positions at senior levels have included systems assurance director, lead safety assessor and head of systems engineering /RAMS, and the safety regulator for a country. He has worked in metro, tram and heavy rail (conventional and high speed) He has expertise in systems engineering, compliance, ISA/NoBo Safety Assessment, RAMS, CENELEC, EN5012X, Yellow Book, Various MIL STDs, ERTMS European interoperability and UK legislation. Techniques used include FMEA, Fault Trees, Event Trees, RCM, simulation and associated software, SIL Allocation. He has produced a range of technical publications and research on railway reliability, safety and risk, refurbishment, condition monitoring and neural networks. He has international experience in the Middle East, Germany, Holland, Brazil, Korea, China, Australia etc. He is commercially astute having conducted extensive business development and lead several successful large bids. Howard's major objective is to bring vitality, intellectual curiosity and innovation to railway engineering.

Shaik Rasool received the Master of Technology in Computer Science & Engineering from Jawaharlal Nehru Technological University in 2011. He is currently working as Assistant Professor in the Department of Information Technology at M.J.C.E.T., Hyderabad, India. He has published eight research papers in the field of Computer Science in various International Journals and a book chapter in IGI. His research interest includes Network Security, Biometrics, Data Mining and Information Security.

Venkata Krishnaiah Ravilla did his Ph.D. at Jawaharlal Nehru Technological University Anantapur in Electronics & Communication Engineering Specialization. He acted as editor for many international journals like Cognitive processing Springer journal. He acted as a reviewer for many international journals like IEEE Transactions on Image Processing. He has published more than 150 research articles. He is doing a Technology development research project of Indian Railways sponsored by Department of Science & Technology, Government of India with a worth of Rs.91,07,000; with three years duration. This was aimed swatch Bharat in Railways. He is a member of Professional Societies like IETE, ISTE, IE and IEEE. He is working with different societies which promote quality education with service aim. He has organized some international conferences and acted as chair for some international conferences. He is a motivator for people who want to serve to the society with their skill set.

M. Alper Selver received the B.Sc. degree from Gazi University, Ankara, Turkey, in 2002, and the M.Sc. and Ph.D. degrees from Dokuz Eylül University (DEU), Izmir, Turkey, in 2005 and 2010, respectively, all in electrical and electronics engineering. He has studied with Medical Informatics Laboratory at FH Aachen, Abt. Juelich, 763 Germany, and the Heffner Biomedical Imaging Laboratory, Columbia University, New York, NY, USA. He is currently an Associate Professor with DEU. His research interest includes medical and industrial image processing, multi-scale and intelligent system design.

Dammika Seneviratne currently works as Post-doctoral researcher in the Division of Operation and Maintenance – Luleå University of Technology, Luleå, Sweden. He holds a B.Sc. degree in Mechanical Engineering from the University of Peradeniya, Sri Lanka, specialized in Production engineering. He received his M.Sc. degree in Mechatronics Engineering from the Asian Institute of Technology, Thailand. After working for a number of years as a Mechanical Maintenance Engineer in various organizations he attained a PhD degree in Offshore Technology from the University of Stavanger. His research interests include condition monitoring, operation and maintenance engineering in railway systems; risk based inspection planning in offshore oil and gas facilities; reliability and risk analysis and managements, and risk based maintenance.

Syed Noorulhassan Shirazi is a research associate in the School of Computing and Communications at Lancaster University, United Kingdom. His current research focuses on anomaly based challenge detection techniques in elastic cloud deployment scenarios. His interests include security and resilience of computer networks and networked systems.

Arun Solanki received his Ph.D. Degree in 2014 in computer science and engineering. He has completed his M.Tech. In computer engineering. Currently, he is working as a faculty associate at the school of ICT, Gautam Buddha University, Greater Noida. He has published more than 20 research papers with national and international publishers.

Kanza Noor Syeda obtained her MSc in Computer Science from Lancaster University, United Kingdom in 2016. Currently she has internship with Digital Rail Ltd, UK as a Data Analyst and working on developing railway safety management system using modern approaches like Natural Language Processing and Machine Learning. Her research interests include big data analytics, security and resilience and incident analysis.

Filip De Turck leads the network and service management research group at IDLab of the Ghent University, Belgium and IMEC. He received his Ph.D. degree from the Ghent University in 2002. He is a full-time professor since October 2006 in the area of telecommunication and software engineering. He is author or co-author of more than 400 refereed papers published in international journals or in the proceedings of international conferences. His main research interests include scalable software architectures for telecommunication network and service management.

Dirk Van Den Wouwer holds a Master's degree in Electronics from KIHA, Antwerp, Belgium. He currently heads the research and development department of Televic Rail. Dirk has been involved in several nationally and internationally funded research projects and has a track record in executing and valorizing scientific research projects. Before joining Televic Rail, he was R&D Director at Gemidis NV – a spin off company from Ghent University. Prior to this, Dirk worked at several technology companies as project manager and system architect, among others.

Avimanyou Kumar Vatsa is a Ph.D candidate and received MS (Computer Science) and minor in statistics from University Of Missouri - Columbia, MO, USA in 2015. He obtained his M.Tech (Computer Engineering) with Hons. from Shobhit University, Meerut and B.Tech (I.T.) from V.B.S. Purvanchal University, Jaunpur, (U.P), INDIA, in 2009 and 2001 respectively. He is working as teaching and research assistant at University of Missouri – Columbia, MO USA and worked as Assistant Professor for more than ten years in several engineering colleges and university in INDIA. He had been member of academic and administrative bodies. During his teaching, he had been coordinated many technical fests and national conference at college and university level. He has worked as software engineer in software industry. He is on the editorial board member and reviewers of several international and national journals in networks and security field. His area of research includes Low and High Dimensional Data (Big Data), Image Processing, MANET (Mobile Ad-Hoc Network), Computer Network and Network Security.

Stijn Verstichel graduated magna cum laude at Ghent University, Faculty of Engineering in Summer 2005. A month later he joined the research group of Piet Demeester, IBCN (Internet Based Communication Networks and Services) to be employed as a Jr. Researcher on two European Projects. The first, Geant2, consists of the development and deployment of a new-generation pan-European Research Network, and corresponding monitoring software. InteGRail, the second project, also focuses on the development of specific semantic software, but this time for the railway industry. Its aim was to create a holistic, intelligent and integrated information and data sharing platform for the European Railway Network. On the

1st of January 2007, he received a Ph.D. grant from IWT, Institute for the Support of Innovation through Science and Technology, to work on his research in distributed reasoning techniques for the Semantic Web. He successfully defended his Ph.D., titled "Distributed Reasoning for Context-Aware Services" on June 15th, 2011. He is currently still with IDLab - IMEC as a post-doctoral researcher, performing research on semantic technologies applied in a variety of domains, such as eHealth, wireless senor networks and transportation as well as being involved in the follow-up of bachelor and master courses at the Faculty of Engineering and Architecture of Ghent University. He is author or co-author of more than 30 papers published in international journals or in the proceedings of international conferences and a regular reviewer for conferences and journals in his research field.

Bruno Volckaert is a professor of advanced programming and software engineering in the Department of Information Technology (INTEC) at Ghent University and a senior researcher at IMEC. He obtained his Master of Computer Science degree in 2001 from Ghent University, after which he worked on his PhD at Ghent University on data intensive scheduling and service management for Grid computing, which he obtained in 2006. His current research deals with reliable and high performance distributed software systems for City-of-Things (IoT for Smart Cities), decision support systems for UAVs, intelligent transportation applications and autonomous resource optimization of cloud-based / micro-service based applications. He has been involved in over 35 national and international research projects, and is co-author of over 85 peer-reviewed publications in international journals or in the proceedings of international conferences.

E. Yesim Zoral received the B.S. degree from Dokuz Eylül University, ˙Izmir, Turkey, in 1990, and the M.Sc. and Ph.D. degrees from the Illinois Institute of Technology, Chicago, IL, USA, in 1993 and 1999, respectively, all in electrical engineering. She is currently a Professor with the Electrical and Electronics Engineering Department, Dokuz Eylül University, Izmir, Turkey. Her current research interests include RF/microwave circuits, computer aided design of RF circuits for wireless and antenna applications, dielectric resonators, and material measurement.

Index

A

AEI Reader 92
API 98, 107, 109, 113, 167, 319
ARGOS 69, 86-87
AWK 206

B

behavioral analysis 134
Big Data 1-4, 6-10, 13-17, 19-23, 35, 40-42, 45, 47, 51-52, 54, 56-57, 67-70, 72, 74-75, 80-81, 89-90, 127-128, 135, 151, 153-154, 158, 179, 210, 217-218, 224-225, 227, 229, 234-236, 240-242, 245, 291, 295-299, 301-302, 308, 311-312, 315, 320-323, 333
big data analysis 40, 42, 47, 51, 56, 158, 224, 227, 229, 234-236, 298
big data analytics 1-4, 13-17, 19-23, 241, 245, 297-298, 302, 320-322
blockchain 32-36, 38-39

C

camera 42-43, 45, 47, 49-53, 56-58, 286-287
collision 41, 186, 204, 273-274
CSI 92

D

data aggregation 218
data feeds 30, 217-219, 291, 295-296, 303, 308, 311-312, 315
data integration 17, 30-31, 35, 107, 210, 213-214
data mining 8, 13-14, 16, 70, 136, 138-139, 145, 163, 210-213, 221-222, 226, 248, 297, 302-303
data processing 8, 15, 40-41, 54, 68, 95, 120-121, 123, 161, 210, 215-218, 222, 297, 303, 320, 323
data science 210, 216, 222
databases 112, 153, 160, 210-212, 218, 222, 250, 341
deep architecture 323, 333
delay 31, 96, 152, 183, 197-202, 209-211, 214-216, 218, 220-222, 227, 230-231, 234-235, 276, 286, 301, 311-312, 315, 320-326, 334
diagnosis 1, 321
disruption 31, 96, 134, 210, 217-218, 222, 224-227, 230, 232-236, 294-295, 298, 301, 303, 306, 311-313, 315
driver support system 56

E

Enterprise Service Bus 30-31, 38
Entities of Interests (EOI) 265
ERRAC 319
evolution 2, 100, 127-128, 189, 219, 269
Extreme Learning Machines 320, 322, 326, 332

F

Facebook 175, 209-210, 215-217, 225, 227, 229-230, 234
framework 7-8, 14-15, 35, 81, 95-97, 99-100, 102-116, 118, 122-123, 157, 160, 163, 179, 240, 249-250, 292, 295, 312, 322-323, 326, 341

G

geotagged 157, 173-174, 176-177
GPSR (Greedy Perimeter Stateless Routing) 206
GyTAR (Greedy Traffic Aware Routing Protocol) 207

H

hash value 32, 38

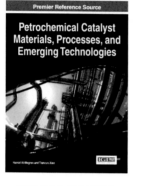
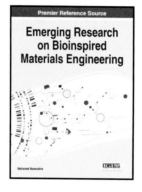

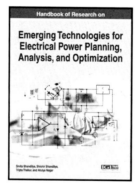

Stay Current on the Latest Emerging Research Developments

Become an IGI Global Reviewer for Authored Book Projects

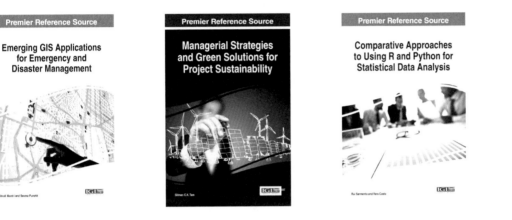

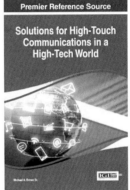

The overall success of an authored book project is dependent on quality and timely reviews.

In this competitive age of scholarly publishing, constructive and timely feedback significantly decreases the turnaround time of manuscripts from submission to acceptance, allowing the publication and discovery of progressive research at a much more expeditious rate. Several IGI Global authored book projects are currently seeking highly qualified experts in the field to fill vacancies on their respective editorial review boards:

Applications may be sent to:
development@igi-global.com

Applicants must have a doctorate (or an equivalent degree) as well as publishing and reviewing experience. Reviewers are asked to write reviews in a timely, collegial, and constructive manner. All reviewers will begin their role on an ad-hoc basis for a period of one year, and upon successful completion of this term can be considered for full editorial review board status, with the potential for a subsequent promotion to Associate Editor.

If you have a colleague that may be interested in this opportunity, we encourage you to share this information with them.

Printed in the United States
By Bookmasters